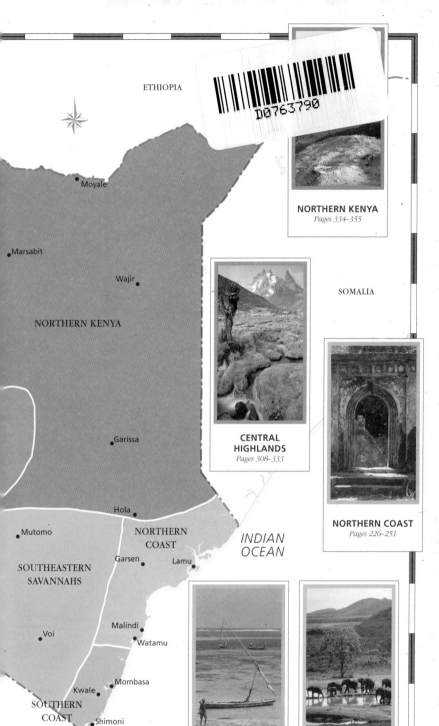

ETHIOPIA

D0763790

NORTHERN KENYA
Pages 334–355

Moyale

Marsabit

Wajir

SOMALIA

NORTHERN KENYA

CENTRAL HIGHLANDS
Pages 308–333

Garissa

NORTHERN COAST
Pages 226–251

Hola

Mutomo

NORTHERN COAST

INDIAN OCEAN

Garsen

Lamu

SOUTHEASTERN SAVANNAHS

Voi

Malindi

Watamu

Kwale

Mombasa

SOUTHERN COAST

Shimoni

SOUTHERN COAST
Pages 198–225

SOUTHEASTERN SAVANNAHS
Pages 176–197

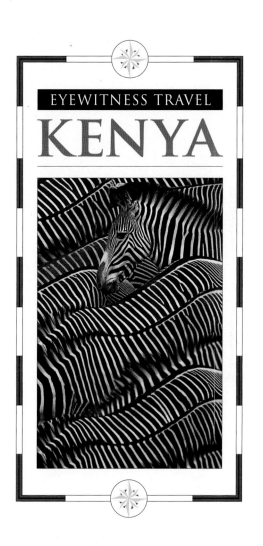

EYEWITNESS TRAVEL
KENYA

WITHDRAWN

EYEWITNESS TRAVEL

KENYA

CONTRIBUTORS: PHILIP BRIGGS AND LIZZIE WILLIAMS

WITHDRAWN

LONDON, NEW YORK,
MELBOURNE, MUNICH AND DELHI
www.dk.com

MANAGING EDITOR Aruna Ghose
EDITORIAL MANAGER Ankita Awasthi
DESIGN MANAGERS Sunita Gahir, Kavita Saha
PROJECT EDITOR Arundhti Bhanot
PROJECT DESIGNER Mathew Kurien
EDITORS Sandhya Iyer, Yasmin Rahman
DESIGNERS Stuti Tiwari Bhatia, Amisha Gupta
SENIOR CARTOGRAPHIC MANAGER Uma Bhattacharya
CARTOGRAPHER Mohammad Hassan
DTP DESIGNER Azeem Siddiqui
SENIOR PICTURE RESEARCH COORDINATOR Taiyaba Khatoon
PICTURE RESEARCHER Shweta Andrews

CONTRIBUTORS
Philip Briggs, Lizzie Williams

PHOTOGRAPHERS
Demetrio Carrasco, Nigel Hicks, Linda Whitwam

ILLUSTRATORS
Chapel Design and Marketing Ltd., Chinglemba Chingtham,
Arun Pottirayil, T. Gautam Trivedi

Reproduced in Singapore by Colourscan
Printed and bound by L. Rex Printing Company Limited, China

First American Edition, 2009
11 12 13 14 10 9 8 7 6 5 4 3 2 1

Published in the United States by DK Publishing,
375 Hudson Street, New York, New York 10014

Reprinted with revisions 2011

Copyright © 2009, 2011 Dorling Kindersley Limited, London
A Penguin Company

Published in Great Britain by Dorling Kindersley Limited.

A CATALOG RECORD FOR THIS BOOK
IS AVAILABLE FROM THE LIBRARY OF CONGRESS.

ISSN: 1542-1554
ISBN: 978-0-7566-7028-3

*Front cover main image: Zebras drinking at a water hole in the
Masai Mara Game Reserve*

MIX
Paper from
responsible sources
FSC™ C018179
www.fsc.org

**The information in this
Dorling Kindersley Travel Guide is checked regularly.**
Every effort has been made to ensure that this book is as up-to-date
as possible at the time of going to press. Some details, however, such
as telephone numbers, opening hours, prices, gallery hanging
arrangements and travel information are liable to change. The
publishers cannot accept responsibility for any consequences arising
from the use of this book, nor for any material on third party
websites, and cannot guarantee that any website address in this book
will be a suitable source of travel information. We value the views
and suggestions of our readers very highly. Please write to: Publisher,
DK Eyewitness Travel Guides, Dorling Kindersley, 80 Strand, London,
WC2R 0RL, Great Britain, or email: travelguides@dk.com.

◁ **A Samburu warrior gazing over the Great Rift Valley**

Lionesses with cubs, Masai Mara

CONTENTS

HOW TO USE THIS
GUIDE **6**

INTRODUCING
KENYA

Elaborate Swahili wooden
door, Lamu town

WILD KENYA

THE SAFARI
EXPERIENCE **58**

HABITATS **80**

FIELD GUIDE **96**

KENYA AREA
BY AREA

Hiking on the picturesque Chogoria
Route leading to Mount Kenya

Traditional sailing dhow,
Lamu waterfront

TRAVELLERS'
NEEDS

Modern skyscrapers dominating
the Nairobi skyline

SURVIVAL GUIDE

The imposing Fort Jesus in Mombasa

HOW TO USE THIS GUIDE

This travel guide helps you to get the most from your visit to Kenya. It provides both detailed practical information and expert recommendations. *Introducing Kenya* maps the country, sets it in its historical and cultural context, and describes events through the entire year. *Wild Kenya* is an extensive guide to wildlife viewing in Kenya and includes practical information on parks and reserves. *Kenya Area by Area* describes important sights, with maps, photographs and illustrations. Restaurant and hotel recommendations can be found in *Travellers' Needs*. The *Survival Guide* has tips on everything from transport to using the telephone system.

WILD KENYA

The Safari Experience focuses on the activities on offer while on a safari and gives tips on locating and viewing wildlife through the year. *Habitats* gives an overview of the landscapes of Kenya. The *Field Guide* is an introduction to the wildlife of Kenya, from the Big Five to all the keenly sought primates, large and small mammals, reptiles and birdlife.

Key Facts provides details for each animal species, including habitat, top places to see and sighting tips.

KENYA AREA BY AREA

In this book Kenya has been divided into eight regions, each of which has a separate chapter. The most interesting places to visit have been numbered on a *Regional Map* at the beginning of each chapter.

Each area of Kenya can be quickly identified by its colour coding, shown on the front flap.

1 Introduction
The landscape, history and character of each region is outlined here, showing how the area has developed over the centuries and what it offers to the visitor today.

2 Regional Map
This map shows the road network and gives an illustrated overview of the region. All the sights are numbered and there are also useful tips on getting around.

Sights at a Glance lists the chapter's sights by category.

3 Street-by-Street Map
This gives a bird's-eye view of the key area in each chapter.

A suggested route for a walk is shown in red.

Stars indicate the sights that no visitor should miss.

The information block provides the details needed to visit each sight. Map references locate the sights on the *Road Map of Kenya* on the inside back cover.

4 Detailed Information
All the important sights in Kenya are described individually. They are listed in order following the numbering on the Regional Map at the start of the chapter.

Features explore themes specific to the region.

5 Kenya's Top Sights
These are given two or more full pages. Historic buildings are dissected to reveal their interiors; national parks have maps showing facilities and trails; museums have colour-coded floorplans to help locate interesting exhibits.

6 Travellers' Needs and Survival Guide
These sections cover areas such as shopping, entertainment, activities, health, security, communications, banking and currency and travel.

Directory boxes give contact information for services and venues mentioned in the text.

INTRODUCING KENYA

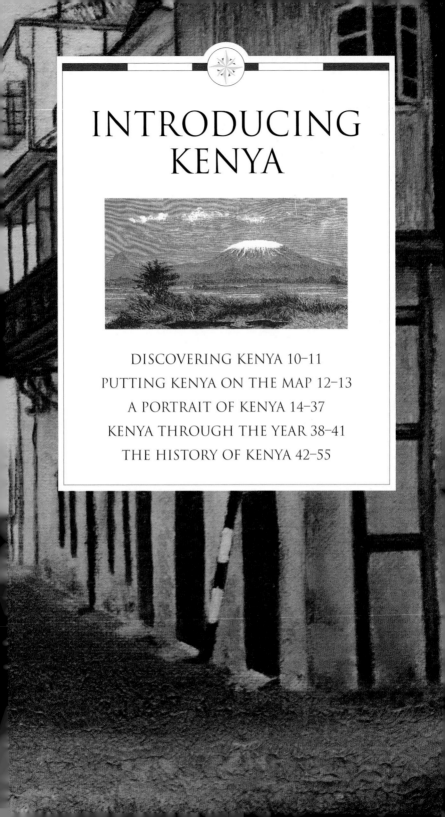

DISCOVERING KENYA

Kenya has an outstanding variety of natural habitats, from tropical forests and shimmering deserts to dazzling beaches and endless savannahs. These host a spectacular biodiversity that is the great draw for most holiday-makers to the country. There are dozens of national reserves, and, increasingly, private ranches, where the ever-popular Big Five – leopard, lion, elephant, rhino and buffalo – can be seen. The splendid tropical coastline is another attraction, where long sunny days can be spent lazing on pristine beaches or exploring the underwater life of the clear azure Indian Ocean.

Superb starling

Visitors will also discover vibrant cities with a number of interesting urban highlights and historical sights, isolated tracts of wilderness, verdant forests, lofty mountains and the warm hospitality of over 40 ethnic groups.

NAIROBI

- Nairobi National Museum
- Carnivore Restaurant
- Game viewing

From a swampy railway camp, Kenya's capital has grown into one of Africa's largest cities. **Nairobi National Museum** *(see pp158–9)* showcases this history and also human evolution in the region. Downtown Nairobi has an eclectic mix of modern and colonial architecture. Shopping, restaurants and nightlife are good and include the exceptional **Carnivore Restaurant** *(see p160)*. **Nairobi National Park** *(see pp162–5)* offers game viewing against a backdrop of the city's skyline, while baby elephants can be seen at the nearby **David Sheldrick Wildlife Trust** *(see p161)*.

SOUTHEASTERN SAVANNAHS

- Tsavo National Park
- Elephant viewing
- Views of Kilimanjaro

Straddling Nairobi–Mombasa Highway, the combined **Tsavo West** and **Tsavo East National Parks** *(see pp182–7)* are the largest protected area in Kenya, and are famed for exceptionally large herds of elephant and buffalo. To the east, **Amboseli National Park** *(see pp194–7)* lies at the base of Kilimanjaro *(see p191)*, the world's tallest free-standing

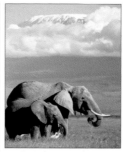

Elephants grazing on the plains of Amboseli beneath Kilimanjaro

mountain. Although it falls over the border in Tanzania, the gleaming snowcapped peaks provide a marvellous setting for game viewing.

SOUTHERN COAST

- Spectacular beaches
- Historic Fort Jesus
- Sable antelopes at Shimba

The palm-backed beaches of the Southern Coast are strewn with starfish and sand dollars and lined with top class resorts. The popular **Diani Beach** *(see p210)* is an impressive picture-perfect swathe of white sand. From here, **Wasini Island** *(see p220)* makes an excellent day trip for snorkelling. The coastal forests are home to monkeys and birds, and **Shimba Hills National Reserve** *(see pp216–19)* harbours the rare sable antelope. The greatest draw on the coast is historical **Mombasa** *(see pp204–209)* with its lovely palm-lined beaches, Swahili houses, mosques and the imposing 16th-century **Fort Jesus**.

NORTHERN COAST

- Elegant Swahili architecture
- Intriguing Gedi Ruins
- Atmospheric Lamu town

There are many distractions on the road along the Northern Coast, including **Arabuko Sokoke National Park and Gedi Ruins** *(see pp234–9)* – a forest sanctuary for a number of rare birds and butterflies, and the

The deep blue waters of the Indian Ocean at Mombasa

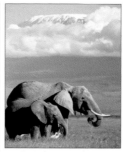
◁ **A contemporary painting by a Kenyan artist depicting traditional houses with fretwork balconies in Mombasa**

Safari vehicles pause to allow visitors a glimpse of the Mara lions

remains of a mysterious 13th-century city. Offshore, **Malindi Marine National Reserve** *(see p232)* harbours an array of interesting marine life that can be viewed by diving, snorkelling or from a glass-bottomed boat. Further north, **Lamu Archipelago** *(see pp244–50)* features mangrove swamps and empty beaches pounded by surf. Lamu town is steeped in Swahili tradition with an ancient warren of alleyways and tightly-packed houses to explore.

SOUTHERN RIFT VALLEY AND MASAI MARA

- **Excellent wildlife sightings**
- **Safaris in Masai Mara**
- **Superb birdlife at Baringo**

Dotted with spectacular lakes and surrounded by grand escarpments, the Rift Valley has a number of attractions. **Lake Naivasha** *(see pp266–9)* is home to large pods of hippo. **Hell's Gate National Park** *(see pp270–71)* has soaring sandstone cliffs and officially permits walking among the wildlife. The habitat of wild fig and acacia trees around **Lakes Bogoria and Baringo** *(see pp280–83)* offer the best bird-watching in East Africa. **Lake Nakuru National Park** *(see pp276–9)* is known for its prolific rhino

and leopard may be spotted in the giant yellow acacia trees. **Masai Mara Game Reserve** *(see pp262–5)*, with the country's highest concentration of game, is Kenya's most popular safari destination and is famous for the wildebeest migration.

WESTERN KENYA

- **Lake Victoria**
- **Beautiful Kakamega Forest**
- **Scenic tea plantations**

The most fertile and populous area of the country, Western Kenya is scattered with market towns, fields and tea plantations. The principal town, **Kisumu** *(see pp298–9)*, lies on the shores of **Lake Victoria** *(see pp302–303)*. The town's open air market has colourful displays of fruits and vegetables from across the region. On the lake, there are upmarket lodges on the islands of **Mfangano** and **Rusinga** *(see pp304–305)*. To the north, **Kakamega Forest National Reserve** *(see pp294–7)* is a tract of rainforest full of small animals, while **Saiwa Swamp National Park** *(see pp290–91)* is home to the rare sitatunga.

CENTRAL HIGHLANDS

- **Game on Laikipia Plateau**
- **Impressive Mount Kenya**
- **Aberdare National Park**

The fertile Central Highlands are dominated by **Mount Kenya National Park** *(see pp322–5)*, which has dense forest and the country's richest farmland at its foothills. There are several routes to the top and the climb takes about 4–6 days. To the north is one of Kenya's greatest conservation success stories, **Laikipia Plateau** *(see pp318–21)*, a huge area with over 9,500 sq km (3,650 sq miles) of private ranches where fences have been taken down and land stocked with game. Excellent accommodation and activities are on offer from ranch lodges. To the west, **Aberdare National Park** *(see pp316–17)* has craggy peaks, deep valleys and crashing waterfalls, while to the east, **Meru National Park** *(see pp330–33)* has riverine forests and various large animals.

NORTHERN KENYA

- **Jade-coloured Lake Turkana**
- **Samburu-Buffalo Springs-Shaba National Reserves**
- **Samburu tribal culture**

Although difficult to travel in, Northern Kenya has a unique landscape that makes it a worthwhile visit. Here are endless deserts, barren mountains and arid scrubland, broken by oases of vegetation and the huge **Lake Turkana** *(see pp352–5)*. The region is home to ethnic groups such as the Samburu, who can be seen leading their camels across the hostile landscape. In the south are **Samburu-Buffalo Springs-Shaba National Reserves** *(see pp342–7)*, where the Ewaso Nyiro river supports desert-adapted animals.

Samburu camels

Putting Kenya on the Map

Flanked by a tropical 480-km (300-mile)
coastline on the Indian Ocean in the
southeast, bordering Sudan, Somalia
and Ethiopia in the arid north
and Uganda and Tanzania in
the southwest, Kenya straddles
the equator. Roughly the size of
France, it covers 586,000 sq km
(226,196 sq miles), of which about
10,700 sq km (4,130 sq miles) is taken
up by Lakes Victoria and Turkana.
Estimated at 38.8 million in 2008, Kenya's
population is likely to cross 40 million in
the next few years, of which 75 per cent
lives in an agricultural belt running north
west from Nairobi to the Ugandan border.
The rest of the population lives in the cities of
Nairobi, Nakuru, Kisumu and Mombasa.

Satellite image of the Nairobi cityscape

INDIAN OCEAN

0 km   125

0 miles   125

KEY

✈	International airport
✖	Domestic airport
⚓	Ferry service
══	Highway
══	Major road
──	Minor road
▬▬	Untarred major road
═ ═	Untarred minor road
──	Railroad
─·─	International border
xxx	Disputed border

ETHIOPIA

SOMALIA

KENYA

Guenale

Dawa

Dolo Bay

Mandera

Luuq

B9

Moyale

A2

Garbahaarrey

Baydhabo

Marsabit

B9

Wajir

Laga Bor

Laga Bogal

Ewaso Nyiro

Mado Gashi

C83

Lago Dera

A3

C81

Equator

Tana

A3

A3

Garissa

B8

Hola

B8

Mutomo

B7

Tiva

Garsen

C112

Pate Island

Lamu Island

Ungwana Bay

Gongoni

Galana

Savo

C103

Malindi

A109

Voi

C115

B8

Watamu

A23

A109

Kilifi

Kwale

Mombasa

C106

C106

A14

Mkomazi

Shimoni

Korogwe

Wete

A PORTRAIT OF KENYA

With outstanding natural beauty, prolific wildlife, a gorgeous tropical coastline and a rich and diverse ethnic tapestry, Kenya has plenty to offer visitors. Thrilling safaris on the broad savannahs of the Rift Valley are the biggest draw, while the palm-backed white-sand beaches along the Indian Ocean coast are ideal for a relaxed holiday.

Covering a considerable chunk of East Africa, Kenya is neatly girthed across the middle by the equator and bisected by the southerly course of the jagged Rift Valley. The country has a varied altitude featuring lofty mountains and escarpments, open plains and stony deserts, fertile rolling hills and forested valleys and a beautiful 480-km (300-mile) tropical coastline. This wealth of natural habitat is protected in over 50 national parks and reserves, and many more private conservancies. Together, these cover about 10 per cent of the 580,400-sq-km (224,000-sq-mile) country. With the exception of the great apes, Kenya is home to a full complement of East African animals and is also one of the best places on the continent for bird-watching. The long sunny days and the azure Indian Ocean, with its colourful marine life, ensure a perfect environment for a laid-back holiday on the coast.

Grey crowned crane

Kenya's character has been shaped by its long history, from the emergence of mankind some 6 million years ago to the colonial days of hunters, settlers and adventurers. Its rich ethnic heritage is evident from the traditionally dressed Maasai and Samburu people tending their livestock, while a long Swahili tradition has left its mark in the architecture and Islamic way of life on the coast and in the Swahili language.

A group of lionesses resting on a tree trunk

◁ Maasai warrior, in trademark red garb, at the Lewa Wildlife Conservancy

Flamingoes congregating in the algae-rich waters of Lake Nakuru

LAND AND ECOLOGY

Kenya is a land rich in biodiversity. Its natural environment is split into many distinct zones, from rainforest, high moorland and wetlands to semidesert, thornbush scrub and grassland savannah. These habitats harbour over 7,000 species of plants and trees, more than 25,000 species of animals and in excess of 1,000 species of birds. This concentration and variety of flora and fauna is greater than that in many other African countries, owing largely to Kenya's two life-giving rainy seasons.

The impact of humans in this region dates back millions of years, and there is archaeological evidence to show the existence of hominids (early man). Over time, they were followed by migrant hunter-gatherer tribes, who roamed across the land in search of resources, and eventually pastoralists, who introduced agriculture. In the late

Rhino calf being fed at Lewa Wildlife Conservancy

19th century, agriculture was boosted by the advent of European settlers, who were attracted by Kenya's climate and fertile soil. They laid out plantations and terraced fields in the verdant western hills and valleys. As a result, wildlife was forced into the agriculturally unproductive savannah, where big-game hunters depleted substantial herds of large animals. By the 1940s, the need to establish national wildlife reserves was recognised, not only to protect big game, but also to protect natural habitats and maintain large areas for water catchment.

Wildlife numbers were further decimated during the poaching scourge that plagued East Africa over the 1970–80s. In 1989, President Moi set alight a huge stock of confiscated ivory (see p165) in a much publicised and successful bid to stamp out poaching; this contributed to a subsequent worldwide ban on ivory trade. Kenya Wildlife Service (KWS) was formed in 1990 to take on the poachers, and it now employs thousands of officers in game management, anti-poaching and conservation activities. Animal numbers have steadily increased in national parks and private conservancies, which have contributed to wildlife protection and increased the mobility of animals on migratory routes.

ECONOMY

On becoming independent in 1963, Kenya had a good transport infrastructure and an economy dominated by agriculture. Today, it is one of the world's leading producers of tea and coffee and also exports exotic vegetables and fresh flowers to Europe. In fact, Kenya is the world's largest exporter of roses, and tea alone generates an income of US$600–700 million.

A tea picker at work near Kericho

In the 1970s, when long-haul destinations grew in popularity with European holiday-makers, tourism became increasingly important to the Kenyan economy. While Kenya once attracted fearless adventurers and big-game hunters, today its wildlife, natural attractions and location – only a 9-hour flight from Europe – ensure that it is East Africa's principal holiday destination with a good tourism infrastructure that supports tens of thousands of jobs. In good years, tourism can earn Kenya in excess of US$800 million, which makes the sector the country's biggest foreign exchange earner. Tourism experienced a slump after the terrorist bombings in Nairobi in 1998 and in Mombasa in 2002, but

Workers cutting roses at a flower farm near Naivasha

the industry recovered quickly and, by 2006, Kenya received a record two million visitors. The sector has continued to expand and visitors now have a greater choice of destinations and activities.

Kenya's economy has experienced a number of cycles of growth followed by downturns and stagnation, caused by anything from drought to political instability and corruption. Nevertheless, given that Kenya does not rely on mineral wealth like other countries in the region and has been under pressure from an influx of refugees, its economic growth has been overall steady. Per capita income grew at least threefold between 1975 and 2006. Kenya was removed from the International Monetary Fund's list of countries requiring debt relief in 2005, and today it is considered a self-sufficient developing nation. Nairobi, the capital, is now the primary communications and financial hub of East Africa. A wide range of foreign firms have branches in the city, and foreign investment in turn further supplements economic growth.

Hot-air balloon floating over the Masai Mara Game Reserve

GOVERNMENT AND POLITICS

Kenya is a republic and multiparty state with a unicameral National Assembly. The president is both head of state and head of government, and appoints the vice president and cabinet. Since independence in 1963, Kenya's politics has been dominated by the terms of two presidents. President Jomo Kenyatta, who governed from 1963 to 1978, is often referred to as the Father of the Nation for his contribution to Kenya's independence and for steering the new republic through a period of economic empowerment. His successor, Daniel arap Moi, governed from 1978 to 2002 and is criticised both for reverting Kenya to a one-party state for a time and for excessive corruption.

In 2002, Mwai Kibaki succeeded Moi as president, but he failed to address his electoral promises. His 2007 election win was reputedly rigged and his main contender, Raila Odinga, was believed to be the legitimate winner. The dispute led to violence across the country, resulting in deaths and a downturn in the economy. The United Nations stepped in and by mid-2008 an agreement between Kibaki and Odinga had been negotiated. A new constitution was passed in 2010 that granted citizens a bill of rights.

Maasai tribesmen performing a warrior dance

PEOPLE AND SOCIETY

The diversity in Kenya's ethnic groups today is derived from a long history of migration, settlement and fusion of older cultures. Thousands of years ago, the Cushite, Bantu and Nilotic peoples roamed East Africa and settled into hunter-gatherer and pastoral communities. The first millennium saw the intermingling of Persians and Arabs with tribes on the coast, which gave rise to Swahili culture, while the 19th and 20th centuries witnessed the arrival of white settlers from Europe and indentured labour from India. Since 2006 refugees from strife-torn, neighbouring Somalia have filtered into Kenya. Some indigenous communities retain a way of life in scattered settlements that has changed little over the centuries. Each group has its own social and political organisation, and a deep sense of kinship that governs individual behaviour, rites of passage and marital customs. By contrast, since the arrival of the colonists, many other ethnic groups have adopted a Western way of life. The

President Mwai Kibaki inspects a guard of honour

result is a multicultural society, and while ethnic Africans dominate, there are pockets of Indian traders, farmers of European descent and a multinational community of businesspeople.

Kenya has one of the fastest rates of population growth in the world – in just 80 years, the population has risen from three million to an estimated 30 million. Settlements are distributed unevenly around the country, with the arid north being more sparsely populated than the fertile west. The urban population, about 25 per cent of the total, is concentrated in the large cities of Nairobi, Mombasa, Nakuru and Kisumu.

Kenya's constitution guarantees freedom of worship, and the majority of Kenyans are actively religious. Christianity was introduced by early missionaries in the 19th century and today some 70 to 80 per cent of the population is Christian. Most are regular churchgoers and Protestant, Anglican and Roman Catholic churches are prolific across the country. Islam

Friday prayers at Jamia Mosque, Nairobi

was introduced during the centuries of trade with the Arabian Peninsula and people on the coast are mainly Muslim. There are also substantial communities of Hindus and Sikhs among the Indian populace in urban areas.

ARTS AND SPORTS

In recent decades, Kenya has produced a number of internationally acclaimed musicians, writers and sportspeople. These include Kikuyu pop star Joseph Kamaru, who has sold over half a million records worldwide, and Ngugi wa Thiong, a noted novelist and playwright since the 1960s.

The introduction of cricket, rugby and golf during the colonial years has made both watching and playing sports a popular activity among Kenyans. They love playing football, although the national team, Harambee Stars, has never qualified for the FIFA World Cup. However, Kenya is best known for its phenomenally successful world-class distance runners. At the 2008 Beijing Olympics, Kenya scooped 13 medals, including a gold in the men's marthon for Samuel Kamau and a silver in the women's marathon for seasoned runner Catherine Ndereba. Kenya also hosts the annual Lewa Marathon (see p402). Other popular sports are as diverse as car rallies, horse racing and deep-sea fishing events.

Athletes celebrating Kenya's victory in the 3000 m steeplechase, 2008 Olympics

The Landscape of Kenya

Kenya's regions all have markedly diverse landscapes. The coast is fringed with coral reefs and islands, backed by a gradually rising dry coastal plain of savannah and thorny bush. The country is neatly bisected from north to south by the Great Rift Valley, which is broad and shallow in the north and deepens further south where it is walled by towering escarpments. The arid north's flat expanse forms three-fifths of Kenya. By contrast, the Central Highlands support the Aberdares, Mount Kenya and many other mountains. Nairobi is located on a 1,500-m (5,000-ft) high plateau. West of the Rift Valley, savannah plains descend to Lake Victoria.

The pristine coral reefs *that stretch along the palm-lined beaches of the coast are among Kenya's biggest attractions.*

INDIAN OCEAN COASTLINE

Kenya's tropical coastline boasts a string of fine, palm-backed beaches with soft white sands, gentle breezes and mangrove forests. The colourful offshore reefs are home to a host of marine life, while the temperate waters offer good diving and snorkelling. A wide variety of wildlife inhabits the coastal forests.

Mangrove forests *cover some 40 per cent of the coast. This salt-tolerant tree is found on sheltered shores and deep into river estuaries.*

Sea turtles *nest at a number of sites along the coast. The females dig holes with their flippers and lay as many as 100 eggs at a time.*

Starfish, *urchins, parrotfish, lionfish and angelfish are some of the more colourful marine species that inhabit Kenya's coral reefs.*

WESTERN ESCARPMENTS

Western Kenya's Rift Valley, characterised by its cliffs and escarpments, is home to several soda lakes fringed with pink thanks to the flocks of flamingoes that feast there on fish and algae. The escarpments give rise to gentle hills and bright green tea plantations, which descend to the sandy shores of Lake Victoria.

The lilac-breasted roller *has a distinctive bold white forehead with a pale purple chest and throat. Fairly common, it can be seen on bare branches in dry, open woodland.*

Tea, *an important export commodity, is grown in the highland areas near the Rift Valley at altitudes above 1,500 m (4,900 ft).*

Yellowwood acacia *is a straight-stemmed evergreen forest tree with broad branches and dense, glossy foliage. It is a popular habitat for leopards.*

NORTHERN DESERTS

The north of Kenya is a region of arid, stony, sun-baked deserts, where the people live a harsh existence. This is Kenya at its wildest. Across the shimmering Chalbi Desert lies Lake Turkana, often called the Jade Sea due to its brilliantly turquoise waters surrounded by a lunar landscape of extinct volcanoes and lava beds.

Camels *are kept by nomadic pastoralists in the north. They are used to carry goods between remote settlements that trucks cannot reach.*

The gerenuk *is one of a number of desert-adapted animals that are not found in the south of Kenya. An unusual antelope, it stands on its hind legs to feed on thorn trees.*

Crocodiles *are abundant in Lake Turkana. The lake's Central Island, in particular, is a favourite breeding ground.*

CENTRAL HIGHLANDS

A temperate plateau of lush agricultural and game-rich land, the Central Highlands lie on the lower slopes of Mount Kenya, Africa's second highest mountain. Laikipia Plateau consists of grasslands and dense cedar and olive forests, while the Aberdares have a landscape of undulating moors and primeval forests.

The giant lobelia *is a plant that only grows at high altitudes on the slopes of East Africa's mountains. When in bloom, it produces numerous greenish-white flowers.*

The bongo *is a shy mountain antelope with a reddish coat that has distinctive white stripes. It lives in bamboo forests and swampy glades.*

Red hot pokers, *with their distinct vibrant colours, can be frequently seen in mountain glades after the long rains.*

SOUTHERN SAVANNAHS

The most popular region for safari trips, southern Kenya has the largest reserves in the country which are home to a full host of East African animals. Tsavo and Amboseli are famous for great herds of elephant while the Masai Mara has gentle undulating hills and riverine forests along the Mara river.

Wildebeest *move around the Masai Mara's southern plains in an annual migration in search of fresh pasture.*

Secretary birds, *often seen on open plains, are named for the plumes on their crest, which resemble quills tucked behind the ears of old-fashioned secretaries.*

Whistling thorn acacia *stud the open grasslands. Ants pierce the thorns with tiny holes, which make a whistling sound when the wind blows through them.*

The Great Rift Valley

A geographical and geological fissure, the Great Rift Valley extends approximately 8,700 km (5,400 miles) from Lebanon to the lower Zambezi River Valley in Mozambique. The valley was formed by a rifting of the earth's crust some 10–20 million years ago, which forced up volcanic activity that altered the landscape. Its width varies from about 30 km (19 miles) to 150 km (93 miles) across. It is an important archaeological site, and fossils of bones of animals and early humans have been found at several places in the Rift Valley; the high alkaline level in the soil and sediments of volcanic ash are ideal components in the process of fossilisation.

KEY

■ The Great Rift Valley

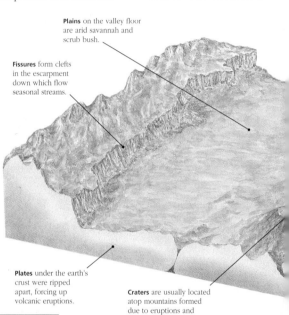

Plains on the valley floor are arid savannah and scrub bush.

Fissures form clefts in the escarpment down which flow seasonal streams.

Flamingoes *are attracted to feed on the algae in the Rift Valley lakes. Many lakes contain high levels of sodium carbonate caused by alkalinity from the surrounding volcanic rock and evaporation.*

Plates under the earth's crust were ripped apart, forcing up volcanic eruptions.

Craters are usually located atop mountains formed due to eruptions and volcanic deposits.

The bubbling geysers and steam jets *that line the shores of Lake Bogoria are caused when water is heated close to boiling point by volcanic gas and hot rocks underground.*

Mount Elgon *is an extinct volcano on the Kenya-Uganda border and, at about 15 million years, is thought to be the oldest volcano overshadowing East Africa's Rift Valley. Of its several peaks, the 4,321-m (14,178-ft) Wagagai is the highest.*

Menengai Crater, *located on the floor of the Rift Valley just outside Nakuru, is a 2,490-m (8,167-ft) high extinct volcano. Its last eruption is thought to have occurred around 7,000 BC.*

TECTONIC ACTIVITY

The earth's crust and lithosphere were pulled apart by violent subterranean forces which forced down chunks of rock below parallel fault lines, and forced up molten rock in volcanic eruptions. The result was cliffs and mountains rimming the valley floor, which over time gradually sank into a low flat plain studded with craters, small scarps and lakes.

Lake Magadi *is a saline lake which produces a dense sodium carbonate brine that can, in places, be up to 40 m (130 ft) thick. Several geothermal hot springs feed the lake.*

Lakes formed as there were no outlets for water in the valley.

Mountain ranges can be found above the escarpment around the valley floor.

Central Island, *a dramatic extinct volcano created by the Rift Valley, rises from the middle of picturesque Lake Turkana. It has three distinct vents, two of which have formed lakes.*

KENYA'S RIFT VALLEY

The Rift Valley neatly divides Kenya down its length from the Ethiopian border in the north to the Tanzania border in the south. The valley is characterised by uninhabitable desert in the north, fertile farmland in the middle and flat arid plains to the south. The valley floor is at its lowest near Lake Turkana where there is virtually no distinction between the Great Rift and the surrounding desert, but as it heads south, the valley walls form sheer inward-facing escarpments rising to a height of 600–900 m (2,000–3,000 ft). A number of active and semi-active volcanoes are evidence of volcanic activity in the valley.

Mount Longonot, *a 2,890-m (9,466-ft) dormant volcano near Naivasha, is lined with spectacular fissures and laval canyons.*

The arid landscape of the northern deserts

The farmlands of the Southern Rift Valley

The plains of the southern savannahs

Indigenous Peoples of Kenya

Maasai shields, made of cattle hide

Kenya has more than 40 major ethnic groups, with several smaller tribes assimilated within them. These tribes range in size from more than seven million Kikuyu people to less than 500 Elmolo. All remain firmly rooted in tribal tradition. They can be broadly divided into three linguistic groups – the Bantu, Nilotic and Cushite. Most arrived in this region in tribal migrations from other parts of Africa from AD 1000. The main groups are the Kikuyu, Kalenjin, Meru, Luhya, Luo, Kisii, Kamba, Maasai, Samburu and Turkana. Since the colonial years, some have imbibed the conveniences of the West while other remote tribes remain untouched by the modern world.

A vibrant canvas depicting the indigenous people of Kenya

KEY

Borana ①	Meru ⑪
Elmolo ②	Rendille ⑫
Embu ③	Samburu ⑬
Kalenjin ④	Turkana ⑭
Kamba ⑤	
Kikuyu ⑥	
Kisii ⑦	
Luhya ⑧	
Luo ⑨	
Maasai ⑩	

DISTRIBUTION OF ETHNIC GROUPS

Thousands of years of migration and displacement caused by colonial land reallocation means that most ethnic groups are centred around specific regions of Kenya. The livelihoods of these groups depend on their environments. Generally, the tribal groups living in the fertile highlands tend to be farmers, while those living on the drier, flat plains of the north tend to be pastoralists.

BORANA

A subgroup of Ethiopia's Oromo people, the Borana *(see p337)* arrived from southern Ethiopia in the early 20th century and settled in the region around Marsabit and Isiolo in Northern Kenya. For this nomadic herding group, life revolves around their livestock. Houses of interwoven branches thatched with grass are built by the women, and villages move as much as 100 km (60 miles) a year to follow fresh pasture and rain. However, conflict with the Rendille and other groups in the region over meagre resources for their cattle has caused the Borana to retreat to safer areas near the towns. Many of their settlements have been abandoned and only armed herdsmen and warriors now accompany their livestock in the wilderness of Kenya's extreme north.

Young Borana in striking attire

Elmolo men building a dried weed hut

ELMOLO

A Cushitic people closely related to the Rendille, Kenya's smallest ethnic group lives on the shores of Lake Turkana at Loiyangalani. The Elmolo *(see p336)* are one of the last hunter-gatherer peoples still in existence, although, through intermarriage, their population has largely been absorbed into the Turkana and Samburu groups. Their livelihoods are largely based on fishing, using nets cast from simple log canoes. Traditionally, villages were made up of clusters of rounded huts built from dried lake weed, but these are gradually being replaced by concrete structures.

EMBU

Traditionally, the Embu occupied the southeastern lower slopes of Mount Kenya around the town of Embu. They are believed to have migrated from the Congo Basin during the 16th century and may have reached as far as the coast, but it is possible that a conflict with the Arab slave traders forced them to retreat to the interior. The family unit is very central to the Embu, and the importance of having daughters suggests that the society was originally matriarchal. They are predominantly agriculturists and well known as bee-keepers.

Embu couple in their colourful clothing

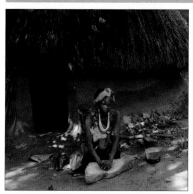
Kalenjin woman outside her thatched mud hut

KALENJIN

Comprising a group of people formerly called the Nandi by the British, the Kalenjin include the Kipsigis, Nandi, Marakwet, Tugen, Keiyo, Pokot, Terik and Sabaot, all of whom mostly speak the same language but in different dialects. While they were formerly known individually, the Kalenjin groups united in response to colonialism to advocate their interests to the British government. The Kalenjin live in small communities of settled farmers mainly clustered on the western edge of the Rift Valley and make up about 12 per cent of Kenya's population. They have been dubbed the running tribe as, since the mid-1960s, the majority of successful Kenyan runners have been Kalenjin (see p293).

KAMBA

This indigenous group generally inhabits the largely semiarid hills north of the Nairobi–Mombasa Highway, between Nairobi and Mount Kenya and eastwards towards Tsavo East National Park. The Kamba were involved in the Omani slave and ivory trade as middlemen in the 18th century due to their proximity to the coast. Today, they are known for their wood carving skills, and for eking out an agricultural living from their relatively unfertile lands.

Young Kamba women working their land

Kikuyu woman with an elaborate headdress

KIKUYU

Believed to have arrived in the area around Mount Kenya during the Bantu migrations between the 14th and 16th centuries, the Kikuyu (see pp310–11) are the largest of Kenya's ethnic groups and make up over 20 per cent of the total population. According to Kikuyu legend, their founder Gikuyu was told by their god Ngai to build a house on the slopes of Kirinyaga (Mountain of Brightness), the Kikuyu name for Mount Kenya. The Kikuyu were the first among the tribes to join the political system. They formed the Kikuyu Association in 1920 and played an active role in Kenya's struggle for independence. Kenya's first president, Jomo Kenyatta, was a Kikuyu.

KISII

Based around the town of the same name in Western Kenya, the Kisii (also known as the Gusii) are a Bantu group which originally migrated from the region that is now the Democratic Republic of the Congo. They ended up in a geographical location unique among Bantu groups in that they were surrounded on all sides by Nilotic-speaking communities. As a result they developed an almost warlike culture to defend themselves against cattle-raiding neighbours, and to this day, have a reputation for being resilient and

Women crafting intricate soapstone figures

very industrious. The region is one of the most economically active in Kenya, blessed with rolling tea, coffee and banana plantations, and the Kisii are well known for fashioning soapstone into outstanding craft items, which are popular as souvenirs with visitors to Kenya.

Luhya woman at the village market

LUHYA

The second largest indigenous group after the Kikuyu, the Luhya make up 17 per cent of Kenya's population. Luhya society is structured around an extremely complex system of clans and subclans. They come from the west between Lake Victoria, Mount Elgon and the Ugandan border, which is one of the most densely populated regions of Kenya. Traditionally agriculturalists, today the Luhya produce a number of cash crops such as tea, cassava and maize. They are also known for their thatching and weaving skills. One of the best known Luhya customs, bullfighting, still thrives today.

LUO

Kenya's third largest ethnic group, the Luo constitute about 14 per cent of its population. They inhabit the far west around the shores of Lake Victoria and are traditionally agriculturists and fishermen. The elders control family compounds. Unlike other tribal groups in Kenya, the Luo were not dispossessed of their land on a large scale during colonial times, and eventually adopted the English language and British-style dress and education. Along with the Kikuyu, with whom they shared major political power in the early years of Kenyan independence, the Luo continue to hold positions of power and political influence in the country.

Luo men in their fishing boats

A Maasai warrior dance

MAASAI

Mostly inhabiting southern Kenya and northern Tanzania, the pastoral Maasai *(see pp254–5)* make up about 2 per cent of Kenya's population and are traditional nomadic herdsmen, although this is getting increasingly difficult in modern times. Their herds dominate all aspects of their lives as they believe that back in time when the earth and sky split, the rain god gave them all the cattle for safekeeping. They have successfully conserved their ethnic identity and continue to wear striking body decorations. Women are famous for their beaded jewellery while men typically wear a red checked *shuka* (robe). A Maasai homestead is a *manyatta (see pp256–7)*, a group of low huts made of bent branches daubed with dried mud.

MERU

Accounting for 5 per cent of the total tribal population of Kenya, the Meru comprise eight subgroups of people who migrated to the northeast side of Mount Kenya around the 14th century. Originally governed together by a council of elected elders, the Meru were perhaps the only democratic society in precolonial Africa. Their complicated mythology shows many similarities to the story of the birth of Christ, leading to the theory that they may have been a lost tribe of Israel. Today, they occupy some of the country's richest farmland and grow several cash crops.

A Meru drummer tapping a rhythm on his log drum

A Rendille elder with his camel

RENDILLE

A pastoralist nomadic people, the Rendille live in small communities in the harsh rocky terrain of northeast Kenya around the Kaisut Desert. Camels are central to most aspects of their lives, and are relied on for many of the Rendille's daily needs, such as milk, food, trade and transport. Traditionally, the Rendille lived in semipermanent villages that were moved several times a year. The area they inhabit is one of the country's most unforgiving regions and drought and overgrazing have turned settlements into wastelands, forcing many Rendille to abandon their nomadic way of life in favour of more permanent settlements. Despite linguistic differences, they maintain kinship and economic cooperation with their Samburu neighbours to the southwest.

SAMBURU

Closely related to the Maasai and with an almost identical language, the Samburu (see p347) inhabit the northern foothills of Mount Kenya in the 21,000-sq-km (8,000-sq-mile) Samburu district. They are seminomadic pastoralists whose mainstay is rearing cows, sheep, goats and camels. Like the Maasai, they have retained their traditional dress and wear striking bright robes, colourful multibeaded necklaces, bracelets and earrings.

Samburu girls wearing bead necklaces

A group dance performed on social occasions

TURKANA

Another pastoralist group, the Turkana (see p337) live a harsh existence around Lake Turkana in arid and hostile Northern Kenya. Their livelihood comes chiefly from raising cattle, camels and goats and fishing in the lake. Of all Kenya's peoples, they are the most isolated and least affected by the modern world. Turkana women often wear plate-like bead necklaces or an aluminium or brass neck ring, while the men cover their hair with mud and ostwrich feathers. Men also carry tiny *ekicholongs* (wooden stools) that are used as simple chairs to sit on the hot sand and also double as headrests while sleeping.

Traditional Dress

There are a myriad ethnic groups in Kenya, many of whom adopted Western clothing during the colonial era. Some, however, retained their ethnic attire. Most notably, these include the Maasai and Samburu, whose bright and colourful robes, beaded jewellery and body decoration leave a lasting impression on any visit to the country. In recent years, there has been some effort to introduce a national dress in order to identify the Kenyan people. For example, some government ministers have swapped their plain grey suits for more traditional African tailored outfits.

A tailor at work over bales of floral printed kitenge cloth

DRESS

On top of their everyday clothing, most Kenyans carry an additional piece or two of cloth, which can be worn in many different ways. These are sold across the country, and open markets especially have colourful reams of cloth hanging from stalls. The two most popular streets in Kenya for cloth shops are both called Biashara Street, one in Nairobi and the other in Mombasa.

The bui-bui, worn by Swahili Muslim women, *is a long black cloak with matching head-dress and veil that covers the body from head to foot.*

The cloth is brightly coloured and decorated with a variety of patterns.

The kanga's border, called *pindo*, has a different design from the cloth's centre (*mji*).

The kanga, *usually worn by women, is a length of cloth that is either tied around the chest or waist or used like a headscarf or baby's sling. The hem is sometimes printed with Swahili proverbs, which can be messages of caution, love, reassurance or just acts of self-expression.*

A shuka *is a red piece of cloth or, in more modern times, a red blanket, worn by Maasai men, wrapped around the waist and then thrown over one shoulder.*

Kikoys, the traditional garb of Swahili men, *are made from a fringed piece of woven cotton, usually in pastel shades and stripes. New ones are washed in the sea to preserve their colours.*

The kitenge *is a multicoloured cotton fabric with a wax-resist print, worn in a similar way to the* kanga. *The various colours, patterns, writings and symbols on the cloth represent a variety of moods, feelings, cultures and traditions.*

ADORNMENT

Many of Kenya's ethnic groups incorporate body or hair adornment in their dress. The combination of beaded jewellery, body paint, intricate hair braiding and decorated clothing can be visually very striking. Some items are also worn to signify certain stages in life.

The jewellery of the Elmolo and Turkana peoples *around Lake Turkana is made of beads and also incorporates items from the lake, such as fish bones and teeth. Unmarried girls wear soft goatskin aprons covered with pieces of ostrich egg.*

Beaded necklaces are a prominent part of a Samburu girl's attire. Given by admirers, these necklaces are accumulated till they form a collar that can support the chin, and only then is a girl deemed old enough to marry. Once married, women carry a metal cross on their headbands.

Elaborate hair braiding *is seen among Samburu warriors, who place great significance on physical appearance. They also use ochre body paint to embellish their skin.*

Akalas *are rugged sandals worn by the Maasai to protect their feet from thorns. Also called "thousand milers", they are made from old car tyres but are surprisingly comfortable.*

Ostrich feather headdresses *are often worn in ceremonies by Maasai moran – warriors who have not yet killed a lion.*

BEADS

Beading symbolises beauty, age, marriage and social status. It dates back to around 1850, when Arab traders imported tiny glass beads to the East African coast. There are some 40 varieties of beadwork and the most common colours are red (the preferred colour of the Maasai), blue (for the sky), white (for milk) and green (for fresh grass). Beads are also used to demonstrate feelings. Girls often give armbands as a sign of love to warriors and brides wear large disc-like necklaces to present their beauty to their new husband. A boy who is to be initiated receives a beaded pendant known as *surutia* from his mother. After the initiation he returns this to her, and she wears it proudly for the rest of her life as a sign of her son's status.

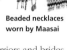

Beaded necklaces worn by Maasai

Large brass-hoop earrings *are worn by Pokot women to signify they are married. Pokot men arrange their hair into a bun and cover it with blue clay.*

Religion in Kenya

Most of the tribes in Kenya worshipped a supreme being known by various names but often referred to as Ngai, who was revered for bringing rain. These traditional religions declined when Christian missionaries arrived in the 19th century. Today, about 80 per cent of Kenya's population is Christian, predominantly Anglican or Roman Catholic, and increasingly, Pentecostal. Along the Swahili coast, much of the population follows Islam, as does most of Kenya's Asian community. There is also a small number who follow Hinduism and Sikhism.

Ethiopian painting in a local church, Kalacha

CHRISTIANITY

The first missionary to arrive in Kenya was Johann Ludwig Krapf in 1846. The East African coast was still under the administration of the Zanzibar Sultanate and Sultan Seyyid Sa'id permitted Krapf to establish a mission station in Mombasa in 1846. The interior was opened up to Christian missionaries with the building of the Uganda Railway from Mombasa to Kampala at the turn of the 20th century. By the 1920–30s churches had been built across the country, and by the 1950s the Bible had been translated into the Luo and Swahili languages.

German missionary Johann Ludwig Krapf *is credited with setting up the Kenya Anglican Church. He compiled the first Swahili dictionary and translated sections of the Bible into this language.*

The Minor Basilica Holy Family Cathedral, *built in 1960, is Nairobi's largest church and the seat of the Archbishop of Nairobi. A modern building with large multipane stained-glass windows, the cathedral houses one main altar and eight chapels, and can seat up to 4,000 people. Mass is celebrated every day.*

Pentecostal churches *have been drawing crowds for evangelical events, especially in Nairobi. The trend is attracting preachers from the USA, who are joining the local clergy in preaching redemption to growing congregations.*

ISLAM

Islam is by and large practised by the Swahili people on the coast, as well as by the Somali people in the northeast of Kenya and Asian immigrants in the cities. It was introduced on the coast in the 8th century by Arab traders and it is believed that many black Africans converted to Islam to avoid being sold as slaves.

Mosques *are prolific in the old trading towns along the coast such as Lamu, which has as many as 40 mosques in just a small grid of streets.*

The Maulidi Festival, *held on Lamu Island each year, celebrates Prophet Mohammed's birthday and is a festival of solemn prayer. There are also colourful processions and other events, such as donkey and swimming races, held on this occasion.*

TRADITIONAL RELIGION

Before the arrival of Christianity, most traditional religions celebrated one god, who was the creator of earth and brought rain, which in turn provided grass, plants, animals and prosperity. People would both pray for good rain and make sacrifices to the god to appease him during drought, famine, disease and death. He, and sometimes she, was manifested in the sun, moon, thunder and lightning, stars, mountains and in trees, especially the wild fig tree, under which sacrifices were made. Another common belief is in spirit beings, who are believed to reside in powerful places, with soothsayers and witch doctors often acting as intermediaries.

The Kikuyu god, *also referred to as Ngai, is said to rest on Mount Kenya when he visits earth. Traditionally, the Kikuyu build their houses with their front doors facing the mountain and the dead are buried with their heads pointing towards the revered peak.*

Cattle *are central to the existence of the Maasai. Legend has it that the earth and sky separated and their god Ngai entrusted all the cattle to the Maasai people to look after. Any pursuit other than a pastoral one is considered insulting to Ngai and demeaning to the Maasai.*

OTHER RELIGIONS

Hinduism is only practised by a small minority in Kenya. The religion was introduced when the British brought indentured labour from India to build the Uganda Railway in the late 19th and early 20th centuries. Today, there are Hindu temples in all the major cities and many Sikh gurdwaras built and run by the Ramgarhia Sikh community of Kenya. Both Mombasa and Nairobi also have ornate Jain temples.

The Shri Swaminarayan Mandir *was built in Nairobi in 1999 using 350 tonnes (385 tons) of yellow stone mined near Rajasthan in India and shipped to Kenya. It has an impressive interior of intricately carved wood.*

The Sikh gurdwara *at Makindu was built in 1926 by Sikh railway workers. Set in a peaceful patch of woodland about 160 km (100 miles) south of Nairobi on the Nairobi–Mombasa Highway, it still serves as a rest house for both pilgrims and occasional visitors to this popular site.*

Mombasa's Jain temple, *completed in 1963, was the first to be built outside India. The temple's dome is topped by a spire of gold and its doors are made of solid silver. Its interior is decorated with sculptures and figures of Jain deities.*

Music and Dance

Kenya's music was originally centred around chanting, drumming and dance, and it played a large role in such ceremonies as initiations and weddings. With the onset of Christianity, these musical traditions were largely replaced by gospel music. The 1950s saw the arrival of the electric guitar, and with it new genres of music and dance. These include Benga music, which has strong elements of social and political criticism, and Congolese pop music, with its distinctive rumba rhythm. Many groups from the Democratic Republic of the Congo made Nairobi their home, and their influence remains a key feature of Kenya's dance music. More recently, hip-hop and rap have become popular.

Popular Kenyan group, Gospel Fathers, at Kikwetu Musical Festival

DANCE IN KENYA

Most Kenyans enjoy dancing at ceremonies and church services. Young Kenyans prefer nightclubs, which are popular in Nairobi and Mombasa. Many hotels along the coast and in the national parks arrange traditional and contemporary dance and acrobatic performances by local troupes.

Acrobats *are very popular in Kenya, performing as roadside buskers and entertainers in hotels. Many travel as part of international professional troupes.*

The Sarakasi Trust *is the largest performing arts organisation in East Africa. It teaches a range of disciplines including acrobatics, cabaret, salsa, drumming and traditional and contemporary dance styles.*

Deep rhythmic chanting *and vertical leaps in the air are part of the* **Engilakinoto,** *a Maasai ceremony that conventionally followed a successful lion hunt.*

TRADITIONAL INSTRUMENTS

Kenya's wide variety of traditional instruments are made from a number of materials including wood, animal hide, horn and reed.

A nyatiti *is an eight-stringed instrument with a curved arm that is plucked. It is similar to a medieval lyre.*

A siwa *is a large curved, ornately carved flute capped with a bull's horn. It is used in Lamu during local festivities and events. Two siwas in Lamu Museum, one of brass and one of ivory, date from the 17th century and are thought to be the oldest musical instruments in East Africa.*

Drums *are mostly large and round with taut cow- or goat-hide skins. They can be played while seated or standing. On the coast, smaller drums are held under the arm and are rapped with a curved stick.*

MUSIC IN KENYA

Modern Kenyan music is the fusion of a number of different styles, including ethnic folk music, lively pop music from Central Africa, as well as eastern and Arabian sounds from the coast. Kenyans enjoy live music and there is no shortage of venues for large concerts in Nairobi and Mombasa.

Benga music *originated in Nairobi and is a mix of Luo folk music and modern instruments. It is characterised by vocals, bass rhythms, clear guitar riffs and percussion.*

The Kisima Music Awards, *held annually in Nairobi, are East Africa's equivalent of the Grammys. The awards night attracts thousands and is broadcast across Africa on television.*

Joseph Kamaru *is one of Kenya's most successful gospel singers. His earlier music made skilful use of Kikuyu proverbs and was often politically charged.*

The African Children's Choir, *comprising young orphaned children aged between 7 and 12, is assembled each year for a world tour of over 50 cities.*

Taarab *is a style of music on the coast that combines poetic Swahili lyrics and Arabian rhythms using percussion instruments and vocals. Modern* taarab *is similar to Bollywood movie music.*

Gospel music *has risen in popularity since the mid-90s. It is sung by large choirs and features African rhythms and melodies and European harmonic influences.*

UNBEATABLE

Kenya's 2002 election victory by Mwai Kibaki's National Rainbow Coalition (NARC) was largely driven by a single song. "Unbwogable", sung by the hip-hop duo Gidi Gidi Maji Maji,

Gidi Gidi at Festival Mundail in Holland

means unbeatable in Luo and was adopted by NARC as the party's campaign anthem. Written in three languages – Luo, English and Swahili – the song has lyrics that call for people to rise up and demand change.

Soukous music *originated in the Democratic Republic of the Congo. In Kenya, it is called Lingala. The music has upbeat danceable rhythms, and is usually accompanied by female dancers.*

Arts and Crafts

Painted gourd

Kenya's earliest art is found in caves and was made by ancient nomads. However, painting and other types of visual art were largely introduced by the colonialists. Body art and adornment are important among some of Kenya's people and emphasise social status as well as stages of initiation and rites of passage. The art of carving has been practised in Kenya for centuries and sculptors use indigenous wood, stone and metal to produce both functional and decorative items.

A display of handicrafts at the African Heritage Centre, Nairobi

Tribal masks *were originally used to ward off evil spirits and scare away enemies. Today, many are produced as decorative wall hangings.*

CARVING

Many carved items such as pots, neck pillows (wooden headrests), walking sticks and chests are used by Kenyans in everyday life. The Kamba people, who have long been known as skilled woodworkers, produce carved animals and masks, which are immensely popular. Carving on the coast is centred on the island of Lamu, where the local people have been influenced by Arab craftsmen to create a unique hybrid of styles.

Lamu's doors *are intricately patterned with carvings. In the Swahili tradition, the greater the wealth and social standing of the inhabitant of the house, the more elaborate the front door. Some date to the late 18th century and are inscribed with Koranic verses.*

Makonde ebony carvings *are black and brown or wholly black. With its origins in Tanzania, this contemporary art specialises in abstract and elongated human figures. A tree of life depicts an entire family in one striking single pose.*

STONE AND CLAY

Soapstone or Kisii stone, was originally carved into vessels as it holds water well. Today, it is fashioned into a wide variety of souvenirs. The quarrying, carving and polishing of the stone are all done by hand. Western Kenya's red earth provides clay to make pots, which are usually made by women using centuries-old methods of shaping, decorating and firing in charcoal ovens.

Clay pots *are used for carrying water, storing millet and cereals, as cooking utensils and even for keeping bees.*

Soapstone decorative boxes *are sculpted by the Gusii people. Designs are created by dyeing the stone with ink, paint, or shoe polish, then sealing the colour with beeswax and finally incising the surface in patterns, which allow the natural lighter colour of the stone to come through.*

TEXTILES AND WEAVING

Textiles produced in Kenya are usually worn as traditional dress *(see p28)*. Women wear two-piece sets of *kangas* as a wrapround skirt and shawl or scarf, while men on the coast wear cotton *kikoys*. Weaving, done by women, is most often used to make baskets, but palm leaves, dyed in shades of purple, are also woven into narrow strips and sewn together to make attractive sleeping mats, as well as place mats and coasters.

Woven baskets, *once made from fibres of baobab and wild fig trees, and nowadays from sisal, were traditionally carried by Kikuyu women behind their heads with the strap across their forehead.*

Batik, *an Indonesian-Malay word for the wax-resist dyeing of fabric, is characterised by deep rich colours and fine crinkly lines, which are the result of breaks in the layers of wax applied to the cloth. This technique arrived on the African coast during the Indian Ocean trade period.*

VISUAL ART

Painting on walls using natural pigments existed for centuries, as witnessed in the many rock paintings found in caves and archaeological sites all over Kenya. The development of painting on canvas, however, only began when foreign artists and missionaries arrived during the colonial era and influenced Kenyan artists to use this medium.

Gakunju Kaigwa's *sculpture,* Wings of Love *(1998), draws its inspiration from traditional and contemporary life in Kenya. The acclaimed artist makes detailed sculptures of people and animals.*

Jimmy Ogonga's *most famous sculpture,* Dancing with the Enemy *(2000), was created using jacaranda wood. As well as sculpture, Ogonga's art includes painting, film, printmaking and photography.*

Peter Beard's collages *of Kenya often feature elephants, crocodiles and rhinos. An avant garde American photographer, he was left an archive of photographs and journals by Karen Blixen (see p169); many feature in his collages.*

JOY ADAMSON'S ART

One of several portraits of Kenya's ethnic people, by Joy Adamson

One of colonial Kenya's best known names, Joy Adamson became famous for her memoir on hand-rearing a lioness named Elsa. Few people know she was also an accomplished self-taught artist and produced many paintings that document much of Kenya's flora. She was commissioned by the government to paint over 600 portraits of Kenya's tribes in their traditional dress. These now hang in Nairobi's State House and the National Museum *(see pp158–9)* and remain an important testament to Kenya's rich cultural history.

Kenyan Literature

In Kenya, the oldest way of passing on stories from one generation to the next is through the narration of (often moralistic) tales. Written literature, in Kenyan languages as well as English, began in the early 20th century when missionaries, and later colonialists, introduced formal education. Many of the white settlers became world-renowned authors, and much has been written about the events and characters of the colonial days. *Out of Africa* by Isak Dinesen – the pseudonym of Karen Blixen – is probably the best known such book about Kenya. Independence in the 1960s unleashed a wave of unrestricted Kenyan writing and today Kenya has literary associations and home-grown book awards that encourage contemporary writing.

The Man-Eaters of Tsavo featuring author J H Patterson on the cover

AFRICAN WRITING

Swahili prose and poetry date back to the early 18th century. The oldest known document in the language is "Utenzi wa Tambuka" (Story of Tambuka), an epic poem penned in a royal palace on Pate Island in 1728. It is about the Byzantine, Arab and Ottoman wars across Europe and Arabia from 628 to 1453. By the middle of the 19th century, the first Swahili dictionary had been compiled and Bible translated.

The first published writings by Kenyan authors were born out of the experience of colonialism and the struggle for independence. One of Kenya's best known authors from this time, Ngũgĩ wa Thiong'o, is also the first

Ngũgĩ wa Thiong'o's epic work *Wizard of the Crow*

East African author to have a novel published. His book, *Weep Not Child,* was published in 1964 and deals with how the lives of Kenya's Kikuyu people changed after independence. In the late 1970s, Ngũgĩ was imprisoned for a year because of his politically outspoken playwriting, of which the Moi government disapproved. In 2006, he published *Murogi wa Kagogo* (Wizard of the Crow), an epic novel written in the Kikuyu language about 20th-century dictatorship in developing countries. Six volumes long, it is the biggest book ever written in an African language.

Former Kenyan Culture Minister and United Nations Ambassador, Grace Ogot, has written several novels and short stories, many of which are set against the scenic backdrop of Lake Victoria and the traditions of the Luo people. Meja Mwangi, assistant director on the movie *Out of Africa*, is another prolific writer who is best known for his gritty urban tale, *Going Down River Road* (1976).

COLONIAL LITERATURE

With the arrival of the hunters and explorers in the mid-19th century, and later the white settlers, several books about

Writer Ernest Hemingway

their fearless escapades in the fledgling colony of Kenya were published. *The Man-Eaters of Tsavo* (see p181) is J H Patterson's account of his battle with a pair of maneless lions who were responsible for the deaths of a number of construction workers on the Uganda Railway (see p299) in 1898. In 1935, well-known American author Ernest Hemingway published *Green Hills of Africa*, based on a hunting safari he took in 1933 in the Chyulu and Tsavo regions, as well as at Lake Manyara in Tanzania. *Out of Africa* (1937) by Danish author Karen Blixen (see p169) depicts her life on a coffee farm from 1917 to 1931 and her relationship with the aristocratic big-game hunter Denys Finch Hatton. Blixen's book is as much a story of Kenya's wildlife and scenic beauty as it is of her emotional journey adapting to an isolated life.

Beryl Markham, a champion horse trainer, aviator and celebrated beauty, recounts her record-breaking solo flight across the Atlantic in *West with the Night* (1942). Elspeth Huxley's *Flame Trees of Thika* (1959), and the sequel *The Mottled Lizard* (1962), portray her life as a coffee grower's daughter in the early part of the 20th century on a farm that she describes as "a bit of El Dorado my father had been fortunate enough to buy in the bar of the Norfolk Hotel".

The colonial literary legacy was explored after Kenya's independence in James Fox's *White Mischief* (1980), dealing with Lord Erroll's murder in 1941 and the Happy Valley set of white settlers (*see p319*) and *The In-Between World of Vikram Lall* by M G Vassanji, winner of the 2003 Giller Prize, exploring the lives of Indian settlers in Kenya (*see p50*). Errol Trzebinski's *The Lives of Beryl Markham* (1994) and *The Life and Death of Lord Erroll* (2000) depict the same period.

CONTEMPORARY BOOKS

Former Italian socialite Kuki Gallmann's *I Dreamed of Africa* (1991) is a vivid account of her life on a ranch on Laikipia Plateau and her subsequent work in conservation. *My Kenya Days* (1994) provides a record of the adventurer Wilfred Thesiger's 30 years in Kenya from 1960, during which time he was an honorary game warden in the

The Italian author Kuki Gallmann, who wrote *I Dreamed of Africa*

northern frontier. John Le Carré's novel *The Constant Gardener* (2001) revolves around a British diplomat in Nairobi whose wife is murdered in Northern Kenya while investigating a drugs trial scandal. Bill Bryson's *African Diary* (2002) is an account of his travels around Kenya at the invitation of CARE International, the charity dedicated to working with local communities to eradicate poverty around the world.

WILDLIFE STORIES

Born Free (1960) is the story of Joy and George Adamson's (*see p333*) successful efforts at rehabilitating Elsa, an orphaned lion cub, into the wild. At the time, it brought a great deal of international

attention and focus to conservation issues in Africa. Other books from Joy and George followed, describing their crucial work with big cats in Kenya. In the last 40 years, Daphne Sheldrick (*see p161*) has written several books on her conservation work with elephants in Kenya, while Richard Leakey's *Wildlife Wars: My Battle to Save Kenya's Elephants* (2001) is an account of his extraordinary, almost warlike, battle with poachers during the late 1980s. Photographers Jonathan and Angela Scott have contributed to a number of wildlife and photography books including the spin-off books from the popular BBC *Big Cat Diaries*, which were all filmed in the Masai Mara.

Elsa being fed from a bottle by George and Joy Adamson

The film *Out of Africa* by Sydney Pollack

SCREEN ADAPTATIONS

Many epic stories set in Kenya have been played out on the big screen and film-makers have fallen in love with Kenya's intriguing colonial history, landscapes and animals. Films adapted from books include *Born Free* (1966), one of the greatest animal stories ever told; *Out of Africa* (1985), starring Meryl Streep and Robert Redford; and *I Dreamed of Africa* (2000), with Kim Basinger in the leading role. Also based on a book is *The Constant Gardener* (2005), starring Ralph Fiennes and Rachel Weisz. Some of it was filmed in Nairobi's Kibera slum as well as in dramatic locations in Northern Kenya. *To Walk With Lions* (1999) follows George Adamson's later life with his lions at Kora National Park and stars Richard Harris as the formidable man. The German-language film *Nowhere in Africa* (2001) is about a Jewish refugee family that escaped Germany for a new life on a Kenyan farm in the 1930s; it won the Oscar for Best Foreign Language Film. *The Flame Trees of Thika* and *Shadow on the Sun*, which is about Beryl Markham, have both been aired as television series.

KENYA THROUGH THE YEAR

Although Kenya is located on the equator, its seasons follow the southern hemisphere's pattern, with spring beginning in September, summer in December, autumn in March and winter in June. Reflecting this natural order is the country's yearly cycle of festivals and events which showcase both local and national cultures as well as the region's many natural wonders.

Dhow race, New Year's Day at Lamu

Owing to the fact that a good part of the population is Christian or Muslim, Christian holidays are observed throughout Kenya, while Islamic festivals are celebrated along the coast and in the northeast. The country also hosts several annual sporting and adventure activities that international visitors can participate in and combine with a safari or beach holiday.

Vintage aircraft display, Nairobi International Air Show

SPRING

The dry spring months from September to November offer good game viewing. The grass is short and wildlife congregates around waterholes. The skies remain clear for Nairobi's spectacular air show as well as a number of other outdoor events.

SEPTEMBER

Schweppes East African Concours d'Elegance (*last week*), Nairobi. Translating as "a gathering of elegance", this popular vintage car and motorcycle fair is held at Nairobi Racecourse. Many of the vehicles on display were used in the colonial years, going as far back as 1910.
Eid-ul-Fitr (*variable*), across Kenya. This Islamic festival falls at the end of the lunar month of Ramadan, when Muslims fast by day and feast by night. Festivities are accompanied by traditional Swahili *taraab* music and dancing (*see p33*).

OCTOBER

Nairobi International Air Show (*1st weekend*), Nairobi. Held at Wilson Airport by the Aero Club of East Africa, the show features fly-bys and air acrobatics by both modern jets and vintage planes.
Diwali (*Oct–Nov*), across Kenya. This Hindu "festival of light" is celebrated by Kenya's Asian community with plenty of fireworks.

NOVEMBER

Kitale Agricultural Show (*early Nov*), Kitale. This farming show takes place in a rich agricultural district. Livestock competitions, produce stands, demonstrations and muscial entertainment make for a lively excursion.
Kenya Music and Cultural Festival (*mid-Nov*), Nairobi. Held at the Kenya National Theatre, this festival showcases school groups from across the country performing theatre, indigenous music, dance, poetry, storytelling, acrobatics and games.
Lamu Cultural Festival (*mid-Nov*), Lamu. A 3-day event focusing on Swahili culture, with food, music, races, crafts and a bridal ceremony. Most activities take place at the waterfront or Lamu Fort.

SUMMER

The short rains begin at the end of November when brief afternoon thunderstorms are followed by bright sunshine. Christmas is a big celebration this time of year. It is also high season on the coast when holiday-makers from Europe take winter breaks.

DECEMBER

Painted statuettes at the Craft Fair

Craft Fair (*early Dec*), Nairobi. Held in time for Christmas shopping, this large craft fair sells home-made items from all over Kenya.
Islamic New Year (*variable*), across Kenya. The first day of Muharram, the first month in the Islamic calendar, is observed quietly with prayers.
Eid-ul-Haj (*variable*), across Kenya. The Islamic festival of the annual pilgrimage, or *haj*, to Mecca, this is held over 3 days of feasting in all Muslim communities.

JANUARY

New Year's Day Dhow Race
(1st Jan), Lamu. Only eight captains are invited to race, so winning is a great honour. Race day is one of skill and showmanship and celebrations last well into the night.

AUTUMN

March to May is the period of the long rains. Vegetation flourishes, providing a surplus of food for the grazers. Animals look their best, but roads become impassable in the wet and it is not usually the best time to go on either a safari or a beach holiday.

FEBRUARY

Kijani Kenya Music Festival
(Feb–Aug), across Kenya. Run by a non-profit organisation, this event features international performing artistes, including those from opera and ballet, to raise money for HIV/Aids and eco-projects.
Maulidi or Milad-un-Nabii Festival *(variable)*, Lamu. The Islamic celebration of Prophet Mohammed's birth is a 4-day event that draws Muslims from all over East Africa. It combines solemn prayer with popular entertainment such as donkey and dhow races, *bao* (a traditional board game) contests and performances of Swahili music and dance. Visitors are welcome but should show respect for local custom.

Muslim men and boys playing the drums at Maulidi, Lamu waterfront

MARCH

Kenya Open Golf Championship *(early Mar)*, Nairobi. Part of the European PGA Tour, the annual tournament is held on the beautiful course at Karen Golf and Country Club. Kenya has over 40 golf courses, making it a great golfing destination.
KCB Safari Rally *(variable)*, Rift Valley. One of the world's oldest and toughest rallies that dates back to 1953, this covers 725 km (450 miles) of open and dirt roads over 3 exciting days.

WINTER

The winter months are dry and not overwhelmingly hot, a good time for outdoor activities. A good number of international visitors arrive specifically to run the Lewa (Safaricom) Marathon. July and August are cool with dry, clear skies, and are therefore considered good months to climb Mount Kenya.

Stranded 4WD being heaved back to firmer terrain, Rhino Charge event

JUNE

Cricket season *(Jun–Feb)*, across Kenya. The long cricket season is dominated by league cricket. The Premier League, played on grass wickets, is considered the most prestigious.
Lewa (Safaricom) Marathon *(late Jun)*, Laikipia Plateau. This is a charity race held in aid of wildlife organisations. The event attracts 600–700 runners, both local and international, for the full and half marathon *(see p402)*. It is paced out on dirt roads and is the only marathon in the world to go through an area inhabited by wildlife.
Rhino Charge *(usually Jun)*, Laikipia Plateau. A gruelling 4WD off-road endurance event through rugged terrain of dense bush, ditches and boulders. The winner of the Rhino Charge is the team that manages to complete the course with the least distance covered, or as close to the path "as the crow flies".

AUGUST

International Camel Derby *(Aug/Sep)*, Maralal. Held over a weekend, this comprises a short amateur race, where camels and riders are assisted by a handler who runs alongside, and a more serious 42-km (26-mile) professional race. Anyone can participate, and for those who have never ridden a camel before it can be a hilarious experience.

The Climate of Kenya

Kenya lies on the equator, so daytime temperatures in most parts of the country are consistently warm all year round. It only really gets cool in winter months in the Central Highlands, and Mount Kenya is perennially snowcapped. The long rainy season usually lasts from March to May, and the short rainy season runs over November and December. While Kenyan safaris are available throughout the year, game viewing is best in the dry winter months from June to August and the warm months of September and October. Early morning game drives can get chilly. On the coast, temperatures soar from mid-December to mid-February.

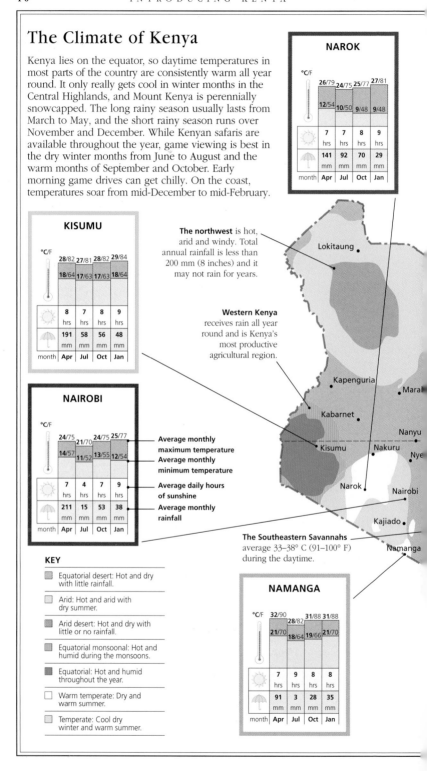

NAROK

°C/F			
26/79	24/75	25/77	27/81
12/54	10/50	9/48	9/48
7 hrs	7 hrs	8 hrs	9 hrs
141 mm	92 mm	70 mm	29 mm
Apr	**Jul**	**Oct**	**Jan**

KISUMU

°C/F			
28/82	27/81	28/82	29/84
18/64	17/63	17/63	18/64
8 hrs	7 hrs	8 hrs	9 hrs
191 mm	58 mm	56 mm	48 mm
Apr	**Jul**	**Oct**	**Jan**

The northwest is hot, arid and windy. Total annual rainfall is less than 200 mm (8 inches) and it may not rain for years.

Lokitaung

Western Kenya receives rain all year round and is Kenya's most productive agricultural region.

Kapenguria

Mara

Kabarnet

Nanyu

Kisumu   Nakuru

Nye

Narok

Nairobi

Kajiado

NAIROBI

°C/F			
24/75	21/70	24/75	25/77
14/57	11/52	13/55	12/54
7 hrs	4 hrs	7 hrs	9 hrs
211 mm	15 mm	53 mm	38 mm
Apr	**Jul**	**Oct**	**Jan**

Average monthly maximum temperature

Average monthly minimum temperature

Average daily hours of sunshine

Average monthly rainfall

The Southeastern Savannahs average 33–38° C (91–100° F) during the daytime.

Namanga

NAMANGA

°C/F			
32/90	28/82	31/88	31/88
21/70	18/64	19/66	21/70
7 hrs	9 hrs	8 hrs	8 hrs
91 mm	3 mm	28 mm	35 mm
Apr	**Jul**	**Oct**	**Jan**

KEY

- Equatorial desert: Hot and dry with little rainfall.
- Arid: Hot and arid with dry summer.
- Arid desert: Hot and dry with little or no rainfall.
- Equatorial monsoonal: Hot and humid during the monsoons.
- Equatorial: Hot and humid throughout the year.
- Warm temperate: Dry and warm summer.
- Temperate: Cool dry winter and warm summer.

MARSABIT

°C/F				
	35/95	33/91	35/95	36/97
	24/75	23/73	25/77	22/72
☀	9 hrs	9 hrs	10 hrs	10 hrs
☂	48 mm	19 mm	9 mm	8 mm
month	Apr	Jul	Oct	Jan

Drenched zebras huddling together as clouds loom over the Masai Mara

MERU

°C/F				
	23/73	22/72	23/73	25/77
	10/50	8/46	8/46	7/45
☀	7 hrs	4 hrs	7 hrs	9 hrs
☂	110 mm	60 mm	60 mm	10 mm
month	Apr	Jul	Oct	Jan

Moyale

Marsabit

Wajir

Dif

siolo

Equator

Meru

Garissa

Kitui

Hola

Lamu

Voi

Malindi

Mombasa

Northern Kenya's daytime temperatures can rise above 37° C (99° F), but rarely fall below 21° C (70° F) at night.

The Central Highlands, with peaks rising over 4,000 m (13,123 ft), are cooler than the rest of the country.

The Northern Coast has warm average temperatures of 35° C (95° F). Afternoon showers offer some relief during the rainy seasons.

0 km   150

0 miles   150

The coast is hot and humid throughout the year but the heat is tempered by cool sea breezes.

LAMU

°C/F				
	32/90	28/82	30/86	31/88
	26/79	23/73	24/75	24/75
☀	8 hrs	8 hrs	10 hrs	9 hrs
☂	135 mm	82 mm	37 mm	7 mm
month	Apr	Jul	Oct	Jan

MOMBASA

°C/F				
	30/86	27/81	29/84	31/88
	24/75	22/72	23/73	24/75
☀	8 hrs	7 hrs	9 hrs	8 hrs
☂	196 mm	89 mm	86 mm	25 mm
month	Apr	Jul	Oct	Jan

THE HISTORY OF KENYA

enya's history dates back to the emergence of mankind, as evidenced by humanoid fossils from 6 million years ago. Arabs and Persians reached the coast in the first millennium, while European explorers arrived in the early 19th century, mapping the way for British colonialism and the era of the white settlers in the first half of the 20th century. Charismatic leader Jomo Kenyatta negotiated independence in 1963, and Kenya remains a cosmopolitan and culturally rich nation today.

Archaeological remains from the Tugen Hills and Lake Turkana region suggest that early ape-like species lived in what is now Kenya about 4–6 million years ago. From evidence unearthed in the early 20th century, it was thought that these developed, about 1.4 to 2.8 million years ago, into the tool-making hominid *Homo habilis*. This species, until recently, was thought to have evolved into the more advanced *Homo erectus* that evolved into modern man. However, it is now suspected that *Homo habilis* did not precede *Homo erectus* after all but came to an evolutionary dead end. In 2001, near Lake Turkana, Maeve Leakey found the complete skull of *Homo erectus* within walking distance of the upper jaw of a *Homo habilis*. Both must have lived in the region at the same time, and are likely to have evolved from another, older common ancestor – a missing link that has not yet been found. By 10,000 BC, it is thought that early man had mastered making stone tools, discovered the use of fire,

Swahili door knocker

developed a basic language and formed communities organised around hunting and gathering.

From 2,000 BC, Cushitic-speaking pastroal nomads from Ethiopia who herded cattle and experimented with agriculture were the first of many migratory peoples to arrive in Kenya. They initially settled around Lake Turkana but later moved south, attracted by the high rainfall and good grazing in the highlands and Rift Valley. The Yaaku or Eastern Cushites followed 1,000 years later and again occupied much of central Kenya. Bantu-speaking groups from Central Africa and Nilotic-speaking groups from Southern Sudan followed between 500 BC and AD 500. Over time, the original hunter-gatherers became part of these new communities.

While the interior was marked by frequent tribal migrations, the coast was greatly influenced by Arabs, Egyptians and Persians, who originally came to the East African coast to trade. From AD 750, the first Arab seafarers arrived and introduced Islam to the coastal communities.

TIMELINE

6,000,000 BC	2,000,000 BC	5,000 BC	AD 1	AD 750

6,000,000 BC Families of apes begin evolving into the earliest ancestors of humans

2,000,000 BC Hominids begin making stone tools

10,000 BC Hunter-gatherers forage for food and hunt live animals

Hand axe

600 BC Egyptians explore the coast

2,000 BC Cushitic-speaking people arrive from Ethiopia

750 AD Arabs introduce Islam to the coast

500 BC Bantu and Nilote migrations start

AD 100–200 Coastal people live in village communities and forge iron

◁ A 19th-century illustration by artist Baraldi Severino of the Sultan of Malindi with his royal entourage, in 1498

The Cradle of Mankind

East Africa has long been considered the "Cradle of Mankind", with archaeological evidence still being uncovered in the region. Discoveries at the Olduvai Gorge in Tanzania, Lake Turkana in Kenya, Hadar in Ethiopia and the Kagera river in Uganda support Charles Darwin's theory that humankind evolved from apes. One species of yet unknown ape eventually evolved into *Homo sapiens* and it is generally believed that it was here that man stood upright. To prove Darwin's hypothesis, Mary and Louis Leakey began pioneering extensive excavations from the 1930s that established many facts about early life in the region.

Charles Darwin, *in his seminal book* On the Origins of Species, *introduced the theories of evolution and natural selection.*

KENYAN SITES

Fossils found around Lake Turkana and Koobi Fora suggest that humans first evolved in Kenya. Other archaeological finds around Lake Victoria and Rift Valley have provided much of the key evidence for human evolutionary studies.

The Millennium Man (Orrorin tugenensis), *about 6.5 million years old, was found in 2000 in the Tugen Hills. Some scholars suggest this could be the earliest known upright hominid.*

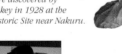

Stone axes *were discovered by Louis Leakey in 1928 at the Kariandusi Prehistoric Site near Nakuru.*

A 930,000-year-old fossilised skull *of a hominid was excavated by anthropologist Richard Potts at Olorgasailie. Its species, however, is unknown.*

Discoveries on the eastern shore of Lake Turkana also unearthed a significant yield of animal fossils.

KENYA'S DINOSAURS

Lake Turkana's ample fossil evidence indicates that the lake's shores were once teeming with wildlife, including prehistoric elephants and three-toed ancestors of the horse. The first scientific dinosaur expedition, undertaken in 2004, collected over 200 fossils dating to the Mesozoic era more than 200 million years ago. This provided the first concrete evidence that dinosaurs inhabited what is now Kenya before humans evolved in the region.

Elephant's fossil bones, Lake Turkana

Turkana Boy *was discovered by Richard Leakey's team near Lake Turkana in 1984. At 1.6 million years old these are believed to be the most complete* Homo erectus *remains found to date.*

EAST AFRICAN SITES

East Africa's most important archaeological site, Olduvai Gorge has yielded many fossils. The gorge was first visited by the Leakeys in 1931, when they found stone tools here. Other sites include Hadar in Ethiopia and Laetoli in Tanzania.

Nutcracker Man (Paranthropus boisei), *the Leakeys' first big find, in 1959, in the Olduvai Gorge, was so named due to its large molars. An early hominid, the fossil is 1.75 million years old.*

The Laetoli footprints, *about 3.6 million years old, were discovered in 1978 by Mary Leakey. Preserved in volcanic ash in the Olduvai Gorge, this is the earliest evidence of hominids walking upright.*

An impressive collection of Plio-Pleistocene hominids was discovered by Richard Leakey at Koobi Fora, starting in 1968.

Handyman, *dating back 1.4 million years, was discovered in the Olduvai Gorge in 1960. Bone fragments suggested it was a new species,* Homo habilis, *an evolved hominid capable of carving stone tools.*

Lucy, *a female hominid dating 2.8 million years, was found in Ethiopia in 1974. The team, led by American paleoanthropologist Donald Johanson, established it was a new species,* Australopithecus afarensis.

HOMINID FOSSIL SITES

1 Kariandusi, Kenya *(see p272)*
2 Koobi Fora, Kenya
3 Lake Turkana, Kenya *(see pp352–3)*
4 Olorgasailie, Kenya *(see p170)*
5 Tugen Hills, Kenya *(see p288)*
6 Hadar, Ethiopia
7 Engaruka, Tanzania
8 Laetoli, Tanzania
9 Olduvai Gorge, Tanzania
10 Kagera river, Uganda

HUMAN EVOLUTION

Orrorin tugenensis, who lived between 6.1 and 5.8 million years ago, is thought to be the second oldest known hominid ancestor that is possibly related to modern human beings.

Paranthropus boisei, an early hominid, lived from 2.6 to about 1.2 million years ago. It is the largest of the *Paranthropus* species.

Australopithecus afarensis, who lived between 3.9 and 2.9 million years ago, is thought to be ancestral to both the *Australopithecus* and *Homo* genera.

Australopithecus africanus, who lived between 2–3 million years ago, split into two lines, *Australopithecus robustus* and *Homo habilis*.

Homo habilis, the first of the genus *Homo*, and the least similar to humans, evolved 2.5–2 million years ago, when it diverged from the *Australopithecines*.

Homo rudolfensis lived around 1.9–1.6 million years ago. It is not confirmed whether another *habilis* or a separate species, *Homo georgicus*, evolved between *Homo habilis* and *Homo erectus*.

Homo erectus evolved 1.8 million–70,000 years ago and was the first hominid to walk upright.

Homo antecessor lived from 1.2 million–50,000 years ago.

Homo heidelbergensis lived about 800,000–300,000 years ago.

Homo rhodesiensis, first discovered in 1921, is believed to have lived around 300,000–125,000 years ago.

Homo neanderthalensis is thought to have existed around 250,000–30,000 years ago.

Homo sapiens, or modern man, is thought to have evolved around 250,000 years ago.

SWAHILI CIVILISATION

It was the monsoon winds that blow along the East African coast from the northeast from December to March and from the southeast from April to November that brought the first sailors to East Africa on ocean-going dhows. While traders from many different nations visited the coast, it was the Arabs who stayed, and from the 8th century they established a string of powerful commercial settlements. These were founded on trade that was carried across the Indian Ocean to as far away as China. Leopard skins, tortoise shells, ivory, rhinoceros horns, gold and slaves were exported from Africa in exchange for metal tools, utensils, swords and daggers. When commodities were not traded, early currencies of beads and cowrie shells were used. Over time, contact between the Arabs and indigenous Bantu cultures on the coast created

Chinese porcelain found at Gedi Ruins

the inimitable Swahili culture, in which the characteristics of both were assimilated, and which was marked by its own unique language and a devotion to Islam. Over the next few centuries Swahili civilisation flourished, and by the 15th century Mombasa, Malindi, Pate and Lamu in Kenya, and Zanzibar, Pemba and Kilwa in modern-day Tanzania had developed into prosperous ports with grand houses and several prolific mosques.

THE PORTUGUESE CONQUEST

The Arabs continued to dominate the coast until they were challenged by the arrival of the Portuguese. Explorer Vasco da Gama, who had been ordered by Portuguese King John to round the Cape of Africa and find the sea route to India, landed at Malindi in 1498. Over the next few decades, more fleets of Portuguese ships arrived, and by 1510, most of the Swahili cities on the coastline south of Mogadishu (in present-day Somalia) had been ransacked. By 1512, Malindi had become the northern headquarters of the Portuguese on the East African coast. Later, in 1593, this was moved to Mombasa, when the Portuguese built Fort Jesus as a garrison, and its ramparts and battlements confirmed their dominance over the coast. Throughout the 17th century, the Arabs attempted to re-establish control over their outposts. Envious of the Portuguese possessions in East Africa, the Sultan of Muscat in Oman, Seif bin Sultan, incited the local Arabs to fight the Portuguese in a series of confrontations. The

Pate Ruins, a predominant 15th-century Swahili settlement along the coast

TIMELINE

800 The first rag and coral structures built in the early coastal trading centres	1000 Cattle-raising and possibly cereal-growing are introduced	
		Gedi Ruins
800	**1000**	**1200**
900 Islamic Arabs occupy Mombasa and other seaports	1200 Swahili culture and language become dominant along the coast	1200–1300 The palace and mosque built at Gedi

A 19th-century lithograph showing Vasco da Gama's exploration of the coast in 15th century

Portuguese downfall finally came in 1698 after a 33-month siege of Fort Jesus. The subsequent Portuguese expulsion from Kilwa and Pemba in 1699 virtually ended their rule in East Africa north of Mozambique, and by 1720 the last remaining Portuguese garrison had left the coast for good.

OMANI RULE

After the Arab victory at Fort Jesus in 1698, the coast fell under the jurisdiction of Muscat but there was a series of conflicts between the local Arabs and the Omanis until the Swahili settlements were finally unified under the rule of Omani Sultan Seyyid Sa'id from 1806 to 1856. He was in control of a profitable slave trade, and moved the capital of his sultanate from Muscat to Zanzibar in 1832. For the first time the Arabs were venturing into the interior of East Africa to capture slaves, who were sold through the slave market in Zanzibar. However, by the early 1800s, the anti-slave lobby in Europe

Omani dagger, 17th century

was gathering momentum, and in 1822 Seyyid Sa'id signed the Moresby Treaty, which deemed it illegal to sell slaves to subjects of Christian countries including Britain and the US. In 1840, the British established a consulate at the sultan's court in Zanzibar in order to monitor the treaty. This casual negotiation marked the beginning of European influence in East Africa. In 1845, Seyyid Sa'id reluctantly signed the Hamerton Treaty, which forbade all slave trading by sea, and after years of pressure, slavery was banned altogether in 1873. Meanwhile, missionaries arrived to lend their support for the abolition of slavery, and to chart the interior at the same time. In 1846, Johann Ludwig Krapf and Johannes Rebmann, two German missionaries, were the first Europeans to venture into the interior of what is now Kenya. Rebmann was the first white man to lay eyes on Kilimanjaro in 1848, and Krapf the first to see the twin peaks of Mount Kenya in 1849.

Hand-coloured engraving by S Hollyer of explorer John H Speke with Lake Victoria in the background

EXPLORATION OF THE INTERIOR

By the mid-19th century, British explorers had ventured inland and the likes of David Livingstone, H M Stanley and Richard Burton mapped much of the East African interior. In 1858, John Hanning Speke discovered the source of the River Nile on what is today the Ugandan side of Lake Victoria. These expeditions revealed a wealth of resources. In 1883, Britain's Royal Geographical Society dispatched Joseph Thomson, a Scottish geologist and naturalist, to the region and with the exception of the northern deserts, he charted almost all of what is today Kenya. His adventurous journey was documented in the 1884 book *Through Masailand*. He travelled from Kilimanjaro across country to Lake Naivasha, then continued up the Rift Valley, climbed the Aberdares, which he named after the then president of the Royal

Count Samuel Teleki von Szek

Geographical Society, and passed Mount Kenya, Lake Baringo and Mount Elgon before returning to the coast via Lake Victoria and the western plains. In 1885, the Austro-Hungarian Count Samuel Teleki de Szek and Austrian naval officer and explorer Ludwig von Höhnel reached Lake Turkana, which they named Lake Rudolph after Austria's crown prince. In the 1890s, Americans Arthur Donaldson Smith and William Astor Chanler surveyed the Tana river and northeastern bush. The land that was to be Kenya was thus mapped out.

THE SCRAMBLE FOR AFRICA

The reports sent back to Europe by these early explorers stoked imperial interests, and Africa was seen as ripe with potential and there for the taking. The large continent seemingly had plentiful natural and mineral resources such as gum, palm oil and copper that could be utilised in Europe as it entered the grimy years of the industrial revolution, whereas Africa was seen as a market for manufactured goods made in Europe's factories. During the carve up of Africa, often dubbed the Scramble for Africa, the European powers laid claim to almost all African territories, and most of these claims were settled at the Berlin Conference of 1884. France claimed the majority of western Africa, Belgium obtained the Congo region, Portugal got Mozambique and Angola, and Britain and Germany received the bulk of southern and eastern Africa. Africans were not invited to attend the conference and did not get sovereignty over their land.

TIMELINE

1858 John Hanning Speke discovers the source of the River Nile

An English ship enforcing the abolition of the slave trade

1873 Slavery deemed illegal in East Africa

1850   1860   1870

1854 Krapf produces a rough map of the interior showing an inland sea – Lake Victoria

Johann Ludwig Krapf

1862 Ahmed Fumoluti al-Nabahani declares himself Sultan of Witu, which briefly becomes an independent state, "Swahililand"

1869 Opening of the Suez Canal increases British accessibility to East Africa

BRITAIN'S SHARE

In London, gunboat diplomacy was avoided when Britain and Germany agreed to share their eastern African territory as far inland as the Great Lakes. The Germans got mainland Tanzania, and the British got the concession for Kenya and Uganda. Britain offered the tiny island of Heligoland in the North Sea, in return for the British protectorate over Zanzibar. Surprisingly Germany agreed, but much later benefited from the deal as Heligoland served as an invaluable naval base for the Germans during both world wars. On the coast, the Sultan of Zanzibar, through treaties leasing his territories in exchange for an annual fee, relinquished power to the British.

Officials of the Imperial British East Africa Company signing a treaty with the Kikuyu people

EAST AFRICAN PROTECTORATE

In Mombasa, in 1887, Britain set up the Imperial British East Africa Company, which administered the new East African Protectorate. The company produced its own money and treaty documents, on which were the seal of the British crown. Between 1888 and 1892, through territorial agreements with local chiefs in exchange for British authority, the East Africa Company established outposts throughout the country and cut a 500-km (310-mile) long dirt road inland from Mombasa to a swampy, flat area called Ewaso Nyarobi (Place of Cold Water), which later became Nairobi. With the colony growing, administration of the protectorate was transferred from the company to the Foreign Office in 1895, and the British opened up the interior further when work on the Uganda Railway from Mombasa commenced in 1896.

A 19th-century lithograph depicting Mombasa coast captured by British cruisers in 1875

British lay claim over Africa

1884 European nations lay claim over African territories

1887 The British negotiate a concession of the Zanzibar sultan's territory for a 50-year period

1895 The British government takes over present-day Kenya

380 | 1890 | 1900

1883 Joseph Thomson is the first European to travel to Maasai country

1889–90 The Imperial British East Africa Company employs army officer Fredrick Lugard to survey a new route from Mombasa to Uganda

1897 The Imperial British East Africa Company negotiates treaties with local chiefs

Lions attacking railway workers' camps in 1898, a 19th-century illustration by W R Stott

THE UGANDA RAILWAY

As Britain's endeavours grew in the interior, the only way to supply the outposts was to build a railway from the coast to Uganda. To help build the railway, the British imported skilled labourers from India, many of whom stayed on in East Africa to form the region's large Asian community. The railway, dubbed the Iron Snake by Africans, was called the Lunatic Line *(see p299)* by a cautious parliament back in Britain because of its tremendous cost of £5 million and the incredibility of its success. Work began in 1896, and 845 km (525 miles), 43 stations and 1,200 bridges later, the railway arrived in Port Florence (now Kisumu) at Lake Victoria in 1901, which at that time was part of Uganda. Not only was it an amazing feat in the history of railway construction but also a long and hazardous task where every conceivable problem arose. Crossing the Rift Valley escarpments was a major technical problem and work was held up at Tsavo for almost a year by two man-eating lions that killed scores of railway workers.

Termites feasted on sleepers, sleeping sickness caused by tsetse flies decimated herds of oxen used to haul material and many workers fell ill or died from malaria. Nevertheless, the railway was hailed as a success and opened up the region to the rest of the world.

GROWTH OF A COLONY

By 1899 the railway had reached the foot of the Kenyan highlands where a camp and depot were established in readiness for the challenge presented ahead by the technically difficult Rift Valley. The site was also chosen because of its network of rivers and for its elevation, as at 1,661 m (5,450 ft) temperatures were too low for the malaria mosquito to survive. The railway's administrative offices were moved here from Mombasa and homes built for the staff, which in turn attracted an influx of Asian merchants to supply goods and services to the railway workforce. Nairobi was born, and by 1905 it had become the seat of the British East

The last peg of the Uganda Railway from Mombasa being driven in at Port Florence

TIMELINE

1898 Construction of the Uganda Railway is delayed in Tsavo; two lions kill 135 railway workers

1899 Railway reaches the foot of the Kenyan highlands

1903 Lord Delamere is one of the first of tens of thousands of white settlers that arrive in Kenya up until the 1950s

1907 A Legislative Council is established with Lord Delamere as one of the settler members

| 1895 | 1900 | 1905 | 1910 |

1901 Railway arrives in Kisumu at Lake Victoria

1902 The border between Kenya and Uganda is adjusted; Kisumu is now in Kenya

1905 Nairobi becomes the capital of the British East Africa Protectorate

Nairobi, 1900s

Africa Protectorate. In 1920, Kenya, named after the territory's highest mountain, was declared a crown colony run by a governor and a Legislative Council, with Nairobi as its capital. Consequently, all ethnic groups were subject to colonial rules and lost their political independence.

Karen Blixen, the famed coffee planter and writer with her Scottish hounds, near Nairobi

WHITE SETTLERS

The railway laid down the infrastructure that opened up the fertile interior. The combination of a pleasant climate and good quality land made the Central Highlands an ideal environment for dairy farming and to grow tea, coffee, tobacco and other cash crops. A call went out to all corners of the British Empire for people to settle in Kenya and so the era of the White Highlands began. One of the first to arrive was British peer Lord Delamere, who acquired large tracts of land in the Rift Valley and was followed by adventurous farmers, mostly from his home territory of Lancashire, who also staked their claims. By 1912 the population of white settlers stood at 3,000 and by the 1930s more than 30,000 of them lived in Kenya. By then a third of the colonial government's revenue was generated from duties on settlers' produce and their goods imported into Kenya. Perhaps the most famous of the settlers were author Karen Blixen, of *Out of Africa* fame, and the Happy Valley set *(see p319)*, a group of British aristocrats who led decadent lifestyles in Kenya during the 1930s, and became embroiled in the mysterious murder of Lord Erroll in 1941.

Kikuyu farmers working on colonial fields

LAND ACQUISITION

New legislation on land tenure favoured the white settlers and they were granted prime agricultural land, while the Africans were herded into native reserves and formally dispossessed of their land, with the Maasai and Kikuyu suffering the greatest losses. The resentment by Africans of colonial rule grew deeper with every acre lost, and so the struggle for independence began. From the early 1920s, increasing numbers of Kenyans, led by the Kikuyu, formed political groups whose primary focus was the return of their land. The first of these was the East African Association founded in Nairobi in 1921 by Harry Thuku, which campaigned to end the *kipande* (identity card) system. However, this was short-lived – Thuku was arrested for his political activity in 1922, and in the demonstrations that followed 25 Africans were shot dead by both police and white civilians. This was the first challenge to the colonial regime.

World War I British troops

1915 African males told to carry identity cards when they leave their native reserves	1918 After World War I, farms are sold to white war veterans for nominal prices	1921 The East African Association is founded in Nairobi by Harry Thuku	
1915		**1920**	**1925**
1914 During World War I, a quarter of the 200,000 Africans recruited by the British die in battle	1920 Kenya is declared a crown colony administered by a British governor	1922 Thuku is arrested, then exiled without charge or trial to the Northern Frontier Province	

Kikuyu tribe members held in a camp by the British government during the Mau Mau Rebellion

ORGANISED RESISTANCE

The East African Association changed its name in 1924 to the Kikuyu Central Association (KCA), and former Nairobi water meter reader Jomo Kenyatta became its secretary in 1927. After failing to get Nairobi's Legislative Council to listen to the grievances of the African people about land issues, he sailed to Britain in 1929 to present the case to the colonial offices of parliament. He returned to London again in 1931, where he remained in exile, campaigning for the Kenyan people until 1946.

Although Britain made a small attempt to appease African protest by appointing the first black Kenyan to the Legislative Council in 1944, they were not prepared for the thousands of soldiers who returned to Kenya after World War II. These war veterans were empowered by new influences they had encountered overseas and angry that they had given their lives and labour on behalf of the British in yet another World War. Yet, even by 1945, their rights in Kenya had not improved. Political and ethnic factions mushroomed and the time was ripe for Kenyatta to return from exile to give a common voice to these concerns under the banner of the new Kenya African Union (KAU). The land issue was paramount – by 1948, 1.25 million Kikuyu were restricted to 5,200 sq km (2,000 sq miles), while 30,000 settlers occupied 31,000 sq km (12,000 sq miles). By 1953, almost half of all Kikuyu had no land claims at all. Thousands migrated into the cities in search of work, and Nairobi's population doubled between 1938 and 1952. The results were worsening poverty and unemployment.

MAU MAU REBELLION

Many Africans began to think that freedom from colonial rule could not be achieved by peaceful means. From 1947, various ethnic groups joined forces under the Kikuyu-dominated

Rebels renouncing their ties to the Mau Mau by licking the blood of a goat off sticks held by a shaman

TIMELINE

Jomo Kenyatta, England, 1937

1927 Kenyatta becomes secretary of the Kikuyu Central Association

1931 Kenyatta goes to England where he remains in exile until 1946

1945 In WW II Britain uses Kenya as a base for operations in Ethiopia

1925	1930	1935	1940	1945

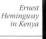

Ernest Hemingway in Kenya

1933 American writer Ernest Hemingway visits Kenya and writes some of his most famous works

1944 Kenya African Union (KAU) formed

1947 Kenyatta becomes KAU leader

Mau Mau banner and swore oaths that they were ready to fight and die for their rights. The violent Mau Mau Rebellion began in earnest in 1952. White settlers and thousands of Africans who collaborated with the white farmers or sympathised

Jomo Kenyatta being sworn in as Kenya's first president

with the government were attacked by Mau Mau gangs. In late 1952, Jomo Kenyatta and six of his colleagues were arrested and sentenced to 7 years imprisonment for supposedly inciting the Mau Mau. A state of emergency was declared in 1952 and troops were brought in to suppress the violence. By the end of 1954, the British had herded 77,000 Kikuyu into concentration camps. The loss of life among the white settlers was perhaps about 100 people; the main victims were some 2,000 other Kikuyu who refused to support the cause and were killed as collaborators, and the Mau Mau themselves, who lost 11,000 people. The crisis neared its end in 1957, when most of the leading Mau Mau leaders were captured in Nyeri. The state of emergency was lifted in 1959, though pockets of fighters remained in the forests until 1963.

INDEPENDENCE

Despite its victory over the Mau Mau, Britain was now reluctant to hang on to an unstable colony. It began to concede political power and give Kenyans self-government, and in 1957, 25 African, 15 Asian and five Arab members were elected to the Legislative Council. The ban on indigenous people growing coffee

was lifted, which led to a dramatic rise in the income of small farmers over the next 10 years. By 1959, freehold land titles in large numbers were issued to Africans, mostly on land of white settlers who had left during the Mau Mau Rebellion, and a campaign was underway to employ landless people. By 1960 Kenya's first African political parties were formed to take part in the developing political process. While still in prison, Kenyatta was elected president of the new Kenya African National Union (KANU), a successor to KAU, which was formed by Tom Mboya and Oginga Odinga. Kenyatta was released in 1961 and went to Lancaster House in London for talks, and the path to full independence was opened. In elections in May 1963 KANU won the majority of seats and at midnight on 12 December 1963, Kenya became independent. In 1964, Kenyatta became president of the new republic and Kenya joined the Commonwealth.

Jomo Kenyatta along with Tom Mboya and Oginga Odinga on a motorcade, Nairobi, 1964 elections

Kenyatta being taken for trial at Kapenguria

1952 Kenyatta imprisoned for 7 years; Mau Mau Rebellion begins

1961 Kenyatta assumes presidency of KANU

1963 Kenya becomes independent; Kenyatta becomes the prime minister

| 1950 | 1955 | 1960 | 1965 |

1955 Africans allowed to form political parties

1960 Kenya African National Union formed

Members of the newly elected government

1964 Republic of Kenya formed; Kenyatta becomes president and Odinga vice president

THE KENYATTA YEARS

Charismatic and pragmatic, Jomo Kenyatta ruled even-handedly, and in his inaugural address he invited all Kenyans to work at nation-building. To diffuse any lingering tribal tensions, he chose his first cabinet from across the ethnic divide to balance all interests in the new government, and he managed to convince the white settlers of his faith in an undivided multiracial Kenya. The first years of the new republic were dominated by restructuring and rebuilding, and the British government funded a programme of land purchases that resettled landless Africans on farms – a scheme that continued for some years at the cost of millions of pounds.

Kenyan currency depicting President Daniel arap Moi

Kenyatta's term featured rapidly improving infrastructure and unprecedented growth in the economy. In the 1970s, Nairobi saw an upsurge of high-rise buildings as foreign investment moved in. The Nairobi–Mombasa Highway was rebuilt, the international airport in Nairobi was extended, the national airline was established, new schools and hospitals were built and large increases in tea and coffee production oiled the country's economy. However, having suffered from ill health since the previous year, the greatly admired Kenyatta died in 1978 and was succeeded by his vice president, Daniel arap Moi.

THE MOI YEARS

Despite having success in improving infrastructure and social welfare, Moi, unlike his predecessor, led an autocratic, authoritarian and repressive government. He stayed in power for 24 years with little tolerance of any form of opposition. After swiftly crushing an attempted coup in 1982 he went on to expel critics from his government and detain opposition leaders. In 1987, he changed the constitution to extend his presidential powers, which included the provision to sack judges if he so wished. By the 1990s, Kenya was floundering economically, there were ominous outbreaks of ethnic violence in the Rift Valley, which left thousands of Kikuyu and Luo dead, and the nation's troubles were compounded by evidence of widespread corruption. The late 1990s witnessed frequent demonstrations for democracy and change, which were more often than not suppressed violently by the authorities.

Kenyatta, Mboya and Kibaki rejoicing over their party's victory in elections

TIMELINE

	1978 Kenyatta dies in office and is succeeded as president by Daniel arap Moi	**1982** Kenya is declared a one-party state by the National Assembly		**1992** Moi is re-elected in multiparty elections; foreign observers report that KANU manipulated the election
1974 Kenyatta re-elected				
1970	**1975**	**1980**	**1985**	**1990**
		1982 Army suppresses air force coup attempt		**1991** Multiparty political system is reintroduced

Women mourning at Kenyatta's funeral

In the 2002 presidential elections, Moi unsuccessfully promoted Uhuru Kenyatta, the son of Kenya's first president, as his successor, but people were ready for change and looked towards the opposition. In the election KANU was opposed by the National Alliance of Rainbow Coalition (NARC), a coalition of 15 parties that had joined forces with a faction which had broken away from KANU. NARC won in a landslide victory, and Moi's former vice president Mwai Kibaki was elected president by a large majority.

Kenyan President Mwai Kibaki and opposition leader Raila Odinga after signing a power-sharing deal

THE KIBAKI YEARS

Initially, Kenya was awash with optimism and the new government had some early successes. However, the popularity of Kibaki's government was short-lived, as it failed to end endemic corruption, revive the country's stalled economy and deliver a new constitution. In 2005, Kibaki held a public referendum on the draft of a new constitution, which the public rejected. Kibaki responded to this by sacking his entire cabinet, to which people reacted angrily. Elections were held at the end of 2007 and Kibaki's main contender was Raila Odinga, son of Kenyatta's first vice president Oginga Odinga, of the Orange Democratic Movement (ODM). However, disputed election results, which initially had Odinga as the legitimate winner and then Kibaki as the leader, led to a violent reaction across the country and several hundred deaths.

International mediators stepped in and by mid-2008 a power agreement was negotiated placing Kibaki as president and Odinga as prime minister.

On 4 August 2010 Kenyans voted overwhelmingly "yes" in a referendum over the adoption of a long-awaited new constitution to improve good governance and accountability.

Kenyatta meeting his supporters post exile

JOMO KENYATTA

Widely regarded as the founder of modern Kenya, or Baba wa Taifa, which means "father of the nation", Kenyatta was born Kamau wa Ngengi in 1889. In the 1920s, Kenyatta adopted this new name, Swahili for "the light of Kenya". He studied economics in Moscow and anthropology in London in the 1930s, and lobbied for Kikuyu land rights during his long exile from Kenya between 1931 and 1946. In 1938, he wrote *Facing Mount Kenya*, an anthropological book about the Kikuyu people. Although not without criticism, he presided over the bloody transition to independence, and for 15 years held his country's fractious tribes together and earned respect for his humanity and statesmanship throughout the world. In later years, up until his death in 1978, he was also affectionately known as *mzee* (old man).

| 1997 Moi wins a further term in widely-criticised elections | 2001 Ethnic violence culminates in clashes in Nairobi's Kibera slum | 2004 Wangari Maathai wins the Nobel Peace Prize | | 2008 Violent clashes across Kenya; Kibaki and Odinga sign power agreement |
| | | | | 2010 Kenyans vote in favour of a new constitution, gaining a bill of rights |

Wangari Maathai

1995	2000	2005	2010	2020

| 1998 Bomb explodes at US Embassy in Nairobi, killing 218 people and injuring thousands | 2002 Mwai Kibaki wins a landslide victory over KANU rival Uhuru Kenyatta | 2003 Government introduces free primary education | 2009 10 million Kenyans face food shortage after drought in Northern Kenya |

A lion gazing over the Mara plains ▷

WILD KENYA

THE SAFARI EXPERIENCE

Some are inspired by the liberating sense of space associated with Kenya's endless plains. Others are overwhelmed by the quality of time-stood-still that seems to inhabit this dusty wilderness. Above all, one cannot help but be captivated by the assortment of wonderful creatures that walk and breathe in this most untrammelled and ancient of landscapes.

Kenya prides itself on being the original home of the safari, a term that is derived from a Swahili word meaning journey, and that came to be associated with trophy hunting expeditions popularised by the likes of Karen Blixen, Hemingway and Finch-Hatton. Sadly, these earliest gun-toting safaris contributed greatly to the demise of East Africa's wildlife, so that by the end of the colonial era a large percentage of the once free-ranging herds were concentrated in state-run wildlife and forest reserves – precursors to the network of national parks and reserves that forms the cornerstone of Kenya's safari industry today.

Dwindling wildlife numbers, increased conservation awareness and the new influx of visitors brought about by the jet age meant that by the end of the 1960s, the hunting safari was largely a thing of the past. Visitors to Kenya arrived not with guns and bullets but with cameras, ushering in the era of the photographic safari. Today, the core components of a safari, that is, the landscapes and wildlife, remain little changed since the 1970s. The industry, however, has diversified greatly, so that accommodation might range from rudimentary camping or tin-roof huts to 100-room monolithic hotels and eco-friendly tented camps that exude safari chic.

Photographing from a 4WD

A legacy of the colonial hunting fraternity is the term used to describe the quarry it considered most dangerous – the Big Five, comprising the lion, leopard, elephant, rhino and buffalo. Sighting them is regarded a virtual rite of passage on safari, and Kenya certainly excels when it comes to this goal. However, be it antelopes locking horns or a dung beetle rolling a ball or widow-birds displaying their plumage, the African bush is a place of limitless adventure and wonder.

Camping in the wilderness, Chyulu Hills National Park

◁ A leopard saunters past a safari vehicle, Samburu National Reserve

SAFARI ACTIVITIES

The most popular activity on safari are daytime game drives, although in some cases it is also possible to explore the bush by boat or balloon, or on foot, usually in the company of a ranger or guide. Whatever the activity, a typical day on safari – unlike most other holidays – will start early. The African bush is at its most scintillating in the hour or two immediately after sunrise, and the earliest

Balloon safari over the Mara

possible start is recommended. This is when secretive nocturnal predators such as leopard or serval are most likely to be encountered, while more conspicuous species such as lion and spotted hyena tend to be most active before the heat of the day kicks in. Other advantages of an early start are the cooler temperatures, the higher level of avian activity and the often sumptuous photographic light.

GAME DRIVES

A typical day on safari is structured around a 3- to 5-hour game drive in the morning and a shorter afternoon drive, returning to camp in between for a leisurely lunch and siesta or splash in the pool. Visitors who want to explore further afield, or need to travel between lodges, will find a full-day drive more appropriate. For those who want a really early start, or who plan to stay out all day, most lodges will provide a packed breakfast on request.

Driver-guides in Kenya can be highly variable in skill. Many have worked as urban drivers or mechanics before moving into the lucrative tourism industry. This technical background can be reassuring when an engine starts grumbling in the middle of the bush, but it also means that a high proportion of driver-guides have little interest in wildlife or affinity for the bush. Higher tips ensure more active participation from the driver-guides, but the onus is

on the individual safarigoer when it comes to emphasising any specific interests or dislikes to the driver-guide, and a proactive role is encouraged when it comes to wildlife spotting, route planning, bird identification and deciding on places for photographic stops.

ON FOOT

There is no more exciting way of seeing wildlife than on foot. Sensibly, however, Kenya Wildlife Service (KWS) has made it illegal for visitors to leave their vehicles in national parks that harbour dangerous wildlife, unless they are at a lodge, rest camp, entrance gate or other designated spots. By contrast, many private reserves and concessions encourage guests to join a guided game walk, which makes for a far more invigorating experience than a game drive, capable of transforming an otherwise relatively mundane sighting into something positively inspirational. Exploring the bush on foot exposes a

Raised wooden walkway at the Safari Walk, Nairobi National Park

wealth of sensory stimuli – sounds, smells and physical textures – that tend to be lost within the confines of a vehicle. Walking with an articulate and knowledgeable guide can greatly enhance one's appreciation of the intricacies and minutiae of the bush, whether it is the traditional medical uses of trees, the opportunity to identify otherwise inconspicuous birds and butterflies, the gigantic spider webs that hang from the branches or a series of S-shaped ripples left by an undulating snake on sandy soil. Several Kenyan parks also offer the opportunity to walk unguided among large wildlife. In conventional game-viewing terms, the pick of these is undoubtedly Hell's Gate National Park *(see pp270–71)*, which has a spectacular setting and supports high densities of impala, zebra, buffalo, giraffe and gazelle, and even the odd large predator. Kakamega Forest National Reserve *(see pp294–7)*, Saiwa Swamp

Minibuses with pop-up roofs on a game drive, Amboseli National Park

National Park *(see p290–91)*
and Mount Kenya National
Park *(see pp322–3)* are also
very pedestrian friendly, and
even the larger and more
popular reserves have a few
sites that are explorable on
foot – Tsavo West National
Park's Mzima Springs area
(see p187), for instance, or
Amboseli National Park's
Observation Hill *(see p194)*.

While most animals are
fairly indifferent to the attire
and actions of safarigoers in
vehicles, they are less relaxed
with pedestrians. Persistent
chatter is therefore a strict
no-no, and it is a good idea
to wear neutral colours and
avoid wearing strong perfume
or aftershave. Trousers, socks
and solid shoes will provide
good protection against bites
and thorns, while a hat and
sunblock will help protect
against direct sunlight. As it is
more difficult to approach
wildlife closely on foot than
in a vehicle, binoculars are
more useful than a camera.

BALLOONS AND BOATS

Although not widely available
in Kenya, balloon and boat
safaris both present a unique
perspective on the bush. The
most popular site for balloon
trips is the Masai Mara Game
Reserve *(see pp262–5)*, where
they can be arranged – for a
hefty price – at most lodges.
All balloon excursions leave
before dawn, often accompanied by spectacular sunrises,

A pod of hippo swimming close to a motorboat on Lake Baringo

and the sensation of drifting
above the open plains and
the immense herds they
support is truly breathtaking.
It is usually all over within an
hour of sunrise, when a lavish
bush breakfast is provided
complete with champagne
and, with luck, a few lions or
elephants looking on.

Kenya does not have any
bona fide boat safaris, but the
Rift Valley lakes of Naivasha
(see pp266–9) and Baringo *(see
pp280–83)* offer boat trips that
are fantastic for bird-watching.

AFTER DARK

Most national parks under the
jurisdiction of the KWS limit
game drives to daylight hours,
a rule that is enforced rigidly
at busy lodges on main tourist
circuits. However, several
small and more isolated bush
camps, especially in private
reserves such as the Laikipia
Plateau *(see pp318–21)*, or in

concessions adjacent to
national parks, offer night
drives – generally late afternoon drives that continue for
an hour or two after sunset –
an opportunity that no wildlife enthusiast will want to
pass up. Come dusk, many
familiar safari favourites bed
down for the night, leaving
the stage open for a cast
of more elusive creatures,
ranging from twitchy-nosed
elephant shrews and bug-eyed
bushbabies, both frequently
picked up in the spotlight, to
the singular and seldom seen
termite-guzzling aardvark.
Carnivores are usually most
active after dark, and night
drives offer a good chance of
seeing leopards, along with
smaller hunters such as civets,
genets and servals.

Even for those who return
to their lodge before dusk,
the African bush can take on
a thrillingly mysterious quality
by night. It is worth spending
a little time simply soaking
this up from the lodge balcony or somewhere else,
away from the lights and
crowds. Especially near water,
the night air comes alive with
a white noise of cicadas and
frogs, punctuated by the occasional eerie yelp of a hyena
or low grunts of rival lions,
providing a compelling
backdrop to a night sky of
mesmerising clarity. This is
the best time to look out for
flashing fireflies, geckoes and
chameleons – the last go
white after dark, a spectral
pigmentation that makes them
easy to spot – and such
spectacular nocturnal birds as
Verreaux's eagle-owl and the
pennant-winged nightjar.

Lions playing under a setting full moon, the Masai Mara Game Reserve

LOCATING WILDLIFE

For those raised on wildlife documentaries, where obliging menageries enact one thrilling natural drama after the other, it is easy to embark on a safari with unrealistic expectations. In reality, many game drives entail long periods of bumping around seeing little but the odd grazing antelope or perching bird, punctuated by an occasional encounter as sudden as it is thrilling – a herd of elephants trumpeting from deep in the bush, or lions devouring a fresh kill, or a cheetah stalking the plains in search of an unsuspecting gazelle. While luck arguably plays the decisive role in what one might see on any given day, perseverance and skill are also key factors, and safarigoers who play an active role in locating wildlife are more likely to strike the jackpot than those who leave wildlife spotting to their driver-guide.

HOW AND WHERE TO SPOT GAME

During the heat of the day, most animals prefer to stand or lie in the shade. In open country, always scan the grass below isolated trees. In denser vegetation, try to look into the thickets rather than at the openings between them. In open-topped vehicles, standing passengers who stick their heads out of the roof will stay more alert than those who sit, and the added height creates a better vantage point for seeing more distant animals.

WATERBODIES

Rivers, reservoirs and lakes are reliable wildlife magnets. Most animals need to drink every day, and watering points attract a steady trickle of thirsty elephant, zebra, giraffe, buffalo and other ungulates from mid-morning onwards, especially in arid climates and

Wading through vegetation in a marsh, Amboseli National Park

during dry seasons. Generally, steep and densely vegetated riverbanks attract fewer transient drinkers than large open reservoirs, but it is surprising how much wildlife emerges after a few minutes of observation at an apparently deserted waterside. A troop of monkeys might leap through the canopy, a crocodile erupt to the surface, a bushbuck or kudu creep quietly from the riverine tangle, or a kingfisher flash past in a blaze of colour.

BEHAVIOURAL CLUES

The behaviour of one animal can alert safarigoers to the presence of another. For instance, vultures characteristically circle or roost in large numbers in the vicinity of a recent kill and attendant carnivores and scavengers. When a troop of baboons or vervet monkeys takes to the trees in noisy agitation, odds are there is a leopard or lion prowling nearby, while similarly jumpy guineafowls or exaggeratedly alert antelope might well be responding to the same stimulus. It is common for small birds to become very agitated and vocal when a predatory snake, owl or goshawk is close to their nest. However, the most frequent indirect evidence of an interesting sighting requires no specialist bush knowledge to interpret – a huddle of safari vans in an area usually means that wildlife has been spotted there.

A pair of young giraffes drinking at a shallow waterhole while the adult keeps watch

FAECAL SPOOR

Even where wildlife appears to be uncommon, the savannah will be littered with spoor. Among the most conspicuous of these are faeces, which include the heavy steaming pats deposited by elephants and rhinos, the elongated scats of lions and jackals, the calcium-rich white droppings of bone-chomping hyenas and the tidy piles of raisin-sized pellets that mark the territorial boundaries of most of the small antelope species.

ANIMAL TRACKS

Sand roads through reserves often host a veritable logbook of animal prints. Most commonly, these will be antelope hoof marks, which consist of two teardrop-shaped segments shaped like an inverted elongated heart. Antelope prints are usually proportionate in size to the creature that made them, ranging from 13–15 cm (5–6 inches) long for an eland to about 2.5 cm (1 inch) for a duiker. Identification can often be narrowed down by looking at habitat and abundance – a solitary trail of medium-sized prints in riparian forest would most likely be a bushbuck, while a muddle of medium-sized prints in light woodland might be an impala herd. A buffalo print is larger and more rounded than any antelope's, while a giraffe print is squarer and up to 20 cm (8 inches) long. The print of a zebra is very horse-like, a hippo's resembles a four-pronged fig leaf, a rhino's is like a compressed head with cauliflower ears, while the plain oval half-a-metre (2-ft) long print of an elephant is recognisable by size alone.

Carnivore prints tend to resemble an inverted heart, topped by a quartet of oblong or circular toe marks. In the early morning, especially, a freshly laid trail will often lead a good tracker to the actual animal. It helps narrow down possibilities to look at size and whether claw marks are visible above the toes, as is the case with all dogs and hyenas, but not in cats except for the cheetah. A clawless 10-cm (4-inch) print is almost certainly a lion's, while a similar print with claw marks would be a spotted hyena's.

Lion footprint in soft sand

IN THE CAMP

After a long day on the dusty road, most safarigoers return to camp ready for a quick nap, or settle down at the poolside bar with a chilled drink. However, lodges and camps often offer a prime opportunity to see smaller creatures such as lizards, squirrels, hyraxes and frogs. Many also offer great bird-watching, especially in the cooler hours of the day, when fruiting trees and flowering shrubs often attract a range of colourful birds that are unlikely to be noticed from a fast-moving vehicle. Many lodges are built alongside rivers, lakes or artificial watering points that attract a steady trickle of transient wildlife. These watering points can be particularly rewarding if they are spotlit at night, when scavenging hyenas and smaller predators visit openly or surreptitiously. The notion of the lodge as a hide is taken to its logical conclusion in Taita Hills and at the so-called "tree hotels" of Kenya's Central Highlands – Treetops, The Ark and Serena Mountain Lodge *(see pp374–5)*, where game drives are rendered almost redundant by the rich variety of wildlife that comes to drink throughout the day and night.

A red-bellied coastal squirrel feeding off a table at Shimba Lodge

URBAN HABITATS

Urban Kenya may not hold much promise for seeing the likes of elephant or lion, but it can be very rewarding for smaller creatures. Downtown Nairobi, for instance, is a prime site for the ungainly marabou stork, while leafier suburbs are still inhabited by leopards and monkeys, as well as colourful turacos and hornbills and elusive giant chameleons. By night, almost every urban wall below an altitude of around 1,500 m (4,921 ft) is likely to host a few bug-eyed geckos, and the eerie nocturnal call of the bushbaby is often heard reverberating through the suburbs. Nairobi National Park *(see pp162–5)* is famed for its improbable juxtaposition of giraffes, gazelles and even big cats against a heat-hazed backdrop of shimmering skyscrapers. With a little forethought and initiative, any enforced urban stopover will present visitors with the opportunity for some low-key wildlife watching.

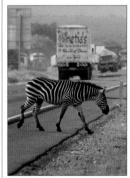
A zebra crossing at the Trans-Africa Highway, Nairobi

CONSERVATION

L ike much of Africa, Kenya has suffered immense loss of natural habitat and a strong decline in wildlife population over the past century. The plight of flagship animals such as the African wild dog and black rhino serves to underscore the deep vulnerability of the country's wildlife. Equally true, however, is that East Africa's national parks and reserves

The vulnerable dugong

are among the last places on this planet where people can witness something akin to the volume and variety of mammals that roamed the planet in prehistoric times. Conservation is a major issue in Kenya, but ultimately for the uplifting reason that, by comparison to almost anywhere else on earth, there are still so many wild places and creatures left to conserve.

Eucalyptus and tea plantations encroaching on the countryside

HABITAT LOSS

The core environmental issue in Kenya is the competition between wildlife and human population that has increased tenfold since the early colonial era. The most significant manifestation of this rising ecological pressure has been the widespread loss of habitat. Indigenous forests rich in biodiversity have been hacked down, making way for sterile pine and eucalyptus plantations or subsistence farms, while large tracts of savannah and other grassland have been replaced with cash crop monocultures. This situation is now more or less contained within most protected areas. Elsewhere, however, the ongoing destruction of biodiversity-sustaining microhabitats such as forest patches and small wetlands – whether directly or as a result of extensive environmental pollution or colonisation by invasive plants of exotic origin – remains a cause for immediate concern.

HUNTING AND POACHING

The immense wildlife herds that formerly coexisted with people in East Africa have suffered extensively from direct persecution over the past century, from the European hunters in the colonial era, from the commercial poaching industry that peaked in the 1980s and, at more sustainable levels, from local tribes. However, since 1990, the prevailing trend among populations of Kenya's large mammals has been positive.

Most national wildlife parks and reserves depleted by the poaching wars of the 1980s are now experiencing significant population growth in many species. In spite of this, some reports suggest that this encouraging trend excludes large predators such as lion and cheetah, which are frequently poisoned or hunted by protective pastoralists in buffer zones bordering Kenya's reserves.

PROTECTED AREAS

The bulk of Kenya's protected areas are state-owned and fall under the auspices of either the Kenya Wildlife Service (KWS) or the Kenya Forest Department (KFD). KWS manages all national parks, marine parks and national reserves (in some cases, on behalf of the district authority), while KFD is responsible for forest reserves. Many of today's key protected areas were initially set aside during the colonial era. This imposed strongly on local communities, who were forcibly relocated to sites outside the park boundary and forbidden from taking

Attending on cheetahs at the KWS headquarters in Nairobi

The endangered African wild dog, a rare sight in Kenya's parks

their livestock to traditional grazing grounds. Furthermore, hunting – whether for food or to protect crops – had abruptly been rebranded as poaching and criminalised.

KWS has taken a different approach in protecting the country's wildlife by involving the local people in the conservation process and encouraging the creation of eco-tourism projects that bring direct benefits to communities living in buffer zones, particularly in the vicinity of national parks such as Tsavo *(see pp182–7)* and Amboseli *(see pp194–7)*. Another important development has been the creation of private reserves, particularly on Laikipia Plateau *(see pp318–21)*, whose agglomeration of small reserves is probably the world's most important stronghold for the black rhino, and also harbours other rarities such as Grevy's zebra, reticulated giraffe and African wild dog.

TOURISM

A healthy tourism industry is probably integral to the long-term survival of Kenya's wildlife. Not only does it generate direct revenue in the form of entrance fees to parks and reserves and private wildlife concessions, it also creates a wide range of relatively well-paid conservation- and tourist-related employment. Furthermore, it serves as a strong deterrent to commercial poachers, who cannot easily go about their clandestine business in areas regularly visited by tourists. For all that, there is much that visitors can do to minimise their impact on protected areas *(see pp72–3)*.

EDGE OF EXTINCTION

Developed by the Zoological Society of London, the EDGE of Extinction project ranks the world's top 100 mammal species in terms of conservation priority as a combination of Evolutionarily Distinct (ED) and Globally Endangered (GE) categories. In other words, an endangered species that is highly distinct in evolutionary terms, such as the long-beaked echidna, would rank higher in the list than a species with many close relatives. Six EDGE mammals are present in Kenya. These are the black rhino (7th), hirola (37th, endemic), golden-rumped elephant shrew (46th, endemic), dugong (53rd), African elephant (77th) and Grevy's zebra (82nd, near-endemic).

CITES

The Convention on International Trade in Endangered Species of Wild Fauna and Flora (CITES) is an international agreement blocking trade in specimens or products of plant and animal species that threaten their survival. Signed in 1963, it currently accords protection to 30,000 species and products, ranging from rhino horns to various dried herbs. Many species present in Kenya have been listed by CITES, but its biggest coup in the Kenyan context was the ban on ivory trade implemented in 1990 and considered the key moment in the reversal of the extinction-threatening slaughter of elephants by poachers.

IUCN RED LIST

Established in 1963, the International Union for Conservation of Nature (IUCN) Red List of Threatened Species uses a set of precise criteria to evaluate the extinction risk of more than 46,000 species and subspecies of flora and fauna. Every animal or plant taxon evaluated is assigned one of the following categories:
- Extinct (EX) – No individuals known to survive.
- Extinct in the Wild (EW) – Survives only in captivity or as an introduced population outside its natural range.
- Critically Endangered (CR) – Extremely high risk of extinction in the wild.
- Endangered (EN) – Very high risk of extinction.
- Vulnerable (VU) – High risk of extinction.
- Near Threatened (NT) – Close to qualifying for or is likely to qualify for a threatened category in the near future.
- Least Concern (LC) – No significant risk of extinction.
- Data Deficient (DD) – Insufficient information available for assessment.
- Not Evaluated (NE).

A rare encounter of a black rhino with a white rhino near Lake Nakuru

WILDLIFE THROUGH THE YEAR

The natural world does not adhere to the rigid calendars that dictate such human events as festivals and public holidays. All the same, it does follow a clear annual cycle, one that will inevitably display slight variations from any given year to the next, but that is also marked by several reasonably predictable events. Pivotal to all this is the length and duration of the wet seasons. These show a

Willow warbler, a
Palearctic migrant

marked regional variation, but usually consist of the short rains from late October into December and the more substantial long rains, which last from late February to late May or early June, generally peaking over April. The short dry spell between the short and long rains usually has little effect on wildlife. However, the main dry season, from June to October, is the toughest time of year for most species.

RAINY SEASON (NOV–MAY)

The arrival of the first rains signals a period of renewal comparable to spring in colder climates. The bush is rejuvenated by the fresh growth of buds, leaves and grass, and the availability of food and water is high. Consequently, this time of year is associated with heightened insect activity, calving and nesting and the arrival of migrant birds from the northern hemisphere.

Cuckoos call (*Nov–Mar*). There is some regional and species-specific variation, but the wet season is when birds are most likely to perform display flights or spend long periods advertising their presence to potential mates with repetitive calls. No sounds so typify the East African bush during this period as the persistent "it-will-rain" call of the red-chested cuckoo and the overwrought "dee-dee-dee-diederick" sound of Diederick's cuckoo, both of

Spotted hyenas keeping watch over their cubs at the den

which are heard everywhere but are seldom seen.
Denning season (*Nov–Mar*). Most dogs and hyenas rear their pups in dens, which are often excavated below termite hills or from old aardvark holes. There is some seasonal and regional variation, but jackals and bat-eared foxes in particular tend to give birth at the start of the rains and to stick close to their dens for the next 2 to 3 months, often offering great opportunities for close-up sightings.
Breeding season for birds (*Nov–May*). Although it varies

greatly from one species to the next, courtship and breeding activity usually starts with the onset of the rains. This is most visible in the many birds who shed their "ugly duckling" camouflage plumage and emerge in full breeding colours. This phenomenon is especially striking among the bright-yellow masked weavers and dazzling red bishops, as well as the temporarily long-tailed widows and whydahs.
Wildlife disperses into bush (*Nov–May*). During the rainy season, the bush is scattered with temporary pools. The area around these pools provides fresh fodder, allowing ungulates and other grazers to disperse over a wide region. The dispersal also allows overgrazed land close to more permanent water-bodies to recover in time for the next dry season.
Insect activity peaks (*Nov–May*). Insects are most active during the rainy season, whether it is the fireflies that light up forest fringes at night, or the myriad colourful butterflies that flit between flowers and faeces to feed. A striking

A masked weaver arriving with building material for his nest

event, often following an afternoon rainstorm, is the irruption of flying ants that frequently attract flocks of hungry raptors, in particular steppe and tawny eagles, black kites and buzzards.
Calving season *(Dec–Feb)*. The window between the short and long rains is the main calving season for wildebeest, plains zebra, gazelle and many other ungulates, particularly in the south. In the Serengeti-Mara system, migrating grazers calve on the Tanzanian side of the border, as do resident populations in Amboseli, Tsavo and the Masai Mara.
Passage migrants leave *(Mar–Apr)*. As the rainy season draws to a close and the northern winter thaws, the millions of migrant birds that overwintered in Africa embark on the long flight to Europe. This can result in exceptional aggregations of certain species – especially swallows – as they pass through Kenya en route from southern Africa, and unexpected species being spotted in the oddest places. By late April, all the migrant birds will usually have departed.

DRY SEASON (JUN–OCT)

Depleted water and food sources in the dry season make it a period when survival rather than reproduction is crucial in the natural world. Ironically, this is also the best time to see

A flock of great white pelicans landing on Lake Nakuru

large mammals, as visibility is improved by the lack of vegetation and animals congregate close to water sources.

Secondary gazelle calving season *(Jun–Aug)*. Although many gazelles calve at the same time as the plains zebra, some calve later on, notably Thomson's in June–July and Grant's in July–August.
Marsh terrapins aestivate *(Jun–Sep)*. Within a month of the last rain, the muddy pools that dot the bush start to dry up. Nomadic marsh terrapins that inhabit such pools will either wander away in search of permanent water or aestivate – that is, bury themselves deep in the cracking mud and shut down most life systems until the next rains, when they re-emerge undaunted.
Wildebeest migration *(Jul–Oct)*. The wildebeest usually cross into the Masai Mara from the Serengeti in late July

or August, and spend the next 3 months grazing the plains bare before they return southwards in October *(see pp124–5)*.
Wildlife congregates near water *(Aug–Oct)*. The dry season really kicks in over this period. Drinking water tends to be restricted to perennial rivers and lakes, which attract high densities of animals. This phenomenon often results in superb game viewing, particularly in Samburu-Buffalo Springs and Amboseli, where the wildlife concentrations can be mind-boggling.
Bushfire season *(Aug–Oct)*. The dry season may offer great game viewing but it also brings plenty of hardship to wildlife (and subsistence farmers), not least in the form of the destructive wildfires that frequently sweep across vast tracts of bush, killing smaller or slower-moving animals such as tortoises and snakes, and attracting birds such as storks and raptors that feed on the fleeing insects. Most African trees are fire-resistant, so the bush recovers quickly, and the fresh shoots that emerge from the burnt grass offer juicy pickings to many grazers.
Passage migrants arrive *(Oct–Nov)*. The first rains at the end of the dry season coincide with the arrival of millions of migrant birds from the Palearctic, some of which continue on to southern Africa while others settle in Kenya for the duration of the northern winter. Raptors, waders, warblers and waterfowl are among the better represented groups.

Wildebeest crossing Mara river during the annual cross-border migration

PRACTICAL INFORMATION

The incredible diversity found in Kenya's national parks and reserves, both in terms of landscape and wildlife, makes for a memorable safari experience. In some respects, booking a safari in Kenya could hardly be more straightforward. The first thing to be decided is the safari destination, and there are plenty of reputable tour operators, both in-country and abroad, that can offer expert guidance. Following

Antelope crossing sign, Aberdare NP

that, budget and personal taste will be key factors in determining what kind of safari – fly-in or road, lodges or campsites – seems most suitable. However, it is important to consider all available options carefully before booking, and the following pages are a guide to that process, from planning and booking to packing and preparation; they also highlight various key aspects of getting the most from the safari once it starts.

CHOOSING AN ITINERARY

The most suitable itinerary depends greatly on how long visitors want to spend on safari, what they hope to see and whether they fly or drive between different reserves. The Masai Mara *(see pp262–5)* is the best starting point for first-time safarigoers in search of the Big Five. By road, it is often combined with the Rift Valley lakes and the tree hotels *(see pp316–17)* of the Central Highlands, but by air it could as easily be twinned with Amboseli National Park *(see pp194–7)*. Samburu-Buffalo Springs *(see pp342–5)* is good for repeat safarigoers, Meru *(see pp330–33)* is the best for untrammelled wilderness and Laikipia Plateau *(see pp318–21)* is great for walking and night drives. It is advisable to prepare an itinerary in liaison

with a reputable tour operator *(see pp404–405)* with a strong specialist knowledge of Kenya.

WHEN TO GO

Kenya's top wildlife attraction is the Serengeti–Mara migration *(see pp124–5)*, when wildebeest arrive in Masai Mara from late July onwards and cross back into Tanzania before November. If catching this event is the top priority, then any time from August to mid-October is reliable. This is peak tourist season, however, and the parks are less overrun with visitors at other times of year. Of the other seasonal parks, Amboseli is at its best at the end of the dry season between October and early November, while wildlife numbers in Samburu-Buffalo Springs tend to be lower during good rainy seasons. Bird-watching is best from November to March,

when resident species are boosted by Palearctic migrants. There is no truly bad time to go on safari, but the risk of game drives being washed out and vehicles getting bogged down in mud is highest at the peak of the long rains (March and April).

TYPES OF SAFARI

There are a number of things to consider when deciding what type of safari to book. These include whether to fly or drive between reserves, whether to travel as part of a group or in a private party and whether to stay in simple campsites, large mid-range lodges or smaller and more upmarket bush camps. To some extent, these decisions come down to choosing between a cheap option and an expensive one – a group driving safari with budget campsites will cost a fraction

Driving through vast herds of wildebeest and zebra on the plains of the Masai Mara

Camping in the wilderness of Amboseli's stark savannah

of a private fly-in safari using exclusive bush camps. Apart from budget, the decision is purely a matter of personal taste. Flying between reserves reduces transit time and places fewer geographic restrictions on the itinerary. However, it creates a greater distance between travellers and the countryside and people of Kenya. Joining a group safari also has its pros and cons – if the group gels well, it can be great fun and the congenial atmosphere will enhance the experience. However, a private safari allows for a greater degree of autonomy, especially for those with special interests.

In some respects, budget camping safaris, though cheap, offer the most hands-on safari experience, especially at night, when campers are separated from the African night by nothing but a flimsy canvas sheet. A more popular option is a lodge-based safari, with two broad accommodation types being available – the large "hotel in the bush" lodge operated by several chains, and the more intimate bush camp offering standing tents or stand-alone chalets. Larger lodges are often the more reassuring option for nervous safari novices, offering secure accommodation, decent restaurant food and a high degree of comfort, but their institutionalised atmosphere tends to neutralise the wilderness, isolating guests from the immense African night sky and sounds. Bush camps tend to be smaller, with anything from 6 to 20 units, and blend into the surrounding wilderness in a

more authentic manner than the larger lodges. Many bush camps are genuinely luxurious, with chic decor, catering almost entirely to fly-in guests, for whom they provide all activities using experienced in-house guides. If the price tag is within range, there is no better way to experience Africa in the wild.

Bookings can either be made through a local ground operator or a tour agency at home. In most cases, a domestic tour operator will possess greater in-depth knowledge of the terrain and can offer more competitive rates. The advantages of using an international agent are that planning an itinerary is easier, the agency will often get a better flight package than an independent traveller would and there is

generally less room for any complications regarding payment and insurance.

Prices are usually inclusive of accommodation, camping gear, services of a vehicle and driver-guide, all meals, park fees and other activities. Drinks and tips are extra. Check what is included in advance.

ENTRANCE FEES

All parks and reserves charge significant entrance fees, ranging from US$60 per person for 24 hours at the more popular reserves such as Amboseli and the Masai Mara to US$10 per person for 24 hours at more obscure ones. Relatively low vehicle entrance fees are charged where appropriate.

A stamped entrance ticket to Meru National Park

At most parks, fees can be paid in US dollars or Kenyan shillings, but others, such as Amboseli, the Aberdares, Tsavo East and West, Nairobi and Lake Nakuru, now operate a smart card system, where visitors can add credit to smart cards and use them instead of cash. These cards function like debit cards that have to be topped up with sufficient cash to cover park fees. In practice, fees are built into safari quotes by the operator, but self-drive safarigoers will need to familiarise themselves with current fees and the smart card system.

Kifaru House's rural façade blending into the surroundings, Lewa Downs

WHAT TO WEAR

The ideal clothing for safari is loose-fitting, lightweight and made of natural fabrics. Pale garments are less likely to attract tsetse flies but they tend to show more dirt, while bright colours can be intrusive when tracking wildlife on foot. The quantity required depends on the duration and type of safari – more changes will be necessary on budget camping safaris than at small, exclusive lodges where anything put in the laundry basket is returned clean within 24 hours. Many Kenyan reserves are at high altitudes, and nights can be cooler than might be expected of tropical Africa, so it is sensible to pack sweat-shirts and a windbreaker. After dark, closed shoes, socks and trousers offer the best protection against mosquito bites. Vehicle-based safaris do not call for special-ised footwear, but decent shoes are essential for walking safaris and mountain ascents.

A backpacker carrying essentials

PHOTOGRAPHING WILDLIFE

Daytime game drives usually offer better photographic opportunities than other activi-ties, because the vehicle doubles as a hide and as a stabilising device for the camera. Ideally, the camera should be supported with a beanbag or even some bunched-up clothing placed firmly on the roof or window edge, and the driver asked to switch off the car and keep as still as possible – the vibration of a running engine or any other slight movement while the shutter is open will almost cer-tainly result in a blurred image. In an open-topped vehicle, the elevation of the roof will often provide the best photographic van-tage point for distant animals and perched birds, but where the sub-ject is at ground level close to the vehicle, a more pleasing result will usually be obtained by shooting from the car window. Some drivers are skilled at lining up vehicles for photog-raphy, others rather less so, and it will almost always help if the photographer provides some guidance. Simplistically, the best result is likely to be obtained by approaching wild-life along a line that places the vehicle directly between the animal and the sun, while avoiding placing any distract-ing vegetation between subject and lens. The most appropriate manner of approach is a mat-ter of judgement – come in too fast and direct, and the animal might be startled away, but an exaggeratedly slow or stop-start approach is likely to make the animal think that it is being stalked.

PHOTOGRAPHIC GEAR

The two most important considerations in obtaining high quality wildlife photo-graphs are lens magnification and support sufficient to prevent camera shake while using a long lens. An SLR camera is preferable to a "point and shoot", and the lowest magnification lens that can realistically be used is 200 mm, though 300 mm or even 500 mm is preferable. Zoom lenses of 70–300 mm are cheaper than fixed lenses, and allow for greater flexi-bility when it comes to composition. However, they tend to lack sharpness and are less useful in low-light conditions – flaws that are exacerbated by the use of a 1.4x or 2x converter.

Photographers with limited experience in the field of wildlife often underestimate the importance of camera support equipment. Tripods, monopods and window clamps can all be used for support, but the most flexible and stable option for shooting out of a vehicle window or roof is a beanbag. This is easy to make at home, and the addition of a zip will allow it to be carried empty on flights and filled with

Photographers taking pictures of flocks of pink flamingoes on the Lake Nakuru shoreline

Hikers with a local guide en route to Sheldrick Falls, Shimba Hills

suitable material, such as beans, rice and corn, at the start of the safari.

It is important to use a camera bag that insulates expensive equipment against the insidious dust associated with most Kenyan game reserves. Digital camera users should make sure they have all the batteries, plugs, connecters and storage devices they will need, as well as a universal adapter. Film users should bring as many rolls as they are likely to need, which will probably range from four to ten per day, depending on their level of interest.

BINOCULARS

Essential for any kind of safari, binoculars help obtain better views of distant wildlife, and are invaluable when it comes to spotting and identifying bird species. The minimal requirement is 8x magnification, but for the steady of hand 10x, 12x or 16x is better. Full-size 8x40 and 10x50 models have a wider field of vision and better colour definition than their compact 8x25 or 10x30 counterparts. However, the latter are more portable, steadier to hold and inexpensive. Obscure brands tend to suffer from poor focusing, distortion and unsatisfactory colour rendition, and gimmicks such as universal focus or zoom are best avoided when selecting a pair.

FIELD GUIDES

A wide selection of field guides covers the wildlife of Africa as a whole and Kenya more specifically. There are several detailed books that will be of use to more dedicated or specialised wildlife enthusiasts. Most are available in bookshops in Nairobi and lodge gift shops, but this cannot be guaranteed and it is advisable to get hold of any book absolutely essential for the safari well in advance.

Among the best mammal guides to this region are *The Safari Companion* by Richard Estes, useful for interpreting behaviour, and *Kingdon's Field Guide to African Mammals* by Jonathan Kingdon, for identification and taxonomic relationships. The comprehensive *Birds of Kenya and Northern Tanzania* by Zimmerman et al. is the first choice for serious bird-watchers, while Stephen Spawls's *Field Guide to the Reptiles of East Africa* and Channing and Howell's *Amphibians of East Africa* are ideal for specialists but bulky for general use.

The field guide on the following pages (*see pp96–145*) will help visitors in putting a name to most mammals and some of the more conspicuous of Kenya's reptiles, amphibians and birds.

OTHER ITEMS TO PACK

Some useful and essential items to take on a trip include sunblock, a hat and sunglasses, a penknife, a torch and an alarm clock. A day pack is useful to carry binoculars and field guides, and it is advisable to pack all the toiletries that might be required. Contact lens users with sensitive eyes might want to carry a pair of glasses for dusty safari conditions. Mosquitoes are present in most reserves and parks, so it is vital to carry a supply of prophylactic drugs.

CHILDREN ON SAFARI

Taking children on safari can be a mixed blessing. Most children are thrilled at the sight of any wildlife, and early exposure to the wildernesses of Africa is a memory that will endure for a lifetime. Equally, Kenya's game reserves can be strenuous for younger children, who may quickly become tired and irritable on long uneventful drives. In general, older children will take better to the whole safari regime, and many private lodges do not allow younger children for safety reasons or even out of consideration to other guests. It will be a gamble to take children along and the safest way to ensure that the trip remains pleasant and within control is to book a private safari, so that game drives can be curtailed as and when boredom sets in, ensuring that the needs of younger children are catered to and other safarigoers remain undisturbed.

Children experiencing wildlife at close quarters, Masai Mara

DISABLED TRAVELLERS

Kenya offers few facilities for disabled travellers, and safaris present a number of additional problems, from the difficulties associated with getting in and out of light aircraft or tall 4WDs to rough roads and lack of wheelchair ramps or other special arrangements at most camps and lodges. On the other hand, Kenyan culture is generally far more accommodating to the elderly and disabled, and the staff at most camps will go out of their way to surmount any logistical obstacles. It is possible for disabled travellers who liase with a reputable tour operator, and are clear about what they can and cannot do upfront, to have a perfectly satisfactory safari in Kenya.

HEALTH

The biggest health risk on safari, as elsewhere in Kenya, is malaria *(see pp412–13)*. The tropical sun can induce dehydration or sunstroke on foot safaris or in open-topped vehicles, so it is best to keep a hat handy, use sunblock and drink plenty of water. Bilharzia, commonly known as snail fever, is borne by freshwater snails and can be contracted while swimming in lakes or rivers in game reserves, although the more overt threat presented by crocodiles should be enough of a discouragement in itself. Apart from mosquitoes, the

Appropriately-dressed hikers on a foot safari with a forest ranger

most dangerous biting creatures are snakes, but these tend to be secretive, and unprovoked attacks are a rarity. The risk of being bitten by a snake, spider or scorpion is greatly reduced by wearing closed shoes and trousers. The most annoying diurnal biters are the harmless tsetse flies and horseflies. After walking in grassy places, skin should be closely checked for ticks, which are easy to remove within an hour or two, but can be difficult to dislodge once firmly attached. Certain tick species can cause tick-bite fever, a debilitating but easily cured disease.

SAFETY AROUND WILD ANIMALS

In many Kenyan parks and reserves, wildlife is habituated to people and vehicles, but this is not the same thing as domestication. The lions that laze around obliviously in front of a cluster of safari vehicles will almost certainly respond differently were one of the passengers to disembark. Most likely, they would run away, but it is also possible that they would attack. Similarly, large herbivores such as elephant, hippo, rhino and buffalo might all bulldoze pedestrians under certain circumstances. Such attacks are rare, but they most often stem from a combination of bad judgement and even worse luck, so it is worth keeping in mind a few rules of thumb. Wildlife should not be approached on foot, except in the company of a reliable guide, and visitors should not get between a hippo and water. Food, especially meat or fruit, should not be left in the same tent where people will sleep. If large predators are encountered while on foot, safarigoers should be aware that there is no more certain way of triggering the instinct to give chase than to run away.

BLENDING IN

Appropriate clothing is important on foot safaris but rather less so in vehicles, as animals generally pay little attention to individual passengers. Pungent perfumes or other strong artificial smells may disturb wildlife or fellow passengers and smoking should be avoided. Far more intrusive – to wildlife and to vehicles in the vicinity – are those whose response to any interesting sighting is to exclaim loudly. Although it has no effect on wildlife, driving around slowly at 20–30 kmph (12–19 mph) makes for a far more involving experience than speeding about in air conditioned isolation.

ENVIRONMENTAL IMPACT

The long list of rules that governs the national parks and reserves in Kenya might seem excessive or restrictive to first-time safarigoers, but most of these rules have been designed to ensure the safety

A curious lioness mauling a camera, Masai Mara Game Reserve

Bushfire ravaging the moorland at Mount Elgon National Park

of wildlife and visitors, and to minimise the environmental impact of tourism. Littering, for instance, is not only unsightly but potentially dangerous to inquisitive wildlife. Discarded matches or cigarette butts are among the most common causes of uncontrolled bushfires. Also forbidden in most reserves is off-road driving, which can cause considerable damage to fragile ecosystems, and hooting or yelling at animals to attract their attention. Likewise, speed limits are in place to prevent accidents on the often unpredictable road surfaces, as well as collisions with unsuspecting wildlife. Feeding wildlife can also have several negative effects, particularly with respect to baboons and monkeys, which quickly learn to associate humans with food and often become dangerous once they do, leading to them being shot. Collecting plants or buying animals is also expressly forbidden, as is the sale or purchase of products of animals or plants specified on the CITES list *(see pp65)*.

On an organised safari, the driver-guides can be expected to take the lead when it comes to sensitive behaviour towards the environment, wildlife and other safarigoers. They will be aware of park rules and of the kind of behaviour that might disturb animals, and can be expected to make their clients conscious of these where necessary. When stopping for a sighting, the driver-guide should switch off the engine, mute the volume on the radio and keep conversation to a hushed minimum so as not to disturb the wildlife or people in other vehicles. Occasionally, however, a driver-guide might contravene park rules – for instance by following a hunting predator off-road, thereby disturbing the hunt, or by provoking an elephant into a mock charge, or driving dangerously fast – in which case the client might want to intervene.

STAFF RELATIONS

Building a good relationship with the driver-guide and other staff, such as a cook on a camping safari, is vital to the success of a safari. Safarigoers should be pro-active and make sure that the driver is aware of any special requirements and interests, and feels like his clients are active participants in wildlife spotting and identification. Most drivers are quite poorly paid and appreciate it when clients cover the cost of a meal or drink. They survive mainly on tips, so be generous. There are no hard-and-fast tipping rules, but most safari companies will advise clients as to what constitutes an average or good tip for a driver-guide. It goes without saying that when it comes to sorting out minor frictions or disagreements, humour will usually get better long-term results than anger.

SPECIAL INTERESTS

Although most first-time visitors to Kenya opt for a general interest safari, a variety of more specialised options are available, ranging from dedicated ornithological tours to camel-back adventures in the remote northern deserts of the country *(see pp404–405)*.

Ranger interacting with tourists at the Chimpanzee Sanctuary, Laikipia

Safari Parks at a Glance

Kenya's astounding wealth of reserves and national parks often dazzles first-time visitors. In reality, however, the safari industry focuses on a handful of more popular reserves, of which Amboseli, Tsavo, Laikipia, Nairobi and the Masai Mara are obvious starting points, ideally broken up with a night at one of the Aberdare tree hotels. For repeat visits, Samburu, Buffalo Springs and Shaba National Reserves stand out for hosting large mammals that are practically endemic to Kenya, while for one of the most thrillingly untrammelled safari experiences in Africa, Meru is an ideal getaway. Saiwa Swamp and Hell's Gate offer the chance to break the regular game drive regimen with walking or cycling, while Lake Nakuru and Kakamega are essential stops for keen bird-watchers.

Lake Nakuru National Park (see pp276–9), *set on the Rift Valley's floor, is popular for its soda lake that supports millions of flamingoes and pelicans.*

Masai Mara Game Reserve (see pp262–5) *is everybody's favourite safari destination in Kenya. Renowned for the spectacular annual migration of the wildebeest, this popular game reserve also hosts a high density of lion, cheetah, spotted hyena and other carnivores.*

Lake Turkana

Turkwel

Suam

Kitale   *Saiwa Swamp National Park*   Marala

Kakamega   *Kakamega Forest National Reserve*   Laikipia Plateau

Nzoia   Nanyuki

Ruma National Park   Nakuru   *Aberdare National Park*   N.
    Homa Bay   Ny

Mara   Naivasha

Narok   Naire

Nairobi National Park

Hell's Gate National Park
(see pp270–71) is one of the few sanctuaries in Kenya that offers game viewing on foot.   Namanga

Amboseli National Park (see pp194–7) *is home to some of East Africa's most impressive giant-tusked elephants. This national park is most beautiful at sunset, with spectacular views of Mount Kilimanjaro, which looms dramatically on the southern horizon.*

Samburu-Buffalo Springs-Shaba National Reserves (see pp342–6) *are contiguous and semiarid. Their austere plains protect a host of dry country species such as the brilliant cobalt-chested vulturine guineafowl. The Ewaso Nyiro river flows through the three reserves, which offer good leopard sightings.*

Tsavo East and West National Parks (see pp182–7) *are home to more than 10,000 elephants, whose trademark red colouration is caused by bathing in red dust. The two national parks are also the best places in Kenya to see the endangered black rhino.*

Meru National Park (see pp330–33), *Kenya's most underrated major park, is an off-the-beaten-track gem. Its lush plains are run through by dozens of palm-lined streams and it is inhabited by large herds of reticulated giraffe, elephant and buffalo.*

Shimba Hills National Reserve (see pp216–19), *an underestimated coastal reserve, is the last Kenyan refuge for the handsome sable antelope. It also has the scenic Sheldrick Falls.*

0 km 100
0 miles 100

Mandera
Moyale
Laga Bor
Laga Bogal
Wajir
Ewaso Nyiro
Laga Dera
Tana
Garissa
Hola
Tiva
Tsavo East and West National Parks
Voi
Malindi
Galana
Taita Hills Wildlife Sanctuary
Mombasa

■ SAFARI DESTINATION	WHAT TO SEE	WHEN TO GO
Aberdare National Park Protecting the Aberdare range, this park is home to a wide variety of forest animals. The upper slopes, covered in open heath and bamboo forest and studded with pretty waterfalls, are well worth visiting *(see pp316–17)*.	All the Big Five. The world's largest wild population of the elusive and endangered mountain bongo. Genet, bushbuck, bushpig, black-and-white colobus, blue monkey.	Treetops and The Ark are accessible all year round. During peak rainy seasons (Nov–Dec and Mar–May), exploration is difficult as the dirt tracks to the upper slopes become impassable.
Amboseli National Park The snow-capped peak of Kilimanjaro dominates the skyline of this small park. Amboseli's dusty savannah and lush swampland are known for their large tuskers, the birdlife and seasonal concentrations of grazers *(see pp194–7)*.	Elephant, lion, cheetah, spotted hyena, plains zebra, wildebeest, gazelle, giraffe, hippo, waterbirds, a wide variety of birds.	Wildlife densities peak near the end of the rains. Migrant waterfowl numbers are highest over Nov–Mar. The park is best visited outside tourist seasons (Mar–May; Oct–Nov).
Hell's Gate National Park Centred upon the dramatic Hell's Gate gorge, this is the only savannah reserve in Kenya where walking and cycling are freely permitted. The plains hold impressive concentrations of grazers and birds *(see pp270–71)*.	Lion, cheetah, elephant, giraffe, buffalo, zebra, wildebeest, gazelle, hartebeest, cliff-dwelling raptors such as Verreaux's eagle and Lammergeyer.	Wildlife concentration is highest in the dry season (Jun–Oct) while bird diversity is greatest in summer (Nov–Mar). An early start is advisable to avoid sunstroke and/or dehydration.
Kakamega Forest National Reserve A celebrated bird-watching site, this reserve – the country's last substantial tract of western rainforest – also harbours primates such as the nocturnal sloth-like potto *(see pp294–7)*.	Black-and-white colobus, red-tailed, De Brazza's and blue monkeys, hammer-headed fruitbat, 300-plus bird species including the great blue turaco, 400-plus butterfly species.	All year round. Walking conditions are pleasant in the dry months (Jun–Oct). Birds are easiest to locate during the mating season (Jun–Oct), when butterflies are also most conspicuous.
Laikipia Plateau The patchwork of conservancies and ranchland on this plateau includes several of Kenya's most exclusive reserves, including Lewa Downs, Ol Pejeta and Solio Ranch. Lodges offer guided walks and night drives *(see pp318–21)*.	Black and white rhinos, lion, cheetah, Grevy's zebra, greater kudu, reticulated giraffe, Lelwel hartebeest, elephant, chimpanzee (introduced to Ol Pejeta).	Throughout the year, though roads can be more challenging and wildlife is more dispersed during the long rains (Mar–May).
Lake Nakuru National Park This small park in the heart of the Rift Valley is known for the waterfowl that congregate on its lake. The park's road circuit is easily covered in half a day, and offers the best chance of seeing white rhino in Kenya *(see pp276–9)*.	Black and white rhinos, buffalo, lion, leopard, waterbuck, giraffe, olive baboon, 400-plus bird species including large flocks of flamingoes and great white pelican.	Throughout the year, although the number and variety of water-associated birds is most impressive in Nov–Mar when resident species are supplemented by Eurasian migrants.
Masai Mara Game Reserve Kenya's famous wildlife destination is a northerly extension of the Serengeti in Tanzania. Its annual wildebeest cross-border migration is one of National Geographic's seven wonders of the modern world *(see pp262–5)*.	Black and white rhinos, elephant, lion, Maasai giraffe, buffalo, gerenuk, gazelle, lesser kudu, Beisa oryx, hippo.	The wildebeest migration typically crosses in from Tanzania in July and returns in October. Exact timings vary from year to year, but big herds can reliably be seen over Aug–Sep.
Meru National Park Located in the lush eastern rainshadow of Mount Kenya, Meru is the most underrated of Kenya's major parks. Game viewing can be superb, however, and it is one of those rare havens from tourist traffic *(see pp330–33)*.	Elephant, lion, cheetah, spotted hyena, plains zebra, wildebeest, gazelle, giraffe, hippo, waterbirds.	Throughout the year. Game viewing peaks near the end of the dry season (Jul–Nov), when the grass is low and wildlife congregates along the park's many perennial streams.

ACCOMMODATION	PRACTICAL INFORMATION
Treetops Lodge The only two lodges are The Ark and Treetops *(see p317)*, both of which offer game viewing. Both operate as annexes of hotels outside the park, with guests being bussed in and out in groups. Three small self-catering camps are operated by KWS, and camping is permitted at a few cleared sites.	160 km (100 miles) NW of Nairobi; 20 km (12 miles) W of Nyeri. *Tel 0722 757746.* ⬭ 6am–7pm daily. ▦ smart card. ▣ 🖉 Ⓐ www.kws.org
The park has at least 10 lodges, ranging from large hotels run by the Serena *(see p364)* chain to luxury tented camps such as Satao and Tortilis on Maasai concessions bordering the park. KWS runs two self-catering guest-houses. Many campsites lie right outside the park managed by Maasai communities. **Satao Elerai Camp**	230 km (142 miles) S of Nairobi via Namanga. *Tel 020 6000 800.* ✗ ⬭ 6am–7pm daily. ▦ smart card. 🖉 Ⓐ www.kws.org
Elsamere, Lake Naivasha Camping is permitted at several sites but otherwise there is no accommodation within the park. However, it is easily visited as a day trip from any one of the dozens of lodges that surround Lake Naivasha, which lies immediately north of the park.	100 km (62 miles) NW of Nairobi; 3 km (2 miles) S of Lake Naivasha. *Tel 050 50407.* ✗ ▦ *to within walking distance of entrance gate.* ⬭ 6am–6pm daily. ▦ ▣ 🖉 Ⓐ www.kws.org
The closest conventional hotel is in Kakamega town. Within the forest, cosy guesthouse accommodation with meals is available at Rondo Retreat *(see p373)* and there are several affordable self-catering and camping options. **Rondo Retreat**	15 km (9 miles) E of Kakamega town. *Tel 056 30603.* ✗ ▦ ⬭ 6am–7pm daily. ▦ ▣ 🖉 Ⓐ www.kws.org
Borana Lodge, Laikipia Dozens of private lodges *(see p375)* are dotted around the plateau. Most of them are small exclusive bush or tented camps offering all-inclusive fly-in packages from Nairobi. Many local tribal concessions offer more basic camping facilities aimed at self-drive visitors.	10 km (6 miles) W of Nanyuki airport. *Tel 020 2166626.* ✗ ⬭ *varies between conservancies, but typically 6am–6pm daily.* ▦ ▣ ▮▮ ▣ 🖉 Ⓐ www.laikipia.org
There are only two proper lodges in the park, of which the best is Lion Hill Game Lodge *(see p371)*, run by the Sarova hotel chain. Also within the park are several self-catering units and campsites managed by KWS. A wide selection of hotels and guesthouses can be found in the adjacent town of Nakuru. **Sarova Lion Hill Lodge**	Outskirts of Nakuru town; 145 km (90 miles) NW of Nairobi. *Tel 051 2217151.* ▦ *to Nakuru town.* ⬭ 6am–7pm daily. ▦ smart card. ▮▮ ▣ ▣ 🖉 Ⓐ www.kws.org
Kicheche Camp Dozens of lodges are scattered in and around the reserve, ranging from chain hotels to exclusive bush lodges. For general game viewing, the best lodges are those situated northwest of the Talek and Mara rivers. Several campsites also operate in and around the park.	265 km (165 miles) SW of Nairobi via Narok. ✗ ▦ ▮▮ 🖉 Ⓐ www.maratriangle.org
Two small upmarket bush lodges operate within the park, namely Elsa's Kopje and Leopard Rock *(see p375)*. KWS also has a few self-catering cottages and there are several campsites. Guesthouse accommodation is available at Maua en route from Meru town. **Elsa's Kopje**	75 km (47 miles) E of Meru town. *Tel 0164 20613.* ✗ ⬭ 6am–7pm daily. ▦ ▮▮ 🖉 Ⓐ www.kws.org

■ SAFARI DESTINATION	WHAT TO SEE	WHEN TO GO
Nairobi National Park The source of numerous publicity shots of wildlife strutting in front of Nairobi's skyscrapers, this remarkable periurban reserve – unfenced except on the city-facing side – protects a wide range of savannah dwellers (see pp162–5).	Lion, leopard, black rhino, buffalo, ostrich, gazelle, eland, giraffe, warthog, wildebeest, zebra, secretary bird.	Game viewing is good all year round. The local zebra and wildebeest migration across Athi Plains makes Jul–Aug particularly worth-while. Eurasian migrants are seen over Nov–Mar.
Ruma National Park Located in the Lake Victoria basin, Ruma protects Kenya's last viable population of roan antelope. The park is also an interesting goal for self-drive safarigoers seeking an off-the-beaten-track experience (see p305).	Roan antelope, leopard, spotted hyena, buffalo, oribi, Rothschild's giraffe, Jackson's hartebeest, a wide selection of birds including the globally threatened blue swallow.	Most of the wildlife is resident all year through, but the park's black cotton soil can make for treacher-ous driving conditions in the rainy season, which peaks from Mar to May.
Saiwa Swamp National Park One of Western Kenya's gems, this tiny, pedestrian-friendly park protects a 3-sq-km (1-sq-mile) large wetland. Its riparian forest harbours a selection of monkeys and birds normally associated with nearby Uganda (see pp290–91).	Sitatunga, leopard, giant forest squirrel, spotted-neck otter, De Brazza's monkey, black-and-white colobus, bushbuck, over 300 bird species including double-toothed barbet.	Game viewing is excellent throughout the year, though a stormy afternoon drenching is likely between March and May.
Samburu-Buffalo Springs-Shaba National Reserves This trio of near-contiguous reserves lies in semiarid country north of Mount Kenya. It gives safarigoers the chance to experience the region's unique dry-country wildlife (see pp342–7).	Leopard, elephant, lion, reticulated giraffe, Grevy's zebra, gerenuk, lesser kudu, Beisa oryx, Somali bee-eater, vulturine guineafowl, golden-bellied starling.	Wildlife is present all year through, but concentra-tions are highest towards the end of the dry season (Jun–Oct) when the Ewaso Nyiro river is the only reli-able water source.
Shimba Hills National Reserve The closest safari destination to Diani and Mombasa, Shimba Hills lies on a lushly forested ridge offering spec-tacular views to the coast. Its grasslands are home to Kenya's only population of the sable antelope (see pp216–19).	Sable antelope, elephant, oribi, bushbuck, buffalo, red-bellied coast squirrel, greater bushbaby, localised coastal forest birds such as the green-headed oriole.	Most of the wildlife is resident, but visibility can be poor and roads are rather muddy during the long rains of Mar–May.
Taita Hills Wildlife Sanctuary This small private sanctuary bordering Tsavo West is best known for its superb Salt Lick Lodge, which allows visitors close-up encounters with elephant. Other wildlife can be seen on diurnal and night game drives (see p188).	Elephant, buffalo, lion, leopard, topi, impala, giraffe, zebra, more than 300 bird species with the ghoulish marabou stork being especially noticeable.	All year round. Elephant concentrations are espe-cially impressive at the end of the dry season (Aug–Nov), when several hundred might swing past the waterhole in one night.
Tsavo East National Park Kenya's largest national park retains a wild atmosphere with its rugged terrain and the palm-fringed Galana, Kenya's second-longest river. Its proxim-ity to the coast makes it a popular trip from Malindi (see pp184–5).	Elephant, buffalo, hirola, lion, cheetah, fringe-eared oryx, gerenuk, gazelle, hippo, crocodile and dry-country birds such as the golden pipit and golden-bellied starling.	Less strongly seasonal than most parks. The Galana and Voi rivers attract large herds of wildlife in the dry season (Jun–Oct), as do waterholes below Voi Safari Lodge and Mudanda Rock.
Tsavo West National Park Slightly smaller than its eastern namesake, Tsavo West is fascinating for geological features such as Shetani Lava Flow and Mzima Springs, which relate to the same volcanic activity that created Kilimanjaro (see pp186–7).	Black rhino, hippo, elephant, buffalo, giraffe, lion, cheetah, lesser kudu, impala, yellow baboon, Kirk's dik-dik.	Game is most visible in the dry seasons, with the best months being Jan, Feb and Aug–Oct. For bird-watchers, the Ngulia area receives immense numbers of pas-sage migrants in Oct–Nov.

ACCOMMODATION	PRACTICAL INFORMATION

Giraffe Manor

Nairobi National Park has no campsites or lodges within its boundaries. It is, however, easily visited as a day-trip out of Nairobi, with the hotels situated in Langata or other locales south of the city centre being particularly convenient.

Main gate is less than 10 km (6 miles) SW of the city centre alongside KWS HQ on Langata Rd. *Tel 020 6000800.* to Nairobi. to Nairobi. to entrance gate. 6am–7pm daily. smart card. www.kws.org

A three-bedroom self-catering guesthouse is operated by KWS, as is the campsite. The closest hotels that offer proper lodging are in the city of Kisumu, which lies on the Lake Victoria shore, while more basic accommodation is available in the nearby town of Homa Bay.

New Victoria, Kisumu

425 km (264 miles) W of Nairobi; 24 km (15 miles) S of Homa Bay. *Tel 020 6000800.* 6am–7pm daily.

Tree Top House

KWS operates a shaded campsite and has also opened a treehouse offering basic self-catering accommodation. There is a pleasant tented camp at Sirikwa, 6 km (4 miles) from the entrance gate. Simple hotel accommodation is available at nearby Kitale.

22 km (14 km) N of Kitale. *Tel 020 6000800.* to Kitale. to within walking distance of the entrance gate. 6am–7pm daily. www.kws.org

At least a dozen lodges *(see pp376–7)* are scattered around the three reserves, ranging from large chain hotels to a handful of remote and exclusive tented camps. There are also several public campsites within the park, and basic guesthouses in Isiolo.

Tents at Larsen's Camp

340 km (211 miles) N of Nairobi; 40 km (25 miles) N of Isiolo. 6am–7pm daily.

Shimba Lodge

An excellent and underutilised "tree hotel" *(see p367)* is situated within the park and there is a good tented camp in the adjacent Mwaluganje Elephant Sanctuary to the north. Self-catering *bandas* and campsites are operated by KWS.

55 km (34 miles) SW of Mombasa via Likoni Ferry; entrance gate at Kwale village. *Tel 020 6000800.* to Kwale. 6am–7pm daily. www.laikipia.org

Two private lodges, Taita Hills Game Lodge and Salt Lick Lodge *(see p364)*, operate within the reserve, jointly managed by the Sarova chain. Salt Lick Lodge, in particular, is most popular as one of the best locations anywhere in Kenya for viewing the magnificent African elephant.

Taita Hills Game Lodge

Entrance gate is 38 km (24 miles) SW of Voi along Taveta Rd. *Tel 043 31271.* access to Taita Hills Lodge is 24-hr. www.sarovahotels.com

Galdessa Camp

The park supports a varied selection of lodges, ranging from exclusive tented camps to larger, blander monolithic hotels. There is plenty of inexpensive accommodation in Voi town, and a few campsites to choose from within the park itself.

Voi Gate is 157 km (98 miles) NW of Mombasa; 232 km (144 miles) SE of Nairobi. *Tel 020 2405957.* to Voi. 6am–7pm daily. smart card. www.kws.org

A variety of lodges includes several exclusive tented camps and a few larger hotel-like lodges. A selection of self-catering *bandas* and campsites are operated by KWS, and there is at least one good hotel in Mtito Andei town.

Voyager Camp

Voi Gate is 157 km (98 miles) NW of Mombasa; 232 km (144 miles) SE of Nairobi. *Tel 043 30049.* to Mtito Andei. smart card. www.kws.org

HABITATS

*K*enya boasts a wide spectrum of habitats. There is a barren
lava desert in the extreme north, the lush tropical rainforest
of Kakamega near the border with Uganda and permanent
glaciers on equatorial Mount Kenya. The coast is lined with palm-
shaded beaches, the mountaintops are swathed in cool forests and
windswept moors while the Rift Valley is studded with beautiful lakes.

If any one habitat can be said to be characteristic of Kenya, it is the loosely defined complex of grassland and scattered trees known to ecologists as the savannah. Moister in the southwest, drier in the north and east, savannah is the predominant habitat of popular game sanctuaries such as Amboseli, Masai Mara, Samburu-Buffalo Springs and Tsavo, and it provides a stage to Africa's most varied cast of safari favourites, from lion and zebra to elephant and gazelle.

The dry-country Euphorbia species

There are some animals, such as the water-loving hippo and fruit-eating parrots, that have very specific habitat requirements. But even more habitat-tolerant creatures display clear ecological preferences. The versatile but secretive leopard, for example, is most common in rocky or bushed areas that offer it plenty of cover, while the thirsty elephant will range widely and relatively indiscriminately for food, but always within daily walking range of drinking water.

Visitors who are keen to see the broadest variety of wildlife should be especially conscious of the significance of microhabitats. Many of Kenya's savannah reserves, for instance, are bisected by belts of lush riverine woodland that support colobus monkeys, turacos and other forest creatures. Likewise, isolated hills and cliffs often support a distinct specialist fauna whose more visible components include gaudy agama lizards, soaring black eagles and scurrying families of rock hyrax. On a smaller scale, creatures as different as dwarf mongoose, tawny eagle, aardvark, hartebeest, red-and-yellow barbet and cheetah all make regular use of termite hills, or are attracted to their edible contents.

Other habitats have a more cyclic or ephemeral nature, for instance the seasonal leafy canopies of coastal forests, or the temporary roadside ponds that provide breeding grounds to frogs and terrapins during the rains.

The pristine palm-lined stretch of Tiwi Beach near Mombasa

◁ The stark landscape of Tsavo East National Park

Habitats at a Glance

Habitat types are determined by a miscellany of climatic, vegetational, geological and other criteria, of which the most important in Kenya are rainfall and altitude. Broadly speaking, altitude and precipitation are highest in the southwest quarter of country, which includes the central and western highlands, much of the Southern Rift Valley, the Lake Victoria basin and the Masai Mara. This relatively small part of the country displays the greatest variation in habitat, ranging from moist savannah and highland meadows to rainforest, vast freshwater lakes, Afro-montane moorland and glacial peaks. Rainfall is quite high along the coast, but otherwise the eastern and northern three-quarters of the country is lower-lying and drier, and supports a relatively uniform cover of dry bush and desert habitats.

Afro-montane habitats (see pp90–91), *comprising high altitude vegetation, are seen on the upper slopes of Mount Kenya, Mount Elgon and the Aberdares.*

Kenya's varied wetlands (see pp92–3) *range from the immense freshwater sprawl of Lake Victoria to smaller aquatic gems such as Lakes Naivasha and Baringo. Rivers such as the Ewaso Nyiro, Tana and Galana feed isolated ribbons of riparian forest through the semiarid plains of the east and north.*

Lokitaung   Ileret

Lake Turkana

Nc
Ho

Lodwar

Loiyang

Turkwel

Barag

Kitale   Maralal   Wam

Eldoret

Kakamega   Kapsabet   Isi

M

Lake Victoria   Kisumu   Nakuru   Na
Mo.

Homa Bay   Naivasha   Emb

Narok   Thika

Nairobi

Nama

Savannah and woodland (see pp84–5) *cover much of the Rift Valley and areas to its south. This includes the lush hills of the Masai Mara, the Lake Victoria basin and the drier thorn scrub of Amboseli and Tsavo. In terms of game viewing, this is the most important habitat in the country.*

KEY

☐	Arid and semiarid
☐	Savannah and woodland
☐	Forest
☐	Wetlands
▨	Afro-montane
☐	Intertidal

Arid and semiarid plains
(see pp86–7) *form over half of Kenya's surface, covering much of the country's interior. Arid and semiarid habitats support a mere fraction of Kenya's human population.*

NICHE HABITATS

Within larger ecosystems exist many microhabitats. A clear example of this is a termite hill, which not only supports its insect creators, but provides shelter to small reptiles, food to aardvarks and barbets and a vantage point for prowling cheetah. Isolated koppies support a unique set of creatures, from klipspringers to agama lizards, while ephemeral puddles might be temporary home to terrapins and waders.

Klipspringers are found in rocky koppies

Seasonal wetlands attract waterbirds

Termite hills house aardvarks

The intertidal zone (see pp94–5) *broadly consists of the stretch of sand and shallow seawater between the upper and lower tide marks. The mangroves seen in this habitat follow some rivers a short distance inland.*

Moyale

Marsabit

Tarbaj

Wajir

Loga bogal

Laga Bor

Dif

Mado Gashi

Ewaso Nyiro

Equator

Tana

Garissa

0 km 100

0 miles 100

Hola

Mutomo

Tsavo

Garsen Lamu

Voi

Galana

Malindi
Watamu
Kilifi

Kwale Mombasa

Closed canopy forest
(see pp88–9) *comprises a tiny proportion of Kenya's surface area, but is known for its rich biodiversity. This habitat is particularly attractive to bird-watchers as it hosts many rare species.*

Savannah Habitats

In its broadest definition, the term savannah can be applied to any wooded habitat with an open canopy. The classic savannah landscapes of East Africa consist of a grassy understorey studded with fire-resistant deciduous trees. This open woodland is often interspersed with lush riparian trees along rivers. Savannah is widely thought to be the climax vegetation type in areas such as the Mara, but some ecologists theorise that it is the product of centuries of burning by pastoralists, who do so to stimulate fresh growth for their cattle. This is Kenya's most important habitat in terms of wildlife, although it is less florally diverse than true forest.

A herd of elephants emerging from a wooded area, Masai Mara Game Reserve

Sycamore Fig
Found in riparian woodlands, this tall evergreen tree has a thick buttressed trunk and wide shady canopy. When in fruit, it attracts a steady stream of monkeys and frugivorous birds.

Thicker woodland is often associated with underground water.

Wag-n-bietjie or wait-a-bit acacia is named for its large thorns that entangle themselves in clothing.

Open grassland often intergrades with more wooded savannah habitats.

Wildebeest and Zebras
The open plains support immense herds of mixed grazers, a term used to describe herbivores that feed mainly on grass as opposed to leaves, fruits or roots.

WHAT FLORA TO SEE

Fireball lily

GRASSLAND

Red oat grass *(Themeda trianda)* is a coarse grass that dominates tall grass plains.

Wire grass *(Pennisetum schimperi)* is a weedlike plant avoided by most grazers.

Wild cucumber *(Cucumis spp)* looks like the common vegetable but is inedible.

Sodom apple *(Solanum incanium)* is a small flowering plant with large yellow fruit. It is closely related to tomatoes, eggplants and potatoes.

Umbrella thorn *(Acacia tortillis)* grows in isolation from other trees and is a favoured food of giraffes.

Fireball lily *(Scadoxus multiforus)* has dazzling red flowers that bloom after the rains.

Euphorbia *(Euphorbia candelabrum)* grows up to 10 m (33 ft) in height. Its stem and leaves exude a white sap that is toxic to most animals, but not to rhinos.

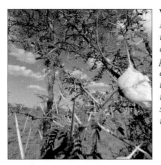

Whistling Thorn
Named for the low whistling sound created by wind passing through the ant galls around its twinned thorns, the whistling thorn is a small tree associated with thick woodland.

Umbrella thorns are medium to tall trees named for their flat shady canopy.

Bateleur Eagle
This unique raptor of the savannah is a snake-eagle with black feathering and a red face mask.

Red oat grass, which gives the plains a golden red hue in low light, provides good feeding for grazers.

Euphorbia candelabrum
A distinctive tall succulent, this species of Euphorbia *often grows on the aerated soil of disused termitaria.*

Wild date palm

Sausage tree pod

THICKER WOODLAND

Whistling thorn acacia *(Acacia drepanolobium)* is a short tree that frequently grows in dense clusters.

Wag-n-bietjie *(Acacia brevispica)* grows up to 5 m (16 ft) in height, providing shade for grazers.

RIPARIAN WOODLAND

Sausage tree *(Kigelia agrucana)* is named for its seedpods, which grow to 50 cm (20 inches) in length. These are used as gourds by the Maasai.

Sycamore fig *(Ficus sycamoros)*, a spectacular riparian tree, grows up to 20 m (66 ft) in height.

Wild date palm *(Phoenix reclinata)* is a beautiful tree with loose wide leaves and a large oval fruit favoured by monkeys. It grows next to rivers and swamps.

Arid and Semiarid Habitats

Much of the Kenyan interior, especially in the north and east, comprises arid and semiarid habitats. Arid plains typically have a short rainy season, when the grey scrubland comes to brief verdant life, but some parts of the north are dry almost around the year. Arid habitats are locally variable, ranging from red earth plains in the east and around the northern base of Mount Kenya to black stony plains that barely support any life. The unsuitability of such areas to human settlement means that many large tracts are protected in reserves such as Tsavo.

Guided walk on a crescent dune, North Horr, Northern Kenya

African Baobab
Often referred to locally as the upside-down tree, the baobab has bare skyward-pointing branches that look like upturned roots.

Gerenuk
Endemic to arid parts of East Africa, the peculiar gerenuk uses its elongated neck to browse goat-like on high leaves (see p132).

The milk bush is named for its toxic white latex.

WHAT FLORA TO SEE

Penwiper plant

SUCCULENTS

Euphorbia (*Euphorbia candelabrum*), with its candelabra-like leaf formation, is often associated with slopes in the more arid parts of Kenya.

Desert rose (*Adenium spp*), also known as the impala lily, is indigenous to East Africa. It is also seen in Northern Kenya, where it is often planted to brighten lodge gardens.

Milk bush (*Euphorbia tirucalli*) is a medium-sized flowering succulent with large yellow fruit.

Turkana aloe (*Aloe turkanensis*), like *Aloe vera*, is one of several aloe species that are used in the making of organic soaps, perfumes and similar products.

Penwiper plant (*Kalanchoe marmorata*) is named for its purple blotched leaves, which

look a little like blotting paper. The erect white flowers grow up to 10 cm (4 inches) in length.

Vulturine Guineafowl
This large game bird with a brilliant cobalt chest is one of the most characteristic birds of the semiarid north, being especially common in Samburu-Buffalo Springs.

Desert Rose
This striking dry-country succulent is shrub-sized with brilliant pink-red flowers.

Tamarind and red pod terminalia are tall leafy trees associated with watercourses and slopes in the semiarid north.

The false umbrella thorn has a flat-topped shape similar to that of the "true" umbrella thorn.

The Turkana aloe, like other aloes, has spiked succulent leaves and orange inflorescences.

Three-thorned acacia

VASCULAR TREES AND SHRUBS

Kenya hyacinth (*Sanseviera parva*), with its long loose leaves, is also known as mother-in-law's tongue.

African myrrh (*Commiphora africana*) is a large thorny shrub that produces a fragrant resin.

Tamarind pods

Red pod terminalia (*Terminalia brownii*) is burnt by women of the Borana tribe as a hair perfume.

African baobab (*Adansonia digitata*) has a bulbous trunk used to store water during periods of drought.

False umbrella thorn (*Acacia reficiens*) is one of many shade-giving acacia species associated with the arid regions of Kenya.

Three-thorned acacia (*Acacia senegal*) is the source of gum arabic, a popular food additive.

Tamarind (*Tamarindus indica*) is a tall leafy tree whose fruit is popular with primates and elephants.

Forest Habitats

Ecologists generally differentiate forest from woodland by the presence of a closed canopy in the former. This distinction is clearly manifested in the inability of sunlight to significantly penetrate the forest interior. The most biodiverse of terrestrial habitats, these tropical forests account for a relatively small part of Kenya's surface area, but harbour a disproportionately high species count and endemism level. There are low-lying and relatively dry coastal forests such as Arabuko Sokoke, sweaty tropical lowland forests around Kakamega and moist Afro-montane forests on the slopes of Mount Kenya, often connected by belts of riparian woodland.

Forest floor covered with moist litter and shade-loving plants

Strangler Fig
This parasitic tree starts life as an epiphyte and gradually extends its roots to the forest floor to envelop the host tree, while its branches grow upward to reach above the canopy.

African mahogany is one of the tallest forest trees, standing up to 45 m (148 ft) high.

Ferns, among the most diverse forest plants, are often seen along streams.

WHAT FLORA TO SEE

Ripe figs, favoured by parrots

CANOPY TREES

African mahogany *(Khaya spp)*, with its wide, buttressed trunk, is often felled for hardwood timber.

Strangler figs *(Ficus spp)*, when mature, can be distinguished by the tall, hollow cylinder left inside the trunk after the host tree dies.

Croton *(Croton megalocarpus)* is a common upper-canopy forest tree

in lowland and montane forests, reaching a height of 40 m (131 ft).

Red stinkwood *(Prunus africana)*, popular as timber, exudes a pungent almond-like smell when freshly cut.

Figs *(Ficus spp)* are common forest trees whose fruits – which are actually modified flowers – attract fruitbats, monkeys and a variety of birds in season.

Large-leaved saucer-berry *(Cordia abyssinica)* has saucer-shaped flowers and large berries that attract many birds. It often grows along forest streams.

Black-and-white Colobus
Forests are the favoured habitat of many monkey species, including the striking black-and-white colobus, which occurs in coastal, Afro-montane and tropical lowland forests (see p112).

TYPICAL WILDLIFE

African green pigeon
Black-and-white casqued hornbill
Blue monkey (see p112)
Bushbabies (see p113)
Bushbuck (see p129)
Duikers (see p132)
Gaboon viper
Leopard (see pp106–107)
Millipedes
Paradise flycatcher (see p145)
Red-bellied coastal squirrel
Rhinoceros beetle
Tree frogs (see p134)
Tree hyrax
Yellow-rumped elephant shrew

White stinkwood *(Celtis africana)* has a grey trunk and grows up to 25 m (82 ft) high in forests.

African rosewood *(Hagenia abyssinica)* is common in high altitude forests.

Flap-necked Chameleon
The second-most important centre of chameleon speciation in the world, East Africa's forests host several endemic species, including the flap-necked chameleon.

Bird's-nest ferns *(Asplenium spp)* are epiphytes that grow on trunks.

Orchids, whether terrestrial or epiphytic, are the most spectacular flowering plants in the forest.

Tree ferns

EPIPHYTIC AND UNDERSTOREY PLANTS

Epiphytic orchids *(Orchidaceae)* are stunning, seasonally flowering plants that grow on the trunks of larger trees.

Tree ferns *(Cyathea spp)* are splendid prehistoric-looking trees

with long fronded leaves and trunks that typically reach up to 3 m (10 ft) in height.

Dragon trees *(Dracaena spp)*, familiar as pot plants, are spectacular leafy shrubs associated with the forest subcanopy.

African violets *(Saintpaulia spp)*, though unrelated to true violets, are popular shade-loving pot plants that

African violets

originate from the understorey Eastern Arc forests of Tanzania and southeast Kenya.

Afro-montane Habitats

Kenya's mountains include several of Africa's tallest peaks, notably Mount Kenya, the Aberdares and Mount Elgon. The unique vegetation associated with them is divided into several altitudinal zones, starting with lower montane forest on slopes below 2,000–3,000 m (6,560–9,840 ft), then rising through bamboo forest, hagenia shrubland and open heath to the Afro-alpine moorland below the snow line. Each mountain effectively forms an evolutionary "island" of Afro-montane habitats, and while the broad floral composition and altitudinal zones are similar throughout, the level of endemism on individual mountains is very high.

Bare slopes and harsh climate above the rocky snow line of Mount Kenya

Sharpe's Longclaw
Endemic to the high grasslands of central Kenya, this pipit-like bird was listed by IUCN as endangered in 2000.

Tussock grass *(Festuca pilgeri)* and mosses *(Bryophyta spp)* are prolific on wet slopes and rocks of the Afro-alpine zone.

The giant lobelia is a spectacular high-altitude plant that grows up to 6 m (20 ft) in height.

The giant groundsel is one of several otherworldly examples of gigantism among Afro-alpine flora.

WHAT FLORA TO SEE

Bamboo forest, the Aberdares

BAMBOO AND HAGENIA ZONES

Bamboo *(Arundinaria alpina)* is a form of grass that grows to spectacular heights on East Africa's mountains.

Old Man's Beard *(Usnea spp)* is a grey-green lichen that hangs from tree branches. Most species are edible and several are used as traditional medicines or as a source of vitamin C.

African juniper *(Juniperus procera)* is an aromatic conifer seen on the northern slopes of Mount Kenya.

East African rosewood *(Hagenia abyssinica)* grows up to 20 m (66 ft) in height and dominates wooded parts of the hagenia zone.

Giant St John's wort *(Hypericum revolutum)* is a dense shrub that dominates more open sections of the hagenia zone.

Podo *(Podocarpus milanjianus)* is a spectacular timber tree that grows up to 46 m (150 ft) in height.

Afro-montane Forest
Generally dank and chilly, montane Afro-forests have trees draped in the wispy lichen known as Old Man's Beard.

The snow line, the upper limit for flora, is under retreat on most Kenyan mountains.

Mountain Bongo
This beautiful, large antelope is thought to number some 100 in the wild (see p129).

Giant lobelia

The giant thistle is endemic to Mount Kenya and the Aberdares.

Pink everlastings (*Helichrysum spp*) have pretty flowers that follow the sun's movements.

The large painted lady (*Gladiolus carneus*) is a tall gladiolus with large pink-red flowers.

Giant groundsel   Red-hot poker

HEATH ZONE

Red-hot poker (*Kniphofia thomsonii*) is found along montane streams. This reed-like shrub is named for its long orange flowers.

African sage (*Artemisia afra*) is a clumped shrub with fern-like leaves and several medicinal uses.

East African sugarbush (*Protea kilimanjaro*) has furry leaves and large cup-like flowers.

AFRO-ALPINE ZONE

Giant lobelia is represented by two species on Mount Kenya, namely *Lobelia telekii* and *L. keniensis*.

Giant groundsel (*Senecio keniodendron*) can survive at high altitudes due to spongy areas between the leaf cells where water freezes without harming the plant.

Giant thistle (*Carduus keniensis*) is recognised by its orange flowers and bristly leaves.

Wetland Habitats

The term wetlands embraces all freshwater and most saline aquatic habitats other than open sea. It includes rivers and lagoons, but is most often used in reference to marshlands and lakes, habitats that are of great significance to the survival of aquatic life, as well as to the majority of terrestrial creatures that depend on them for drinking water. Kenya is well endowed with lakes, ranging from the inland seas of Victoria and Turkana to the more confined Baringo and Nakuru, while the rivers form life-sustaining ribbons of green through drier habitats.

Riparian thickets surrounding the meandering Mara river

Raffia palm often grows tall on the edge of rivers and lakes.

Otters
These secretive aquatic carnivores feed on tilapia and other fish in most of Kenya's larger rivers and lakes.

Wild date palm grows in riverside clumps with multiple curved stems.

Papyrus is a 2–3 m (6–10 ft) high plant that forms dense clumps in shallow water.

Water hyacinth *(Eichhornia crassipes)* is an invasive species that has colonised parts of Lake Victoria.

White water lilies are found in still freshwater habitats.

African Jacana
This pretty orange, blue, black-and-white bird has splayed claws that enable it to walk on floating plants.

WHAT FLORA TO SEE

Nile cabbage

REED-LIKE FRINGING VEGETATION

Common reed *(Phragmites australis)* is used as a site for nests – and also as nest-building material – by many weavers, bishops and allied bird species.

Papyrus *(Cyperus papyrus)*, also known as paper reed, is a giant sedge that was used to make paper by the ancient Egyptians.

Sedges *(Cyperus spp)* are tall grass-like plants associated with the margins of East African lakes.

FLOATING VEGETATION

White water lily *(Nymphaea nouchali)* can be distinguished from the invasive hyacinth by its white rather than blue flower.

Nile cabbage *(Pistia stratiotes)*, a floating perennial with tint flowers

and thick, foot-long leaves, is common on parts of Lake Victoria.

Blue-green algae *(Spirulina platensis)*, a microscopic resident of saline inland waters, is the main diet of flamingoes at Lake Nakuru.

Hippopotamus

The most iconic of Africa's wetland mammals, hippos can be very vociferous at night. Mainly associated with freshwater habitats, they also occasionally venture into saline waters.

TYPICAL WILDLIFE

African fish eagle *(see p140)*
Cape clawless otter *(see p110)*
Dragonflies
Elephant *(see pp114–15)*
Frogs *(see p134)*
Hippopotamus *(see pp116–17)*
Marsh mongoose *(see p111)*
Marsh terrapin *(see p137)*
Nile monitor *(see p135)*
Pied kingfisher *(see p145)*
Pond skaters
Sitatunga *(see p129)*
Waterbuck *(see p131)*
Whirligig beetle
Yellow-billed stork

The fever tree, a yellow-barked acacia, grows by marshes and lakes.

The waterberry *(Syzygium guineense)* stands up to 15-m (49-ft) tall and has edible leaves and fruits.

The common reed is the dominant plant in Kenya's wetland habitats.

The bulrush, *(Typha spp)* is a common invasive species in the wetlands.

Tilapia

This varied group of cichlid fish is associated with most freshwater and some saline habitats in Kenya.

Fever trees

WATERSIDE TREES

Toothbrush tree *(Salvadora persica)* is a small riverine tree with fibrous wood, which is traditionally used as a toothbrush in many African cultures.

Fever tree *(Acacia xanthophloea)*, with its jaundiced bark and preference for low

Wild dates

swampy habitats, is so named because early colonial settlers thought it propagated malaria.

Wild date palm *(Phoenix reclinata)* is a small palm with large, fleshy, yellow, clustered fruits.

African Olive *(Olea capensis)*, common in riverine forests, is also

known as ironwood due to its hard, fine-grained wood, which is used to make high-quality furniture.

Raffia palm *(Themeda trianda)* is the favoured nesting site of Kenya's palmnut vulture, which feeds on its fruit.

Intertidal Habitats

This zoologically rich habitat consists of the narrow stretch of tidal water that divides the beachfront and fringing vegetation from offshore coral reefs. It is popular with visitors who come to swim in the warm surf, which is protected by the reefs at high tide. At low tide, the beaches drain of water, leaving behind sand and rock pools frequented by small fish, marine invertebrates and wading birds. This zone supports a limited flora, although one niche habitat included within its confines are the mangroves that run along coastal creeks and other inlets.

The palm-lined beach at low tide, Kipungani village, Lamu

Mangroves

The intertidal flats, estuaries and creeks of the Kenyan coastline support prolific mangrove ecosystems, comprising a select group of plants whose roots can absorb water and oxygen in saline conditions.

Seaweed, essentially a spread of multicellular algae, can float in water and occasionally infests the beaches of Kenya.

Mangrove roots often protrude from the mudflats at low tide to absorb oxygen directly from the air.

WHAT FAUNA TO SEE

Sea urchin

MANGROVES

Mangrove kingfisher *(Halcyon senegaloidesis)* is a brilliant blue bird associated almost exclusively with mangroves.

Hermit crabs *(Paguroidea)* are colonial decapods that live in "borrowed" shells. Despite their name, they are not closely related to true crabs and several species are terrestrial.

Mudskippers *(Oxudercinae)* are amphibious fish whose unique adaptations to intertidal habitats means they are very active on exposed mangrove mudflats.

TIDAL POOLS

Sea urchins *(Echinoidea)* are the marine equivalent of hedgehogs. These small spiky invertebrates are often seen clinging to rocks in tidal pools.

Starfish *(Asteroidea)* are radially symmetrical predators with extraordinary regenerative powers.

Crabs, with their thick exoskeleton and sharp pincers, are common in rock pools and on most beaches.

Giant Coconut Crab
The largest terrestrial arthropod in the world, the giant coconut crab weighs in at 4 kg (9 lb) and can crack open a coconut with its strong pincers.

TYPICAL WILDLIFE

Bottlenose dolphins
Devil firefish
Dugong
Green turtle *(see p137)*
Hammerhead shark
Humpback whale
Jellyfish
Leatherback turtle *(see p137)*
Moray eel
Octopus
Sperm whale
Squids
Stingrays
Swordfish
Whale shark

Casuarinas *(Casuarina cunninghamiana)* are tall, conifer-like trees that were introduced to Kenya and are now invasive along the coast.

The coconut palm *(Cocos nucifera)*, though non-indigenous to Kenya, is well adapted to the saline coastal sands and is widely cultivated for fruit, fronds and wood.

Offshore Coral Reefs
Hundreds of fish species and an even greater diversity of invertebrates make their home in coral reefs off the Kenyan coast.

Marlins
Often known as spearfish, these fish have spiked snouts and powerful torsos that enable them to glide through the water at up to 80 kmph (50 mph).

Mussels

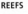

Portuguese man-of-war *(Physalia physalis)* is also known as bluebottle. This is a floating jellyfish-like invertebrate whose sting is excruciatingly painful and very occasionally fatal.

Mussels *(Mytilidae)* and other shelled bivalve molluscs frequently cling to the sides of permanent rock pools.

REEFS

Clownfish *(Amphiprion spp)* are dazzling yellow, orange and black reef fish that live symbiotically with sea anemones.

Parrot fish *(Scaridae)* are pastel-hued pink and blue fish. They are so named for their parrot-like "beaks" formed by their teeth.

A pair of clownfish

Blue-streaked cleaner wrasse *(Labroides dimidatus)* is a fish that feeds on the parasites of other fish.

Moorish idol *(Zanclus cornutus)* is a stunning yellow, black and blue fish with a vertically compressed body and long trailing dorsal fin.

FIELD GUIDE

K enya's superb network of national parks and other protected areas harbours a quite extraordinary diversity of wildlife. This is one of Africa's premier destinations for the Big Five as well as a number of other favourites, ranging from the greyhound-like cheetah to several elegant antelope species. Yet these mammalian icons represent a mere fraction of what Kenya has to offer – with over 500 reptile and amphibian species and an astonishing checklist of birds.

Most safaris to Kenya focus on the southern parks bordering Tanzania, namely Amboseli, Masai Mara and Tsavo East and West National Parks, as well as the splendid string of lakes that runs along the floor of the Rift Valley. This vast southern wilderness, home to the enigmatic Maasai pastoralists, seems almost to have been designed to fulfil the expectations of first-time visitors to Africa. The game viewing here can include groups of tusk-heavy elephants gathering at a waterhole in the red plains of Tsavo; the thousands of braying wildebeest that swarm across the Mara river every July; zebras rolling in the ultra-fine dust of Amboseli below the snow-capped peaks of Kilimanjaro; or the white rhinos that graze earnestly on the floodplain of Lake Nakuru in sight of millions of bright pink flamingoes.

The iridescent agama lizard

If southern Kenya stands as one of Africa's great conventional safari destinations, the rest of the country is rich in less celebrated but equally fantastic wildlife-viewing opportunities. The semiarid plains of the north, protected in Samburu-Buffalo Springs, are host to numerous dry-country rarities, ranging from the quirky gerenuk antelope and majestic oryx to the near-endemic reticulated giraffe and Grevy's zebra. The forests of the coastal belt form part of one of the world's greatest biodiversity hotspots, home to several endemic birds and monkeys. The central and western forests, such as the Aberdares and Kakamega, show unexpected zoological affinities with the rainforest of Central Africa in the form of bongos, giant forest hogs and numerous colourful forest birds.

Lake Nakuru with its vast flocks of pelicans and flamingoes

◁ A migrating herd of wildebeest crossing the swollen Mara river

Endemic Animals

By definition, endemic animals are peculiar to a single, generally restricted range, and are especially vulnerable to localised habitat destruction and hunting. Kenya's most important centre of endemism is the eastern coast, whose forests harbour at least four large mammal and half a dozen bird species found nowhere else in the world. Also important are the forested Central Highlands and isolated massifs such as the Taita Hills and Mount Marsabit.

FIELD GUIDE ICONS

☐ Diurnal
☾ Nocturnal
🐾 Savannah
🌵 Arid and Semiarid
🌲 Forest
⛰ Afro-montane
🌾 Wetland
🏖 Intertidal

TANA RIVER RED COLOBUS
(SPECIES: PROCOLOBUS RUFOMITRATUS)

BEST SEEN: Tana River Primate Reserve

    CR

The only Kenyan representative of a group of rainforest monkeys associated with West and Central Africa, the Tana river red colobus has a distinct ginger cap and fringe, a long tail and a grey-brown coat. Isolated from other red colobus populations by several hundred kilometres, it is restricted to marshy forested habitats about 75 km (47 miles) upstream of the mouth of the Tana river, where recent estimates suggest that the total population is no more than 800.

The medium-sized, long-limbed Tana river red colobus

The ash-grey mangabey with orange-red chest and belly

TANA RIVER MANGABEY
(SPECIES: CERCOCEBUS GALERITUS)

BEST SEEN: Tana River Primate Reserve

    EN

Sharing its range with the Tana river red colobus, the eponymous mangabey is the only Kenyan representative of a family of large arboreal Cercopithecid monkeys associated with low-altitude rainforest in Central and West Africa. Endemic to riparian woodland along a 60-km (37-mile) stretch of the Tana river, it was listed as one of the world's 25 most endangered primate taxa in 2000, but a subsequent survey showed that the population stands at 2,070 individuals, an increase of 18 per cent since 1974.

CLARKE'S WEAVER
(SPECIES: PLOCEUS GOLANDI)

BEST SEEN: Arabuko Sokoke NP

☐ 🏡   EN

The most localised of many dozens of weaver species found in Kenya, Clarke's weaver is endemic to the Arabuko-Sokoke Forest and immediate surrounds, where it is almost exclusively associated with brachystegia woodland. It is often seen in large flocks that mingle with helmet-shrikes. The global population is estimated to be fewer than 1,000.

This chameleon species varies from black to bright green

JACKSON'S THREE-HORNED CHAMELEON
(SPECIES: CHAMAELEO JACKSONI)

BEST SEEN: Nairobi NP, Aberdare NP, Mount Kenya

    NE

Common in the forest suburbia of Nairobi, this striking 0.3-m (1-ft) long chameleon is named for the trio of impressive horns that grow on its snout. With the exception of one racially discrete population on Tanzania's Mount Meru, it is endemic to the Central Highlands of Kenya, where it spends most of its time in the trees.

Clarke's weaver, mostly yellow with an all-black head

IUCN status CR: Critically Endangered; EN: Endangered; VU: Vulnerable; NE: Not Evaluated

HIROLA
(SPECIES: BEATRAGUS HUNTERI)

BEST SEEN: Tsavo East NP, Arawale Hirola Reserve

 CR

Also known as Hunter's hartebeest, the hirola is similar in appearance to other hartebeests, but is much smaller, has impala-like horns and distinctive white "spectacles". It is naturally confined to an area of dry grassland in southern Somalia and the Northern Coast of Kenya, but is now almost certainly extinct outside Kenya, where its population plummeted to fewer than 1,000 in the late 1990s as a result of drought and competition with livestock. This decline led to the creation of the 530-sq-km (205-sq-mile) Arawale Hirola Reserve, about 100 km (62 miles) northwest of Lamu. Two herds introduced to Tsavo East have adapted well to its semiarid habitat, and small herds are occassionally seen on the plains south of Voi and Aruba Dam.

The white spectacle-like marks identify the hirola

TAITA THRUSH
(SPECIES: TURDUS HELLERI)

BEST SEEN: Taita Hills

 CR

Confined to three fragmented pockets of cloud forest covering a total area of less than 4 sq km (2 sq miles), this handsome black, red and white thrush is endemic to Taita Hills. The total population was estimated at 1,350 in 1997, but it has probably declined in the interim due to further habitat loss and fragmentation. Within its restricted range, the Taita thrush is a shy skulking bird associated with leaf litter, and its song is yet to be identified.

Taita thrush, with distinctive red beak and eye-ring

A long nose and yellow rump distinguish this shrew

GOLDEN-RUMPED ELEPHANT SHREW
(SPECIES: RHYNCHOCYON CHRYSOPYGUS)

BEST SEEN: Arabuko Sokoke NP, Gedi Ruins

 EN

The golden-rumped elephant shrew is the largest and most vulnerable member of the ancient African order Macroscelidea, consisting of roughly 15 species of peculiar rodent-sized creatures – known as elephant-shrews or sangis – that hop around like miniature kangaroos and possess absurdly elongated and perpetually twitchy noses. Confined to the coastal Arabuko Sokoke National Park and its immediate vicinity, the golden-rumped elephant shrew is one of the few diurnal members of the order. It is often glimpsed from footpaths through the Gedi Ruins, which border Arabuko Sokoke. Comparable in size to a rabbit, it weighs 500 g (18 oz) and is dark russet-brown in colour but with a bright yellow-gold rump and throat. It feeds on the forest floor, scratching noisily through the leaf litter to locate its prey of crickets, millipedes and other medium to large insects with its sensitive nose.

Hinde's babbler, with scaly feathering and red eyes

HINDE'S BABBLER
(SPECIES: TURDOIDES HINDEI)

BEST SEEN: Mwea NR

VU

Endemic to the eastern slopes of the Central Highlands, Hinde's babbler is a black, brown and white bird distinguished from other members of the babbler family by its bold red eyes. A major quarry for bird-watchers in Kenya, it has a limited distribution and some estimates place the population at 1,500, which means it is unlikely to be seen unless actively sought.

Key to Field Guide icons *see p98*

Cats

Secretive and solitary, the cats of the family Felidae are the most stealthy and efficient killers among carnivores. Also the most strictly carnivorous, they feed exclusively on other warm-blooded creatures, from sparrows and mice to buffalo and giraffe. Although they differ greatly in coloration and size, all cats have a similar body plan to their familiar domestic counterpart, with an elongated body, long tail, small head, sensitive whiskers, prominent canines and keen bifocal vision. Much wild felid behaviour will be familiar to the average cat owner.

FAMILY

Kenya's seven felid species, traditionally split between three genera, are *Felis*, with small- to medium-size cats; *Panthera*, with big cats distinguished by a larynx modification enabling them to roar; and *Acinonyx*, with the cheetah, the only felid with non-retractable claws.

AFRICAN WILD CAT
(SPECIES: FELIS SILVESTRIS)

BEST SEEN: Masai Mara GR, Tsavo NP, Samburu-Buffalo Springs NR

LC

The smallest African felid, and the most elusive of those associated with savannah habitats, the African wild cat is closely related to its much rarer European counterpart. DNA evidence suggests that it is the sole wild ancestor of the domestic cat, which was first domesticated in North Africa some 10,000 years ago. Very similar in appearance to a domestic tabby but with markedly longer legs, it is a versatile hunter of rodents, birds and insects. It has a high habitat tolerance, which means that it is the most widely distributed of all African predators, being absent only from rainforest interiors and true deserts. Although seldom seen, it remains very common away from human habitation. Its genetic integrity, however, is under increasing threat as a result of interbreeding with the feral domestic cats that are occasionally seen in East Africa's game reserves.

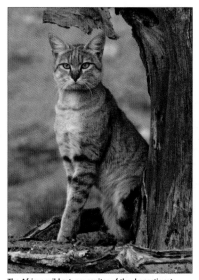

The African wild cat, progenitor of the domestic cat

Small rounded ears are the most obvious physical difference between the golden cat and caracal.

GOLDEN CAT
(SPECIES: FELIS AURATA)

BEST SEEN: Aberdare NP, Arabuko Sokoke NP, Mount Kenya

NT

The rainforest counterpart to the caracal, the golden cat is similar in general appearance and overall build, but richer in colour, with black spotting on the belly, light striping on the tail and non-tufted and relatively small ears. Essentially a species of the Congolese rainforest, its range extends to suitable habitats in East Africa, where it is uncommon and very secretive. It has been sighted in Western Kenya and in the Arabuko Sokoke forest. Among the least studied of the African carnivores, the golden cat is extremely unlikely to be observed, even in the few localities where it is known to be present.

The golden cat, named for its lustrous tawny-gold coat

IUCN status NT: Near Threatened; LC: Least Concern

CARACAL
(SPECIES: FELIS CARACAL)

BEST SEEN: Masai Mara GR, Tsavo NP, Buffalo Springs NR

▶ ⚲⚲ ♣ LC

The largest and most powerful of Africa's "small cats", the caracal bears a strong resemblance to the Eurasian lynx, and the two were long thought to be conspecific. However, genetic studies suggest that the caracal is more closely allied to the serval and golden cat than to any non-African species. A male can be 1 m (3 ft) in length from head to tail and weigh up to 20 kg (44 lb); females are usually a lot smaller. The caracal has a fairly uniform tan coat with light spotting sometimes distinguishable on the paler belly, and long tufted ears whose dark colouration is referred to in Turkish as *karakulak* (black ear) from which the cat gets its name. It is exceptionally sharp of hearing, even by felid standards, thanks to this tufting and some 20 muscles that control ear direction. A versatile hunter, it is particularly skilled at hunting birds in flight, and its agility and preference for rocky habitats means that it presents the greatest threat to hyraxes after Verreaux's eagle. Like other small cats, the caracal is a solitary nocturnal hunter, seldom observed by day or night. For all that, it is widespread in Kenya, and probably very common, generally favouring more arid and rocky habitats than the serval.

Caracal, the cat most strongly associated with dry habitats

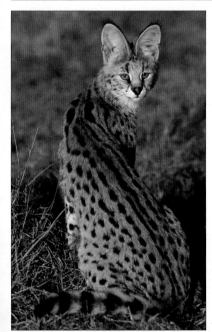

The serval is the smallest of Africa's spotted cats

SERVAL
(SPECIES: FELIS SERVAL)

BEST SEEN: Masai Mara GR, Meru NP, Aberdare NP

▶ ⚲⚲ LC

Superficially similar to the larger cheetah, the serval is a sleek spotted cat associated with rank grassland and other non-forested habitats offering good access to water. It can be distinguished from the cheetah by its proportionately shorter tail (about one-third of its body length), and the most common colour morph has streaky as opposed to circular black-on-gold spots, although speckled and melanistic morphs are also seen in some areas. It has the longest legs in relation to body size of any felid, and very large ears – adaptations that help it locate prey in its preferred habitat of tall grassland. It feeds mainly on small mammals and birds, which it pounces upon with a spectacular high spring, delivering the fatal blow by striking the victim swift and hard with one of its powerful claws. The serval will also occasionally catch fish and pounce on frogs. Diurnal serval sightings are not commonplace, but it is the most readily seen of the smaller felids, especially during the first 30 minutes after sunrise.

Key to Field Guide icons *see p98*

Lion

The largest terrestrial predator in Africa, the lion is the most sociable and least secretive of the world's 36 cat species. It is unusual among felids in that it seldom takes to the trees, and that an adult male sports a regal blond or black mane. For most people, the charismatic "king of the jungle" is the ultimate African safari icon, so much so that it is often easy to forget that lions once ranged widely across Eurasia. Though common and conspicuous in several Kenyan reserves, lions are in decline elsewhere, with Africa's lion population having seen a 75 per cent decline since 1990.

Lions are remarkably indolent *creatures, spending up to 20 hours a day at rest. Though seldom active in the heat of the day, they often cover long distances at night.*

FAMILY AND BREEDING

The most sociable of cats, the lion lives in prides of five to ten animals, including an adult male, a few adult females, and their offspring. Larger prides are seen in the Serengeti-Mara ecosystem, where they are presided over by two or more adult male siblings. Prides are active in defending their territories, which typically cover 20–200 sq km (8–77 sq miles). Takeover battles are often fought to the death, and if successful, result in the usurper killing all existing cubs, thereby encouraging the females back into oestrus sooner. Lions undergo an extraordinary mating ritual. A male and female pair off, mating briefly but violently at gradually increasing intervals of 12–25 minutes for up to 3 days, after which they return to their pride.

Females in a pride give birth more or less simultaneously *and rear their cubs cooperatively. Large prides consist of up to half a dozen lionesses and their offspring. Females usually stay with their birth pride, but young males are forced out by the dominant male when they reach sexual maturity.*

WHAT YOU MIGHT SEE

The first lion sighting often results in disappointment, as the animals loll disinterestedly in the shade. Observe them for a while, however, and one is bound to see exciting interactions. It is always worth staying with an isolated female and male pair, as they may well start mating; and if a lioness is lying low in the grass, looking intently into the distance, odds are she is part of a hunt.

Rivalry between adult males *can be intense and fights are often to the death.*

Grooming and social licking *are an important part of the daily ritual in any lion pride.*

IUCN status VU: Vulnerable

FEEDING

Hunting is normally a team effort undertaken by females, who rely on stealth more than speed. A common strategy is for one or two lionesses to herd their prey in the direction of other pride members lying hidden in tall grass. Males seldom take part in a hunt but are quick to exercise their feeding rights once a kill is made. Favoured prey includes antelope, and large prides can even bring down a giraffe or a buffalo.

A large male lion takes first pickings on a fresh giraffe kill

COMMUNICATION AND VOICE

Adult lions are most active around dusk and dawn, but cubs interact throughout the day, playing and mock fighting for hours on end. Subordinate individuals frequently stop to greet or groom dominant pride members, especially when they reunite after a period apart. The most common call, made by females as well as males, is a series of far-carrying moaning grunts that first increase in volume, then fade away. As dominant males often move separately from the main pride (regrouping after a kill), this characteristic sound of the African night has the dual purpose of advertising the caller's presence to the pride and warning rivals off its territory.

A cub displays submissiveness to one of the adult males in the pride

Name: *Panthera leo*
Swahili: *Simba*

 Size Shoulder height: 100–130 cm (40–51 inches); Weight: up to 280 kg (617 lb).

Lifespan 12–15 years in the wild.
Population in Kenya 2,000–3,000.
Conservation status VU.
Gestation period 105–112 days.
Reproduction Females reach sexual maturity at 3 years and give birth to litters of two to six cubs every 18 months.

 Habitat Most often in savannah, but range into all habitats except desert and rainforest.

A group of Maasai hunters

 Top places to see
Masai Mara Game Reserve (*see pp262–5*), Nairobi NP (*see pp162–5*), Tsavo NP (*see pp182–7*).

Sighting tips
Look out for resting prides during the day – it is worth returning to the spot at dawn or dusk to catch them in action.

Friends and foes
Contrary to the popular belief that lions are regal hunters and hyenas craven scavengers, lions feeding on a carcass are as likely to have stolen it from a hyena as to have killed it themselves.

Facts and trivia
Traditionally, the only form of hunting permitted by the pastoral Maasai is the Olamayio lion hunt, a form of group hunting held as an initiation ritual.

The main diet *of lions in Kenya comprises ungulates such as zebra, buffalo and antelope.*

Cubs *spend a large part of their day mock fighting and playing with each other, and sometimes with adults.*

A mating bout *often lasts for less than a minute and is accompanied by growling and hissing.*

Cheetah

The world's fastest runner, the cheetah can reach 115 kmph (71 mph) in short bursts, accelerating from standstill in four seconds. It is anatomically distinct from true big cats, with a greyhound-like build, disproportionately small head and unique semiretractable claws catering to its specialist pursuit of sprinting. Once widespread in Asia, Arabia and Africa, it has suffered a massive range retraction in recent times, and is now practically endemic to sub-Saharan Africa.

The king cheetah, *a rare mutant, has a striped coat. Prone to unusual colour morphs, cheetahs have included all-black and all-white individuals, as well as those with unspotted golden coats or tawny or blue-grey spots on a creamy coat.*

FAMILY AND BREEDING

Though not as sociable as lions, cheetahs are less solitary than most cats. The highly territorial adult male is generally solitary, although coalitions of two to three brothers are often seen. Females are solitary except when rearing cubs, and related females often have overlapping territories. The cheetah follows a protracted courtship ritual, which leads to the female coming into oestrus after 1–2 weeks. Mortal fights between competing males are common during this period. Litters consist of four to five cubs, born blind and hidden away for the first few months of their life. Even so, the cub mortality rate is high, partly due to the harsh habitat, and partly because the mother is unable to ward off predators. The surviving cubs stay with the mother for about 18 months, and are unique among felids in that they need to be taught how to hunt.

Cubs often stay together *after they are abandoned by their mother, honing their hunting skills as a pack before they eventually separate to fend for themselves.*

WHAT YOU MIGHT SEE

Almost always associated with open country, cheetahs have a more restless temperament than other large predators. They are most often seen trotting through the grass with a distinct air of determination, breaking step only to climb on a tree trunk or termite mound that presents itself as a lookout post. They are also more likely to be seen hunting in daylight than other cats.

Cheetahs regularly sharpen their claws, *which are only partly retractable.*

The black "tear marks" *that run down a cheetah's face help differentiate it from a leopard.*

IUCN status VU: Vulnerable

FEEDING

Where most feline predators combine hunting with scavenging, cheetahs feed solely on fresh meat. A diurnal and crepuscular hunter, the cheetah usually creeps to within 15–31 m (50–100 ft) of its prey before opening chase at immense speed, eventually knocking down its victim and suffocating it with its mouth. High tourist concentrations can adversely affect a cheetah's hunting habits – safari vehicles often alert prey to its presence – although some individuals have turned the tables by using parked vehicles as cover to stalk gazelles and other prey.

Devouring a freshly killed gazelle, while keeping an eye out for predators

COMMUNICATION AND VOICE

The cheetah differs from true big cats such as the leopard and lion in several respects, one of which is that the cheetah lacks the ability to roar. The most common vocalisation, often made by a mother looking for her cubs, is a peculiar high pitched twitter called yipping, which sounds more like a small bird or bat than a large carnivore. In common with other cats, a cheetah will purr when content or when it meets a familiar individual, and will growl, hiss and yelp when threatened or annoyed.

Cheetahs communicate with a wide repertoire of sounds such as growling, hissing and spitting

KEY FACTS

Name: *Acinonyx jubatus*
Swahili: *Duma*

Size Shoulder height: 80 cm (31 inches); Weight: 41–60 kg (90–130 lbs).

Lifespan 6–12 years in the wild.
Population in Kenya Below 1,000.
Conservation status VU.
Gestation period 3 months.
Reproduction Females reach sexual maturity at around 2 years and give birth to up to five cubs a year thereafter.

Habitat Thinly-vegetated plains and open or broken grassland.

Resting on a safari vehicle

Top places to see
Masai Mara GR *(see pp262–5)*, Tsavo NP *(see pp182–7)*, Nairobi NP *(see pp162–65)*, Ol Pejeta *(see p320)*.

Sighting tips
If a cheetah on the hunt is sighted, maintain some distance from it – overzealous guides frequently ruin the event by driving too close and chasing off the cat's intended prey.

Friends and foes
Easily intimidated, a cheetah will wolf down a fresh kill before it can be chased off by nearby scavengers, consuming up to 10 kg (22 lb) in 15 minutes.

Facts and trivia
Striped cheetahs were thought to be a local superstition until 1926, when British zoologist R I Pocock was shown the pelt of one.

Cheetah cubs *are very playful but also wary, and will often flee into a burrow when disturbed.*

A short high-speed chase, *generally over open grassland, is the hallmark of the cheetah's hunting strategy.*

Cheetahs often ascend trunks *or termite mounds to scan the area for rivals and potential prey.*

Leopard

Paradoxically the most abundant and the most elusive of Africa's large predators, the leopard is distinguishable by its rosette-patterned coat, powerfully pugilistic physique and preference for dense cover. This determinedly nocturnal cat is the supreme solitary hunter, capable of creeping to within a few feet of its prey before it pounces. Despite widespread persecution, the global leopard population remains in good shape, comprising an estimated 500,000 individuals ranging across sub-Saharan Africa, the Middle East and tropical Asia.

The melanistic leopard, *popularly known as a panther, is less proportionately common in Africa than in Asia. The exception is in highland areas, notably Aberdare National Park, where melanistic individuals are regularly reported.*

FAMILY AND BREEDING

The leopard is among the most solitary and territorial of cats. Adults live alone in well-marked territories that are never shared with individuals of the same sex, although males and females frequently have partial territorial overlap. Even so, a chance meeting between two individuals is usually accompanied by real or feigned aggression. Far smaller than males, female leopards come into oestrus every 6–7 weeks. At this time, males from bordering or overlapping territories will often fight to the death for coupling rights. Mating itself is an ill-tempered and abruptly executed affair, and the male has no involvement in rearing the cubs. Females give birth to litters of two to three cubs in a sheltered cave or thicket, and keep a close watch over them for the next 10–14 days, when the cubs' eyes open. Infant mortality is high; it is unusual for more than one cub to survive to adulthood. Cubs can fend for themselves at around one year, but usually stay close to their mother for another 6–12 months before becoming fully independent.

Leopard cubs *typically have greyer pelts than the adults. Leopards are famously solitary, and two individuals keeping peaceful company will almost certainly be a female and her cub.*

WHAT YOU MIGHT SEE

For most safarigoers, the leopard is the most ardently sought of the Big Five. It is most likely to be seen resting up in a tree, in which case it is often worth waiting to see whether there is a kill secured nearby, or if it decides to descend to the ground. Even more thrilling is to catch a leopard on the move, showing off its sleek yet pugilistic build to the full.

A creature of shadow, *cover and darkness, the leopard is most active after dark.*

Sharpened claws *are essential components in this cat's hunting and defensive arsenal.*

IUCN status LC: Least Concern

FEEDING

The leopard is an adaptable and opportunistic hunter, feeding on anything from medium-sized antelope to hares, birds, baboons, hyraxes and insects. It depends almost entirely on stealth, stalking silently through thick vegetation before emerging at the last possible moment to pounce and strangle its prey with its powerful jaws. In rainforests and other habitats where lions are absent, the leopard is typically the apex predator, and adults tend to be notably heavier than their savannah counterparts. A leopard will frequently carry a large kill high into the canopy, where it is safely out of the reach of less arboreal scavengers such as lion, hyena and jackal.

Leopard dragging prey, often three times its weight, into the canopy

COMMUNICATION AND VOICE

As might be expected of such a potentially fearsome creature known for its ability to survive in close, near-spectral proximity to humans, the leopard is not given to extensive vocalisation. Males in particular advertise their presence with a repetitive rasping cough that sounds not unlike wood being sawed. Purring has also been recorded, probably to indicate contentment when feeding. Territorial clashes between males are accompanied by snarling and hissing. However, the most remarkable feature of the leopard remains the capacity for furtiveness that ensures that the species still persists, although barely detected, in peri-urban areas such as Karen Forest on the outskirts of Nairobi.

Display of affection between leopards, seldom observed in unrelated adults

KEY FACTS

Name: *Panthera pardus*
Swahili: *Chui*

 Size Shoulder height: 70–80 cm (28–32 inches); Weight: up to 90 kg (198 lb).

Lifespan 20 plus years.
Population in Kenya Unknown – probably several thousand.
Conservation status LC.
Gestation period 3–4 months.
Reproduction Females reach sexual maturity at 2–4 years, when they come into oestrus.

 Habitat Shows high habitat tolerance and might occur anywhere.

Leopard stalking a baboon

 Top places to see
Samburu-Buffalo Springs NR (*see pp342–5*), Masai Mara GR (*see pp262–5*), Laikipia Plateau (*see pp318–21*).

Sighting tips
Leopards often take refuge in the branches of tall trees, where they may be detected by a tail flickering below the canopy.

Friends and foes
Leopards are the only large cats that regularly prey on baboons, which therefore react hysterically to the cat, issuing a distinctive panicked alarm call that human trackers can recognise.

 Facts and trivia
The leopard's name reflects an ancient belief that it is a hybrid between a lion (*leo*) and a panther (*pardos*).

The leopard is compulsively clean *and spends much of the day grooming itself.*

Although highly adaptable, *leopards favour habitats that offer them plenty of cover and camouflage.*

Leopards frequently spend their day *lying quietly in the branches of the upper canopy.*

Dogs and Hyenas

Cats aside, the two major families of large carnivore in Kenya, Canidae (dogs) and Hyaenidae (hyenas), are exciting to see in the wild. Indeed, spotted hyenas are probably the most socially complex of the region's carnivores, and it is riveting to watch clan members meet and greet at a den. Jackals, foxes and wild dogs are also at their most confiding and inquisitive while denning, offering plenty of opportunity to watch the pups at play.

FAMILY

Dogs and hyenas, though similar in appearance, split evolutionarily about 45 million years ago – the suborder Feliformia has cats, mongooses and hyenas; Caniformia has seals, bears, otters, pandas and dogs.

Young jackals often play in a puppy-like manner

BLACK-BACKED JACKAL
(SPECIES: CANIS MESOMELAS)

BEST SEEN: Masai Mara GR, Tsavo NP

     LC

The most common of three closely-related small dog species in East Africa, the black-backed jackal lives in pairs rather than packs. It is most active at dusk and dawn, and its shrill yelping is a characteristic sound of the African night. It has a shoulder height of 40 cm (16 inches), and an ochre coat offset by a prominent silver-flecked black saddle. An opportunistic feeder, it subsists on small mammals, birds and carrion, and is often seen lurking near lion kills.

The least distinctively marked of the three jackal species

GOLDEN JACKAL
(SPECIES: CANIS AUREUS)

BEST SEEN: Masai Mara GR, Samburu-Buffalo Springs NP

LC

Also known as the common jackal, this northern hemisphere species is the only jackal whose range extends north of the Sahara – where it was revered by ancient Egyptians as the jackal god Anubis – and into Eurasia. The golden jackal is widely but thinly distributed throughout Kenya, with the Serengeti-Mara ecosystem forming the southern extreme of its global range. More or less uniform in colour, it is more diurnal in habit than the black-backed jackal, and equally vocal.

SIDE-STRIPED JACKAL
(SPECIES: CANIS ADUSTUS)

BEST SEEN: Masai Mara GR, Tsavo NP

LC

Associated with brachystegia woodland rather than acacia woodland, the unobtrusive side-striped jackal is more strictly nocturnal and less vocal than the other two jackal species. It is similar in general colouration to the black-backed jackal, but with an indistinct pale stripe along the flanks. An adaptable omnivore seen singly or in pairs, it supplements a diet based on meat with fruit, grain and carrion.

A white-tipped tail identifies the side-striped jackal

BAT-EARED FOX
(SPECIES: OTOCYON MEGALOTIS)

BEST SEEN: Masai Mara GR, Amboseli NP, Tsavo NP, Samburu-Buffalo Springs NP

LC

Easily distinguished from any jackal by its uniform silver-grey coat, huge ears and black eye-mask, this small canid is not a true fox. A number of peculiarities – up to 50 sharp teeth, for instance – have led to it being placed in its own genus. Exclusively insectivorous, it tends to be nocturnal during the hot months and diurnal in the cooler ones. Pairs and small family groups can be seen throughout the year.

The large ears help detect subterranean insect activity

IUCN status EN: Endangered; NT: Near Threatened; LC: Least Concern

The blotchy brown coat of the spotted hyena

SPOTTED HYENA
(SPECIES: CROCUTA CROCUTA)

BEST SEEN: Masai Mara GR, Aberdare NP, Tsavo NP, Samburu-Buffalo Springs NP, Amboseli NP

   LC

Africa's second largest predator stands 1 m (3 ft) high at the shoulder, and weighs about 70 kg (154 lb), with females being larger than males. The most common and conspicuous large predator in many reserves, it is most often seen at dusk and dawn. Though highly vocal at night, its famous "laugh" is less commonly heard than a haunted whoooo-whoop that ranks as perhaps the definitive sound of the African night. The hyena has a complex social structure, living in wide-ranging clans of five to 25 animals that follow a strict matriarchal hierarchy and perform an elaborate ritual when two members meet. Powerfully built, it has a characteristic sloping back, bone-crushingly powerful jaws and a dog-like face and snout. Routinely portrayed as a giggling coward whose livelihood depends on scavenging from the noble big cats, it is actually an adept hunter, capable of killing an animal as large as a wildebeest.

AFRICAN WILD DOG
(SPECIES: LYCAON PICTUS)

BEST SEEN: Laikipia Plateau, Masai Mara GR

    EN

Africa's largest canid, also known as the hunting or painted dog, is small in comparison to a Eurasian wolf, and is distinguished from similar species in the region by its black, brown and cream coat. It typically lives in packs of five to 50 animals that hunt cooperatively, literally tearing apart prey on the run. Once so common that it was treated as vermin, it has suffered enormous losses in recent decades, partially through direct persecution and partially through the packs' susceptibility to infectious diseases spread by domestic and feral dogs. It is now Africa's second-most endangered large carnivore, with a total wild population of around 5,000, of which 5 per cent is centred in Kenya. Once common in the Serengeti-Mara ecosystem, the species is now extremely rare, although recent sightings of this legendarily nomadic creature are cause for hope that it may yet recolonise the area.

African wild dog packs may include up to 50 animals

The aardwolf is jackal-sized but hyena-shaped

AARDWOLF
(SPECIES: PROTELES CRISTATUS)

BEST SEEN: Tsavo East NP, Samburu-Buffalo Springs NP, Masai Mara GR

    LC

A lightly built and strictly nocturnal Hyaenid, the aardwolf (literally, earth wolf) weighs 10 kg (22 lb) and is often confused with jackals, from which it differs in appearance by having a soft creamy striped coat and prominent dorsal mane. It is exclusively insectivorous, feeding almost entirely on two specific termite genera, and its distribution, generally in drier areas, is linked strongly to the presence of suitable nests, into which it burrows nose-first to feed.

STRIPED HYENA
(SPECIES: HYAENA HYAENA)

BEST SEEN: Masai Mara GR, Tsavo NP, Samburu–Buffalo Springs NP

NT

Essentially a northern hemisphere species, this was the hyena known to ancient Mediterranean civilisations, who believed it to be hermaphroditic and capable of changing sex at will. Much smaller than the spotted hyena, it has a pale brown or grey coat with black streaks, and a luxuriant dorsal mane. It occurs alongside the spotted hyena in dry parts of East Africa, but is thinly distributed, shy and seldom observed.

Striped hyena, less sociable than its spotted namesake

Key to Field Guide icons *see p98*

Small Carnivores

Kenya supports a wide diversity of small carnivorous mammals, some very conspicuous and easily observed, others highly secretive and elusive. Falling firmly into the first category are the mongooses of the family Herpestidae, several species of which are likely to be seen in the course of any safari. The nocturnal viverrids and mustelids are generally less likely to be seen, although genets often become very tame in lodges where they are regularly fed.

FAMILY

Genets and civets belong to the most ancient of carnivore families, Viverridae, which is confined to Africa and Asia. Mustelidae, by contrast, is the most diverse carnivore family, represented by 55 species and 24 genera worldwide.

CAPE CLAWLESS OTTER
(SPECIES: AONYX CAPENSIS)

 LC

Arguably the largest of "small" carnivores, weighing as much as 35 kg (77 lb) in some cases, the Cape clawless otter is a dark brown piscivore with a bold white collar. While seen in any suitable wetland habitat, it is most common in waters where it can evade crocodiles.

SPOTTED-NECKED OTTER
(SPECIES: LUTRA MACULICOLLIS)

 LC

Seldom weighing more than 6 kg (13 lb), the spotted-necked otter appears all brown from a distance, but has a lightly spotted throat. Absent from alkaline or saline aquatic habitats, or those with poor visibility, it is most likely to be seen on Lake Victoria's shores.

HONEY-BADGER
(SPECIES: MELLIVORA CAPENSIS)

 LC

The honey-badger, or ratel, has a fearless temperament and pugilistic build, with a black body bisected by an off-white stripe down its back, a deceptively puppyish face and heavy bear-like claws. An opportunistic feeder, its diet includes snakes, scorpions and the soft parts of tortoises.

AFRICAN CIVET
(SPECIES: CIVETTICTIS CIVETTA)

 LC

Larger and heftier looking than the related genets, the African civet is a long-haired omnivore with a black, white and gold coat. It feeds on small animals, including certain snakes, but will also eat fruits and roots. It is seen on night drives, pacing deliberately with its nose to the ground as if following a scent.

COMMON GENET
(SPECIES: GENETTA GENETTA)

 LC

Also known as the small-spotted genet, this is the most familiar member of a genus of cat-like predators represented by some eight species in sub-Saharan Africa, to which it is endemic. It regularly visits lodges at night, especially in Samburu-Buffalo Springs, but is seldom seen otherwise.

BLOTCHED GENET
(SPECIES: GENETTA TIGRINA)

 LC

Similar in appearance to the common genet but with a black-tipped tail instead of a white-tipped one, the blotched or large-spotted genet has a slender low-slung torso, spotted black on gold coat and a long striped tail. It is a frequent nocturnal visitor at The Ark in the Aberdares.

IUCN status LC: Least Concern

PREDATOR AND PREY

Small carnivores are often undiscerning feeders, snaffling up anything from insects to small rodents and birds, as well as fruit and carrion. The honey-badger is famed for its symbiotic relationship with the greater honeyguide, a bird which leads it to beehives and feeds on the scraps as the hive is torn apart. The Herpestidae mongooses are known to prey on snakes, but this behaviour is more common in Asia than in Africa, where they prey on small animals that are less well equipped to bite back.

The banded mongoose feasting on egg

BANDED MONGOOSE
(SPECIES: MUNGOS MUNGO)

 LC

The most common of several mongoose species in Kenya, the banded mongoose is a slender cat-sized carnivore whose dark brown coat bears a dozen or so faint black stripes along the back. Highly sociable and diurnally active, it is typically seen in family bands of ten to 20 members.

DWARF MONGOOSE
(SPECIES: HELOGALE PARVULA)

 LC

The diminutive and highly social dwarf mongoose has a shoulder height of 7 cm (2.8 inches). It is a light brown predator often seen in the vicinity of the termite mounds and hollowed dead branches that it uses as a home. Family members can sometimes be seen interacting near the den.

SLENDER MONGOOSE
(SPECIES: HERPESTES SANGUINEUS)

 LC

A widespread species, the slender mongoose divides its time between foraging terrestrially and arboreally. Though quite variable in shade, it is almost always uniform grey or brown in colour with an elongated body and tail, the latter with a diagnostic black tip.

WHITE-TAILED MONGOOSE
(SPECIES: ICHNEUMIA ALBICAUDA)

 LC

About the size of a badger with a bushy white tail, this is the largest African mongoose. One of the most strictly nocturnal and solitary species, it is often observed by spotlight on night drives, and is also a regular visitor to "tree hotels" in the Central Highlands.

MARSH MONGOOSE
(SPECIES: ATILAX PALUDINOSUS)

 LC

This large grizzled brown mongoose tends to be solitary and is mainly, though not exclusively, nocturnal. Most numerous in papyrus swamps and other moist habitats, it feeds on aquatic creatures such as molluscs and lungfish, obtained by filtering mud through its slender fingers.

STRIPED WEASEL
(SPECIES: POECILOGALE ALBINCHA)

 LC

A widespread but uncommon resident of open grassland, the striped weasel is mostly black below and white on top, with an all-white tail. With its very short legs and almost cylindrical body shape, it could almost be mistaken for a snake at first glance. It preys almost exclusively on small rodents.

Key to Field Guide icons *see p98*

Primates

Intelligent, hyperactive and graceful, monkeys are among the most entertaining of creatures. Most Kenyan species are Cercopithecids, an adaptable family of omnivores that fill many ecological niches from swamp forests to semi-arid plains. This group includes the vervet and baboon, the most commonly seen primates on safari. By contrast, the leaf-eating colobus monkeys are strongly arboreal and live in forests within 12 degrees of the equator.

The blue monkey, identifiable by its white throat

BLUE MONKEY
(SPECIES: CERCOPITHECUS MITIS)

BEST SEEN: Aberdare NP, Mount Kenya, Arabuko Sokoke NP

⬜ 🐒　　　　　　　　　　　　　LC

The most widespread of African forest primates, the blue monkey shows a high level of racial variability, and is also known as diademed, white-throated, Sykes and samango monkey. Seen mainly in forest margins, it lives in troops of up to ten animals that willingly travel riparian corridors through savannah habitats. The races in Kenya typically have a grizzled blue-grey coat, a rustier hue on the back and a white throat extending along the chest or collar.

BLACK-AND-WHITE COLOBUS
(SPECIES: COLOBUS GUEREZA)

BEST SEEN: Aberdare NP, Mount Kenya, Kakamega Forest NR

⬜ 🌳　　　　　　　　　　　　　LC

The most beautiful of Kenya's primates, this colobus is almost exclusively arboreal and can cover up to 31 m (100 ft) in one leap. Larger than other forest monkeys, it weighs up to 12 kg (26 lb), feeds solely on leaves and is associated with highland and mid-altitude forests. It is typically seen in troops of three to ten adults with a couple of albino-white babies in tow.

A striking albino-white colobus baby with its mother

The red-tailed monkey, usually seen high in the canopy

RED-TAILED MONKEY
(SPECIES: CERCOPITHECUS ASCANIUS)

BEST SEEN: Kakamega Forest NR and other forested areas in the Uganda border area

⬜ 🐒　　　　　　　　　　　　　LC

This lightly built and strongly arboreal monkey is named for its coppery-red tail, but is more easily recognised by the striking heart-shaped white blob on its nose. It is more omnivorous than most monkeys and unusually unsocial, living singly or in pairs that frequently feed alongside other monkey species.

DE BRAZZA'S MONKEY
(SPECIES: CERCOPITHECUS NEGLECTUS)

BEST SEEN: Saiwa Swamp NP

⬜ 🐒 🌿≈　　　　　　　　　　LC

Associated with swampy forested habitats, De Brazza's monkey is confined in East Africa to a handful of localities near the Kenya-Uganda border, and is only seen in Saiwa Swamp National Park *(see pp290–91)*. A spectacular thicket and dark grey-brown guenon, it has a reddish-brown patch around its eyes, a white band across its brow, and is rendered unmistakeable by its white moustache and beard.

The swamp-loving De Brazza's monkey

IUCN status LC: Least Concern

The sociable vervet spends long stretches grooming

VERVET MONKEY
(SPECIES: CHLOROCEBUS AETHIOPS)

BEST SEEN: Masai Mara GR, Lake Naivasha, Meru NP

 LC

Delightful or mischievous, depending on its level of familiarity with people, the vervet monkey is one of the true characters of the African savannah. It lives in troops of 30–75 animals that are constantly engaged in entertaining interaction, whether fighting, grooming, carrying their young on their chest, clambering around branches, or raiding a lodge's lunch buffet. It is thought to be the world's most numerous primate species (apart from humans) and is mainly terrestrial, although it seldom strays too far from trees. Smaller and lankier than any baboon, it has a grizzled light-olive or grey coat offset by a black face, white ruff and pale belly, though this rather dull colouration is offset in the male by a gaudy blue scrotum. It is highly intelligent, boasting an array of alarm calls that has been likened to a rudimentary language.

The patas has a streamlined runner's build

PATAS MONKEY
(SPECIES: ERYTHROCEBUS PATAS)

BEST SEEN: Laikipia Plateau, Samburu-Buffalo Springs NR

 LC

The dry-country equivalent of the vervet, the patas monkey is thinly distributed in Kenya in the semiarid plains and mountains northwest of Mount Kenya. It is the spindliest of African monkeys, longer limbed and more russet in colouration than the vervet or baboon, and can attain a speed of 48 kmph (30 mph), making it the world's fastest-running primate.

OLIVE AND YELLOW BABOONS
(SPECIES: PAPIO ANUBIS AND P. CYNOCEPHALUS)

BEST SEEN: Masai Mara GR, Lake Nakuru NP, Tsavo NP

 LC

Weighing up to 45 kg (99 lb), the baboon is the largest primate in Kenya, and is recognised by its inverted U-shaped tail and dog-like head. Two species with marginally overlapping ranges occur in Kenya: the bulkier and darker olive baboon of the west, and the lankier yellow species of the east. Like the equally sociable vervet, the baboon is behaviourally fascinating, living in large, perpetually squabbling, and sex-obsessed matriarchal troops, with the dominance-seeking males moving between troops. Adaptable omnivores, baboons steer clear of people but can become very aggressive around campsites and lodges that they associate with food. In such circumstances, they should be treated with caution.

Though mainly terrestrial, baboons feel safest near trees

BUSHBABIES
(FAMILY: GALAGONIDAE)

BEST SEEN: Aberdare NP, Laikipia Plateau, Shimba Hills NR

LC

Closely related to the lemurs of Madagascar, bushbabies are endearing creatures with wide round eyes and agile bodies that enable them to leap from tree to tree. Several species are recognised, but most are difficult to distinguish except by call, and are only likely to be seen if sought with a spotlight.

The large eyes are an adaptation to a nocturnal lifestyle

Key to Field Guide icons *see p98*

African Bush Elephant

The world's largest land animal, the African elephant is one of the most enduringly exciting creatures encountered on safari, not only for its imposing bulk, but also for its complex social behaviour. Elephants are notable for two unique adaptations – a long trunk that combines immense strength with the sensitivity to isolate and tear out a single blade of grass, and outsized tusks that grow throughout its life, sometimes reaching lengths in excess of 3 m (10 ft).

Bloody combat *between male elephants is unusual, since breeding rights are generally established within the community through mock fights which involve trunk locking and tusk clashing.*

FAMILY AND BREEDING

Elephants are intensely sociable creatures. Females and youngsters move around in close-knit matriarchal clans. Females typically come into oestrus between one and 5 years after giving birth. Once impregnated, they give birth about 22 months later. Unlike their female kin, males are generally booted out of their birth group in their early teens, after which they roam around singly or form bachelor herds, often tailing the larger breeding herds with which they share a territory. Males periodically come into musth, a sexually-related condition characterised by a fifty-fold increase in testosterone levels; such elephants are unpredictable and best treated with caution by other elephants and humans alike.

Adult females maintain a vigilant watch *over their young until they are old enough to deter predators. A female gives birth to a 100-kg (220-lb) calf every 5 to 10 years. Each calf thus represents a major genetic investment for the matriarchal herd, and is raised communally. Matriarchal herds comprise up to four generations of sisters, daughters and granddaughters, dominated by the oldest female.*

WHAT YOU MIGHT SEE

Elephants are interactive and great entertainers. Their tusks are versatile tools, used to dig for salt or water, tear bark, and even in defence. The trunk is employed to place food in the mouth, to suck up water and is wielded threateningly in displays of dominance. When an elephant raises its trunk in your direction, trumpeting and stamping its feet, it is best to retreat.

Ears flap continuously *in hot weather to cool circulating blood below the thin skin.*

Faced with a potential threat, *a herd "periscopes" – moves its trunks around to investigate.*

IUCN status NT: Near Threatened

FEEDING

A versatile feeder, the African elephant is a mixed grazer-browser that spends up to 15 hours daily chomping some 200 kg (440 lb) of vegetable matter. It drinks up to 200 litres (53 gallons) daily, arriving at a waterhole a few hours after sunrise and often lingering on until late afternoon to play in the water or spray itself. Herds range widely in search of food, but concentrated populations in protected areas often cause serious environmental degradation by uprooting trees.

The trunk, used to reach high branches or dislodge ripe fruit

COMMUNICATION AND VOICE

Elephant herds interact physically the whole time, but it was long thought that their aural communication was limited to the occasional bout of irate trumpeting. Only in 1987 did researchers in Amboseli National Park discover that the elephant's main means of communication in fact consists of subsonic rumblings, well below or at the very edge of human perception, that can travel through the earth for several miles. These are picked up by the skin on the trunk and feet, allowing dispersed herds to coordinate their movements over a vast area. Elephants also have an exceptional sense of smell and good eyesight.

Elephants use their feet to sense the distant subsonic rumblings of a peer

Name: *Loxodonta africana*
Swahili: *Ndovu*

Size Shoulder height: 2.5–4 m (8.2–13 ft); Weight: up to 6,300 kg (13,890 lb).

Lifespan 65 years.
Population in Kenya 30,000.
Conservation status NT.
Gestation period 22 months.
Reproduction Typically, females first conceive in their early teens and give birth at 5-yearly intervals until their late 50s.

Habitat All habitats except the northern deserts.

On safari in Amboseli National Park

Top places to see
Amboseli NP *(see pp194–7)*, Tsavo NP *(see pp182–7)*, Masai Mara GR *(see pp262–5)*.

Sighting tips
A trail of steaming football-sized dung and vegetation destruction are sure signs that elephants have passed by.

Friends and foes
The elephant's droppings are festive material for dung beetles, which feed almost exclusively on fecal matter.

Facts and trivia
The legend of elephant graveyards has a factual basis. Old elephants whose last set of teeth has worn down gather in marshes to feed on waterlogged vegetation until even that gets difficult and they die of starvation.

Tusks and trunk *are both used to dig for subterranean water in riverbeds during the dry season.*

The trunk *is regularly used to tear juicy branches from the canopy and manoeuvre them into the mouth.*

Elephants spray themselves *with water or dust to help cool down under the hot tropical sun.*

The white rhino can easily be identified by its square mouth

WHITE RHINOCEROS
(SPECIES: CERATOTHERIUM SIMUM)

BEST SEEN: Lake Nakuru, Laikipia Plateau, Meru NP

NT

Bulkier than the black rhino, the white rhino is held to be the world's heaviest non-marine mammal after the elephant, weighing up to 3,600 kg (7,937 lb). Misleadingly named, it has smooth grey skin – the misnomer "white" derives from the Dutch word *weit* (wide) and refers to the square lips it uses to crop grass so efficiently. Prehistoric Saharan rock art and skeletal remains indicate that the white rhino once occurred throughout Africa, but its historical range comprises two geographically and racially discrete populations, neither of which occurs naturally in Kenya. The southern race, saved from the brink of extinction in the early 20th century, now numbers some 12,000 animals in the wild, all descended from a bottleneck population of fewer than 30 individuals in South Africa's Imfolozi Game Reserve. The northern race, however, is now the rarest and most endangered of all living rhino taxa.

COMMON HIPPOPOTAMUS
(SPECIES: HIPPOPOTAMUS AMPHIBIUS)

BEST SEEN: Lake Naivasha, Masai Mara GR, Nairobi NP

VU

The most characteristic resident of Africa's rivers and freshwater lakes is the common hippo, whose purple-grey hairless hide, pink undersides and cheeks, barrel-like torso and stumpy legs render it unmistakeable. Ears, eyes and nostrils are placed high on the skull, allowing it to spend most of its time submerged in the shallows. It feeds terrestrially, however, emerging between dusk and dawn to crop grass with its wide mouth, often ranging far from water in the process. The hippo is highly gregarious, living in pods of up to 30 members, and very territorial, with fights for dominance between males often resulting in serious injury or death. Contrary to appearance, the hippo is highly mobile on land and can easily attain a speed of above 32 kmph (20 mph). It can be very dangerous to humans, as it typically heads straight to the safety of the water when disturbed, mowing down anything in its path. The fantastic communal grunting of the hippo, a characteristic sound of waterside lodges, can be heard by day as well as after dark.

Hippos are poor swimmers, tending to stick to shallow water

IUCN status EN: Endangered; VU: Vulnerable; NT: Near Threatened; LC: Least Concern

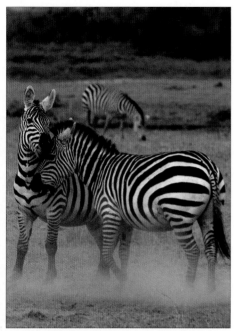

The striping on a plains zebra reaches right under the belly

PLAINS ZEBRA
(SPECIES: EQUUS QUAGGA)

BEST SEEN: Amboseli NP, Masai Mara GR, Meru NP

 LC

Placed in the same genus as their domestic counterparts, zebras resemble a striped hybrid between a horse and an ass, with each individual possessing a stripe pattern as unique as a human fingerprint. The most common of the two Kenyan species is the plains zebra, or Burchell's zebra, a grazer whose natural distribution ranges from Ethiopia to South Africa. The plains zebra is often seen in large ephemeral herds, but its core social unit is an aggressively defended non-territorial herd comprising one stallion, up to five mares and their respective foals. The purpose of the zebra's stripes is often cited as camouflage, breaking up the animal's outline in long grass, but this fails to explain their benefit in arid habitats. It is more likely that the striping is visually confusing to predators when the herd scatters.

The stripe pattern seen on Grevy's zebra is dense and narrow

GREVY'S ZEBRA
(SPECIES: EQUUS GREVYI)

BEST SEEN: Samburu-Buffalo Springs NR, Laikipia Plateau, Sibiloi NP

 EN

This magnificent dry-country equivalent to the plains zebra is the world's largest wild equid, standing 1.5-m (5-ft) tall at the shoulder and weighing up to 430 kg (948 lb). It is distinguished by its narrower striping, white belly and bear-like round ears. Grevy's zebra move in smaller herds than the plains zebra and a stallion generally enjoys exclusive mating rights with any female passing through its territory. Once widespread in the Horn of Africa, it is now practically endemic to Northern Kenya, whose estimated population of 1,500–2,000 is concentrated in Lewa Downs and Samburu-Buffalo Springs National Reserve.

African Buffalo

Africa's only wild ox, the African buffalo is similar in appearance to the Indian water buffalo and closely related to domestic cattle. Powerfully built, with a bulk of up to 800 kg (1,764 lb) and heavy splayed horns, it is famed for its unpredictable temperament. Indeed, the "great white hunters" who coined the term Big Five regarded this ox as the most dangerous of foes. Buffalo are the most numerous of the Big Five, with a continent-wide population estimated at over 1 million, and are highly conspicuous on most Kenyan safaris.

Affectionately known as Daga Boys *after a local African word meaning mud, elderly male buffaloes tend to live singly or in small bachelor herds and have a reputation for grumpiness, as well as for being quicker to charge than individuals in breeding herds.*

FAMILY AND BREEDING

The African buffalo is highly gregarious and non-territorial, generally moving in mixed-sex herds of ten to 50 animals, with one dominant male and a hierarchical structure binding the adult females and non-dominant males. Females come into oestrus at the start of the rainy season and give birth to a single calf, or more occasionally twins, almost exactly a year later. Tensions between males run high during the mating season, with dominant bulls trying to pull rank and subordinate males fighting to challenge their breeding rights. The imposing bulk of an adult buffalo ensures that it has few natural enemies, and a strongly bonded herd will cooperate to chase away predators. Nevertheless, buffaloes are regularly preyed upon by larger lion prides in national parks such as Masai Mara Game Reserve, with the lion occasionally coming off second best.

Aggregations of more than 1,000 buffalo *can still be seen during the rainy season in some parts of Kenya, especially the Masai Mara and Tsavo East National Park.*

WHAT YOU MIGHT SEE

Buffaloes are less visibly interactive than certain other sociable animals. When a vehicle approaches a buffalo herd, the mass response will often be to stare down the vehicle or even to close in on it. While this can be quite intimidating, it signals curiosity – and chronic myopia – more than anything sinister. Buffaloes often support hitchhiking birds – cattle egrets, oxpeckers and starlings.

Rival males *often lock horns during the mating season, but serious injuries are rare.*

Buffaloes take to a wallow *during the day more so than even rhinos and elephants.*

IUCN status LC: Least Concern

FEEDING

Primarily a grazer, the African buffalo requires a significant proportion of grass in its diet, although it can supplement this by browsing on low trees and shrubs. Large herds are common in most grassland habitats, while forests support smaller herds.

Buffalo herds gathering at a waterhole to drink and wallow

The buffalo feeds throughout the day, but will readily adopt a nocturnal feeding pattern in areas where it is repeatedly disturbed. It must drink at least once every 24 hours – and also enjoys wallowing – so herds seldom stray more than 10–15 km (6–9 miles) away from a reliable water source.

COMMUNICATION AND VOICE

The African buffalo is generally far quieter than its mooing domestic counterpart when it comes to day-to-day communication. However, upon sighting a predator, it makes an explosive snorting alarm call that swiftly mobilises the rest of

the herd into defensive mode. A threatened animal may also grunt aggressively. The buffalo has an acute sense of smell and exceptional hearing, but poor eyesight, for which reason a herd may often stand and stare myopically at a perceived intruder.

Buffalo herds tend to walk in a single file when covering long distances

Name: *Syncerus caffer*
Swahili: *Nyati* or *Mbogo*

Size Shoulder height: 1.2–1.7 m (4–6 ft); Weight: up to 500–800 kg (1,102–1,764 lb).

Lifespan 20–25 years.
Population in Kenya 80,000.
Conservation status LC.
Gestation period 11–12 months.
Reproduction Females mature at the age of 4–5 years and give birth to a single calf at the start of the rainy season.

Habitat Mostly non-arid environments.

Grazing herds near a safari vehicle

Top places to see
Tsavo East NP *(see pp184–5)*, Masai Mara GR *(see pp262–5)*, Samburu-Buffalo Springs-Shaba NR *(see pp342–6)*.

Sighting tips
The buffalo is still present in many habitats where hiking is permitted such as in the forested zones of Mount Kenya and Hell's Gate National Park.

Friends and foes
Cattle egrets flock around herds of buffalo to feed on insects that are disturbed as the mammals move through the grass.

Facts and trivia
The Maasai taboo on eating wild animals recognises two exceptions, buffalo and eland. This ancient belief accurately reflects the close kinship between domestic cattle, eland and buffalo.

A courting male buffalo *will rest his head on the female's rump as a prelude to mating.*

Female calves *stay with their birth herd, but males may be forced out upon reaching sexual maturity.*

The large packs of lion *in the Masai Mara routinely try to prey on buffalo, with mixed success.*

Black Rhinoceros

With its armoured grey hide, massive bulk, fearsome horns and irascible disposition, the black rhino is one of the most ancient surviving branches of the ungulate line. It stands on the brink of extinction, with its continental population having plummeted from 100,000 to 2,500 over 20 years prior to the early 1990s. The situation has improved slightly since then, but the black rhino remains among the most critically endangered of African animals. Kenya, supporting more than 20 per cent of the global total, is now possibly the best place to see it.

The rhino and oxpecker *were long thought to have had a symbiotic relationship, with oxpeckers cleansing the rhino's skin of ticks and other pests. It is now known that oxpeckers also suck blood from cuts and wounds in their host's hide.*

The bond between mother and calf *is generally strong and lasts for 3–4 years. During the first 12 months, the calf is vulnerable to predation from lions and hyenas, and is protected aggressively by its mother. The female will eventually terminate the relationship once another calf is imminent.*

FAMILY AND BREEDING

Adult black rhinos are essentially solitary, though not especially territorial. Both sexes are aggressive towards unfamiliar individuals but equable towards rhinos with neighbouring or overlapping territories, sometimes even pairing off temporarily. The bond between a mother and calf, however, is more enduring. Courtship between black rhinos is a protracted affair. The female scrapes her territorial dung piles vigorously, and the first male to pick up the scent trails behind her trying to cover it up with his own faeces. Prior to mating, the pair often indulge in noisy mock-sparring. Once the male is accepted, the two stay together for days or even weeks. A single calf weighing up to 50 kg (110 lb) is born 15 months later, and is fully mobile within 3 days.

WHAT YOU MIGHT SEE

Black rhinos are reclusive animals, and most safarigoers consider themselves lucky to see one in the wild. The solitary nature of these beasts means that most sightings involve no interaction. Visitors may occasionally locate a mother and calf, or a few adults assembled at a wallow. Black rhinos have a proclivity to charge when disturbed, so it is necessary to stay alert.

IUCN status CR: Critically Endangered

An adult male defecates *at a communal dung post, signalling his passing to other rhinos.*

Rhinos enjoy wallowing in mud, *whose colour often alters their own appearance.*

FEEDING

The black rhino is a dedicated browser, utilising leaves, branches and fruits of at least 200 plant species. This behaviour is indirectly accountable for the misleading names of black and white rhinos – the original Dutch name *weit* (wide), later mistranslated to "white", was an allusion to the square grass-cropping mouth of the white rhino *(see p116)*; the black rhino received its name by default. The black rhino feeds most busily in the early morning and late afternoon, ideally retiring to a wallow or waterhole at midday, though it can go almost a week without drinking water if need be.

Plucking twigs with its prehensile upper lip

COMMUNICATION AND VOICE

Vocalisations, though complex and varied, are seldom observed during a casual rhino encounter. When two individuals meet, they may growl or trumpet to signal aggression, but will more likely snort in amicable greeting. Rhinos give a high-pitched alarm call when moderately threatened, and emit a loud pig-like squeal when seriously alarmed. Indirect communication between neighbours includes the sharing of common dung heaps at waterholes and feeding places, which allows every individual to know which other rhinos have passed by recently. In contrast to its acute sense of smell, the black rhino has poor sight, with a focal range of less than 10 m (33 ft).

The awesome sight of two adult males locking horns in combat

Name: *Diceros bicornis*
Swahili: *Faru*

Size Shoulder height: 1.4–1.8 m (4.6–5.9 ft); Weight: up to 1,400 kg (3,086 lb).

Lifespan 40–45 years.
Population in Kenya 550–600.
Conservation status CR.
Gestation period 15 months.
Reproduction Typically, females mature sexually at 5 years and give birth to a calf every 3–4 years.

Habitat Well-wooded and open savannah.

Relocating a rhino to a sanctuary

Top places to see
Tsavo West NP *(see pp186–7)*, Lake Nakuru NP *(see pp276–9)*, Meru NP *(see pp330–33)*, Masai Mara GR *(see pp262–5)*.

Sighting tips
Rhinos are fond of rolling on their sides in mud wallows, which are therefore good places to spot these elusive animals.

Friends and foes
The black rhino is the third largest animal in Africa and a full-grown adult has little to fear from predators, but it is sometimes chased away by peeved elephants.

Facts and trivia
The primary cause of the modern decline in Africa's rhino population is the mistaken belief that its horn has medicinal properties.

Rhinos are solitary creatures *and seldom interact with each other or with different species.*

A rhino might charge *at the slightest provocation, and can quickly accelerate to a terrifying 55 kmph (34 mph).*

Individual rhinos return daily *to favoured rubbing posts, gradually polishing the top smooth.*

Small Mammals

Kenya is best known for its rich megafauna, but the country also supports a fascinating variety of smaller and more obscure mammals. These range from diverse and highly conspicuous orders such as the rodents and bats, which keen observers are likely to encounter on a daily basis, to the more quirky and elusive giant forest hog, aardvark and pangolin, all of which come close to topping the wish list of seasoned safarigoers.

FAMILY

Many of these animals are evolutionary one-offs. For instance, the aardvark is the only living member of the order Tubulidentata. By contrast, pigs belong to the same order as giraffes, camels and antelopes.

The pangolin with its thick armour-plated scaling

PANGOLIN
(FAMILY: MANIDAE)

BEST SEEN: Widespread but seldom seen

                              Most species: NT

Also known as scaly anteaters, pangolins are unobtrusive nocturnal insectivores whose name derives from the Malay *penguling*, a reference to their habit of curling into a tight ball when disturbed. The savannah-dwelling ground pangolin is the more widespread of the two Kenyan species, while the 35 kg (77 lb) giant pangolin is confined to the forests of the west. Both animals are rarely seen in the wild.

HYRAX
(ORDER: HYRACOIDEA)

BEST SEEN: Hell's Gate NP, Masai Mara GR, Tsavo NP

                              All species: LC

Endemic to Africa, hyraxes are dwarfish relics of a once-prolific near-ungulate order more closely related to elephants than any other living creature. The widespread rock hyrax *Procavia capensis*, a conspicuous resident of rocky outcrops and mountains, lives in territorial family groups of up to 20 individuals. The forest-loving tree hyrax *Dendrohyrax arboreus* is seldom seen, but often heard emitting a terrifying banshee wail that rips through the night air.

Hyraxes spend long periods basking in the sun

Aardvarks use clawed feet to dig into termite mounds

AARDVARK
(SPECIES: ORYCTEROPUS AFER)

BEST SEEN: Laikipia Plateau, Masai Mara GR, Tsavo NP

                              LC

One of the most peculiar of African mammals, the aardvark – a Dutch name meaning earth pig – weighs up to 80 kg (176 lb). It is a shy, strictly nocturnal insectivore with pinkish skin, a heavy tail not unlike a kangaroo's and long upright ears. It uses an elongated snout and long retractable sticky tongue to snaffle up as many as 50,000 termites in one night.

PORCUPINE
(FAMILY: HYSTRICIDAE)

BEST SEEN: Widespread but seldom seen

                              Both species: LC

The largest African rodent, weighing up to 27 kg (60 lb), the porcupine is represented in Kenya by two almost indistinguishable and seldom seen species, both coated in long black and white quills that occasionally betray the animal's presence by rattling as it walks.

The long quills of the porcupine are modified hair

IUCN status NT: Near Threatened; LC: Least Concern

Fruitbats generally roost in colonies in trees

BATS
(ORDER: CHIROPTERA)

BEST SEEN: Kakamega Forest NR

 Most species: Variable

Chiroptera (bats) is the second-most successful mammalian order, with 1,000-plus species globally. Although widely feared, no African bat sucks blood, and they play a vital ecological role in controlling flying insect populations. Small insect-eating bats are often seen hawking at dusk throughout Kenya, but larger fruitbats tend to prefer wooded habitats. The largest African mainland species, the hammer-headed fruitbat *Hypsignathus monstrosus*, is distinguished by the distended head sac it uses to broadcast a far-carrying booming mating call through the western Kenyan rainforests.

The tusks of the warthog are the largest in any swine

WARTHOG
(SPECIES: PHACOCHOERUS AFRICANUS)

BEST SEEN: Masai Mara GR, Lake Nakuru NP, Tsavo NP

 LC

The most common and conspicuous of Kenya's wild pigs, the warthog is a long-legged slender-bodied swine that stands 80 cm (32 inches) high at the shoulder and weighs up to 150 kg (331 lb) in exceptional cases. It has an almost hairless grey coat, a long dorsal mane, upward-curving tusks and a trio of callus-like "warts" on its face. Family groups, a regular sight in many savannah reserves, are often seen trotting briskly away with long, thin tails stiffly erect. The warthog is an unfussy omnivore whose favoured food consists of roots and bulbs. It defends itself against predators by reversing into a burrow with tusks facing out aggressively. The remote northeast of Kenya is home to the desert warthog *Phacochoerus aethiopicus*, a similar-looking species, which is IUCN red-listed as Least Concern, and is most likely to be seen in the vicinity of Marsabit and Turkana.

BUSHPIG
(SPECIES: POTAMOCHOERUS LARVATUS)

BEST SEEN: Aberdare NP, Mount Kenya

 LC

Larger, more hirsute and shorter-legged than the warthog, the bushpig is the other widespread Kenyan swine. It is less conspicuous as a result of its strictly nocturnal habits, its secretive nature and a preference for dense riverine and forested vegetation. The bushpig has small tusks but can be quite aggressive when cornered. It displays a high degree of colour variation, ranging from grey-brown to chestnut. Sightings are almost guaranteed when staying overnight at a tree hotel in Aberdare National Park or Mount Kenya.

The bushpig, with its pale grey dorsal crest

GIANT FOREST HOG
(SPECIES: HYLOCHOERUS MEINERTZHAGENI)

BEST SEEN: Aberdare NP, Mount Kenya

 LC

Measuring up to 2 m (6 ft) in length and weighing around 250 kg (551 lb), the giant forest hog is the world's largest swine, and the only one that can be described as magnificent. Bizarrely, despite its monstrous proportions, this mighty porker eluded Western science until 1904, when a specimen was shot in the Congo rainforest. Dark grey-brown in general colouration, this hog is a very hairy creature, with a naked face, wide snout and fairly large tusks, and normally moves in pairs or small family parties. A nocturnal and strictly vegetarian animal, it is typically associated with western lowland rainforests, but the eastern race occurs in montane forests in Kenya. Unlikely to be seen elsewhere, it is a regular nocturnal visitor to Serena Mountain Lodge (*see p375*) on Mount Kenya.

Unable to root like most pigs, this hog digs with its tusks

Key to Field Guide icons *see p98*

The Wildebeest Migration

One of the world's greatest natural spectacles, the annual migration of up to two and a half million ungulates through the Serengeti-Mara extends over approximately 40,000 sq km (15,500 sq miles) of wilderness in southern Kenya and northern Tanzania, making it Africa's largest intact migratory ecosystem. The cycle breaks up into three distinct periods of migratory motion – the march between the southern and western Serengeti, the north-ward trek across the Grumeti and Mara rivers towards the Masai Mara, and the return leg to southeastern Serengeti's short grass. These are punctuated by two periods of dispersal – into the Masai Mara (August–October) and the southeastern Serengeti (December–April).

Wildebeest herds stretch across the plains below a hot-air balloon

MIGRATING HERDS
Moving in a deafeningly braying column that can reach up to 40 km (25 miles) in length, the cross-border migration covers over 800 km (500 miles) annually, following a fairly predictable annual cycle dictated by local rainfall patterns. Numerically, the migration is dominated by up to two million wildebeest, but fellow travellers include plains zebra, Thomson's gazelle, Grant's gazelle, topi, Coke's hartebeest and eland.

The arrival of the short rains (October–November) *is the signal for the migration to head south from the Masai Mara to the plains of the southeastern Serengeti and western Ngorongoro Conservation Area. It is here that the wildebeest calve over January and February, replenishing the population.*

The westward migration begins *as the long rains draw to a close, usually in May. The dispersed wildebeest march northwest into the Serengeti's Western Corridor, amassing along the south banks of the Grumeti river (May–June), sometimes coming almost to the shores of Lake Victoria.*

At the start of the northward trek to the Masai Mara, *the wildebeest must cross the deep and wide Grumeti river, a tense but spectacular event that takes place in early June. Many animals drown in the crossing, or are taken by the massive crocodiles that lurk in the river's muddy waters.*

THE MIGRATORY ROUTE

KEY

— May–June
→ June
→ July–August
→ August–November
→ December–April
■■■ International border
☐ Serengeti-Mara plains

The Masai Mara is carpeted with wildebeest *for the 2 to 3 months that divide the treacherous northward and southward crossings of the Mara river. About half of the two million migratory beasts are dispersed across the reserve's green plains, while the remainder spread out into the remote northwest of the Serengeti.*

Many thousands of zebra, gazelle and antelope *join the wildebeest in the Serengeti-Mara migration. These large herds of ungulates are followed by an entourage of well-fed predators, most conspicuously lion and spotted hyena.*

The crossing of the Mara river into Kenya *claims the lives of several hundred animals annually. The first herds to cross run the greatest risk of being devoured. For this reason, tens of thousands of animals will congregate by the river, often waiting for a week or two before the first brave individual takes the plunge. The rest of the herd follows in its wake.*

Giraffe

The world's heaviest ruminant and the tallest land mammal, the giraffe is instantly recognisable by its elongated neck and attractively patterned coat. It is common in most Kenyan national parks and reserves. Three distinct regional races are represented, with the common Maasai giraffe of the south and east being replaced by the handsome, more endangered reticulated giraffe further north, and Rothschild's giraffe in the west.

Distinct coat patterns *distinguish the three races of giraffe found in Kenya. The reticulated giraffe* (top) *has chestnut-coloured polygonal spots with bright white outlines, the Maasai giraffe* (bottom) *has ragged spots on a coat of yellow-fawn, and the Rothschild's giraffe is intermediate.*

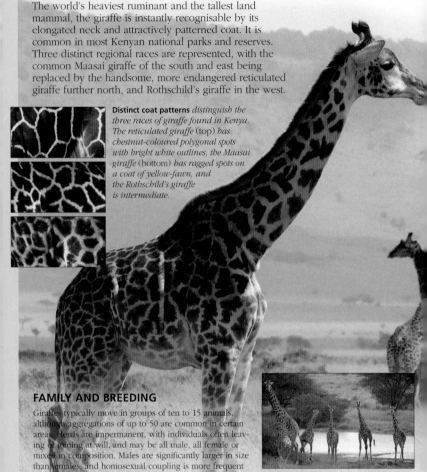

FAMILY AND BREEDING

Giraffes typically move in groups of ten to 15 animals, although aggregations of up to 50 are common in certain areas. Herds are impermanent, with individuals often leaving or joining at will, and may be all male, all female or mixed in composition. Males are significantly larger in size than females, and homosexual coupling is more frequent than heterosexual coupling. The social structure is polygynous, and a male might have several female partners, guarding them against approaches from other bulls during oestrus. Females normally have one calf, more occasionally twins, and give birth standing, allowing the newborn to drop up to 2 m (7 ft) to the ground. The calf gets up on its feet immediately and might start suckling within 30 minutes.

Giraffes are usually seen in loose herds *that might consist of anything from five to 20 individuals, though ten to 15 is most normal in Kenya. In addition to bachelor herds and their all-female counterpart, crèche herds consisting solely of sub-adults are sometimes encountered.*

WHAT YOU MIGHT SEE

Giraffes are one of the iconic sights of the Kenyan savannah, and it is fascinating to watch their feeding habits, splay-legged drinking stance and extraordinary running gait – rather clumsy yet oddly graceful. Although they are herd animals, physical interaction is relatively infrequent, so it is always worth sticking with a pair of necking males to see how the situation will develop.

The long neck of the giraffe *forces it to splay its legs wide and even bend at the knees when it drinks.*

A running giraffe *can move at speeds of up to 55 kmph (34 mph).*

IUCN status LC: Least Concern

FEEDING

The giraffe is a highly specialised canopy feeder, browsing on high-grade leaf foliage at heights of up to 6 m (20 ft), although it will occasionally eat grass too. At least 100 different tree species are utilised, but the various acacias are strongly favoured. The combination of a long neck and versatile tongue allows a giraffe to reach leaves that no other species can. It mostly feeds in the early morning and late afternoon, retiring into the shade to chew the cud during the hottest hours of the day.

Browsing on acacia leaves, savannah grassland

COMMUNICATION AND VOICE

Giraffes are often thought to be mute, but do occasionally bleat, bellow or emit a high-pitched whistle and make a snorting alarm call when threatened. It is now thought that most of their communication occurs at low frequencies that are inaudible to the human ear. Males often engage in a behaviour called necking – intertwining their necks and heads and occasionally dealing out heavy blows. This has various functions, ranging from combat to a prelude to homosexual mounting.

A display of affection between adult giraffes

 Name: *Giraffa camelopardalis*
Swahili: *Twiga*

 Size Shoulder height: 3–4 m (10–13 ft); Weight: up to 2,000 kg (4,400 lb).

Lifespan 25 years.
Population in Kenya At least 10,000.
Conservation status LC.
Gestation period 15–16 months.
Reproduction Females reach sexual maturity at 3–4 years of age and give birth every 2 years.

 Habitat Open savannah and woodland.

Bulbous stems of whistling thorn acacia

 Top places to see
Masai Mara GR *(see pp262–5)*, Amboseli NP *(see pp194–7)*, Lake Nakuru NP *(see pp276–9)*, Meru NP *(see pp330–33)*, Samburu-Buffalo Springs NR *(see pp342–5)*.

Sighting tips
It is worth waiting to watch a giraffe that is heading towards water – the sight of it bending over to drink is truly astonishing.

Friends and foes
Giraffes seldom eat from the whistling thorn acacia because of the plant's relationship with the *Crematogaster* ant, which nests at the base of the thorns and inflicts a nasty bite on browsers.

 Facts and trivia
The myth that a giraffe will die if it lies down probably derives from its limited sleep requirements of about 30 minutes a day.

Giraffes do lie down – *contrary to myth – but only where they can see predators from afar.*

Giraffes are not averse to mingling *with zebras, antelope and other ungulates, but will seldom move with them deliberately.*

Necking between males, *a dramatic sight, is often a sign of aggression in giraffes.*

Spiral-horned Antelopes

Endemic to Africa, spiral-horned antelopes of the tribe Tragelaphini are medium to large bovids with dark grey- or chestnut-brown coats, white spots or vertical stripes on their flanks and pronounced dewlaps or spinal crests. Six species are present in Kenya, and most display considerable sexual dimorphism, with the male generally sporting magnificent twisted or spiralled horns and being larger and darker than the hornless females.

FAMILY

The Tragelaphines are less closely related to other antelope than to buffaloes and cows. This genetic affinity is most apparent in the eland, which looks like a cross between a kudu and a domestic cow.

COMMON ELAND
(SPECIES: TRAGELAPHUS ORYX)

BEST SEEN: Masai Mara GR, Samburu-Buffalo Springs NR, Laikipia Plateau

 LC

Also known as the Cape eland, Africa's largest antelope has a maximum shoulder height of 1.8 m (6 ft) and can weigh almost 950 kg (2,094 lb). The most overtly cow-like of the spiral-horned antelopes, it is light tan in colour, with faint white vertical stripes, small unisex horns and a hefty dewlap. It moves in groups of about ten animals, but larger parties are also seen. The eland was revered by the hunter-gatherers who once inhabited East Africa and often depicted the animal on the rock paintings they left behind.

The eland has relatively short, straight horns

The male greater kudu has the only horns that go into a full double spiral.

An adult male kudu sporting well-developed horns

GREATER KUDU
(SPECIES: TRAGELAPHUS STREPSICEROS)

BEST SEEN: Lake Bogoria, Laikipia Plateau

 LC

The most magnificent of African antelopes, the greater kudu is second in stature only to the eland. It stands up to 1.5 m (5 ft) high and has a greyish coat with up to 10 vertical white stripes on each side. Males have massive double-spiralled horns. Small family parties are seen in dense woodland along dry-country watercourses. An accomplished jumper, it can clear fences twice its shoulder height. The kudu was hammered by rinderpest in the late 19th century in East Africa, and remains localised.

LESSER KUDU
(SPECIES: TRAGELAPHUS IMBERBIS)

BEST SEEN: Samburu-Buffalo Springs NR, Tsavo West NP, Meru NP

NT

An East African dry-country endemic whose range is centred on Kenya and southern Ethiopia, the lesser kudu is a predominantly nocturnal inhabitant of semiarid thornbush, where it is often seen in the denser vegetation following watercourses. As its name suggests, it looks very much like a miniature of the greater kudu, and the two often occur alongside each other. The lesser kudu's grey coat is typically marked by at least 11 vertical white stripes as well as a pair of white throat patches, and the male's horns are far less impressive. Thinly distributed, it might be seen in any dry-country reserve, but will most often flee before it can be observed closely.

The lesser kudu is very shy and skittish

IUCN status NT: Near Threatened; LC: Least Concern

A lone bushbuck grazing in a forest-clearing

BUSHBUCK
(SPECIES: TRAGELAPHUS SCRIPTUS)

BEST SEEN: Shimba Hills NR, Masai Mara GR, Aberdare NP

 LC

The closest thing in East Africa to a Bambi lookalike, the bushbuck is a widespread medium-sized antelope of forest and riparian woodland. It is likely to be present in such habitats in any ecosystem, even outside of protected areas. It is very attractive, with a coat that is regionally variable. The male is usually dark brown or chestnut in colour and has relatively small horns, while the more petite female is generally pale red-brown. Both sexes have similar white throat patches to the lesser kudu, and a variable combination of white spots and sometimes stripes on the coat. The bushbuck usually moves singly or in pairs, and although it is common in suitable habitats, it tends to be rather furtive.

SITATUNGA
(SPECIES: TRAGELAPHUS SPEKEII)

BEST SEEN: Saiwa Swamp NP, Kingwal Swamp

 LC

The semiaquatic sitatunga is a widespread but infrequently observed inhabitant of swampy habitats from Botswana to Sudan. It is similar in appearance to a bushbuck, but the male in particular is significantly larger and more shaggy coated, with more prominent striping and duller overall colouration. Most often seen singly, more occasionally in pairs, it communicates with loud barking cries that often carry long distances at night. It feeds primarily on rush, sedge and other typical marsh vegetation, with its head held low and legs spreadeagled. Its most obvious adaptation to a semiaquatic lifestyle is the uniquely splayed hooves that allow it to move easily through swamps and marshes, but make it look rather clumsy on dry land. It can swim well, too, but generally only takes to water to avoid predators.

The sitatunga, associated with waterside vegetation

MOUNTAIN BONGO
(SPECIES: TRAGELAPHUS EURYCERUS)

BEST SEEN:
Aberdare NP

 CR

A subspecies of the more widespread and common forest bongo of West and Central Africa, the mountain bongo (*T. e. isaaci*) is a massive heavyset antelope whose deep chestnut coat is marked with a dozen bold white vertical stripes. Weighing up to 400 kg (882 lb), it is bulkier even than the greater kudu and has short but heavy black horns with prominent ivory tips. This bongo has been regarded as an effective Kenyan endemic since 1914, when the last Ugandan specimen was shot on Mount Elgon. Its wild population is now estimated at 100 inhabitants in isolated montane forest pockets in the Aberdares and Mau Escarpment. A few dozen individuals bred at the Mount Kenya Safari Club on the northwest footslopes are in the process of being reintroduced to Mount Kenya National Park.

The forest-dwelling mountain bongo, primarily a browser

Key to Field Guide icons *see p98*

Large Antelopes

Antelopes are a constant of Africa's wild places, thriving in every habitat from rainforest to semidesert. Although they range in size from the diminutive duikers to the horse-like roan antelope, most members of this group are medium sized, as typified by the gazelles and impala that move in ubiquitous herds through the open savannah. Highly photogenic and socially fascinating, it is arguably the antelope that defines the safari experience.

FAMILY

Antelope are not related to deer. Indeed, deer form a separate family, whose most distinguishing feature is the growth of bony seasonal antlers, unlike the antelope's permanent non-bony horns.

The impala, a fast runner and prodigious jumper

IMPALA
(SPECIES: AEPYCEROS MELAMPUS)

BEST SEEN: Tsavo NP, Masai Mara GR, Lake Nakuru NP

 LC

A relative of the wildebeest, this elegantly proportioned antelope has a chestnut coat with black-and-white stripes on the rump and tail. Males have magnificent black annulated horns. Impalas are usually seen in herds of over 100, dominated numerically by females and young. They are agile jumpers, and herds often jump in all directions to confuse predators.

SABLE ANTELOPE
(SPECIES: HIPPOTRAGUS NIGER)

BEST SEEN: Shimba Hills NR

 LC

Among the largest and most handsome of antelopes, the male sable has a jet black coat offset by a white face, underbelly and rump. Its splendid decurved horns reach up to 1.4 m (4.6 ft) in length. The female is less striking, with a chestnut-brown coat and shorter horns. Common in certain other parts of Africa, the sable is confined to a single protected area in Kenya, whose population of around 120 animals is quite conspicuous on game drives.

The handsome sable antelope, Shimba Hills

ROAN ANTELOPE
(SPECIES: HIPPOTRAGUS EQUINUS)

BEST SEEN: Ruma NP

 LC

Similar in proportions to the sable, the roan has short decurved horns, a fawn-grey coat with a pale belly and a light mane. Although common elsewhere in Africa, it is rare in Kenya, where a few herds of five to ten animals survive near Lake Victoria. There is currently talk of reintroducing it to the Masai Mara.

Roan antelope, often seen in densely-wooded savannah

COMMON ORYX
(SPECIES: ORYX GAZELLA)

BEST SEEN: Samburu-Buffalo Springs NR, Tsavo NP, Laikipia Plateau

 LC

This dry-country antelope has a shoulder height of 1.2 m (4 ft) and striking horns that sweep straight back from the skull at the same angle as the forehead and muzzle. Seen in nomadic herds of up to ten animals, it can go without water for almost as long as a camel, obtaining all its needs from the plants it eats.

The ash-grey oryx with bold black face markings

Blue wildebeest at the Mara river during the migration

BLUE WILDEBEEST
(SPECIES: CONNOCHAETES TAURINUS)

BEST SEEN: Masai Mara GR, Amboseli NP,
Tsavo NP

LC

The blue wildebeest is common in southern
hemisphere grassland habitats, such as the
Serengeti-Mara, but is totally absent north of the
equator. It is highly gregarious, with up to two
million animals undergoing a spectacular annual
migration *(see pp124–5)*. The wildebeest's
dark grey-brown coat precludes confusion
with other antelope, but it could be mistaken
for a buffalo at a distance, although its slighter
build and shaggy beard are diagnostic.

The topi's dark coat distinguishes it from the hartebeest

TOPI
(SPECIES: DAMALISCUS LUNATUS)

BEST SEEN: Masai Mara GR, Tsavo NP,
Ruma NP

LC

Known as the tsessebe or tiang elsewhere in
its range, the topi comes across as a darker
and glossier variation of the Coke's hartebeest,
with which it shares similar habits and a habitat preference for open grassland. It is dark
brown in general colouration, with some black
on the flanks and snout, and striking yellow
lower legs. Widespread but thinly and patchily
distributed, small herds are especially common
in the Masai Mara ecosystem.

WATERBUCK
(SPECIES: KOBUS ELLIPSIPRYMNUS)

BEST SEEN: Lake Nakuru, Masai Mara GR, Crescent
Island

LC

The waterbuck is the largest, most distinctive
member of the kob family, and is recognised
by its shaggy grey-brown to chestnut coat, the
male's large lyre-shaped horns, and its bold
white rump markings. As its name suggests,
the waterbuck is seen in the vicinity of standing water, with herds of up to ten individuals
lorded over by an aggressive dominant male.
Two races are known: the Defassa waterbuck
of the Rift Valley and Western Kenya is more
chestnut and has a full white rump, while the
eastern race has a white U on its rump.

Male waterbucks lock horns in aggressive combat

COKE'S HARTEBEEST
(SPECIES: ALCELAPHUS BUSELAPHUS)

BEST SEEN: Masai Mara GR, Samburu-Buffalo
Springs NR, Amboseli NP

LC

One of the more conspicuous large antelopes
in Kenya's grasslands, Coke's hartebeest – also
called the kongoni – is similar in height to the
related blue wildebeest, with large shoulders,
a backward sloping back, slender torso, pale
yellow-brown coat, smallish unisex horns and
a narrow heart-shaped face alluded to in its
Dutch name. Males frequently climb on termite hills to scan, as a display of territorial
dominance. Usually seen in parties of up to
eight animals, Coke's hartebeest (*A. b. cokei*)
is replaced by the stubbier horned Jackson's
hartebeest (*A. b. jacksoni*) in the far north.

The slender hartebeest, set apart by its narrow face

Key to Field Guide icons *see p98*

COMMON DUIKER
(SPECIES: SYLVICAPRA GRIMMIA)

BEST SEEN: Masai Mara GR, Tsavo NP, Amboseli NP

 LC

The least typical but most widespread and conspicuous of Africa's 18 duiker species, the common or grey duiker is a variably coloured resident of wooded savannah habitats that may be seen almost anywhere in Kenya apart from forest interiors and deserts. Most often seen in pairs, it could be confused with steenbok, but it is generally greyer. The duiker has a unique identifier in the form of a black tuft of hair that divides its horns.

BLUE DUIKER
(SPECIES: PHILANTOMBA MONTICOLA)

BEST SEEN: Arabuko Sokoke NP, Tana River Primate Reserve

 LC

A widespread but shy resident of coastal forests, the blue duiker is the smallest Kenyan antelope, with a height of about 35 cm (14 inches) and a weight of 5 kg (11 lb). It is one of a group of hunch-backed forest-dwellers that rank as perhaps the least well understood and most elusive of East African antelopes. Seldom seen, it can be distinguished by its white under-tail, which it flicks regularly.

HARVEY'S RED DUIKER
(SPECIES: CEPHALOPHUS HARVEYI)

BEST SEEN: Aberdare NP, Mount Kenya, Shimba Hills

 LC

The 46-cm (18-inch) tall Harvey's red duiker is among the more widespread of a cluster of red duiker species, most of which are deep chestnut with a white tail and black snout patch. The duiker most likely to be observed in Kenya, it is usually seen in forest clearings. It is replaced by Peter's red duiker in Western Kenya and by the critically endangered Ader's duiker in Arabuko Sokoke.

SUNI
(SPECIES: NEOTRAGUS MOSCHATUS)

BEST SEEN: Arabuko Sokoke NP, Tana River Primate Reserve

 LC

The suni is a small antelope of coastal forests and thickets whose posture, colouration and habits make it easy to confuse with a duiker. It has a more freckled coat than any duiker, however, and on close inspection it can also be distinguished by its backward sweeping horns, large and almost rabbit-like ears, pronounced facial glands, and habit of flicking its black-and-white tail from side to side, rather than up and down.

GERENUK
(SPECIES: LITOCRANIUS WALLERI)

BEST SEEN: Samburu-Buffalo Springs NR, Meru NP, Tsavo NP

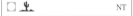 NT

As reflected in its Swahili name *swala twiga* (gazelle giraffe), the gerenuk is distinguished from the otherwise similar gazelle and impala by its strikingly long neck. It makes the most of this feature when it feeds, standing goat-like on its hind legs with its neck at full stretch to nibble at leaves that other antelope cannot reach. Endemic to East Africa, it lives in small family herds and is strongly associated with dry acacia thornbush.

KLIPSPRINGER
(SPECIES: OREOTRAGUS OREOTRAGUS)

BEST SEEN: Lake Nakuru NP, Mount Kenya, Tsavo West NP

 LC

A relict of an ancient antelope lineage, the klipspringer (rock jumper) boasts several unusual adaptations to its mountainous habitat. Binocular vision enables it to gauge jumping distances accurately, it has a unique ability to walk on hoof tips, and its hollow fur insulates at high altitude. Pairs bond for life, and both sexes have a grizzled grey-brown coat, short forward-curving horns and an arched back.

IUCN status NT: Near Threatened; LC: Least Concern

THOMSON'S GAZELLE
(SPECIES: EUDORCAS THOMSONII)

BEST SEEN: Masai Mara GR, Amboseli NP, Nairobi NP

 LC

One of the most familiar East African antelopes, Thomson's gazelle, or "Tommy", has a tan-brown coat with white belly, bold black horizontal patch on the flank and small horns. Swift and graceful, it usually occurs in small herds in open grassland habitats, often alongside other grazers such as the wildebeest and zebra. Endemic to East Africa, its range is centred on the Serengeti-Mara ecosystem.

GRANT'S GAZELLE
(SPECIES: NANGER GRANTI)

BEST SEEN: Samburu-Buffalo Springs NR, Masai Mara GR, Tsavo NP

 LC

Although it occurs alongside the Tommy, Grant's gazelle can easily be distinguished by its much larger size and lack of a black side stripe. It also has larger horns, which reach extraordinary dimensions in the racially discrete northern population in Samburu-Buffalo Springs. It lives in smaller herds than Thomson's gazelle and is less numerous where their ranges overlap, although it is far more widespread.

REEDBUCK
(GENUS: REDUNCA)

BEST SEEN: Aberdare NP, Masai Mara GR, Lake Nakuru NP

 LC

Two species of reedbuck occur in Kenya, both pale, lightly built and rather skittish grassland-dwellers with white underbellies and small horns. The Bohor reedbuck is a lowland and mid-altitude species with short forward-curving horns, while the chunkier and greyer mountain reedbuck is almost exclusively associated with grassy and rocky mountain slopes. Both species are common in their habitats, and are seen in pairs or trios.

ORIBI
(SPECIES: OUREBIA OUREBI)

BEST SEEN: Ruma Hills NP, Masai Mara GR, Shimba Hills

 LC

A patchily distributed small- to medium-sized antelope, the oribi has a shoulder height of around 50 cm (20 inches) and small straight unisex horns. It has a sandy coat with a white belly and can be recognised by the diagnostic round black glandular patch below its ears. Typically seen in pairs or small herds in tall open grass, it tends to draw attention to itself with a trademark sneezing alarm call before rapidly fleeing.

STEENBOK
(SPECIES: RAPHICERUS CAMPESTRIS)

BEST SEEN: Masai Mara GR, Tsavo NP, Amboseli NP

 LC

Somewhat resembling a scaled-down version of the oribi, the steenbok is a small antelope with tan upperparts, white underbelly and short straight horns. It tends to prefer thicker vegetation than the oribi, however, and its smaller size means it is more likely to be mistaken for a duiker. The name steenbok is Afrikaans for stone buck and refers not to the animal's habitat, but to its habit of "freezing" when disturbed.

DIK-DIK
(GENUS: MADOQUA)

BEST SEEN: Samburu-Buffalo Springs NR, Meru NP, Tsavo NP

 LC

Two species of this group of small, pretty antelopes are present in Kenya – Kirk's in the south and Guenther's in the north. Their ranges overlap in Samburu-Buffalo Springs, where a degree of hybridisation may occur. Usually seen in pairs, the two species are difficult to tell apart by sight, but either is readily distinguishable from other antelopes by their grey-brown coat, white eye circles and twitchy, elongated nose.

Key to Field Guide icons see *p98*

Amphibians and Reptiles

Amphibians and reptiles tend to get a lot of bad press, and not entirely without reason, considering the Nile crocodile kills dozens of villagers annually and several snake species can inflict lethal bites. However, most reptiles are harmless to people and of great ecological value. These cold-blooded creatures maintain their body heat using external sources, for instance by basking in the sun. They are therefore prolific in warm climates and tend to be poorly represented at high altitudes.

FAMILY

DNA and fossil evidence indicate that crocodiles are more closely related to birds than to lizards or snakes. As such, the class Reptilia is an artificial construct, one that would only gain scientific validity were it to include birds.

AFRICAN BULLFROG
(SPECIES: PYXICEPHALUS ADSPERSUS)

 LC

Among the most common and vocal of Kenya's 100-odd species of frog, which are mostly nocturnal, the African bullfrog is also the largest and can weigh up to 1 kg (2 lb). After the rains, safarigoers are frequently treated to an evening medley of guttural croaks and ethereal whistles.

TREE FROGS
(FAMILY: HYPEROLIIDAE)

 Variable

Africa's most diverse frog family, found in moist woodland habitats, tree frogs are small and brightly coloured, with long broad-tipped toes used to climb trees and reeds. A common species is the bubbling kassina, whose popping chorus is among the most wondrous of African sounds.

SKINKS
(FAMILY: SCINCIDAE)

 Variable

Represented in Kenya by about two dozen species, skinks are small fleet-footed lizards with slender bodies, long tails and dark scaling. Among the more visible species are the variable, striped and rainbow skinks of the genus *Mabuya*, most of which are associated with rocks.

GECKOES
(FAMILY: GEKKONIDAE)

 NE

The most diverse African lizard family, geckoes have lidless bug-eyes suited to nocturnal hunting and adhesive toes that allow them to run upside-down on smooth surfaces. Most familiar is the common house gecko, a translucent white lizard that can be seen in most safari lodges.

CHAMELEONS
(FAMILY: CHAMAELEONIDAE)

 NE

Kenya has about a dozen chameleon species, including four endemics. These charismatic lizards are known for their colour changes (influenced by mood rather than background), independently swivelling eyes and long sticky tongues that uncoil to lunge at insect prey.

AGAMAS
(FAMILY: AGAMIDAE)

 NE

Agamas are medium to large lizards with bright plastic looking scales – blue, purple, red or orange, depending on the species. The flattened head is generally differently coloured from the torso. Particularly spectacular are the male red-headed agamas that are often observed basking on rocks.

IUCN status LC: Least Concern; NE: Not Evaluated

HARMLESS SNAKES

Of the 200 snake species recorded in East Africa, all but 45 are entirely harmless. Among the more common of these benign slitherers, snakes of the genus *Philothamnus* are generally bright green with large dark eyes, and are often seen near water. The widespread rhombic egg-eater, sometimes mistaken for the venomous puff adder owing to its cryptic mottled skin, can dislocate its jaws to swallow an egg whole, regurgitating the crushed shell in a neat little package.

Rhombic egg-eater, a non-venomous snake

AFRICAN ROCK PYTHON
(SPECIES: PYTHON SEBAE)

 NE

Africa's largest snake, this python can reach lengths of 6 m (20 ft), and may be seen on safari. It is non-venomous, wrapping its body around its prey, swallowing it whole and slumbering for weeks or months while the digestive juices do their work.

MAMBAS
(GENUS: DENDROASPIS)

 NE

Mambas are fast-moving and widely feared snakes that generally attack only when cornered. The 4 m (12 ft) black mamba, Africa's largest venomous snake, has a distinctive coffin-shaped head. The eastern green mamba is smaller and shyer. Bites are rare but the venom is fatal.

COBRAS
(GENUS: NAJA)

 NE

Cobras are long snakes – up to 3 m (10 ft) – whose trademark hoods open in warning when they raise their head to strike or spit venom into the target's eye. Bites can be fatal. Spitting, though it can result in temporary blindness, causes little long-term damage if the venom is diluted with water.

BOOMSLANG
(SPECIES: DISPHOLIDUS TYPUS)

 NE

As its Afrikaans name suggests, the boomslang (tree snake) is almost exclusively arboreal. It is generally green in colour, but may also be brown or olive. Theoretically the most toxic of Kenyan snakes, it is back-fanged and passive, and, aside from snake handlers, it has never inflicted a fatal bite.

ADDERS AND VIPERS
(FAMILY: VIPERIDAE)

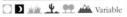 Variable

The sluggish disposition of the puff adder means that it is more frequently disturbed than other snakes. A thickset and cryptically marked species, it is outranked in size and beauty by the Gaboon viper, whose geometric gold, black and brown scaling blends perfectly with its habitat.

MONITORS
(FAMILY: VARANIDAE)

 NE

Africa's largest lizard, the Nile monitor can grow to be 3 m (10 ft) long, and is often seen along river margins, while the closely related savannah monitor is marginally smaller in size. Both species feed on meat and carrion, and though not normally dangerous, can inflict a nasty bite if cornered.

Key to Field Guide icons *see p98*

NILE CROCODILE
(SPECIES: CROCODYLUS NILOTICUS)

BEST SEEN: Masai Mara GR, Tsavo East NP,
Lake Turkana

☐ 🌿≋   LC

The hide of dark, heavy
scales is valued by
commercial poachers to
make handbags, shoes
and other leather goods.

A crocodile can stay
submerged in water
without drawing breath
for 45–60 minutes.

A Nile crocodile has about 80
teeth which are shed and
replaced twice annually.

Crocodiles have lurked in the lakes and
rivers of Africa for at least 150 million years,
and are the nearest thing alive to a relict of
the Jurassic Era, being more closely related
to dinosaurs than to any living creature.
Kenya is home to the Nile crocodile, which
is Africa's bulkiest and longest-lived predator,
growing to a maximum recorded length of
8 m (26 ft), weighing up to 1,000 kg (2,205
lb) and boasting a lifespan similar to that of
humans. It occurs naturally in non-montane
freshwater habitats, basking open-mouthed
on the sandbanks before it slips, sinister and
silent, into the water on the approach of a
boat. Lake Turkana harbours the world's
densest population of Nile crocodile, with
up to 15,000 individuals breeding on its
islands. A female lays up to 100 hard-
shelled eggs in a small hole, covers them to
protect them from predators, then returns
3 months later to carry the hatchlings to the
water, where she leaves them to fend for
themselves. The Nile crocodile feeds mainly
on fish, but occasionally drags a mammal as
large as a lion into the water; in fact, mammals form the main prey of crocodiles in the
Mara river, as seen to grisly effect during the
wildebeest migration *(see pp124–5)*.

Crocodiles make for a primeval sight as they bask on a bank

Like other reptiles, the leopard tortoise has scaled skin

TORTOISES
(FAMILY: TESTUDINIDAE)

BEST SEEN: Masai Mara GR, Tsavo NP,
Samburu-Buffalo Springs NR

☐ 🏔 ♣   Most species: Variable

The term tortoise is used to describe
any terrestrial chelonian, an order of
shelled reptiles that also includes freshwater terrapins and marine turtles. The
most visible species on safari is the leopard tortoise, which is Kenya's largest
terrestrial chelonian, occasionally weighing as much as 40 kg (88 lb). It can
be recognised by the tall domed gold-
and-black mottled shell after which it
is named. Often seen making its way
slowly along game reserve roads, the
leopard tortoise has a lifespan of 50
years and few natural enemies, but its
lack of mobility makes it susceptible
to fast-spreading bush fires. It is also
frequently hunted by local people.
Kenya also has two hinged tortoise
species, which are smaller and have a
hinged shell, and the peculiar flat-
shelled pancake tortoise, which is
placed in its own genus and spends
much of its time tucked away in rock
fissures or below boulders.

IUCN status CR: Critically Endangered; EN: Endangered; LC: Least Concern

The long muscular tail is used to propel and steer through the water.

TERRAPINS
(FAMILY: PELOMEDUSIDAE)

BEST SEEN: Meru NP, Nairobi NP, Lake Turkana

 Most species: LC

Kenya is home to five freshwater terrapin species, including the endemic Lake Turkana hinged terrapin. The region's terrapins are generally flatter and a plainer brown than its tortoises, and are usually seen in or close to water, sunning on partially submerged rocks or dead logs, or peering out from roadside puddles. Probably the most common species is the marsh terrapin, which inhabits waterholes, puddles and other stagnant waterbodies in savannah habitats, but often wanders considerable distances on land in rainy weather. It aestivates during the dry season, burying itself deep in mud only to re-emerge after the first rains – hence the local legend that terrapins drop from the sky during storms.

Hinged terrapins basking in the sun

Hawksbill turtle swimming gracefully through the reefs

MARINE TURTLES
(FAMILY: CHELONIOIDEA)

BEST SEEN: Watamu, Kisite-Mpunguti Marine Park, Malindi

Most species: CR or EN

Five of the world's seven turtle species occur along the East African coast, and all are much larger than any indigenous tortoises or terrapins. The green turtle, named for the colour of its fat, breeds along the beaches of Kenya, as does the scarcer hawksbill. An individual turtle lays several hundred eggs in the sand every season. After 2 months of incubation in the sand, the hatchlings make their way towards the sea, whose temperature will affect the sex of the hatchlings – the cooler it is, the higher the proportion of males. In the late 19th century, marine turtles remained common to abundant throughout their natural habitat, with some populations numbering well into the millions. Today, as a result of poaching and pollution, all but one of the world's seven species are on the IUCN Red List, and the hawksbill and leatherback are both listed as Critically Endangered.

Key to Field Guide icons *see p98*

Birds

With a national checklist of 1,136 species, Kenya has the second most varied avifauna in Africa. Birds are a prolific feature of the landscape, especially in Kakamega Forest, the Rift Valley lakes and reserves such as the Masai Mara, where enthusiasts may easily see up to 120 species in a day. Avian diversity is greatest from September to April, when migrants arrive and resident species shed their drab plumage to emerge in brilliant breeding colours.

FAMILY

A growing body of genetic and fossil evidence suggests birds are most properly placed with crocodiles as the only living members of the Archosauria, a group that also includes the extinct dinosaurs.

The marabou with a unique fleshy neck pouch

MARABOU STORK

(SPECIES: LEPTOPTILOS CRUMENIFERUS)

RELATIVES: saddle-billed stork, yellow-billed stork, open-billed stork

 LC

A fabulously ungainly omnivore that stands 1.5 m (5 ft) tall, the marabou is identified by its scabrous bald head and inflatable flesh-coloured neck pouch. The most common and habitat-tolerant of eight resident stork species, it may be seen near water, alongside vultures at a kill or even in urban environments, particularly in the vicinity of rubbish dumps.

HADEDA IBIS

(SPECIES: BOSTRYCHIA HAGEDASH)

RELATIVES: sacred ibis, glossy ibis, African spoonbill

 LC

A characteristic bird of suburban lawns, hotel gardens and grassy wetlands, the hadeda is best known for its harsh onomatopoeic cackle, most often emitted on take-off or in flight. Like other ibises, it is a robustly built bird that spends the day using its long decurved bill to probe the soil in search of snails and other invertebrates. Also common is the black-and-white sacred ibis, which was revered and frequently mummified in ancient Egypt, but is extinct there today.

Hadeda ibis, known for its raucous "ha-ha-hadeda" call

Egyptian goose, seen in large lakes and open water

EGYPTIAN GOOSE

(SPECIES: ALOPOCHEN AEGYPTIACUS)

RELATIVES: spur-winged goose, yellow-billed duck, white-faced whistling duck

 LC

East Africa's lakes support 14 resident species of waterfowl, of which the largest is the spur-winged goose, but the most conspicuous is the ubiquitous Egyptian goose – a large rufous-brown bird that is very assertive and perpetually honking. Waterfowl populations tend to be densest during the European winter, when the residents are joined by ten migrant species.

AFRICAN DARTER

(SPECIES: ANHINGA RUFA)

RELATIVES: white-breasted cormorant, long-tailed cormorant, African finfoot

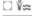 LC

Frequently seen perching on bare branches overhanging rivers and lakes, the African darter or snakebird looks like a distended cormorant, with a kinked serpentine neck almost as long as its torso and striking russet patches that glow off-gold in the right light. The gregarious, boldly marked white-breasted cormorant and the more solitary long-tailed cormorant are also common.

The snake-like neck is distinctive when fully stretched

IUCN status LC: Least Concern

Pelicans often roost communally on lakeshores

GREAT WHITE PELICAN
(SPECIES: PELECANUS ONOCROTALUS)

RELATIVES: pink-backed pelican

☐ ∭≋ LC

Easily recognised by their bulk, enormous wingspan and larder-like bills, Kenya's two pelican species are its largest water-associated birds. Most common is the great white pelican, an almost all-white bird with a large yellow pouch hanging from its long bill and black underwings that are clearly visible in flight. The smaller and more sparsely distributed pink-backed pelican has a pink-grey back and dark grey flight feathers. Both species can be seen bobbing along the surface of Rift Valley lakes such as Nakuru, often forming synchronised flotillas of around six to 12 individuals.

Goliaths have the largest wingspan of any African heron

GOLIATH HERON
(SPECIES: ARDEA GOLIATH)

RELATIVES: black-headed heron, great white egret, cattle egret

☐ ∭≋ LC

The herons and egrets of the Ardeidae family are among the most distinctive waterbirds in Kenya. Most are tall and long-necked, and use their elongated sharp bills to spear fish, frogs and other prey. The star of the group is the goliath heron, which stands up to 1.5 m (5 ft) tall and is common on Lake Baringo. The familiar Eurasian grey heron, black-headed heron and cattle egret are, however, more common.

GREATER FLAMINGO
(SPECIES: PHOENICOPTERUS ROSEUS)

RELATIVES: lesser flamingo

☐ ∭≋ LC

Represented by two species in Kenya, both of which are abundant on the soda lakes of the Rift Valley, flamingoes are pink-tinged birds that feed on algae and microscopic fauna, which are sifted through filters in their unique down-turned bills. They are very sensitive to water levels and chemical composition, and will easily relocate. The greater flamingo is the larger of the two species found in Kenya, but is usually outnumbered by the lesser flamingo, which is much pinker, especially on the bill.

Flamingoes, the most gregarious of waterbirds

GREY CROWNED CRANE
(SPECIES: BALEARICA REGULORUM)

RELATIVES: black-crowned crane

☐ ∭ ∭≋ LC

The 1-m (3.2-ft) high crowned crane is a beautiful grey, white and chestnut bird with a bristly golden crown and red neck wattle. Pairs and small parties are often seen in Masai Mara and Western Kenya. Its courtship dance is a riveting, albeit rather comic display that involves plenty of agitated flapping and whack movements. It has a distinctive and boomingly nasal two-note call, usually issued in flight.

A grey crowned crane has an elaborate courtship dance

Key to Field Guide icons *see p98*

The lappet-faced vulture is usually seen singly or in pairs

LAPPET-FACED VULTURE
(SPECIES: TORGOS TRACHELIOTOS)

RELATIVES: white-backed vulture, hooded vulture, palmnut vulture

                                                    VU

Africa's largest raptor is a truly impressive bird, with a bald pink head, a massive blue-and-ivory bill and heavy black wings that spread open like a cape reinforcing its menacing demeanour. It often shares kills with the region's five other carrion-eating vulture species, squabbling and squawking over the spoils. Capable of soaring on thermals for hours on end, this vulture ranks among the world's most powerful fliers, and its vision is practically unmatched in the animal kingdom. It is also unexpectedly fastidious, and will spend hours preening itself after feeding.

Augur buzzard, seen in Central Highlands and Rift Valley

AUGUR BUZZARD
(SPECIES: BUTEO AUGUR)

RELATIVES: yellow-billed kite, chanting goshawk, harrier hawk

                                                    LC

Among the most common raptors in Kenya, this buzzard is a handsome, medium to large bird with a black back, a variable (black, white or intermediate) breast and a bright orange-red tail. Like other buzzards, it has long broad wings, a relatively short tail and stocky build that makes it look rather like an eagle when it perches. It is probably outnumbered by the duller migrant steppe buzzard in March and October, when migrants flying between Europe and southern Africa pass through Kenya.

AFRICAN FISH EAGLE
(SPECIES: HAKLIAEETUS VOCIFER)

RELATIVES: martial eagle, bateleur, Verreaux's eagle

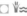   LC

Among the most evocative sounds of the bush is the far-carrying call of the African fish eagle, a high, piercing banshee wail delivered in duet, with both birds throwing back their heads dramatically. This strongly monogamous eagle is visually distinctive and striking, with black-and-white feathering against a rich chestnut belly and hooked yellow bill. It is a conspicuous resident of rivers and lakes, perching high in the branches of tall fringing trees, or soaring above the water for long periods, sweeping down occasionally to scoop a fish into its talons. It might be confused with two other water-associated raptors, the palmnut vulture and osprey.

African fish eagles perch openly in the vicinity of water

VERREAUX'S EAGLE-OWL
(SPECIES: BUBO LACTEUS)

RELATIVES: barn owl, spotted eagle-owl, scops owl

                                                    LC

Also known as the giant eagle-owl, Africa's largest nocturnal bird is most often seen near the large acacia trees in which it likes to breed. It is identified by its black eyes with pinkish eyelids that it closes during diurnal rest, and distinguished from the similarly proportioned Pel's fishing owl by its grey-brown feathering, crested ears and bold black facial disk marks. Usually unobtrusive, it is sometimes heard hooting at night. As with other owls, it is feared as a harbinger of death in many East African cultures.

Verreaux's eagle-owls stand more than 60 cm (2 ft) tall

IUCN status VU: Vulnerable; LC: Least Concern

The secretary bird, the world's most atypical raptor

SECRETARY BIRD
(SPECIES: SAGITTARIUS SERPENTARIUS)

RELATIVES: no close relatives, affinities uncertain

 LC

A bizarre grassland bird with long skinny legs, a slender grey torso, long black tail and bare red face mask, the 1.5-m (5-ft) tall secretary bird may have been named for its flaccid black crest, which recalls the quills used by Victorian secretaries. It is also claimed that "secretary" is a corruption of the Arabic *saqr-et-tair* (hunting bird). The monotypic family to which it belongs is thought to be ancestral to all modern eagles, buzzards and vultures. A terrestrial hunter, it feeds on snakes and lizards, which it stamps to death in a flailing dance ritual. It roosts in trees, but otherwise flies only when disturbed.

The flightless ostrich is associated with open landscapes

COMMON OSTRICH
(SPECIES: STRUTHIO CAMELUS)

RELATIVES: Somali ostrich

 LC

At a height of 2 m (7 ft) and weighing more than 100 kg (220 lb), ostriches are the world's largest birds. Two species are recognised, and their ranges overlap in Kenya. The pink-legged common ostrich is a familiar resident of protected grassland areas in the south and the blue-legged Somali ostrich is more thinly distributed in the semiarid north. In both species, the larger male has a handsome black-and-white plumage, while the female is smaller and duller. They are farmed in certain areas for their feathers, eggs and low-cholesterol meat.

SOUTHERN GROUND HORNBILL
(SPECIES: BUCORVUS CAFER)

RELATIVES: black-and-white casqued hornbill, Abyssinian ground hornbill, silvery-cheeked hornbill

 LC

Ground hornbills are rather fantastic turkey look-alikes, with black feathers, white under-wings, large casqued bills, conspicuous throat and eye wattles and long fluttering eyelashes. They are typically seen marching along in small family parties in open habitats, probing the ground for the large insects that form their main diet. Despite their terrestrial habits, they are strong fliers. Their low booming call is most often heard shortly after dusk. The southern ground hornbill, whose wattles are red, is replaced in the far northwest by the Abyssinian ground hornbill, a slightly larger species with blue eye wattles and a blue or red neck wattle.

The southern ground hornbill with large red wattles

KORI BUSTARD
(SPECIES: ARDEOTIS KORI)

RELATIVES: Denham's bustard, black-bellied bustard, Hartlaub's bustard

LC

Loosely related to cranes but more sturdily built, bustards are medium to large ground birds associated with open habitats. The most conspicuous species is the kori bustard, the world's heaviest flying bird, weighing up to 12.5 kg (27.6 lb) and standing about 1.3 m (4.3 ft) tall. Usually rather measured and stately in demeanour, it performs a manic courtship dance, raising and fanning its tail and flapping its wings up and down in apparent agitation.

The large size of the kori bustard renders it unique

Key to Field Guide icons see p98

HELMETED GUINEAFOWL
(SPECIES: NUMIDA MELEAGRIS)

RELATIVES: yellow-necked spurfowl, coqui francolin

                  LC

Endemic to Africa, guineafowls are large, gregarious ground birds with spotted white-on-grey feathers and blue heads. The helmeted guineafowl, the most common of three Kenyan species, is regularly seen scurrying along dirt roads. The star of the family, however, is the vulturine guineafowl, a dry-country bird with a brilliant cobalt chest draped in lacy black-and-white feathers.

HAMERKOP
(SPECIES: SCOPUS UMBRETTA)

RELATIVES: no close relatives, affinities uncertain

                  LC

Belonging to a monospecific family, the hamerkop is a rusty brown, rook-sized bird whose long, flattened bill and angular crest combine to create its hammer-headed appearance. This proverbial odd bird's massive and amorphous nest is normally constructed untidily over several months in a tree fork close to the water, and is made of litter, branches, mud and other natural and artificial objects.

AFRICAN JACANA
(SPECIES: ACTOPHILORNIS AFRICANUS)

RELATIVES: blacksmith plover, pied avocet, crowned plover

   LC

Also known as the lily-trotter, the African jacana is one of East Africa's most characteristic waterbirds, usually associated with lily pads and other floating vegetation on which it is able to walk thanks to its exceptionally far-spreading toes. A totally unmistakeable and very attractive bird, it has a rich chestnut torso and wings, white neck, black cap and blue bill and frontal shield.

NORTHERN RED-BILLED HORNBILL
(SPECIES: TOCKUS ERYTHRORHYNCHUS)

RELATIVES: African grey, Von der Decken's, yellow-billed hornbills

                  LC

Typical savannah hornbills of this genus are large birds with heavy decurved bills, often seen in lodge gardens. The northern red-billed hornbill is one of the more common species. Most nest in holes in tree trunks: the female plasters the entrance to seal herself in for the incubation period, while the male feeds her through a slit until the eggs hatch.

AFRICAN GREY PARROT
(SPECIES: PSITTACUS ERITHACUS)

RELATIVES: orange-bellied parrot, Fischer's lovebird, Narina trogon

                  NT

African parrots tend to be elusive in the wild, calling attention to themselves with a series of explosive screeches, then flapping out of view with their characteristically direct flight. Particularly vociferous, the African grey parrot is a familiar red-rumped bird whose Kenyan range is limited to the vicinity of Kakamega Forest, though it is often kept caged at coastal resorts.

AFRICAN HOOPOE
(SPECIES: UPAPA AFRICANA)

RELATIVES: green woodhoopoe, forest woodhoopoe, common scimitar-bill

                  LC

The African hoopoe is a handsome orange, black-and-white bird whose crest is very striking when held erect. Seen singly or in pairs, it is most common in park-like habitats and hotel gardens, where it feeds on the lawn, poking around for insects with its long, curved bill. Its closest relatives are woodhoopoes, glossy-black birds with long tails and decurved bills.

IUCN status NT: Near Threatened; LC: Least Concern

HARTLAUB'S TURACO

(SPECIES: TAURACO HARTLAUBII)

RELATIVES: great blue turaco, barefaced go-away bird, Ross's turaco

 LC

Endemic to Africa, turacos and go-away birds are large vocal frugivores with elongated bodies, long tails and prominent crests. The lovely Hartlaub's turaco of the Central Highlands forests has a green back, blue wings, red underwings and white face patches. The go-away birds, named for their explosive onomatopoeic call, are common in savannah habitats.

LILAC-BREASTED ROLLER

(SPECIES: CORACIUS CAUDATA)

RELATIVES: broad-billed roller, Eurasian roller, Abyssinian roller

 LC

One of the most popular and recognisable safari birds, the lilac-breasted roller is a robust jay-like bird with a lilac chest, sky-blue underparts and gold back. It is often seen perching on an acacia branch, then swooping down to hawk on its prey. Four similar-looking rollers occur in Kenya's savannahs, all of whom indulge in the agile aerial displays to which their name refers.

LONG-TAILED WIDOWBIRD

(SPECIES: EUPLECTES PROGNE)

RELATIVES: Jackson's widowbird, red bishop, golden bishop

 LC

Related to the smaller weavers, this is a black bird with red-and-white shoulder markings and an extraordinary long droopy tail that gives it a total length of up to 80 cm (31.5 inches) during the breeding season. It is often seen flying low and ponderous over reedy marshes and grassland, where it occurs alongside several other attractive but less dramatic widows and bishops.

CARMINE BEE-EATER

(SPECIES: MEROPS NUBICUS)

RELATIVES: little bee-eater, white-throated bee-eater, blue-headed bee-eater

 LC

A vivid red bird with turquoise head markings, the carmine bee-eater is the most stunning member of a family of dashing colourful insectivores whose sleek profile is determined by an upright stance, long wings and tail and long decurved bills. Bee-eaters are easy to observe, perching openly on bare branches, sporadically darting off to catch an insect before returning to the perch.

FORK-TAILED DRONGO

(SPECIES: DISCRURUS ADSIMILIS)

RELATIVES: square-tailed drongo

 LC

A characteristic savannah and woodland passerine, the fork-tailed drongo is an all black insectivore that tends to hawk its prey from an open perch below the canopy. It is a bold and assertive character, and emits a wide array of indignant nasal calls. It is sometimes confused with black cuckoos, male black cuckoo-shrikes and black flycatchers, but none of the above have a comparably deep fork in their tail.

WHITE-BROWED COUCAL

(SPECIES: CENTROPUS SUPERCILIOSUS)

RELATIVES: red-chested cuckoo, yellowbill, Diederick's cuckoo

 LC

The white-browed coucal is a large, clumsy bird seen in rank grassland, marsh and lake margins. It has a white eye-strip and streaked underparts. It is most visible before rainstorms, which it tends to predict with a dove-like bubbling that gives it the name of rainbird. The coucal is related to cuckoos, which are common but secretive in African habitats.

Key to Field Guide icons see p98

AFRICAN FIREFINCH
(SPECIES: LAGONOSTICTA RUBRICATA)

RELATIVES: common waxbill, pin-tailed wydah, purple grenadier

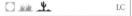 LC

Bright red with light spotting on the flanks, this ubiquitous but unobtrusive gem frequents gardens and lodge grounds. It is one of several colourful seed-eaters in the family Estrildidae, most of which are smaller than a sparrow and have conical bills whose waxen sheen gives it the common name of wax-bill. They are parasitised by the related colourful wydahs.

COMMON BULBUL
(SPECIES: PYCNONOTUS BARBATUS)

RELATIVES: spotted nicator, rufous chatterer, mountain greenbul

 LC

Among the first birds likely to be seen in Kenya, this cheerful and habitat-tolerant small bird is a common resident of gardens and lodge grounds in the Central Highlands and elsewhere. A restless but confiding character with a bright tuneful song, it is most common in the canopy of forest margins, and is also known as the yellow-vented bulbul after its most conspicuous field character.

MALACHITE SUNBIRD
(SPECIES: NECTARINIA FAMOSA)

RELATIVES: golden-winged sunbird, Hunter's sunbird

 LC

Sunbirds are small restless nectar-eaters with long decurved bills. Most species are sexually dimorphic, with the rather dowdy females being smaller and less conspicuous than the iridescent males. The malachite sunbird, long-tailed and dazzling metallic green in colour, is arguably the most beautiful of these, and is associated with aloes and other flowering shrubs.

MASKED WEAVER
(SPECIES: PLOCEUS INTERMEDIUS)

RELATIVES: red-billed quelea, golden weaver, white-headed buffalo-weaver

 LC

The *Ploceus* weavers are surely the most characteristic of African bird genera, and the masked weaver is among the more common species in Kenya. The dexterous male builds intricate ball-shaped nests at the end of a thin hanging branch, which is stripped of leaves as protection against snakes. Once completed, the nest is inspected by the female, who deconstructs it ruthlessly if she deems it unsatisfactory.

AFRICAN PIED WAGTAIL
(SPECIES: MOTACILLA AGUIMP)

RELATIVES: yellow wagtail, golden pipit, yellow-throated longclaw

 LC

Frequently observed walking along the edge of rivers, lakes and swimming pools, the African pied wagtail is named for its bold black-and-white markings and incessantly bobbing tail. It is Kenya's most common resident wagtail, but is outnumbered in some areas by the yellow wagtail, one of three migrant species, during the northern winter. The colourful longclaws and duller pipits are closely related.

SPECKLED MOUSEBIRD
(SPECIES: COLIUS STRIATUS)

RELATIVES: blue-naped mousebird, white-headed mousebird

 LC

This scruffy frugivore is the most widespread member of the order Coliidae, which is endemic to Africa, and consists of half-a-dozen long-tailed and prominently crested species. Generally seen in flocks of around five to eight birds, the name mousebird refers to their habit of shuffling nimbly along branches, though it might equally apply to their grey-brown colouration. Four species occur in Kenya.

IUCN status LC: Least Concern

OLIVE THRUSH
(SPECIES: TURDUS OLIVACEOUS)

RELATIVES: Cape robin-chat, common rock thrush, stonechat

 LC

The Turdidae is a diverse family of medium-to-small insectivores, represented by about 50 species and 20 genera in Kenya. Among the most recognisable is the olive thrush, which is often seen hopping around hotel lawns. The family also includes robin-chats, a group of orange, blue, black and white birds that are also common in gardens, but tend to prefer thicker cover.

AFRICAN PARADISE FLYCATCHER
(SPECIES: TERPSIPHONE VIRIDIS)

RELATIVES: silverbird, chin spot batis, common wattle-eye

 LC

This hyperactive leaf-gleaning flycatcher tolerates most habitats other than true desert, and might be seen anywhere, although local abundance is affected by complex seasonal intra-African movements. Usually bluish with an orange tail, it also has black-and-white and intermediate morphs. The male's tail can be up to three times the body length.

PIED KINGFISHER
(SPECIES: CERYLE RUDIS)

RELATIVES: Malachite kingfisher, giant kingfisher

 LC

Probably the most numerous and visible of Kenya's water-associated kingfishers, this black-and-white bird has a unique hunting method that involves hovering above open water then diving down sharply to spear a fish with its dagger-like bill. Other water-associated species range from the gem-like, finch-sized malachite kingfisher to the crow-sized giant kingfisher.

RED-AND-YELLOW BARBET
(SPECIES: TRACHYPHONUS ERYTHROCEPHALUS)

RELATIVES: double-toothed barbet, red-fronted tinkerbird, cardinal woodpecker

 LC

One of the most striking birds in dry-savannah habitats is the red-and-yellow barbet, pairs of which frequently perch conspicuously to perform a comic and very loud duet. Seldom seen but very vocal, tinkerbirds are sparrow-sized barbets that tend to perch high in the forest canopy, tirelessly repeating a piping one-note call for hours on end.

SUPERB STARLING
(SPECIES: LAMPROTORNIS SUPERBUS)

RELATIVES: red-winged starling, violet-backed starling, red-billed oxpecker

 LC

Common and colourful, with a glossy green back and rufous belly separated by a narrow white line, the superb starling is mainly a savannah bird. It is the most visible of several beautiful Kenyan starlings, including the plum-coloured violet-backed starling of riverine woodland and thornbush, the cliff-dwelling red-winged starling and the utterly breathtaking golden-breasted starling, a dry country special.

TROPICAL BOUBOU
(SPECIES: LANIARIUS AETHIOPICUS)

RELATIVES: long-tailed shrike, black-headed gonolek

 LC

Boubous are handsome but furtive shrike-like birds who betray their presence with tightly synchronised duets that involve the male singing a short series of loud antiphonal notes and the female replying with a harsh click or chirr sound. The black-and-white tropical boubou, often known as the bellbird in reference to its ringing call, is common in the Central Highlands, but is replaced by the slate-coloured boubou in savannah habitats.

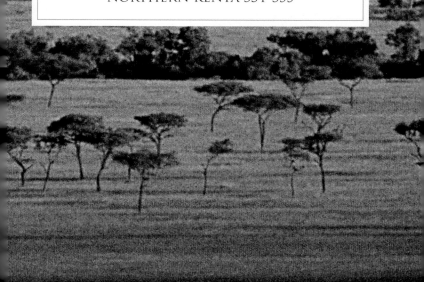

KENYA
AREA BY AREA

Kenya at a Glance

Kenya's diverse terrain and topography afford it a magnificent array of landscapes. On the coast, white sandy beaches are backed by dense forests, and intriguing alleyways and mosques in the ancient towns reveal the coast's history. The Southeastern Savannah's burnt grasslands host East Africa's big game. Further inland, Nairobi has plenty of urban attractions, good shopping and nightlife. Volcanoes and lakes dot the Rift Valley, and above it lie Western Kenya's fertile hills and escarpments. To the south the Masai Mara, part of Africa's greatest ecosystems, supports a wealth of wildlife. The Central Highlands feature dense forests and moorland. By contrast, the north is empty with stony sun-baked deserts.

Mount Kenya (see pp322–5) *straddles the equator and is Africa's second tallest mountain. The ring road around it offers sweeping views of its peaks towering over the forest.*

Kakamega Forest National Reserve (see pp294–7), *north of Kisumu, is Kenya's last remaining patch of indigenous rainforest that once spread over most of central Africa. Its pathways wind beneath a rich canopy of trees full of monkeys, birds and clouds of butterflies.*

0 km   150

0 mile   150

WESTERN KENYA *(see pp284–307)*

SOUTHERN RIFT VALLEY AND MASAI MARA *(see pp252–283)*

NAIROBI *(see pp150–*

Masai Mara (see pp262–5) *is Kenya's best known reserve. Its highlight is the annual migration of the wildebeest that cut across the savannah tracking rain and new pastures, with predators in hot pursuit.*

The Karen Blixen Museum (see p168) *is dedicated to the celebrated author of* Out of Africa. *The period house, located in Nairobi, gives a fascinating insight into the lives of Kenya's early aristocratic white settlers when the city was in its infancy.*

◁ Savannah grassland and beautiful acacia trees that comprise the Masai Mara landscape

Samburu-Buffalo Springs-Shaba National Reserves (see pp342–6) *to the north of Isiolo are fed by the Ewaso Nyiro river with the lush narrow stretch of palms and woodland surrounded by arid scrubland. These reserves are the best places to encounter some of the more unusual desert adapted animals such as the oryx and gerenuk.*

Lamu (see pp248–9) *is the principal town of the Lamu Archipelago, where donkeys wander the maze of narrow alleyways and white-sail dhows drift past the waterfront. Steeped in Swahili coastal culture, this town has remained unchanged for centuries and is now a UNESCO World Heritage Site.*

NORTHERN KENYA
(see pp334–355)

Mount Kenya

CENTRAL HIGHLANDS
see pp308–333

SOUTHEASTERN SAVANNAHS
(see pp176–197)

NORTHERN COAST
(see pp226–251)

SOUTHERN COAST
(see pp198–225)

Diani Beach (see p210), *south of Mombasa, stretches for 20 km (12 miles) and is one of Kenya's best beaches with pristine white sand, palm trees, clear turquoise sea and a coral reef full of colourful marine life.*

Amboseli National Park (see pp194–7), *on the Tanzanian border, is most famous for its giant-tusked elephants. Game viewing is especially rewarding here against the superb backdrop of Kilimanjaro.*

NAIROBI

Kenya's capital, Nairobi, has grown rapidly since its foundation as a railway camp in 1899. Today, it is the economic, commercial and transport hub for East Africa and a gateway for safaris across the game-rich region. Nairobi is also Kenya's one-stop destination for entertainment and shopping, and offers a number of attractions for visitors before or after a long safari.

The word Nairobi is a corruption of the Maasai name Ewaso Nyarobi (Place of Cold Water), a reference to the swampy patch of land where the Maasai brought their herds to drink. Originally a humble settlement of rickety shacks, Nairobi began to attract European explorers, white settlers and big game hunters when the railway from Mombasa reached it in 1899. The area was the last piece of flat ground before the railway's hard climb up the eastern shoulder of the Rift Valley. This allowed the construction of many stone buildings including the legendary Fairmont the Norfolk Hotel *(see p362)*. By 1905, Nairobi was large enough to become capital of the British East Africa Protectorate. It gained city status in 1950.

After independence the city grew steadily into East Africa's most prosperous and important economic centre. Today, it is home to multinational organisations, diplomatic missions, universities and NGOs, and is also a strategic base for the United Nations. Throughout its history, Nairobi has attracted a steady influx of rural people looking for work.

The city now has an estimated population of 4 million. There are pockets of upmarket residential areas in spacious leafy suburbs, but most of the population lives in congested slums, some of which are home to nearly a million people.

The city centre is a grid of modern, gleaming tower blocks. The streets have a lively and energetic atmosphere with trading stores, curio shops and hawkers, markets and traffic. For the visitor, there are good museums and galleries, nightclubs and casinos, upmarket hotels, parks and wildlife attractions in the suburbs. The city is one of the few in the world with a national park right on its doorstep.

Old steam locomotives stationed in the grounds of Nairobi's Railway Museum

◁ The hub of commercial buildings near City Square

Exploring Nairobi

Divided into a number of districts, Nairobi covers some 680 sq km (260 sq miles). Government buildings are scattered around City Square off City Hall Way, with skyscrapers cluttered on Standard and Kaunda streets. To the west are the Uhuru and Central parks and the leafy Nairobi Hill district. Most of the outlying sights, such as Bomas of Kenya and AFEW Giraffe Centre, are southwest of the city off Langata Road as it heads past Nairobi National Park towards the upmarket suburb of Karen. To the west of Karen are the undulating Ngong Hills with marvellous views of the Rift Valley.

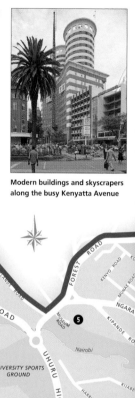

Modern buildings and skyscrapers along the busy Kenyatta Avenue

SIGHTS AT A GLANCE

Museums and Public Buildings

Bomas of Kenya ⑪
Karen Blixen Museum ⑮
Nairobi National Museum pp158–9 ⑤
National Archives ②
Railway Museum ④

Gardens, Parks and Sanctuaries

AFEW Giraffe Centre ⑭
August 7th Memorial Park ③
City Park ⑦
David Sheldrick Wildlife Trust ⑫
Nairobi Arboretum ⑥
Nairobi National Park pp162–5 ⑩
Uhuru Gardens ⑧

Restaurants

Carnivore Restaurant ⑨

Towns, Neighbourhoods and Markets

Athi River ⑱
City Market ①
Machakos ⑲
Nairobi Mamba Village ⑬

Archaeological Sites

Olorgasailie Prehistoric Site ⑳

Areas of Natural Beauty

Lake Magadi ㉑
Ngong Forest Sanctuary ⑯
Ngong Hills ⑰
Nguruman Escarpment ㉒

For additional map symbols *see back flap*

GETTING AROUND

The city centre is compact enough to be explored on foot. However, visitors need to be cautious while walking around Downtown Nairobi. Taxis, found on just about every street corner, are relatively inexpensive and should always be used after dark. Any tour operator can arrange a day tour of Nairobi National Park combined with the attractions to the immediate southwest of the city. Visitors with private cars can also find these sights as they are clearly signposted off Langata Road.

Zebras at Nairobi NP, with Nairobi skyline in the background

SEE ALSO

- *Street Finder* pp172–5
- *Where to Stay* pp362–3
- *Where to Eat* pp382–4

AROUND NAIROBI

LAVINGTON
NGONG ROAD
KIBERA
LANGATA RD
Wilson Airport
KALOLENI
UHURU HIGHWAY
Jomo Kenyatta International Airport
5 km (3 miles)
DAGORETTI RD
KAREN
LANGATA
BOGONI RD
MAGADI RD

KEY

■ Area of the main map

KEY

▨ Street-by-Street map
 see pp154–5

✈ International airport

☒ Domestic airport

🚉 Railway station

🚌 Bus station

ℹ Visitor information

✚ Hospital

✝ Church

✡ Synagogue

C Mosque

🛡 Police station

P Parking

⊠ Post office

━ Highway

━ Major road

━ Minor road

— Railway

CITY PARK

Mathare
FOREST ROAD
FOREST ROAD
FOREST LANE
MSHALE
OCHHA LANE
DESAI ROAD
SOIT OLOLOL RD
AURA RD
MURANG'A ROAD
LOME ROAD
PARK ROAD
DESAI ROAD
BILESHA ROAD
KINSHASA ROAD
SIMBI ROAD
TINGIRA RD
BAJUNI ROAD
MUHINGU RIVA
CHANAN SINGH ROAD
NGARA ROAD
RAMESH GAUTAMA
MUSINDI ROAD
JODONGO ROAD
Nairobi
NGARA ROAD
RING ROAD PUMWANI
KILOME ROAD
LOWER KIRINGAYA ROAD
KIRINYAGA ROAD
KEEKOROK ROAD
NGARIAMA ROAD
RIVER ROAD
TOM MBOYA
DUBOIS ROAD
TSAVO RD
RIVER ROAD
CROSS RD
ACCRA ROAD
DURUMA RD
GABORONE LANE
LUTHULI AVENUE ROAD
SHEIKH KARUME RD
MAMA NGINA ST
RONALD NGALA STREET
TOM MBOYA ST
MOI AVENUE
MANGO RD
RACECOURSE ROAD
CITY HALL WAY
TAIFA ROAD
HAILE SELASSIE AVENUE
HARAMBEE AVENUE
TUMBO AVE
PATE ROAD
STATION ROAD
KBS Bus Station
KBS Bus Station
Railway Station

0 metres 500
0 yards 500

0 km 5
0 miles 5

Street-by-Street: Downtown Nairobi

Nairobi began life as a swampy railway camp, but after more than a century of development its compact downtown area now comprises imposing skyscrapers, colonial buildings and Asian-style architecture with shops set back under long, covered walkways. As the capital of Kenya, it houses government buildings, banks and large hotels, including the modern Hilton Hotel and the historic Fairmont The Norfolk. The centre is a commercial hive and it is not unusual to see an executive in a suit walk down the same street as a Maasai warrior in full regalia. Neatly bisected by the Uhuru Highway, the centre's main thoroughfares are the Kenyatta and Moi avenues. Purple blooms of jacaranda trees colour the streets in December.

The skyline of Downtown Nairobi, dominated by skyscrapers

Jamia Mosque
Kenya's leading mosque and one of its most impressive religious structures, the Jamia Mosque has a pillared façade, imposing twin minarets and gleaming silver domes.

Kenyatta Avenue runs through the heart of the city and is a hub of commercial activity.

★ City Market
With a huge range of good quality art, curios and tribal artifacts from all over Africa, this market is very popular with visitors to Kenya. It also has a café that offers authentic African cuisine ❶

KENYATTA

KAUNDA

UHURU HIGHWAY

The Minor Basilica Holy Family Cathedral, built in 1960, is the seat of the Archbishop of Nairobi. It is also the city's largest church, with a seating capacity for 4,000 people.

STAR SIGHTS

- ★ City Market
- ★ August 7th Memorial Park
- ★ City Square

| 0 metres | 200 |
| 0 yards | 200 |

KEY

— — — Suggested route

Kenyatta International Conference Centre
Built in 1974, this 30-storey towering building has hosted many important international conferences.

STANLEY HOTEL

Now a modern tower block, the Stanley first opened its doors in 1902 as a boarding house on Victoria Street before moving to the present location in 1909. The site of Nairobi's first stock exchange, the hotel was very popular with visitors in the 1960s for its legendary Thorn Tree Café, where travellers would pin messages and letters for fellow travellers to the trunk of an acacia tree. The hotel has hosted famous stars such as Gregory Peck, Clarke Gable and Grace Kelly.

The grand façade of the iconic Stanley Hotel, Nairobi

National Archives
Housed in the former Bank of India building, the archives hold an excellent collection of tribal and contemporary art, documents and reference material ❷

Stanley Hotel

MOI AVENUE

MANGINA ST

TY HALL WAY

Kenyatta International Conference Centre

City Hall

HARAMBEE AVE

★ August 7th Memorial Park
The site of the 1998 US Embassy bomb attack that killed 218 people and left thousands injured, this tranquil park has a black granite memorial commemorating the victims of that fateful day ❸

Parliament House is the seat of Kenya's government. It is housed in a 1950s building with an impressive clock tower.

★ City Square
Dominated by the statue of Jomo Kenyatta, Kenya's first president, this paved 705-sq-m (7,585-sq-ft) courtyard has ornamental fountains, gardens and flag poles and is flanked by the City Hall and law courts.

City Market ❶

City Map 1 B3. Koinange St. 🚌
🕐 *8am–6pm Mon–Sat.* 🔴 *public holidays.* ♿

Housed in an aged Art Deco building and spread over two levels, Nairobi City Market is crammed full of compact and colourful stalls. Fruit and vegetables are stacked high in mounds and flower sellers arrange their blooms in giant buckets, while outside, around the edge of the market, shops sell fresh meat, fish and seafood and dairy products. There are a number of inexpensive crafts and curios for sale such as batiks, Kisii soapstone, sisal mats and baskets, the famous Kenyan *kiondo* bags and wood carvings – the herds of wooden giraffes standing to attention are particularly eye-catching. Prices are negotiable and there is an opportunity for a bout of good-natured haggling with the local traders. For fabrics, including cheap *kikoys*, *kangas* and Maasai blankets, visitors should cross Koinange Street to Biashara Street, to the northeast of the market, where there are many Asian shops specialising in textiles.

National Archives ❷

City Map 2 D3. Corner of Moi and Luthuli Aves. *Tel 020 2228959.* 🚌
🕐 *8.15am–4.15pm Mon–Fri, 8.15am–1pm Sat.* 🔴 *public holidays.*
📷 ♿

With its impressive columned façade, Kenya's National Archives is housed in the

Plaque bearing the names of people killed at the US Embassy bomb attack

former Bank of India building, which was built in 1906 and is one of Nairobi's oldest stone buildings. The ground floor has a lobby and gallery that display historical photographs of Nairobi, paintings and handicrafts. Among the displayed items are some superb pieces from the private collection of Joseph Murumbi, avid art collector and former vice president of Kenya. These include Persian carpets, Indian furniture and a number of drums and other tribal artifacts gathered from across Africa. When Murumbi died in 1990, it was discovered that he had collected some 50,000 books. Along with his art collection, approximately 8,000 rare pre-1900 books were bequeathed to the National Archives.

The first floor of the building has reading rooms that house a vast number of documents relating to the country's history since its colonial days. Also in this area are collections of photographs of former presidents Jomo Kenyatta and Daniel arap Moi during their term in office and on travels abroad.

The distinctly colonial edifice housing the National Archives

August 7th Memorial Park ❸

City Map 2 D4. Corner of Moi and Haile Selassie Aves. *Tel 020 341062.*
🚌 🕐 *7am–6pm daily.* 📷 ♿
www.memorialparkkenya.org

On 7 August 1998, a terrorist bomb attack on Nairobi's US Embassy resulted in the death of 218 people and seriously injured thousands more. The explosives, loaded on to the back of a truck, were intended to be driven into the embassy's basement car park. However, security guards stopped the truck at the gates, at which point the terrorists detonated the bomb. The explosion ripped through the building and killed many on the street. Simultaneously, a terrorist strike was unleashed upon the US Embassy in Dar es Salaam, Tanzania, killing 11 people. The Memorial Gardens were opened on the site on 7 August 2001. It is a quiet area with benches for contemplation, a statue made of debris from the attack and a granite wall bearing a plaque of the names of those who died here. An information centre displays photographs of that tragic day.

Railway Museum ❹

City Map 1 C5. Station Rd. 🚖 *up to Station Rd. A dirt track directly ahead of it leads to the museum.* *Tel 020 221211.* 🕐 *8.15am–5pm daily.* 📷 ♿

Anyone with an interest in Kenya's history will thoroughly enjoy the informative Railway Museum. Here, the full and fascinating story of the building of the Uganda Railway, dubbed the Lunatic Line *(see p299)*, unfolds through a series of displays of old memorabilia, photographs and original rolling stock. Here a poster of early colonial administrator, Sir Charles Eliot, is inscribed with his memorable quote, "It is not an uncommon thing for a [railway] line to open a country, but this line literally created a country". Another exhibit of interest is the railway coach christened Kima Killer. It was from this coach that, in 1900, a lion dragged out and killed railway superintendent Charles Henry Ryall at Kima Station. Crockery and silverware used by Queen Elizabeth II on the Royal Train in 1959 are also on display. Smaller items include brass lanterns, beautiful clocks, old-fashioned telephone heads and typewriters used in trains and ships. Just outside the building are several restored locomotives and carriages built between 1923 and 1955 that visitors can clamber over. These include one that the former US President Theodore Roosevelt rode to take pot shots at unsuspecting wildlife during a hunting safari in 1909, and the steam train used in the film *Out of Africa* (1985).

The old Kenya Railways logo

Nairobi National Museum ❺

See pp158–9.

Nairobi Arboretum ❻

Arboretum Rd, off State House Rd.
🚌 ⓘ *Tree Centre, 020 2725471.*
⭘ *sunrise–sunset.* 🎫 *last Mon of each month.* ♿ www.nature kenya.org

With a network of walking and jogging trails and shady picnic sites, the 80-acre (32-ha) Nairobi Arboretum is home to over 350 species of trees. Rimmed by high-rise buildings, it has been regenerated in the last few years and is now transformed into a green and vibrant public space popular with families and courting couples. Originally open grassland scattered with a few hardy acacia trees, the arboretum began life in 1907 as a trial area to see if exotic and fast growing softwood trees, which were needed to fuel wood-burning steam trains, could survive in Nairobi's climate. Many species from Australia and the Americas did survive and went on to become commercially valuable in Kenya. In the 1930s, indigenous trees were introduced to the arboretum and today there is a sizable collection of the country's 800 or so species. All trees are clearly labelled, mentioning the year in which they were planted as well as their commercial use. In the case of exotic trees, the country of origin is also given.

Picknickers under a bougainvillea at the City Park

City Park ❼

Main entrance on Limuru Rd. 🚌
⭘ *sunrise–sunset.* ♿ 🍴

Laid out in 1904 as Nairobi's first recreational area, the 300-acre (121-ha) City Park has magnificently landscaped gardens with flowerbeds, trees and shrubs, a sunken garden with ponds full of fish, a canal and a nursery. The Boscawen Collection here houses rare and unusual plants, including orchids. The adjacent war cemetery has 97 graves from both World Wars, while a maze and an early-20th-century bandstand bear testament to the colonial days. Thick patches of indigenous forest in the park harbour birds such as the hadeda ibis and black-and-white hornbill, as well as Sykes and vervet monkey and clouds of butterflies. The open-air restaurant adds to the park's popularity with picnickers.

A steam locomotive on display at Nairobi's Railway Museum

Nairobi National Museum ❺

Established in 1930, the Nairobi National Museum presents an overview of Kenya's culture and natural history. It was greatly expanded in the 1950s and in 2008 reopened after a 2-year modernisation. The museum documents much of Kenya's ethnology, plus the country's flora and fauna. It also has an impressive prehistory section, which also includes displays of fossils uncovered by the Leakeys. Outside in the well-forested grounds are a number of attractions, including a glass mosaic garden and a snake park that houses most of the reptilian species found in Kenya. A walk along the well-tended paths offers views of the Nairobi river at the bottom of Museum Hill. The museum has craft shops and a café.

The *abuu*

Spiral stairwell with a suspended column of old Nairobi photographs

Ahmed the Elephant
In the courtyard stands a replica of Ahmed, the famous tusker who was put under armed protection in the 1970s to demonstrate Kenya's commitment to eradicating poaching.

Asian African Heritage gallery

★ **Tower of Gourds**
This impressive tower is the central feature of the Hall of Kenya. Assembled from about 42 ethnic groups, the gourds symbolise the diversity of cultures in Kenya. Gourds are traditionally used as drinking vessels and for storage.

GALLERY GUIDE
The ground floor galleries include the Hall of Kenya, with displays relating to the ethnic groups, a collection of East African birds and a hall dedicated to the history of evolutionary finds in Kenya. Upstairs are displays of artifacts, ancient rock art and two galleries of photographs.

STAR EXHIBITS

★ Tower of Gourds

★ Cradle of Humankind

Mother and Child
Among the many statues scattered around the grounds is this piece sculpted by Francis Nagenda from trachyte, a volcanic rock.

Great Hall of Mammals
On the central podium is a selection of some key large mammals, along with the skeleton of Ahmed the elephant complete with extra-long tusks. There are also displays on the evolutionary history and characteristics of several animals.

KEY

- The Hall of Kenya
- Great Hall of Mammals
- Cradle of Humankind
- History of Nairobi National Museum
- Birds of East Africa
- History of Kenya
- Cycles of Life
- Ecology Gallery
- Asian African Heritage
- Temporary Exhibitions
- Non-exhibition space

First floor

★ Cradle of Humankind
This gallery showcases human evolution. The central display shows a reconstruction of early humans who lived millions of years ago, including Homo erectus.

Statue of Louis Leakey
The History of Nairobi National Museum gallery contains a larger-than-life bronze of Kenya's famous archaeologist who was the museum's honorary curator from 1941 to 1961 before he opened his Centre for Prehistory and Paleontology in the same grounds.

Snake Park

Ground floor

Snake Park
Started in 1959 to facilitate research on reptiles, the snake park was opened to the public in 1961. The park houses many snake species found in Kenya, including cobras, puff adders, mambas and large African rock pythons.

Uhuru Gardens ❽

Langata Rd, just after the turnoff for Wilson Airport. 🚌 ◯ *sunrise–sunset daily.* ♿

Located to the west of Uhuru Highway, the Uhuru Gardens are home to two monuments dedicated to Kenya's struggle for independence. Built in 1983 and marking 20 years of the country's independence, the soaring obelisk-like 24-m (79-ft) granite-and-marble **Uhuru Monument** is built on the spot where the end of British rule was declared at midnight on 12 December 1963. At its base are a pair of clasped hands, a dove of peace and a statue depicting a group of freedom fighters raising the new Kenya flag.

Across the car park, a more abstract granite-and-black marble structure built in 1988 also commemorates Kenya's independence. The gardens themselves are bare and unremarkable but provide an open space for Nairobi residents to picnic at weekends. In 2005, they were the site of the burning of 3,800 illicit small arms and light weapons confiscated from the public by the police. The event was overseen by the Ministry of Justice and Constitutional Affairs to highlight a campaign against illegal firearms being used in civilian society.

Roasting meat on Maasai swords at Carnivore Restaurant

Carnivore Restaurant ❾

Off Langata Rd, behind Uhuru Monument. **Tel** 020 6005933. 🚗 ◯ *noon–2.30pm daily, 7pm–10.30pm daily.* ♿ 🅿
www.tamarind.co.ke

Acclaimed as one of the best restaurants in East Africa, Carnivore is most famous for serving a set menu of a variety of excellent roast meat. Its signature dish *nyama choma*, Swahili for barbecued meat, is roasted on traditional Maasai swords over a huge charcoal pit. A typical meal begins with soup, before waiters set down hot cast-iron plates, salads, sauces and relishes. Each table has a small white flag and as long as it is upright, the waiters carve sizzling

Uhuru Monument in Uhuru Gardens

slices of meat off the Maasai swords on to the plates. Leg of lamb and pork, rump and sirloin steak, spare ribs, sausages, chicken wings, and game meat such as ostrich and crocodile are all served. The meal is only over when diners lower the flag. Another Carnivore speciality is *dawa*, Swahili for medicine, and is made by stirring lime, sugar and vodka into crushed ice.

The adjacent **Simba Saloon** offers lighter meals, and from Wednesday to Sunday hosts a popular nightclub. In the car park to the left of Carnivore's main entrance, the upmarket gallery **African Heritage** sells quality crafts, textiles and traditional beaded jewellery.

Nairobi National Park ❿

See pp162–5.

Sculpture of freedom fighters raising the Kenyan flag, Uhuru Monument, Uhuru Gardens

For hotels and restaurants in this region see pp362–3 and pp382–4

Bomas of Kenya ⓫

Forest Edge Rd, 10 km (6 miles) SW
of Nairobi, off Langata Rd.
Tel 020 891391. 🚌 ⬜ 2.30–4pm
Mon–Fri, 3.30–5.15pm Sat–Sun and
public holidays. 🖼 🎫 ♿ 🖥
www.bomasofkenya.co.ke

Established in 1971 by the
government specifically to
preserve Kenya's fast dimin-
ishing traditional culture, the
Bomas of Kenya showcases
the country's major tribal
groups. In 11 mock-up
villages of *bomas* (homesteads), guides explain the
traditional way of life,
including craft-making, family
structure and cooking and
social living arrangements.

Among the highlights here
are the colourful dance performances, acrobatics and story
telling, which are presented
every afternoon. The massive
circular amphitheatre has a
central stage where Kenya's
only resident dance company,
the Harambee Dancers, perform a selection of the 30 or
so Kenyan tribal dances in
their repertoire. Many of the
dances presented here are no
longer commonly performed
in Kenya. The centre offers a
comprehensive introduction
to traditional dancing styles,
such as the mesmeric Kalenjin
and Maasai warrior dances,
with perhaps the most striking

Dancers in traditional regalia enacting a hunting scene, Bomas of Kenya

being the Samburu warriors
leaping vertically into the air
with twirling spears in a bid to
win the hearts of their maidens.

David Sheldrick Wildlife Trust ⓬

Mbagathi Gate, Nairobi National
Park, Magadi Rd. **Tel** 020 2301396.
🚗 access only by a private vehicle or
on a guided tour. ⬜ 11am–noon
daily. 🖼 🎫 **www**.sheldrickwildlife
trust.org

A nonprofit conservation trust
established after the death of
David Sheldrick in 1977,
Daphne Sheldrick's unique
elephant orphanage on the
edge of Nairobi National Park
(see pp162–5) provides an
important refuge for lost,
orphaned or abandoned baby
elephants. The trust's patient
and attentive keepers, who
are experts on hand-rearing
baby elephants and duplicate
a natural mother's role of
nurturing, teach the orphans
how to suckle and bathe and
use their trunks and ears.

Every morning visitors can
watch the baby elephants at
play, while a keeper tells the
story of each individual and
explains the process of
bringing up the babies until
they are old and self-sufficient
enough to be rereleased into
the wild in Tsavo National
Park, as the closer Nairobi
National Park is too small to
sustain them. It is an
endearing sight to watch the
young elephants trot after
their keepers, chasing each
other, splashing in the
waterhole and being fed from
giant milk bottles. On
occasion, the trust also cares
for orphaned rhino.

Daphne with one of the elephants

THE SHELDRICKS

David Sheldrick was
the founder warden of
Tsavo National Park,
when it was established
in 1948. He remained
the park's warden for 28
years and developed its
infrastructure of over
2,000 km (1,250 miles)
of roads for game view-
ing, dams, causeways, boreholes and windmills to provide
water for the animals. He also embarked on a long and
pioneering study on the behaviour of elephants and was the
first person to hand-rear these animals. Since his death in
1977, his wife Daphne has continued to raise and rerelease
animals into the wild. She was the first person to perfect
the milk formula for elephants dependant on infant milk –
essential for their survival, as a calf under 2 years old can
die within 24 hours without milk. The trust has released over
70 elephants into Tsavo National Park, while Daphne continues to promote wildlife conservation worldwide through
books, articles, lectures and television appearances.

Baby elephant wallowing in mud,
David Sheldrick Wildlife Trust

Nairobi National Park ⑩

Established in 1946, the 117-sq-km (45-sq-mile) Nairobi National Park lies within sight of Nairobi's suburbs, and animals can sometimes be seen stalking through the grass against a backdrop of city skyscrapers. Characterised by open grassy plains studded with acacia, Kenya's first national park is home to over 80 game and 400 bird species. Larger animals include buffalo, the big cats and antelope. On the southern boundary is the Athi river, home to hippo and crocodile. The park is best known for its large population of black rhino who were moved here from remote parts of the country to protect them from poaching. The notable exception is elephant as the park is too small to sustain them, but baby elephants can be seen at the David Sheldrick Wildlife Trust on the edge of the park.

Kenya Wildlife Service HQ
Located at the park entrance, the headquarters offers information on Kenya's national parks and loads the smart cards that provide access to parks and reserves.

Narogoman Dam, an artificial dam and the largest in the park, has a rich variety of birdlife.

★ **Safari Walk**
A boardwalk takes visitors through a patch of indigenous forest with around 150 species of local trees, home to white rhino, giraffe and unusual animals such as the albino zebra and bongo antelope.

Nairobi 5 km (3 miles)

Wilson Airport

Main Gate

Hyena Dam

Ivory Burning Site

Langata Gate

Narogoman Dam

Olomanyi Dam

White Grass

Banda Gate

David Sheldrick Wildlife Trust

Kisembe

Mokoyeti

C58

Mbagathi Gate

Lion Corner

Hyrax Valley

Songor

Magadi 100 km (62 miles)

Python Pool

Maasai Gate

M G

★ **Animal Orphanage**
Opened in 1964, the orphanage is a refuge for injured animals from all over Kenya. The animals are either released back into the wild or transferred to the Safari Walk.

Hyrax Valley, an area of open plains, is good for spotting grassland game such as giraffe, impala and buffalo.

STAR SIGHTS

★ Safari Walk

★ Animal Orphanage

★ Athi River Track

Black Rhinos
Nairobi National Park is one of Kenya's most successful rhino sanctuaries in terms of breeding. Rhinos are relocated from here to former habitats where they once occurred naturally.

Athi Plains and Kitengela Corridor
This region is where wildebeest and zebra follow the annual migration in and out of the park to the dispersal area on the southern boundary in March and July, and again in November and January.

GETTING AROUND

There is a well-maintained network of dirt roads and adequate signage to picnic sites and waterholes. Visitors with private transport should allow half a day to explore the park. Alternatively, Nairobi's tour operators offer half-day guided excursions into the park. No walking is allowed except at the nature trail at the Hippo Pool. The Safari Walk and Animal Orphanage are at the main entrance of the park and can be visited separately. The park has no accommodation.

VISITORS' CHECKLIST

Road Map C5. 5 km (3 miles) SW of Nairobi on Langata Rd. ✗ ℹ️ *020 6000800 (Kenya Wildlife Service HQ).* ◯ *6am–7pm daily.* 🎫 *local tour operators offer half-day tours.* ♿ 🍴 🖥 📷 www.kws.go.ke
Safari Walk ◯ *8am–6pm daily.* 🎫 📷 ♿ **Animal Orphanage** ◯ *8am–6pm daily; feeding time 2.30pm daily.* 🎫 ⬆

KEY

✈	International airport
✗	Domestic airport/airstrip
ℹ️	Visitor information
☀	Viewpoint
▬	Major road
══	Minor road
═ ═	Unpaved motorable road
──	Railway
─ ─	Park boundary

Kitengela Corridor

Jomo Kenyatta International Airport
5 km (3 miles)

Embakasi Plain

Middle Ridge

Sosian

Athi Plains

A104

Athi Basin Dam

Boma Valley

Leopard Cliff

Athi

Hippo Pool

★ **Athi River Track**
Located in the south of the park, the track leads past some good distractions such as picnic sites, viewpoints over escarpments and cliffs, artificial dams and a walking trail at the Hippo Pool.

Mombasa
450 km (280 miles)

0 km		2
0 miles		2

Namanga
135 km (84 miles)

Baboon Escarpment
An impressive viewpoint on the southern border of the park, Baboon Escarpment looks down over dense vegetation and cliffs. It is home to the comical rodent-like rock hyrax and, of course, the ever inquisitive baboon.

Exploring Nairobi National Park

The open grassy plains of the national park, dotted with acacia trees and man-made dams, offer rewarding game viewing only a 15-minute drive from Nairobi's city centre. There is an extensive network of gravel roads, and apart from a few steep ones in the hilly south, most are navigable in an ordinary car. A map can be bought at the Main Gate with detailed numbered points that match road junctions in the park. Staff at this gate provide information on where to locate the park's wildlife, especially lion and cheetah, which are monitored closely. It takes 3–4 hours for visitors to see most of the park, its picnic sites and the nature trail at the Hippo Pool on the Athi river.

Rhino sculpture at the entrance to Nairobi National Park

Main Gate

Off Langata Rd. ⏰ 6am–7pm daily.
🅿️ 🍴 ♿ ⚿

While there are several gates into the park, Main Gate, located just beyond Wilson Airport, is the most suitable point of access. The headquarters of Kenya Wildlife Service (KWS) and the office of the Safety and Communication Centre (see p414) are both located in a cluster of buildings here. Visitors will also find a park information centre in this complex, along with such facilities as a car park, cafés, the Ranger's restaurant and a shop that sells gifts and maps of the park. Two of the park's most popular attractions, the Safari Walk and the Animal Orphanage, are situated near Main Gate. To the left of the gate is the office where travellers pay for and top up their smart card (see p69).

The **Conservation Heroes Monument** in the car park lists all the names of KWS employees who have lost their lives working for KWS since it was formed in 1990. Some died in accidents when

relocating animals and others in armed battles with poachers. Poaching was at its critical high in 1990, and since then, all KWS employees have been armed.

🦌 Safari Walk

Main Gate. **Tel** 020 6000800.
⏰ 8am–6pm daily. 📷 ♿ 🍴
www.kws.go.ke

Opened in 2006 and funded by the European Union, this is a fantastic walk through 40 acres (16 ha) of forest that is home to some 150 indigenous species of trees and plants, which in turn attract plenty of birds. The walk starts on a paved path and rises into the forest on a wheelchair-friendly boardwalk that eventually winds its way to overlook a waterhole. Visitors can hire a guide at the gate, or make their own way around by reading the very informative notice boards that not only describe the animals but also provide information about human-animal conflict in the wild. Animals inhabit

spacious grassy mounds that are separated by moats and single electric fencing. Despite this, the atmosphere is anything but zoo-like. Residents include the big cats, buffalo, monkey, pygmy hippo, rhino, plains zebra, hyena, ostrich, two unusual albino zebras and the rare bongo antelope. Lions can be seen behind a glass barrier at grass level in a sunken hide, while leopards can be viewed from above, at tree level. At the cheetah enclosure, visitors are permitted to enter and pat the cat and take photographs. At the beginning of the walk is a time capsule earmarked to be opened in 2050. Inside are messages from local people about what improvements they would like to see for the welfare of wildlife in Kenya.

🏠 Animal Orphanage

Main Gate. **Tel** 020 6000800.
⏰ 8am–6pm daily; feeding time 2.30pm daily. 📷 📷 ♿

With spacious enclosures, the Animal Orphanage provides a refuge for sick and orphaned animals. Some of these animals are brought here from the country's various national parks for cure and care, while others, such as baby cheetahs that were captured to become pets, have been rescued from poachers by KWS staff. Whenever possible, animals are reintroduced into the wild. When this is not possible, the orphanage becomes their home for the rest of their lives. Informative boards narrate the stories of each individual animal, and when there are cubs

Viewing platform above the leopard pen at the Safari Walk

The Athi river wending its way through the spectacular gorge between Leopard Cliffs, Nairobi National Park

resident, visitors are permitted into the enclosures for a close up photograph. Although the orphanage was established in 1964, the enclosures are regularly added to and improved upon, including the one for a leopard that has been built around a tree.

The distinctly bovine eland, Africa's largest antelope, on the Athi Plains

🐾 Athi Plains

While the western, northern and eastern sides of Nairobi National Park are fenced to keep wildlife out of Nairobi's residential areas and off the Nairobi–Mombasa Highway, the southern boundary is unfenced and provides access to the Athi Plains. Owned by group ranches and private land owners, this dispersal area covers approximately 1,000 sq km (385 sq miles) and is an essential component of the park's ecosystem, particularly because it serves as a natural open corridor for migrating wildlife. Many herbivores migrate to the Athi Plains during the rainy season that starts in November. They move back to the park's

permanent waterholes during the dry season from July to August. Large populations of giraffe, zebra, wildebeest, eland and Thomson's gazelle can be seen grazing across the seemingly endless plains. A number of birds, including the strutting secretary bird, crested crane and ostrich, are also plentiful during this time.

🐾 Athi River and Hippo Pool

One of the most magnificent areas of the park is along its southwestern boundary, which has steep valleys created by streams joining the Athi river. The Athi enters the park in the southeastern corner, and forms a natural boundary along the

park's southern edge. Hyraxes are plentiful on the rocks and the sure-sighted may even spot a klipspringer or mountain reedbuck. The Athi's park side is favoured by zebra. A stretch on the river's southern boundary known as the Hippo Pool is a popular picnic spot. There is a ranger post here, allowing people to leave their vehicles. An armed warden will accompany visitors on the short, shady walk through a riverine forest well populated with vervet monkey. Pigeons, barbets and starlings feed on the fig trees here, while the acacia trees are a favourite roost for white-backed and Ruppell's griffon vultures.

IVORY BURNING SITE

On 18 July 1989, 12 tonnes (13 tons) of confiscated ivory, thought to be worth 60 million KSh, were burnt on a site just inside Nairobi National Park in an attempt to stop the mass slaughter of African elephants by poachers. The fire was lit by the then President Moi and the event was televised across the world in a plea to end the trade in ivory. It subsequently contributed to the worldwide ban on ivory trading imposed by the Convention on International Trade in Endangered Species of Wild Fauna and Flora (CITES). At independence, there were an estimated 170,000 elephants in Kenya, but by 1989, they numbered only 16,000 and some 1,000 elephants a month were being killed by poachers. In 1990, KWS declared war on the poachers and imposed a shoot-to-kill policy. Elephant numbers improved dramatically and the population today is put at around 28,000.

Memorial built at the ivory burning site

Zebras in Nairobi National Park with city skyscrapers in the background ▷

Nairobi Mamba Village ⑬

North Langata Rd, Karen.
Tel *020 2486201.* 🚌 *to Karen.*
🕐 *9am–5.30pm daily; feeding time*
4.30pm Sun. 📷 🍴 🛒 🏪
www.nairobimambavillage.com

A popular family getaway, Nairobi Mamba Village is laid out around a man-made lake with manicured gardens that are dotted with interesting sculptures and picnic sites. The restaurant here offers a lunchtime buffet on the lawn and transforms into a disco at night. Visitors interested in semiprecious stones will find it worthwhile to stop in at the **Mamba Art Gallery**.

In keeping with its name – *mamba* meaning crocodile in Swahili – the resort is home to around 60 Nile crocodile. While motionless for most of the day, these reptiles come alive at feeding time when attendants toss meat chunks into their eager jaws. A footpath leads to the other side of the lake where a spacious pen houses many ostriches that can be hand fed. The lake also attracts several waterfowl species. Boats and fishing rods are available for hire here.

AFEW Giraffe Centre ⑭

Koitobus Rd, Karen. **Tel** *020 891658.*
🚌 *to Karen.* 🕐 *9am–5.30pm daily.*
📷 🛒 🏪 **www**.giraffe
center.org

Established in 1983 to protect Rothschild's giraffe, the African Fund for Endangered Wildlife (AFEW) Giraffe Centre is one of Nairobi's most popular

The colonial Karen Blixen Museum amid its beautifully maintained gardens

excursions. At the time it was set up, there were only 130 Rothschild's giraffe left in the wild in Western Kenya and their habitat was constantly shrinking due to heavy cultivation. Funds were raised to move three of the wild herds to Lake Nakuru National Park *(see pp 276–9)*, Mwea National Reserve *(see p329)* and Ruma National Park *(see p305)*, while a dozen or so animals were established at the AFEW Giraffe Centre.

A particular favourite with children is the circular viewing platform built on stilts, which allows them to feed pellets to the giraffe at eyeball height. The platform also has a lovely view of the nearby **Giraffe Manor** *(see p363)*, a luxury hotel which has giraffe stalking across its lawns. Guides are available to walk visitors through the centre. Across the road from the main entrance is a small patch of forest with a nature trail.

Old tractor, Karen Blixen Museum

Karen Blixen Museum ⑮

Karen Rd, Karen. **Tel** *020 8002139.*
🚌 *to Karen.* 🕐 *9.30am–6pm daily.*
📷 ♿ 🏪 **www**.museums.
or.ke

Danish-born Karen Blixen is best known for her book *Out of Africa*, which she wrote under the pseudonym Isak Dinesen *(see p36)*. This autobiographical work recounts her days on a coffee farm in Kenya where she lived from 1914 to 1932. Located in Nairobi's suburb of Karen, her farmhouse with its wide verandas and redtiled roof has been converted into a museum. It features original furnishings and props from the movie *Out of Africa (see p37)* as well as photographs relating to Blixen's life. Guides are on hand to take visitors around the clutch of rooms, which give an insight into the privileged lives of Kenya's white settlers. Outside, there are a few antique farming implements on display. The house is surrounded by a tranquil garden that provides splendid views of Blixen's beloved Ngong Hills. The museum shop sells handicrafts, postcards, books, including *Out of Africa*, as well as souvenirs. The **Karen Blixen Coffee Garden** restaurant *(see p383)* is further along Karen Road adjacent to another former settler's house.

Rothschild's giraffes at the viewing platform, AFEW Giraffe Centre

For hotels and restaurants in this region see pp362–3 and pp382–4

Serene grasslands carpeting gently undulating slopes, Ngong Hills

Ngong Forest Sanctuary ⑯

Kibera Rd, 6 km (4 miles) SW of Nairobi. **Tel** 020 2113358. 🚻
🕐 sunrise–sunset. 📷🔗
www.ngongforest.org

The 5-sq-km (2-sq-mile) Ngong Forest Sanctuary serves as an important green lung for Nairobi. A lush tract of indigenous forest covered by a network of paths, streams and dams, the reserve is home to several butterfly species and some small, shy mammals such as duikers. Some 120 species of birds have been identified here, including a variety of shrikes, cuckoos and waxbills. The forest has persistently been under threat of habitat loss as local people from the adjoining Kibera area – Nairobi's largest slum – collect firewood and medicinal plants from it. Currently it is under the protection of Ngong Forest Sanctuary Trust, which has raised funds to completely fence the perimeter. The trust also runs regular guided birdwatching walks, which need to be booked in advance.

Ngong Hills ⑰

Road Map C5. Ngong village, 8 km (5 miles) from Ngong Rd and Langata Rd Junction. 🚍 to Ngong.
🕐 sunrise–sunset.

Located on the southwestern edge of Nairobi, the hills take their name from the Maasai word *ngong* (knuckles), which refers to the hills' four-peaked ridge. From Nairobi they seem to be of an unassuming height, but on the western side they drop to the Rift Valley floor some 1,200 m (3,950 ft) below, which is scattered with small Maasai settlements. The rolling grassy slopes are studded with shrubs and command grand views. Although good for walks, the slopes can only be experienced in the company of armed rangers, who can be hired from the KWS office in Ngong. A trail runs along the top of the hills and on a clear day Mount Longonot can be seen in the north, while Kilimanjaro may be spotted on the southern horizon. The eastern slopes overlooking Nairobi National Park hold the grave of Denys Finch Hatton – believed to be the lover of Karen Blixen – marked by an obelisk and a small garden.

KAREN BLIXEN

"I had a farm in Africa at the foot of the Ngong Hills", is Karen Blixen's immortal opening line to her famous autobiography *Out of Africa*. Born in Denmark in 1885, she went to the British colony of Kenya in 1914 with her husband Baron Bror von Blixen-Finecke to farm coffee. However, the couple

Karen Blixen at her farm in Kenya

divorced in 1925 and Karen was left to run the financially troubled farm on her own. She began a long affair with English aristocrat and safari hunter Denys Finch Hatton. In 1931, Hatton died when his Gypsy Moth crashed in Tsavo. A distraught Karen returned to Denmark where her writing career began in earnest – *Out of Africa* was published in 1937. Beautifully written with evocative descriptions of the people, animals and landscape, *Out of Africa* is not so much a story of Karen's life in Kenya as it is of her love of Africa. Much of the eponymous and much-acclaimed 1985 movie was filmed at her former home. Karen remained in Demark until her death in 1962.

Lush and dense vegetation, Ngong Forest Sanctuary

Athi River ⑱

Road Map C5. 25 km (16 miles) SE of Nairobi on the A109. 🏚 *22,000.* 🚌 **Maasai Ostrich Farm** Namanga Road from Athi River, turn off 10 km (6 miles) from Kitengela. 🚗 *Tel 020 2700688.* ⬜ *7am–6pm daily.* 🎫 💳 🍴 📷 🌐 www.mericagroup hotels.com/ostrich

The town of Athi River is a sprawling urban centre to the southeast of Nairobi on the Nairobi–Mombasa Highway. It is, at present, expanding significantly, with some 5,000 houses expected to be built, along with retail and commercial facilities. The town gets its name from the Athi river, which flows through it after crossing the Athi Plains to the south of Nairobi National Park *(see pp162–5)*. Beyond the town the river is met by the Nairobi river and goes northeast to Thika.

The notable attraction in the area is **Maasai Ostrich Farm**, which is set in 200 acres (81 ha) of rolling grassland on the Athi Plains. Visitors to the farm will see both juvenile and adult ostriches, and ostrich rides are offered. A shop here sells painted egg shells and ostrich leather products, such as handbags and wallets. Popular for weekend day trips from Nairobi, the farm also has a garden restaurant that serves *nyama choma*, which includes grilled ostrich meat. Its resort has five spacious rooms and ten tented cabins with facilities such as a swimming pool, sauna and tennis court.

The terraced slopes and verdant countryside around Machakos

Machakos ⑲

Road Map C5. 70 km (43 miles) SE of Nairobi. 🏚 *144,110.* 🚌

Ringed by the pleasant, green Ukambani Hills, Machakos is a simple country town to the south of Nairobi. This region is home to the Akamba people who, long before the arrival of the Europeans, were great traders, organising caravans to take ivory to Arab merchants in Mombasa in exchange for copper, bracelets, beads, rolls of cloth and salt. These goods were brought back to Akamba trading posts in the interior.

The original name of the town was Masaku, after a local chief, but the British found it difficult to pronounce and it ended up as Machakos. It was Britain's first upcountry administrative centre and it

remained so for a decade, until the administration moved to Nairobi in 1899. In 2002, Machakos was the site for the signing of a peace agreement between the Sudanese government and the Sudan People's Liberation Army, who were fighting for a separate state in southern Sudan. Negotiations were led by the then-president of Kenya, Daniel arap Moi, and the treaty came to be known as the Machakos Protocol.

Today, subsistence farming sustains the region, and terraced fields cover every hill. Its tree-lined streets give Machakos a rustic charm. The only structure of note here is the square, concrete clock tower at the town centre erected in honour of a visit by Princess Margaret in 1956.

Olorgasailie Prehistoric Site ⑳

Road Map B5. 64 km (40 miles) S of Nairobi. *Tel 020 3742161.* ⬜ *8am–6pm daily.* 🎫 💳 🌐 ℹ️ www.museums.or.ke

Skull from Olorgasailie

Archaeologists first began exploring the Stone Age Olorgasailie Prehistoric Site on Magadi Road in 1919. It was further excavated by Mary and Louis Leakey *(see p349)* in the 1940s, and there are still digs here today. Located within the basin of an ancient lake that drained perhaps over one million years ago due to tectonic

Visitors inspect the hominid dig site from the boardwalk at Olorgasailie

activity, the site is rich in fossils thanks to heavy falls of alkaline ash from surrounding volcanoes, including Mount Suswa and Mount Longonot. It is thought that the lake attracted a number of animals, which were followed by early hunters, who fashioned the stone tools discovered at the archaeological sites.

Olorgasailie also has a museum with a wooden boardwalk over the fossils and displays of the finds. These include numerous hand axes and cleavers made by *Homo erectus* around half-a-million years ago, as well as fossils of elephants, hippos and baboons. Excursions to the actual sites can be arranged at the museum. Basic accommodation is available in *bandas* (huts). Camping is also an option, but it can get intolerably hot here.

Lake Magadi ㉑

Road Map B5. End of the C58, 110 km (68 miles) S of Nairobi.

Nestled in a low-lying basin on the floor of the Rift Valley near the border with Tanzania and covering 104 sq km (40 sq miles), Lake Magadi is located in one of the hottest and driest places in Kenya. From a distance, it shimmers in the heat haze and is surrounded by sparse, open bushland where Maasai may be seen herding their livestock. Several hot springs, mostly to the south of the lake, feed it with a constant supply of alkaline soda – *magadi* being the Maasai word for soda – which in turn attracts a number of wading birds including storks and flamingoes. After the rainy season, the pinkish lake fills with dense sodium carbonate brine, but this evaporates quickly in the sun, leaving behind a vast expanse of white salt that can be 15–30 m (50–100 ft) deep in places.

Located on the eastern shore of the lake is a factory that produces soda ash from the salt. It is, in fact, the second

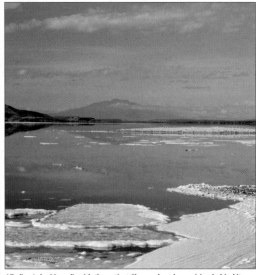
Alkaline Lake Magadi, with the extinct Shompole volcano rising behind it

largest producer of soda in the world, and the small settlement of Magadi has grown around it. A causeway over the lake leads to the Nguruman Escarpment area to the west, but people crossing over it need to wear sunglasses as the reflections off the soda surface can be blinding.

Nguruman Escarpment ㉒

Road Map B5. 140 km (87 miles) S of Nairobi. 4WD.

Beyond Lake Magadi, the 2,300-m (7,550-ft) high Nguruman Escarpment rises dramatically above the floor of the Rift Valley and forms its western wall. From the escarpment, stupendous views can be had back over the lake and over the Ewaso Nyiro River Valley, which becomes the Engare Ngiro Swamp before it reaches Lake Natron in Tanzania. Wild and remote, the area has no roads, but tracks are negotiable by 4WD. This is good trekking country and a number of tour operators *(see p405)* can organise treks with Maasai guides. The Ewaso Nyiro river, shaded by wild fig trees,

Yellow-billed stork at Lake Magadi

is an especially scenic place to walk and paddle in. The escarpment is topped by the **Loita Hills**, which level out to the Masai Mara Game Reserve *(see pp262–5)* to the east.

Wildlife viewing has improved considerably in this area with the establishment of the 140-sq-km (40-sq-mile) Shompole Conservancy and its super-luxury eco-lodge *(see p363)*. Jointly managed by the local Maasai and private developers, this sanctuary lies to the south of the Nguruman Escarpment and provides a dispersal area for game along the Tanzanian border.

The cascading Olasurr Falls, in the remote Loita Hills

NAIROBI STREET FINDER

Map references given in this guide for entertainment venues, shopping areas and other attractions in Nairobi refer to the Street Finder map on the following pages. Map references are also provided for leading Nairobi hotels *(see pp362–3)* and restaurants *(see pp382–4)*. The first figure in the map reference indicates which Street Finder map to

A *matatu* that plies on the streets of Nairobi

turn to and the letter and the number which follow refer to the grid reference on the map. The map below shows central Nairobi and around, as well as the main highways to the suburbs. Symbols used for sights and other useful information are displayed in the key below. The index on the opposite page lists most of the important streets and avenues located in central Nairobi.

KEY

Major sight		Police station	
Place of interest		Post office	
Other building		Parking	
Railway station		Synagogue	
Bus station		Mosque	
Visitor information		Church	
Hospital		Gurdwara	

SCALE OF MAPS 1–2

0 metres   250

0 yards   250

View of Nairobi from Kenyatta International Conference Centre

STREETWISE IN NAIROBI

Nairobi's city centre is a neat grid arranged in square blocks of streets and buildings. With the installation of close-circuit televisions and better policing, security is constantly improving here. Although street crime does occasionally occur, a few precautions could prevent such instances. Visitors need to be vigilant in crowded areas. Do not carry valuables and avoid walking alone after the shops have closed or on Sundays. After nightfall, hire a taxi and steer clear of deserted areas.

Areas to avoid are isolated spots near Uhuru Highway and Uhuru Park and the streets near River Road to the east of Moi Avenue, which are frequented by petty thieves jostling the passengers off the *matatus* and buses. Koinange Street is perfectly fine for walks in the daytime, but transforms into Nairobi's red-light district late at night.

It is wise to withdraw cash only during the day and to use ATMs that have a security guard or are located within the bank premises.

Carjacking and traffic light robberies can occur, so exercise caution if driving at night. Traffic can be quite congested, but roads are well signposted and traffic police are generally present.

Street Finder Index

SOUTHEASTERN SAVANNAHS

*S*tudded with rocky outcrops, flat-topped acacias and spectral baobabs, the semiarid plains that slope eastwards from Nairobi support exceptional concentrations of wildlife. There are jewel-like crater lakes and broken lava flows so fresh that they remain bare of vegetation, while towering above it all, the majestic snowcapped outline of volcanic Kilimanjaro dominates the southern skyline.

Owing to the region's inherent aridity, settlements are few and far between, and tend to be somewhat insubstantial. With the exception of the fertile Taita Hills, the area is poorly suited to cultivation, although hardy sisal plantations cover large tracts of land bordering Tsavo. Most of the Southeastern Savannahs is given over to low-density pastoralism or is protected in national parks and private reserves.

Nevertheless, the region supports a rich mosaic of rural cultures. Oloitokitok and Namanga are important bases for the pastoralist Maasai. The Akamba, famed for their honey and wood carvings, inhabit the area between Tsavo and Nairobi, while industrious Taita farmers cultivate terraced smallholdings near Wundanyi.

Much of the area is hot and dry, but the open plains are interspersed with some striking manifestations of geologically recent volcanic activity.

For added drama, there is Kilimanjaro, the world's tallest freestanding mountain. The great mountain is an important watershed, feeding most of the surface and underground streams and rivers that run through the region's main reserves to join the mighty Galana river.

Wildlife is the key attraction for visitors to this vast wilderness. All of the Big Five are well represented, along with other safari favourites such as zebra, giraffe and gazelle. The contiguous Tsavo East and West National Parks collectively form the country's largest protected area, and are flanked by several smaller private reserves. Further west, Amboseli, Kenya's busiest national park, is famed for its giant tuskers. The plains, bisected inland of Mombasa by one of East Africa's most celebrated colonial legacies, the Lunatic Line railway, were also the site of pivotal battles between British and German troops during World War I.

Giraffes on the vast plains of Amboseli with the mighty Kilimanjaro in the backdrop

◁ Elephants walking past a waterhole in the semiarid Tsavo West National Park

Exploring the Southeastern Savannahs

The region's major reserves, Tsavo and Amboseli, are
best visited on an organised safari. Tsavo East, thanks
to its proximity to Malindi, is a popular destination for
those who want to punctuate their beach holiday with
a day or overnight safari. Sites that are more accessible to independent travellers include the lovely
Lake Chala, embedded in an extinct caldera outside
Taveta, and the lush and little-explored Taita Hills,
while the starker Chyulu Hills National Park offers
some excellent but relatively demanding hiking in an
area rich with game. Located at the base of Taita Hills,
Taita Hills Wildlife Sanctuary offers close-up sightings
of elephant and buffalo.

KEY

Area illustrated

SEE ALSO

- **Where to Stay** pp364–5

- **Where to Eat** pp384–5

Elephants drinking at Salt Lick Lodge, Taita Hills Wildlife Sanctuary

KEY

━━━ Major road

══ Minor road

═══ Untarred major road

═══ Untarred minor road

--- 4WD track

━━━ Major railway

━━━ Minor railway

▬▬▬ International border

△ Peak

Kalikuyu

Kakya

Thiunguni

hyali   *Tbua*

South Kitui National Reserve

umarela

Ndia
Ndasa   *Tiva*

Tsavo East National Park

Kalinzo Plain

Yatta Plateau   *Galana*   Koito
ani   C103
Sala

bolobo

Ndara
Ndara Plains   *Voi*
Ndara   *Dika Plains*
8 m   *Maungu Plains*
Hills   NAIROBI-MOMBASA HIGHWAY   Mwanatibu
Taita Ranch
a
Rukinga Ranch   Mombasa
asigau
641 m
Kilibasi

Safari 4WD on a red dirt road in Tsavo West National Park

SIGHTS AT A GLANCE

Towns

Makindu ❶

Mtito Andei ❸

Namanga ⓰

Oloitokitok ⓭

Taveta ❾

Voi ❺

National Parks

Amboseli National Park pp194–7 ⓯

Chyulu Hills National Park ❷

Tsavo East and West National Parks pp182–7 ❹

Wildlife Sanctuaries

Kimana Wildlife Sanctuary ⓮

Lumo Community Wildlife Sanctuary ❽

Taita Hills Wildlife Sanctuary ❼

Areas of Natural Beauty

Lake Chala ⓬

Lake Jipe ⓫

Taita Hills ❻

Historical Buildings

Grogan's Castle ❿

0 km   25

0 miles   25

GETTING AROUND

The overwhelming majority of people who visit the Southeastern Savannahs do so on an organised road or fly-in safari, taking in one or more of the major national parks and private reserves in various combinations. The most important trunk road in the region connects the country's two largest towns, Nairobi and Mombasa, and is flanked by Tsavo East and West National Parks. This highway consists of just one lane in either direction for most of its length of 490 km (304 miles). Bus and other road transport are plentiful, but the passenger trains that run thrice-weekly along the parallel railway line are a safer prospect. Adequate surfaced or dirt roads connect the Nairobi–Mombasa Highway to Taveta, Wundanyi and Namanga, but other roads in the region tend to be rough, frequently potholed and therefore slow going.

Façade of the Sikh temple at Makindu

Makindu ❶

Road Map C6. 165 km (103 miles) SE of Nairobi. 🏃 *2,500.* 🚌 🚲 🛒 *Mon.*

Located on the Nairobi–Mombasa Highway, the small town of Makindu was founded during the construction of the Lunatic Line *(see p299)* to Uganda. It is home to the most revered and possibly the oldest Sikh temple in the East African interior. Set in peaceful flowering gardens on the north side of the highway, the main temple building dates to 1926, but its tin-roofed predecessor, built by Sikh railway workers in 1902, still stands alongside it. Makindu is an important pilgrimage site for Nairobi-based followers of Guru Nanak Dev, the founder of Sikhism. However, visitors of all religious affiliations are accorded a warm welcome. A 24-hour facility offers accommodation and food to travellers for a donation. A more attractive place to break the journey is **Hunter's Lodge**, a colonial-era hotel set in lush gardens overlooking the Kiboko river.

The Makindu Handicrafts Workshop, located 13 km (8 miles) away in Mbuinzau, is a good place to watch Akamba tribal woodcarvers at work.

🏨 Hunter's Lodge
Kiboko, 5 km (3 miles) NW of Makindu. **Tel** *0722 926685.*

Chyulu Hills National Park ❷

Road Map C6. 22 km (14 miles) S of Makindu via Kibwezi. **Tel** *045 622483.* 🚙 *4WD.* ⏰ *6am–7pm daily.* 🌐 🅰 **www**.kws.go.ke

Extending over 741 sq km (286 sq miles), this finger-shaped park was gazetted in 1983 to protect the Chyulu Hills, a vital catchment area that runs around 80 km (50 miles) northwest of a shared boundary with Tsavo West National Park *(see pp186–7)*. One of the world's youngest mountain ranges, Chyulu formed as recently as 500 years ago, and its jagged black rocks and ashen lava flows pay testament to the violence of its volcanic origin. The park supports a selection of wildlife that is similar to neighbouring Tsavo West's, and includes populations of elephant, buffalo, giraffe, zebra and eland. However, their natural densities are relatively low and the animals tend to be shy. The old lava flows are sparsely vegetated, but a spine of forested land along the upper slopes harbours 37 species of flowering orchid.

The **Kisula Caves** lie 15 km (9 miles) from the entrance gate, along a rough track that can be explored in a 4WD. Also of interest is the 13-km (8-mile) long **Leviathan Cave**, the world's largest known lava tube when it was discovered in 1975, although it has since been relegated to second place by Hawaii's Kazumura Cave. A limited infrastructure makes this national park most suitable for adventurous hikers, who can explore the untrammelled slopes in the company of an armed ranger.

Volcanic hills rising dramatically beyond Chyulu Hills National Park

Mtito Andei ❸

Road Map D6. 75 km (47 miles) SE of Makindu. 🏃 *4,700*. 🚗 🚌

Flanking the main highway, halfway between Mombasa and Nairobi, Mtito Andei (Forest of Vultures) is of interest mainly as a gateway to the adjacent Tsavo West National Park. It is also the country's most important truck stop, and is well equipped with filling stations, eateries, hotels and guesthouses, such as the Tsavo Inn *(see p365)*.

Tsavo East and West National Parks ❹

See pp182–7.

Rows of sisal at a plantation, a familiar sight around Voi

Voi ❺

Road Map D6. 80 km (50 miles) SE of Mtito Andei. 🏃 *20,000*. 🚗 🚌

By far the largest town on the Nairobi–Mombasa Highway, Voi is named after its reputed founder, Kivoi, a 17th-century chief of the Akamba tribe. The town emerged as an important centre of local commerce and sisal agriculture after the railway was built linking it to Mombasa in 1898. Voi also stands at the junction of the main road to the Taita Hills and the border town of Taveta. However, few visitors stop here unless they are en route to Tsavo East National Park *(see pp184–5)*, whose main gate lies just 7 km (4 miles) from the town centre. Good lodges can be found near the park's entrance, while the town is well equipped with filling stations, Internet cafés, shops, restaurants and ATMs.

The verdant slopes and scrubland of the Taita Hills

Taita Hills ❻

Road Map D6. 50 km (31 miles) W of Voi. 🚗 *4WD*.

Not to be confused with the eponymous wildlife sanctuary that lies in its shadow, Taita Hills is the most northerly of the Eastern Arc Mountains, a series of Precambrian massifs rich in endemic life. Home to the local Taita people, the hills' fertile slopes are covered in lush tropical cultivation and montane forests. The highest point in the range is the 2,208-m (7,244-ft) **Vuria**, recognisable from afar by its numerous satellite towers and aerials.

The main attraction of Taita for bird-watchers is the lovely Taita thrush *(Turdus helleri)*, a montane forest endemic, whose total population is estimated at 1,350 individuals.

The thrush's range is now confined to three forest patches, of which the most accessible is **Ngangao**, 13 km (8 miles) from Wundanyi via **Maghambinyi**. Also endemic to Taita are the Taita apalis *(Apalis fascigularis)* and Taita violet *(Saintpaulia teitensis)*.

Near the gateway town of Wundanyi is a site called **Ngomenyi** (Cave of Skulls), just 2 km (1 mile) along the Mbale Road, but difficult to find without local guidance. The exhumed skulls of ancestral chiefs are displayed on a small overhanging rock. Also on this road is **Shimoto Rock**, from where suspected witches were thrown to their death in precolonial times. **Mbale** itself is the site of a pretty church founded in 1906 by Father Maynard, known locally as *mlete* (tall man).

MAN-EATERS OF TSAVO

Historical photograph of the man-eating lion from Tsavo

In March 1898, construction of the railway bridge across the Tsavo river was brought to a virtual standstill by a pair of man-eating lions who devoured at least 28 Indian labourers – and possibly as many as 140 – before they were shot dead that December, by hunter, author and army man J H Patterson *(see p36)*. The maneless lions are almost certainly the most dedicated man-eaters on record, and their legend has lived on in books and movies such as *Bwana Devil* (1952) and *The Ghost and the Darkness* (1996). It is now thought that their taste for human flesh was acquired as a result of their scavenging improperly buried bodies of malaria victims associated with the railway. Patterson kept the lions' skins as floor rugs until the 1920s, when he sold them to the Chicago Field Museum in the USA, where they remain on display to this day.

Tsavo East and West National Parks ❹

Kenya's largest, second oldest and arguably wildest national park, Tsavo was gazetted in 1948 to protect a 21,812-sq-km (8,420-sq-mile) tract of savannah that remained largely unsettled as a result of limited water resources. An untrammelled wilderness larger than Wales, it was subsequently split into Tsavo East and West, which are administered separately. The smaller Tsavo West protects a hilly volcanic landscape overlooked by Kilimanjaro, while Tsavo East comprises open semiarid plains stretching 200 km (124 miles) north of the Nairobi–Mombasa Highway. Together, they support Kenya's largest elephant population and plenty of lions as well, although the latter tend to lack the long manes of their Masai Mara counterparts. Cheetah, gerenuk, oryx and hirola are more common in Tsavo East, while black rhino and lesser kudu are more likely to be seen in Tsavo West.

KEY

☐   Tsavo East and West National Parks

★ Shetani Lava Flow

This solidified lava flow, perhaps the bleakest of the many volcanic features that scar the hills and plains of Tsavo West, was deposited some 200 years ago. The cataclysmic event is still recalled in local folklore.

Chaimu Crater

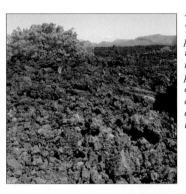

★ Mzima Springs

A short trail through the lush forest that encloses freshwater pools fed by Mzima Springs is one of the few places in Tsavo West where visitors can walk unguided and see large mammals.

0 km   25

0 miles   25

STAR SIGHTS

★ Shetani Lava Flow

★ Mzima Springs

★ Mudanda Rock

Lake Jipe

Located on the border with Tanzania, whose North Pare Mountains provide its scenic backdrop, the shallow Lake Jipe is renowned for bird-watching and at times it also attracts plenty of elephants.

Galana River
Fed by tributaries that originate in Kilimanjaro and the Central Highlands, Kenya's second longest river is the most important perennial water source in Tsavo East, and its palm-lined banks support hippo, buffalo and lesser kudu.

Ngulia Rhino Sanctuary is the last stronghold for Tsavo West's once numerous black rhino.

Lugard Falls is a set of rapids named after Lord Frederick Lugard, a colonial administrator who passed through the area en route to Uganda in 1890.

KEY

✕	Domestic airport/airstrip
ℹ️	Visitor information
🏠	Lodge
Ⓐ	Campsite
▬▬	Major road
═══	Minor road
▪ ▪	Unpaved major road
= =	Unpaved motorable road
——	Railway
– –	Park boundary
▬▪	International boundary

Yatta

Plateau

A109

Tsavo Gate

Galana

C103

Manyani Gate

Mbololo

Ⓐ Sala Gate

Ⓐ

TSAVO EAST NATIONAL PARK

ills

Voi Gate

🏠 Ⓐ

Aruba Dam

anyi

Voi

A23

Sagala

🏠

Dika Plains

Mwatate

Sagala Hills

Maungu

Maungu Plains

NAIROBI–MOMBASA HIGHWAY A109

Buchuma Gate

Mwatate

Rukanga

Mombasa 100 km (62 miles)

★ Mudanda Rock
This heavily striated quartzite formation, which towers in magnificent isolation above a small waterhole, stands a few miles east of the Nairobi–Mombasa Highway between the Mtito Andei and Voi gates. It can be accessed from Tsavo Gate by a good dirt road.

Golden-breasted Starling
The semiarid thorn scrub of Tsavo East is brightened up by several colourful birds more often seen in Northern Kenya, including the golden-breasted starling and golden pipit.

GETTING AROUND

Tsavo East and West are separated by the Nairobi–Mombasa Highway. Several entrance gates to both parks lie along this road, including the widely used Voi Gate (to Tsavo East) and Mtito Andei Gate (to Tsavo West). Despite their vast size and the presence of several lodges and camps, these parks carry a relatively low tourist volume and the most popular areas for game drives are the developed Kilaguni-Ngulia area of Tsavo West and the Voi river route through Tsavo East.

Exploring Tsavo East National Park

Sign, Voi Safari Lodge

Even without its westerly neighbour, Tsavo East National Park stands out as the largest of Kenya's national parks, covering 13,747 sq km (5,307 sq miles) of semiarid scrubland cut into two unequal parts by the perennial flow of the palm-fringed Galana river. The northern two-thirds of Tsavo East is rarely toured by casual visitors, which means that the park looks larger on a map than it feels on the ground. Even so, it is a vast tract of African wilderness, notable for its overwhelming sense of space, but also for the wildlife that concentrates seasonally along the Galana and Voi rivers, both of which are serviced by a network of good game-viewing roads. The main points of access are the Voi Gate when coming from the Nairobi–Mombasa Highway, the Manyani Gate when arriving from Nairobi or Tsavo West National Park and the Sala Gate when driving from Malindi.

The striking black-flecked yellow-throated francolin seen in Tsavo

⚓ Voi Safari Lodge

10 km (6 miles) N of Voi, 4 km (2 miles) by road from Voi Entrance Gate. **Tel** 043 30019. 🏨 ✍
www.safari-hotels.com

The clifftop Voi Safari Lodge, situated less than a 10-minute drive from Voi Gate, makes for an excellent first stop in the park, with its commanding position above the scrubby flatlands that run towards the distant Galana river. Below the lodge, a muddy waterhole frequently attracts thousand-strong buffalo herds, while a slow scan of the interminable plains almost invariably reveals herds of elephants grazing below shady trees or making their way to drink at the waterhole. Visitors can watch the wildlife action over a drink at the bar or follow a well-marked footpath down to a small hide for close-up photographs of antelope, baboon and storks alongside the waterhole. The grounds of the lodge support rich and varied birdlife, with Alpine swift and red-winged starling being particularly conspicuous, along with the colourful red-headed agama lizards and oddball hyraxes that scurry across the rocks.

Sign, Voi Entrance Gate

🦌 Voi River Route

The park's most accessible and reliable game-viewing circuit follows the Voi river east from Voi Gate to **Aruba Dam**. Impala, zebra and gazelle are common in this area, and it is a good place to look for the localised gerenuk and Besia oryx, as well as striking dry-country birds such as golden pipit, vulturine guineafowl, golden-breasted starling and Somali ostrich. The trademark maneless lions of Tsavo East are often seen lounging below trees in the vicinity of Aruba Dam, while cheetahs inhabit the open country around the entrance gate. The dam, constructed in 1951 to create a near-permanent water source in this otherwise arid locale, has an attractive setting below low hills. It generally supports a wide selection of waterbirds and wildlife, except when it dries up in years of severe

Voi Safari Lodge, overlooking the sweeping savannah grassland

The Galana river meandering through Tsavo East National Park

drought. The lush **Kanderi Swamp**, which lies south of the main game-viewing road between Voi Road and Aruba, is another near-perennial source of water.

Galana River

Running through the heart of Tsavo East before it flows into the Indian Ocean a short distance north of Malindi, this 390-km (242-mile) river, also known as the Sabaki, is the second longest in Kenya. Its 70,000-sq-km (27,000-sq-mile) catchment area runs from the foothills of Kilimanjaro to the Athi Plains outside Nairobi. Two popular tented camps lie on the river's southern banks, which are lined with doum palms and lush riverine vegetation. The most significant landmark along the Galana is the misleadingly named

Lugard Falls, a series of white-water rapids running across a potholed bed of black dolomite striated with quartzite. A short distance downriver, there is a viewpoint over a pool where hippos and crocodiles are almost always in residence. A public game-viewing road follows the southern bank of the Galana as far east as Sala Gate, through an area of dense scrubland inhabited by large numbers of elephants and buffaloes. The area to the north of the Galana has re-opened after being closed since the 1980s, when it was overrun with poachers.

Mudanda Rock

10 km (6 miles) S of Manyani Gate.
Often compared to a scaled down version of Australia's famous Ayer's Rock, Mudanda

Rock, a 2-km (1-mile) long inselberg, rears impressively from the surrounding plains, offering excellent views across to the distant Galana river. The name Mudanda (Strips of Drying Meat) refers to the near vertical quartzite striations that run through the rock like multicoloured veins. The crest of Mudanda Rock, which can be reached from a clearly signposted car park via a set of concrete stairs, overlooks a small natural waterhole where large numbers of elephant and other animals, including buffaloes, frequently gather to drink and wallow. The area is also known for its dense leopard population, but these elusive cats are seldom seen in daylight hours.

A visitor climbing down the steep incline of Mudanda Rock

POACHING IN TSAVO

As recently as the 1970s, Tsavo supported an estimated 6,000 black rhinoceros, the largest concentration anywhere on the continent. At its peak, the park also provided refuge to over 20,000 elephants, an unsustainable density of around one individual per square kilometre that prompted intensive debate about the implementation of a culling programme. However, this debate was rendered moot by Somali poachers who started crossing into the area in the early 1970s. Initially, their main quarry was Tsavo's prodigious elephant population, with ivory fetching around US$300 per kilogram on the open market. Soon, however, the rhinoceros also became a target, and, by the mid-1980s, had been poached to virtual extinction, while elephant were being lost at a rate of several thousand individuals annually. Fortunately, the trend was reversed in the early 1990s. Key turning points included the CITES *(see p65)* ban on international ivory sale and the unification of the country's disparate conservation bodies into the Kenya Wildlife Service (KWS) under Richard Leakey *(see p349)*. As a result, poaching is almost a thing of the past in Tsavo – the elephant population has nudged back above the 10,000 mark and rhinoceros are also slowly recovering, up from a mere three confirmed individuals in 1986 to over 100 today.

Elephants ambling across Tsavo East National Park

Exploring Tsavo West National Park

Although Tsavo West sprawls over an impressive 7,065 sq km (2,728 sq miles), the main tourist circuit is relatively compact, focusing on the volcanic landscapes to the north of the Tsavo river. The dense bush means that wildlife is less easily spotted than in some other national parks, and predator sightings are rather hit and miss. Among the more commonly seen large mammals are zebra, elephant, buffalo, impala and gazelle. The Ngulia Rhino Sanctuary within Tsavo West is the best place in Kenya to look for black rhinoceros, and the park is also good for the skittish lesser kudu. This area is accessible from the Nairobi–Mombasa Highway via Mtito Andei Gate and the more southerly Tsavo Gate, while visitors coming from Amboseli can use the Chyulu gate.

Entrance gate, Ngulia Rhino Sanctuary

🐾 Shetani Lava Flow
3 km (2 miles) NW of Chyulu Gate.

A relict of the most recent major volcanic eruption in the Tsavo area, Shetani is a solidified stream of magma that erupted from the southern end of the Chyulu Hills *(see p180)* about 200 years ago. According to local oral tradition, many people and animals were buried alive by the fast flowing stream of fiery lava, accounting for its Swahili name of Shetani, which means devil. The site is strewn with jagged tar-coloured rocks that look like they might have been deposited recently thanks to the sparse vegetation. The site can be explored on foot in the company of an armed ranger, although the treacherous caves that undercut some of the rocks probably pose a far greater threat than any wildlife, so it is best to tread very carefully.

🦏 Ngulia Rhino Sanctuary
25 km (16 miles) by road from Tsavo Gate, close to Ngulia airstrip.
⏲ 4–6pm daily.

Established in 1986 to protect Tsavo West's last few remaining black rhinos, this 62-sq-km (24-sq-mile) fenced sanctuary near Ngulia Safari Lodge *(see p365)* harbours an estimated 55–60 individual rhinos, a threefold increase since the early 1990s. A dedicated anti-poaching unit provides round-the-clock protection to these rare creatures, while electric fencing ensures that poachers are kept out and the rhinos stay in. Incidental beneficiaries of this high security have been the elephants that happened to be trapped within the fence when it was erected. By late 2005, an unsustainable population of around 150–160 elephants was confined within the sanctuary, leading to serious degradation of the wooded environment. Since then, the ecological balance has been restored with the relocation of almost 60 elephants from within the sanctuary to elsewhere in the national park.

The sanctuary is serviced by a limited road network and five waterholes. While animal sightings are not guaranteed, a population density of about one black rhino per square kilometre means that Ngulia Sanctuary now offers the best chance anywhere in Kenya of spotting this elusive browser.

Solidified expanse of lava at the foot of the Chyulu Hills

Mzima Springs, surrounded by a canopy of trees inhabited by birds

Mzima Springs

48 km (30 miles) SW of the Mtito Andei Gate.

A freshwater oasis in the heart of Tsavo West's dry savannah, Mzima Springs is a fascinating geological phenomenon. Fed by water that drains from the slopes of Kilimanjaro and Chyulu into a network of subterranean streams that flow above the non-porous Precambrian bedrock, the spring surfaces some 50 km (31 miles) east of its source. Having undergone a process of natural filtration via the porous volcanic rocks of the Chyulu Hills, this sparkling water emerges into a series of crystal clear pools at a daily rate of more than 200 million litres (53 million gal), some 10 per cent of which is diverted along an artificial pipeline to form the main source of water for Mombasa and its environs.

A unique feature of the largest pool is an underwater observation chamber built at the end of a small wooden pier in 1969 to offer spectacular subsurface views of hippos in their aquatic milieu. Not surprisingly, the hippos have since retreated to a more private location at the other end of the pool, but a swirl of fish is visible through the windows, with giant carp-like golden mudsuckers being especially common.

A walking trail through the lush palm and fever-tree thickets that surround Mzima might take anything from 15 minutes to an hour, depending on how often the walkers stop. The birdlife here can be excellent. The liquid song of the pretty black-headed oriole reverberates through the canopy, while more secretive woodland species include the African paradise flycatcher and Narina trogon. Fish eagles and African darters perch on overhanging branches, while pied kingfishers hover above the surface ready to feast on their favoured prey of small fish. Hippos and crocodiles are resident, antelope such as eland and lesser kudu frequently come down to drink from the pools, while bushbuck and duikers haunt the forest undergrowth.

Chaimu Crater

5 km (3 miles) E of Kilaguni Lodge.

This volcanic hill rises in stark isolation from a setting of solidified lava flows, forming an almost perfect conical pyramid whose coal black ashy slopes support a meagre cover of yellow grass on one side, and are totally denuded on the other. The natural equivalent of a giant slagheap, the honeycombed hill can be climbed via a steep, soft and shadeless path to the rim, which offers fantastic views over the surrounding plains. The hot, dusty ascent is best taken in the relative cool of the early morning, keeping an eye open for snakes and resting mammals.

The conical Chaimu Crater rising above its ashy slopes

NGULIA BIRD-RINGING PROJECT

Situated along one of the world's busiest avian migration routes, the Ngulia Hills have acquired something close to legendary status among ornithologists for the large number of birds attracted to Ngulia Lodge during the peak migration months of October and November. Millions of Eurasian migrants pass this way annually, representing several dozen species. For this reason, Ngulia is the site of Africa's foremost bird-ringing project, which has ringed more than 300,000 individual birds since 1969. More than 100 migrant and resident species have been ringed, with the most prolific being marsh warbler, river warbler, red-backed shrike, sprosser and common whitethroat.

Marsh warbler, distinguished by its yellowish buff breast

A view of Taita Hills from the *bandas* of Salt Lick Lodge

Taita Hills Wildlife Sanctuary ❼

Road Map D7. 37 km (23 miles) SW of Voi along the Taveta Rd. **Tel** 043 31271. 🚌 *buses run past the entrance gate but not into the reserve.* 🚗 *4WD.* 🎨 🍴 🛏 🏪 🌐

Established in 1972, Taita Hills Wildlife Sanctuary is a private reserve extending over approximately 110 sq km (43 sq miles) of thorny savannah set below the craggy volcanic peaks of Taita Hills (*see p181*). The sanctuary shares an unfenced border with Tsavo West National Park (*see pp186–7*), allowing wildlife free movement in and out of the national park, but an electric fence runs along the northern boundary to prevent elephant and buffalo from damaging crops in the neighbouring villages.

More than 50 mammal and 300 bird species have been recorded at the sanctuary. However, populations tend to fluctuate according to season, with elephant and buffalo in particular being densest towards the end of the dry season (June to November). Resident within the reserve are three lion prides as well as small populations of leopard and cheetah.

The main attraction of the wildlife sanctuary is a stilted construction – **Salt Lick Lodge** (*see p364*), whose Germanic architecture is said to resemble bunkers, in recognition of the World War I battles fought in the vicinity. The lodge offers fine views over a waterhole, which attracts a steady stream of thirsty wildlife – there is no finer place in Kenya for close-up views of elephant, which gather here in their hundreds on busy nights.

Visitors can explore the sanctuary in their own vehicles as the area is too small to pose any real danger of getting lost. Guided game drives are also offered along the well-maintained network of internal roads, where giraffe and Coke's hartebeest are among the more common ungulates. Also popular in the wildlife sanctuary are night drives. Owing to the sanctuary's small size, the night drives offer a good chance of spotting nocturnal species such as hyena, leopard, honey badger, genet and white-tailed mongoose.

Lumo Community Wildlife Sanctuary ❽

Road Map D6. 50 km (31 miles) W of Voi along the Taveta Rd. 🚌 🚗 *4WD.* 🕐 *6am–6pm daily.* 🎨 🚗 🌐

Formed in 1993, when the tribal lands of the Lualenyi, Mramba and Oza communities were united, this 450-sq-km (174-sq-mile) sanctuary bordering Tsavo West supports the Big Five, except rhino. It is named after the Lumo people, a Taita clan of these plains. Visitors with private transport are permitted to explore the reserve under their own steam, but most stay at **Lion Rock Safari Camp** (*see p364*), a spectacularly sited eco-lodge that offers guided day and night drives and walks through the tangled scrub.

Entrance to the Lumo Community Wildlife Sanctuary

Taveta ❾

Road Map C6. 110 km (68 miles) W of Voi. 🏃 *11,500.* 🚌 🚤 *Wed & Sat.*

Named for the Bantu-speaking Taveta people of the area, this modest border town comes to life on the bi-weekly market days, when villagers from both Kenya and Tanzania arrive to trade fresh produce and smuggled or imported goods. The town's facilities include hotels, restaurants and banks, but it is of interest primarily as a base to explore the Chala and Jipe lakes. The **Taveta Military Cemetery** houses the graves of 123 soldiers from the World War I campaign against what was then German East Africa.

The graves of World War I soldiers, Taveta Military Cemetery

Grogan's Castle ❿

Road Map C6. 10 km (6 miles) S of Taveta along the Jipe Rd. 🚌 🚗 *4WD.*

Perched imperiously on a tall volcanic plug that looms above the dirt road to Lake Jipe, this building was constructed as the home of Ewart Grogan, a Scottish settler, best known for his pioneering foot journey from the Cape to Cairo, undertaken from 1898 to 1900. Combining Swahili style arches and courtyards with contemporary 1930s European flourishes, the whitewashed building feels more like a monastery than a castle, with the windows offering grand views across the plains of Tsavo to Lake Jipe, the Pare Mountains and Kilimanjaro. The building is superficially rundown but structurally sound, and there have been long-standing talks of converting it into a hotel.

Placid Lake Jipe, with the Pare Mountains rising from its furthest shores

Lake Jipe ⓫

Road Map C6. 25 km (16 miles) S of Taveta. 🚌 🕐 *6am–7pm daily.* 📷 🌊 🏕 *The northern shore lies outside Tsavo West and can be explored on foot without paying park entrance fees.* **www**.kws.go.ke

Located partially within the southern sector of Tsavo West, Lake Jipe is a shallow, papyrus-lined freshwater body set within a natural sump that runs along the border with Tanzania for 10 km (6 miles). It is a magnificent spot, with the Pare Mountains rising above the Tanzanian shore and Kilimanjaro, the lake's main source of water, hulking over the northern skyline. Wildlife is usually visible, especially during the dry season, when elephants come to drink and bathe at the lake. Hippos and crocodiles are plentiful, and the reedy shore harbours local birds such as African water rail and pygmy goose. Local fishermen can usually be persuaded to take visitors out onto the lake for a fee.

The presence of an endemic fish, *Tilapia jipe*, suggests a long history of isolation from other wetlands. There are indications that the lake is becoming shallower and choked with papyrus, probably due to an increase in silt washed down from Kilimanjaro as a consequence of deforestation and associated erosion.

Lake Chala ⓬

Road Map C6. 8 km (5 miles) N of Taveta. 🚌

Straddling the Kenyan border near the southern footslopes of Kilimanjaro, this spectacular circular lake has a diameter of 3 km (2 miles). Despite that, it remains practically invisible until the tall rim of the volcanic crater in which it is nestled is reached. The lake's still and calm waters are hemmed in by sheer cliffs draped in tropical greenery, and can be reached via a rather steep path from the grounds of the disused Lake Chala Hotel on the eastern rim. From the rocky shore, translucent waters plunge almost vertically to undetermined depths. Once a popular spot for a dip, Lake Chala is no longer considered safe, following a fatal crocodile attack on a British volunteer in 2002. The lake supports an abundance of waterbirds and a species of endemic cichlid fish, named *Oreochromis hunteri*.

Lake Chala, confined by the steep walls of a crater

A Maasai giraffe in Kimana Wildlife Sanctuary

Oloitokitok ⑬

Road Map C6. 100 km (60 miles)
N of Taveta. 🚶 10,500. ✕ 🚌 🛳
Tue & Sat.

This small and little visited border town has the distinction of being the closest place to Kilimanjaro anywhere in Kenya. Set at a warm, dusty elevation of 1,700 m (5,580 ft), it feels more like the plains than the mountains. Weather permitting, the town centre and surrounding country roads offer stunning views of the snow-capped Uhuru Peak, little more than 20 km (12 miles) distant as the crow flies. The poor state of roads on this side of the border means that Oloitokitok probably has closer economic links with Tanzania than the rest of Kenya. Indeed, if it were not for visa and other border complications, it would be far quicker to drive here from Taveta (see p189) along the partially surfaced road through Marangu in Tanzania.

Equipped with one small bank, a filling station and a plethora of budget lodgings and eateries, this unassuming town is an important trading centre for the local Maasai, who come from surrounding villages on both sides of the border on the twice-weekly market days. It offers a splendid opportunity to interact with these tribes people. Local touts might be willing to set up Kilimanjaro climbs from Oloitokitok, but the legality of these is highly questionable given that the upper slopes of the mountain all lie within Tanzania.

Kimana Wildlife Sanctuary ⑭

Road Map C6. 30 km (19 miles)
SE of Amboseli. ✕ 🕐 6am–7pm
daily. 🎒 🎫 🌐 www.african
safariclub.com

Founded in 1994 and opened to visitors 2 years later, this 60-sq-km (25-sq-mile) sanctuary lies on Maasai land along the Kimana river, where it forms part of an important wildlife migration corridor between the Amboseli and Tsavo ecosystems. Although day visitors are welcome, the sanctuary operates as a private ranch for the UK-based **African Safari Club**, which runs three lodges here, flying in clients from its coastal properties on daily charters. The Kimana river is teeming with crocodiles and hippos, while the fringing woodland, dominated by ficus and fever trees, hosts large resident populations of bushbuck, giraffe, wildebeest, zebra and numerous other bird species. Lion sightings are guaranteed

here, counting a trio of caged individuals, but large carnivores are thin on the ground, while elephant, buffalo and eland tend to be highly transient, with numbers varying from one week to the next.

Amboseli National Park ⑮

See pp194–7.

Namanga ⑯

Road Map C6. 170 km (106 miles)
S of Nairobi. 🚶 5,500. ✕ 🚌

Set in the heart of Maasailand, Namanga will be passed through by visitors driving down to Amboseli National Park from the capital, and it is also probably Kenya's busiest border town, situated on the surfaced road between Nairobi and Tanzania's "safari capital" of Arusha. Tourism is pivotal to the local economy, and the road to the border post is lined with stalls and street vendors selling everything from beaded Maasai jewellery to chilled sodas.

The hectic border-town atmosphere notwithstanding, Namanga has a pretty riverside location below the striking Ol Doinyo Orok (Black Mountain), and offers impressive views of Mount Meru and Kilimanjaro. Set in lush riverside gardens, **Namanga River Lodge** (see p364) is the best place for a break before embarking on the insanely rutted road to Amboseli.

Row of street stalls in the border town of Namanga

Kilimanjaro

The 5,891-m (19,330-ft) Kilimanjaro is not only the highest mountain in Africa, but also the world's tallest free-standing mountain, rising about 5 km (3 miles) from the dusty plains below. Its upper slopes stand within Tanzania, but for non-climbers the best views are obtained from Kenya's Southeastern Savannahs, with Amboseli being the most popular vantage point. Among the most breathtaking sights on the continent, the snowcapped peak is often hidden in clouds, which usually clear around dusk and dawn. The origin of its name is obscure – *kilima* is Swahili for "little mountain," but *njaro* could derive from the Chagga word for "trade caravan", or from the Maasai *ngare* meaning water, or the name of a Swahili demon of cold. Others claim it is a distortion of *kilema kyaro* (impossible journey), the initial Chagga response to European queries about ascending the peak.

Known as Ol Doinyo Naibor (White Mountain) to the Maasai, Kilimanjaro was believed to be protected by evil spirits that froze anybody who tried to ascend it.

Dubbed the Roof of Africa, the 5,891-m (19,330-ft) Uhuru Peak is the highest point on the continent.

Mawenzi

Kibo

KILIMANJARO RANGE

Volcanic in origin, Kilimanjaro is a relatively young mountain, having first erupted about one million years ago as a result of the same tectonic activity that formed the Great Rift Valley *(see pp22–3)*. It has not displayed any serious volcanic activity recently, and is now considered dormant.

The ice cap and glaciers *that cover Kilimanjaro have retreated drastically as a result of global warming since the first recorded ascent by Hans Meyer and Ludwig Purtscheller in 1889.*

Mawenzi Peak *rises to 5,149 m (16,893 ft). Chagga legend has it that Mawenzi and Kibo are sisters. One day, in a fit of anger, Kibo beat her junior Mawenzi over the head, leading to her jagged shape today.*

Kilimanjaro's montane forest *lies between 1,800 m (5,906 ft) and 3,000 m (9,843 ft) and displays high biodiversity, including black-and-white colobus monkey, the endangered Abbott's duiker and 40 Afro-montane forest birds.*

Amboseli National Park ⑮

Amboseli is a land of giants. Practically unscathed by ivory poaching in the 1980s, it still harbours some of the region's oldest and bulkiest elephants, sporting tusks whose dimensions have been consigned to history elsewhere in the area. Towering above the park is the jagged dome of Kilimanjaro, the highest point in Africa and the tallest free-standing mountain in the world. An ever mutating patchwork of dusty plains and marshland, this wildlife-rich park is not a self-contained ecological unit but the unfenced and watery core of a more expansive semiarid ecosystem protected in buffer reserves on Maasai land. A game reserve since 1899, Amboseli was made a national park in 1974.

KEY

☐ Amboseli National Park

★ Lake Amboseli
Dominating the western third of the park, Lake Amboseli is most often a dustbowl, going years on end without holding significant quantities of water. However, when it does fill up, it attracts large volumes of game.

Observation Hill
One of the few places in Amboseli where visitors are permitted to leave their vehicle, the isolated volcanic plug, known to the local Maasai as Noomotio, offers superb views of the surrounding plains and marshland and the wildlife that thrives here.

0 km | 3
0 miles | 3

STAR SIGHTS

★ Lake Amboseli

★ Kilimanjaro from the Amboseli Plains

★ Ol Okenya Swamp

Enkongo Narok Swamp
Fed by subterranean springs that rise on Kilimanjaro, this vast and ever-changing morass of marsh and open water is an important feeding and drinking point for large mammals in the dry season.

★ **Kilimanjaro from the Amboseli Plains**
Eulogised by authors such as Ernest Hemingway and Robert Ruark, the inspirational sight of Kilimanjaro's snowcapped peak towering some 5 km (3 miles) above the Amboseli plains provides a superb backdrop for the park's prodigious wildlife.

VISITORS' CHECKLIST

Road Map C6. 230 km (142 miles) S of Nairobi via Namanga. ✕ ℹ️ *020 6000800.* 🕕 *6am–7pm daily.* 🏛️ ⛺ 🅰️ www.kws.go.ke

KEY

✕	Domestic airport/airstrip
ℹ️	Visitor information
🏛️	Lodge
🅰️	Campsite
🔆	Viewpoint
═	Minor road
═ ═	Unpaved motorable road
▪ ▪	Park boundary
▲	Peak

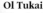

Ol Tukai
The site of the park's headquarters and two lodges, Ol Tukai lies at the very heart of the national park. The shady yellow fever trees that cover the area provide a sharp contrast to the surrounding plains and marshes, and harbour plenty of monkeys and woodland birds.

★ **Ol Okenya Swamp**
Elephants are often very common in the vicinity of Ol Okenya Swamp, which lies a few minutes' drive from the Ol Tukai park headquarters. When not feeding by the shore, they are generally seen semisubmerged and foraging in the water itself.

GETTING AROUND

The somewhat rutted main road through the park runs southeast from Meshanani Gate to Kimana Gate, passing through Ol Tukai about halfway through. Meshanani Gate is the main point of access coming from Nairobi, while Kimana Gate leads on to Tsavo West National Park and Taveta. Most visitors arrive via Namanga at lunchtime, when the park's scenic qualities are muted below the glare of the midday sun. Game-viewing circuits are compact, so the best time to explore is shortly after sunrise or before sunset, when the sun is refracted orange through a suspension of fine volcanic dust, and the clouds that typically hover on the southern horizon dissipate to reveal Kilimanjaro.

Exploring Amboseli National Park

Souvenir plate from Amboseli

Like most major national parks, Amboseli is not accessible by public transport but is reached through an organised safari or self-drive visit. Standalone fly-in and drive-in safaris operate out of Nairobi, 230 km (140 miles) away, but poor road conditions between Namanga town and Namanga Gate make it a bumpy 5-hour drive. The park extends over a relatively compact 150 sq miles (390 sq km), and a full day is adequate to explore its main road circuits, with 2–3 days being the recommended minimum duration for a safari. The park is often included in more wide-ranging safari itineraries such as to Tsavo West National Park.

Blue wildebeest at Lake Kioko, with Observation Hill in the background

Ol Tukai

Set in the heart of Amboseli National Park, this oasis of greenery consists of a ground-water forest of yellow fever trees that contrasts strikingly with the surrounding plains and shallow marshes. Visible from miles away, Ol Tukai is the site of the park's headquarters and one of its oldest lodges, **Ol Tukai Lodge** *(see p364)*. The site is a popular starting point for game drives as well as a good place to break up drives with a leg stretch and cold drink. The fauna here differs from that in the rest of the national park, with monkeys, especially baboons and woodland birds being particularly conspicuous.

Observation Hill

10 km (6 miles) W of Ol Tukai.
This isolated rocky outcrop is situated along a road that skirts the marshy northern verge of **Lake Kioko** – almost certainly a corruption of the Swahili word *kiboko* (hippo). The short but steep footpath to the hill's crest leads to a shelter offering a grandstand view of the surrounding plains and marshes, most spectacular at dawn and dusk, when Kilimanjaro provides an eye-catching backdrop. Elephants can be seen at the lake during the day, and grazers kick up dust as they march across the open savannah, sometimes in thousands. Observation Hill is known as Noomotio meaning "a rocky depression that holds water", in the local Maa tongue, probably in reference to its black porous rock, a product of the same Pleistocene volcanic activity that created Kilimanjaro.

Amboseli Plains

Kilimanjaro does not merely provide Amboseli with a splendid backdrop. The extinct volcanic mountain is arguably the defining influence on the park's ecology and landscape. The very name Amboseli derives from the Maasai *empusel*, a reference to the insinuating layer of grey saline volcanic ash that was deposited by Kilimanjaro during its volatile infancy. The plains support an abundance of large herbivores, with wildebeest, Burchell's zebra and Grant's and Thomson's gazelles most characteristic of the open areas, while impala and Maasai giraffe browse amid stands of *Acacia tortillis*.

Predators are scarce, having been hunted down in protest by the Maasai who were evicted from the park when it was gazetted. However, numbers are said to be on the rise, and there is a fair chance of seeing wildlife such as lion, cheetah, spotted hyena and jackal. The open plains also support a variety of birdlife including the secretary bird, yellow-necked spurfowl and the localised Pangani longclaw, while the woodland has Von der Decken's hornbill, white-bellied go-away bird, red-and-yellow barbet and steel-blue wydah.

Maasai herders in their colourful robes, on the stark plains of Amboseli

Elephants wading through swathes of swamp vegetation, Amboseli National Park

Ol Okenya and Enkongo Narok Swamps

Visitors arriving at Amboseli during the dry season are bound to wonder at the large numbers of game living in Amboseli's desert-like conditions. This phenomenon was first noticed in 1883 by Scottish geologist and explorer Joseph Thomson on his long dusty trek through Maasailand. The reason lies with Kilimanjaro, whose molten snow and spring water vanish below ground on its upper slopes, forming a network of subterranean streams that re-emerge at the base of the mountain to feed Amboseli's ceaselessly mutating network of lakes and marshland.

By far the most important swamps are Ol Okenya, which lies to the east of Ol Tukai, and the much larger Enkongo Narok Swamp, to the west. These perennial wetlands provide a reliable source of drinking water to the immense herds of grazers that congregate on Amboseli towards the end of the dry season (August to October/ November), only to disperse widely outside its borders as soon as it rains. Likewise, the elephants that converge on the marshes by day often wander outside the park to graze at night.

The marshes of Amboseli are one of its principal attractions. Towards the end of the rains, game viewing can be truly fantastic, the highlight of which is the elephant population that can be seen wading deep into the marsh to forage on the soft

vegetation, while mud-stained buffalo look on from the reedy fringes. Bird-watchers are well catered for, with some 50 water-associated species likely to be recorded by enthusiasts, ranging from the long-toed lapwings and greater jacanas that mince through the vegetated shallows of the swamps, to the pelicans, cranes and herons that stand and feed on the edge of the waters.

Lake Amboseli

Maps of the park show Lake Amboseli as a vast blue tract covering much of the park's western third. In reality, this immense pan has only filled with water on a few occasions in the past century. More often, it is a barren expanse of cracked clay, swept across by swirling armies of dust devils and the occasional herd of wildebeest or zebra.

Swamps in Amboseli National Park

AMBOSELI ELEPHANT RESEARCH PROJECT

Founded by Cynthia Moss in 1975, the Amboseli Elephant Research Project (AERP) is the world's longest running study of a wild elephant population. The project has compiled three decades' worth of births, deaths and kinship within a community of 50 elephant families totalling more than 1,000 individuals. Today, much of what is known about elephants is owing to AERP, whose work has been

Elephants crossing a road within proximity of a safari van

accorded recognition through many fascinating documentaries. Due to their efforts, the local elephant population was spared the attention of poachers who were so active in East Africa in the 1980s. As a result, they have little fear of vehicles, making this park arguably the finest place in Africa to observe elephants at close quarters.

SOUTHERN COAST

The sultry south coast of Kenya is lined by a seemingly endless succession of white sandy beaches lapped by the warm blue waters of the Indian Ocean. At its heart lies the historic port of Mombasa, the country's second largest city. Kenya is widely regarded to be the quintessential land of the safari, but the south coast ensures that it also holds its own as a world-class beach destination.

About 2,000 years ago, the Bantu-speaking ancestors of the coastal Swahili arrived on the southern shores of Kenya. By around AD 1000, they had a well-established maritime trade network with Arabia and Asia, which led to the settlement of many Shirazi Arabs and their integration into the Swahili community through intermarriage. This is reflected in the large stone cities constructed at ports such as Mombasa, which was founded at least 800 years ago, and in the growth of Islam as the main religion. Immediately inland lies the territory of the "nine tribes" of the Mijikenda, whose ancestors migrated southwards from the Somali border region in the 17th century.

Although a sequence of foreign incursions has left its mark on the south coast – beginning with the Portuguese in the early 16th century, Omani Arabs in the 19th and, more recently, the British – the mood remains predominantly Swahili. Fishing, subsistence agriculture and other traditional occupations drive this region's rural economy, but Mombasa, serviced by the country's deepest seaport, remains an important centre of international trade and commerce. In recent years, tourism has had a strong impact on the coastal economy, particularly on the holiday resorts closest to Mombasa.

Along with dozens of beach resorts, the south coast of Kenya is studded with enigmatic jungle-bound ruins and time-warped fishing villages that evoke millennia of maritime trade with Arabia. The area is steeped in history, with atmospheric old towns and remnants of Portuguese architecture. Wildlife enthusiasts will be drawn to the offshore reefs protected along the coast's five marine reserves, and to the opportunity of elephant and buffalo sightings in the forested environs of Shimba Hills National Reserve.

Omani House built in the late 18th century, Fort Jesus, Mombasa

◁ Local fishermen with their dhows, in the tranquil waters of the Indian Ocean, Mombasa

The Portuguese at the Coast

Portuguese explorers first sailed south along the Atlantic coastline of Africa in search of a maritime route to the source of the Indian spice trade in 1420. Only in 1488, however, did Bartolomeu Dias round the Cape of Good Hope, followed a decade later by Vasco da Gama, who crossed the Indian Ocean to finally reach India in 1498. Within a decade, the East African coastline was effectively under Portuguese control, leading to the collapse of a centuries-old economy based on the gold and ivory trade with ships from Arabia and Asia. For two centuries Portugal remained the dominant force, but under increasing pressure from other European powers and the Sultanate of Oman it finally left Kenya in 1728.

The formidable seaward bastion of Fort Jesus, Mombasa

ALLIANCE WITH MALINDI

Vasco da Gama, following a hostile reception from the Sultan of Mombasa, was eagerly entertained by his archrival at Malindi in 1498. This alliance persisted throughout the Portuguese era, when the court at Malindi relocated to Mombasa to enjoy the protection of Fort Jesus.

Vasco da Gama Cross *stands sentinel on the Malindi waterfront. This tall cross, made of stone, was erected by Vasco da Gama in 1499 for navigational purposes and as a gesture of appreciation for the Sultan of Malindi.*

DA GAMA'S ROUTE AROUND AFRICA

Vasco da Gama set sail from Lisbon with a fleet of four ships in July 1497. Following a route pioneered by Dias a decade earlier around the Cape of Good Hope, he headed into the – from a European perspective – *mare incognita* of the Indian Ocean. Da Gama rounded the Cape in December and sailed north to Mombasa and Malindi, before crossing the Indian Ocean to arrive at the Indian port of Calicut on 20 May 1498.

Lisbon

Goa

Calicut

Malindi
Mombasa

INDIAN OCEAN

ATLANTIC OCEAN

Maputo

St Helena Bay

0 km   2000

0 miles   2000

THE PORTUGUESE CONQUEST

Sailing from Lisbon in March 1505, Dom Francisco de Almeida's 22-ship armada was decisive to the Portuguese conquest of the Swahili coast. With over 1,000 soldiers at his disposal, Almeida razed or captured a succession of prominent ports, including Mombasa, Kilwa, Zanzibar and Mozambique Island.

Drawings on the walls of Fort Jesus *by Portuguese soldiers, dated to 1639 or earlier, illustrate the conquest of the East African coast by this heavily armed power. The Omani navy's 33-month siege, from 1696 to 1698, ended Portugal's long tenure over Fort Jesus.*

An extravagant bronze throne and the royal entourage display the prosperity of Malindi at the time of Vasco da Gama's arrival.

Dom Francisco de Almeida *was the architect of the Portuguese conquest of East Africa. In 1505, assisted by Portugal's ally, the Sultan of Malindi, he plundered and torched Mombasa, killing more than 1,500 islanders.*

THE PORTUGUESE LEGACY

Although it endured for two centuries, the Portuguese occupation left a limited mark on coastal cultures north of Mozambique. A few Portuguese words have been incorporated into the Swahili language, some ruins still stand, but the most enduring legacy is the introduction of crops that revolutionised local agricultural output.

The Sultan of Malindi offered Vasco da Gama the services of a Swahili or Arabian sailor to help him navigate his way to India across the Indian Ocean.

Published in 1646, this Portuguese map *of Mombasa Island shows Fort Jesus during the Portuguese years guarding the Mombasa harbour and a wall protecting the rest of the town.*

Corn, *locally known as maize, was one of the New World crops introduced to Africa by the Portuguese. It now forms the basis of ugali, the local staple in most parts of East Africa.*

Porcelain, *made in China, was carried by Portuguese ships from the 16th century onwards to East Africa and Europe, where it was first manufactured successfully as recently as 1708.*

Exploring the Southern Coast

The urban highlight of this region is undoubtedly Mombasa's Old Town, which spreads northwards from the imposing walls of historic Fort Jesus. Also of historical interest are the ruined medieval Swahili towns of Jumba la Mtwana and Mnarani and the more southerly Shimoni caves. More contemporary sites include Ngomongo village and Bombolulu Cultural Centre, which lie just north of Mombasa. Wildlife enthusiasts can visit the Shimba Hills and adjacent Mwaluganje Sanctuary, as well as the offshore reefs that run the length of the coast around Mombasa and offer some of the world's most scintillating snorkelling and diving.

The crumbling doorway of a mosque at Mnarani, near Kilifi

SIGHTS AT A GLANCE

Villages and Towns
Gazi **8**
Kilifi **23**
Mombasa pp204–209 **1**
Mtwapa **20**
Shimoni **10**
Shirazi **9**
Takaungu **22**

National Reserves
Mombasa Marine National Reserve **16**
Shimba Hills National Reserve pp216–19 **6**

Wildlife Sanctuaries and Marine Reserves
Haller Park **17**
Kaya Kinondo **5**
Kisite-Mpunguti Marine Reserve **12**
Mwaluganje Sanctuary **7**

Archaeological Sites
Jumba la Mtwana **21**

Historical Bridge and Buildings
Bombolulu Workshops and Cultural Centre **14**
Kongowea Junction **13**
Rabai National Monument **2**

Beaches and Islands
Bamburi and Shanzu Beaches **19**
Diani Beach **4**
Kenyatta Beach **18**
Nyali Beach **15**
Tiwi Beach **3**
Wasini Island **11**

Holiday-makers relaxing at Diani Beach

*Map labels:* Gc, Mgamb, Silanoni, Mt, Maruvesa, Mbo, Samburu, Maji Ya Chumvi, Mny, Voi, A109, NAIROBI–MOMBASA HIGH, Kinagoni, Mari, C107, Matumbi, Mtaa, Kituu, Shambini, Banga, MWALU SANCT **7**, Mwamandi, Kinango, Mwardimu, Gulanze, SHIMBA HILLS NATIONAL RESERVE **6**, C106, Mkomba, C108, Mwangulu, Ramisi, Kikoneni, Mafisini, Mavena, Kisimacha, Mrima, A14, SHIRAZI **9**, Lunga-Lunga, Kanana, Majoreni, Limba, Kisiwani Island, Jambe, Ft, **10** SHI, Vanga, WASINI ISLAND **11**, **12**, KISITE-MPUNGU MARINE RESERV

SEE ALSO

• *Where to Stay* pp366–8

• *Where to Eat* pp385–6

0 km   15

0 miles   15

A lesson in sea kayaking at Nyali Beach

KEY

— Major road

＝ Minor road

▬▬ Untarred major road

=== Untarred minor road

--- 4WD track

— Major railway

▬ International border

GETTING AROUND

Most visitors to the coast land at Moi International Airport, which lies on the mainland about 10 km (6 miles) west of the Mombasa city centre. For those who have not arranged a hotel transfer, taxis are available for charters to the city centre or any of the beach resorts to the north or south – the latter involving an hour's wait for the Likoni Ferry. Good surfaced roads connect most resorts and points of interest along the coast south to Shimoni and north to Kilifi, and public transport is plentiful, as are charter taxis.

Mombasa ❶

A mask for sale

Kenya's second largest city and most important port occupies a small offshore island linked to the mainland by bridges to the north and west, and the Likoni Ferry to the south. The town was a prosperous trade centre for the best part of a millennium; today, local tourism is centred on the beaches north and south of the island, and many visitors spend a week or more here without setting foot in the city proper. One reason is that Mombasa's considerable vintage is not reflected in the plethora of old buildings and ruins one might expect. Noteworthy exceptions are Fort Jesus and Old Town, the destinations of most day tours from the beach resorts.

The colonial façade of the Municipal Council office, Treasury Square

♣ Treasury Square

Nkrumah Rd. ♿

Surrounded by stately colonial buildings, including the historic **City Hall** and several international banks, Treasury Square has long lain at the financial and administrative heart of Mombasa. Today, complete with neat flowerbeds, tall trees, a few park benches and an intermittently functional fountain, the square provides an attractive enclave of tropical greenery in the otherwise built-up city centre. It is also the site of a monument commemorating Allidina Visram, an Indian merchant who established a trade network into the East African interior prior to his death in 1916.

🏛 Old Law Courts

Nkrumah Rd, adjacent to Fort Jesus.
⏰ 8am–6pm daily. 📷 🎫

Situated between Treasury Square and Fort Jesus (see pp208–209), the Old Law Courts, which opened in 1902, is one of the city's most impressive colonial edifices. Restored by the Kenya Museum Society, the building now houses a museum dedicated to Swahili culture and local history, as well as occasional art exhibitions.

⛪ Anglican Cathedral

Nkrumah Rd and Cathedral Rd.
Tel 041 2230502.

This impressive cathedral, the oldest in Mombasa, could be mistaken for a mosque, thanks to its tall domed roof, arched entrances and other Moorish architectural flourishes. The interior is pleasant, and a plaque close to the main door commemorates 150 years of Anglicism in Mombasa, dating from the arrival of J L Krapf (see p30) in 1844.

CENTRAL MOMBASA

Anglican Cathedral ③
Jain Temple ④
MacKinnon Market and
   Biashara Street ⑤
Old Law Courts ②
Shri Swaminarayan Temple ⑥
Treasury Square ①
Uhuru Gardens and
   Giant Tusks ⑦

The bustle outside MacKinnon Market

🏛 Jain Temple
Langoni Rd, off Digo Rd. ⬤ 10am–
12.30pm daily.
Consecrated in 1963, the Jain
Temple in Mombasa is the
oldest outside India. The
temple's fantastic interior is
decorated with statues of
deities and paintings from
floor to ceiling. Founded in
India in the 6th century BC,
Jainism places great emphasis
on reincarnation, *karma* and
the attainment of a state of
salvation referred to as *moksha*.
In keeping with the Jain belief
that all life is sacred, the courtyard is home to a large flock
of plump feral pigeons, and
all shoes and leather clothing
must be removed before
entering the temple.

KEY

Street-by-Street area:
see pp206–207

Key to Symbols see back flap

🏛 MacKinnon Market and Biashara Street
Digo Rd, along the western fringe of
the Old Town. ⬤ 7am–3pm daily.
Mombasa's oldest municipal
market is named after Sir
William MacKinnon, the
Scotsman who founded the
Imperial British East Africa
Company by royal charter in
1888. Not at all touristy, the
relatively sedate covered
market is dedicated mainly to
fruit and vegetable stalls and
an amazing variety of tropical
produce. Outside, a confusion
of other stalls spills out on to
the surrounding streets and
alleys, selling everything from
electrical goods to clothing.
   A block to the north,
Biashara (Commerce) Street is
the centre of the local textile
retail industry, although these
days the shops selling unremarkable imported fabrics far
outnumber those that specialise
in *kitenge* (woven sarongs)
and other local cloths.

🏛 Shri Swaminarayan Temple
Haile Selassie Rd. **Tel** 041 2227448.
One of the oldest and most
striking Hindu temples in East
Africa, this three-storey edifice
near the railway station is
reminiscent of a gigantic
brightly decorated wedding
cake. The interior is, if anything, even more ornately
decorated, with numerous
idols and religious scenes
carved or painted on the
walls. Non-Hindu visitors are
warmly welcomed and will
often be given a free guided
tour, although a donation
might be expected.

♣ Uhuru Gardens and Giant Tusks
Moi Ave.
Mombasa's best known
landmark is a quartet of giant
artificial tusks constructed to
commemorate the coronation
of Queen Elizabeth II in 1953.
Situated on Moi Avenue,
where they coincidentally form
an "M" shape, the tusks are not
worth going out of the way to
see, but can be combined with
a visit to the adjacent Uhuru
Gardens, whose centrepiece is
a fountain and pool decorated
with a large, multicoloured
and rather outdated political
map of Africa.

Two of the four sculpted giant
tusks, Mombasa's leading landmark

⌂ Mbaraki Pillar
Mbaraki Rd.
This 7-m (23-ft) tall pillar
tomb is situated on the industrial south of Mombasa Island,
a 5-minute walk west of
Likoni Ferry. If, as some
authorities believe, the pillar
was erected in the 14th
century, it must be the most
substantial surviving relic
of medieval Mombasa yet
identified. However, local
legend has it that the coral-
rag pillar marks the burial
spot of a 17th-century
Mijikenda chief from the
facing mainland.

Street-by-Street: Old Town

An intricately carved door

The compact maze of narrow Old Town alleys lends itself to casual exploration. Most of its buildings date from 1870 to 1930, and the architecture combines British colonial influences with more ornate Indian flourishes. This historic area possesses a tangible sense of community, and while it may be less overtly Swahili than old Lamu, many of its predominantly Islamic residents can trace family roots back to the 19th century. Today, the Old Town carries an aura of rejuvenation, due to the efforts of conservationists and to the tourist boom that prompted the reinvention of many old houses as boutiques, galleries or craft shops.

An atmospheric Old Town house by the Mbarak Hinawy Road

The Bohra Mosque, originally dating to 1901, was replaced in the 1980s by a replica of a famous mosque in Yemen.

Leven Steps
Built by Lieutenant James Emery in 1824, when Mombasa was briefly a British protectorate, these steps offer a good view across the old dhow harbour to the Krapf Memorial.

The White House was built by an Indian trader. Occupied by the ladies of the Church Missionary Society in the 1890s, it became Kenya's first American Consulate in 1915.

0 metres   100
0 yards   100

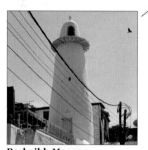

Basheikh Mosque
Claimed locally to have been founded in the 13th century, Basheikh Mosque is probably Mombasa's oldest, and is topped by a plain but appealingly tall and curvaceous whitewashed minaret.

STAR SIGHTS

★ Ndia Kuu Road

★ Fort Jesus

★ **Ndia Kuu Road**
Originally known as Main Road, Ndia Kuu is flanked by 19th-century homesteads notable for their fretwork balconies and wooden Zanzibari doors, many still recognisable from photographs from Victorian times.

Government Square
The administrative and commercial hub of Mombasa in the 1890s, this concrete square on Mbarak Hinawy Road is surrounded by period buildings such as the original post office, the Old Customs House and the fish market.

KEY

- - - Suggested route

The Old Post Office was built in 1899 so that the Indian railway workers could send their money home.

Mandhry Mosque

MBARAK HINAWY ROAD

UU

NKRUMAH ROAD

Mombasa Club

Treasury Square

Old Police Station and Mombasa Club
The open square in front of Fort Jesus is lined with early colonial buildings, including the original 1898 police station, which now houses Ali's Curio Market, and the Mombasa Club, a members-only club since it opened in 1897.

★ **Fort Jesus**
The most important historic landmark in Mombasa, Fort Jesus resisted and succumbed to many lengthy sieges over the three centuries following its construction by the Portuguese in 1593 (see pp208–209).

Mombasa: Fort Jesus

Standing sentinel over Mombasa harbour, Fort Jesus was built for the Portuguese by an Italian architect in 1593. Expanded and renovated several times since, it was the Swahili coast's most strategic building for three centuries. The fort changed hands more than a dozen times, usually with considerable violence. The most protracted battle in its history, a 33-month siege by the Omani navy from 1696 to 1698, claimed at least 6,000 lives. The fort's significance diminished during the colonial era, when it served as military barracks and then a prison. It is now the region's most popular museum.

The arched entrance gate to Fort Jesus, dating back to the 16th century

★ Omani House
An Omani trader built this house circa 1800 on the gun platform where the Portuguese made their last stand in 1698 before the fort's Captain was shot and beheaded.

The cistern, excavated in 1603 by the Portuguese to collect rainwater from the church roof via a system of covered drains, was in use till 1790.

★ Site Museum
The site museum displays an impressive collection of artifacts unearthed during excavations of the fort, ranging from Chinese porcelain to Arabic earthenware. There are also displays about Swahili and Mijikenda culture.

STAR FEATURES

★ Omani House

★ Site Museum

★ Portuguese Graffiti

Seaward Bastion
Fort Jesus is most imposing from the seaward side. The tall walls are made of 3-m (10-ft) thick blocks of coral stone, and rise a full 16 m (52 ft) from the coral base to the fortified turrets.

Views

The seaward side of Fort Jesus offers lovely views over the palm-lined harbour, while the other walls look over the town of Mombasa.

VISITORS' CHECKLIST

Nkrumah Rd. **Tel** 041 472213. ◯ 8am–6pm daily.

www.museums.or.ke

★ Portuguese Graffiti

A Portuguese sailor painted this vivid panel with ships, human figures, fish and other animals around 1639.

The fort was built on a coral ridge at the harbour entrance.

Bastion of San Matheus
Depicted in plans dating to 1610, this seaward bastion was named after San Matheus (St Matthew).

PLAN OF THE SITE

Church
Elliptical Bastion
Entrance
Captain's House

PERIODS

▢	Portuguese before 1632
▢	Later Portuguese
▢	Arab
▢	Modern

Barracks Stores

Museum
Barracks
Angle Tower

Warden's House

0 metres 25
0 yards 25

Rabai National Monument ❷

Road Map E7. 30 km (19 miles) NW of Mombasa. 🚌 ⬜ *8am–6pm daily.* 📷 ✔ ♿ ✝ *7.30am (English), 9.30am (Swahili) Sun.*

Perched on an escarpment inland of Mombasa, Rabai National Monument is the site of the earliest Christian mission in the East African interior, established in 1846 by Dr J L Krapf. The original church, built in 1848, is now a museum dedicated to this founding father of the Anglican Church of Kenya. Krapf also compiled the first Swahili dictionary and grammar, and was the first European visitor to Mount Kenya (*see p322–5*).

St Paul's Church, constructed in 1887, is still in active use, and contains several artifacts imported by Krapf and his colleague Johan Rebmann, including a church bell and a piano. Krapf and Rebmann's houses are still standing and the mission staff will show visitors around. Behind them is a cemetery where several early missionaries and their children are buried.

Mazeras, the junction town for Rabai, has a church of similar vintage, a Methodist edifice built in 1893. Of greater interest is the sprawling **Mazeras Botanical Garden**, founded in the 1940s and now managed as a nursery by the Mombasa Municipality. Unfenced and rather rundown, the garden holds a residual charm, with its impressive strangler figs, lily-covered ponds, troops of vervet monkeys and varied birdlife.

The unspoiled palm-fringed expanse of Diani Beach

Tiwi Beach ❸

Road Map E7. 20 km (12 miles) S of Mombasa. 🚌 📷 🛒

One of the most alluring beaches near Mombasa, Tiwi Beach is great for snorkelling. It is studded with low-key accommodations including Twiga Lodge, a legendary backpacker's haunt since the 1970s. About 20 km (12 miles) to its north is **Likoni Ferry**, the only traffic conduit south of Mombasa Island that must be used by all vehicles heading from Mombasa city centre or Moi International Airport. **Shelly Beach**, a short distance east of the mainland ferry terminal, is the closest beach to Mombasa, but tourist development is limited and conditions are not ideal for swimming.

Diani Beach ❹

Road Map E7. 13 km (8 miles) S of Tiwi Beach via Ukunda Junction. 🚌 🍴 🛏 📷 🛒 ⬛

The focal point of Kenya's seaside destinations, Diani Beach is a long, idyllic stretch of palm-fringed white sand, with dozens of resort hotels offering all-inclusive deals in the midrange to upmarket bracket. The surfaced road linking the resorts has shops and malls offering all manner of products and services, such as tour operators, diving shops, restaurants, DVD rental stores, Internet cafés, craft markets and launderettes. A variety of activities are on offer, including short safaris to Tsavo East National Park (*see pp184–5*), Shimba Hills National Reserve (*see pp216–19*) and Taita Hills (*see p181*), and water sports, such as diving, snorkelling, windsurfing and game fishing.

The landward side of Diani Road supports patches of native forest, with Sykes and vervet monkeys as well as forest birds such as the raucous trumpeter hornbill. It also hosts an estimated 500 Angola colobus monkeys, about 10 per cent of the East African population. Founded in 1997 after several monkeys were killed by speeding cars, the NGO **Colobus Trust** erected "colobridges" of wire and plastic casing at 26 strategic points, allowing the monkeys to cross the road aerially.

Colobus Trust
Diani Beach, 6 km (4 miles) S of Ukunda Junction. *Tel 0711 479453.* ⬜ *8am–1pm, 2–5pm daily.* 📷 ✔ *Mon–Sat.* **www**.colobustrust.org

Disembarking from Likoni Ferry at Mombasa Island

Snorkelling and Diving

The warm equatorial waters of the Indian Ocean support a rich and diverse marine fauna, and make Kenya's coast one of the world's premier diving and snorkelling destinations. For snorkellers, the main attractions are the off-shore reefs that run the length of the coast, allowing the most nervous of novices access to a kaleidoscopic world of multihued coral formations and reef fish. More experienced divers

A colourful reef dweller

combine exploration of the reefs with forays into the open sea, where the deeper waters host a wonderful cast of turtles, squid, dolphins, sharks, dugongs, rays and billfish. Underwater excursions can be arranged on the spot through the beach resorts. Among the prime sites are Watamu, Malindi, the Kisite-Mpunguti Marine Reserve at Wasini near Diani and the Kiunga Marine Reserve near Lamu.

UNDERWATER SPORTS

Kenya's offshore barrier reefs are among the most rewarding sites for first-time divers and snorkellers. For those with diving experience or the desire to take a full course of several days, there are exciting deep-sea and wreck dives on offer.

Wreck diving, *available at Diani, Bamburi and Watamu, is a popular alternative to visiting natural reefs. The artificial habitat is a good place to spot large fish, such as grouper, barracuda and cornetfish.*

The attraction of reef diving *is that larger marine creatures, such as rays, sharks, turtles and the eagerly sought whale shark, might be seen alongside the guaranteed array of brightly coloured reef fish.*

The best site for snorkelling *in Kenya is Watamu, where the coral outcrops are protected within calm clear waters hemmed in by the main barrier reef.*

MARINE LIFE

Thousands of vertebrate and invertebrate species inhabit the offshore coral reefs of Kenya, occurring in a dazzling variety of shapes and colours, ranging from whales and seahorses to squids and rays.

The bottle-nosed dolphin *is one of several marine mammals resident in the warm waters of Kenya.*

The whale shark, *the world's largest living fish, is harmless to divers, being a plankton feeder.*

The clown triggerfish, *measuring up to 50 cm (20 inches), is among the largest and most distinctive of the numerous bright-hued fish that inhabit the reefs.*

The blue ribbon eel, *although not electric, is an aggressive species and can inflict a nasty bite if provoked.*

Camel rides along the alluring white-sand beach in Mombasa ▷

Cattle grazing on the grassy fringes of the sacred Kinondo forest

Kaya Kinondo ❺

Road Map E7. 13 km (8 miles) S of Diani Beach. **Tel** 0722 446916. 🚌 8am–5pm Mon–Sat. 🚫 on the Digo holiday of Chipalata, which falls every fourth day, the most sacred sites cannot be visited; call in advance to check. 📷 🎥 🚫 forbidden at a few specific sacred spots.

The coastal belt south of Mombasa (see pp204–11) is dotted with 38 *kayas*, patches of indigenous forests that have been held sacred by the Mijikenda peoples, a group of nine Bantu-speaking tribes, for centuries. Gazetted as national monuments, these ancient forests were also inscribed as a UNESCO World Heritage Site in 2008. Traditionally, outsiders were not permitted to enter a *kaya*. However, that changed in 2001 with the opening of the 74-acre (30-ha) Kaya Kinondo as a community-based ecotourism project initiated by the local Digo tribe, a subgroup of the Mijikenda.

Sign, Kaya Kinondo Sacred Forest

Once inhabited by the Mijikenda, most *kayas* today are maintained as ceremonial shrines, where ancestral spirits can be worshipped and medicinal plants collected. The Mijikenda place strict taboos on non-medicinal use of vegetation and hunting in their *kayas*, which account for more than 10 per cent of Kenya's coastal forest, offering refuge to several rare plant and bird species. Kaya Kinondo alone harbours at least 187 plant, 45 butterfly and 48 bird species, including the endangered spotted ground thrush and charismatic black-and-white casqued hornbill. The most conspicuous mammals found here are Angola colobus and other monkeys. The forest is also home to Ader's duiker and Zanj elephant shrews.

A guide is mandatory to enter the forest. Visitors can choose between a 45-minute or 2-hour trail, followed by a visit to a tribal medicine man and the school in Kinondo village.

Shimba Hills National Reserve ❻

See pp216–19.

Mwaluganje Sanctuary ❼

Road Map E7. 45 km (28 miles) SW of Mombasa. **Tel** 041 5485121. 🕕 6am–6pm daily. 📷 🎥 🍴 🏧 🛍️

This 36-sq-km (14-sq-mile) northern extension of Shimba Hills operates as a community project, with its proceeds going to the 200 Mijikenda families who volunteered the land as a sanctuary in 1995. Although it protects terrain similar to Shimba, its lushly vegetated hills are more densely studded with baobabs and cycads, and are bisected by the perennial Manalo river.

Elephants are the main wildlife attraction in the sanctuary. The estimated population of 150 is composed mainly of bulls, as family herds tend to prefer the thicker forests of Shimba. The odds of an elephant sighting are far greater here than in Shimba proper, although other large mammals such as buffalo, leopard, zebra, waterbuck, warthog and sable antelope are relatively uncommon.

While the sanctuary has a small network of roads, the most reliable game-viewing site, **Travellers Mwaluganje Elephant Camp**, lies 9 km (6 miles) from the entrance gate. This underrated tented

Low-lying area around Manalo river dominated by baobab trees, Mwaluganje Sanctuary

camp overlooks a small waterhole that attracts a steady stream of thirsty elephants and plenty of birds. The camp also offers day visitors drinks and lunch. A traditional *kaya* lies within the sanctuary and can be visited on foot by prior arrangement.

⚑ **Travellers Mwaluganje Elephant Camp**
Tel 041 5485121 (for reservations).
🍴 💻 🌊

Gazi ❽

Road Map E7. 20 km (12 miles) S of Diani via Ukunda. 👥 1,000. 🚌

Historically, the sleepy fishing village of Gazi was known as the headquarters of Mbaruk bin Rashid, a notorious slave trader who claimed descent from the Mazrui dynasty ousted by the Omani capture of Fort Jesus *(see pp208–209)* in 1828. A strong opponent of British colonisation, Mbaruk masterminded the Mazrui Rebellion of 1895, an ill-fated enterprise that led to his eventual defeat and death in exile in neighbouring German East Africa. The palatial residence built for Mbaruk in the 1850s still stands on the outskirts of the village. It subsequently served as a courthouse and a school when its top floor was decapitated to make way for a corrugated iron roof, but it has been abandoned since the early 1990s.

A more compelling reason to visit this historic village is the **Gazi Women's Mangrove Boardwalk**, a community project opened in 2006 to protect the mangroves that line Gazi Bay. Six different species of mangrove can be seen from the 300-m (984-ft) boardwalk. Wildlife includes mudskipper crabs, the dazzling kingfisher and various marine birds.

Gazi Women's Mangrove Boardwalk
🕐 daylight hours. 📷 🎫 www. mangroveactionproject.org

Outer walls of a ruined medieval mosque amid thick foliage, Shirazi

Shirazi ❾

Road Map E7. 15 km (9 miles) S of Gazi. 🚌 🍴 🌊

This tiny fishing village, also known as Kifunzi, meaning Little Funzi, is named for its close-knit Shirazi people. The community traces its ancestry to the city of Shiraz in Iran, birthplace of many of the medieval traders who settled on the Swahili coast. The only relic of this ancient link is a venerable coral rag-rock mosque lying in partial ruins in the rambling gardens of **Paradise Lost**, a by-appointment-only seafood restaurant

Detail, ruined medieval mosque

that caters to the odd passing sightseer. The restaurant also arranges dhow trips out to sea or canoe trips to see dolphins, crocodiles and tropical birds at Ramisi Creek.

Offshore, **Funzi Island** is a wonderful tropical beach accessible by boat at high water or by wading across when the tide is out from the village of Bodo, just to the southwest of Shirazi. Situated on the island in glorious isolation, **Funzi Keys** *(see p366)* is an idyllic beach lodge built in an inspired Swahili style that offers various activities such as snorkelling and scuba diving.

Paradise Lost
Tel 040 3203513. 🔲 by appt. 🎫
🍴 www.paradiselostkenya.com

PALM TREES AND THEIR TRADITIONAL USES

Makuti-roofed bandas, made from palm fronds

So ubiquitous is the coconut palm, *Cocos nucifera*, in Kenya that it may come as a surprise to learn that it is exotic to East Africa, having arrived there from Asia or South America several centuries ago. Since then, it has become one of the region's most diversely used plants. The young coconuts provide a refreshing alternative to bottled soft drinks, while the flesh of older coconuts is a popular snack, a source of cooking oil and an essential ingredient in Swahili cuisine. The fibrous husk that encloses the nut is twined to make rope or matting, or dried for fire fuel. Palm fronds can be made into a disposable shopping basket with just a few deft strokes of the hand, and they are also used to create the *makuti* thatching characteristic of the roofs along the coast. Finally, the sap and flower are brewed together to make palm wine, a popular drink in coastal parts of Kenya.

Shimba Hills National Reserve ❻

Gazetted as a state forest in 1903 and upgraded to national reserve status 65 years later, Shimba Hills runs along the table escarpment that rises sharply from the coastal flats about 20 km (12 miles) inland of the popular Diani and Tiwi beaches. Extending over a scenic 250 sq km (97 sq miles), the reserve is dominated by rolling green grasslands, but it also supports part of Kenya's second largest coastal forest after Arabuko Sokoke National Park. Shimba is best known as the last Kenyan stronghold of the sable antelope, hosting an estimated population of 200 of these magnificent creatures, while other large mammals include giraffe, leopard, zebra, warthog, several monkey species and substantial populations of elephant and buffalo.

KEY

☐ Shimba Hills National Reserve

★ **Sable Antelope**
Shimba Hills is the last Kenyan refuge for the handsome sable antelope, small herds of which are frequently seen in the open grassland in the northern part of the reserve.

Makadara Forest is the best place in the reserve to see the forest's birdlife.

Pengo Hill is the highest point in the reserve.

Makadara Forest

Pengo Hill ▲
450 m

Shimba Forest
Shimba and various contiguous forest reserves support Kenya's second largest coastal forest, although this habitat is interspersed with moist undulating grassland.

Mkanda

Kidongo Gate

GETTING AROUND

Less than an hour's drive from Diani or Mombasa, Shimba Hills is most often visited on an all-inclusive package. Day and overnight trips can be arranged at short notice through any coastal tour operator. The village of Kwale at the park entrance is connected to Diani and Mombasa by a good road and public transport. Private transport is not required for the guided walk offered by the Shimba Forest Guides Association (SHIFOGA) but it is necessary for entering the park itself.

STAR SIGHTS

★ Sable Antelope

★ Shimba Lodge

★ Giriama Viewpoint

Crested Guineafowl
Shimba is home to a number of forest birds including the crested guineafowl, which differs from the more familiar helmeted guineafowl in having a shaggy black hairdo.

★ **Shimba Lodge**

The closest thing to Treetops (see p317) near the coast, this lodge offers its overnight visitors plenty of game viewing with wildlife, ranging from gargantuan elephants to cute bushbabies.

VISITORS' CHECKLIST

Road Map E7. 55 km (34 miles) S of Mombasa. 020 6000800. to Kwale. 6am–7pm daily.
www.kws.go.ke

KEY

ⓘ	Visitor information
⚠	Lodge
⚠	Campsite
☀	Viewpoint
═	Minor road
═ ═	Unpaved motorable road
▪ ▪	Park boundary
▲	Peak

Kwale
Warden's Office
C106
Shimba Lodge Gate
Kwale Gate
Kivunoni Gate
Elephant Lookout
Railway Mwagandi

0 km 2
0 miles 2

Kwale Gate

The main access point to the national reserve, Kwale Gate lies at the northern edge of the park to the south of Kwale village.

★ **Giriama Viewpoint**

Perched on the escarpment that runs along the eastern boundary of Shimba, Giriama Viewpoint is one of several spots that offer magnificent views around Diani on a clear day.

Sheldrick Falls

This pretty waterfall is worth seeing in its own right, but the walk to it is also notable for the opportunity to glimpse elephant, buffalo and other forest creatures, as well as for the view back towards the beaches.

Exploring Shimba Hills National Reserve

A wonderfully peaceful bush retreat, Shimba Hills tends to be viewed as an extension of the coastal tourist trade rather than as part of any safari circuit. The climate, though far from chilly, is noticeably cooler than the coast below, and thoroughly refreshing. So too, coming from the human overload of the popular resort beaches, is a sense of being in a relatively untrammelled vista of African bush. Day or overnight trips offer the opportunity to see sable antelope, elephant, buffalo and forest specialists such as Angola colobus, Sykes monkey, blue duiker, suni, bushbuck and the exquisite red-bellied coast squirrel. A wealth of rare plants includes primeval cycads, flame lilies, terrestrial and epiphytic orchids and an endemic evergreen tree *Diospyros shimbaensis*. More than 250 butterfly and 200 bird species have been recorded here, several of them localised forest dwellers.

Dark timber façade of the atmospheric Shimba Lodge

🏠 Shimba Forest Guides Association (SHIFOGA)

Edge of Kwale village, towards park entrance gate. **Tel** *072 4227224.*
⏰ *6am–6pm daily.* 📷 ✂ 🍴
Established in 2004, Shimba Forest Guides Association (SHIFOGA) is a community project on the outskirts of Kwale, operating a guided nature trail through a patch of secondary forest donated to the association for that purpose by Kenya Wildlife Service (KWS) and the Forestry Department. The guided walk takes around 45 minutes – although dedicated bird-watchers might need longer – and runs through a patch of forest where a troop of Sykes monkeys comes to feed on most days. The best time to look for monkeys is after 10am, but birds are more active earlier in the day, and include the colourful Fischer's turaco and loudly duetting tropical boubou. The project provides employment to about 10 villagers, who can also be hired as guides on game drives into the park. A limited selection of *kangas* (*see p28*) and T-shirts are sold at the office and cold drinks and food are available in Kwale, which is serviced by sporadic public transport from Mombasa and Diani.

🏨 Shimba Lodge

2 km (1 mile) from Shimba Gate.
Tel *072 2200952.* 🍴 ✉ **www.** aberdaresafarihotels.com
One of the most underrated lodges in the country, Shimba Lodge – a rambling, overgrown treehouse – is under the same management as the world-famous Treetops Lodge in the Aberdares (*see pp316–17*). The lodge feels like an extension of the luxuriant jungle that surrounds it, and the waterhole below its dining area regularly attracts groups of elephants and other big game. The lodge offers one of Africa's best "small game" experiences, with red-bellied coast squirrels clambering around its wooden frames by day, while the night shift is taken by a multitude of bug-eyed greater bushbaby.

An elevated walkway through the forest offers the opportunity to watch troops of Sykes and Angola colobus monkeys swing between the trees, and provides good views into a canopy inhabited by green barbets, Fischer's turacos, forest batises, palm-nut vultures, olive sunbirds and dark-backed weavers. Overnight visitors will find that a deafening chorus of insects and frogs gives the forest an almost physical presence. Even day visitors will find it worthwhile to stop by for lunch or a drink.

📷 Giriama and Ocean Viewpoints

Situated 2 km (1 mile) apart from each other on the crest of a ridge overlooking Diani

Elephants drinking at a waterhole, Shimba Hills National Reserve

Hiking to Sheldrick Falls across the forested slopes of Shimba Hills

Beach, Giriama and Ocean Viewpoints offer superb views over verdant hills to the distant Indian Ocean, although conditions are often rather hazy. There is a shelter and a small information display at Ocean Viewpoint.

Makadara Forest and Pengo Hill

About 10 km (6 miles) south of the main gate, the game-viewing road passes through Makadara Forest. This is regarded as the top site in the park for forest birds, which are most easily seen from a cleared picnic site where visitors are allowed to step out of their vehicles. The main attraction here is the green-headed oriole, a vociferous and pretty coastal forest endemic at the very north of its restricted range. The area supports various other birds, including the Narina trogon, brown-breasted barbet, trumpeter hornbill and four-coloured bush-shrike. At the forest's southern end, the road climbs to Pengo Hill, the highest point in the reserve at 450 m (1,476 ft). On a clear day, it offers views all the way to the Taita Hills and Kilimanjaro.

Sheldrick Falls

10am & 3pm daily.

On the same ridge as Giriama Viewpoint, but further south, **Elephant Lookout** is the starting point for the 2 km (1 mile) descent to Sheldrick Falls, a 90–120 minute round hike that can only be taken at specified times with a mandatory armed ranger. Appropriately named, the lookout is a good place from which to spot elephants.

The hike to Sheldrick Falls passes through forested and occasionally steep slopes where Sykes monkey, buffalo and elephant are observed with some regularity, particularly during the early hours of the day. The trail also provides superb views towards the ocean. The waterfall plunges 21 m (69 ft) over a rock shelf into a cool forest-fringed pool where swimming and picnicking are permitted. The falls are named after the late David Sheldrick, the founder-warden of Tsavo East National Park *(see pp184–5)*, and husband of the celebrated elephant researcher, Daphne Sheldrick.

Grassland Game Drives

Shimba has a well-maintained, well-signposted network of game-viewing roads, centred on the grassland south of the main gate. The major road network can easily be covered in 2–3 hours, with vehicles generally being thin on the ground. The most productive time to do the drive is early morning or late afternoon. Wildlife might literally be seen anywhere, but the muddy wallow between markers 4D and 4E often hosts a herd of contented buffalo, and the surrounding slopes are good for the indigenous herds of sable antelope. Elephant are best seen on the forest margins, as are the striking bushbuck. The grassland has a limited variety of birds, but the red-necked spurfowl, yellow-throated longclaw and black-bellied bustard are worth looking out for.

Heavy clouds and hazy weather at Giriama Viewpoint

Shimoni ⑩

Road Map E7. 80 km (50 miles)
S of Mombasa. 🚶 *2,400.* 🚌

Only 10 km (6 miles) from
the Tanzanian border as the
crow flies, the attractive fishing village of Shimoni served
as the headquarters of the
Imperial British East Africa
Company before Kenya was
formally colonised in the late
19th century. Shimoni is dotted with relics from that
period, including a ruinous
former District Commissioner's
residence and the grave of
Captain F E Lawrence, a victim
of the 1895 Mazrui Rebellion.
On the outskirts of Shimoni
is a coral forest that supports
troops of Sykes and vervet
monkeys and the rare Angola
colobus. Another interesting
natural feature are the hundreds of little swifts that
breed on the jetty.

Shimoni translates as "place
of the hole" in Swahili, in
reference to the eponymous
Shimoni Caves, which reputedly extend inland for up to
20 km (12 miles) and are held
sacred by local Digo people.
During the slave trading era,
this gloomy coral and limestone labyrinth was used to
incarcerate captives from the
interior before they could
be shipped for sale at the
Zanzibar slave market. The
beachfront entrance through
which the slaves were led is
now silted up, but the caves
can be entered via a staircase
located above the caves. A
guide will point out where
chains and hooks are embedded into the walls, as well as

District Commissioner's house made from coral stone, Shimoni

the natural well of semisaline
water from which the slaves
were forced to drink.

Several operators run day
trips from Diani to Shimoni
and Wasini, and the small
village is often overrun with
tourists around 9–10am.

Shimoni Caves
🕐 8.30–10.30am & 1.30–6pm. 🏞 🎫

Wasini Island ⑪

Road Map E7. 1 km (half a mile) SE
of Shimoni. 🚤 🎫 🍴 🛏 🛍
www.wasini-island.com

Separated from Shimoni by a
narrow channel, this 5-sq-km
(2-sq-mile) island is named for
the Chinese – called *wa-cini*
in Swahili – who used to visit
it regularly to trade porcelain
for mangrove poles and other
local products. Located on the
baobab-studded landward
shore, the main village is
surrounded by old walls and
graves, including a pillar tomb
inset with Ming porcelain.
The island boasts a couple of
seafood restaurants, including

the legendary **Charlie Claws**
(see p386). Though busy
at midday, when tours from
Diani arrive for lunch, it is
very quiet at other times.

Wasini's star attraction is a
boardwalk that runs through
its **Coral Garden**, a stark landscape of coral outcrops
interspersed with sand flats
and mangroves where mud-
skippers and hermit crabs
scuttle past. Late afternoon
and overnight visitors might
well be rewarded with sightings of the spectacular
coconut crab, the world's
largest terrestrial crustacean.

Coral Garden
🕐 8am–5pm daily. 🏞 🎫 🛏

Kisite-Mpunguti Marine Reserve ⑫

Road Map E7. HQ opposite Shimoni
Jetty. 🚤 *organised day trips from
Diani or locally hired boats from
Shimoni.* 🏞 🎫 www.kws.go.ke

Protecting 40 sq km (16 sq
miles) of open sea, islands
and reefs, Kisite and Mpunguti
were gazetted in 1973 and
1978 respectively, to control
over-fishing and trophy collection around Kisite Island, a
waterless coral outcrop 8 km
(5 miles) from Shimoni. The
area harbours the richest
marine life of any Kenyan
reserve. Boat trips to the
island are a good opportunity
to see one of the five dolphin
species. Diving and snorkelling
are especially good by the
Mpunguti ya Juu, Mpunguti ya
Chini and Liwe la Jahazi coral
islets. The Shimoni headquarters has a short nature trail
through a forest patch.

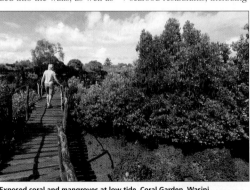

Exposed coral and mangroves at low tide, Coral Garden, Wasini

The 19th-century Slave Trade

Two main factors lay behind the 19th-century boom in the slave trade out of East Africa. One was the reduction in the transatlantic traffic out of West Africa, following the abolition of the slave trade there. The other was the takeover of the Swahili coast in 1828 by Omani settlers. By 1840, they were exporting over 40,000 slaves annually. The effects on the interior were devastating. A few tribes became powerful by serving as porters and organising slave raids. Others had their villages ransacked for able-bodied men and women, and the young and old killed or left to die. This terrible flow of human booty was stemmed in 1873, when a naval blockade allowed Scottish explorer John Kirk to persuade Sultan Barghash of Zanzibar to outlaw the slave trade in exchange for British protection.

**Strong chains,
Shimoni Caves**

Omani Arabs, who colonised the East African coast in the 1830s, were the driving force behind the 19th-century slave trade.

David Livingstone, *the famous explorer, was one of slavery's most outspoken critics. His funeral became the catalyst for the blockade that led to the abolition of Zanzibar's slave trade.*

SLAVE RAIDS IN EAST AFRICA

Thousands of East Africans were sold into slavery during the 19th century. Perhaps twice as many died of disease or exhaustion on the long march to the coast, and nobody knows how many old, young and infirm Africans died as a result of murderous slave raids.

Slaves were captured in the interior and sold to Omani traders at coastal villages before being shipped to the Great Slave Market at Zanzibar.

Fresh captives were herded into a stockade *by one of the local tribes, who collaborated with the Omani Arabs, terrorising parts of the interior with their brutal slave raids.*

Shimoni Caves *were an important holding dungeon for slaves en route to Zanzibar, where an estimated 50,000 African captives were sold annually at the Great Slave Market.*

William Wilberforce, *British politician and philanthropist, was the most influential figure in the abolition of slavery in the British Empire and the curtailment of the slave trade out of Africa.*

The main building at Bombolulu Workshops and Cultural Centre

Kongowea Junction ⑬

Road Map A6. Immediately SE of Nyali bridge, off Mombasa Island.

Located on the mainland off Mombasa Island is Kongowea Junction, formerly known as Freretown (pronounced Freetown) after Sir Bartle Frere, who played a major role in negotiating the abolition of the slave trade with the Sultan of Zanzibar in the 1870s. Between 1874–88, around 1,400 freed slaves were settled in Freretown to form a thriving self-reliant Christian community under the leadership of William Salter Peel, the first Anglican Bishop of East Africa.

South of the junction is **Freretown Bell**, which once warned the community of imminent danger, and gave the area the nickname Kengeleni (Place of the Bell). This town was formally disbanded in the 1920s, but many local residents trace their ancestry to the freed slaves who built the attractive **Emmanuel Anglican Church** by the Freretown Bell in 1889.

About 3 km (2 miles) south of the bell, the **Krapf Memorial** is a 6-m (20-ft) tall stone cross commemorating the works of German missionary Dr J L Krapf *(see p210)*, who lived in Kenya between 1844–81. Below the memorial, a low stone wall encloses the graves of his wife and child.

Spanning the west end of the old harbour, the 400-m (1,300-ft) long Nyali Bridge is the only road conduit between Mombasa Island and the coast

further north. Built in the early 1980s, it replaced what was then the world's longest pontoon bridge, the remains of which are still visible from the mainland and the island.

Bombolulu Workshops and Cultural Centre ⑭

Road Map A6. 4 km (1 mile) N of Mombasa via Nyali bridge. **Tel** 041 471704. ▦ free bus service from the north coast hotels. ○ 8am–6pm Mon–Sat, 10am–3pm Sun. 🎨 📷 ⑪ 🖼 🏠 www.bombolulu.org

Founded by the Association of the Physically Disabled of Kenya (APDK) in 1969, the Bombolulu Workshops and Cultural Centre is a highly regarded crafts centre, manufacturing a wide selection of good quality leatherwork, basketry, wood carvings and jewellery, which is sold both on site and further afield. Visitors are encouraged to visit the five workshops set up here, each of which specialises

in a different type of craftwork. The cultural centre consists of rural homesteads from all over Kenya, and puts on traditional dance performances several times a day. Set in grounds that were formerly part of a botanical garden, the leafy complex also houses an open-sided buffet restaurant serving traditional Swahili lunches and a large craft shop. In total, the centre generates employment for more than 150 disabled people.

Nyali Beach ⑮

Road Map B6. 7 km (2 miles) N of Mombasa. ▦ ⑪ 🖼 🏠 🥽

One of the loveliest beaches around Mombasa, Nyali is lined with prestigious hotels and resorts including the pioneering Nyali Beach Hotel, which kick-started the Mombasa beach tourism industry when it opened in 1946. Running down to the beach, the **Nyali Golf and Country Club**, founded in 1956, boasts the only 18-hole course on the coast north of Mombasa, one of the finest in Kenya, although conditions can be tricky when the oceanic winds are up. The club is also famous for the vervet monkey and other wildlife that inhabit its leafy glades.

Directly opposite the Nyali golf course, and easily recognised by the gigantic sculpted crocodile that guards the entrance, **Mamba Village Centre** claims to be the largest crocodile farm in Kenya. The centre also has a snake park, spider house, botanical garden,

Beachgoers walking past colourful sailboats at Nyali Beach

Racing to the ocean across Kenyatta Beach

horse-riding facilities and aquarium. The restaurant specialises in crocodile meat and houses one of the most popular discos in Kenya, with a capacity of 5,000 people.

Nyali Golf and Country Club
Links Rd. *Tel* 041 471589.

Mamba Village Centre
Links Rd. *Tel* 020 3549303.
8am–6.30pm daily.

Mombasa Marine National Reserve ⓰

Road Map B6. Off the coast of Mombasa. *Tel* 041 2312744.
www.kws.go.ke

The developed coastline north of Mombasa is protected in the 200-sq-km (77-sq-mile) stretch of the Mombasa Marine National Reserve, including the eponymous 10-sq-km (4-sq-mile) national park. The reserve is often used for water sports; details are available at most hotels. The offshore coral gardens support a wealth of colourful reef fish and invertebrates, and are excellent for diving and snorkelling.

Haller Park ⓱

Road Map A6. 7 km (4 miles) N of Nyali Bridge. *Tel* 041 2101000.
8am–5pm daily. Hippos are fed at 4pm and giraffes at 11am & 3pm daily.

Formerly known as Bamburi Nature Trails, Haller Park is a small private reserve, named after the Swiss agronomist Rene Haller, who engineered its exemplary ecological transformation from barren limestone quarry 30 years ago to verdant nature sanctuary today. The highlight of this idyllic little park is a relaxed nature trail that takes around 90 minutes to complete, passing enclosures inhabited by hippo, Rothschild's giraffe, crocodile, buffalo, bushbuck, suni antelope, vervet monkey and other introduced wildlife.

The woodland and streams naturally support a diverse assortment of birdlife, including the conspicuous African fish eagle, pied kingfisher and white-browed robin chat. Other attractions include a thatched butterfly pavilion, where colourful indigenous butterflies are bred, a reptile park housing numerous snakes and crocodiles, a palm garden, a good restaurant and mountain-biking facilities.

Kenyatta Beach ⓲

Road Map B6. 7 km (4 miles) N of Nyali, off the main Mtwapa Rd opposite Haller Park.

Named after Jomo Kenyatta, Kenya's first president, Kenyatta Beach is the only public beach on the coast north of Mombasa, and it tends to be a lot busier with Kenyans than with tourists, especially at the weekend. Swimming is pleasant at high tide, and this is a good place to arrange excursions in glass-bottomed boats to the nearby Mombasa Marine National Reserve. Low tide is the ideal time to explore rock pools and coral outcrops. The main attraction on this beach is an establishment called **Pirates**, which functions as a family-friendly waterslide park by day and transforms into a hectic beach bar and disco by night.

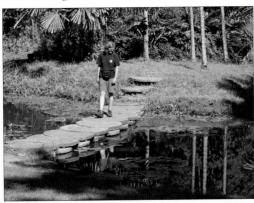

Frog trail, one of many paths winding through the woodlands of Haller Park

Pristine palm-fringed white-sand beach at Bamburi

Bamburi and Shanzu Beaches ⑲

Road Map B6. 10 km (6 miles) N of Nyali Bridge. 🚌 🍴 🖥 📷 🛍
Note: *beach access is easiest through one of the upmarket hotels; visitors are required to dress appropriately to use hotel facilities.*

Running northward from Kenyatta Beach to Mtwapa Creek, Bamburi and Shanzu beaches form a near-continuous 10-km (6-mile) stretch of classic Indian Ocean coastline – white sand, swaying palms and turquoise blue water hemmed in by offshore reefs. Around a dozen upmarket beach hotels serve the area and offer a range of seaside activities, from swimming and sunbathing to snorkelling, windsurfing and scuba diving. Other facilities in the area include a scattering of restaurants and banks. A short distance inland, **Shanzu Workshop** is a Girl-Guide affiliated NGO founded in 1992 to train and educate disabled young women to find employment or generate an income. Tailoring, leatherwork and jewellery design are among the various trades taught here. An on-site gift shop stocks a fabulous selection of clothes, bags and other items made from colourful *kikoy* fabrics (*see p395*).

Souvenir, Shanzu Workshop

Around the corner is **Ngomongo Village**, a reclaimed limestone quarry that has been planted with casuarinas and other indigenous trees, and developed as one of the country's most unusual cultural attractions. A 2-hour guided tour through the shady coastal thicket leads past ten traditional villages, each of which represents the diversity of Kenya's many tribes, including the Maasai, Mijikenda, Akamba, Pokot and Luo. Each village consists of reconstructed homesteads surrounded by crops and livestock associated with the relevant tribe. Informative rather than sensational, Ngomongo feels more authentic than it sounds, and includes visits to a Kikuyu witch doctor and a lively display of traditional dances from around the country. Visitors can also see ostriches and crocodiles, which are kept in enclosures, as well as monkeys that frequently pass through the village.

🏛 **Shanzu Workshop**
20 km (12 miles) W of Nyali Bridge; 2 km (1 mile) E of Mtwapa Rd along the road to the Serena Hotel. **Tel** *041 2223078.* ◯ *9am–5pm daily.* 📷 ♿

🏠 **Ngomongo Village**
20 km (12 miles) W of Nyali Bridge, clearly signposted from Shanzu Workshop. **Tel** *0718 939434.* ◯ *9am–5pm daily.*
📷 📷 🍴 📷

Traditional Akamba dwelling, Ngomongo

Mtwapa ⑳

Road Map B6. 20 km (12 miles) N of Mombasa. 🚶 *24,000.* 🚐

Set above the mangrove-lined north shore of Mtwapa Creek, this small but rapidly expanding town has a lively yachting, restaurant and nightlife scene that attracts Mombasa residents at weekends. The creek is an Indian Ocean inlet, perfect for waterskiing and game fishing. On weekdays, Mtwapa is an unremarkable coastal settlement, but there is no shortage of affordable hotels and eateries to choose from.

Mtwapa's chief tourist attraction is dining by the creek shore. **La Marina** (*see p386*) has a romantic setting on the north shore of the creek and, as well as lunch or candlelit dinner, offers the option of dhow cruises with on-board entertainment. **The Moorings** floating restaurant (*see p386*), further along the creek, offers great seafood at more modest prices.

Jumba la Mtwana ㉑

Road Map B6. 4 km (3 miles) along a side road running E of Mtwapa. ◯ *8am–6pm daily.* 📷 📷 **www. museums.or.ke**

The most impressive Shirazi ruin along the Kenyan coast south of Gedi (*see pp238–9*), Jumba la Mtwana has a beautiful beachfront location a short distance north of the mouth of Mtwapa river. Cooled by constant sea breezes and blessed with an ample supply of fresh water, this ruin was probably once a substantial settlement. The site is now rather overgrown, with gigantic fig and baobab trees erupting from the old coral-rag walls. Excavated by British archaeologist James Kirkman in 1972, the site was cleared and gazetted as a national monument 10 years later. Among the buildings that remain in a recognisable state are four houses, an inscribed tomb and three mosques, of which the **Mosque by the Sea** is interesting for its arched doorways and well-preserved mihrab.

The enigmatic aura that permeates the ruins is reflected in its absence from all historical records. Based on Chinese porcelain unearthed by Kirkman, the town is thought to have been founded circa 1350 and abandoned a century later, for reasons that remain unclear. Its original name is unknown, and the modern appellation Jumba la Mtwana is obscure in origin. Although it is translated as "mansion of the slave", no link with the slave trade *(see p221)* has been established.

Takaungu ㉒

Road Map E7. 6 km (4 miles) from Kibaoni on the Mtwapa-Kilifi Rd. ⚑ 1,500. 🛥 🚌 🛕 *important pilgrimage site during Maulidi (variable).*

This sleepy and little-visited fishing village, set on a low cliff above the south bank of Kivukoni Creek, may come across as the consummate coastal backwater, but it has quite a historical pedigree. One of the region's oldest slave trade centres, it is where the ruling Mazrui family of Mombasa re-established itself after Fort Jesus was captured by the Omanis in 1828. In

1844, the missionary J H Krapf visited this "hospitable village" before settling on Rabai *(see p210)* further inland as the site of his first mission. Scattered relics of the village's 19th-century incarnation include a deep coral-rag well, the crumbling slave market and an old mosque overgrown with strangler figs. A 10-minute walk from the town centre, the beach consists of a steep incline flanked by tall coral outcrops. Utterly idyllic by day, it is claimed to be haunted by the ghosts of slaves after dark.

Tomb detail with Arabic inscriptions, Mnarani Ruins, Kilifi

Kilifi ㉓

Road Map E7. 50 km (31 miles) N of Mombasa. ⚑ 30,390. 🚌

Kilifi Creek is known as one of the safest natural harbours on the East African coast, and the **Kilifi Boatyard**, about 1 km (half a mile) inland, has long served as a focal point for the

country's yachting community. Day visitors are also welcome and the seafood is excellent. That aside, the town itself offers little of interest to visitors, though they can still see the semisubmerged ferry that once provided the only access from Mombasa prior to the opening of the modern Kilifi bridge in 1991.

From the 13th to 16th centuries, Mnarani was the most important settlement on the creek. Its ruins, set on a cliff above the south bank, are now protected as **Mnarani National Monument** and can be reached via a steep flight of 104 concrete steps. Mnarani means "place of the pillar" in reference to an engraved 13th-century pillar tomb that marks the grave of an important sultan. First excavated in the 1950s, two well-preserved mosques adorn the site; one is inscribed in an Arabic script yet to be translated and known elsewhere only in Kilwa Kisiwani in Tanzania. The ruins also include one of the deepest wells found along the Southern Coast. An impressive natural feature at Mnarani is an 800-year-old baobab credibly claimed to be the largest in Kenya.

Kilifi Boatyard
www.kilifiboats.com

🏛 **Mnarani National Monument**
200 m (656 ft) W of the main Mtwapa–Kilifi Rd, on the south bank of Kilifi Creek. ◷ 9am–6pm daily. 🎫 🌐 www.museums.or.ke

Mosque by the Sea, one of the few remaining mosques in Kenya from the 15th century, Jumba la Mtwana

NORTHERN COAST

Running from the picturesque Kilifi Creek to the remote Somali border, Kenya's north coast is a stretch of palm-lined beaches and atmospheric ruins, and with some exceptions, is refreshingly unspoiled by urbanisation. The area is profoundly Swahili in character. Life in this coastal haven unfolds at a reassuringly slow pace and visitors are made to feel at home by the local hospitality.

Interred within the humid depths of the Northern Coast's forests are the crumbling mosques and palace walls of the Gedi Ruins, Kenya's very own lost city. Abandoned in the 16th century, these medieval relics of a once-wealthy trading port, whose name has been lost in the mists of time, stand witness to the 2,000-year-old Swahili coastal culture. A far less enduring, though still notable, presence on the Northern Coast came in the form of the Portuguese empire. Vasco da Gama stopped off at Malindi in 1498 on his way to India, paving the way for the Portuguese invasion of 1505. Following their loss of Fort Jesus at Mombasa, in 1729, the Portuguese abandoned the area entirely in favour of present-day Mozambique.

More recently, popular holiday resort destinations have developed at Malindi and Watamu, which lie along a lovely stretch of Indian Ocean coastline notable for its fantastic coral outcrops. Sun-worshippers are catered for by a seemingly endless succession of bone-white beaches scattered with great beach resorts that offer a broadly comparable experience to the south coast, while the offshore reefs offer superlative diving and snorkelling. The open sea off Watamu has also retained its charm as a game fishing destination, first popularised by the American author Ernest Hemingway. Despite its development as a resort destination, this region still holds on to traditional Islamic values.

Culturally, the undoubted travel highlight of the Northern Coast is the Lamu Archipelago, which boasts superb sightseeing opportunities and some beautiful beaches. This is where the various strands of the Swahili coast, past and present, intertwine to form a satisfying whole, epitomised by the lovely laid-back authenticity that permeates the alleys of Lamu town, a UNESCO World Heritage Site.

Traditional sailing vessels lining the picturesque Lamu waterfront

◁ The atmospheric Gedi Ruins, a Swahili town abandoned in the 17th century

The Swahili Coast

Swahili comb

The name Swahili derives from the Arabic *sawahil* – meaning edge or coast – and Islam has been the predominant religion here for many centuries. The Swahili language, by contrast, forms part of the indigenous Bantu linguistic group, but has a liberal peppering of Arabic words. It is difficult to say when these exotic and indigenous elements first fused into a distinct Afro-Islamic culture, but as early as the 12th century, the coast was studded with stone-walled city-states recognisably Swahili in character. Many such cities, including Mombasa and Malindi, survive to the present day.

The commanding Lamu Fort, built in the mid-19th century

The Swahili settlement of Mombasa *dates back at least 800 years, but the multistorey buildings that line the narrow alleys of the present-day Old Town mostly date to the 19th century.*

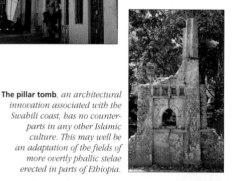

Arches, one of several Arabic features associated with Swahili architecture, are amply used.

The pillar tomb, *an architectural innovation associated with the Swahili coast, has no counterparts in any other Islamic culture. This may well be an adaptation of the fields of more overtly phallic stelae erected in parts of Ethiopia.*

ARCHITECTURAL INFLUENCE

Swahili harbour towns such as Lamu show a clear Arabic influence in architectural style. The whitewashed coral-rag buildings typically span two or three storeys, and line a maze of narrow alleys to form a compact high-rise settlement.

Zanzibari doors, *made of heavy wood, are often seen in old Mombasa and Lamu. The spikes served as protection against war elephants – a practice that originated in medieval India, where tuskers were used to ram down doors.*

The medieval ruins *on Pate Island date to when the Swahili coast was a hub of international trade. Gold transported to the coast via the Zambezi Valley was sold at the now ruined city of Kilwa.*

SWAHILI CULTURE

A strong unifying factor in Swahili culture is Islam, which first took hold in the region in the 10th century or earlier. Many other aspects of Swahili culture demonstrate a strong Arabic influence, ranging from the traditional dress and forms of body adornment to the spicy cuisine.

Maulidi *is one of the most important events in the Islamic calendar of the Swahili. It is celebrated most ardently in Lamu where men move in procession along the waterfront.*

Most Swahili men *wear ornamental amulets containing Koranic verses around their necks as protection against evil spirits known as jinns or djinns in Arabic and Swahili.*

Lamu town, declared a World Heritage Site by UNESCO in 2001, has a number of old houses with ornately carved timbered doors.

Swahili cuisine *reflects the cosmopolitan history of the coast, with Indian and Arabic spices complimented by the trademark Swahili ingredient of grated coconut flesh or coconut milk.*

The bui-bui, an all-black veiled dress, is the most common female attire in more conservative Swahili settlements.

Taarab music *fuses Swahili lyrics with Arabic-style melodies. An evolving art form, it combines traditional instruments such as the lute-like* udi, darbuk *drums and zither-like* gannon *with the likes of guitar and violin.*

Henna painting, *traditionally reserved for special occasions, is now accepted as day-to-day adornment of the hands and feet.*

SWAHILI PROVERBS

The Swahili language is rich in proverbs, many of which are inscribed on the *kanga* cloths worn by women and inform contemporary Swahili rap music. Popular sayings include *Haraka haraka haina baraka* (Hurrying brings no blessing) and *Baraka zitasimama tukimsahau mama* (Blessings will stop if we forget Mother).

Vibrant *kanga* **fabric with printed Swahili proverbs**

Exploring the Northern Coast

The most popular bases for exploration are Watamu and Malindi, both of which cater to the all-inclusive beach package market. The most worthwhile day trip in the area is Gedi Ruins near Arabuko Sokoke National Park, off the main road to Watamu. This site is particularly recommended to keen walkers and bird-watchers, who can visit it in conjunction with Mida Creek. The more remote, but equally rewarding, Tana River National Primate Reserve and scenic Hell's Kitchen near Marafa are difficult to reach without an experienced local guide. To the north lies the Lamu Archipelago. Visitors will require a full week to soak in the time-warped atmospheric Lamu town and Pate Island, including a full-day dhow trip to the Manda Toto reefs and the medieval Takwa Ruins.

The fantastic rock formations at Hell's Kitchen north of Malindi

Aerial view of the palm-fringed Old Town, Lamu

SIGHTS AT A GLANCE

Towns and Islands
Lamu Archipelago pp244–50 **8**
Malindi pp240–41 **5**
Watamu **1**

National Parks and Reserves
Arabuko Sokoke National Park and Gedi Ruins pp234–9 **3**
Malindi Marine National Reserve **2**
Tana River National Primate Reserve **7**

Areas of Natural Beauty
Hell's Kitchen **6**
Mida Creek **4**

SEE ALSO

KEY

- ▬▬ Major road
- ═══ Minor road
- ▬▪▬ Untarred major road
- ═▪═ Untarred minor road
- ▪▪▪ 4WD track
- ▬▬ International border

The remnants of the Great Mosque, Gedi Ruins

Kolbio

Boni
National Reserve

Arosen

Dodori

Dar Es Salaam

Milimani

Mangai

Kiunga

Manbore

Kiungamwina
Island

Bodhei

Dodori
National Reserve

Majengo

Duldul

Kiduruni

Bargoni

Mongani Creek

Siyu Channel

Dondo

Kiwaiyu

Kisingitini

Siyu

Pate
Island

Hindi

Pate

Hidio

Mokowe

Manda Island

Mkunumbi

Lamu

Takwa

Milinga

LAMU ARCHIPELAGO

Kiongwe

Mpeketoni

Kipini

INDIAN OCEAN

| 0 km | 25 |
| 0 miles | 25 |

GETTING AROUND

A good surfaced road and plenty of public transport connects Mombasa to Malindi and Watamu, and offers ready access to sites such as Arabuko Sokoke National Park, Gedi Ruins and Mida Creek. All roads are clearly signposted. The drive from Mombasa, the closest international airport to Malindi, takes less than two hours, though it can be longer using public transport. Malindi airport, a 20-minute drive from Watamu, is serviced by regular domestic flights from Mombasa and Nairobi. The Lamu Archipelago has poor road connectivity, and public transport is slow and infrequent, so most visitors fly in to Lamu town from Malindi, Mombasa or Nairobi.

The pristine Vasco da Gama Cross standing sentinel over the Malindi coast

The eye-catching coral outcrops at Turtle Bay

Watamu ●

Road Map E6. 55 km (34 miles)
N of Kilifi. ⛰ 2,000. ✈ ⛽
www.watamu.net

Blessed with one of the most inspiring coastal settings in East Africa, the Swahili fishing village of Watamu lies at the northern end of Turtle Bay. The bay's 7 km (4 miles) of sandy beach overlooks shallow turquoise waters interrupted by a succession of fantastically ragged coral outcrops that explode from the water like giant surrealist mushrooms. The village itself is something of an oddity, with its combination of Swahili traditionalism and overt commercialism. It is, however, a pleasant place, and visitors are rarely hassled. The focus is inevitably the beach, which is a gem, whether as a place to pull up a deckchair and relax below the swaying palms or to snorkel and dive among the kaleidoscopic array of reef fish that inhabit the magnificent offshore coral gardens. Another of Watamu's assets is its proximity to the Arabuko Sokoke Forest and Gedi Ruins *(see pp234–9)*, which lie within a 10-km (6-mile) radius.

Located outside Watamu, the **Bio-Ken Snake Farm** houses the largest collection of snakes in East Africa, most of them acquired through the free "remove a snake" service it offers to locals. Almost all of the region's venomous species are on display here, including various cobras, vipers and all three mambas, and are regularly milked for antivenin for regional distribution. It is a fascinating place, and the staff show a clear commitment to eradicating ignorance about these often reviled but ecologically important reptiles. It is necessary to call ahead to find out about day outings to look for snakes in the wild and any upcoming evening talks at one of the nearby resorts.

> **🏠 Bio-Ken Snake Farm**
> 5 km (3 miles) N of Watamu.
> **Tel** 042 2332303. 🕙 10am–noon, 2–5pm daily. 🎫 📷 ♿
> **www**.bio-ken.com

Malindi Marine National Reserve ●

Road Map E6. 10 km NE of Watamu Beach. **Tel** 042 2335684. ⛽ 🎫

Africa's oldest marine reserve was gazetted in 1979 to protect a 213-sq-km (82-sq-mile) expanse of coastline, offshore reefs and open water running from Mida Creek to Malindi via Watamu. The reserve incorporates the smaller **Malindi** and **Watamu Marine National Parks**, which offer some of the finest snorkelling and diving opportunities in Kenya,

Coral reef exposed at low tide, Watamu Marine National Park

with over 300 recorded species of reef fish and a daunting variety of marine invertebrates and birds. The reserve is a breeding site for hawksbill and green turtles, and olive ridley and leatherback turtles have also been recorded. Most diving and snorkelling excursions from hotels in Watamu and Malindi take place in the reserve, and entrance fees are usually incorporated into the cost of the activity.

Arabuko Sokoke National Park and Gedi Ruins ●

See pp234–9.

Mida Creek ●

Road Map E6. 6 km (4 miles) S of Watamu Junction. ⛽ 🕙 sunrise–sunset. 🎫 📷

The 6-km (4-mile) long Mida Creek, located at the southern end of the Watamu peninsula, is renowned for its coastal birdlife. Recent counts of over 6,000 waders have been made along its sandy shore. It is of particular significance as a wintering site for Palearctic migrants, such as the eagerly sought crab plover. Besides this, some 70 other aquatic species have been recorded, with the likes of greater sand-plover, lesser sand-plover, mangrove kingfisher, grey plover, greater flamingo and dimorphic egret among the more commonly seen residents and visitors.

The offshore **Whale Island** hosts thousands of breeding pairs of roseate and sooty terns between June and October, while the dense coastal scrub around the creek hosts several interesting non-aquatic birds, ranging from the spectacular carmine bee-eater to the threatened Sokoke pipit and chestnut-fronted helmet-shrike.

In 2003, a local community group constructed a 260-m (853-ft) suspended wooden boardwalk through the surrounding mangroves to a hide overlooking the sand flats.

Spectacular rock formations at Marafa Depression, popularly known as Hell's Kitchen

The community project is run by enthusiastic local guides. The quality of birding from the boardwalk and hide depends strongly on tidal factors, so it is best to call a day ahead to ask about timings. The creek's calm waters are ideal for most aquatic activities, which can be arranged through any hotel in Watamu.

Malindi ❺

See pp240–41.

Hell's Kitchen ❻

Road Map E6. 35 km (22 miles) NW of Malindi. 🚐 ◯ *6am–6pm daily.*
🅿 📷

Reminiscent, in a scaled-down way, of the Grand Canyon in the USA, Hell's Kitchen is the popular name for Marafa Depression, a valley of spectacularly eroded sandstone pillars, known as demoiselles, that stand up to 30 m (98 ft) tall. According to local folklore, Marafa was formerly inhabited by a Giriama tribe so wealthy that its people washed their bodies with milk rather than water. The gods punished this ostentatious behaviour by brewing up a mighty overnight storm that caused the area to sink and all its human inhabitants and livestock to be washed into the Sabaki river.

Impressive at any time of day, the valley is stunning in the early morning, when the soft light makes the layered columns look like they have been sprinkled with pink

icing sugar. Now managed as a community project, the gorge is overlooked by a fenced car park and can be reached via a footpath that runs about 3 km (2 miles) through its base.

Tana River National Primate Reserve ❼

Road Map E5. 50 km (31 miles) N of Garsen, on Malindi–Garissa Rd.
Tel 046 62270. 🚐 ◯ *6am–7pm daily.* 📷 📷 🅿 🅰 www.kws.go.ke

This far-flung and little-visited reserve runs for about 35 km (22 miles) along the forested course of the Tana, Kenya's largest river. The area was gazetted in 1976 to protect the last remaining habitat of the Tana river red colobus and Tana mangabey, a pair of endemic monkeys that show a strong affiliation to Congolese species, suggesting that the forests were linked in the Miocene Era. Neither monkey is thought to number

more than 1,000 individuals in the wild, and both are critically endangered, though they are quite easily seen within the confines of the reserve.

In addition to being of great interest to primate enthusiasts, this area supports a native population of the endangered hirola antelope, and a variety of avifauna, including Pel's fishing owl, Fischer's turaco, east coast akalat and brown-breasted barbet. It is also the only known habitat of the Tana river cistocola – not seen in the wild since the 1970s – and the elusive white-winged apalis, feared by some biologists to be extinct.

Difficult to reach by public transport, this remote reserve is very pedestrian friendly. Organised overnight tours based at the upmarket **Delta Dunes** *(see p369)*, can be booked in Malindi.

The Tana river delta, which sprawls southward from the reserve, is an important breeding site for birds, but large areas of it are rendered inaccessible by marshy conditions.

The muddy Tana river delta meets the Indian Ocean

Arabuko Sokoke National Park and Gedi Ruins ❸

Extending over 420 sq km (162 sq miles) northwest of the main coastal road between Kilifi and Watamu, Arabuko Sokoke National Park protects the largest remaining tract of coastal forest in East Africa. The area is well known as a stronghold for six globally threatened birds, among a recorded 230, while at least four of its 250 recorded butterfly species occur nowhere else in the world. A popular goal for day trips here is the ruined city of Gedi just outside the park's boundaries. This is the most extensive and atmospheric of the many medieval ruins along the Kenyan coast, and a walking trail to the old city walls is a good introduction to the forest itself.

★ Forest Paths
Guided walks through Arabuko Sokoke's network of paths offer hikers the opportunity to see plenty of forest wildlife.

Whistling Duck Pond
Covered in beautiful blue water lilies, this small forest-ringed pond on the Nyati Trail is named for the white-faced whistling duck, one of several waterfowl sometimes seen here. Although seldom seen, the buffalo and elephant that drink here in the dry season often leave conspicuous spoor.

★ Sokoke Scops Owl
Arabuko Sokoke Forest is renowned among ornithologists for its selection of rare and endemic coastal birds, including the endemic Sokoke scops owl and five other globally threatened birds.

KEY

✕	Domestic airport/airstrip
ℹ	Visitor information
▲	Campsite
⋔	Ruin
☀	Viewpoint
▬	Major road
═	Minor road
≡	Unpaved motorable road
– –	Trail
– –	Park boundary

STAR SIGHTS

★ Forest Paths

★ Sokoke Scops Owl

★ Gedi Ruins

For hotels and restaurants in this region see pp368–9 and pp387–8

★ Gedi Ruins

The best known archaeological attraction in the vicinity of Arabuko Sokoke, the ruined city of Gedi is an impressive relic of one of the most important Islamic medieval trade centres along the Swahili coast of Kenya.

VISITORS' CHECKLIST

Road Map E6. Mida Gate is 2 km (1 mile) W of the junction for Watamu. 🗙 🚌 ℹ️ *020 2335801.* 🕐 *6am–7pm daily.* 📷 📹 🅰️ **www**.kws.go.ke

0 km   5

0 miles   5

Giriama Dancers

The Giriama people of the Arabuko Sokoke area are not traditionally Islamic, and many adhere to animist beliefs. Living on the outskirts of Gedi Ruins, they can be seen performing dances in their traditional attire.

Kipepeo Butterfly Farm

This community-based eco-project, founded in 1993, encourages local subsistence farmers to breed the pupae of some of the 250 butterfly species found in Arabuko Sokoke for export.

Watamu, with its stunning bays and coral cliffs, is a popular stopover for beach-lovers.

Colourful Tree Frogs

The forest pools and trees of this national park are home to a wide variety of reptiles and amphibians, including several species of tree frog. These are most easily tracked after dark by their distinctive and repetitive calls.

GETTING AROUND

One of Kenya's most important protected areas in terms of global biodiversity, the forest is best explored on foot, following a network of well-maintained tracks that emanate from the forest headquarters alongside the main Mombasa–Malindi Highway. Guides are mandatory. The forest can be explored as a day trip from Malindi or Watamu, or from the campsite at the headquarters. The self-guided trail around the old city walls of Gedi also provides a good introduction to the park.

Exploring Arabuko Sokoke Forest

The national park is accessible by public transport and it is permitted to explore on foot, although a vehicle, ideally a 4WD, will allow visitors to cover far more ground and to go deeper into the forest. All visitors must report to the main gate, on the north side of the Mombasa–Malindi Highway about 2 km (1 mile) west of the junction for Watamu, the closest base for visits. Park fees are collected at the gate, where local guides are also available – the latter highly recommended but not mandatory. A good network of walking trails runs northeast from the main gate, though the route through Mida Gate to Whistling Duck Pond and Nyati Viewpoint is preferable by vehicle. Dedicated bird-watchers will want to deviate to Komani track and Dakacha to seek out the rare Sokoke scops owl and Clarke's weaver.

probably the park's most worthwhile bird habitat, supporting busy mixed flocks whose numbers include the Sokoke pipit, chestnut-fronted helmet-shrike, little yellow flycatcher, Amani sunbird and occasionally Clarke's weaver.

Whistling Duck Pond, a pretty lily covered expanse enclosed by tall forest, often hosts a selection of waterfowl, and forms an important drinking hole for buffalo and elephant in the dry season. The track then passes through dense *Cynometra* woodland, where wildlife is scarcer, although this is the preferred habitat of Sokoke scops owl and Ader's duiker, and buffalo and elephant spoor are also much in evidence. About 5 km (3 miles) after the pond, the track ascends a low ridge to Nyati Viewpoint, which offers sweeping views across the woodland canopy to the coastline between Malindi and Mida Creek.

A 4WD manoeuvres through a narrow dirt track, Nyati Trail

🐾 Nyati Trail

The 14-km (9-mile) motorable track running from Mida Gate to **Nyati Viewpoint** probably offers the best introduction to Arabuko Sokoke National Park's main habitats. For those without a vehicle, the first 8 km (5 miles) is a flat stretch and can easily be undertaken as a return walk, turning back at **Whistling Duck Pond**.

The first part of the track passes through a lovely patch of mixed evergreen forest, notable botanically for the prehistoric-looking cycad *Encephalartos hildebrandtii*. The spiky fronds of this fern-like shrub are often stripped bare by the forest's furtive population of around 120 elephants – elusive and seldom seen creatures, whose distinctive large pats are often splattered along the road. Vehicle-bound bird-watchers can step out to walk part of this stretch, looking out for east coast akalat, forest batis,

blue-mantled flycatcher and various greenbuls – some difficult to locate without a recording of the bird's calls, which a guide can provide.

After about 4 km (2 miles), the mixed forest gives way to deciduous *Brachystegia* woodland, which sheds its leaves between January and March, and supports an interesting assortment of epiphytic creepers, orchids and lichens. The open canopy here is

🐾 Arabuko Swamp and Treehouse

Running along the eastern boundary about 5 km (3 miles) from the Mombasa–Malindi Highway, Arabuko Swamp is the park's largest wetland, hemmed in by tall forests in the west and open cultivated land in the east. A varied selection of herons and other waterbirds is present, and a 2-km (1-mile) walking trail leads around the south shore to a fabulous treehouse, a viewing platform perched atop a colossal baobab. En route, visitors pass through a mixed woodland that hosts a similar

Lilies on Whistling Duck Pond, a favourite haunt of the white-faced duck

The dense expanse of forest canopy, Arabuko Sokoke forest

selection of bird species to the first stretch of the Nyati Trail, along with Sykes and vervet monkeys, though other large mammals are scarce due to encroaching cultivation.

🦎 Komani Track

This rough track runs for about 5 km (3 miles) west of Arabuko Swamp to a patch of *Cynometra* thicket where, ideally around 6.30pm, the guides from the Visitor Centre can reliably locate the Sokoke scops owl. This endangered small owl, which comes in grey and russet morphs, was first described in 1965 and was thought to be endemic to Arabuko Sokoke until an individual was netted in Tanzania's East Usambara in 1992. The owl rests up in holes in trees by day, and is very unlikely to be seen unless spotted by somebody very familiar with its nesting sites. The presence of this nocturnal insectivore is documented or suspected in a few other small Kenyan forests, but Arabuko Sokoke remains its main stronghold, supporting up to 80 per cent of the estimated global population of 2,000–3,000.

A butterfly with speckled wings

🦎 Dakacha

An obvious extension to any ornithological visit to the forest, the Dakacha area lies a short distance outside the park's northern boundary, and is the most reliable site for Clarke's weaver, arguably the most alluring of the many rare birds associated with Arabuko Sokoke. With a global population estimated at around 2,000, this bright yellow Kenyan coastal forest endemic is listed as endangered by the world conservation union IUCN, and its numbers remain in slow decline as a result of habitat destruction. Although the weaver is regularly recorded in *Brachystegia* woodland within Arabuko Sokoke from August to November, it is less common at other times and vanishes almost entirely over the breeding season (April–July). It is thought that the weaver's main breeding site is around Dakacha, where it is quite easily seen throughout the year, provided that visitors are accompanied by a knowledgeable local guide.

Kipepeo Butterfly Project

Outside entrance gate to Gedi Ruins.
🕐 8am–5pm daily. 📷 🅿 ♿
www.kipepeo.org

This community-based eco-project was founded in 1993 to discourage local subsistence farmers from chopping down indigenous trees used as breeding sites by the 260 butterfly species associated with Arabuko Sokoke. Today, pupae are bred by more than 800 individual farmers for export to the USA, Europe and South Africa, where they are hatched for live greenhouse exhibits. As an offshoot, the project now also supports a community mushroom farming enterprise and breeds silkworms, while a beekeeping enterprise produces honey sold locally to various beach resorts and marketed more widely under the Kipepeo label. It is an admirable and educational set-up, but visitors may feel a bit disappointed, for most often the only butterflies present are the ones still cocooned in their pupae.

A butterfly catcher working for Kipepeo Butterfly Project

Mzee Randu's Giriama Dancers

Tel 0726 047697. 📷

The Giriama are among the most traditional of the Mijikenda tribes, and this amiable family troupe, based immediately outside Gedi Ruins, will perform their traditional dances at short notice. Propelled by a trio of drummers and a panel of corrugated iron that plays a similar percussive role to a tambourine, the performance involves about a dozen male and female dancers, and can last anything from 10 minutes to an hour, as requested.

Exploring Gedi Ruins

Arguably the most important archaeological site on the coast, Gedi is also the most impressive, both for its brooding enigmatic atmosphere and its well-preserved Swahili architecture. Its name, from the Oromaic Gede (Precious), alludes to the abundant water of its deep stone wells. It is generally regarded to have been founded in the 13th century, but some excavations have traced its origins to two centuries earlier. At its peak, Gedi spread over 49 acres (20 ha) with a population of 3,000 people and at least eight mosques. Yet, its very existence goes undocumented in any surviving Swahili, Arabic or Portuguese source. Archaeological evidence suggests that it was abandoned after the destruction of Mombasa by the Portuguese in 1529.

★ Pillar Tomb
One of the several Islamic pillar tombs of the Swahili coast, this tomb has a phallic form that is disputed locally, and may have been inspired by tombstones from Ethiopia or Madagascar.

The Women's Court is so named because it holds traces of a kitchen.

Audience Court
Located on the north side of the palace, this court was most probably used by the sultan to address his subjects at ceremonial events and in times of crisis.

★ Great Mosque
Built in the mid-15th century, when Gedi was at its economic prime, this was the largest of the city's eight mosques, with six doors and a thick roof that was supported by 18 pillars. A 15-m (50-ft) deep well stands outside.

Great Mosque

STAR FEATURES

- ★ Pillar Tomb
- ★ Great Mosque
- ★ Palace

GETTING AROUND

The best starting point is the museum, which offers a good introduction to Gedi. From here, a footpath leads through the original town centre, passing the Dated Tomb, the Great Mosque, the Tree Platform and the Palace. Another path runs through the forest to the inner and outer city walls, passing many crumbling structures en route and offering the chance to spot the peculiar yellow-rumped elephant shrew and a variety of secretive forest creatures. Watch out for the vicious safari ants underfoot.

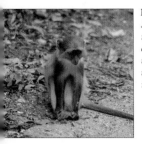

Blue Monkeys
Small troops of blue monkey are often seen clambering along the old walls in the late afternoon, while bird activity peaks in the early morning.

VISITORS' CHECKLIST

Road Map E6. 1 km (half a mile)
N of Watamu alongside Gedi
Village. 🚌 ℹ️ *020 2040001.*
🕐 *7am–6pm daily.* 🎫 📷 ♿
📷 www.museums.or.ke

Tree Platform
Built in the canopy of a massive baobab, this bird-watching platform also offers a great aerial view over the ruined city.

The Reception Court was reached through a fine arched doorway that still stands today.

Stone wells, some still usable today, provided fresh water to the people of Gedi.

★ Palace
Dating to the 15th century, the palace covers 900 sq m (9,700 sq ft) and was used by three generations of sultans. It features a large court and an annexe for the sultans' many wives.

PLAN OF THE SITE

KEY
ℹ️ Visitor information
🅿️ Parking
••• Footpath
☐ Area illustrated

0 metres   125
0 yards   125

Tree Platform
Palace
Great Mosque
Tomb of the Fluted Pillar
Museum
🅿️
ℹ️
Dated Tomb
House of the Dhow
Large House
Mosque of the Sarcophagi

Malindi ⑤

Kenya's second largest coastal settlement, Malindi is one of the oldest ports along the Swahili coast. The town enjoyed its greatest era of prosperity in the early 16th century, when it entered into alliance with Portugal against Mombasa, but the modern town is essentially a 19th-century entity, one that has since prospered as the country's leading urban beach resort. The town centre boasts a rather limited selection of historical landmarks, but it is well endowed with tourist facilities. A string of resort hotels running south of town caters to water sport enthusiasts. Malindi is well placed for day trips to Gedi, Arabuko Sokoke and Hell's Kitchen, and for short safaris to Tsavo East National Park.

Mango baskets for sale

Uhuru Gardens, a pleasant retreat in the heart of Malindi

🌿 Uhuru Gardens

Cnr Tsavo and Mama Ngina Rds. 🏛
Named Uhuru, which means freedom, shortly after independence, this small park-like enclave of shady trees is a good place for visitors to get their bearings before embarking on further exploration of Malindi. A couple of good craft shops run along the west side of the park. The fabulously rundown balconied double-storey building to the east of the park was built in 1890 as a combined residence and workplace for Malindi's first British district officer, J Bell Smith. Designated a national monument a century later, the building still functions as a District Office today.

The modest concrete construction in front of the office is the **Henry the Navigator Monument**, erected by Portugal in 1960 to commemorate the voyages of global exploration initiated by that 16th-century monarch.

🏛 Friday Mosque and Pillar Tombs

Mama Ngina Rd. 🏛
Situated to the south of Uhuru Gardens, the old town of Malindi suffers in comparison to its counterpart in Lamu or even Mombasa, in large part thanks to the destructive fires that have swept through it at

Friday Mosque on the seafront, the town's principal mosque

several points in its history. Indeed, the only Islamic monument of historical significance is the pair of pillar tombs that stand in front of the large seafront Friday Mosque. The larger tomb stands about 5 m (16 ft) high and dates to the 15th century, but the smaller may be more recent. The tombs can only be reached by entering a side door into the mosque compound and treading carefully and respectfully through the rows of rectangular graves outlined by coral stones.

🏛 Malindi Tourist Market

Lamu Rd. 🕐 9am daily. 🔲 🏛
Located opposite the Friday Mosque, this conglomeration of at least 50 stalls sells curios and crafts from all over Kenya, ranging from locally made batiks and paintings to beaded jewellery and sandstone carvings from Western Kenya. Inconvenience levels are low, and bargaining is undertaken with typically laid-back good humour. Open daily, many stalls only kick into action later in the day.

🏛 Malindi Museum

Mama Ngina Rd. **Tel** 042 213 1479.
🕐 8am–6pm daily. 🎫 includes same-day entry to the Portuguese Chapel and Vasco da Gama Cross. 🎫
Webb Memorial Library
🕐 8am–5pm Mon–Fri.
This interesting little museum opened in 2004 in the House of Columns, a three-storey waterfront building that began life as the trading store of Adulhusein Gulamhusein sometime before 1891. The building served as a hospital for several decades until 1952 and was later the local headquarters of the Department of Wildlife. It was acquired by the National Museums of Kenya in 1999 and restored in 2004.

Displays on the ground floor include a stuffed 77-kg (170-lb) coelacanth, a remarkable fish regarded by anatomists to be something of a living fossil. The highlight on the first floor is a collection of rare *vigango* (wooden burial totems) carved by the Gohu society of the coastal Giriama tribe, and believed by them to represent a link between the

The bell-shaped Vasco da Gama Cross at the northern end of Malindi

VISITORS' CHECKLIST

Road Map E6. 115 km (71 miles)
N of Mombasa. 70,000.
042 20747.

living and the dead. The top floor is given over to the **Webb Memorial Library**, which includes several out-of-print volumes dedicated to the history and culture of East Africa.

Portuguese Chapel

Mama Ngina Rd. 8am–6pm daily.
www.museums.or.ke
There is an appealing simplicity to this small thatched coral-rag building, which has overlooked the waterfront since before 1542, the year in which St Francis Xavier visited Malindi. In a ruinous state for much of the 17th and 18th centuries, the chapel was restored in the early 1890s. Most of the graves surrounding the chapel are unmarked – some may be Portuguese – although it is known that J Bell Smith was buried here in 1894.

Vasco da Gama Cross

Casuarina Rd. 8am–6pm daily.
www.museums.or.ke
One of the oldest surviving European monuments in equatorial Africa, this large limestone *padrao* (cross) was erected by the Portuguese navigator Vasco da Gama in 1499 to commemorate his historical landing at Malindi. It originally stood outside the Sultan of Malindi's palace, but its overt Christian connotations were considered offensive by local Muslims, and as a compromise it was relocated to its present out-of-town site in the 16th century. Visible from the town centre, the cross, which is a 10-minute walk past the Portuguese Chapel, has a splendid location on a windswept coral outcrop overlooking the bay and tidal flats that are inhabited by flocks of small waders.

Falconry of Kenya

Behind Lamu Rd. **Tel** 072 234 6491.
9.30am–5.30pm daily.
Somewhat misleadingly billed as Kenya's only falconry, this admirable rehabilitation centre for injured and orphaned raptors sometimes houses no birds at all, since it has a policy of returning healthy birds back to the wild. However, there is usually a wide variety of *Accipiters*, ranging from owls and harrier-hawks to lizard buzzards and eagles. There is also a small reptile park, where visitors can see green and black mambas, crocodiles and tortoises, as well as a pair of bushbabies.

MALINDI

Falconry of Kenya ⑦
Friday Mosque and
  Pillar Tombs ②
Malindi Museum ④
Malindi Tourist Market ③
Portuguese Chapel ⑤
Uhuru Gardens ①
Vasco da Gama Cross ⑥

Malindi Bay

OLD TOWN

Malindi Marine
National Park
5 km (3 mile)

0 metres   800

0 yards   800

Key to Symbols see back flap

Traditional dhows and Swahili-style ocean facing buildings at Lamu waterfront ▷

Lamu Archipelago � 8

The least conventional resort destination on the Kenyan coast, the Lamu Archipelago consists of a trio of large offshore islands – Pate, Manda and Lamu – and several smaller islets nestled in a sheltered bay midway between the Tana river mouth and Somali border. Soporific, steeped in Swahili tradition and defiantly isolated from mainstream modern Kenyan culture, the islands boast their fair share of idyllic beaches, but their main attractions are cultural and historical. The focal point is Lamu town, whose distinct architecture and overwhelming sense of cultural integrity make it unique among comparably sized settlements anywhere along the Swahili coast, resulting in its inscription as a UNESCO World Heritage Site in 2001.

Swahili women in their
traditional black *bui buis*

KEY

✕	Domestic airport/airstrip
⛴	Ferry port
ℹ	Visitor information
🅰	Lodge
⌂	Ruin
▪▪▪	Untarred major road
═══	Minor road
═ ═	Unpaved motorable road
▪ ▪	Trail

★ Nabahani Ruins
The Lamu Archipelago, in particular Manda and Pate islands, is dotted with Islamic ruins dating to the prime of the medieval maritime trade along the Swahili coast.

Kilv

Mtangaw

Lamu Waterfront
The attractive waterfront is lined by 19th-century houses and shops, most of which are in the traditional Swahili style, spanning two or three storeys and with white-washed coral-rag walls.

Malindi
210 km
(130 miles)

Hindi

Manda Bay

Mokowe

Man
Ras Kilindini

Mwana
Mariyamu

*Manda
Island*

Matondoni

Lamu

Lamu Island
is the main
sightseeing
focus of the
archipelago.

*Lamu
Island*

Shela

Kitau

Kipungani

*Lamu
Bay*

★ Shela Beach
This attractive beach is the most popular recreational beach on Lamu Island, stretching along miles of semi-deserted coastline.

STAR SIGHTS

★ Nabahani Ruins

★ Shela Beach

★ Dhow Trips

For hotels and restaurants in this region see pp368–9 and pp387–8

Manda Toto Island
The best snorkelling destination within day-trip distance of Lamu town, Manda Toto is often visited in conjunction with Manda, the larger island that houses the Takwa Ruins.

Kiwaiyu Island is the smallest and most remote in the archipelago.

Ndau Bay

Kiwaiyu Island

Uvondo Island

Ndau Island

Kiwaiyu

Kiwaiyu Bay

Kisingitini

Tundwa

Bajumwali

ate Island

Sylph Channel

★ Dhow Trips
The most pleasant way of getting between Lamu, Manda, Pate and the smaller islands is by the traditional dhows that have sailed along the Swahili coast for centuries.

Faza lies surrounded by the ruins of several mosques, including the beautiful Mbwarashally mosque built in the 18th century.

GETTING AROUND

The first destination of most visitors to the archipelago, Lamu town, which has plenty of hotels and eateries, can easily be explored on foot (aside from donkeys, no practical alternative exists). Shela is within reasonable walking distance of Lamu, but other sites on the main island are only accessible by donkey or dhow. Motorised dhows run daily between Lamu town and Pate Island, requiring that at least one night be spent on Pate. For those with limited time, private dhows can be chartered to visit either Manda or Pate, usually as a day trip.

0 km 5

0 miles 5

Siyu
The largest structure on Pate Island, Siyu Fort was built in the mid-19th century to protect what was then one of the most important sultanates on the Swahili coast from Omani occupation. The town diminished greatly in importance since it was absorbed into the Omani Sultanate of Zanzibar in 1863.

Exploring Lamu and Manda Islands

Most visitors to the archipelago base themselves in Lamu town, which is serviced by scheduled flights from Nairobi, Mombasa and Malindi. All flights land at the airstrip on Manda Island, from where motorised dhows ferry visitors across the channel to Lamu itself. It is worth dedicating at least one full day to the old town of Lamu, which is easily explored on foot. It is also possible to walk or catch a dhow ferry to nearby Shela without making prior arrangements. Other excursions are best organised a day in advance through a hotel or local guide. The most popular day option is the snorkelling trip to Manda Toto and the Takwa Ruins by motorised dhow, followed by the donkey excursion to Matondoni.

The minaret of the Friday Mosque towering over Shela town

Lamu Island

Separated from the tiny mainland port of Mokowe by a 3-km (2-mile) wide channel, Lamu Island takes its name from the eponymous town on its eastern shore. The Lamu archipelago's largest settlement, **Lamu** (*see pp248–9*) seems at once an anachronism and oddly cosmopolitan in mood, having adapted to tourism without sacrificing too much of the time-warped atmosphere on which its charm relies.

A 30–45 minute walk from Lamu town, and connected to it by regular passenger dhows, **Shela** overlooks the archipelago's most accessible and popular beach. A fabulous arc of bone-white sand, Shela Beach runs for more than 10 km (6 miles) in the other direction to town. Swimming here is generally safe, even though it is one of the few Kenyan beaches to lack a protective reef. However, it is inadvisable to wander alone along the beach too far

out of eyeshot as occasional muggings are reported. The main focus of beachfront tourist activity is the upmarket **Peponi Hotel** (*see p368*) at the east end of Shela, which has been in the same family for 40 years. There are also a couple of other restaurants dotted along the sandy shore.

Shela village itself is a far more venerable settlement than its modest proportions might seem to indicate. Founded around 400 years ago by refugees from the ruined city of **Takwa** on Manda Island, it is the site of two important mosques. Most striking is the whitewashed **Friday Mosque**, whose conical minaret, built in 1829, towers to a height of 18 m (59 ft) above the surrounding houses, and has an internal spiral stairwell of 58 steps. Separated from this tall edifice by a sand dune, the disused **Wa Deule Mosque** has an intricately carved mihrab dated to 1848.

A popular day trip from Lamu town, the small village of **Matondoni** is most easily reached on donkeyback, following a flat path across the island's dry interior to the mainland-facing shore. The village's cluster of brick and thatch huts bears little resemblance to the archipelago's more ostentatious settlements, but it is an important centre of dhow building, and the local residents are willing to demonstrate this and other traditional crafts to visitors. On the whole, a visit to Matondoni is one of the instances where the journey is more memorable than the

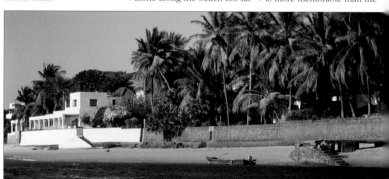

The scenic and tranquil waters of Shela Beach

For hotels and restaurants in this region see pp368–9 and pp387–8

The unusual pillar tomb at the Friday Mosque, Takwa Ruins

destination, with the added bonus of observing interesting birdlife in the form of colourful rollers and bee-eaters that hawk from the low coastal shrub.

Kipungani, a village with a population of 300 people, lies on the far southwestern shore of Lamu Island, overlooking the mangrove-lined channel that divides the island from the mainland. The main attraction here is **Kipungani Explorer** (see p368), which ranks among the most wonderfully remote upmarket beach retreats anywhere in Kenya. Its clients are generally ferried direct by motorised dhow from the airstrip on Manda Island or from Lamu town. There would be nothing preventing independent travellers from heading to Kipungani by donkey or dhow, but tourist facilities are limited.

Passenger dhow in Lamu town

Shela
3 km (2 miles) SE of Lamu town.

Matondoni
7 km (4 miles) W of Lamu town.

Kipungani
10 km (6 miles) SW of Lamu town.

Manda Island
2 km (1 mile) E of Lamu.
Separated from Lamu town by a mile-wide channel, Manda, the smallest of the archipelago's three main islands, is the site of Lamu's only airstrip. The island is otherwise

practically uninhabited due to the absence of potable water. It was not so 500 years ago, however, when the Swahili trading centre of Takwa stood on the narrowest part of the island, a site that was probably chosen for defensive reasons, as the surrounding shallow water would have made it difficult for a hostile ship to approach in safety. It is thought that the city was abandoned in the early 17th century, due to the increased salinity of the water supply and ongoing fighting with the rival port of Pate (see p250). The substantial **Takwa Ruins** can still be visited on the far side of the island to Lamu, about 5 km (3 miles) from the airstrip, and include a striking Friday Mosque with a large pillar tomb rising from its wall. The tomb is probably that of an important sheikh,

and it remains the site of a biannual pilgrimage from Shela, many of whose inhabitants claim descent from the 17th-century Takwa refugees.

Manda Toto, literally "child of Manda", is a small uninhabited coral island that juts out from the channel dividing Manda from the mainland. Surrounded by reefs, it is easily the best snorkelling site in the Lamu area, with a plethora of colourful reef fish likely to be seen alongside more occasional visitors such as the immense whale shark, schools of dolphin and marine turtles.

An important nesting site for marine birds, the island is most easily visited by dhow together with the Takwa Ruins as part of a day package from Lamu town.

Takwa Ruins
9am–6pm daily.
www.museums.or.ke

A secluded beach at Manda Toto, off the northeast coast of Manda

Lamu: Old Town

If any one place represents a clear continuum between the Swahili coast past and present, it is Lamu, whose old town has changed little since the 18th century, and whose profusion of traditional architecture makes it the best-preserved of East Africa's old Swahili towns. Lamu homesteads typically rise to two or three storeys, featuring shaded inner courtyards and verandas, elaborately carved wooden doors and high plastered ceilings supported by poles of mangrove timber. The town is a compact labyrinth of alleyways and whitewashed buildings that lends itself to pedestrian exploration. The maze of alleys can be disorientating, but the predictable terrain, sloping towards the waterfront, makes it impossible to be lost for very long.

Riyadha Mosque
Built by the Yemenite settler Sharif Habib Salih in 1900, this is the most prestigious mosque in Lamu and an important pilgrimage site during the Maulidi festival.

The German Post Office Museum was established in 1888 to service the German Protectorate at Witu.

Riyadha Mosque

German Post Office Museum

★ Lamu Fort
Built between 1813 and 1821 with the assistance of Sultan Seyyid Sa'id of Oman, this imposing two-storey stone structure now doubles as a community centre and a museum and gallery.

Pwani Mosque, founded circa 1370, is the oldest of Lamu's 23 mosques, although nothing of the original building remains now.

0 metres   50

0 yards   50

STAR SIGHTS

★ Lamu Fort

★ Lamu Museum

★ Lamu Waterfront

Harambee Avenue
This avenue ran along the seafront prior to the mid-19th century. It is now the busiest thoroughfare through Lamu, lined with small shops, boutiques, cafés and restaurants.

For hotels and restaurants in this region see pp368–9 and pp387–8

Swahili House Museum
This restored 18th-century house, centred around a typical Lamu courtyard, is furnished in period style, with ornate hardwood furniture and four-poster beds.

VISITORS' CHECKLIST

Road Map F6. Eastern shore of Lamu Island facing Manda Island. 17,000. *Maulidi (variable), Lamu Cultural Festival (Nov).* **www**.lamuheritage.com **Lamu Museum** 9am–6pm daily. *fee includes Lamu Fort, Swahili House Museum and the German Post Office Museum.* **www**.museums.or.ke

Lamu Donkey Clinic
The clinic was set up by the International Donkey Protection Trust to treat the island's innumerable working donkeys.

★ Lamu Museum
Built in 1891 as a residence for colonial governors, Lamu Museum houses a selection of traditional Swahili musical instruments, notably two ancient Siwa horns. It also has displays on the historical evolution of Lamu town, and non-Swahili coastal cultures such as the pastoralist Orma and Pokomo.

★ Lamu Waterfront
The 2-km (1-mile) long waterfront took its present shape in the mid-19th century as a result of land infill. It is very pleasant to stroll along it or relax at one of the laid-back restaurants and watch the traditional dhows sail past.

Exploring Pate and Kiwaiyu Islands

Two other islands in the Lamu Archipelago are of great interest to visitors, albeit in a wildly contrasting manner. The most northerly is a serpentine sliver of sand called Kiwaiyu, which offers snorkelling from a pair of isolated beach lodges. For the adventurous, however, a more challenging goal is the larger island of Pate, notable for its three small towns as time-warped and absorbing as any in East Africa. Getting to Pate is easy, whether by chartering a boat or by surrendering to the combination of tides, winds and whimsy that dictate the schedule of the daily water taxis between Lamu town and Mtangawanda. For all that, Pate remains resolutely off the beaten track. No formal accommodation exists, although it is easy to arrange to sleep in a local homestead.

The imposing Siyu Fort sitting dramatically on the waterfront

Pate Island

32 km (20 miles) NE of Lamu. 🚤
Siyu Fort 🕐 9am–6pm daily. 🎫 📷
www.museums.or.ke

East Africa's oddest urban anachronism, Pate town was founded in the 9th century by Omani refugees and peaked in influence during the 12th–15th centuries under the Nabahani dynasty. The "modern" town centre, which rises phoenix-like from the more expansive ruins of its medieval precursor, took shape in the 18th century, when Pate enjoyed a second golden age as a prosperous centre of Swahili arts and crafts. Today, Pate has the disorientating labyrinthine quality of a traditional city centre. However, when viewed from the rooftops of its characteristic three-storey stone buildings, it becomes clear that this urban enclave consists of no more than 100 houses, isolated on one side by thick mangroves, and on the rest by tall palms rising from the crumbling walls of the Nabahani Ruins.

About 8 km (5 miles) north of Pate town, the modern town of **Siyu** is less architecturally impressive than Pate, but has a welcoming atmosphere. Although scarcely credible today, little more than a century ago Siyu was described as "the pulse of the whole district" by Fredrick Holmwood, Vice Consul of Zanzibar. Only 50 years before that it was a renowned centre of Islamic scholarship, whose population of 20,000 remained aloof from regional political machinations until the Omani occupation of 1847, and only succumbed to Omani rule in 1863.

The outskirts of the town are dotted with ancient walls and imposing tombs, but the most notable building is the immaculately preserved **Siyu Fort**, constructed in the mid-19th century to safeguard the town from Omani attacks. Further afield, about a 45-minute walk from the town, are the sprawling but elusive **Shanga Ruins**, containing more than 100 homesteads and 300 tombs dating from the 11th century. These are best visited with a local guide.

Located on the northern shore of Pate Island, **Faza** is its largest town and dates to medieval times. The island boasts relatively few antiquities, having been razed to the ground during a military attack by Pate in the 15th century and again by a 650-strong Portuguese army from Goa a century later. The site was briefly settled by the Portuguese, who built a church here, though no trace of it remains today. The town was revived as a Swahili trade centre in the 18th century, when the Shala Fatani Mosque, now an architecturally intriguing ruin, was built.

Kiwaiyu Island

16 km (10 miles) N of Pate Island.
✈ www.kws.go.ke

Kiwaiyu is the largest landmass in the Kiunga Marine Reserve, which protects a 60-km (37-mile) stretch of coastline and more than 50 calcareous reefs and islands running northwards of Pate. Serviced by two exclusive lodges and an airstrip, the island is a wonderfully remote and relaxed base for diving, snorkelling and game fishing. It has some fine beaches too. Marine life includes the rare dugong and several species of marine turtle, while herds of elephants are sometimes seen on the facing mainland, which is protected in gazetted national sanctuaries.

Makuti-roofed houses flanked by palm trees, Siyu

For hotels and restaurants in this region see pp368–9 and pp387–8

Dhows of the Swahili Coast

There are few sights more characteristic of East Africa's Swahili coast than that of a traditional fishing dhow sailing past the shore, white sail billowing in the wind, as it might have done at any time in the past thousand or so years of trade with Arabia. It may come as a surprise to learn that the term dhow – applied

Detail of carved dhow prow

by Europeans to practically any traditional East African seafaring vessel – is neither Arabic in origin, nor is it used in Swahili to describe a specific type of boat. More likely, dhow is a corruption of *não*, a Portuguese term that covers any small local seafaring vessel, possibly via the Swahili *kidau*, a particular type of small boat.

Most large dhows are now powered with motors in addition to or instead of sails.

The sail, when not in use, is rolled up to rest at a 90 degree angle to the mast.

SAILING VESSELS

Dhows range in size from small fishing craft to large ocean-going vessels. The international nature of coastal trade is reflected in their names – *dengiya*, for instance, is thought to be the root of the English word dinghy, while the *jahazi*'s alternative name of *jalbut* derives from the English "jolly boat" or Indian "gallevat".

The jahazi, *the largest traditional sailing vessel to remain in wide use in East Africa, has changed little in design since medieval times. It measures up to 20 m (66 ft) and is used to carry cargo or up to 100 passengers across long tracts of open water.*

The mashua, *smaller than a jahazi but similar in appearance, design and purpose, measures up to 10 m (33 ft) from bow to stern. It typically has a capacity of 25 passengers and is used for offshore fishing expeditions, as well as for long distance transport between ports.*

The dugout-like mtumbwi, *used to fish in protected waters, is the most rudimentary boat used on the Swahili coast. It is made from a hollowed tree trunk, a design replicating the very first boats crafted by humans.*

The ngalawa *consists of a long dugout supported by two narrow outriggers, a design that is sufficiently stable to be propelled by a sail in calm conditions. Unsuitable for the open sea, it is mainly used by local fishermen in protected waters.*

SOUTHERN RIFT VALLEY AND MASAI MARA

he classic African savannah of the Southern Rift Valley and Masai Mara forms the heart of Kenya's popular safari industry. Superb Big Five viewing is practically guaranteed in the Masai Mara, home to the country's densest wildlife populations, while the Southern Rift Valley also offers plentiful wildlife viewing in a setting of blackened volcanic outcrops, severe basalt cliffs and sparkling lakes.

Widely regarded to be the cradle of mankind, the East African Rift – part of an immense tectonic chasm that stretches from the Red Sea to the Zambezi river – is scattered with a wealth of paleontological sites associated with our earliest hominid ancestors. These ancient soils have supported human habitation for millions of years, most recently by the pastoral Maasai, who migrated into the area in the 18th century, and whose ferocity in battle ensured it was one of the last parts of East Africa to be explored by Europeans.

Staunchly traditionalist, the Maasai today adhere to pastoralist ways. Elsewhere, much of the Southern Rift Valley is given over to large-scale agriculture, while smaller pockets of land are protected in a network of national reserves. Urbanisation levels are low and towns are mostly very small, the only obvious exception being Nakuru, the country's fourth largest city.

The main attractions of this dramatic stretch of the Rift are its natural assets. The Rift Valley floor supports a quintet of beautiful lakes, ranging from freshwater Naivasha and Baringo, with their profusion of fish, hippo and birds, to alkaline Bogoria and Nakuru, whose hypersaline waters host up to two million flamingoes. For wildlife, the Masai Mara, most rewarding over August–October when migrant wildebeest swarm across its hills, offers peerless big cat sightings, while Lake Nakuru National Park is a stronghold for flamingoes and the endangered rhino.

A hot spring fountain at Loburu, on the shore of Lake Bogoria

◁ Migrating wildebeest dotting the rolling grasslands of the Masai Mara

The Maasai

The archetypal East African pastoralists, the Maasai migrated from the Sudanese Nile to the Kenya-Tanzania border area in the 18th century. A reputation as fearsome warriors ensured that the Maasai were avoided by the slave caravans and European explorers who penetrated the interior in the 19th century. European settlement brought disaster in the form of a rinderpest epidemic that killed most of the Maasai's cattle and caused large tracts of their territory to be made into game reserves and settler farms. The central unit of Maasai society is the age-set, which changes every 15 years or so following the initiation of a new generation of *ilmoran* (warriors).

Maasai woman adorned with colourful beaded jewellery

The calabash is made from the pod of a sausage tree.

Multicoloured jewellery offsets the bright shawls worn by the Maasai people.

The spiralled horn of a greater kudu, *an antelope that is now rare in Kenya, is used to summon the next generation of* ilmoran *to the Eunoto ceremony that marks their coming of age as warriors.*

A **Shuka** is the red robe worn by Maasai men.

MAASAI GROUPS

Social interaction between neighbouring families and distant relations is integral to Maasai culture, since their communities – like those of other pastoralists – tend to be more dispersed than their agricultural cousins. During key events such as Eunoto, families belonging to the same clan will travel long distances to be present at the initiation of an *ilmoran*, carrying a range of gifts for the celebrations.

Family wealth *is measured in terms of children and cattle – a herd of 50 cattle is respectable, the more offspring the better, and a man with plenty of one but not the other is considered poor. This means that even inherently wealthy families live on the poverty line – most have several children and converting a household's cattle to cash would demean its standing.*

Every teenage boy *must undergo initiation by circumcision before being accepted as an* ilmoran. *This ritual is performed without anaesthetic. Should the initiate cry out, his post-circumcision ceremony is cancelled and he will be rejected by his peers for several years before being forgiven.*

Sticks are used as defence against animals and for ritual stick fights.

Bleeding the cattle *is a tradition practised by the Maasai. Blood, drained painlessly and harmlessly from a nick in the cow's jugular vein, is mixed with milk and fermented in a calabash for several days before being drunk. This is the main diet of the Maasai who feed almost exclusively off their cattle, shunning wildlife, vegetable matter or fish.*

Beef *is seldom eaten by the Maasai, as a living cow is more valuable to them than a dead one. However, a cow will be slaughtered, grilled and eaten – with immense relish – on special occasions.*

Ochre dye is used to redden the hair of the Maasai.

Maasai dancing *resembles pogoing and an individual's skill is measured by how high the dancer is able to jump.*

Slipper-like shoes are made of leather, or sometimes rubber from old car tyres.

Maasai warriors *are easily recognisable, with their toga-like red* shuka, *ochre hair styled in a manner that has been compared to a Roman helmet, ear lobes cut away from the main part of the ear, and trademark wooden poles or spears.*

OL DOINYO L'ENGAI

The Ol Doniyo volcano spewing red-hot lava

The Maasai believe in a single deity called Engai, but it possesses a dualistic nature, characterised as the benevolent Engai Narok (Black God) and vengeful Engai Nanyokie (Red God). This deity is said to live on the Tanzanian shore of Lake Natron in the crater of Ol Doinyo L'Engai (Mountain of God), a volcano that most recently erupted in 2008.

The Maasai Manyatta

The Maasai customarily live in family compounds known as *manyattas*. A single *manyatta* will normally be inhabited by a nuclear family, which can amount to many dozens of people. As Maasai society is polygamous, an elder can take as many wives as he can afford and father as many children as possible. Conventionally, a Maasai man of the active *ilmoran* (warrior) age-set is forbidden from marrying or from starting his own *manyatta* until the next *ilmoran* generation is initiated, when he and his peers – typically in their early to mid-30s – become junior elders, the group responsible for political and legislative decisions. Women, by contrast, are usually married off in their teenage years, leading to a large age discrepancy between a man and his wives.

Children peeking from the doorway of a traditionally constructed hut

The manyatta is often set amid acacia trees.

The manyatta *is normally designed to form a circular pattern for defence purposes. Huts are arranged around the perimeter to guard the livestock pens in the centre.*

THE MANYATTA LAYOUT

The *manyatta* typically consists of a protective outer fence made of spiked branches or euphorbia trees. Within this lies an outer circle of huts, one of which is reserved for the man of the family and one apiece for each of his wives and their younger offspring. The stock pens form the inner circle, affording maximum protection to the precious cattle and goats.

The bare dirt floor of a *manyatta* is usually pounded and baked hard by hoof prints and the sun.

Making fire *is part of the immense bush craft of the Maasai. Rural manyattas still depend less on shop bought gadgets than on traditional techniques such as the impressive feat of starting a fire simply by rubbing two sticks together furiously until they spark.*

Traditional Maasai huts, *with some regional variations, are typically made by first creating a frame of strong sticks. The huts are then plastered with smooth mud or by mixing it with grass. The low flat ceilings are usually made with thatch, although these too may be regularly strengthened with the mud-mixture.*

The thatched roof of a Maasai hut is usually low and flat.

A single entrance is guarded by *ilmoran* at night to prevent cattle rustling and predation by lions.

Cooking *is done by the women in a chimney-free hut that is easily recognised by its smoky smell. The classic Maasai diet is strongly centred on protein derived from cows and other livestock and is usually supplemented by ugali (maize porridge) and other local staples.*

Stock pens, like the outer walls, are made with acacia and other thorny branches.

Tending livestock *is a job for boys that have yet to become* ilmoran. *Younger children look after goats and sheep, while teenagers are given the far greater responsibility of cattle-herding. Even today, many Maasai households prefer their children to tend livestock than to attend school.*

Cattle are milked usually by the women, *either in the early morning before the cattle are taken out to graze for the day or in late afternoon after they are brought back. Milk and cattle blood form an important part of the Maasai diet, but it is regarded as insulting to the cattle to consume milk and meat – the living and the dead – on the same day.*

Exploring Southern Rift Valley and Masai Mara

Apart from the great draw of the wildlife-rich Masai Mara Game Reserve, this region is most popular for its lakes, in particular Naivasha and Nakuru. The former has superb birdlife and offers the exciting opportunity to hike or cycle unguided through the spectacular plains at Hell's Gate, while the latter is famous for its large flocks of flamingoes and the near certainty of close-up encounters with rhinos. Lakes Bogoria and Baringo are equally popular for their relaxed atmosphere and varied birdlife. Located near the scenic Naivasha Road, Mount Longonot National Park is pedestrian-friendly and offers a unique perspective on the region's turbulent geological past. Further north, excavated sites at Hyrax Hill and Kariandusi offer a glimpse of hominid history.

A tusker on the eastern plains of the Masai Mara

Flamingoes feeding beside an erupting geyser, Lake Bogoria

GETTING AROUND

The main trunk road through the Southern Rift Valley is the A104, which connects Nairobi to Nakuru via Naivasha. It is well served by buses and *matatus*, but the little-used railway service has been discontinued. From Nakuru, the B4 is a good surfaced road running north to Baringo, with sufficient public transport. The B3/C12 to Masai Mara via Narok runs south from the A104. Given that it is one of the busiest tourist routes in the country, this road is appallingly corrugated in parts, and flying is a better option. Public transport to Masai Mara extends along the B3 up to Narok, from where private transport is required to complete the last leg of the journey.

0 km   20

0 miles   20

Kam

Eld

Ea

Sorget

Limule
2,565 m

Londiani

Kec

B1

*Southwestern
Mau Forest*   *Ea*

Ilare *Kipsonot* *Kan*

Chemosit

C23

Litein   Koiwa   Olengu

C24   *Mara
Forest*

Yaganek   Tenwek

Kisii   Keroka   C15   Bomet   B3   Longisa

Masimba   Ndanai   *Chepalungu
Forest*   Kapkimo

Nyangusu   Gorgor   C14

Monianku   C16   C14   Olo.

Kilgoris   Kaboson   Ngorengo

*Moita
2,037 m*   C17   C13   Lemek

Mara   *Eregero
2,273 m*

C13   Lolgorien   Aitong   *Loita Plai*

Ntimaru   *Esoit Oloololo Escarpment*   C12

MASAI MARA
GAME RESERVE

Talek   Bakitabu

Mara   D301

Sand

One of the towering cliffs of Hell's Gate National Park

SIGHTS AT A GLANCE

Towns
Naivasha ⑥
Nakuru ⑫
Narok ①

Parks and Reserves
Hell's Gate National Park pp270–71 ⑧
Kigio Wildlife Conservancy ⑨
Lake Nakuru National Park pp276–9 ⑮
Masai Mara Game Reserve pp262–5 ②
Mount Longonot National Park ⑤

Areas of Natural Beauty
Lake Elmenteita ⑪
Lake Naivasha pp266–9 ⑦
Lakes Bogoria and Baringo pp280–83 ⑯
Mau Escarpment ③
Menengai Crater ⑭
The Naivasha Road ④

Archaeological Sites
Hyrax Hill Prehistoric Site ⑬
Kariandusi Prehistoric Site ⑩

SEE ALSO
- *Where to Stay* pp369–72
- *Where to Eat* p388

KEY

━━	Major road
══	Minor road
∎∎∎	Untarred major road
═══	Untarred minor road
---	4WD track
━━	Major railway
──	Minor railway
△	Peak
▬▬	International border

Narok ❶

Road Map B5. 140 km (87 miles) W of Nairobi along the B3.
🚶 24,000. ✕ 🚌

This small but fast growing district capital is the last town of substance along the main road from Nairobi to Masai Mara Game Reserve. A popular refuelling and refreshment stop, Narok offers good facilities, including the last bank, ATM and relatively affordable Internet access that Mara-bound travellers are likely to encounter for a few days. On the Mara side of town, the Kenol Filling Station, where most tour groups stop for a few minutes, has well-stocked curio and grocery shops and an efficient garden restaurant.

Narok's most prominent, indeed only, attraction for visitors is the **Maa Museum**. Housed in a former community centre on Narok's eastern outskirts, it has several displays relating to Kenya's Maa-speaking people, which include the Maasai, Samburu and Njemps. It may soon relocate to a new site past the Kenol Filling Station in the direction of the Masai Mara. The small museum includes displays relating to traditional and contemporary Maasai culture. These include some exceptional ethnographic portraits painted by Joy Adamson in the early 1950s, along with a gallery of more recent photographs taken with disposable cameras by Maasai women to depict day-to-day events in the *manyattas (see pp256–7)*. It is likely that the museum will expand in size and scope when it relocates to the new site west of the town centre.

🏛 **Maa Museum**
Signposted at entrance to Narok coming from Nairobi. 🕐 *9am–6pm daily.* 📷 ♿ www.museums.or.ke

Masai Mara Game Reserve ❷

See pp262–5.

Tracts of farmland and forest at the western edge of Mau Escarpment

Mau Escarpment ❸

Road Map B4.

Rising to an altitude of 3,100 m (10,170 ft), this rather inaccessible mountain range runs for more than 100 km (60 miles) along the western Rift Valley Escarpment north of Narok. Seldom visited, the Mau Escarpment is one of East Africa's greatest ecological treasurehouses. Its crest supports the region's largest existing block of montane forest, extending over 900 sq km (348 sq miles), and is home to the only remaining wild population of mountain bongo outside Aberdare National Park *(see pp316–17)*. Other rare or localised forest dwellers include the yellow-backed duiker, golden cat, giant forest hog, black-and-white colobus and a primate known as the potto. About 173 montane bird species have been recorded, several with very localised distributions.

With its heavy rainfall, the Mau Escarpment is an important watershed, feeding dozens of streams and rivers that eventually empty into Lakes Victoria, Nakuru and Natron. Five forest reserves have been gazetted and a sixth earmarked for the future. Mau is a stronghold for Kenya's oldest ethnic group, the Okiek, who have traditionally practised a sustainable hunter-gatherer lifestyle within these forests. Since colonial times, however, their presence has been perceived to be at odds with conservation, leading to several controversial, and so far only partially successful, attempts to evict them from the forests their ancestors inhabited for millennia.

The Naivasha Road ❹

Road Map C5.

The main road from Nairobi to Naivasha and Nakuru is one of the busiest and best in Kenya. The scenic 90-km (56-mile) drive normally takes about 90 minutes. The largest town on the way is **Limuru**, birthplace of Kikuyu novelist Ngũgĩ wa Thiong'o *(see p36)*, and site of the country's largest shoe factory. This breezy highland town lies off the main road, and the main draw here is a large swampy reservoir to the right of the road. The reservoir is a rewarding place for those who are interested in waders and other waterbirds.

The spectacular descent into the Rift Valley starts a few kilometres past Limuru, and it is *de rigueur* to stop at one of

A diorama of Maasai life at Narok's Maa Museum

For hotels and restaurants in this region see pp369–72 and p388

The vast northern slopes of Mount Longonot rising dramatically from the Rift Valley floor

several viewpoints offering fabulous panoramic views over a stretch of the valley floor dominated by the dormant volcanoes **Longonot** and **Suswa**. Several curio stalls along the route offer a wide range of items, white sheepskins being the local speciality.

Mount Longonot National Park ❺

Road Map C5. 60 km (37 miles) NW of Nairobi, entrance at Longonot village on the old Naivasha Rd. 🚌 ⬤ *9am–6pm daily (though it is inadvisable to attempt the ascent after 2pm).* 🎟 📷 **www.kws.go.ke**

This 52-sq-km (20-sq-mile) park protects the majestic Mount Longonot, a dormant volcano that rises sharply from the Rift Valley floor southeast of Lake Naivasha to an altitude of 2,776 m (9,108 ft). Dominating the landscape for miles around, Longonot last erupted in the 1860s, and until recently its floor was alive with steam vents, although this evidence of subterranean activity appears to have declined of late. Longonot derives from the Maasai name Olo Nong'ot, meaning "mountain of many spurs", a reference to the dozens of deep ravines incised into the ashy soil of the starkly vegetated slopes.

For visitors who are fairly fit, Mount Longonot is ideal for a wonderful day hike, although the lack of cover makes it advisable to leave

in the early morning to avoid overexposure to the sun. The ascent from the park entrance gate to the crater rim takes about 90 minutes, and is best undertaken in the company of a ranger. En route, there is good chance of encountering gazelle, zebra, giraffe and other wildlife. Almost perfectly circular, the caldera is fully intact and the view over its 3-km (2-mile) wide forest floor is spectacular, as are the views across the Rift Valley to Naivasha. It is possible to hike the full circumference of the crater rim in 3 to 4 hours, and adventurous travellers have also been known to descend into the crater, although the path down is rather treacherous and the buffalo that inhabit the floor have a reputation for aggression.

Naivasha ❻

Road Map B4. 90 km (56 miles) NW of Nairobi on the new Naivasha Rd. 🏛 *32,000.* ✈ 🚉 🚌

The compact market town of Naivasha is most often visited en route from Nairobi to Lake Naivasha *(see pp266–9)*, which is a short drive to the southwest of the town. Naivasha is well equipped with several filling stations, good Internet facilities, banks and ATMs, a few reasonably stocked supermarkets and – in the form of the long-serving **La Belle Inn's** *(see p370)* covered balcony – at least one highly agreeable

spot for an alfresco drink or snack. A short drive north of town is the **White Heat Art Gallery**. This is a worthwhile diversion for visitors who are interested in crafts. The gallery sells an unusual range of items, which are crafted from recycled metal, along with beadwork, pottery, paintings, prints and beautifully carved Swahili furniture. Most of these items are made on-site and stand several rungs above the usual souvenirs sold to visitors in terms of quality and originality. The gallery is a tranquil spot for a break from the Rift Valley highway.

🏛 **White Heat Art Gallery**
5 km (3 miles) S of Naivasha.
Tel *0724 636990.* ⬤ *9am–5pm Mon–Fri, 9am–noon Sat & Sun (by appt).* 🍴 ♿ 📷

The colourful façade of a streetside shop, Naivasha town

Masai Mara Game Reserve ❷

Balloon safaris, a popular activity

The 1,510-sq-km (583-sq-mile) Masai Mara Game Reserve is Kenya's most celebrated wildlife reserve, and arguably its best. Gazetted in 1968, it is dominated by open grassland, but as implied by the Maasai name Mara, meaning spotted, it is interspersed with rocky hills, acacia woodland and riparian forest. The Mara is rewarding not just for predators such as leopard and cheetah, but spotted hyena, bat-eared fox and black-backed jackal as well. Elephant and buffalo are common, and around three dozen black rhinos still survive. Other ungulates include impala, eland and reedbuck. A checklist of 450-plus birds includes raptors and ground birds such as ostrich and ground hornbill.

★ Wildebeest Migration
The legendary wildebeest migration, which streams across the Mara river from the Serengeti Plains in Tanzania, forms one of the world's greatest wildlife spectacles.

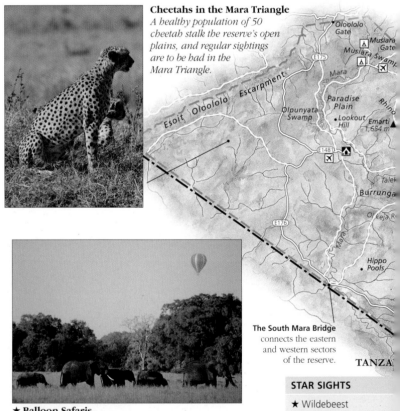

Cheetahs in the Mara Triangle
A healthy population of 50 cheetah stalk the reserve's open plains, and regular sightings are to be had in the Mara Triangle.

Esoit Oloololo Escarpment

Ololololo Gate

Musiara Gate

Musiara Swamp

E175

Mara

Paradise Plain

Rhino

Olpunyata Swamp

Lookout Hill

Emarti 1,654 m

E148

Talek

Burrunga

Ol keja R

E176

Hippo Pools

The South Mara Bridge connects the eastern and western sectors of the reserve.

TANZA

★ Balloon Safaris
A highlight of any visit to the Masai Mara is an early morning balloon safari, which offers the opportunity to have a bird's-eye view over the plains and their wildlife in the haunting dawn light. Flights are usually rounded off with an alfresco champagne breakfast.

STAR SIGHTS

- ★ Wildebeest Migration
- ★ Balloon Safaris
- ★ Lion Sightings

For hotels and restaurants in this region see pp369–72 and p388

★ Lion Sightings

An estimated 250–300 lions have territories within the Masai Mara. This is one of the highest densities anywhere in Africa and good sightings are practically guaranteed daily, especially in the open plains.

KEY

✕	Domestic airport/airstrip
ℹ	Visitor information
⛰	Lodge
⚠	Campsite
═══	Minor road
= =	Unpaved motorable road
- -	Park boundary
━ ∙	International boundary
▲	Peak

0 km _____ 5
0 miles _____ 5

Hippo Pools

The Mara river and its various tributaries support several permanent hippo pools, where pods of these engaging beasts can be seen lazing around in the muddy water.

Eastern Plains now have all-weather roads with a new route from Talek to Sekenani Gate.

GETTING AROUND

The road from Nairobi to the Masai Mara makes heavy demands on drivers unused to the local conditions, so it is easiest to visit on an organised fly-in or drive-in safari. Those who prefer the self-drive safari should note that there is only one bridge across the Mara river within the reserve, and one each across the Mara and Talek outside the northern boundary. Seeing the Mara on public transport is not possible. Game viewing is exceptional through the year, but it peaks over August to October during the wildebeest migration.

Ngama Hills

Standing out like a beacon from an otherwise rather flat landscape, the Ngama Hills are a useful landmark for those navigating themselves around the unsignposted dirt tracks of the Mara.

Exploring the Masai Mara Game Reserve

The reserve can be divided into three distinct parts. The eastern sector runs southeast from the Mara and Talek rivers to the Ngama Hills, the central sector lies cupped between these two rivers north of their confluence and the western sector is flanked by Oloololo Escarpment and the Mara river. The east carries the heaviest traffic, which can detract from the wilderness atmosphere. Bear in mind that game drives are generally confined to the same sector as the lodge or campsite. Visitors with more than 3 nights at their disposal could divide their time between lodges in different sectors. It is easiest to visit the Masai Mara on an organised safari from Nairobi, but self-drive safaris are also an option. However, internal roads are rough and signposts non-existent.

Lionesses keeping watch over their cubs at the Masai Mara Game Reserve

🐾 Ngama Hills and the Eastern Plains

Accounting for about half of the reserve, the eastern sector of Masai Mara is the closest to Nairobi and the most visited. Dozens of campsites and lodges are set within its boundaries or lie immediately outside them. The most prominent geographical landmark, the quartzite Ngama Hills tower above the main Sekenani Entrance Gate and are visible from all corners. The smaller Ol Opelagonya and Ololoitikoshi hills both lie in the far southeast towards Ololaimutiek Gate. The rock-strewn grassland of these hills does not support the wildlife volumes associated with the plains below, but its dense thicket patches are a favoured haunt of the reserve's last few dozen remaining black rhino, while the margins harbour buffalo, dik-dik and impala.

The flatter plains that run from the base of the Ngama Hills to the banks of the Mara river form the classic East African landscape of short grassland interspersed with a parsimonious scattering of acacia and other trees. The main roads through this part of the reserve are somewhat rutted and the relatively heavy traffic seems to be a deterrent to wildlife, so it is generally more productive to stick to the maze of regularly intersecting tracks that run between them. Lion and cheetah are common in this area, along with topi, gazelle, eland, ostrich and kori bustard. The park supports a much higher elephant density than expected in such open terrain. On self-drive visits, the distinctive eastern outline of the towering Ngama Hills and the more distant Oloololo Escarpment help visitors maintain their bearings. Other landmarks include the long-serving **Keekerok Lodge** *(see p372)*, which is the launch site for early morning balloon trips. Further south, the seasonal Sand river more or less follows the Tanzanian border west towards its confluence with the Mara. Practically at the border, the South Mara Bridge is the only crossing point between the reserve's eastern and western sectors, and overlooks a hippo pool that is a popular picnic spot.

🐾 Mara and Talek Rivers

The Mara river and its tributary the Talek are the only perennial waterways to flow through the Masai Mara Game Reserve. Dotted with dozens of deep hippo pools, the Mara river supports a varied aquatic wildlife that includes hippo, crocodile and otter, along with riverine birds such as hamerkop and African darter. The lush ribbon of riparian forest that follows both rivers for much of their length is densely populated with leopard, vervet monkey and bushbuck, as well as a selection of birds that is strikingly different from those in the rest of the park. This includes the brilliantly coloured Schalow's and Ross' turacos and the melodic white-browed robin-chat.

Giant herds of wildebeest staggering across the swift Mara river

Mixed herd of wildebeest and zebra at a waterhole near the eye-catching Oloololo Escarpment

One of the most spectacular events in the Serengeti–Mara migration is the wildebeest crossing of the Mara river. This might happen several times during the migrant wildebeest's 3-month Masai Mara tenure. There are eight major crossing points, of which the four most regularly-used lie along a 5-km (3-mile) stretch of the Mara upriver of its confluence with the Talek and overlooked by the **Mara Serena Safari Lodge** *(see p372)*. Often, wildebeest will congregate in their thousands on the banks for days before one impatient individual takes the plunge, triggering a lemming-like stampede that provides rich pickings for the waiting crocodiles. An estimated 3,000 wildebeests perish annually while crossing the Mara, but numbers are readily replenished by the average of 400,000 calves born in the Serengeti every January to February.

Central Plains
Located in the heart of the reserve and serviced by a handful of upmarket camps, the untrammelled plains of the central Masai Mara – flanked by the Mara river to the west and the Talek to the south – offer exceptionally reliable game viewing, particularly when it comes to big cats. Dominated by a long succession of thick-maned males, the legendary "marsh lion" pride hangs around the grassy verges of **Musiara Swamp** and Governor's Camp, and is habituated to vehicles. The open grassland around

Paradise Plain is arguably the best place in Kenya to look for cheetah, while several generations of habituated leopard inhabit the vicinity of **Leopard Gorge**, a short drive outside the reserve from the Musiara Gate. By contrast, the prominent **Rhino Ridge** overlooking Paradise Plain seldom lives up to its name.

Crisscrossed by motorable tracks, the short grass plains north of Rhino Ridge are densely excavated with aardvark holes that now serve as dens to spotted hyena, bat-eared fox and black-backed jackal. Two localised birds associated with this part of the park are Denham's bustard and the lovely rufus-bellied heron that inhabits Musiara Swamp. The central plains are spectacular from August to October when zebra and wildebeest congregate there in their tens of thousands. The best place to view large numbers of hippo and wildebeest – and with luck the occassional river crossing – is **Lookout Hill**, located opposite Serena Lodge.

Mara Triangle
This most westerly sector of the Masai Mara is also the oldest, having first been gazetted as a 510-sq-km (197-sq-mile) game reserve in the late 1940s. It is the most scenically dramatic part of the reserve, set below the 400-m (1,312-ft) tall **Oloololo Escarpment** and studded with isolated granite hills known as koppies. The open grassland supports dense seasonal concentrations of migrant zebra and wildebeest.

The Mara Triangle is good for spotting big cats and other members of the Big Five, although rhino are not very common. Roan antelope and African wild dog were once common here, but have not been seen since the late 1980s, although plans are afoot to reintroduce the former from Ruma National Park *(see p305)*, their only extant haunt in Kenya. The Oloololo Escarpment along the western boundary is a good place to spot the dainty klipspringer antelope, the rock hyrax and spectacular Verreaux's eagle.

Cheetah, not so elusive in the Masai Mara Game Reserve

Lake Naivasha ❼

A popular first stop out of Nairobi, this near-circular and shallow freshwater lake has a beautiful Rift Valley setting, with the distinctive volcanic outline of Mount Longonot rising to the south. The name Naivasha is a corruption of the Maasai *enaiposha* (restless water), in possible reference to the rough waves that often sweep its surface in the afternoon. The Gilgil and Malewa rivers flow into Naivasha's swampy northern shore, but there is no known outlet and the water most probably stays fresh due to a subterranean outlet that emerges at Lake Magadi. First documented by Scottish geologist Joseph Thomson in 1884, the lake typically extends over 130 sq km (50 sq miles) but has experienced several inexplicable fluctuations in level, almost drying out in the late 1940s.

The African fish eagle, a vocal lakeshore resident

★ Green Crater Lake

Nestled at the base of a lush volcanic crater, this small, beautiful lake forms the centrepiece of a private wildlife sanctuary whose attractions include colobus monkeys, giraffes and flamingoes.

Oserian Wildlife Sanctuary
This private sanctuary offers the best game viewing around Naivasha, with naturally occurring populations of leopard, cheetah, plains zebra and various grazers, as well as introduced herds of white rhino and Grevy's zebra.

STAR SIGHTS

★ Green Crater Lake

★ Elsamere

★ Bird-watching

★ Elsamere

This former home of Joy Adamson is now a centre dedicated to the preservation of the lake's ecology, and also offers insights into Adamson's life.

Crescent Island Wildlife Sanctuary
Originally the rim of an extinct volcanic crater, as can be clearly seen from the air, Crescent Island encloses the deepest part of Lake Naivasha and supports a variety of wildlife, including waterbuck and giraffe.

VISITORS' CHECKLIST

Road Map B4. 4 km (2 miles) SE of Naivasha town then SW on the Moi South Lake Rd.

KEY

✕	Domestic airport/airstrip
▲	Lodge
△	Campsite
☆	Viewpoint
▬	Major road
═	Minor road
= =	Unpaved motorable road
– –	Park boundary

Naivasha 2 km (1.2 miles)

Nairobi 80 km (50 miles)

Entrance Gate · Elmenteita Weavers

Sanctuary Farm

Karagita

MOI SOUTH LAKE ROAD

Elsa's Gate

al Park

0 km ⟶ 2

0 miles ⟶ 2

Lake Naivasha Country Club
Now a hotel, the club was a popular party venue in the colonial era for the decadent Happy Valley set (see p319).

GETTING AROUND

The lake is encircled by the Moi South and North Lake roads. The southern road is surfaced for most of its length and serviced by regular public transport. The unsurfaced northern road is erratic in quality, and little traffic runs beyond the entrance to Crater Lake Game Sanctuary. Bicycles are available for rent from the many lakeside camps and are a good way to explore the lake's environs, particularly around Hell's Gate. Weather permitting, boat rides offer a chance to spot birdlife. Visitors are advised not to do the 5-km (3-mile) walk from Kongoni to Crater Lake Game Sanctuary alone.

★ **Bird-watching**
Renowned as one of Kenya's ornithological high points, Lake Naivasha supports around 500 bird species, with large flotillas of the handsome great white pelican being particularly conspicuous.

Exploring Lake Naivasha

A bromeliad in bloom, Elsamere gardens

Lake Naivasha is easily reached from Nairobi, although travellers using public transport need to change vehicles in Naivasha town. It is a popular stop on tours to the Masai Mara and an excellent base for freshly landed independent travellers with enough activities to keep them occupied for several days. Access to the lake is along the surfaced Moi South Lake Road, which runs southwest out of Naivasha town along the southern shore for about 30 km (19 miles) before veering northward as far as Kongoni Junction, where it becomes the Moi North Lake Road. This northern road is unsurfaced and erratic in quality, with little traffic, especially after the entrance gate to Crater Lake Game Sanctuary.

A loose herd of wildebeest grazing on the plains of Crescent Island

Southeastern Shore

Fringed by lush papyrus beds and a fever tree forest giving way to drier plains dotted with euphorbia and acacia scrub, the southeastern shore is the closest part of the lake to Naivasha town. The shore is well developed for tourism, with a number of upmarket hotels, self-catering complexes and campsites. Some of the finest bird-watching in Kenya is along this stretch, and most hotels welcome day visitors. Of particular interest is the stately **Lake Naivasha Country Club** *(see p370)*, which opened in 1937 as a staging post for the flying boat service from the UK to South Africa, and stands in massive lakeshore grounds inhabited by hundreds of bird species, as well as monkeys and hippo. This is a good place to call in for afternoon tea. The club also features a

swimming pool, which is open to club members and casual customers. Visitors may easily see some 30 species of water-associated birds in the space of 10 minutes here. For anyone interested in handicrafts, there is **Elmenteita Weavers**, which stocks a wide selection of beautiful handcrafted tapestries, carpets, clothing and much else besides.

Elmenteita Weavers
8 km (5 miles) SW of Naivasha town on Moi South Lake Road. *Tel 050 2030115.* 9am–5pm daily.

Crescent Island Wildlife Sanctuary
9 km (6 miles) SW of Naivasha town on Moi South Lake Rd. *boat trips are offered by all hotels along the lake's southwestern shore.*
Shaped rather like a leaping dolphin, Crescent Island Wildlife Sanctuary consists of

the western rim of an extinct volcanic caldera whose floor is submerged within Naivasha to form the deepest point of the lake at around 20 m (66 ft). A popular half-day outing, the island is connected to the mainland by a marshy causeway that dries up completely when the lake is low. As there are no predatory animals, visitors are permitted to walk freely among the abundant wildlife, which includes giraffe, zebra, waterbuck, Thomson's and Grant's gazelle and buffalo, as well as a profusion of waterbirds.

Elsamere
25 km (14 miles) S of Naivasha town on Moi South Lake Rd. *Tel 020 2050964.* 10am–6pm daily. www.elsamere.com
The home of Joy Adamson *(see p333)* from 1966 until she was murdered in Shaba National Reserve in 1980, Elsamere lies on the southwestern shore of Naivasha, in pretty landscaped gardens surrounded by a fever tree forest. The house is maintained as a museum with its original furnishings intact. The walls are hung with Adamson's paintings of local tribespeople, and several of her personal possessions are on display, along with a selection of first editions of her books in various languages. Visitors with an hour or two to spare can watch a detailed video dedicated to her life and works. A lavish all-day tea buffet

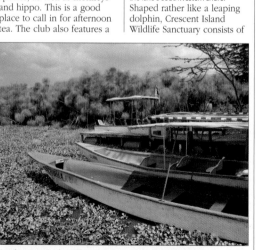

Tour boats moored at Fisherman's Camp, Lake Naivasha

is included in the entrance fee and homely accommodation is also available.

Guided nature trails through the grounds and surrounding woodland are offered here. More than 200 bird species have been recorded in the immediate vicinity, and a troop of the lovely black-and-white colobus monkey passes through the garden frequently, while hippo regularly graze the lawn at night. All proceeds go towards a Field Study Centre established in 1989 to increase ecological awareness among locals and to offer them educational opportunities in the environmental field.

The emerald waters of Green Crater Lake, Crater Lake Game Sanctuary

🏠 Oserian Wildlife Sanctuary

30 km (19 miles) SW of Naivasha town on Moi South Lake Rd. *Tel 050 2020792.* 📷 🚗 🍴 🏊 **www. oserianwildlife.com**

Bordering the road to the west of Lake Naivasha, shadowed by the Mau Escarpment (see p260), is the Oserian Wildlife Sanctuary, a 100-sq-km (40-sq-mile) private sanctuary established in 1996 and serviced by exclusive accommodation units, including the excellent **Chui Lodge** (see p370).

As a connecting game corridor between Hell's Gate National Park and Lake Naivasha, Oserian naturally supports a wide range of wildlife, including leopard, topi, cheetah, buffalo, greater kudu, spotted hyena and various smaller antelope, along with small herds of Grevy's zebra

Luxuriant pastures and forest at the Mau Escarpment

Road sign, Oserian Wildlife Sanctuary

and Beisa oryx introduced from Northern Kenya. A herd of six white rhino, introduced in 1996, had increased to 13 by 2007, and in 2010 all five females were pregnant. A checklist of 300 bird species includes the largest known population of the endangered grey-crested helmet-shrike. Game drives in open vehicles and exciting bush walks are conducted by well-informed guides. Day visitors are not permitted in the sanctuary.

🦌 Lake Oloiden

Past Elsamere, the Moi South Lake Road passes through a wilder landscape of towering forests of fever trees and spiky euphorbia sloping down towards the alkaline shores of Lake Oloiden. Formerly part of Lake Naivasha, Oloiden is now separated from its southwest shore by a stretch of elevated land. There is plenty of wildlife to be seen from the road here. Giraffe are particularly common, gliding serenely through the trees, as well as zebra, waterbuck, impala and various gazelle.

🏠 Crater Lake Game Sanctuary

5 km (3 miles) NE of Oserian on Moi South Lake Rd. *Tel 050 2020613.* 📷 🚗 🍴 🏊

A short distance northeast of Oserian, this 50-sq-km (20-sq-mile) fenced sanctuary is one

of the underrated gems of the Rift Valley region in Kenya. The reserve's centre-piece is a small but spectacular crater lake whose water is shaded green by a dense concentration of the algae *Spirulina* and, with a pH of 11.5, is too alkaline to support fish or any other subaquatic fauna. Local Maasai call the lake Songasoi (Sterile Bull) in reference to its lifelessness, but they also recognise the algae-rich water as having curative properties for cattle with worms and other intestinal problems.

Overlooked by a wonderful tented camp, where day visitors are welcome, the forested crater floor supports a rich assortment of birdlife. Lesser flamingo feed on the lake's algae, with the largest aggregations being present over June–August. Troops of black-and-white colobus monkey are seen from the camp daily, along with vervet monkey, eland, waterbuck and bushbuck. Leopard and spotted hyena are resident in the crater but are seldom observed. An outstanding choice of activities includes guided game walks, bird walks around the crater rim, horseback excursions and game drives by day and night. The property was formerly part of the Ndabibi Estate that belonged to Lady Diana Delamere of *White Mischief* fame, and it contains the hill-top grave where she was buried in 1987 alongside her third and fourth husbands.

Hell's Gate National Park ❽

This most overtly volcanic of Kenyan landscapes is protected within a 68-sq-km (26-sq-mile) national park whose name refers to a dramatic steep-sided valley carved by a former outlet of Lake Naivasha. The region's past geological instability is testified to by ancient lava plugs, steam vents and dormant volcanoes, but it is most popular with visitors for the chance to walk or cycle among big game. Hell's Gate was once famed as a breeding site for the lammergeyer, an endangered cliff-nesting vulture that is now an irregular visitor; however, Egyptian vultures and augur buzzards are often seen soaring above the cliffs. Other cliff-associated wildlife includes rock hyrax, klipspringer and Chanler's mountain reedbuck.

River running through the bottom of Hell's Gate Gorge

★ **Main Cliffs**
The facing pair of 120-m (394-ft) tall basaltic cliffs for which Hell's Gate is named are most beautiful in the late afternoon and early morning, when they are burnished by the golden sunlight.

Ol Karia Gate

Ol Koria Geothermal Power Station

Hobley's Volcano

Elkarian Forest

Ma Pi S

Ranger's Post

Narasha Gate

Oloorkarian Maasai Centre

Ol Njorowa

★ **Cycling Tours**
Hell's Gate is one of the few places in Kenya where it is permitted to cycle or walk unguided through herds of big game – Thomson's gazelle, Grant's gazelle, buffalo, wildebeest, giraffe, impala and eland are all likely to be spotted.

Central Tower
Towering conspicuously above the picnic site at Maiben, the imposing volcanic plug referred to as Central Tower has the more memorable and enigmatic Maasai name of Ol Basta (The Horse). As with other cliffs in the park, it forms a breeding site for several species of raptor.

STAR SIGHTS

★ Main Cliffs

★ Cycling Tours

★ Fischer's Tower

★ Fischer's Tower
The park's most famous landmark is the jagged 25-m (82-ft) tall volcanic plug that stands sentinel over Elsa's Gate. A Maasai tradition, reminiscent of the Biblical story of Job, claims the formation to be a petrified bride who defied tradition by looking back at her home before her wedding.

KEY

✈	Domestic airport/airstrip
🛈	Visitor information
🏕	Campsite
⚜	Viewpoint
= =	Unpaved motorable road
- -	Park boundary

Airstrip
10 km
(6 miles)
✈

Naivasha
20 km (12 miles)

🛈 Elsa's Gate

0 km   2
0 miles   2

🏕

🏕 Twiga Loop

Buffalo Circuit
⚜

Grazing Zebra
The plains zebra is one of the more conspicuous mammals in Hell's Gate. However, buffalo, giraffe, leopard, cheetah and spotted hyena are also resident, as are baboons and rock hyraxes.

Obsidian Cave
Set in a narrow valley at the end of Twiga Loop, Obsidian Cave is named after a type of black igneous rock commonly found in the Rift Valley. This glassy rock, used by early man to create cutting tools, is associated with lava flows that cooled too quickly for crystallisation.

GETTING AROUND
The most rewarding route entails following the 12-km (8-mile) road through the flat valley floor between Elsa's Gate and Maiben, returning the same way. It is a 3-hour walk or 1-hour cycling trip in either direction. A dawn start is recommended for the best game viewing and to avoid over-exposure to the midday sun. It is essential to take along a hat, sunscreen and plenty of drinking water. From Maiben, a 2-km (1-mile) walking trail leads into the lower gorge, which is riddled with steam vents. Cultural tours are available at Oloorkarian Maasai Centre. Visitors with a vehicle could continue west from Maiben to the little-visited Ol Koria Geothermal Power Station, and explore the eastern Twiga Loop.

Kigio Wildlife Conservancy ⑨

Road Map B4. 20 km (12 miles) NW of Naivasha. **Tel** 020 2091026. 🖼️ 🚗 🚣 **www**.kigio.com

Formerly a cattle ranch, this small fenced wildlife conservancy lies alongside the perennial Malewa river a few kilometres before it empties into Lake Naivasha. Its cover of tangled acacia scrub interspersed with open grassland supports a wide variety of naturally occurring and introduced wildlife such as zebra, gazelle, warthog and eland. A herd of eight endangered Rothschild's giraffes translocated from Lake Nakuru in 2003 has since produced several calves. The conservancy is served by the boutique **Malewa Wildlife Lodge** (see p370) fronting onto the Malewa river. The absence of dangerous wildlife means that guided walks are offered along with the usual day and night game drives.

Kariandusi Prehistoric Site ⑩

Road Map B4. 30 km (18 miles) NW of Naivasha. 🖼️ ⭕ 8am–6pm daily. 🖼️ 🚗

Excavated by Louis Leakey (see p349) from 1928 to 1931, Kariandusi was inhabited by Stone Age people between one million and 700,000 years ago, when it probably stood alongside the shore of a vast lake that encompassed the present-day Lakes Naivasha, Elmenteita and Nakuru. Hundreds of bolas, Acheulean hand-axes and several other stone artifacts have been unearthed at the site, which may have served as a workshop for the production of tools. Most of the tools are made from lava rocks sourced in situ, but cutting tools were fashioned from sharp-edged obsidian glass transported from nearby Mount Eburu.

A guided tour of the site takes around half an hour, and requires a fair degree of mobility. The small site museum is also worth a visit.

Secluded Lake Elmenteita, one of the Rift Valley's soda lakes

Alongside a tour of Kariandusi, it is possible to visit a diatomite quarry. Diatomite is a soft silica-based rock composed of a layer of diatoms, microscopic shelled algae that were deposited on the floor of the extinct lake and then compressed to form a chalky strata of crumbly white rock. It is mined for use as a water filter and insecticide.

Stone axe, Kariandusi Prehistoric Site

Lake Elmenteita ⑪

Road Map B4. 3 km (2 miles) E of Kariandusi on the opposite side of the Naivasha–Nakuru Rd. 🖼️ 🍴 🚣

The smallest of Kenya's Rift Valley lakes, the 18-sq-km (7-sq-mile) Elmenteita is also the least visited, since the entire shore lies within the privately-owned Delamere Estate and there is no accommodation with lake frontage. From the main Nakuru Road, there are adequate viewpoints over Elmenteita, as well as to the striking volcanic outcrops that the Maasai refer to as **Elngirigata Ol Morani** (Sleeping Warrior), and the colonials nicknamed "Delamere's Nose", after the British aristocrat who founded the estate in 1906.

For a closer look, visitors can follow the network of motorable tracks running west from the main road to a conspicuous hilltop cairn erected in memory of the Irish settler, the fourth Earl of Enniskillen, in 1929. From here, there are splendid views across the fever tree forest that encloses the lake to the marshy northern shore, whose alkaline algae-rich shallows often host a large concentration of flamingoes. Set back from the lake, the former Enniskillen homestead is now the **Lake Elmenteita Lodge** (see p370), which offers guided walks and horseback trips to the lakeshore.

Nakuru ⑫

Road Map B4. 70 km (44 miles) NW of Naivasha. 🚶 220,000. ✈️ 🚉 🚌

Few visitors spend any time in Kenya's fourth largest city, preferring instead to head straight to the adjacent Lake Nakuru National Park (see pp276–9). However, Nakuru is a pleasant town, and quite attractive in November when its jacaranda-lined avenues bloom purple below a mountainous horizon. It has good facilities, including a number of banks, ATMs, Internet cafés, restaurants, hotels and shops. There is also a very lively daily market in front of the railway station. Students of colonial

A diatomite mine cut into the hillside below Kariandusi Prehistoric Site

An early morning view across Menengai Crater near Nakuru

architecture will find rich pickings in this town around the junction of Moi and Kenyatta avenues. They should also make an effort to seek entry into the members-only **Rift Valley Sport Club**. Built in 1907 on Club Road, this club is still redolent with an Edwardian smoking room atmosphere. Aside from the national park, the town is also a good base for visits to Hyrax Hill and Menengai Crater.

Hyrax Hill Prehistoric Site ⑬

Road Map B4. 4 km (3 miles) E of Nakuru, clearly signposted. **Tel** 051 2217175. ▦ ◯ 8am–6pm daily. ▨ ◪ www.museums.or.ke

Named after the rock hyraxes that once thrived here, this important Neolithic site on the outskirts of Nakuru was discovered by paleontologist Louis Leakey in 1926 and excavated by his wife Mary Leakey starting in 1937. It was inhabited between 5,000 and 2,000 years ago and has thrown up some of the region's oldest Iron Age artifacts, including metal tools and iron bracelets, along with cutting instruments fashioned from glass-like obsidian rock. A more recent occupation, within the last millennium, is represented by the hollowed floors of Sirikwa tribe's cattle pens. More difficult to date are the 13 bao games that have been cut into rocks on the site. Bao is a highly complex game that involves

shifting small pebbles between indentations on a wooden board, or in this case, a rock. It has been played throughout Africa for millennia, so these carved examples could as easily be 100 years old as they might be several thousand.

A Neolithic burial mound on the site contains 19 decapitated male skeletons, probably the remains of warriors who were killed in battle and given a ceremonial burial. A small site **museum** displays various artifacts from this and other Rift Valley sites.

Menengai Crater ⑭

Road Map B4. The rim is 8 km (5 miles) from Nakuru town centre along Menengai Drive and Crater Climb. ◮

The gently sloping mountain on Nakuru's northern horizon is Menengai, a massive shield

volcano that rises to an altitude of 2,278 m (7,474 ft) from the Rift Valley floor. The spectacular nested caldera at its summit is one of the largest in the world, with an average diameter of 8 km (5 miles) and nearly 500 m (1,640 ft) deep in places. The rim is accessible by a rough dirt road out of Nakuru, offering superb views across the crater and back towards Lake Nakuru. The presence of fumaroles, cinder cones and steam vents on the crater floor indicate that the volcano is dormant rather than extinct, although geological evidence suggests it has not erupted within the last 6,000 years, and the relict lava flows on its flanks support a fair cover of vegetation.

The origin of the Maasai name Menengai is disputed. It can be translated as "bottomless pit" or as "place of corpses", since the crater was the site of a violent confrontation between two Maasai clans in the 1850s. More likely, similar to its Kikuyu name Kirima kia Ngoma (Devil's Mountain), Menengai means "place of demons", in reference to the evil spirits associated with the steam vents that rise from the crater floor. Either way, locals treat the crater with suspicion, and narrate numerous stories of people taking suicidal plunges from the rim, wandering lost for days around the floor or being killed by Menengai's malevolent spirits.

Visitors considering walking to the crater are advised to hike in a group as muggings have been reported.

The museum at Hyrax Hill Prehistoric Site, near Nakuru

◁ Flamingoes flying over Lake Nakuru, Lake Nakuru National Park ▷

Lake Nakuru National Park ⑮

Small in size but rich in biodiversity, Lake Nakuru was gazetted as a national park in 1968. It is best known for its birdlife, with more than 500 species listed. The avian highlights are the millions of flamingo that gather along its shore and the pelican that cluster on the southern floodplain. Nakuru is a stronghold for both of Africa's endangered rhino species, and there is probably no better place in East Africa to observe the white rhino. While flamingo and rhino top most visitors' wish list, Nakuru offers excellent bird-watching and game viewing, with all the Big Five present, alongside giraffe, waterbuck, gazelle and baboon.

White pelican at the mouth of the Enderit river

★ Rhino Sightings
A dozen white and 20 black rhino were translocated to Lake Nakuru in the 1990s and have since bred to form populations of around 50 of each species. The white rhino in particular is common on the lake's southern floodplain.

Acacia Forest
The southern part of the park supports a cover of lush acacia woodland dominated by the fever tree, so named because early European settlers associated its jaundiced bark with malaria. This is the best place to look for black rhino, lion, leopard and woodland birds.

0 km ▭▬▬ 3
0 miles ▭▬▬ 3

STAR SIGHTS

★ Rhino Sightings

★ Baboon Cliff

★ Flamingoes on Lake Nakuru

Map labels
B4
NAKURU
Eldoret
150 km (93 miles)
Main Gate
Warden's House • Park HQ
Njoro
Baboon Cliff
Lake N
Pelican Point
Enasoit Hill
Zakalia Gate
Naishi HQ
Makalia Falls

★ Baboon Cliff
The superb Rift Valley scenery of this park is capped by the spectacular Baboon Cliff, which offers panoramic views over the lake and its hinterland.

For hotels and restaurants in this region see pp369–72 and p388

Rothschild's Giraffe

Lake Nakuru is an important stronghold for Rothschild's giraffe, a rare western race that has thrived since its introduction to the park in the 1980s. The Nakuru population of this giraffe is the second largest in the world after Murchison Falls National Park in Uganda, and the largest in Kenya.

VISITORS' CHECKLIST

Road Map B4. 5 km (3 miles) from the city centre along Flamingo Rd on the outskirts of Nakuru town. 🚌 to Nakuru town. 🛈 *051 2217151 (Main Gate).* 🕐 *6am–7pm daily.* 🎫 *KWS smart cards are only available at the Main Gate at the edge of Nakuru town, not at Lanet or Enderit gates.* 🛈 🚻 🍴 🛍 🅰 **www**.kws.go.ke

Euphorbia Forest

The Rift Valley escarpment rising to the southeast of Lake Nakuru supports Kenya's largest concentration of the cactus-like euphorbia, a striking tree-sized succulent whose thick sap is poisonous to most animals.

GETTING AROUND

Lake Nakuru is among the most easily explored of Kenya's national parks. The main entrance gate lies in the north of the park within walking distance of Nakuru town centre. The park's proximity to the town and the good state of its compact circuit of dirt roads means that many travellers visit this park as a half-day trip by taxi, which is sufficient to view the lake and its flamingoes. However, it is better to stay overnight in the park and explore it over several game drives, which greatly improves the odds of seeing scarcer species such as the black rhino, lion and leopard.

KEY

🛈	Visitor information
🔺	Lodge
🅰	Campsite
🌟	Viewpoint
▬	Major road
═	Minor road
= =	Unpaved motorable road
—	Railway
- -	Park boundary
▲	Peak

★ Flamingoes on Lake Nakuru

The flocks of up to two million flamingoes that aggregate periodically on Lake Nakuru were proclaimed "the most fabulous bird spectacle in the world" by renowned American ornithologist Roger Tory Peterson.

Exploring Lake Nakuru National Park

Most people visit Lake Nakuru on an organised safari, often en route between the Masai Mara and Samburu-Buffalo Springs. While the most productive area for a game drive is the open floodplain south of the lake, visitors with more time can also explore the relatively untrammelled southern half of the park. Most roads in the park, although unsurfaced, are in good condition and a 4WD is not required except after exceptional rains. Of Kenya's major wildlife-viewing destinations, Lake Nakuru is the most accessible due to its proximity to Nakuru town, which is easily reached from Nairobi or elsewhere by rail, bus or *matatu*. Once there, it is easy to arrange game drives into the park with taxis or any of several tour operators dotted around the town. As with other reserves in Kenya, walking is forbidden within the park.

Salt encrusted on the shores of Lake Nakuru

🐾 Lake Nakuru

The focal point of the national park is Lake Nakuru itself, whose shallow turquoise-green waters are highly alkaline and support dense concentrations of the algae *Spirulina platensis*. Enclosed by mountains and hills, the lake is fed by three major rivers, the Makalia, Njoro and Enderit. This inflow is supplemented by a series of springs that rise along the shore, treated water from the town sewage works and possibly also some untreated urban effluent. Despite no known outlet, Nakuru's relatively small catchment area has made it the most fluctuation-prone of the Rift Valley lakes, varying in area from 5 to 62 sq km (2 to 24 sq miles). To some extent this follows an annual pattern, with large areas of soda-encrusted flats usually being exposed during the dry seasons (July–October and January–February). However, longer cycles may also come into play; indeed, in the 1990s it was feared that Lake Nakuru

might dry up altogether, but water levels have been consistently higher since the El Niño flooding of 1998.

The most conspicuous feature of Lake Nakuru is the immense concentration of lesser flamingo that thrive in its shallows, consuming algae at an estimated rate of 250 tonnes per hectare (110 tons per acre) of surface area annually. The total flamingo count varies from year to year and season to season, but it frequently stands at about two million,

with lesser flamingo outnumbering greater flamingo a hundredfold. During the 1990s, the recession of the lake's waters caused a flamingo exodus to Bogoria, Elmenteita and elsewhere, but numbers have seldom dropped below 500,000 in recent years. This avian migration is utterly mesmerising to behold, especially when a flock of several hundred birds rises above the general squawk-and-chatter to reveal, in flight, a harmony of bright pink, black-fringed under-wings. Surprisingly, Nakuru is only a feeding ground for this multitude of flamingoes, which breed at Lake Natron in Tanzania, leading to a slight dip in numbers at the Kenyan lakes over October and November.

The alkaline waters of Nakuru do not naturally support any fish, and its ecology has changed significantly following the introduction of an alkali-tolerant tilapia from Lake Magadi in 1953. The tilapia has thrived in this new environment, leading to an influx of piscivorous birds such as the pelicans that congregate at the mouth of Enderit river.

🐾 The Lakeshore Circuit

The park's most popular game drive involves looping along the well-maintained dirt road that encircles Lake Nakuru in its entirety, a distance of around 35 km (22 miles) that takes in several contrasting habitats. Heading clockwise from the Main Gate in the north, the road passes through a patch of dense riparian yellow fever forest

Mother and baby white rhino in Lake Nakuru National Park

Pelicans flying over Lake Nakuru with a flock of flamingoes in the background

that offers restricted views of the lake, but is often good for baboon and waterbuck, and is also a popular haunt for the ever-secretive leopard. After about 5 km (3 miles), a short side road to the right leads to a marshy reed-fringed stretch of shore known as **Hippo Point**. Despite the name, hippo are uncommon here, but buffalo often wallow in the mud, and visitors can easily spot some water-associated birds, ranging from the jewel-like malachite kingfisher to the African spoonbill.

African spoonbill

The road following the eastern lakeshore is too densely wooded to offer many clear views over the lake, but it is superb buffalo country, and the immense euphorbia forest that runs up the rocky slopes south of **Lion Hill Game Lodge** (see p371) is very striking. At the first main junction, visitors should keep to the right, crossing the Enderit river at Muya's causeway – a great spot for ducks, teals, plovers and sandpipers – before emerging on the open grassland that extends along the lake's southern floodplain. This is a great area for white rhino – on a busy day, visitors may see as many as three or four pairs – along with antelope, zebra and other grazers. A rough 2 km (1 mile) track through the grass northeast to the Enderit river mouth reveals large

flocks of lesser and greater flamingo, along with great white pelican, yellow-billed stork and various waders.

The western shore supports a mixture of woodland and grassland habitats, and wildlife is usually plentiful. Another must-do hike along this road is the short but steep ascent to **Baboon Cliff**, which offers a superb view over the lake and surrounding mountains. It is also from here that the full scale of the flamingo phenomenon is most apparent, with the individual birds blending into a solid shimmering pink band that separates the green-blue alkaline water from its bleached rim.

Southern Savannah

The southern half of the park sees far less tourist traffic than the north, particularly in the early morning when visitors may drive for hours without seeing another vehicle. The area can be explored reasonably thoroughly over the space of one lengthy game drive. The flattish terrain here supports a park-like mix of open grassland and acacia woodland, the latter dominated by the lovely fever tree, suggesting a very high water table throughout. The thick woodland of the south is the favoured haunt of the critically endangered black rhino, but in comparison to white rhino, these secretive creatures are very seldom seen.

One landmark worth aiming for is **Enasoit Hill**, a thickly vegetated volcanic plug that rises in splendid isolation from grassland north of the park's Naishi subheadquarters. This is the best area for lions, which are often found hidden away in the tall grass or lazing on one of the rocky perches at the hill's base. Between this outcrop and the subheadquarters is a holding pen for rhinos – usually empty, but occasionally used to hold a sick or soon-to-be translocated individual. About 3 km (2 miles) further south on the park boundary, a gushing waterfall is formed by the Makalia river as it plunges over a 10-m (33-ft) high cliff. The lush woodland here is ideal for birds and monkeys, and is the most likely site in the park for spotting a leopard, in the early morning or late afternoon.

Makalia Falls cascading down the cliff, southern end of Lake Nakuru

Lakes Bogoria and Baringo ⑯

The hot and low-lying Rift Valley north of Nakuru provides a rewarding scenic and ecological taster for the arid badlands that run towards the Ethiopian border. This climatic austerity is, however, alleviated by a pair of beautiful but very different lakes – southerly Lake Bogoria, a saline sump whose alkaline algae-rich waters support high densities of flamingo, and freshwater Lake Baringo, with its prolific crocodile and hippo. The area is a favourite with ornithological tours for its wealth of waterbirds and dry-country specials at the southern limit of their range. It is also of considerable scenic interest – it was after his 1892 visit to the forbidding Baringo cliffs that the Scots geologist John Gregory coined the name Rift Valley.

The red-and-yellow barbet, common around Lake Baringo

Kampi Ya Samaki
Kampi ya Samaki is a small but rapidly growing village on the western shore of Lake Baringo. It boasts several small guesthouses and restaurants, and forms a good base for boat trips.

Marigat is the largest town in the vicinity of Baringo and Bogoria.

★ **Boat Trips**
Crossing by boat to Ol Kokwe – the largest island on Baringo and site of the popular Island Camp – offers a good opportunity to see some of the numerous waterbirds and other creatures that thrive in this freshwater habitat.

[Map labels: C77, Loruk, B4, Rongena Island, Lake Baringo, Hot Sulphur Springs, Baringo Cliffs, Samatian Island, Ol Kokwe Island, Parmalok Island, Marigat, C51, E461, B4, Nakuru 90 km (56 miles)]

STAR SIGHTS

★ Boat Trips

★ Flamingoes on Lake Bogoria

★ Loburu Hot Springs

Hippo Sightings
The largest resident of Lake Baringo, the hippo can be seen – and heard – grazing nocturnally on the lawns of the lakeshore hotels and campsites.

Greater Kudu
Recognisable by its long spiralled horns, the greater kudu can be seen on the shallow shores of Lake Bogoria. This handsome antelope is uncommon elsewhere in Kenya.

VISITORS' CHECKLIST

Road Map B3. Lake Bogoria National Reserve is 111 km (69 miles) N of Nakuru; Lake Baringo is 116 km (72 miles) N of Nakuru via Marigat. 🚌 ℹ 051 2211987 (Lake Bogoria National Reserve). ⏰ 6am–7pm daily for Lake Bogoria National Reserve; 24 hrs for Baringo. 🎫 📷 ✅ *Bogoria only.* 🍴 🛏 *Baringo only.* 🛶 ⛺

KEY

ℹ	Visitor information
🛏	Lodge
⛺	Campsite
▬	Major road
═	Minor road
= =	Unpaved motorable road
- -	Park boundary

Njemps Fisherman
The lakeshore Njemps people of Baringo are close linguistic affiliates of the Maasai but subsist very differently. Their main food is fish caught from light balsa dugout canoes.

★ Flamingoes on Lake Bogoria
Rich in algae, Lake Bogoria almost always supports large flocks of flamingoes, sometimes even outnumbering Lake Nakuru when conditions are suitable.

0 km   5
0 miles   5

GETTING AROUND

Access is along the B4, the road that runs northwards from Nakuru to Kampi Ya Samaki on the shore of Lake Baringo, passing en route through Marigat, the junction town for Lake Bogoria. The road is surfaced for most of its length but a couple of washed-away bridges en route can create impassable obstacles after heavy rain. Normally, however, both lakes are accessible in any saloon car with reasonable clearance. There is also plenty of public transport to Kampi Ya Samaki and Marigat, though not to Bogoria itself.

★ Loburu Hot Springs
The boiling geysers that erupt from the western shore of Bogoria are a reminder of the high level of recent tectonic activity that shaped this stretch of the Kenyan Rift Valley.

Exploring Lakes Bogoria and Baringo

Bogoria peaked as a tourist destination in the mid-1990s, when it took over from Lake Nakuru as the most popular feeding site for the Rift Valley's million-strong flocks of flamingo. Today, flock-size varies greatly on both lakes as the birds move en masse from one lake to the other. There is no transport to the lake itself, but the occasional *matatu* runs to the village of Loboi at the main entrance gate, and it is permitted to walk or cycle unguided from there as far as Loburu hot springs. A 4WD is needed to explore deeper into the park. Baringo has regular minibus connections from Nakuru to the lakeside village of Kampi ya Samaki, and is a regular fixture on organised safaris, especially with ornithologists. Once there, the shore and cliffs can be explored on foot, and boat trips to the lake's islands can be arranged through a hotel.

Jets of sulphuric steam erupt from the geysers at Loburu Hot Springs

🦌 Lake Bogoria National Reserve

This 107-sq-km (42-sq-mile) national reserve protects Lake Bogoria, which lies in a basin-like trench at the base of the sheer 600-m (1,968-ft) high cliffs of the eastern Laikipia Escarpment, along with a band of dry acacia woodland around its circumference. Bogoria was formerly known as Lake Hannington, after the Scottish bishop who first documented its existence in 1885, prior to being killed by the King of Buganda. The reserve was created in 1973, and was included in the Ramsar List of Wetlands of International Importance in 2000.

Extending over 34 sq km (13 sq miles), Lake Bogoria is fed by the Sandai and Emsos rivers, together with at least 200 hot springs spread across three main sites. The water is highly saline and alkaline, thanks to the rapid rate of evaporation and lack of any known outlet, and cannot support fish, crocodiles or hippos. However, it is rich in the *Spirulina* algae fed upon by flocks of lesser flamingo, which are almost always present in large numbers, regularly topping the million mark in the 1990s. The handsome fish eagle is also common around the lakeshore, where – in lieu of fishing – it has acquired the unusual habit of preying and feeding on flamingoes and other large wading birds.

The national reserve protects 18 geysers, the largest such concentration in Africa. The most impressive of these are to be found on the western lakeshore at **Loburu Hot Springs**, where a trio of geysers bursts from below the earth in a haze of sulphuric steam to form an ever mutating series of multihued pools and streams that drain into the lake. It is a thrilling, primeval sight, but one best approached with caution, as the edges of the streams and pools are prone to crumbling, and the seething water has claimed more than one fatality.

Despite its protection in a national reserve, the dense semiarid acacia scrub surrounding the lake clearly suffers from overgrazing, and livestock is more conspicuous than wildlife. With luck, however, the road between the entrance gate and springs should throw up the odd impala, dik-dik or warthog. More alluring is one of Kenya's few remaining populations of greater kudu, a shy but magnificently horned antelope that is most numerous along the eastern shore of the lake, but might also be glimpsed along the northwest shore, especially towards dusk.

Flamingoes flock in large numbers to feed in the shallows of Lake Bogoria

For hotels and restaurants in this region see pp369–72 and p388

The Island Camp's landing point on Ol Kokwe Island

Lake Baringo

Like Bogoria, Lake Baringo is fed by a combination of river water and hot springs, has no surface outlet and experiences high rates of evaporation, but it differs in that its water is fresh rather than saline. First described by the explorer Joseph Thomson in 1883, the lake extends over some 130-170 sq km (50-66 sq miles), depending on the water level, which is less prone to fluctuation than others in the Rift Valley. Baringo is home to the Njemps people, who number fewer than 20,000 and speak the same language as the Maasai and Samburu, but specialise in fishing rather than pastoralism. The Njemps fish in Baringo using small flimsy-looking boats made from balsa sticks grown on the eastern shore.

Njemps fishing boat made of saplings

Situated about halfway up the western shore, the centre of activity on Baringo is the small but rapidly expanding Njemps village of **Kampi ya Samaki**, which translates, somewhat prosaically, as "fishing camp". It is a scruffy little place, but well equipped with budget lodgings and eateries, and the excellent and long-serving **Lake Baringo Club** and **Roberts Campsite** (see p369) lie along the lakeshore immediately to its south.

Lake Baringo is not afforded official protection, but it supports a varied aquatic fauna, most strikingly the outsized crocodiles, gigantic monitor lizards and grunting hippos that are easily seen from the western shore around Kampi ya Samaki. The avian checklist for Baringo and its immediate vicinity stands well above 500, and includes a wide selection of water-associated birds along with dry-country species normally associated with sites further north. An abundance of fish includes one endemic species of tilapia, which is claimed locally to keep the lake's substantial crocodile population too well fed for them to trouble people, although this is an assertion visitors are advised not to put to the test. It is well worth taking a boat out on to the lake to visit some of the islands, of which the largest is **Ol Kokwe**, the peak of an extinct volcano whose slopes are still dotted with hot springs. En route, the boatmen take visitors past papyrus beds teeming with hippos, crocodiles and birds. Usually, they will also lure some of the lake's prodigious fish eagles by throwing fish into the lake for the bird to swoop down and catch as it hits the surface – a thrilling sight and a great opportunity to photograph, although one has to be quick to catch it. A rocky outcrop off Ol Kokwe's shores, known locally as Gibraltar, once hosted a breeding colony of 20 pairs of goliath heron, but while this impressively bulky bird is still common around the lake, breeding has been sporadic in recent years.

Baringo Cliffs

Set back about 2 km (1 mile) west of the lakeshore, this tall basaltic escarpment is easily ascended on foot by following the tar road back from Kampi ya Samaki to the junction with the B4. The view from the top is immense, taking in Baringo in its entirety, as well as the soaring cliffs behind it and the 1,477-m (4,850-ft) high peak of volcanic **Mount Korosi** on the northern lakeshore. Seen here are the dik-dik, klipspringer and rock hyrax. A local guide might well be able to locate a few scorpions and snakes. The walk through the gorge below the cliffs is worth a couple of hours, offering a good chance of sighting the spectacular Verreaux's eagle, along with dry-country specials such as the localised Hemprich's and Jackson's hornbill, white-crested turaco and bristle-crowned starling.

Semiarid and scrub vegetation covers the cliffs near Lake Baringo

WESTERN KENYA

With its mild climate and fertile land, Western Kenya offers a scenery of terraced farmland, bright green tea plantations, verdant forests and lovely hills with panoramic views. The region also has Kenya's share of Lake Victoria, Africa's largest lake, as well as Kakamega forest, the only tropical rainforest in East Africa, and Mount Elgon, the country's second tallest mountain.

Ripe for agricultural use, the hills that rise above the western arm of the Rift Valley have been home to the Luo, Gusii and Luhya peoples for centuries. Today, it is the most densely populated rural region of Kenya. In 1901, the railway reached Port Florence (now Kisumu), and since then the town developed as a port serving the communities around Lake Victoria and is now the country's third largest city. Fast-growing Eldoret with its textile mills and other industries is also increasingly becoming an important regional centre for economic activity and is a major service centre for transport along the busy Nairobi–Kampala Road.

With many hours of sunshine and frequent rain, farming is the mainstay of Western Kenya. Fruits, vegetables and flowers are grown commercially for export to the rest of the country and beyond. Tea was introduced from India during the colonial period and the southern hillsides are blanketed in plantations. Other cash crops include sorghum, maize, wheat, sugar cane and cassava. The entire region is dotted with small, agriculture-orientated service towns and industries, such as paper mills and sugar-processing plants.

Western Kenya receives few visitors and as such accommodation and facilities are more basic here than in other parts of the country. Nevertheless, a loop through Western Kenya's tranquil forests, gentle hills and patchwork of fields gives real insight into the country's rural way of life. Attractions here include a couple of interesting museums depicting the lives of the local people and archaeological finds in the area, plus forested parks and reserves that harbour birds, monkeys and butterflies. Around Lake Victoria, there are small fishing villages where local canoes can be hired to explore the papyrus reed beds to see hippos and birds.

A view of Koitobos Peak, the summit of Mount Elgon, Mount Elgon National Park

A lush expanse of tropical rainforest broken by grassland and acacia scrub, Kakamega Forest

Exploring Western Kenya

Some 50 km (31 miles) northwest of Nakuru, the centre of
Kenya's tea industry lies in the undulating hills around Kericho
and Kisii in the Rift Valley. To the north of this area are Kisumu,
the lakeside capital of the region, and Kakamega Forest National
Reserve, which harbours a beautiful canopy of giant trees and
tangled vines full of birds and small mammals. Further north
are Kitale, the springboard town to hiking in the Cherangani
Hills, Mount Elgon National Park, where the extinct volcano
straddles the border with Uganda, and Saiwa Swamp National
Park, which protects the rare sitatunga antelope. Also popular
are drives through the panoramic Tugen Hills and Kerio Valley
and, more to the west, through Kapsabet and Nandi Hills.

SIGHTS AT A GLANCE

Towns and Cities
Eldoret **4**
Homa Bay **16**
Kabarnet **2**
Kakamega **11**
Kapenguria **8**
Kendu Bay and Simbi
  Nyaima **15**
Kericho **23**
Kisii **21**
Kisumu pp298–9 **13**
Kitale **5**
Tabaka **22**

Areas of Natural Beauty
Chagaik Dam and
  Arboretum **24**
Cherangani Hills **9**
Kapsabet and Nandi Hills **10**
Kingwal Swamp **3**

Tours
*Tugen Hills and
  Kerio Valley Drive p288* **1**

National Parks and Reserves
*Kakamega Forest National
  Reserve pp294–7* **12**
Mount Elgon National Park **6**
Ruma National Park **19**
Saiwa Swamp National Park **7**

Lakes and Islands
Lake Victoria pp302–303 **14**
Mfangano Island **17**
Rusinga Island **18**

Archaeological Sites
and Museums
Thimlich Ohinga **20**

The tropical rainforest at Kakamega Forest National Reserve

Kongelai
Ortum
B4
Lomut
Chipkorniswa
Sondang 3,206 m
nyarkwat
A1
CHERANGANI HILLS
Chemnirot 3,581 m
Kolowa
Kapedo
Chepbotet 3,369 m
9
Kalelaigelat 3,350 m
8 🏛
KAPENGURIA
Kaibichbich
Tot
B4
Kito Pass
toboss
Kitum Cave
SAIWA SWAMP
7 NATIONAL PARK
Labot
Chepkum
Nginyang
ITALE 5
🏛
C48
Chepkesin
Kiminini
Cherangani
Cheptongei
B4
Bartabwa
koiwa
Moiban
Bugar
Kamnarok National Reserve
C42
B2
C50
Iten
Nzoia
Soy
C51
Bartolimo
Lake Baringo
Turbo
A104
ye
Biretwo
hepterwai
ELDORET 4
KABARNET
Marigat
Awanza
TUGEN HILLS AND KERIO VALLEY DRIVE
1
2 🏛
C51
KINGWAL
3
MEGA
SWAMP
Chebloch
C54
Cheplembus
Nyaru

SEE ALSO

• *Where to Stay* pp372–4

• *Where to Eat* pp388–9

AMEGA REST IONAL SERVE
12
KAPSABET AND
10 NANDI HILLS
Ainabkoi
Kaputi 2,799 m
C36
Ndurio
Nabkoi
C37
Nyando
Nandi Hills
Equator
JMU
C34
Songhor
Tinderet 2,640 m
Limute 2,565 m
Muhoroni
Nakuru
Awasi
A1
B1
Tunnel
C35
B1
Kapsoit
CHAGAIK DAM
24 AND ARBORETUM
sa
Sondu
C25
23
ondu
KERICHO
Chemosit
Itare
C23
Litein
anga
Yaganek
eumbu
B3
C15
Keroka
Narok
Ndanai

Sitatunga antelope in Saiwa Swamp National Park

KEY

━━ Major road

═══ Minor road

▪▪▪ Untarred major road

═ ═ ═ Untarred minor road

--- 4WD track

━━ Scenic route

━━ Major railway

━━ Minor railway

✕ Pass

△ Peak

▨▨▨ International border

0 km   25

0 miles   25

GETTING AROUND

Daily scheduled domestic flights operate between Nairobi and both Kisumu and Eldoret. The network of roads is extensive and most roads linking the towns are tarred and in fairly good condition with few potholes. Local *matatus* run between the settlements along the main roads, and long distance buses from Nairobi and Nakuru serve the principal towns. Few tour operators run scheduled tours to the region, but tailor-made trips can be arranged.

Tugen Hills and Kerio Valley Drive ❶

Heading into Western Kenya, the Nakuru to Eldoret
route offers panoramic views of the Rift Valley. The
steep hills and escarpments are dotted with neat
terraced smallholdings, dense pine, cedar and giant
gum forests and cascading waterfalls. Near Marigat,
the road climbs through the rolling Tugen Hills to
Kabarnet on a series of switchbacks. It then drops
dizzyingly 1,000 m (3,280 ft) into the dramatic Kerio
Valley, also dubbed Kenya's Grand Canyon. Across
the Kerio river, the road zigzags up to Elgeyo
Escarpment offering sweeping views of the valley,
and flattens out through pine plantations to Eldoret.

TIPS FOR DRIVERS

Starting point: The C51 begins
at Marigat, near Lake Baringo.
Length: 119 km (74 miles) from
Marigat to Eldoret.
Road conditions: The C51 is in
good condition, but the detour to
Lake Kamnarok requires a 4WD.

KEY

☒ Domestic airport

☆ Viewpoint

▬ Major road

▭ Minor road

── Railway

── Park boundary

Kerio View ⑥
This popular bar and restaurant is an ideal
lunch stop and its wide glass frontage offers
a splendid broad view of Kerio Valley and
the Tugen Hills.

Iten ⑤
From Tambach, the road
winds up through a series
of hairpin bends to Iten, a
tiny village on the Elgeyo
Escarpment, with a pan-
oramic view of the valley.

Torok Falls ④
A short distance from the village of
Biretwo, spectacular views of Torok
Falls can be had from the highway.
The falls originate high up on the
Elgeyo Escarpment and are about
a half-day's hike from the C51.

**Lake Kamnarok and Kerio
Valley National Reserves** ②
The two reserves lie along
the Kerio river. The dry
thorn bush hosts wild-
life, while various
waterbirds inhabit
Lake Kamnarok.

0 km   6

0 miles   6

Chebloch Gorge ③
The Kerio river
plunges through a
narrow fissure of
rock into the steep-
sided Chebloch
Gorge beyond the
point where the C51
crosses the river.

Tugen Hills ①
The hills run north to south for about
100 km (65 miles). A viewpoint after
the Kabarnet road's last hairpin bend
offers stunning views of Lake Baringo.

The colonial façade of the Kabarnet Museum

Kabarnet ❷

Road Map B4. 94 km (58 miles) N of Nakuru. 9,600.

The little town of Kabarnet sits on the eastern tree-clad edge of the plunging Kerio Valley. Despite its scenic location, it is little more than a tiny administrative centre for the Baringo district, with a bank, a clutch of shops and a petrol station. Its claim to fame is that it is the hometown of former president Daniel arap Moi.

Set in lush botanical gardens with labelled trees and shrubs, **Kabarnet Museum** is worth stopping for. Housed in what used to be the District Commissioner's residence, the small museum's four galleries have displays highlighting the culture of the local Samburu, Keiyo, Pokot, Marakwet and Nandi peoples, and exhibits on the area's colonial history. The museum also provides information about nearby Lake Baringo (see pp280–83).

🏛 **Kabarnet Museum**
Hospital Rd. **Tel** 053 21221.
◷ 8am–6pm daily.
www.museums.or.ke

Kingwal Swamp ❸

Road Map B4. 24 km (16 miles) S of Eldoret.

Between Kasabet and Eldoret the road skims the eastern edge of an unprotected wetland area, the Kingwal Swamp, that is home to a variety of wildlife. Hemmed in on all sides by farms and cereal fields, the swamp stretches across some 40 hectares (100 acres) of

valley floor and is a refuge for the second-largest population in Kenya of the extremely rare semiaquatic sitatunga antelope (see p129). Kenya's largest population of sitatunga is found in Saiwa Swamp National Park (see pp290–91). Visitors can spot these beautiful animals late in the evening or early in the morning when they emerge to graze. The middle of Kingwal Swamp is dense with beautiful papyrus and is also a good site for bird-watching. Swamp-adapted *Syzygium* (myrtle) trees have been planted on the fringes of the swamp to limit encroachment of agriculture. However, large areas of former swampland have already been planted with Eucalyptus trees to drain the land for agriculture, which is leading to a loss of habitat.

Eldoret ❹

Road Map B4. 53 km (33 miles) W of Kabarnet on the C51. 194,000. Uganda Hwy.

Western Kenya's largest and most prosperous town, Eldoret straddles the Kenya–Uganda

Highway. The town has an unusual history. It was originally founded in 1908 by a group of Voortrekers from South Africa, emigrants who belonged to the farming community of Cape Colony. This particular group had sailed to Mombasa and then trekked inland. The place where they settled was dubbed "64" as it was 64 miles from the newly built Uganda Railway railhead at Kibigori. In 1910, it was renamed Eldoret after the Maasai *eldore* (stony river), a reference to the nearby Sosiani river.

Eldoret has gained importance as a busy service centre for goods trucks heading to Kampala and beyond, with many factories and plants scattered around town for light industries as diverse as textiles, tanning, woollen mills and mushroom cultivation. The town is also the collection and distribution point for much of the fresh produce grown in Western Kenya and the ornamental flowers and exotic vegetables that are exported from Eldoret Airport. **Moi University** and its training hospital are also located here, giving the town a fairly youthful feel. Like other Western Kenyan towns, Eldoret has produced many successful Kenyan athletes.

There are few attractions in Eldoret, and the architecture of multistorey breeze block buildings is unremarkable, but the town centre boasts prolific banks, shops, Internet cafés, petrol stations, trading stores and all the other facilities expected of a town.

A busy street in the town centre, Eldoret

Farmland near Kitale resplendent with sunflowers

Kitale ❺

Road Map A3. 69 km (43 miles) NW of Eldoret. 🏘 63,250. ✈ 🚌

Founded in 1920 by white settlers and expanded when the railway arrived here in 1925, Kitale is an agricultural town surrounded by a patchwork of burnt-orange fields and acres of greenhouses that are used to grow flowers, which are exported to Europe. With a clutch of supermarkets and banks, it is the last sizable settlement before the A1 highway heads into the remote north.

Set in a patch of indigenous riverine tropical forest, the **Kitale Museum** is well worth a visit. The museum has natural history and ethnographical displays, including replicas of traditional homesteads of the Bukusu, Luo, Turkana, Maasai and Elgon peoples. The museum sells locally made handicrafts. There is also an agroforestry centre, set up to educate local farmers, and a snake park. An interesting nature trail leads to a number of picnic spots in the forest, which is home to the rare De Brazza's monkey, and which offers a good chance of spotting black-and-white colobus monkeys and a number of birds.

Antelope, Kitale Museum

🏛 **Kitale Museum**
1 km (half a mile) SE of the bus station on Main St. **Tel** 054 30996. 🕐 8am–6pm daily. 🖼 📷

Mount Elgon National Park ❻

Road Map A3. 11 km (7 miles) NW of Kitale. 🖼 🛏 ⛺ www.kws.go.ke

With a huge intact caldera and distinctive flat top, Mount Elgon straddles the Kenya-Uganda border. Despite its 4,321-m (14,177-ft) high Wagagai peak being located in Uganda, it is recognised as Kenya's second tallest mountain. From Kenya, the mountain can be visited in the 169-sq-km (65-sq-mile) Mount Elgon National Park, a wild and intact wilderness with breathtaking scenery of cliffs, caves, waterfalls, gorges and impressive mountain peaks. The park's vegetation varies with altitude and the lower slopes feature thick-canopied forests of giant Elgon teak and cedar trees, while higher altitudes support bamboo zones,

Entrance to Kitum Cave surrounded by forest, Mount Elgon National Park

tussock grasslands, heath moorlands and unusual vegetation such as the giant lobelia. The park provides habitat to elephant, buffalo, leopard, several species of monkeys, giant forest hog, various types of antelope and over 240 species of birds. There are various vehicle circuits and three short self-guided nature trails to Kitum Cave, Makingeni Cave and the Elephant Bluff, best undertaken by 4WD.

Mount Elgon also offers excellent climbing and trekking opportunities. No special climbing gear is required, except for warm clothes, and the park can also arrange for a guide. The 4,155-m (13,632-ft) high Koitobos peak, the highest on the Kenyan side, can be hiked in about 2 hours from the road's end.

Saiwa Swamp National Park ❼

Road Map B3. 22 km (14 miles) NE of Kitale. 🕐 6.30am–6pm daily. 🖼 ⛺ www.kws.go.ke

Located to the north of Kitale and below the Cherangani Hills, the tiny 3-sq-km (1-sq-mile) Saiwa Swamp National Park is the smallest in Kenya. It was established to protect the rare semiaquatic sitatunga antelope, distinguished by its long, splayed hooves, which are well adapted for walking through the muddy, vegetated swamp fed by the Saiwa river. The park features riverine forest and patches of grassland dotted with acacia trees, and is also home to De Brazza's and black-and-white colobus monkeys, otter, bushbuck and grey duiker. Only accessible on foot, the park has well-maintained trails, plus four observation towers and a basic campsite at the gate.

Kapenguria **8**

Road Map B3. 40 km (25 miles) N of Kitale. 🚌 🏛 *13,000.*

Lying in an area of steep hills and grazing lands, Kapenguria is a small town of red dusty streets, squat buildings with corrugated tin roofs and little infrastructure. The road from Kitale is tarred and in good condition, but beyond Kapenguria it drops down a steep escarpment with sharp bends and potholes. A 4WD is essential to head anywhere further north.

The town rose to fame during Kenya's struggle for independence, when, in 1952, the colonial authorities arrested six leading Kenyan nationalists here, including Jomo Kenyatta *(see p55)*. They became known as the Kapenguria Six and were tried and imprisoned in Kapenguria for being involved in the Mau Mau Rebellion *(see pp52–3)*. They were finally released in 1961 and Kenyatta became president of newly independent Kenya in 1963. Today, the one-storey prison they were held in is the small **Kapenguria Museum**. Displays include photographs, documents and

The verdant slopes of the Cherangani Hills

books relating to the era and visitors can also look at Kenyatta's small cell. There is a very good display of photographs of the Pokot people, who farm millet and sorghum on the Cherangani foothills, and are shown in their traditional dress. There is also a mock-up of a Pokot homestead outside the museum.

🏛 **Kapenguria Museum**
Near Kapenguria district offices.
🕙 9am–6pm daily. 🖼 📷
www.museums.or.ke

Cherangani Hills **9**

Road Map B3. 90 km (56 miles) NE of Kitale.

To the north of Kapenguria, the dramatic and lofty peaks of the Cherangani Hills form a natural barrier between the fertile western highlands and the stony deserts in Northern Kenya. The highest point is

the 3,517-m (11,539-ft) Nagen Peak in the north of the range, which is the fourth highest mountain in Kenya. The hills are riddled with small villages, dirt tracks and streams. Most of the slopes are undemanding at high altitude, and the verdant hills offer perfect walking country for self-sufficient and adventurous hikers.

Wild, closed-canopy forest, tracts of bamboo, alpine meadows and heath-covered moorland can be found on the higher slopes. The birdlife here is rich and varied and lammergeyers are often seen drifting on the thermals.

There are numerous tracks into the hills, some of them accessible by vehicle, but most are rough and tortuously steep, including the paved A1 highway that runs north through the region. Visitors can book a guided tour with a safari company specialising in treks in this region.

diorama depicting the Pokot way of life, Kapenguria Museum

SALT MINING ELEPHANTS OF MOUNT ELGON

Mount Elgon National Park features a series of four caves – Kitum, Makingeni, Chepnyalil and Ngwarisha. The caves are best known for their frequent night visitors of convoys of elephants that come to mine and lick the caves for salt – they

Elephants mining for salt in Mount Elgon National Park

use their tusks to gouge out the rich deposits. With its steep slopes and heavy rainfall, much of Elgon's salts have been leached away. The cave walls are the most concentrated salt source in the area and by bringing their calves to the caves, the salt mining technique is passed on to the next generation.

The lush slopes of Nandi Hills near Kapsabet, carpeted by tea plantations

Kapsabet and Nandi Hills ❿

Road Map B4. 48 km (30 miles) SW of Eldoret. ✈ 🚌

A small regional settlement, Kapsabet is a one-street town of mud homes and a row of concrete traders' buildings. The region is famed for producing some of Kenya's most successful long-distance runners, and in the 1930s, it was here that ex-President Moi went to junior school.

Just to the west is **South Nandi Forest**, a patch of canopy forest that was once contiguous with Kakamega Forest National Reserve *(see pp294–7)*. South Nandi and Kakamega are still no more than a few miles apart at their closest points.

At the tiny settlement of Nandi Hills, to the south of Kapsabet, the old British Nandi Bears Golf Club is one of the most scenic in the country and hosts several annual golf tournaments. It has a colonial clubhouse dating from 1928 and wide fairways that provide sweeping views over the hills.

The Nandi Hills are famous as the site where Nandi warriors clashed with British colonial forces over the building of the Lunatic Line *(see p299)*. The altitude range of 1,800–2,500 m (5,900–8,200 ft), a cool and wet climate and rich volcanic soil create the ideal environment for growing tea. Verdant plantations blanket the upper slopes while sugar cane grows on the valley floors.

Kakamega ⓫

Road Map A4. 106 km (66 miles) SW of Eldoret. 🚶 *73,000*. ✈ 🚌

The small town of Kakamega lies in green fertile country and serves as a springboard to the nearby Kakamega Forest National Reserve. In the 1930s, the town briefly attracted a mini-gold rush of prospectors, but not enough gold was found to sustain a mining industry. About 3 km (2 miles) south, on the Kakamega–Kisumu Road, is the **Weeping Stone of Shinyalu**. A large granite boulder resting on top of a pillar of rocks that rises to a height of 8 m (26 ft), it resembles a solemn head falling on weary shoulders. From the top a constant stream of spring water flows down the sides and the stone is stained from many years of "weeping".

Kakamega is the heartland of the Luhya people *(see p26)*, who are known for their traditional bullfighting. Spurred on by horn-blowing, excited supporters, the two bulls lock horns and fight until one turns and runs. The victorious bull's owner wins money and a good deal of local gambling rests on the outcome.

NANDI BEAR

Nandi and Tugen legends speak of the Nandi Bear – a large, hairy carnivorous animal that can walk upright, with high shoulders and a sloping back. It is believed to attack livestock during the night and only eats the heads of its victims. There were many reputed sightings of the "bear" during the 1800–1900s. Early colonial settlers also claimed to have encountered the beast, giving further credence to the myth. In reality, the hyena is the most likely candidate for the Nandi Bear's true identity. Although hyenas are scavengers by nature, they are known to occasionally attack animals. However, local people would have recognised the hyena, and their descriptions of the bear do not match the physical attributes of a hyena. Perhaps the Nandi Bear could be a type of undiscovered giant hyena that has still not been identified or even a prehistoric survivor – the myth lives on.

The giant Weeping Stone of Shinyalu, just south of Kakamega

The Runners of Western Kenya

Kenya has more world-record holders and Olympic medallists in athletics than any other country. Over the last 40 years, Kenyans, especially the Kalenjin of Western Kenya, have become the world's most successful long- and middle-distance runners in various international track events.

Many highly successful long-distance runners have been born in or near Kapsabet, including Bernard Lagat, Peter Rono, Martin Lei and Nancy Langat. Their achievements have been so extraordinary that they have fascinated sports physiologists and sociologists around the world.

SETTING THE PACE
Running exceedingly long distances at high altitudes, a diet rich in carbohydrates as well as conducive landscape and climate are believed to be among the reasons behind the powerful presence of Kenyan athletes in world track and field events.

Runners in training *can be seen pounding along the dirt roads or climbing the hills in the tea plantations of Western Kenya. Former Kenyan athletes have opened several high-altitude training camps that also attract international athletes.*

Pamela Jelimo and Janeth Busienei, *both from villages around Kapsabet, clinched the gold and silver medals respectively in the women's 800 metres at the Beijing 2008 Olympics.*

Kenya's Wilfred Bungei, *from Kabirirsang near Kapsabet, won the gold in the men's 800 metres at the 2008 Olympics, while Asbel Kiprop from Kaptinga won the silver in the men's 1,500 metres. Kenya won a total of 14 medals at the Beijing Olympics.*

The history of Kalenjin long-distance running *began at the 1968 Olympics in Mexico City when Kipchoge Keino won the gold medal for the 1,500 metres event. Despite suffering acute stomach pains, Kipchoge won by a 20-m (66-ft) lead, and a Kenyan athletic dynasty was born.*

Kakamega Forest National Reserve ⓬

The only tropical forest left in Kenya, Kakamega Forest National Reserve is a 230-sq-km (90-sq-mile) swath of beautiful rainforest in the heart of an intensively culti-vated agricultural region. The forest once joined the Guineo-Congolan equatorial belt of forest that covered all the land from the Rift Valley to the Atlantic Ocean some 400 years ago. Protected since the 1930s, Kakamega is presently managed by both the Kenya Wildlife Service (KWS) and a community forestry group. The forest features towering ancient hardwood trees, tangled vines and a dense and richly green forest floor of ferns and orchids. It is inhabited by a diverse range of birds, insects, butterflies and small mammals.

A path running through lush vegetation, Kakamega Forest

★ Buyangu Viewpoint

A 4-km (2-mile) drive from the forest station, Buyangu Hill gives a bird's-eye view of the forest canopy. On a clear day there are views over the Nandi Hills and Mount Elgon in the north.

GETTING AROUND

There are two gates to the park – Buyangu in the north and Isecheno in the south. Both offer basic campsites and accommodation. Two dirt roads link the A1 main road to the C39 through the southern part of the forest. The park is best explored on foot and trails vary in length from 1 km (half a mile) to 7 km (4 miles). The Isiukhu Trail connects Isecheno to Isiukhu Falls. Driving is also an option, although roads are rough and the engine noise can scare the wildlife away. Rainfall is heaviest in April and May; January and February are the driest months.

Hammer-headed Fruit Bats
Resident in Kakamega Forest, these nocturnal animals are the largest bats in Africa, with a wing span just under 1 m (3 ft).

KEY

✈	Domestic airport/airstrip
ℹ	Visitor information
🏠	Lodge
⬛	Campsite
☀	Viewpoint
▬	Major road
═	Minor road
= =	Unpaved motorable road
- -	Trail
- -	Park boundary
▲	Peak

STAR SIGHTS

★ Buyangu Viewpoint

★ Isiukhu Falls

★ Isecheno Forest Station

For hotels and restaurants in this region see pp372–4 and pp388–9

Kisere Forest Reserve
Separated from the main reserve, Kisere is a dense area of ancient trees, including the giant Elgon olive, and is home to the exceedingly rare De Brazza's monkey.

VISITORS' CHECKLIST

Road Map A3. Buyangu Gate in the northern part of the forest is 2 km (1.2 miles) off the main A1 road; the turn-off is 15 km (9 miles) N of Kakamega town. Isecheno Gate in the south is 15 km (9 miles) off the A1 from Kakamega town via Shinyalu village. 🛈 056 30603 (KWS HQ). ❎ ⭘ 6am–7pm daily. 🗺 🎫 🥾 Ⓐ

★ Isiukhu Falls
An easy excursion from the Kenya Wildlife Service Forest Station at Buyangu, the Isiukhu Falls are best seen during the rainy season when a torrent of foamy water spills down a rocky escarpment.

★ Isecheno Forest Station
A number of labyrinthine jungle trails emanate from this forest station. It offers the services of self-trained guides who take visitors along the trails under the beautiful canopy. The indigenous trees are identified by signs with their local and Latin names.

0 km   3

0 miles   3

Gaboon Vipers
This brown, patterned sluggish snake is among many rare species of reptiles found in Kakamega reserve.

FOREST BIRDS OF WESTERN KENYA

Kakamega Forest Reserve is well known for its diverse birdlife. Over 300 species of birds, including some very rare ones, have been identified in the reserve. These include the grey parrot, great blue turaco, blue-headed bee-eater, chestnut wattle-eye and black-and-white casqued hornbill. Other birds seen in this region include cuckoos, nightjars, owls, kingfishers, tawny eagles and hornbills.

Casqued hornbill

African grey parrot

Blue-headed bee-eater

Exploring Kakamega Forest National Reserve

A superb stretch of virgin tropical forest, Kakamega Forest is easily accessed from Kakamega town along the Kakamega–Eldoret Highway. The southern part of the forest is accessed at Isecheno by a dirt road, which can be slippery when wet, going 15 km (9 miles) east from Kakamega along the A1 via the village of Shinyalu. The reserve has two forest stations – the KWS station at Buyangu in the north of the forest and the Kakamega Environmental Education Programme (KEEP) at Isecheno that administers the southern part of the reserve. Although some of the forest tracks are car-worthy, the best way to explore the beauty of the forest is on foot.

Buyangu viewpoint across Kakamega Forest National Reserve

Buyangu

19 km (12 miles) NE of Kakamega. **i** 056 30603 (KWS headquarters).

On the A1, a turn-off to the right signposted Kakamega Forest National Reserve leads a further 3 km (2 miles) to the KWS Forest Station at Buyangu, the northern area of the forest. A number of paths through the cool of the forest begin just beyond the forest station, where it is also possible to hire a guide. The climate is generally drier here than further south, such that there is a greater diversity of habitat, which includes areas of scrub, marshland and young and ancient forest. The oldest part of the forest, this area supports diverse birdlife such as great blue turacos and a variety of hornbills as well as black-and-white colobus and red-tailed monkeys. The many colossal trees here bear plaques that invite visitors to guess their girth, and the correct answers are inscribed behind the trees.

A 5-km (3-mile) walk from the KWS Forest Station, the **Buyangu Hill** viewpoint is a worthwhile excursion. A short scramble to the top leads to a viewpoint offering spectacular panoramic views across the top of Kakamega's canopy of trees and east to the Nandi Escarpment. This is the highest point in the forest, and on a clear day it offers great views of Mount Elgon to the north. At the top is a picnic site with a thatched shade.

Another popular excursion from the forest station is to **Isiukhu Falls**, a 7-km (4-mile) walk following the Isiukhu river. The falls themselves are rather feeble, except after rain, but the walk goes under some lush canopies of foliage.

Isecheno

18 km (11 miles) SE of Kakamega via Shinyalu village. **forest road** from Chepsonoi on the C39. **www**.columbia.edu/cu/e3b/conservation/KEEP

The southern region of Kakamega Forest, Isecheno is maintained by the community-based KEEP, which operates a forest station here. KEEP is instrumental in protecting the forest and educating the local population about ecological awareness, conservation and tree planting. It provides extensive information about the different animal and plant species found in the forest reserve. A plant nursery here produces seedlings used to patch the unnecessary glades in the forest, and also sells medicinal plants to the local communities. A small butterfly farm has been set up to breed local butterflies.

At the forest station, visitors can hire guides who are know-ledgeable and well versed in the Latin names of the fascinating flora and fauna of the reserve, and who are especially good at pointing out birds in the high trees. If staying overnight, the station also offers night walks along the many trails with flashlights to locate nocturnal creatures.

Not far from Isecheno, **Lirhanda Hill** rises steeply over the lush canopy of trees and provides excellent views of the surrounding countryside and forest. The trail to the hill starts near the **Rondo Retreat** guesthouse (see p373) on the road towards Chepsonoi. Visitors starting from the forest station will need approximately 2 hours to get there.

The tree nursery at the KEEP headquarters, Isecheno

Flora and Fauna of Kakamega

Kenya's only vestige of equatorial rainforest, Kakamega harbours an immense biodiversity. This richly tropical environment is home to a variety of small mammals, birds, primates, insects and reptiles, some of which are not seen elsewhere in East Africa. The forest has an estimated 380 species of woody trees, vines, shrubs, ferns, herbs and flowers. Some 360 species of birds have been identified, 36 of which are

A cinnamon chested bee-eater

endemic to the forest. There are over 400 species of butterflies – representing 45 per cent of all recorded butterflies in Kenya – as well as the shiny black goliath beetle, various ants, leaf insects, spiders and dragonflies. Although shy and rarely seen, there are as many as 40 species of snakes as well as numerous lizard and frog species. The wealth of forest mammals includes seven species of primates.

FLORA

The forest glade is home to ferns and flowering plants such as flame lilies and dracaenas. The deeper forest comprises dense tracts of ancient hardwood trees such as Elgon teak.

The forest floor is resplendent with many conspicuous flowers and orchids.

Figs are parasitic trees that start growing on branches of other trees from seeds left by birds or fruit bats.

African pencil cedars can reach upwards of 30 m (98 ft) and are often festooned with wild orchids.

FAUNA

Kakamega's best-known primates are the black-and-white colobus, bushbaby and red-tailed and blue monkeys. Also commonly seen are the duiker, dik-dik, genet, serval, flying squirrels and bats. The forest floor shelters reptiles such as the Gabon viper and monitor lizard.

The charaxe, *Africa's fastest flying butterfly, feeds off fallen fruit.*

The red-tailed monkey *stores food in its cheek pouches while it travels through the forest.*

The potto *is a large nocturnal sloth-like creature unique to rainforests. It sleeps in the canopy during the day and rarely descends to the forest floor.*

The goliath beetle *can grow as big as a man's hand and feeds mainly on tree sap and fruit.*

Nile monitor lizards *can grow up to 2 m (7 ft) in length, and live off the forest's birds and eggs, which they obtain by stealing nests.*

Kisumu ⑱

A Luo sailing canoe at Dunga

Kenya's third largest town and the administrative centre for Western Kenya, Kisumu lies on the edge of Lake Victoria. It began as a railhead known as Port Florence in 1901, and grew steadily into a busy port with connections to other ports in Uganda and Tanzania. Since the 1970s, however, there has been a decline in trade by boat across the lake – road transport being more favoured – and Kisumu is not as prosperous as it once was. One delightful feature of Kisumu is the many thousands of *boda-bodas* (bicycle taxis) that throng the streets. These are fun to ride, but first-timers need to be cautious. Dunga village, just to the south, offers the best views of the lake, its hippo and rich birdlife.

🏛 Kisumu Museum
Nairobi Rd. **Tel** *057 2020332.*
⬤ *9am–5pm daily.* 🎟 🎥
www.museums.or.ke

An interesting regional museum dedicated to the Luo, Luhya, Kipsigis and Nandi peoples, this is set in a pretty patch of greenery. The trees are labelled, and this is a good place to look out for weavers' nests hanging precariously from branches.

The central hall of the museum has a number of traditional artifacts such as jewellery, cooking pots and utensils, fishing baskets, pipes and weapons. There are also stuffed animals and birds, the most impressive of which is a lion pouncing on a wildebeest.

The grounds house a snake house containing a few of Kenya's most poisonous snakes behind glass, such as

A graphic display of predator-prey interaction, Kisumu Museum

Gaboon vipers, cobras and mambas from Kakamega Forest, while the tiny aquarium has a few small fish from Lake Victoria, such as tilapia. There are also several small fenced ponds containing Nile crocodiles, which are fed on Monday afternoons.

🛒 Market
Nairobi Road, off Jomo Kenyatta Ave.
⬤ *8am–6pm daily.*

Kisumu is home to Western Kenya's largest market, which sells just about anything from flip flops and fish to fresh produce and furniture. Stalls display colourful pyramids of fruits and vegetables, and tilapia fish from the lake, which are split open, salted and dried in the sun.

Although a tad chaotic, the market is surprisingly well organised, with similar items being clumped together in the same lanes. Locally produced sisal rope, clay pots and soapstone souvenirs are popular here. The *mitumba* (second-hand clothes) section of the market consists of clothes sent to East Africa from the USA, Europe and the Far East, so visitors will find plenty of familiar brands and some designer labels as well.

🕌 Jamia Mosque
Otieno Oyoo Street.

The first Muslims arrived in Kisumu with the railway, mostly as indentured labour from India, and many stayed on to become traders. The Railway Mosque was built by them in 1905, but as Arabian traders arrived from the coast and local Africans converted to Islam, the Railway Mosque was felt to be too small and was replaced by the Jamia Mosque. Built in 1919, this features two elegant minarets, three impressive silver

The centre of Kisumu, one of Kenya's largest towns

For hotels and restaurants in this region see pp372–4 and pp388–9

domes and a weathervane.
The mosque holds 1,000
people during prayer time, and
runs a Muslim school as well.
Muslim visitors are welcome
and non-Muslim males may
be allowed in the grounds.
For others, there are good
views of the green and white
building with its striking roof
from Otieno Oyoo Street.

Resident impalas at the Impala Sanctuary near Kisumu

🎣 Dunga

Dunga, 5 km (3 miles) S of town centre.

Dunga is a ramshackle village
reached by a wobbly ride on a
boda-boda (bicycle taxi). It is
known for the **Kiboko Bay Resort** *(see p374)*, which has
lovely views of the lake.

🏠 Impala Sanctuary

Harambee Rd, 2 km (1 mile) S of
town centre. ⬤ 8am–6pm daily.

The Impala Sanctuary was
created in the 1980s to protect
the last population of impala
in the area. Today, many of
these graceful antelope can
be seen wandering freely in
this tiny reserve. Some
animals are housed in
enclosures. These include
baboons, silverback jackals, a
spotted hyena, a leopard and
an elderly male lion. The
reserve has a museum, a
nature trail and picnic sites.

THE LUNATIC LINE

In 1901, the railway from Mombasa
reached what is now Kisumu; it was
then called Port Florence after Florence
Preston, the wife of a railway engineer.
The railway was called the Lunatic Line
at the time of its construction by Liberal
British politicians who objected to a
railway being built at great expense in
what they considered to be the middle
of nowhere. The line was later renamed
the Uganda Railway, and it went on to
become the communications artery for
Kenya. It opened up the highlands for agriculture and
towns sprang up alongside the tracks. It was dubbed the
Lunatic Express in author Charles Miller's popular 1971
book of the same name.

The Lunatic Express **by Charles Miller**

VISITORS' CHECKLIST

Road Map A4. 50 km (31 miles)
from Kakamega. 332,000.
3 km (2 miles) NW of Kisumu
on the B1. small boats
can be hired at Dunga fish market to nearby sights of interest.

🎣 Hippo Point

Hippo Point, 3 km (2 miles) S of
town centre.

This viewing area on Lake
Victoria is a great place to
watch sunsets over the
lake. Hippos can be seen
occasionally.

KISUMU

Jamia Mosque ③
Kisumu Museum ①
Market ②

Key to Symbols *see back flap*

Luo fishing boats on the eastern shore of Lake Victoria in the early hours of the morning ▷

Lake Victoria ⑭

Straddling the equator, Africa's largest lake covers 68,800 sq km (26,550 sq miles) and is the second largest freshwater lake in the world after Lake Superior in North America. The lake has a catchment area of over 184,000 sq km (71,000 sq miles). It was first sighted by Europeans in 1858 when the British explorer John Hanning Speke reached its southern shore and named it after his queen. The lake borders Kenya, Tanzania and Uganda, and supports some 30 million people living in the lakeside communities. In Kenya, fishing for tilapia and Nile perch provides a living for many of the Luo people living on the lakeshore. The lake once had abundant hippo and crocodile but their numbers are now much reduced.

LOCATOR MAP

☐ Lake Victoria

★ **Rusinga Island**
Attached to the mainland by a causeway, this peaceful island is home to fishing settlements and the luxurious Rusinga Island Lodge (see p374). It is also the birth and burial place of Tom Mboya, who was tipped to become the president of Kenya before his assassination in 1969.

0 km 15

0 miles 15

GETTING AROUND

The A1, the main highway that runs west between Kisumu and Kenya's border with Tanzania, is in good condition, but many of the minor roads leading to the lakeshore are in a poor state, so a 4WD is advised. Although there are no formal ferry services on the lake, it is possible to negotiate a ride with local fishermen.

STAR SIGHTS

★ Rusinga Island

★ Mfangano Island

★ Kisumu

★ **Mfangano Island**
Isolated from the mainland by a short stretch of water that is crossed in a 90-minute boat trip between Mbita Point and Sena, Mfangano Island is noted for its ancient cave paintings believed to be 1,000 to 4,000 years old.

For hotels and restaurants in this region see pp372–4 and pp388–9

★ Kisumu
The principal port on the Kenyan shore, Kisumu has wide boulevards and leafy avenues that were laid out during the colonial era. Among the town's few distractions is the interesting Kisumu Museum (see p298).

Ndere Island National Park, a 4-sq-km (2-sq-mile) island, protects populations of hippo and birds and a small herd of recently introduced impala.

VISITORS' CHECKLIST

Road Map A4. 2 km (1 mile) W of Kisumu. 🛪 Kisumu. 🚌 from Kisumu, Kisii and Kericho. 🚢 small boats run between the lakeshore villages.

KEY

🛪	Domestic airport/airstrip
⛴	Boat service
☀	Viewpoint
▬	Major road
═	Minor road
= =	Unpaved motorable road
──	Railway
- -	Park boundary
▬▪	International border
▲	Peak

Dunga
Located on the eastern lakeshore, Dunga is a small fishing village with boats, nets and fishermen's homes. It is possible here to arrange a trip on the lake in a wooden handcrafted ssese canoe.

LAKE VICTORIA'S ECOLOGICAL DEGRADATION

Over the past few decades, Lake Victoria has experienced drastic environmental changes. The lake's water levels have been affected by high rates of evaporation and consumption, limited river inflow and silting. In places it is now only some 40 m (130 ft) deep. In the 1950 and 1960s, Nile perch was introduced as a game fish, but massive growth in the populations of this giant predator resulted in many species of the endemic chilid fish becoming extinct. By the end of the 1990s, an additional threat was posed by water hyacinth that had clogged almost 40 per cent of the lakeshore. This problem is currently being addressed with the introduction of two small weevils of the *Neochetina* genus that have an insatiable appetite for the hyacinth.

Nile perch, driving most local species to extinction

Homa Bay
Located at the base of the volcanic massif Got Asego, this friendly market town serves as a starting point for trips to Ruma National Park (see p305).

A view of the verdant slopes of Mount Homa rising above Homa Bay

Kendu Bay and Simbi Nyaima **⓮**

Road Map A4. 70 km (44 miles) SW of Kisumu.

A small fishing village of mud houses centred around one main street, Kendu Bay lies on the shores of Lake Victoria. The local Luo people often venture offshore to fish with their fishing nets in tiny wooden canoes.

The lake Simbi Nyaima, literally "the village that sank", is a 45-minute walk west of the village on Homa Bay Road. It is a bright green patch of algae-filled water in a volcanic crater, with no known inlet or outlet, and with shores that are devoid of vegetation. The local people believe it to be unlucky and it is not fished. Luo legend claims that it was created when the Simbi people were celebrating at the chief's house. A weary old woman turned up looking for shelter and food but was denied these. In vengeance, she induced a flood that sank the village and created a lake. Today, there is a footpath around its rim where greater and lesser flamingoes can be seen feeding off the algae.

Homa Bay **⓰**

Road Map A4. 58 km (36 miles) W of Kisii.

Located near Lake Victoria, Homa Bay is a ramshackle market town along two main streets, with a covered market and facilities including a bank and post office. Once a bustling port, its shores are now infested with water hyacinth. Above the town rises Mount Homa, a 1,751-m (5,745-ft) massif, known by the Luo as Got Asego (Famous Mountain), which is the highest of many extinct volcanic plugs in the region. Although it is a tough scramble to the top along goat tracks that go through thick thorn bushes, it offers superb views over Lake Victoria, the patchwork of fields and Luo huts. Beyond Homa Bay, the road heads to **Mbita Point**, a small rural community and a collection point for boats to the lake's islands.

Mfangano Island **⓱**

Road Map A4. 8 km (5 miles) offshore. ✈ charter flights. ⛴ from Mbita Point.

The largest of Lake Victoria's islands in Kenya, Mfangano has a rocky shoreline and rugged terrain covered in fig trees. The island also has a few black sand beaches. The highest point on Mfangano is the 1,694-m (5,558-ft) high Mount Kwitutu. Local fishermen and subsistence farmers once got around the island by foot or boat, but a road has now been built circling Mfangano so that the island is now accessible by car and bicycle as well.

An hour or two's walk into the interior from **Sena**, the island's capital, brings visitors to a high bluff with good views over the island's northern coast. An overhang here has cave paintings of white and reddish spirals. The paintings are thought to be 1,000–4,000 years old, and have been traced back to Twa pygmies from the Congo Basin who are believed to have sheltered in this cave. It has been suggested that the white

Prehistoric rock art in a cave near Ukula village on the northern coast of Mfangano Island

The southern stretch of Rusinga Island with Lake Victoria in the distance

spirals represent the moon and the red ones the sun. The Twa may have believed that the paintings could invoke rain.

Rusinga Island ⑱

Road Map A4. Just offshore of Mbita Point. ✕ *charter flights.* 🚌 *to Mbita Point.* 🖰 **www**.rusinga.com

Connected to the mainland by a causeway, Rusinga Island has a rocky shoreline and is home to populations of giant monitor lizard, spotted-neck otter, hippo and over 100 species of birds. The best places to spot these are from **Hippo Bay** or the small offshore **Bird Island**, which is a short boat-ride from **Rusinga Island Lodge** (*see p374*). The goat-grazed interior of the island is, however, rather desolate as many of its trees have been cut down for firewood. There is at present an initiative to restore the greenery of Rusinga and thousands of trees have been planted on the island.

Rusinga is also the final resting place of Tom Mboya, a leading politician during Kenya's fight for independence. His mausoleum, which has a cone-shaped roof, stands behind his grave on family land in the north of the island, approximately 7 km (4 miles) from Mbita on a dirt road.

Rusinga is also rich in fossils and the skull of *Proconsul heseloni*, a 5-million-year-old anthropoid ape, was found here by anthropologist Mary Leakey in 1947.

Ruma National Park ⑲

Road Map A4. 24 km (15 miles) W of Homa Bay. 🚗 *4WD.* 🕐 *sunrise–sunset daily.* 🖼 🅰 **www**.kws.go.ke

Only accessible by 4WD vehicles, the little visited 120-sq-km (46-sq-mile) Ruma National Park in the Lambwe Valley lies 10 km (6 miles) east of Lake Victoria. The park was established in 1966 to protect Kenya's last and only population of roan antelope (*see p130*). More recently, it has been stocked with several introduced animals including Bohor's reedbuck, Jackson's hartebeest, Rothschild's giraffe, zebra and buffalo. Leopard and hyena are also present but remain elusive. The landscape is a mix of grassy savannah on rolling hills, with a few tracts of woodland that attract a number of birds including the endangered blue swallow that migrates between here and southern Tanzania. The park has three rough gravel tracks for game viewing, but these become impassable in wet weather because of the sticky dark mud known locally as black cotton soil. There is no accommodation in the park, although camping is permitted in certain areas. However, there are no facilities available and visitors to the park need to be totally self-sufficient.

A roan antelope bull in the grasslands of Ruma National Park

TOM MBOYA

Politician Tom Mboya at Embakasi Airport

Tom Mboya was an influential politician during the early years of independent Kenya. In 1957, he became the first African to win a seat on the colonial Legislative Council. His People's Congress Party merged with other political parties in 1960 to form the Kenyan African National Union (KANU), with Mboya as secretary general during the period when independence was negotiated. After independence, he became Minister for Economic Planning and Development. In 1969, Mboya was shot dead on a street in Nairobi at the age of 39. The assassin, who was arrested and hanged, was quoted as saying, "Why don't you go after the big man?" The identity of the "big man" has never been revealed, but the incident sparked speculation that someone in government played a part in Mboya's death, as he was considered a contender for president against Jomo Kenyatta. The inscription on Mboya's mausoleum reads, "Go and fight like this man, Who fought for mankind's cause, Who died because he fought, Whose battles are still unwon."

A banana plantation in the rich soils near Kisii

Thimlich Ohinga ⑳

Road Map A5. 181 km (112 miles) S
of Kisumu. 🚗 *from Migori, take the
A1 towards Isebania. Turn right after
4 km (3 miles), on to a rough murram
road at the junction of Muhoro Bay.
Take the first right after the depot for
55 km (35 miles).* ⏲ *8.30am–6pm
daily.* 🖥 **www**.museums.or.ke

Hidden in the bush, the Iron
Age site of Thimlich Ohinga is
the remains of a 15th-century
stone enclosure thought to be
built by an early Bantu group
whose history has been forgotten. The main enclosure,
around 150 m (490 ft) across,
has many houses within it
along with pens for livestock,
a forge for smelting iron and
what is believed to have been
some form of athletic playing
field. The walls are 1–4 m
(3–13 ft) high, 1–3 m (3–10 ft)
wide and built of loose stones
without mortar. Although other
groups have lived there since,
and the area was still inhabited
at the beginning of the 20th

century, few alterations have
been made to the structures
and they are some of the best
preserved Iron Age remains in
East Africa. Despite its protection as a national monument,
however, Thimlich Ohinga is
isolated and rarely visited.
There are no visitor facilities
and travellers require private
transport to get here.

Kisii ㉑

Road Map A4. 120 km (75 miles)
S of Kisumu. 🏠 *25,400.*
🚌 *Moi Highway.*

Straddling the A1 that runs
from Kisumu into Tanzania,
Kisii is the main urban and
commercial town of the Gusii
Highlands. It is a small rambling market town surrounded
by picturesque undulating hills
of terraced smallholdings.
The region is dissected by
rivers flowing west into Lake
Victoria, notably the Kuja and
Mogusi rivers. The town has a

colourful market crammed
with burgeoning fruit and
vegetable stalls, which serve
as a reminder of how fertile
this area is with its abundant
sunshine and rainfall. Local
cash crops include oranges,
bananas, maize, beans, millet
and potatoes.

The town has a number
of Indian and Kikuyu traders,
but the population is largely
made up of the Gusii people.
This group is one of the most
rapidly growing populations in
Kenya – the average woman
bears nine children – so the
Gusii Highlands is one of the
country's most heavily populated rural areas, with some
70–80 per cent of the land
under cultivation. A couple of
supermarkets, a petrol station,
bank, dozens of cheap board
and lodgings and the sprawling open market can be found
on Moi Highway, which runs
through the town. This over-
crowded, and often muddy,
road also serves as one long
matatu stage with vehicles
clustered along the length of it.

Tabaka ㉒

Road Map A4. 24 km (10 miles)
W of Kisii. 🚌 ▢

The settlement of Tabaka is
home to Kenya's soapstone
quarries and the Gusii community here are renowned
for their artistic skill as carvers. Soft pliable stone from
these quarries is fashioned
into all sorts of items for practical use such as bowls and
plates, or tourist items such as
animal statues, chess sets and

The bustling streets in central Kisii

For hotels and restaurants in this region see pp372–4 and pp388–9

abstract figures. In the village, the carvers sit outside on the white dusty soapstone rubble, where visitors can watch them work with chisels. Some may offer a chisel and a piece of rock to let visitors have a go at carving themselves. People can observe the workers smoothening the soapstone with sandpaper and water and polishing the finished products with wax. The soapstone comes in a variety of colours from pale cream – the softest – to deep red – the hardest. Finished carvings are sold in some half a dozen shops in Tabaka. These items are also exported all over the country and can be found in most tourist markets and shops.

An artisan carving soft soapstone using a simple chisel, Tabaka

Kericho ㉓

Road Map B4. 107 km (67 miles) NE of Kisii. 🏠 30,000. 🚌

Thanks to the consistent weather of sunny mornings and rainy afternoons, Kericho is the heart of Western Kenya's tea industry. The origin of the town's name is under some dispute. It could have been named after Ole Kericho, an 18th-century Maasai chief who was killed in the area, or after John Kerich, an early British tea planter. Commercial production of tea was established by the British in the region after World War I. Many of the estates have now been reallocated to small farmers and operate under the Kenya Union of Small Scale Tea

Owners (KUSSTO), although the area is dominated by giant tea plantations owned by international companies such as Brooke Bond. The best place to try a cup of Kenyan tea is on the manicured lawns of the charming colonial **Tea Hotel** *(see p373)*, which also organises tours of the plantations.

In town, most amenities are spread along the main road, Moi Highway. The layout is very orderly with a town square called Chai Square, a village green and the beautiful stone- and ivy-clad British-built **Holy Trinity Church**, constructed in 1952.

Chagaik Dam and Arboretum ㉔

Road Map B4. 8 km (5 miles) E of Kericho on the B1 towards Nakuru. 🚌

Located by the shores of a small lake, which is covered in water lilies and surrounded by clutches of bamboo, the Chagaik Dam and Arboretum is a lovely picnic spot. The arboretum is an easy 5-minute walk from the dam. Hemmed

The picturesque lake at Chagaik Dam, an excellent picnic spot

in by tea plantations, the formal gardens of tropical trees and well-manicured lawns were originally laid out by tea planter Tom Grumbley in the 1940s. Across the lake is a small tangled clutch of sprawling trees and undergrowth that is home to a troop of black-and-white colobus. Bird-watchers should look out for the yellow-spotted barbet, snowy-headed robin-chat, banded and white-chinned prinia and black-billed weaver. Visits to this area can be arranged through the guides at the Tea Hotel in Kericho.

KENYA'S TEA STORY

Tea was introduced in Kenya from India in 1903. Now, with more than 1,100 sq km (425 sq miles) of land devoted to its cultivation, Kenya is the world's third largest producer of tea, with an annual output of 245,000 tonnes (270,000 tons). The country's main plantations are in the highland areas on either side of the Rift Valley, at altitudes of 1,500–2,700 m (4,900–8,850 ft) above sea level. The tea bush is an evergreen grown in tropical climates, so that bushes are harvested throughout the year and tea is picked on a continual cycle of 7–14 days. Only the choicest upper two leaves and a bud are plucked each time. The majority of Kenyan tea is sold through auctions in Mombasa, with Pakistan, the UK and Egypt being the biggest buyers.

Tea plantations dominating the rolling countryside around Kericho

CENTRAL HIGHLANDS

Blessed with fertile volcanic soils and generous rainfall, and dominated by the imposing jagged peaks of Mount Kenya and the Aberdare Range, the Central Highlands rank among the most densely populated and cultivated areas in Kenya. In addition to being the national breadbasket, the region is also home to the politically and economically influential Kikuyu people.

Although they share a similar ecology, Mount Kenya and the Aberdares represent extremes of antiquity. The latter is among the most ancient ranges in East Africa, dating to before the age of dinosaurs. By contrast, Mount Kenya, Africa's second highest mountain, is a geological infant, having erupted into existence long after our earliest bipedal ancestors first strode through the region.

The Central Highlands have long been home to agricultural communities such as the Kikuyu, Meru, Embu and Akamba. Heavily settled by European farmers during the colonial era, the highlands lay at the centre of the notorious Happy Valley *(see p319)* scene of the 1930s, while its forests provided shelter to the Mau-Mau movement that would strike effectively against colonial rule two decades later. Today, the area is studded with easygoing and well equipped but generally unremarkable towns, while the sprawling agricultural estates of colonial times have been replaced by a patchwork of low-key *shambas* (small-holdings) planted with papayas, bananas, coffee and other crops.

Forming an elevated grassy saddle between Mount Kenya and the Aberdares, this area supports the bulk of Kenya's remaining highland forest. Protected within national parks, the mountains support a rich diversity of habitats and an impressive volume of wildlife, ranging from large mammals, such as elephants and lions, to colobus monkeys and chameleons. Other key wildlife areas include the underrated Meru National Park, set in the eastern rainshadow of Mount Kenya, and the agglomeration of private reserves sprawling northwards from the Central Highlands across the Laikipia Plateau.

Moorland vegetation against the spectacular backdrop of the Aberdare Range

◁ View of Mount Kenya from Teleki Valley on the Naro Moro Route, Mount Kenya National Park

The Kikuyu

The Kikuyu are Kenya's most populous ethnic group, comprising 22 per cent of the national population. In common with the other Bantu-speakers of the region, the ancestral Kikuyu migration eastwards from West Africa took place about 2,000 years ago. They finally settled in the fertile highlands north of Nairobi – their present homeland. Oral traditions suggest that they abandoned their original hunter-gatherer lifestyle for agriculture and pastoralism after their arrival. Today, the Kikuyu are prominent both in business and national affairs, and most individuals dress in a Western style and practise Christianity rather than traditional beliefs.

British officials and Kikuyu people signing a land acquisition treaty

The elaborate traditional attire *of Kikuyu women includes beads, animal skin headdresses and white body paint.*

THE KIKUYU WAY OF LIFE

The traditional Kikuyu way of life in the Central Highlands is based on agriculture, though pastoralism and hunting are also practised. During the colonial era Europeans who settled on Kikuyu land enforced a feudal system of dependency. In the long term, this close association with the colonists has led to the Kikuyu becoming the most educated and Westernised of Kenya's tribes.

Ostrich feathers form an impressive part of the traditional Kikuyu headdress.

Most rural Kikuyu *are subsistence farmers, growing a variety of fruit and grains in smallholdings known as* shambas.

KIKUYU RELIGION

The Kikuyu traditionally worship a single god known as Ngai (The Provider), though they also place a high premium on ancestor worship. Partly owing to the high missionary presence in the region and partly because they are predisposed to monotheism, the Kikuyu today are predominantly Christian and most individuals actively shun traditional beliefs.

Residing in the glacial peaks of Mount Kenya *is the Kikuyu god Ngai. Traditionally, Kikuyu homesteads always face the sacred peaks, a custom referred to in the title of former President Jomo Kenyatta's autobiography,* Facing Mount Kenya.

About 75 per cent of the Kikuyu *identify themselves as Christians and are regular churchgoers. Most practise Protestant faiths.*

EMINENT KIKUYUS

The Kikuyu are Kenya's most politically and economically influential community, probably as a result of their traditional homeland's proximity to Nairobi, and a higher than average level of education.

Wangari Maathai, *a well-known environmental activist, became the first African woman to win a Nobel Peace Prize in 2004, for "her contribution to sustainable development, democracy and peace".*

Jomo Kenyatta, *the first president and founding father of independent Kenya, was a few months shy of 70 when he was elected in 1963. He served as president of Kenya until his death in 1978.*

Mwai Kibaki *has been active in parliament since the Kenyatta era. He became Kenya's third president, succeeding Daniel arap Moi in 2002. He remains in power today, despite the controversial outcome of the 2007 election.*

Dedan Kimathi *was the commander-in-chief of the Mau-Mau Rebellion. When it petered out, Kimathi was captured by the colonial army in Nyeri in October 1956, and was later hanged.*

Soldiers patrolling near Nyeri during the Mau-Mau uprising, 1955

THE MAU-MAU REBELLION

By 1950, settler farms covered some 10,000 sq km (3,850 sq miles) of the Central Highlands, an area six times larger than that allocated to the country's million-plus rural Kikuyu. The resultant sense of displacement led to the formation of Mau-Mau, a Kikuyu-dominated guerilla army that hid out in the forests of Mount Kenya and the Aberdares, attacking colonial government targets and settler farms from 1952 to 1956. Repeated attacks on civilian targets led to the Mau-Mau being portrayed as blood-thirsty savages by the colonial authorities. However, the number of settlers killed was just a fraction of the 10,000–50,000 Kikuyu civilians who were killed by the authorities or died whilst they were interred in unsanitary concentration camps. A military failure, the rebellion nevertheless did much to hasten the end of colonial rule, and it was a former Mau-Mau leader, Jomo Kenyatta, who led Kenya to independence and served as the country's first president.

Exploring the Central Highlands

Highland towns offer an agreeable way of experiencing the less touristic side of Kenya. Nyahururu is notable for the spectacular Thomson's Falls, and Nyeri for its association with Lord Baden-Powell of scouting fame. Meru has a worthwhile museum, and Thika offers easy access to Ol Doinyo Sabuk National Park. Few organised safaris linger beyond an overnight stop at one of the tree hotels on the slopes of Mount Kenya or the Aberdares. Those seeking an off-the-beaten-track wildlife experience can try Meru National Park or one of the upmarket camps on the Laikipia Plateau. The region's major draw is Mount Kenya, which offers enough hiking opportunities to last weeks.

Wooden exterior of the popular Mountain Lodge near Mount Kenya

Camping on the grassy slopes of Mount Kenya

KEY

═══	Highway
▬▬	Major road
═══	Minor road
●●●	Untarred major road
═ ═ ═	Untarred minor road
- - -	4WD track
━━	Major railway
───	Minor railway
△	Peak

A herd of Burchell's zebra grazing in Meru National Park

GETTING AROUND

The Central Highlands are well suited to independent travel, whether in a private vehicle or using the plentiful public transport between all towns. The surfaced Ring Road around Mount Kenya, linked to Nairobi by a trunk route through Thika and Karatina, connects Nyeri, Naro Moru, Nanyuki, Meru, Chogoria and Embu, while another surfaced road runs from Nyeri to Nyahururu. There is no public transport to the Laikipia Plateau or Meru National Park, but guests at the tree hotels of Aberdare National Park are shuttled there from Nyeri by the lodge management, and hikes up Mount Kenya can easily be arranged on the spot at Naro Moru, Chogoria and most other towns in the vicinity.

SEE ALSO

- *Where to Stay* pp374–6

- *Where to Eat* p389

The secluded Thomson's Falls on the outskirts of Nyahururu

SIGHTS AT A GLANCE

Towns and Cities

Embu ⑬

Meru ⑪

Nanyuki ⑩

Naro Moru ⑨

Nyahururu ⑥

Nyeri ④

Thika ①

National Parks and Reserves

Aberdare National Park pp316–17 ⑤

Meru National Park pp330–33 ⑫

Mount Kenya National Park pp322–5 ⑧

Mwea National Reserve ⑭

Ol Doinyo Sabuk National Park ③

Areas of Natural Beauty

Fourteen Falls ②

Laikipia Plateau pp318–21 ⑦

0 km   25

0 miles   25

Thika ❶

Road Map C5. 45 km (28 miles)
N of Nairobi. 🚶 83,000. 🚉 🚌

Linked to Nairobi by a rare
dual carriageway, this bustling
and rapidly growing highland
town is best known outside
Kenya as the setting of
Elspeth Huxley's novelistic
account of her colonial child-
hood, *The Flame Trees of
Thika* (1959), which was
adapted as a television series
in the 1980s. Thika is not
quite the rustic outpost it was
in Edwardian times; today, it
practically functions as a satellite of Nairobi. Any flame
trees that may have survived
are outnumbered by smoking
matatus and introduced coni-
fers. The council motto "Your
Industrial Town" more realistically describes the town, with
a dozen-odd textile, cigarette
and food processing factories
scattered around the periphery comprising its industry.

A more worthwhile stop
than Thika is the **Blue Posts
Hotel** (*see p376*), which lies
in pretty flowering grounds
on the northern outskirts of
town. Having celebrated its
centenary in 2008, Blue Posts
claims to be older than Thika
itself, and the ivy-clad period
architecture in the hotel
ensures that it still exudes a
faint aura of the colonial era
commemorated by Huxley.
The Chania and Thika rivers
both flow through the well-
wooded grounds of the hotel,
tumbling over a pair of attractive waterfalls in the process,
and there is plenty of birdlife

Mists cover the summit of Ol Doinyo Sabuk

around too. The small zoo in
the hotel grounds is inhabited
by wildlife such as crocodiles,
bushbabies and several species of monkey. It is also the
one place in Kenya where
visitors can be certain of
seeing a porcupine.

Fourteen Falls ❷

Road Map C5. 25 km (16 miles)
SE of Thika on Graissa Rd. 🚌
⏰ 9am–5pm daily. 🌀 🅿 🅰

Managed by the Thika Town
Council, this pretty waterfall
is formed by the Athi river as
it splits into several small
streams before tumbling over
a wide rock lip close to the
base of Ol Doinyo Sabuk (Big
Mountain). The main drop is
not especially high, no more
than 10 m (33 ft), and the
name is slightly misleading as
the water may form a single
sheet or be broken up into
more than 14 mini-cataracts,
depending on the seasonal
strength of the flow. A group
of local teenagers often hang

round the site and in order to
earn some money will dive
over the waterfall to the pool
below – an activity that is best
not encouraged. The site is
generally most impressive in
April and December when the
water level is highest. At any
time of year, it is worth looking at the small hippo pool, a
5-minute walk up the river.

Ol Doinyo Sabuk National Park ❸

Road Map C5. 28 km (17 miles) SE
of Thika. **Tel** 020 2062503. 🚌
🚗 4WD. ⏰ 6am–7pm daily. 🌀 🅿
🍽 🅰 www.kws.go.ke

This scenic but little visited
national park protects the
isolated 2,145-m (7,050-ft)
mountain known to the
Maasai as Ol Doinyo Sabuk, a
name that seems a little ironic
given its proximity to the far
taller Mount Kenya and Aberdare Range. A 10-km (6-mile)
long dirt road leads uphill
from the entrance gate, passing through forested slopes

The roaring waters of Fourteen Falls, near Thika

that are home to blue monkey, bushbuck, leopard and numerous highland birds. It climbs to the grassy summit, which offers great views on clear days. About 3 km (2 miles) before reaching the top of the mountain, the road passes the grave of Sir William McMillan, a wealthy settler whose immense bulk foiled the tractor that was meant to carry his coffin to the summit and forced the burial to take place en route. The road requires 4WD and may be impassable in rain. Walking is permitted, but given the irritable reputation of local buffalo, only in the company of an armed ranger.

Nyeri ❹

Road Map C4. 135 km (84 miles) NW of Nairobi on the road to Nyahururu. 🏙 100,000. ✖ 🚌
🛏 Baden-Powell's birth anniversary (22 Feb).

Despite its status as Kenya's eighth largest town as well as administrative capital of Central Province, Nyeri retains a small-town feel, with a compact centre surrounded on all sides by leafy suburbia and densely planted smallholdings. The town centre has good facilities, including several banks, hotels, eateries, supermarkets and Internet cafés. However, the main focus for visitors is **The Outspan Hotel** (see p376), a smart colonial-era edifice that also serves as the official springboard for overnight forays to the legendary Treetops Lodge in Aberdare National Park (see pp316–17). The hotel is a pleasant place, and visitors can follow a short downhill walking trail to the forest-fringed Chania river or visit the Kikuyu cultural village where there are daily dance performances.

Nyeri has produced several Kenyans of note, including current President Mwai Kibaki, Nobel Peace Prize winner Wangari Maathai and marathon runner Catherine Ndereba. The most famous former resident, however, is Lord Robert Baden-Powell, whose cottage

Farmers working in the fertile fields near Nyeri

on the grounds of the Outspan is now a small museum. He is buried next to his wife in the colonial **St Peter's Cemetery** near the Anglican church. Each year, on Baden-Powell's birth anniversary, up to 30,000 boy scouts and girl guides march from the Outspan to his grave.

Aberdare National Park ❺

See pp316–17.

Nyahururu ❻

Road Map B4. 100 km (60 miles) NW of Nyeri. 🏙 25,000. ✖ 🚌

Kenya's highest settlement, Nyahururu is perched at an altitude of 2,360 m (7,750 ft) on the edge of the Laikipia

Plateau (see pp318–21). It is otherwise a rather humdrum market town, with adequate amenities but few distinguishing features. The main point of interest is **Thomson's Falls**, which sees the Ewaso Nyiro river plummeting 75 m (246 ft) in one single drop over a volcanic ledge on its course from the Aberdares to Samburu-Buffalo Springs National Reserves (see pp342–6). A footpath leads from the gardens of the distinctly colonial-era **Thomson's Falls Lodge** (see p376) to the base of the waterfall, which is named after Scottish explorer Joseph Thomson, who was in this area in 1883. A tract of riparian woodland follows the river below the falls and supports a selection of highland forest birds along with black-and-white colobus monkey.

The Baden-Powells, circa 1910

LORD ROBERT BADEN-POWELL

Born in London on 22 February 1857, Robert Baden-Powell served in the British army in India and Africa between 1876 and 1910, becoming Lieutenant-General and winning several medals for his heroic efforts, most famously in the Siege of Mafeking in the Anglo-Boer War of 1899–1902. He is best known posthumously as the founder of the Boy Scout movement, an event usually dated to the publication of his book *Scouting for Boys* (1908). He retired from the military at the request of King Edward VII in 1910 to promote scouting. Two years later, he met his future wife Olave, later in charge of the Girl Guide movement started by Baden-Powell in 1910. He was knighted in 1921. Baden-Powell and Olave moved to Nyeri in 1939, where they lived in a specially commissioned one-bedroom bungalow called Paxtu on the grounds of the Outspan Hotel. He died on 8 January 1941 and was buried in Nyeri, facing Mount Kenya. Olave was buried alongside him in 1977. The joint grave is now a national monument.

Aberdare National Park ❺

This 767-sq-km (296-sq-mile) national park protects a 75-km (47-mile) long, 4,000-m (13,100-ft) tall mountain range that rises from the Rift Valley escarpment above Lake Naivasha to form the western buttress of the Central Highlands. It was named by Joseph Thomson in 1884 after Lord Aberdare, then president of the Royal Geographic Society, but the local Kikuyu call it Nyandurua (Drying Hide) after its resemblance to a pegged-out animal skin. The Aberdare bedrock is more ancient than volcanic Mount Kenya, but both mountains are ecologically similar, with forested lower slopes leading to more open vegetation. Wildlife includes golden cat, giant forest hog and dozens of montane and forest bird species.

Bamboo forest between the montane and moorland belts

★ **Afro-alpine Moorland**
Set at altitudes of above 3,000 m (9,843 ft), the misty belt of Afro-alpine moorland supports open vegetation scattered with otherworldly giant lobelias, groundsels and heathers.

*Nyahururu
30 km (19 miles)*

Shamata Gate

Rhino Gate

Chebuswa
3,364 m ▲

Engore Ngobit

Ol Doinyo Lesatima
4,001 m ▲

Ol Doinyo Lesatima, the highest peak in Aberdare has a Maasai name meaning "bull-calf mountain".

Table Mountain
3,791 m ▲

Aberdare Range

Maratini Hill
3,698 m ▲

Ch

Karura Falls
Seldom visited by tourists, the upper moorland of the Aberdares is dotted with pretty waterfalls, many accessible along rough dirt roads that become mud baths after heavy rain.

Gura Falls is Kenya's tallest waterfall, plunging 300 m (984 ft) into a deep ravine.

*Naivasha
50 km (31 miles)*

Matubio Gate

*Nyandarua
3,906 m*

*Elephant Hill
3,590 m*

STAR SIGHTS

★ Afro-alpine Moorland

★ The Ark

★ Treetops

Elephant Sightings
With an estimated 2,000 individuals resident in the park, the African elephant is probably the most conspicuous of the Big Five animals here, although leopard, buffalo and black rhino are also present.

VISITORS' CHECKLIST

Road Map C4. Ruhuruini Gate is 160 km (99 miles) NW of Nairobi on Nyeri Rd. ⓘ 061 2300142 (Park Headquarters). ◯ 6am–7pm daily. 🖼 📷 🛍 Ⓐ www.kws.go.ke
Note: visitors need to apply to the warden in advance to enter the northern sector of the park.

★ **The Ark**
The more modern of Kenya's tree hotels, this attractive wooden edifice has a waterhole that is visited by rhino, elephant and buffalo, with leopard also making sporadic appearances.

★ **Treetops**
Like The Ark, Treetops offers nightly game viewing from its own waterhole. The hotel made headlines in 1952, when it hosted the young Princess Elizabeth on the night that King George VI died and she awoke the uncrowned Queen of England.

GETTING AROUND

The most accessible part of the park is the Aberdare Salient, a mid-altitude eastern extension of the main north-south axis running towards Nyeri via Ruhuruini Gate. The only part of the park serviced by all-weather roads, the Salient is home to the legendary tree hotels – Treetops and The Ark. To the southwest, the other popular gate – Matubio Gate leading towards Naivasha – is located at the higher altitudes of the park where hiking is only permitted in the company of an armed ranger. In addition to spectacular highland scenery, these rarefied altitudes offer the opportunity to encounter park specials such as the melanistic leopard and mountain bongo.

THE TREE HOTELS OF ABERDARE NATIONAL PARK

The concept of a tree hotel – a game lodge that doubles as a hide – was pioneered in 1934, when a rudimentary treehouse-like structure called Treetops opened on the forested Aberdare Salient. The expanded Treetops and The Ark, a similar hotel, now form a popular break between the Rift Valley and Samburu-Buffalo Springs. The drill at both lodges is similar – lunch at a base outside the park (Aberdare Country Club for The Ark, Outspan Hotel for Treetops), then a bus ride across for the night to watch animals drink at the waterhole. Treetops, with its association with Queen Elizabeth II, boasts the greater sense of history, but The Ark surpasses it in terms of game viewing.

KEY
ⓘ Visitor information
🏠 Lodge
Ⓐ Campsite
☼ Viewpoint
▬ Major road
= = Unpaved motorable road
- - Park boundary
▲ Peak

Laikipia Plateau ❼

Extending over 9,500 sq km (3,670 sq miles) northwards from Mount Kenya, Laikipia is a mid-altitude plateau of semiarid plains punctuated by basalt outcrops, forested slopes and spectacular gorges hemming the Ewaso Nyiro and Ewaso Narok rivers. The plateau was split between ranch-land and community land during the colonial era, when the wildlife was frequently persecuted, but decreased profitability of ranching coupled with greater eco-awareness led to most of the plateau being turned into a patchwork of private and community-based wildlife sanctuaries. Collectively, this so-called Ewaso Ecosystem is larger than any protected area in Kenya other than Tsavo. It supports wildlife densities second only to Masai Mara, including about 6,000 elephant, plenty of predators and more than half the country's black rhino.

★ **African Wild Dog**
Laikipia provides sanctuary to 70 per cent of the global population of Grevy's zebra, and the only viable African wild dog population in the northern hemisphere.

Walking Safaris
The focal point at most conservancies and lodges in northern Laikipia is walking safaris, which are usually led by local Samburu or Pokot scouts, and provide the thrill of seeing wildlife without the barrier of a vehicle.

GETTING AROUND

The plateau can be visited by road en route between the Aberdares and Samburu-Buffalo Springs, in which case it is advisable to pick one of the less remote lodges or to charter a flight from Nanyuki. There is no public transport to the plateau, but Solio Ranch and Ol Pejeta are readily accessible from the main road in a private 4WD, and day visitors are welcomed. It is also easy to get to Nanyuki Airport on public transport and fly to a lodge from there.

STAR SIGHTS

★ African Wild Dog

★ Ol Pejeta Chimpanzee Sanctuary

★ Night Drives

★ **Ol Pejeta Chimpanzee Sanctuary**
An observation tower at Ol Pejeta allows visitors to observe Kenya's only chimpanzees – an introduced community of orphaned animals from war-torn Burundi.

For hotels and restaurants in this region see pp374–6 and p389

HAPPY VALLEY

Happy Valley was a hedonist community of aristocrats, farmers and socialites whose promiscuous lifestyle was centred on the Kenyan highlands in the 1930s. Today, it is best remembered for the murder of the 22nd Earl of Erroll, shot dead in his car in 1941. The police initially arrested

White Mischief, on the murder of Josslyn Hay, Earl of Erroll

Sir Henry "Jock" Delves Broughton, whose wife had had a dalliance with the Earl, but he was later acquitted, as immortalised in the movie *White Mischief*. More recent evidence suggests that the Earl was executed by British military intelligence due to his links with the British Fascist movement.

KEY

⊠	Domestic airport/airstrip
🛖	Lodge
🅰	Campsite
▬	Major road
═	Minor road
= =	Unpaved motorable road
− −	Trail
▪ ▪	Park boundary
▲	Peak

Horseback Safaris
Reticulated giraffe and other ungulates will often let people on horses approach them far more closely than they would a vehicle or a human pedestrian.

★ Night Drives
The private conservancies of Laikipia mostly offer night drives, which come with an excellent chance of seeing nocturnal creatures such as the genet, leopard, aardvark and the bushbaby.

Solio Game Ranch
This is Kenya's most important rhino breeding facility. From a population of around 40 introduced in the 1970s, it now supports 135 rhinos, and another 100 have been translocated to other reserves.

Exploring Laikipia Plateau

Laikipia differs from other conservation areas in Kenya in that it consists of dozens of autonomous private or community-owned conservancies, although it is overseen by the Laikipia Wildlife Foundation (LWF), a non-profit organisation which was formed in 1992 and includes all stakeholders in Laikipia – some 20 ranches and a similar number of community groups representing tribes as diverse as the Maasai, Kikuyu, Samburu and Pokot. Each ranch is managed as an exclusive and self-contained entity, and the experience offered is strikingly different to any national park. Game drives are almost invariably run by the reserves using their own skilled driver-guides. Also on offer are activities usually forbidden in official parks, such as guided walks and spotlighted night drives.

outbreak of civil war. Today, Ol Pejeta supports and nurses back to health around 40 orphaned and traumatised chimpanzees, which are split across two communities living in the forest along either side of the Ewaso Nyiro river. As it is a chimpanzee refuge rather than a conservation project, the female chimpanzees are sterilised on arrival to prevent breeding.

Mobile tented camp at the lush Solio Game Ranch

🅜 Ol Pejeta Conservancy and Sweetwaters

25 km (16 miles) NW of Nanyuki on the C76. **Tel** 020 2033240. 🕐 7am–7pm for day visitors. 🅟 🚻 🍴 🚭 www.olpejetaconservancy.org

Formerly a cattle ranch, Ol Pejeta extends over 365 sq km (140 sq miles) of semiarid grassland and acacia thornbush flanking the upper reaches of the Ewaso Nyiro river in southern Laikipia. In 1988, a quarter of the ranch was set aside as the **Sweetwaters Game Reserve and Rhino Sanctuary**, and this was extended to include the entire ranch after it was bought by the UK-based conservation organisation Fauna and Flora International. Ol Pejeta is now the largest individual rhino sanctuary in East Africa, supporting populations of more than 70 black and at least nine white rhino. The tame black rhino, Morani, died in 2008; a successor, the blind orphan rhino Baraka, is being habituated to visitors.

SWEETWATERS
TENTED CAMP
2KM

Logo, Sweetwaters tented camp

Lion, leopard, cheetah, buffalo, reticulated giraffe and elephant are also present, while a varied selection of antelope includes the localised gerenuk, Jackson's hartebeest and Beisa oryx. More than 500 bird species have also been recorded.

The conservancy is known for its high standard of guiding, with night drives and guided walks offered in addition to the usual daytime game drives. Other activities on offer include lion tracking with the Sweetwaters research team, and visits to *manyattas* (see pp256–7).

Following the establishment of a chimpanzee sanctuary in 1993, Ol Pejeta supports the country's only population of chimpanzees, a species that does not naturally occur in Kenya (see p318). The sanctuary was created to provide a natural refuge for orphaned chimpanzees formerly housed at the Jane Goodall Institute in Burundi prior to the

🅜 Solio Game Ranch

33 km (21 miles) N of Nyeri along the Nyahururu Rd. **Tel** 020 20513166. 🕐 6am–6pm daily. 🅟 🚻 🅐

This 70-sq-km (27-sq-mile) sanctuary on the Solio Cattle Ranch was founded in 1970, primarily as a breeding centre for rhinos. The first introduced breeding populations of 23 black and 16 white rhino have bred with spectacular success, and the ranch now supports estimated populations of 50 black and 85 white rhino, while another 100 individuals have been translocated out of Solio to Lake Nakuru (see pp276–9), Tsavo West (see pp186–7), and Aberdare (see pp316–17) National Parks, along with various other locations in Laikipia. The fenced reserve also protects about 600 zebra, 350 buffalo, 55 giraffe and unspecified numbers of eland, Beisa oryx, waterbuck and impala. Wildlife such as lion, cheetah, leopard and spotted hyena are either resident or pass through regularly, and smaller predators such as black-backed jackal, dwarf mongoose and genet are common. Self-drive visits are encouraged, although 4WD

A visitor with the tame black rhino Morani, Ol Pejeta ranch

vehicles may be required after rain. Guided game walks are also on offer at the ranch.

Lewa Wildlife Conservancy
7 km (4 miles) from the main Nanyuki-Isiolo Rd along a dirt track; signposted 4 km (2 miles) N of the junction to Meru. **Tel** 064 31405.
during the rainy seasons of 1 Apr–30 May & 21 Oct–30 Nov.
www.lewa.org

Like so many other sanctuaries on the Laikipia Plateau, Lewa was established as a colonial cattle ranch in the 1920s. A portion was set aside as a wildlife sanctuary in 1983, and the remainder of the 263-sq-km (102-sq-mile) ranch followed 10 years later. More recently, the wildlife sanctuary was also awarded guardianship of the contiguous state-owned **Ngare Ndare Forest Reserve**.

Lewa is one the most important strongholds for the endangered Grevy's zebra, with an estimated 400 individuals representing some 20 per cent of the global wild population, and it also harbours more than 55 black and 35 white rhino. This is a good place to see the very localised sitatunga antelope, which has thrived since being translocated from Saiwa Swamp National Park to a permanent swamp in Lewa in the 1980s. Aside from these specials, Lewa offers good general game viewing, with up to 300 elephant regularly recorded in the reserve, along with reticulated giraffe and a wide variety of antelope. A 2009 predator census estimated a population of 19 resident and up to 15 transient lion, along with 25 spotted hyena, ten leopard, one partially resident pack of wild dogs and nine cheetah.

Expertly guided day and night game drives are available, along with guided bush walks. Lewa also houses an important Acheulean hand-axe site, where an abundance of hand tools made from volcanic rocks have been found, dating to around 800,000 years ago. Lewa is run as a non-profit-making organisation, with proceeds going into conservation, local community projects and economic development.

Northern Laikipia
70 km (43 miles) NW of Nanyuki.
4WD. **Note:** *not all private conservancies are open to day visitors.*

The northern part of the Laikipia Plateau is covered with a patchwork of small community and private conservancies, most of which offer frontage to the Ewaso Nyiro river. The bush here is thicker and scrubbier than in southern Laikipia, and the area is more notable for its pristine atmosphere and wild riverine scenery than great densities of game. One animal that is common here is the stately greater kudu, a spiral-horned antelope seldom seen elsewhere in Kenya. This expanse of wilderness is most rewardingly explored on foot, and guided walks rather than game drives tend to be the main activity, with the exciting possibility of coming across buffalo, elephant and other members of the Big Five. The area's rich avian diversity means that bird-watchers will be in their element. The premier properties in this area are **Sabuk**, **Loisaba** and **Kioja Starbeds** *(see p375)*, which also offer activities such as horse riding, bush walking and camel trekking.

An alfresco lunch in the bush organised by Loisaba group

CHIMPANZEE RESERVE

Denizens of the West African rainforest, chimpanzees do not naturally occur in Kenya, although it is possible that they inhabited forested sites such as Kakamega in prehistoric times. However, the excursion to see the introduced community of orphans from Burundi is one of the most popular attractions at Ol Pejeta, almost as exciting as seeing these primates in the wild. Their crescendo of communal pant-hoot calls allow chimpanzees within earshot to identify which other chimps are also in the vicinity. Interaction between them is also fascinating to observe, and includes plenty of grooming, display of affection as well as regular shows of dominance. More rarely seen is their ability to use tools, for instance to "fish" for termites in termite mounds.

Chimpanzee searching for termites, Ol Pejeta

The endangered Grevy's zebra, Lewa Wildlife Conservancy

Mount Kenya National Park ❽

In clear weather, the jagged peaks of Mount Kenya – considered by the Kikuyu, Meru and Akamba to be the abode of their gods – dominate the skyline of the Central Highlands. While its existence was first reported in 1849 by the missionary Ludwig Krapf, the first person to summit was Sir Halford Mackinder in 1899. An extinct volcano, Mount Kenya was most active some 2.5–3 million years ago. Today, it hosts a diverse flora, with forest on the lower slopes and rising through bamboo forest, montane heath and Afro-alpine moorland to its barren glacial peaks. Its upper slopes are protected in a 715-sq-km (275-sq-mile) national park and the middle slopes in a 2,100-sq-km (810-sq-mile) forest reserve, jointly inscribed as a UNESCO World Heritage Site in 1997.

Blue monkey, a resident of Mount Kenya's forest zone

The Sirimon Route, although less often used, offers better game viewing than the alternatives.

Timau
11 km
(7 miles)

Sirimon Gate

Mount Kenya National Reserve

Sirimon

Global Atmo Watch Statio

Likii

Sirimon Route

Mackinder Valley

Shipton Cave

Nelio 5,189

Batian 5,199 m

Austr Hut

Burguret Route

Naro Moru

Meteorological Station

Naro Moru Route

Lake Höhnel

Park HQ

Park Gate

Naro Moru
16 km
(10 miles)

Höhnel Valley

Nyamindi

Peak Circular Path

Kamweti Route

Embu
45 km
(28 miles)

★ Serena Mountain Lodge
This forest-enclosed tree hotel on the southern slopes offers the best wildlife viewing in the vicinity of Mount Kenya.

Batian and Nelion Peaks
The name Kenya derives from the Akamba word Kiinya, meaning "mountain of the ostrich", a reference to the Batian and Nelion peaks' resemblance to a black-and-white ostrich tail feather.

STAR SIGHTS

★ Serena Mountain Lodge

★ Abseiling at Lewis Glacier

★ Afro-alpine Moorland

★ Abseiling at Lewis Glacier
The mountain's dozen glaciers, all of which are in recession as a result of global warming, are popular with adventurous climbers.

For hotels and restaurants in this region see pp374–6 and p389

★ **Afro-alpine Moorland**
Although less rich in wildlife, the higher altitude Afro-alpine moorland of Mount Kenya supports an unusual cover of low pastel-shaded heathers and grassy tussocks interspersed with giant lobelias, groundsels, aloes and other odd plants.

Meru 38 km (24 miles)

Meru 30 km (19 miles)

Meru Route

Lake Rutundu

Lake Alice

Mount Kenya National Park

Ithanguni 3,894 m

Mutonga

Lake Ellis

Chogoria Route

Nithi Valley

Chogoria 22 km (14 miles)

Mount Kenya National Reserve

VISITORS' CHECKLIST

Road Map C4. 140 km (87 miles) NE of Nairobi. 061 55645 (Park Headquarters). 6am–7pm daily. www.kws.go.ke

KEY

ℹ️	Visitor information
🏠	Lodge
⛺	Campsite
= =	Unpaved motorable road
- -	Trail
- -	Park boundary
▲	Peak

0 km   5

0 miles   5

Chogoria Route
Rated as the most scenic of the main routes up Mount Kenya, Chogoria offers a rather gradual ascent along a track that is still reputedly the highest motorable track in Africa. This track was first explored by car in 1929 to as high as the 4,260-m (14,000-ft) contour.

Lenana Point
Lenana is the highest point on Mount Kenya that can be reached without special mountaineering equipment and experience.

GETTING AROUND

Although there are several trails leading to Mount Kenya's twin peaks of Batian and Nelion, in practice only three are commonly used. The shortest of these is Naro Moru Route, while the most beautiful is the Chogoria Route. The Sirimon Route passes through wide swathes of moorland, home to a number of rare mammals. Less-used trails include the Meru, Burguret and Kamweti routes. The Timau Route can only be hiked with a special permit. Guides and porters are not usually available at the park gates and need to be hired in the nearest town. The park charges entry fees for the anticipated period of a visitor's stay.

Exploring Mount Kenya National Park

A giant lobelia plant

Several thousand people climb Mount Kenya annually, although most go no higher than Lenana Point, the highest peak that can be reached without specialist rock-climbing gear. Several routes are available, but whichever is used, the ascent is not to be taken lightly. Subzero temperatures carry a risk of hypothermia, the rapid ascent often induces altitude sickness and occasional blizzards can lead the unwary away from their routes. Hikes must be arranged with a reputable operator and be equipped with a good local guide and adequate mountain gear. The upper slopes of Mount Kenya are inaccessible to non-hikers, but the forest zone can be accessed at several points, most notably from the Serena Mountain Lodge.

hyraxes, mole-rats and various birds, although zebra, eland, buffalo and even elephant are seen from time to time. With an early start from the camp, it is possible to ascend Lenana and return to the trailhead at the Meteorological Station in one long day. For those who wish to spend more time in the glacial zone, **Austrian Hut** is the highest permanent structure in the mountain, and well positioned for the ascent of Lenana, while the more immediate vicinity is notable for its sparsely vegetated lava formations and views over the **Lewis Glacier**, especially at dusk.

Naro Moru Route

The Meteorological Station is 25 km (16 miles) E of Naro Moru town.

The shortest, easiest and most popular path up Mount Kenya approximates the route taken by the British geologists Halford Mackinder and John Gregory in the 1890s, following the Naro Moru river uphill from Naro Moru town to its source on the western base of the glacial peaks. The round hike can be completed in 3 days, using the **Meteorological Station** as a starting point, but allowing an extra day would greatly reduce the risk of altitude-related illness. It is normal to spend the first night at the station, which lies above the forest line, so hikers on this route will only see the forest and its wildlife from behind a car window unless they opt to walk some or all of the way from Naro Moru. From the station, the hike to **Mackinder's Camp** takes around 6 hours, passing first

Hiking up the popular Naro Moru Route to Mount Kenya

through a steep marshy area known as the Vertical Bog before entering the Teleki Valley, which offers superb views to the peaks in clear weather. The valley is studded with giant lobelias and other floral oddities associated with the Afro-alpine zone. Wildlife here includes rock

Chogoria Route

66 km (41 miles) S of Meru town.

Widely regarded to be the most beautiful hiking route up Mount Kenya, and the longest of those in regular use, Chogoria was pioneered by the aptly named Edward Carr, who drove a Model-T Ford along it as far as the 4,260-m (14,000-ft) contour in 1929, the same year that mountaineer Eric Shipton undertook the second ascent of the peaks. The ascent starts at the **Chogoria Mission Station**, and most people drive at least some of the way through the extensive forest and bamboo zones using the renovated Carr's Road, still said to be the highest motorable track in Africa. Scenic highlights of the upper slopes include **Hall Tarns** and the Afro-alpine moorland of the **Nithi Valley**, both of which are crossed en route to **Minto's Hut**, the base for the final climb to Lenana. At least 4 days and ideally 5 or more

Meru Mount Kenya Lodge on Chogoria Route, Mount Kenya National Park

For hotels and restaurants in this region see pp374–6 and p389

Mount Kenya's snowcapped peaks towering above hikers on the Sirimon Route

should be set aside for this route, descending via the Naro Moru Route to save time.

Sirimon Route

10 km (6 miles) S of the main Timau Road, after a turn-off signposted 16 km (10 miles) NE of Nanyuki.

A very beautiful and rather gradual ascent from the northwest, the little used Sirimon Route offers a relatively unhurried and untrammelled 5-day hike to the peaks, descending via Naro Moru. The northwest slopes receive a significantly lower precipitation than other parts of the mountain, which makes this route particularly attractive during the rainy season. Passing through more extensive moorland than any other route, Sirimon is excellent for Afro-alpine flora and is regarded as the best route for encounters with zebra, klipspringer, elephant, eland and other large mammals. Weather permitting, the moorland also offers fine views to the peaks, particularly from the spectacular Mackinder Valley.

Timau, Burguret and Kamweti Routes

These three ascent routes require special permission from KWS, have limited facilities and are seldom used these days. The most alluring is the Timau Route, a leisurely and scenic approach from the northeast that connects with the Sirimon Route at Shipton's Hut, and is best undertaken over 6 to 7 days. The Burguret Route is a former mule trail that starts in **Gathiuru**, north of Naro Moru, and runs parallel to the North Burguret river for most of its length. This route is of interest for its bamboo forest and for access to caves formerly used as Mau-Mau *(see pp52–3)* hideouts. It is most suitable from January to March, before the start of the long rains. The practically unused Kamweti Route is a very long ascent from the south, starting in Kamweti village and passing through extensive montane forest as it follows the Nyamindi river uphill.

The tree hyrax, Mount Kenya

Serena Mountain Lodge

Similar in conception to the iconic tree hotels of Aberdare National Park *(see pp316–17)*, but if anything superior, Serena Mountain Lodge has a perfect setting overlooking a small waterhole encircled by tall gallery forest, with Mount Kenya's peaks emerging at dusk to loom above the canopy. Unlike the Aberdare Tree Hotels, there is no shuttle from outside the park, which makes it possible to spend all day in the lodge and surrounding forest to enjoy the chattering monkeys, colourful birds and cacophonous wail of the silvery-cheeked hornbill. At night, a white noise of insects and frogs is punctuated by the explosive, heart-stopping braying of tree hyraxes from deep in the forest. Elephant and buffalo pass by daily, while rhino, leopard and lion are more occasional. The undoubted mammalian star is the giant forest hog, a hirsute outsized animal more easily seen here than in any other African forest locality.

The rustic ambience of the restaurant at Serena Mountain Lodge

The formidable southeastern face of Mount Kenya ▷

Plantations are prolific around the luxuriant countryside near Meru

Naro Moru ❾

Road Map C4. 30 km (19 miles) N of Nyeri on the A2. 🏘 *2,700.* ✈ 🚌

This small market town is named after, and lies on the banks of, the Naro Moru river, a chilly tributary of the Ewaso Nyiro that rises in the glacial peaks of Mount Kenya. Naro Moru is the starting point for the most popular hiking route up Mount Kenya, and a good base for the casual exploration of its forested western slopes. However, hotels aside, the town is lacking in most visitor facilities.

The most upmarket base is the **Naro Moru River Lodge** *(see p376)*, which is set in lovely wooded grounds, and has been arranging reliable hikes for decades. A more affordable option, about 10 km (6 miles) out of town along the road to Naro Moru Entrance Gate, the **Mount Kenya Youth Hostel** *(see p376)* has a wonderful setting on the fringe of the forest zone, making it ideal for forest birding and day walks.

Nanyuki ❿

Road Map C4. 30 km *(19 miles)* N of Naro Moru on the A2. 🏘 *32,000.* ✈ 🚌

Founded in 1907 by English settlers, Nanyuki is the administrative capital of Laikipia and the main gateway to the district for travellers visiting by road. The town has a military association dating back to colonial times, and it remains the country's most important air force base, as well as being the site of a long-serving training centre maintained by the British army. The main road attains a moderate degree of architectural distinction by virtue of its colonial-era storefronts, but otherwise it is a typically unassuming highlands town, with more to offer in the way of facilities – banks, hotels, restaurants, Internet cafés and filling stations – than tourist attractions.

Woven bag from Nanyuki

Wildlife enthusiasts passing through Nanyuki should definitely make the effort to visit the **Mount Kenya Wildlife Conservancy**, which forms part of the prestigious **Mount Kenya Safari Club** *(see p376)* but welcomes day visitors. The main attraction here is the world's largest herd of captive-born mountain bongo, an endangered and beautifully marked antelope that is significantly bulkier than its more common lowland West African cousin. Once common in the forests of Mount Kenya, a wild mountain bongo has not been recorded there since 1994, meaning that its natural range is now confined to Aberdare National Park *(see pp316–17)* and the Mau Escarpment. The sanctuary protects various other species associated with Mount Kenya, including the colobus monkey, eland, serval and caracal cat, tame bushbuck and crowned crane.

🎦 **Mount Kenya Wildlife Conservancy**
Mount Kenya Safari Club, 8 km (5 miles) SE of Nanyuki. ⏱ 10am–5pm daily. 🈂 🎫 ♿ 🍴 ✉ www.animal orphanagekenya.com

Meru ⓫

Road Map C4. 75 km (47 miles) E of Nanyuki along the A2 and B6. 🏘 *126,000.* 🚌

The largest town in the Central Highlands and seventh largest in Kenya as a whole, Meru sprawls seemingly interminably along the main road circling the northeast footslopes of Mount Kenya. It receives a higher rainfall than the towns on the mountain's

The Mount Kenya Youth Hostel near Naro Moru

western slopes, and the surrounding bountiful countryside is densely cultivated, forming an important centre for fruit, timber, coffee, bean and tea production. It is also the most important area in Kenya for growing khat, a popular leafy stimulant known locally as *miraa*. A wonderful selection of fresh produce is sold at the sprawling municipal market, and the town is also well-equipped when it comes to amenities such as banks, ATMs, hotels, Internet access, restaurants and supermarkets.

The town is named after the local Meru people, Bantu-speaking agriculturists who share strong affinities with the more populous and politically influential Kikuyu. The Meru form the main subject of the **Meru National Museum**, which, since 1976, has occupied the town's oldest building, a rehabilitated District Commissioner's office originally built in 1916. The museum has three galleries, of which the most interesting is an outdoor display of medicinal shrubs and herbs traditionally used by Meru healers. Also of interest, 13 km (8 miles) outside the town along the same road as Meru National Park, is the *njuuri* (a traditional high court) constructed in 1962 at Ncheke. It is still used occasionally by the council of tribal elders.

🏛 Meru National Museum
Main Rd, opposite Meru Country Hotel. **Tel** *064 32482.* ☐ *9am–6pm daily.* 🖼 📷 **www**.museums.or.ke

The ranger's office at Mwea National Reserve

Meru National Park ⓬

See pp330–33.

Embu ⓭

Road Map C4. 140 km (87 miles) S of Meru along the B6.
🏠 *32,000.* 🚌

Linked to Meru by a madly winding road that clings precipitously to the lushly scenic eastern foothills of Mount Kenya, this moderately proportioned but lively town was founded in 1906 by English settlers. Today, it serves as the administrative headquarters of the Eastern Province and main trading centre of the Bantu-speaking tribe for which it is named. There is very little to distinguish Embu from other similarly sized towns in the Central Highlands, but it has a relaxed leafy feel, and is rather pretty during October and November when its jacaranda

trees start to bloom. The most impressive building in town is the African-themed **Catholic Cathedral** built in 1986 when Embu was recognised as a diocese separate from Meru.

Mwea National Reserve ⓮

Road Map C4. 45 km (28 miles) S of Embu along the B7. **Tel** *068 20301.* ✈ *airstrip at Masinga Resort, 13 km (8 miles) outside the entrance gate.* 🚌 *to within 2 km (1 mile) of the entrance gate.* ☐ *6am–7pm daily.* 🖼 📷 ⚠ **www**.kws.go.ke

Little known and somewhat out of the way, this 42-sq-km (16-sq-mile) reserve protects the unspoiled rolling woodland that runs north from the Kamburu Reservoir at the confluence of the Tana and Thiba rivers. Although small in area and fenced in its entirety, the reserve harbours a variety of large mammals, with impala, waterbuck, elephant, buffalo and Grant's gazelle among the regularly sighted species. The rare Rothschild's giraffe has been introduced to Mwea, and this is one of the better places in Kenya to see the localised lesser kudu. Despite its proximity to Mount Kenya, whose peaks are visible on a clear day, the reserve has a dry climate more typical of the lowlands. Hippo, crocodile and a varied selection of waterbirds can be seen at **Hippo Point**, while the riverine forest supports bushbuck, Sykes monkey, Pel's fishing owl and white-crowned night heron, and is the best habitat for the endemic Hinde's babbler.

Cyclists make their way down a quiet street in Embu

Meru National Park ⑫

One of East Africa's best-kept wildlife secrets, Meru National Park extends over 870 sq km (335 sq miles) of moist savannah in the eastern rainshadow of Mount Kenya and Nyambeni Hills. It lies at the core of a more extensive ecosystem comprising the contiguous Bisanadi, Mwingi and Rahole National Reserves and Kora National Park. In the early 1980s, this was one of Kenya's star attractions, with up to 40,000 visitors annually, and famous for its high densities of buffalo, elephant, lion and other wildlife. The park became a target for poachers in the late 1980s, and fell off the tourist map following the 1988 slaughter of several white rhinos and the rangers guarding them, and the fatal attack on conservationist George Adamson a year later. The park has been safe since the mid-1990s, and wildlife numbers are on the increase.

Vulturine guineafowl in the open grassland

Mulika Swamp is a good place to spot buffalo and elephant.

★ Rhino Sanctuary

Reintroduced from Lake Nakuru National Park and other protected areas in Kenya, some 65 black and white rhinos inhabit the western part of Meru National Park, in a large fenced-off area.

★ Rojewero River

The largest of several fast-flowing streams that run through the park after rising in Mount Kenya, the Rojewero river is fringed by riparian forest and supports several hippo pools.

STAR SIGHTS

★ Rhino Sanctuary

★ Rojewero River

★ Elsa's Grave

Doum Palms

A highly conspicuous component of Meru's flora are the tall doum palms whose narrow trunks and branches run in silhouette along the park's many watercourses.

Reticulated Giraffe
Meru National Park is a good place to see Northern Kenyan "specials" such as the stretch-necked gerenuk, the skittish lesser kudu and the magnificent reticulated giraffe.

KEY

✈️	Domestic airport/airstrip
ⓘ	Visitor information
🔼	Lodge
🔼	Campsite
= =	Unpaved motorable road
▪ ▪	Park boundary

(map showing Bisanadi National Reserve, hwango Swamp, Rojewero, Bisanadi National Reserve, Elsa's Grave, Mwingi National Reserve, Adamson's Falls, Kora National Park, Tana)

★ **Elsa's Grave**
This affecting stone memorial, situated in a forest clearing in the south of the park, is something of a pilgrimage site for devotees of conservationist Joy Adamson's bestselling book Born Free *(see p333).*

Elsa's Kopje
With its swimming pool area overlooking a vast plain, the exclusive hilltop Elsa's Kopje (see p375) is one of the most scenically located lodges in Kenya.

GETTING AROUND

Meru is most easily visited as part of an organised safari, with both fly-in and drive-in options available. There is no access by public transport, but Meru can also be visited in a private 4WD. The internal road network is well maintained and junctions are numbered, both on the ground and on maps, making it easy to navigate. The park's lodges employ specialist guides to take visitors around.

Tana River
Although it lies some distance south of the main wildlife-viewing circuit, the Tana river is the largest waterway in the Kenya and it is well worth making a diversion there for the scenery and birdlife.

Exploring Meru National Park

Although wildlife is quite plentiful, Meru National Park's greatest attraction is undoubtedly its atmosphere of uncrowded wilderness, which ensures that most sightings retain an aura of exclusivity rare in more popular reserves. The Big Five are all present, with elephant and buffalo being particularly conspicuous throughout. A cover of tall grass and dense bush makes predators other than lion difficult to see. An ideal destination for a first game drive is the rhino enclosure, which comes with a near-guarantee of rhino sightings. Elsewhere, wildlife concentrations are mobile and unpredictable, and there is a lot to be said for just exploring the park's mesmerising patchwork of grassland and riverine forest.

Mulika Swamp

Site of the now defunct Meru Mulika Tourist Lodge, Mulika Swamp lies near Junction 35, a short distance inside the entrance gate. It is particularly worth a diversion in the dry season, when large numbers of animals congregate there to drink. Unlike the narrower streams that cut through the park, the swamp is well suited to elephants seeking a midday splash. It also attracts herds of several hundred buffalo, accompanied by flapping flocks of cattle egrets. Giraffe, zebra and impala are frequent visitors, while Bohor reedbuck and waterbuck are resident in the vicinity. The swamp is home to an abundant birdlife that includes grey and purple heron, blacksmith plover and pied kingfisher.

Pied kingfisher

Riverine Forests

A striking feature of Meru National Park is the series of clear and fast-flowing freshwater rivers that rise in the **Nyambeni Hills** in the west, cutting through the grassy plains before they converge with the Tana river along the southern boundary. Most of the rivers support a lush ribbon of riparian forest, whose most conspicuous component is tall doum palms, their narrow trunks and branches standing in stark silhouette against the clear blue sky and providing a playground – and refuge from predators – to the park's numerous olive baboons and vervet monkeys.

The largest of these rivers is the **Rojewero**, which flows through the heart of the park before running along the eastern boundary with the adjacent **Bisanadi National Reserve**, to its confluence with the Tana. An excellent goal for a game drive is the deep hippo pool and nearby group of rapids reached along a road between Junctions 72 and 75. A family of eight to ten hippo is resident here, and the slope of the bank allows for a safe eye-level view of these bumptious creatures. A short drive further along is a viewpoint consisting of a wooden boardwalk overlooking a wide stretch of river above a set of rapids. This is a good site for spotting the endemic golden palm weaver and for observing other riverine species such as the elusive African finfoot, eagerly-sought Pel's fishing owl and spectacular giant kingfisher.

An African elephant in the riverine forests of Meru National Park

Rhino Sanctuary

In the early 1980s, Meru was renowned for its rhinos. Large numbers of black rhino were resident through the park, while a herd of white rhino introduced from South Africa hung around the park headquarters and campsite. These endangered animals were

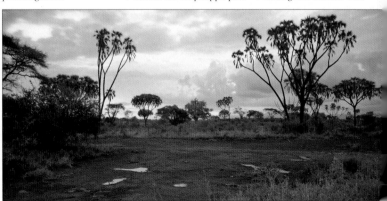

Doum palms tower above the vegetation surrounding Mulika Swamp

Open-fronted thatched cottage with its pool, Elsa's Kopje

the biggest victims of the poaching war that took place in the park, and by 1990 it is thought that none remained. However, as part of a KWS initiative to draw tourists back to Meru, some 55 rhino – mostly black but also white – were reintroduced between 2005 and 2007, and several more calves have been born in the reserve, bringing the total population to around 65. In order to prevent them falling victim to poachers, the rhinos are contained within a large fenced enclosure running south from the main entrance gate past the Mururi Swamp. The relatively dense rhino population within this small area means that the animals are quite easily spotted, and visitors are likely to run into one on a game drive. However, the low traffic means that they are quite skittish compared to their counterparts in Nakuru. Mururi Swamp, set within the fenced sanctuary, is also a favoured haunt of elephant and buffalo.

🦌 Eastern Plains and Tana River

Away from the rivers, the eastern plains of Meru support a cover of lush swaying grass and tangled acacia woodland. Wildlife densities tend to be lower than in the west, but reticulated giraffe, gerenuk, impala, zebra and Somali ostrich are likely to be encountered on a regular basis. The area is dotted with

landmarks related to the tenure of George and Joy Adamson. These include **Elsa's grave**, a simple but affecting stone memorial situated in a forest clearing alongside the Ura river south of Junction 87, as well as the grave of Pippa the cheetah near Junction 13. **Elsa's Kopje** *(see p375)*, an upmarket tented camp on an isolated hill near **Mughwango Swamp**, overlooks one of the earliest campsites of the Adamsons. Somewhat more remote but well worth the effort for those with a few

Pippa's gravestone at Meru

days in the park is the stretch of the Tana river along the southeastern boundary with **Mwingi National Reserve**. This is one of the few areas where Kenya's largest river is easily accessible to travellers. Its forested banks support plenty of wildlife and birds. Spectacular rapids run along the black volcanic bedrock close to Junction 96, while **Adamson's Falls** – named after George, who had a camp in the area after his separation from Joy – lie just across the border with **Kora National Park**.

JOY AND GEORGE ADAMSON

Joy and George at Kora National Park

Meru became a safari destination in the 1960s thanks in part to its association with conservationists Joy and George Adamson, whose pioneering success in releasing captive-raised lions into the wild was immortalised in the book *Born Free*. Mainly known for her work with lions, Joy was also an accomplished artist whose evocative portraits of tribal Kenyans are on display at the National Museum *(see pp158–9)*. Born Friederike Gessner in Austria-Hungary, she moved to Kenya with her first husband to escape World War II. She was nicknamed Joy by her second husband. She married her third husband, India-born George Adamson, then working as a ranger in Northern Kenya, in the early 1940s. The Adamsons acquired *Born Free's* leonine star Elsa in 1956 and released her into Meru 2 years later. Subsequent experiments with a cheetah, Pippa, and leopard, Shaba, also met with success. The couple separated in 1970, but still spent Christmas together every year. Tragically, both met violent deaths – Joy was murdered by a former employee in January 1980, and George was shot dead by Somali poachers in August 1989.

NORTHERN KENYA

*R*emote, thinly inhabited and practically unknown to outsiders, Northern Kenya is one of Africa's last great wilderness areas. An uncompromising desert landscape of scrubland and rocky plains, it is home to some of East Africa's most charismatic pastoralist tribes. This stretch of badlands is broken by one of the largest lakes in the world, Lake Turkana, which runs south from the border with Ethiopia.

Fossil discoveries near Lake Turkana suggest that Northern Kenya has been inhabited by hominids for at least 2.5 million years. Paradoxically, its current occupants are relatively recent arrivals, with ancestral roots in present-day Sudan, Somalia and Ethiopia. Northern Kenya was one of the last parts of Africa to be penetrated by outsiders, remaining terra incognita until 1888, when Count Samuel Teleki, a Hungarian aristocrat, trekked north from Lake Baringo to Turkana. It would be another 7 years before explorer Arthur Donaldson-Smith became the first Westerner to reach Marsabit mountain *(see p348)*. The last of the region's cartographic blanks was filled in 1909, when British colonial administrator Major Chauncey Stigand crossed the Chalbi Desert.

Culturally and economically, there is little about Northern Kenya today that could be described as Westernised.

Pastoral societies such as the Samburu, Turkana and Borana remain staunchly traditionalist, herding cattle, goats or camels for a living, and many people still practise a seminomadic lifestyle. There are few towns of any substance and cultivation is almost non-existent.

Northern Kenya supports several unique mammal and bird species, most of which can be viewed in the popular complex of national reserves near Isiolo. Otherwise, the region boasts few recognised attractions for visitors, with brooding Lake Turkana forming the main goal of most trips further north. For aficionados, however, it is the fantastically empty landscapes en route to the lake, and their stoic pastoralist inhabitants, that impress themselves most firmly on the imagination. Any expedition into these ancient badlands is best viewed as being primarily about the thrillingly unpredictable journey rather than the ultimate destination.

A gathering of camels on the harsh, arid expanse of Chalbi Desert

◁ A view from the top of Teleki's volcano looking to the southern end of Lake Turkana

Nomads of the North

Culturally, Northern Kenya is probably the closest thing to "unchanged Africa" that exists on a comparable scale anywhere on the continent. It is inhabited by a thin scattering of livestock-farming communities who shun modernity and cultural homogenisation in favour of an uncluttered lifestyle bequeathed by generations of stoic desert-dwelling ancestors. Among the tribes here are the Samburu, Borana, Turkana, Gabbra, Rendille and Elmolo. Each tribe has its own traditional culture, dress and customs which are usually adhered to, although a certain degree of intertribal exchange takes place in settlements such as Loiyangalani, where the Rendille, Samburu and Turkana coexist alongside each other.

Fetching and storing water, a major occupation among desert dwellers

NOMADIC LIFESTYLE

By tradition, the tribes of Northern Kenya are nomadic pastoralists. This means that they move regularly from one place to another and depend on livestock (rather than hunting or agriculture) for a living. Prior to the 20th century, the northern nomads had fluid tribal territories, but intertribal boundaries became more entrenched under colonial rule, and remain so today.

Camels are often found in drier areas of the north, replacing cattle that are the popular livestock in most parts of Kenya.

"Singing" wells, *found around the Marsabit area, are named for the Borana's custom of singing communally as the men hoist up buckets of water from the pool in the well's deep base.*

Traditional dance and music *play important social roles among the northern nomads. In most cultures, dances are accompanied by chanting, clapping and competitive pogoing – pride of place goes to whoever jumps highest.*

THE ELMOLO PEOPLE

The oldest inhabitants of the region, the Elmolo differ from their neighbours in lacking a strong tradition of nomadism. They depend on fishing in Lake Turkana, a diet supplemented by hippo or crocodile.

Elmolo women, *like their pastoralist neighbours, are fond of colourful cloths and bead-work jewellery.*

An island near Loiyangalani *is the main centre of the Elmolo, who are said to be Africa's least numerous tribe, consisting of a mere 500 individuals.*

The domed reed-and-cloth huts *built by the Gabbra around Kalacha bear no resemblance to other East African homesteads, yet show strong affinities to huts built by inhabitants of other African deserts such the Sahara and Kalahari.*

The Gabbra *display an ancient Arabic influence both in their complicated calendar (which has allowed them to maintain a very precise oral history) and in their dress of long, flowing white or coloured robes.*

The nomadic lifestyle makes camels the most suitable pack animals as they are capable of carrying heavy loads despite harsh desert conditions.

Nomads generally travel light *and carry few possessions, though calabashes – water containers – are an essential item when they travel long distances.*

THE BORANA NOMADS

The Borana or Boran – of which the Gabbra form a subgroup – are the most widespread and numerous of East Africa's desert nomads, with a territory that covers vast swathes of Northern Kenya and southern Ethiopia. They are closely affiliated to the Oromo of Ethiopia, and speak a mutually intelligible Cushitic language that is known as Afaani Boraana.

THE TURKANA PEOPLE

Northern Kenya is home to about 350,000 Turkana people. They are Nilotic-speaking camel-herders whose territory centres around the lake with which they share a name. Though pastoralists by tradition, many Turkana people have now also taken to fishing.

The attire of Turkana women *is particularly impressive, comprising striking beaten hides and beaded jewellery topped by a dreadlocked Mohican dyed with henna. Many women also wear a goatee-like lower lip plug.*

Turkana houses *are neat and impermanent structures made entirely of thatch and wood, often built by the women of the tribe.*

Notable for their unique hairstyle, *Turkana men cover their heads with mud. They seldom travel far without a spear and the dual-purpose stool that also serves as a headrest when they sleep outdoors.*

Exploring Northern Kenya

The most regularly visited place in Northern Kenya is the Samburu-Buffalo Springs-Shaba complex of reserves near Isiolo, offering exceptional wildlife viewing. Independent travellers can also explore the extraordinary forests of Marsabit mountain and the Samburu stronghold of Maralal. One of the most exciting and remote trips to be done anywhere in Africa starts from Samburu to Marsabit, veers west through the Chalbi Desert to Loiyangalani on the shores of Turkana, and then north, exploring the islands and lakeshore. This expedition can take over a week, but offers a fuller view of Northern Kenya's extraordinary landscapes and people.

KEY

▨ Area Illustrated

Glittering waters of the vast Lake Turkana

SIGHTS AT A GLANCE

Towns
Baragoi ⑤
Isiolo ①
Maralal ④
Marsabit ⑦
Moyale ⑨
South Horr ⑥

National Reserves
Samburu-Buffalo Springs-Shaba National Reserves pp342–6 ②

Areas of Natural Beauty
Chalbi Desert ⑧
Lake Turkana pp352–5 ⑩
Matthews Range ③

SEE ALSO

• *Where to Stay* pp376–7

• *Where to Eat* p389

KEY

▬ Major road
≡ Minor road
▰▰ Untarred major road
=== Untarred minor road
--- 4WD track
▬▬ International border
✕✕✕ Disputed border
△ Peak

Camels at Kalacha, an oasis in the stark Chalbi Desert

0 km   50

0 miles   50

GETTING AROUND

Roads are mostly unsurfaced and in poor condition, none more so than the corrugated Trans-Africa Highway as it runs north from Archer's Post to Moyale via Marsabit. Public transport is extremely limited. There are occasional buses as far north as Marsabit, and minibuses connect Nyahururu to Maralal. A handful of Nairobi-based operators run overland truck trips to Turkana, usually of 6 to 12 days in duration depending on the route used. Otherwise the only practical option is a self-drive expedition or bespoke safari – ideally in convoy, as rescue may be a long way off in the case of a breakdown or any other emergency.

Isiolo

Road Map C4. 80 km (50 miles) N of Nanyuki. 🚶 29,000. 🚍

Heading northwards from the Central Highlands along the A2 to Isiolo, the transition from grassy upland meadow to low-lying acacia scrub is both abrupt and striking. The main urban gateway to Samburu-Buffalo Springs National Reserves and other places further north, Isiolo has a dusty frontier-town feel, which is still further accentuated by the relatively widespread use of traditional clothing among the people.

Founded at the close of World War I as a resettlement camp for former Somali soldiers, the town retains a strong military presence, with three army training corps and a tank unit being based here.

Culturally, Isiolo is a melting pot, home to numerous Somali, Samburu, Rendille and Borana, as well as many Kikuyu and other Bantu-speaking traders from the highlands. It is predominantly Muslim, with around 15 mosques scattered through the town. There is also a large Catholic church. The main highlight for most visitors is the bustling market, which is a good place to buy the handcrafted bead and metal jewellery characteristic of the region. The market is an important centre for trading in *miraa* (khat) leaves as well as the cattle and other livestock that form the lifeblood of the north's limited economy. Isiolo

One of several beautiful mosques in the small town of Isiolo

has several small hotels and campsites, eateries, banks and filling stations, and its supermarkets provide a last opportunity to stock up on manufactured foodstuffs before hitting the open spaces of the north.

Samburu-Buffalo Springs-Shaba National Reserves ②

See pp342–6.

Matthews Range ③

Road Map C3. The gateway town of Wamba is 55 km (34 miles) E of Maralal on the Samburu-Buffalo Springs Rd. 🚍 📷 🍴 🛍 ⛺

Known as Ol Doinyo Lenkiyio by the local Samburu people, the Matthews Range stretches for about 150 km (93 miles)

along a north-south axis and rises to a maximum altitude of 2,688 m (8,819 ft) at **Warges Peak**, near the southern end of the range. The rocky slopes support extensive stands of an endemic species of prehistoric cycad, while the peaks support a cover of dense fragrant juniper forest. A significant portion of the range is now protected by Namunyak Wildlife Conservation Trust, a community-based organisation established in 1995 to protect the area's once prodigious number of large mammals and promote ecotourism in a manner that benefits local communities. More than 1,000 elephant are thought to be resident or to pass through the area seasonally, and other wildlife includes buffalo, lion, leopard, cheetah, African wild dog, black rhino, greater kudu, Grevy's zebra, eland and various smaller antelope. The area is also rich in butterflies and birds. For the independent traveller, the best base for exploration is **Wamba**, an overgrown village situated at the range's southern end.

Maralal ④

Road Map C3. 125 km (78 miles) N of Nyahururu. 🚶 16,500. ✈ 🚍 🐪 *International Camel Derby (Aug).*

The self-styled capital of the Samburu people, Maralal is a lively town whose modern facilities belie the strongly traditional feel of its populace and its spiritual significance in Samburu culture – its name

The densely forested slopes of the Matthews Range, near Parsaloi

Impalas grazing peacefully in a grove at Maralal Wildlife Sanctuary

literally means "house of god". Another important springboard for travel in the arid north, the town confounds all expectations with its breezy highland setting at an altitude of 1,965 m (6,450 ft) on the northern edge of Laikipia Plateau. The town centre boasts few notable landmarks, the main exception being **Jomo Kenyatta House**, the tin-roofed bungalow where Kenyatta, who would later become Kenya's first president, was detained by the colonial authorities in 1961. Maralal was also home to the author Wilfred Thesiger until 1994. The entertaining and exciting International Camel Derby (*see p39*), usually held in August, has become a popular social event with both foreign visitors and Kenyans.

The town lies near the unfenced **Maralal Wildlife Sanctuary**, where zebra, eland, baboon, impala, spotted hyena and the occasional leopard can be seen at the waterhole overlooked by **Maralal Safari Lodge** (*see p377*) only 3 km (2 miles) from the town centre.

🏛 **Jomo Kenyatta House**
Maralal. ⭕ *9am–6pm daily.*

Baragoi ❺

Road Map C3. 150 km (93 miles) N of Maralal on the Turkana Road. 👥 *1,000.* 🚌

The small town of Baragoi, founded in the 1930s, is the major trade centre of an eponymous district that supports a thin population of traditional pastoralists – mainly Samburu but also Turkana, Rendille and Somali. The most important feature, on the outskirts of the small town centre, is a daily livestock market that attracts sellers and buyers from all over the district, many of whom walk for days to get there. Aside from camels, cattle and goats, the leisurely market has sections dedicated to fresh produce, and local jewellery and handicrafts.

Coming from Baragoi, after about 80 km (50 miles) the road passes through Poror, from where a 5-km (3-mile) track leads west to the so-called **World's End Viewpoint**. Here, the Losiolo Escarpment plunges more than 2,000 m (6,562 ft) to the base of the Suguta Valley, forming the highest single drop along the Rift Valley Escarpment.

South Horr ❻

Road Map C2. 40 km (25 miles) N of Baragoi. 👥 *1,000.* 🚌

Set in a valley flanked by the northern base of the Ndoto Hills and southern base of **Ol Doinyo Mara** (Speckled Mountain), the pleasant and atypically lush Samburu settlement of South Horr is a popular overnight stop between Maralal and Lake Turkana. The town is named after the perennial river that runs through it – *horr* means river – and supports shady rows of fever trees along with cultivated stands of bananas and papayas.

South Horr is a good place for visitors to familiarise themselves with traditional Samburu ways. The forest-clad Ndoto Hills offer some excellent and under-subscribed walking and bird-watching opportunities. These are best explored from the out-of-town **Desert Rose** (*see p377*). The demanding day hike to the 2,682-m (8,800-ft) high **Nyiro Peaks** usually offers good wildlife sightings, including buffalo, as well as sterling views north to Lake Turkana.

Explorer and author Wilfred Thesiger in Kenya

WILFRED THESIGER

From 1980 to 1994, Maralal was home to Sir Wilfred Thesiger, an inveterate traveller and prolific author known for his fascination with people of deserts and other arid environments. The son of a British diplomat, Thesiger was born in Addis Ababa, Ethiopia, in 1910 and returned there 20 years later to attend the coronation of Emperor Haile Selassie. In 1933, he became the first European explorer to return alive from the Danakil area of Ethiopia's Rift Valley (whose Afar residents were known for their custom of killing male intruders), in the process establishing that the mighty Awash river evaporated in the saline lake Abbé on the border with Djibouti. He later travelled extensively in Arabia and North Africa, and published several classic books including *The Danakil Diary*, *The Marsh Arabs* and *My Kenya Days*, the last a fascinating account of his 14-year sojourn in Maralal. Thesiger returned to England in 1994 and died in a home for the elderly in 2003, aged 93.

Samburu-Buffalo Springs-Shaba National Reserves ❷

The one part of Northern Kenya that attracts visitors in significant numbers is this trio of ecologically affiliated and unfenced reserves, which collectively protect 440 sq km (170 sq miles) of semiarid savannah flanking the Ewaso Nyiro river. Their ecology is defined by the contrasting habitats of riverine forest along the Ewaso Nyiro and austere acacia scrub and rocky slopes extending outward from it. The reserves probably offer the best chance of sighting leopard in Kenya, and lion, elephant and buffalo are also quite common. The main attraction, however, is a host of dry country specials absent or rare in most other East African parks. This includes mammals, such as Beisa oryx and gerenuk, and a long list of birds of which the cobalt-chested vulturine guinea fowl is the most spectacular.

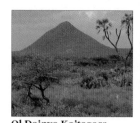

Ol Doinyo Koitogorr
This pyramidal hill is a conspicuous landmark in Samburu. Game drives on its scrub-covered slopes come with a near guarantee of sighting gerenuk, dik-dik and various dry-country birds.

★ **Ewaso Nyiro River**
Sustaining this complex of dry-country reserves is the Ewaso Nyiro river, a near-perennial river that rises in the Aberdares and provides a vital source of water for elephants and other large mammals.

Archer's Post Gate, named after the nearby village, is the main entry point to Samburu National Reserve.

Samburu National Reserve

Ol Doinyo Koitogorr 1,244 m

West Gate

Ewaso Nyiro

Uaso Gate Samburu HQ
Upper River Circuit

Buffalo Springs National Reserve

Ranger's Post

★ **Buffalo Springs**
Another important perennial water source are the Buffalo Springs, which bubble from below the earth a short drive south of the river and attract a steady stream of thirsty gazelles, giraffes, zebras and other ungulates.

| 0 km | 5 |
| 0 miles | 5 |

STAR SIGHTS

★ Ewaso Nyiro River

★ Buffalo Springs

★ Grevy's Zebra

★ **Grevy's Zebra**
Larger than the more widespread plains zebra and with a narrower stripe pattern, the endangered Grevy's zebra is more or less endemic to Northern Kenya.

GETTING AROUND

Samburu and Buffalo Springs form a block to the west of the Trans-Africa Highway, respectively running along the north and south banks of the Ewaso Nyiro. Most lodges are located along the north bank, but the two reserves are connected by a bridge near Samburu Game Lodge. Shaba lies east of the highway, on the south bank of the river. All three can be explored from each other, with Samburu-Buffalo Springs offering the best game viewing and Shaba the more untrammelled atmosphere.

VISITORS' CHECKLIST

Road Map C3. Entrance gates to Shaba, Samburu and Buffalo Springs all lie 40 km (25 miles) N of Isiolo near Archer's Post. 🖂 ℹ 0721 729036 (warden). ◐ 6am–6.30pm daily. 💳 admission fee covers all three reserves. 🍴 🛶 🛖

Joy's Camp (see p377), an exclusive upmarket lodge, stands on the campsite where Joy Adamson raised a leopard called Penny – the heroine of her last book, *Queen of Sheba*.

Chanler's Falls
Gafarsa Gate
Dudubata 881 m ▲
Natorbe Gate
ffalo Springs
kaa Gate
Shaba National Reserve
Shaba Gate
Shaba Hill 1,624 m
A HIGHWAY

KEY

🖂	Domestic airport/airstrip
ℹ	Visitor information
🏠	Lodge
⚠	Campsite
�045	Viewpoint
▬▬	Major road
▪ ▪	Unpaved major road
═ ═	Unpaved motorable road
▬ ▬	Park boundary
▲	Peak

Shaba Hill
A conspicuous landmark in Shaba National Reserve, the 1,624-m (5,350-ft) high Shaba Hill stands in isolation on the southern boundary.

Leopard Sightings
The riverine forest in the eastern half of Buffalo Springs is renowned for its excellent leopard sightings due to the presence of several individuals that have become habituated to vehicles.

Exploring Samburu-Buffalo Springs National Reserves

Originally a single reserve in 1948, Samburu and Buffalo Springs were regazetted as separate entities in 1963. They are separated by the Ewaso Nyiro river and connected by a solitary low bridge in the west, close to the warden's office and Samburu Game Lodge. The bridge may flood occasionally after heavy rain, when the only safe crossing is on the main Trans-Africa Highway south of Archer's Post. Normally it is easy to cross between the two reserves for game drives, making it possible to explore Samburu-Buffalo Springs in its entirety by using a single lodge as a base. The dirt roads within the park are in good condition, but a 4WD may be essential after the rains, particularly on the loose sandy soils that characterise the eastern plains of Buffalo Springs.

Ewaso Nyiro River

The centrepiece of Samburu-Buffalo Springs is the Ewaso Nyiro river, which rises in the Aberdares and arcs through the Laikipia Plateau (see pp318–21) before eventually emptying into the expansive Lorian Swamp in Kenya's remote northeast. Although it has been known to cease flowing in very dry years, the river is essentially perennial and its name, which means muddy water or brown water, refers to the rich red-brown top soil it carries down from Laikipia. Within the reserves, the river supports a lush ribbon of palm-studded riparian forest that contrasts pleasingly with the surrounding aridity. In the dry season, it forms the most important source of drinking water for miles around, and mammal concentrations in Samburu-Buffalo Springs tend to be far higher at this time than after the rains, when the

Signpost in Samburu Reserve

wildlife disperses deep into the desert and meets its drinking needs there using temporary pools.

For visitors with limited time, the well-maintained tracks that run parallel to both the north and south banks of the river are undoubtedly the most rewarding focus for game drives. Hippo and crocodile are resident and easily seen, as are a host of water-associated birds such as the African fish eagle, African spoonbill, water thick-knee, yellow-billed stork and chestnut-bellied kingfisher. The riverine vegetation also attracts plenty of elephant and buffalo. Waterbuck, Burchell's zebra and reticulated giraffe are common, and flocks of orange-bellied parrot often attract attention with their lively screeches. Samburu-Buffalo Springs has a reputation for certain leopard sightings, based largely on the fact that several lodges used to bait these elusive

creatures with fresh meat. This practice has now been outlawed on ecological grounds. The individual leopards that used to benefit from it remain habituated to people and vehicles, as do their offspring, and the odds of an extended leopard sighting are better here than in any other part of Kenya. The best place to look for them is in Buffalo Springs, following the network of tracks that run through the riparian forest on the south bank of the river. Good sightings can sometimes be had in Samburu, on the north bank.

Gerenuk in the foothills of Samburu's Ol Doinyo Koitogorr

Ol Doinyo Koitogorr and the Northern Scrubland

North of the river, Samburu National Reserve protects a far more undulating terrain than Shaba or Buffalo Springs. The skyline is dominated by the impressive 1,250-m (4,100-ft) high Ol Doinyo Koitogorr. The rocky slopes here support a tangled cover of dry thorn scrub, dominated by stunted acacia trees, their branches laden with untidy nests built by buffalo-weaver and sparrow-weaver colonies. These are interspersed with impressive termite towers that stand taller than a person, and often host colonies of the endearing dwarf mongoose, or provide a stage for brightly coloured pairs of D'Arnaud's or red-and-yellow barbet to perform their striking duets.

Wildlife concentrations are lower away from the river, but the emphasis is on species associated specifically with the badlands of Northern Kenya. The rubber-necked gerenuk is common here, and family parties are often seen

The forested banks of the Ewaso Nyiro in Samburu National Reserve

For hotels and restaurants in this region see pp376–7 and p389

foraging on acacia canopies. Pairs of the diminutive Guenther's dik-dik scurry twitch-nosed along the roadside, and larger antelope such as eland, impala, lesser kudu and Grant's gazelle are also very visible – the last with much larger horns than the more southerly race of the Masai Mara and Serengeti. The area is good for cheetah, too, but some luck is required for a decent lion sighting.

This northern scrubland is especially rewarding for visitors who are on the lookout for dry-country birds. Two of the more eye-catching species are the vulturine guineafowl and yellow-throated spurfowl, both of which spend much of their time scurrying around on the ground along the margins of the road. Also a common sight are the blue-legged Somali ostrich, the localised Egyptian vulture and the dazzlingly colourful golden pipit and golden-breasted starling. Somewhat more drab, but no less interesting to serious bird-watchers, are such dry-country endemics as the Abyssinian scimitar-bill, black-capped social weaver, white-headed mousebird, Somali bee-eater and bristle-crowned starling.

Buffalo Springs and the Southern Plains

Flatter and more lightly vegetated than its northern counterpart, Buffalo Springs is characterised by thin claylike soils that support a cover of open grassland interspersed with low greyish stands of whistling thorn and isolated flat-topped umbrella thorns.

Entrance gate to Samburu National Reserve

Grevy's zebra, Beisa oryx and Grant's gazelle seem especially drawn to this open environment. It is also good for a number of large ground birds such as the comically eyelid-fluttering ground hornbill, the mincing secretary bird and a variety of bustards, including the kori bustard, a contender for the accolade of the world's heaviest flying creature. The more common predators are present in small numbers, with cheetah and striped hyena being something of a local speciality.

Away from the river, the game-viewing centrepiece is the eponymous springs in the east of the reserve near Buffalo Springs Shimba Lodge. There are in fact three springs, although the largest is hidden behind a nondescript concrete wall from where sprouts a trio of tall palm trees. Another spring is used to feed a warm swimming pool, although swimming is no longer permitted. The third spring has

Samburu woman at Archer's Post

been left as is, and it forms a major magnet for thirsty wildlife in the dry season, leading to heavy overgrazing in the immediate vicinity. Whatever the season, groups of oryx and reticulated giraffe are almost always present, but buffalo are relatively scarce.

Archer's Post

Straddling the main road between Samburu-Buffalo Springs and Shaba, Archer's Post is an important trading centre for the Samburu people of the region, whose colourful traditional attire stands in striking contrast to the arid surroundings. The village offers campers a last chance to stock up on basic foodstuffs before they enter the park, and even boasts a couple of basic guesthouses and eateries aimed at safari drivers but occasionally used by intrepid backpackers. While informal interaction with the Samburu is likely for visitors spending time in Archer's Post, the small town is also surrounded by semiformal cultural villages aimed at safarigoers who want to learn more about traditional Samburu ways. Village visits of this sort are the one occasion when photographing the normally camera-shy Samburu is tolerated. These visits normally culminate in an exciting display of singing, ululation and pogo-style dancing – a memorable addition to any safari, and one that ensures some of the money generated by tourism goes straight to grassroots communities.

A group of oryx on the open arid plains of Buffalo Springs

Exploring Shaba National Reserve

Gazetted as a reserve in 1974, Shaba made headlines in 1980 as the site of the murder of Joy Adamson *(see p333)*, and served as the setting for the American reality show *Survivor: Africa* in 2001. More recently, the reserve attracted global attention when a resident lioness, nicknamed Kamuniak (Blessed One) by local Samburu, adopted a succession of half a dozen oryx calves over a two-year period. Despite being almost as large as Samburu and Buffalo Springs combined, Shaba has rather little wildlife, and tours based at its solitary large lodge tend to conduct most game drives in Buffalo Springs. Tourist traffic is, therefore, very low, and visitors can often drive for hours through the magnificent semiarid scenery without seeing another vehicle.

A herd of impala grazing while the dominant male keeps watch

🐾 Ewaso Nyiro River

As with Samburu-Buffalo Springs, the Ewaso Nyiro river is the major geographic feature in Shaba. The river flows eastwards along the park's northern boundary for some 35 km (22 miles) and supports a lush ribbon of riverine forest dominated by doum palms, sycamore figs, fever trees and camelthorns. One of the best access points is the **Sarova Shaba Lodge** *(see p377)* on the western boundary. The verdant grounds of this lodge are fed by freshwater springs that run through a sequence of streams and ponds into the river, so the riverine forest here is especially luxuriant and rattling with monkeys, baboons and birds such as the handsome bristle-crowned starling. Numerous outsized crocodiles and monitor lizards frequent the shady southern banks of the river, and a variety of storks and smaller waders can usually be seen picking their way along the northern banks. Game-viewing roads east of the lodge also offer several views of the river.

🏞 Western Game-viewing Circuit

The main game-viewing loop through the western half of Shaba entails following the main track east of the entrance gate for about 3 km (2 miles), then veering northeast along a series of tracks that run parallel to the river for about 16 km (10 miles) before cutting back south again to the main road at **Dudubata Hill**. It is a very scenic drive, with the palm-fringed river often visible, and the sheer basaltic cliffs of **Ol Doinyo Sabache** – site of a rare breeding colony of Rüppell's vulture – rising to an altitude of 1,880 m (6,168 ft) above the northern bank. Several hot springs rise in the area, but otherwise the habitat is very open, consisting of a mosaic of lava-strewn plains, grassland and dry thornbush. A good variety of dry-country mammals are seen here, including Beisa oryx, gerenuk and Grant's gazelle, but population densities are rather low. The birdlife, by contrast, is superb, with a strong emphasis on species associated with very dry habitats, such as coursers, sandgrouse and bustards, as well as the gorgeous rosy-patched shrike and golden-breasted starling and the very localised masked lark. Visitors take at least 3 hours to cover this loop, more if they are serious about birds.

🏞 Eastern Game-viewing Circuit

The eastern plains of Shaba are scenically reminiscent of the west, with the river and Ol Doinyo Sabache visible to the north and the 1,624-m (5,350-ft) high **Shaba Hill** dominating the southern horizon. However, this area is even more untrammelled, thanks to its relatively remote location. A major landmark is the campsite where Joy Adamson raised the heroine of her last book, a leopard called Penny, and was murdered in 1980. Originally adorned with a simple memorial plaque, this is now the site of an exclusive tented lodge called **Joy's Camp** *(see p377)* overlooking a spring-fed waterhole that attracts a steady stream of buffalo, reticulated giraffe, elephant, Grevy's zebra and lion. The untidy fields of black lava that characterise this harsh landscape are home to the ultra-localised Williams lark.

Further afield, it is possible to make a day trip following the Ewaso Nyiro river for about 32 km (20 miles) beyond the park's eastern boundary to the remote **Chanler's Falls**, named after William Astor Chanler, the American explorer.

The cascading waters of Chanler's Falls, near Shaba National Reserve

The Samburu People

Samburu National Reserve is named after the Samburu people, close cultural affiliates of the Maasai, with whom they share a common language called Maa. The two tribes migrated together from their original homeland in Ethiopia or Sudan but split near the Turkana area in the 17th century, with the Samburu settling on the fringe of the Central Highlands and northern deserts, and the Maasai continuing southwards. Pastoralists by tradition,

Warrior's headgear

the Samburu cling staunchly to the ways of their forefathers. The social system is based around three male age-sets, namely *ilayoik*, uncircumcised boys who tend livestock, *ilmoran*, circumcised warriors who defend the clan, and *ilpayiani*, elders who are responsible for administration and lawmaking. For the Samburu, the idea of God is strongly associated with large mountains, and elders are customarily buried facing such a location.

Samburu huts are temporary structures, constructed to suit the nomadic lifestyle of the Samburu.

Most Samburu people still dress in traditional attire, adorning themselves with an elaborate selection of beaded and other jewellery.

THE SAMBURU WAY OF LIFE

The Samburu people are nomadic pastoralists by custom, moving from one temporary camp to the next in search of water and grazing for their livestock. Their homes reflect this lifestyle, being simple and somewhat impermanent structures of mud, wood and thatch.

The men are striking in their customary dress of red chequered blankets.

Traditional forms of dancing *are an important part of Samburu life. The dancers employ a pogoing technique very similar to that of the Maasai.*

The main diet of the Samburu, *who seldom hunt and eat meat only on special occasions, is a fermented mix of cow's milk and blood, sometimes sweetened with honey.*

Loibor Kineji, *literally "people of the white goats", is another name for the Samburu.*

The warrior tradition *is still very much part of Samburu culture, and an* ilmoran *is seldom seen without a spear in hand.*

Marsabit

Road Map D2. 300 km (186 miles)
N of Isiolo. 🕌 *14,000.* 🚌

An isolated massif rising to a
lofty 1,700 m (5,600 ft) from
the surrounding plains, Mount
Marsabit is a long-dormant
basaltic shield volcano whose
slopes support one of the few
towns of any substance in the
northern deserts. The mountain has an oasis-like quality,
and the cool moist highland
air for which it is named –
Marsabit means "cold place" –
provides welcome relief from
the parched terrain below.
Climate and setting aside,
Marsabit is much like other
towns in this area, although it
does support a diverse mix of
Somali, Rendille, Samburu,
Turkana, Borana, Gabbra and
Burji peoples, as well as businesspeople from the Central
Highlands and immigrants
from neighbouring Ethiopia.
    The lower-lying badlands
outside town are protected in
the **Marsabit National
Reserve**, which hosts small
populations of reticu-
lated giraffe, Grevy's
zebra, gerenuk and
even lion and chee-
tah. The area is
studded with extinct
volcanic craters and
Borana "singing"
wells. Adjacent to the town,
the forested **Marsabit National
Park** is a real treat. Its game-
viewing centrepiece is a
beautiful forest-ringed crater
lake overlooked by **Marsabit
Lodge** *(see p377)*. Elephants
pass by the lake daily, and
the birdlife is wonderful, with
fish eagles and falcons soaring
above the waders and storks

**Painting at the
church in Kalacha**

gathering in the shallows.
Deeper in the park is **Lake
Paradise**, another lovely crater
lake, while the **Bongole Crater**
graces the mountain's summit.
    Marsabit's most famous
resident was Ahmed, an elephant whose ground-scraping
3-m (10-ft) long tusks earned
him 24-hour armed protection
by presidential decree until his
death in 1974. The tusks are
on display at the Nairobi
National Museum *(see pp158–
9)*. While few Marsabit elephants can match this today,
their tusks are notably larger
than in most parts of Kenya.

🦌 **Marsabit National Park**
Outskirts of Marsabit town.
Tel *069 2028.* 🕐 *6am–7pm daily.*
🖼 🍴 🚗 🅰 www.kws.go.ke

Chalbi Desert ❽

Road Map C2. 100 km (62 miles)
NW of Marsabit.

Traversed by the only
motorable track between
Marsabit and Turkana, the
startling Chalbi Desert
is an expanse of flat,
cracked, treeless earth
inhabited by ostriches
that run away in hys-
terics at the approach
of a vehicle, and
herds of domestic
camel that are only slightly
more habituated. It is practically uninhabited, although in
wet years the entire desert
becomes a shallow water-
filled pan attracting thousands
of waterbirds. The one permanent settlement is **Kalacha**, a
small Gabbra village set
around a perennial freshwater
spring that has supported

The cracked arid landscape of the
Chalbi Desert near Kalacha

human habitation for centuries.
Excavations nearby have
revealed ancient skeletons
averaging over 2 m (7 ft) in
height, supporting local legends that an extinct race of
giants dug the deep wells that
dot Marsabit and built the massive burial cairns found
throughout the region. The
village's main attraction is its
small church, with walls
covered in Ethiopic paintings.

Moyale ❾

Road Map D1. 250 km (155 miles)
NW of Marsabit. 🕌 *14,000.* 🚗

Straddling the Ethiopian border
at the end of a long stretch of
corrugated road running north
from Marsabit, Moyale is not
a destination that is easily
accessible. Historically, its one
claim to fame is that both the
Kenyan and Ethiopian sides
were taken by Italy in 1940
during World War II and
recaptured by Allied Forces
a year later. Both sides of
town are inhabited by Borana
and Somali majorities, but
are otherwise quite different
in character, with architecture
typical of their respective
countries. However, the
Kenyan side offers visitors
from the south an intriguing
first taste of Ethiopia's unique
cuisine – a fiery red *wat*
sauce eaten with *injera*, a
vast sour pancake. Those
heading across the border
will find that the road is surfaced almost all the way to
Addis Ababa. The lava desert
of **Dida Galgalu** between
Marsabit and Moyale is the
main stronghold of the
endemic Williams lark.

The forest-fringed Lake Paradise, Marsabit National Reserve

For hotels and restaurants in this region see pp376–7 and p389

The Leakey Family

Born in 1903 and 1916 respectively, Louis Leakey and his wife Mary were arguably the leading paleontological figures of the 20th century. They excavated dozens of sites in East Africa, ranging from Acheulean stone tool repositories at Olorgasailie and Kariandusi to the Kondoa rock art of Tanzania. The Leakeys' most groundbreaking discovery, a 1.75 million-year-old *Paranthropus* skull unearthed at Olduvai Gorge in 1959,

Reconstructed hominid skull

provided the first concrete evidence that human evolution stretched past the million-year mark. The family tradition was continued by their son Richard, whose 1970s discoveries at Koobi Fora included the 1.6-million-year-old Turkana Boy and the 2.5-million-year-old Black Skull. Richard retired from paleontology to head up Kenya Wildlife Service in 1989, but his wife Meave and daughter Louise remain active in the field at Koobi Fora.

LOUIS AND MARY LEAKEY
The founders of Kenya's most famous paleontological dynasty, Louis and Mary Leakey have contributed significantly to the study of human evolution, and their work has provided compelling evidence to support Charles Darwin's assertions that human beings evolved in Africa.

Jane Goodall's pioneering chimp study *and Dian Fossey and Birute Galdika's parallel research on gorillas and orang-utans respectively were initiated by Louis Leakey in the belief that ape behaviour would shed light on early human society.*

This partial Homo Habilis skull *was unearthed in 1972. One of several key hominid fossils from Koobi Fora, it is believed to be 1.9 million years old.*

Richard Leakey, *like his father Louis, made his name in the field of paleontology. He is, however, better known for his work as a conservationist and his outspoken anti-corruption stance during the Moi era.*

The mother and daughter team of Meave and Louise Leakey *unearthed a 3.5-million-year-old skull in the vicinity of Lake Turkana in 2001. This belonged to a previously undescribed hominid Kenyanthropus platyops – literally "flat-faced man of Kenya".*

The classic book The Making of Mankind *(1981) is among prolific writer Richard Leakey's popular works on human evolution.*

Lake Turkana ⑩

Immortalised in John Hillaby's classic travel account *Journey to the Jade Sea*, Turkana is the undisputed jewel of Northern Kenya. This 6,400-sq-km (2,450-sq-mile) inland sea is ranked as the largest alkaline lake in the world, and the largest lake of any kind to be set in a desert. The Samburu call it Asso Narok (Black Lake); it was known as Lake Rudolf during the colonial era and was renamed Turkana after the local people post independence. Primordial yet eerily beautiful, Turkana lies in a barren hinterland of volcanic rock swept by a brutally incessant dry southeaster. Its annual rainfall is below 200 mm (8 inches), so vegetation is sparse and can be viciously spiky to the touch. The lake's three islands are a stopover for migrant birds and a breeding site for crocodile and hippo.

A Turkana woman in bright traditional dress, Elmolo Bay

North Island

Formed several million years ago but still riddled with fumaroles and other signs of latent activity, North Island consists of a nested volcano rising to 140 m (459 ft) above the lake surface.

Central Island National Park

The three crater lakes on this island are the main breeding site for Turkana's crocodile population of 15,000–20,000.

STAR SIGHTS

★ Sibiloi National Park

★ Loiyangalani

★ South Island National Park

Fishing on Lake Turkana

The lake supports a thriving population of tilapia and other fish, as attested to by its Turkana name Anam Ka'alakol, literally "sea of abundant fish".

★ **Sibiloi National Park**
This park protects some wildlife, but is more famous for the paleontological treasures unearthed at sites such as Koobi Fora. It lies at the core of a UNESCO World Heritage Site inscribed in 1997.

VISITORS' CHECKLIST

Road Map B1. Loiyangalani is 270 km (168 miles) W of Marsabit. 🚌 🍴 🛶 ⛺
www.kws.go.ke

GETTING AROUND

Loiyangalani on the southeastern shore is accessible by organised truck trips from Nairobi. From here, South Island can be visited by boat. The rest of the eastern shore has dirt roads and is accessible only by 4WD. Limited public transport is available to Kalokol on the western shore; from here boat trips to Central Island are easily arranged.

KEY

✈	Domestic airport/airstrip
🏠	Lodge
⛺	Campsite
━━	Major road
══	Minor road
= =	Unpaved motorable road
- -	Park boundary
━•━	International boundary
✕✕✕	Disputed border
▲	Peak

KENYA

Sibiloi
National
Park

Alia
Derati

Gajos

★ **Loiyangalani**
Although it is the largest settlement on the eastern lakeshore, Loiyangalani remains little more than an overgrown village, and most of its residents – Turkana, Samburu and Elmolo – still live in traditional grass huts.

Porr
670 m
Elmolo
Elmolo
Bay
Loiyangalani
Kulal ▲
2,293 m
South
Island
(77)
Von Höhnel
Bay
Maralal
120 km
(75 miles)
Kalolenyang
1,067 m
Andrew's Volcano
1,067 m
Loriu Range
Kerio
Suchorugwai Desert

★ **South Island National Park**
Like the other islands in Turkana, South Island is volcanic in origin, as evident by the presence of 16 craters. Oral traditions and the existence of non-vegetated lava flows suggest it probably last erupted in the early 19th century.

Exploring Lake Turkana

Its serpentine shape determined by the steep contours of the Rift Valley, Lake Turkana once extended southwards as far as modern-day Baringo, and stretched northwards to feed a tributary of the Ethiopian Blue Nile. Today, fed primarily by Ethiopia's Omo river, it no longer has a surface outlet and the alkaline water, though drinkable, is soapy, saline and saturated with algae, which gives it the blue-green shade alluded to in the nickname "Jade Sea". Most driving safaris to Turkana end up at Loiyangalani; although the eastern lakeshore is not serviced by public transport, private vehicles occasionally head up here from Maralal and will offer travellers a seat at a negotiable rate.

Barren South Island and the vast Lake Turkana

Loiyangalani

270 km (168 miles) W of Marsabit.

Locals refer to Loiyangalani as Turkana City with a mixture of affection and facetiousness. The largest settlement anywhere on Turkana's eastern lakeshore and the main travel gateway of the region, Loiyangalani consists of a few dozen concrete buildings surrounded by a sprawl of about 500 traditional reed huts inhabited by Rendille, Samburu and Turkana pastoralists. It is a truly unique and wonderful place to visit, a distinctly Wild West outpost that owes less to the presence of Lake Turkana than to the freshwater springs that bubble to the surface here. Dress codes and body ornamentations are defiantly traditional, ranging from the striking red robes and colourful beaded jewellery favoured by the Samburu to the henna-dyed Mohican hairstyles and goatee-like lip plugs of the Turkana women.

A popular excursion from Loiyangalani is a half-day boat trip to **Elmolo Bay**, where the last few hundred members of the piscivorous Elmolo tribe eke out an existence on a small island they share with hippos, crocodiles and waterbirds. By contrast, the glittering quartzite rocks and semiprecious stones hawked around the small town come from **Mount Kulal**, whose main volcanic peak soars 2,293 m (7,500 ft) above the lakeshore immediately east of Loiyangalani. A UNESCO International Biosphere Reserve since 1978, Mount Kulal is a worthwhile climb for well-equipped hikers. The upper slopes offer stunning views across the lake to the opposite wall of the Rift Valley. The mountain is the only known locale for the endemic Kulal white-eye bird.

Yellow-billed stork, South Island

South Island National Park

16 km (10 miles) SW of Loiyangalani. 6am–7pm daily. www.kws.go.ke

The largest of three uninhabited volcanic islands that rear up from the deep floors of Lake Turkana, South Island is also sometimes known as Höhnel Island, after Lieutenant Ritter von Höhnel, a member of the 1888 Teleki expedition to Turkana, who witnessed a small eruption off its shore. Ancient lava flows can still be seen at the north end of the island. Local oral tradition talks of fire rising from the peaks, but no evidence of a more recent eruption exists.

Gazetted as a national park in 1983, South Island consists of 16 volcanic craters aligned on a 12-km (8-mile) long ridge that rises steeply to around 320 m (1,050 ft) above the lakeshore. Like Turkana's other islands, it supports large numbers of crocodile, but its main point of zoological interest is as a breeding point for resident and migratory birds, with a maximum count of 220,000 waterbirds and 84 species recorded in 1992. Birds such as the pink-backed pelican, greater flamingo, spur-winged plover, Caspian plover and little stint are seasonally common, while resident species include the African fish eagle, fox kestrel, goliath heron, saddle-billed stork and African skimmer.

Tourist boat on Lake Turkana, Loiyangalani

For hotels and restaurants in this region see pp376–7 and p389

✈ Sibiloi National Park

125 km (78 miles) N of Loiyangalani.
Tel 0721 282125. ☐ *6am–7pm daily.*
🔲 📷 🍴 ⚠️ www.sibiloi.com

Gazetted in 1973, the remote 1,570-sq-km (606-sq-mile) Sibiloi National Park extends along the northeast shore of Lake Turkana. Named after the volcanic Mount Sibiloi, the park is best known as the site of **Koobi Fora**, whose rich sedimentary rocks have yielded more than 10,000 vertebrate fossils – including more than 350 specimens of *Australopithecines* and other extinct hominids – since it was first excavated by the Leakeys (*see p349*) in 1968. Specific areas of interest here include a Stone Age burial site marked by the basaltic **Jarigole Pillars**, a 12-million-year-old fossil forest on Sibiloi Mountain overlooking Alia Bay and the in situ excavated skeletons of extinct elephant, tortoise and crocodile species – the latter measuring almost 15 m (49 ft) long.

Sibiloi also protects a rich desert fauna and flora, ranging from the pink-flowered desert rose and sky-scraping euphorbia trees to a variety of dry-country larks, bustards and raptors. The open plains and *Commiphora* woodland harbour Grevy's zebra, lesser kudu and Beisa oryx, along with thinly distributed populations of cheetah, lion, striped hyena and bat-eared fox.

The jade waters of Lake Turkana provide the perfect scenic counterpoint to the barren terrestrial landscape, as does the Karsa Waterhole, a drinking point for wildlife, and the Hasuma Forest along the seasonal Alia river.

Flamingoes and other waders, Lake Turkana

🐦 North Island

25 km (16 miles) NW of Koobi Fora.

The smallest and least accessible of Turkana's three volcanic islands, North Island is also the only one yet to be accorded national park status. It consists of several nested tuff cones and rises to about 140 m (460 ft) above the surface of the lake. Although the main volcano is thought to be more than 3 million years old, it still displays regular signs of latent activity. Exactly when it last erupted is unknown, but two non-vegetated lava flows run down to the shore, suggesting it was sometime in the last few hundred years, and fumaroles run along the main fault ridge. Crocodiles are common along the shore, and a wide selection of waterbirds is present seasonally.

🐦 Western Turkana

Kalokol is 380 km (235 miles) N of Kitale via Lodwar. 🍴 🍽 ⚠️

More accessible than the eastern shore for those dependent on public transport, western Turkana is not so wild and remote in character, although reaching the lake

itself can be difficult following a drop in water levels and significant retreat of the shore in the 1990s. Access to west Turkana is via Kitale in Western Kenya, and entails passing through the medium-sized town of Lodwar en route to Kalokol, the largest settlement anywhere on the lake, and the only one accessible by public transport. Kalokol no longer lies on the lakeshore, but a jetty about an hour's walk away is the best place to cross to Central Island. The nearby **Ferguson's Gulf** and more distant **Eliye Springs** are more attractive bases for exploring the western shore, but the sandy access roads require a 4WD.

✈ Central Island National Park

9 km (6 miles) E of Kalokol.
☐ *6am–7pm daily.* 🔲
www.kws.go.ke

Also known as Crocodile Island, Central Island was accorded national park status in 1983 in recognition of its significance as the main breeding site for the lake's estimated 15,000–20,000 Nile crocodiles, the largest population in Africa. The island consists of 15 volcanic craters and cones, of which three contain permanent lakes and one is periodically inundated. Birds are also plentiful, with thousands of lesser flamingo congregating on the lake at times, and the lava-strewn ground, with its sparse cover of spiny grass, is evidently a serpentine paradise, with the venomous puff-adder, Egyptian cobra and saw-scaled viper all common.

The Koobi Fora research centre overlooking Lake Turkana

TRAVELLERS' NEEDS

WHERE TO STAY

Kenya's accommodation varies from lavish lodges and camps, with impeccable service, gourmet food and swimming pools in the popular tourist areas, to basic board and lodging, consisting of a bare room with a bed and an often erratic water supply in the small towns. Safari lodges range from large blocks of rooms catering to tour groups to smaller intimate camps made up of temporary tents erected on platforms. Wildlife parks also have campsites, which attend to self-sufficient visitors and campers on organised budget safaris. Alongside some good-value accommodation and a few luxurious beach hideaways ideal for honeymooners, Kenya's sublime coastline also offers all-inclusive resorts to package holiday-makers. Accommodation on Lamu Island is often in old atmospheric Swahili houses decorated with antiques. Nairobi boasts plenty of international hotel chains. Other large towns usually have at least one adequate mid-range hotel, some of which retain the old colonial charm.

Ornamental knocker, Old Town, Lamu

Swahili-style seating and a plunge pool, Lamu Guest House

CHOOSING ACCOMMODATION

While there is a star grading system in Kenya, the classification is based on facilities provided and not ambience or quality of service. The standard of accommodation is generally determined by its price. All visitors to the game-viewing parks are broadly going to have a similar experience, but the price of a safari depends on the type of accommodation offered. At the top end are small tented camps, less expensive are the larger safari lodges, while at the budget end are basic campsites. Likewise, all visitors can equally enjoy the beach, whether they prefer to be bussed in from the airport to spend a week in a fully inclusive luxury resort, or rent a cheaper self-catering cottage or house. The latter work out more economical for a family or group. Away from the main tourist areas, most towns have at least one mid-range hotel aimed at local business travellers, which may often be dull but comfortable enough. There are dozens of places offering very basic board and lodgings for under US$10 a night, but budget travellers using these must always inspect the room first to see that the facilities are functioning, bedding is clean and that the door locks.

When enquiring about accommodation in local areas, visitors must note that the word *hoteli* in Swahili means a venue for food and drink only, not accommodation; instead use the word *guesti*, which means guesthouse. Self-sufficient campers with their own or hired vehicles can get around Kenya utilising campsites in the parks and rural areas, some of which have additional *bandas* (huts).

PRICING

There is a two-tier pricing system for accommodation in Kenya and visitors or non-residents are required to pay almost double that of Kenyan residents. Most rates for non-residents are published in US dollars but can also be paid in Kenyan shillings – however, it is worth checking that the hotel offers a competitive rate of exchange. Hotels in cities and towns aimed at business travellers generally keep the same room rates all year round, while in the parks and on the coast rates are seasonal. Low season in Kenya is from April to June when rates drop considerably, in some cases to half, but holidays during this time are hampered by the long rains. High season is mid-December to mid-February when rates are at their highest. Some coastal resorts add an extra surcharge over Christmas and New Year. Out of high season, walk-in rates, especially along the coast, can be lower than published rates, although there is no guarantee of a room. The upmarket establishments accept credit cards, while low-budget accommodation only accept Kenyan shillings for payment.

FACILITIES

Mainstream international hotels in Nairobi, such as the Hilton and InterContinental, and the coastal resorts have the usual facilities such as

◁ **Hot-air balloon safari over the scenic Masai Mara Game Reserve** air conditioning, satellite TV, Internet access, swimming pools, restaurants and bars, and additional recreational facilities. Smaller hotels often have a simple restaurant and bar serving some form of Continental cuisine, while at basic board and lodgings a plate of local food and beer may be on offer. Safari lodges and tented camps are very comfortable and the more expensive ones have lovely decor and spacious rooms in commanding positions. In remote regions, many hotels rely on solar power and bore-hole water, but nevertheless facilities are not compromised by this. Mosquitoes can pose a problem, so ideally a room should have an air conditioner, a fan or a mosquito net and at the very least mosquito netting in the windows. If travelling in a vehicle, visitors must enquire about parking facilities on offer.

BOOKING

Reservations made through a European or North American travel agent may be more expensive than contacting the lodge or hotel directly. Increasingly, establishments in the tourist regions of Kenya are becoming more easily accessible on the Internet. The website of **African Travel Resource** displays all major hotels and lodges in Kenya. In the case of extended safaris using a variety of accommodation, good deals can be done through the tour operators who get accommodation at wholesale prices.

Rothschild's giraffes on the lawns of the Giraffe Manor, Nairobi

CHILDREN

Kenya is generally a good destination for families, especially on organised tours. While some exclusive safari lodges do not accept children at all, others are child-friendly. Beach lodges are mostly family-orientated and offer adjoining rooms or discounts to children under 12 sharing a room with their parents, and often under fives go free. Some have children's entertainment or clubs such as **Bamburi Beach Hotel** and the **Heritage Hotels** group, which offer special children's guides to the parks and organise bush experiences and engaging activities for children.

HOTEL GROUPS

Kenya has a vast range of reputable chains such as **Fairmont Hotels**, **Sopa Lodges**, **Serena Hotels**, **Heritage Hotels** and **Sarova Hotels**, all of which offer international standards in terms of facilities and service. Most hotels in Nairobi have conference and business centres and the bars and restaurants are focal meeting places for its residents. The five-star Nairobi Serena Hotel (see p363) is regarded as the best of the modern hotels, set in lush gardens with fine views of the city's soaring skyline. There are some historical hotels in the city, including the atmospheric Fairmont The Norfolk Hotel (see p362), whose previous guests have included dignitaries such as Winston Churchill and Theodore Roosevelt, or the charming Karen Blixen Coffee Garden and Cottages (see p363). One of the more unusual places to stay is The Giraffe Manor (see p363) where it is not uncommon for a giraffe to look through a bedroom window or stick its head through a doorway.

There are some good value mid-range hotels around the city centre, but furnishings and décor tend to be a little dated and service often slow in the adjoining restaurants and bars. The same can be said for the principal hotels in other towns, which can be bland and old-fashioned, but nevertheless offer the best accommodation outside the more tourist-orientated parks. There are, however, some fine country hotels, such as the Lake Naivasha Country Club (see p370) set in spacious grounds full of giant yellowwood acacia trees on the lakeshore, and Mount Kenya Safari Club (see p376), which oozes plenty of old-world charm and is set in landscaped gardens in the foothills of Mount Kenya.

The lush garden of Sarova Lodge, Shaba National Reserve

Meru Mount Kenya Lodge, Mount Kenya National Park

BUDGET LODGING

Most towns in Kenya have several cheap hotels referred to as board and lodgings. A careful scrutiny of these is needed as they sometimes double up as local bars and brothels and are not wholly clean. Nevertheless, they offer cheap accommodation at under US$10 a night. Visitors must ensure that the door locks, there is a fan that works, water runs from the tap and the bedding is clean. Guests must also enquire about the availability of food and hot water. Nairobi has many of these places, mostly concentrated around River Road, which is not an especially safe area of the city. However, the capital also offers a few good alternatives to budget travellers in the way of campsites and backpacker-style accommodation with dormitories and double rooms located in converted houses and bars, where non-Kenyan food is available.

SELF-CATERING COTTAGES AND HOMESTAYS

In the national parks, **KWS** (Kenya Wildlife Service) offers a number of accommodation options in guesthouses or *bandas*, which usually cater to four people but can accommodate up to 18. In each, linen and bedding is provided and there are fully equipped self-catering kitchens, though in some cases guests have to bring their own drinking water and firewood. On the coast, houses and cottages are available for hire, and usually provide cooking and eating utensils, but sometimes guests have to bring their own bedding and towels. Some provide personal staff such as a cook or maid. These tend to be old and simply furnished, but the advantage is staying in a peaceful and relatively private location near the beach away from the glitzy resorts. They are ideal for families and groups of friends. Local people do the rounds of the cottages on bicycles selling fresh fish and seafood, fruit and vegetables, and sometimes, home-made bread. Homestays on private farms and ranches, usually owned by the descendents of settler families, are becoming popular, especially on the Laikipia Plateau. These take just a handful of people in and communal meals are taken with the hosts and other guests. **Holiday Homes Kenya** offers a wide range of fully-equipped homes in Kenya.

BEACH RESORTS

Fully self-contained beach resorts line the coast to the south and north of Mombasa. While some are arranged in lines of concrete blocks, others have been designed to blend in with the landscape with thatched roofs and chalets

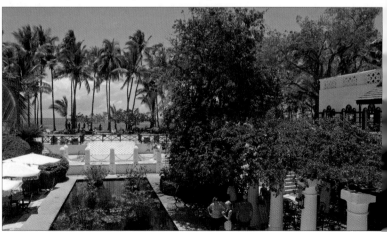

The upscale palm-fringed Serena Beach Hotel, Mombasa

Voi Safari Lodge with a rock-cut swimming pool overlooking the landscape

hidden in the coastal forest. The larger resorts have several swimming pools, including ones for children, landscaped gardens with sun-loungers, a choice of bars and restaurants and additional discotheques (some open air), shops, health and sports facilities and live entertainment. A few are adjoined to a golf course or casino. At a short notice, a full range of watersports can be organised, including snorkelling, scuba diving and, for those who do not want to get wet, trips on glass-bottomed boats are on offer. There is also the option of going on day trips to Wasini Island or Shimba Hills National Reserve *(see pp216–19)* or overnight trips to one of the parks such as Tsavo. Most of the resorts are aimed at package holiday-makers staying for the week, with flights included in the cost of their holidays, and all take reservations directly.

ON SAFARI

Most tour operators *(see pp404–5)* offer a similar safari experience with early morning and late afternoon guided game drives and the opportunity to camp in the wild. It is important to consider the options available before planning a safari trip to Kenya *(see pp68–73)*. The cost of a safari depends on the type of accommodation availed. For a 3-day safari from Nairobi to the Masai Mara, an expensive option could be to fly directly to an intimate luxury tented camp, a medium-priced one would be to drive or fly to a large safari lodge and a budget one would be to drive to and stay at a campsite. Tented camps only take a few guests at a time and provide excellent personalised service and luxury. Spacious, permanently erected shade-cloth or thatch tents have an attached bathroom where water is heated by solar power, and there is a central dining and lounge area. Less expensive are larger safari lodges that sleep up to 150 people, have high standards but are more impersonal. These are either in blocks, or individual units grouped around a waterhole or swimming pool, with central restaurants and bars. All parks have campsites and some have pre-erected tents, shared showers, camp beds and toilets and a kitchen hut. More basic campsites include a long drop toilet, with tour operators providing equipment needed, cooks and camp assistants. For information, bookings and permits contact Let's Go Travel *(see p405)*, **Cheli and Peacock**, **Private Wilderness** and **The Safari and Conservation Co.**

An exclusive tented camp in the Masai Mara Game Reserve

Choosing a Hotel

Most of the hotels and lodges in this guide have been selected across a wide price range for their good value, excellent facilities and prime location. Hotels are listed by area and arranged alphabetically within the same price category. For map references see pages 172–5 for Nairobi and the inside back cover for all others.

PRICE CATEGORIES
The price ranges are for a standard double room per night, including tax, service charges and breakfast.

⑤ Under US$50
⑤⑤ US$51–$125
⑤⑤⑤ US$126–$250
⑤⑤⑤⑤ US$251–$450
⑤⑤⑤⑤⑤ Over US$450

NAIROBI

DOWNTOWN Milimani Backpackers ⑤
Milimani Road **Tel** *020 2343920* **Rooms** *11*

A friendly budget hotel set in a 1940s colonial house, with dormitory beds and double cabins, plus camping and secure parking in the garden. Facilities include hot showers and a bar with a fire pit. The hotel restaurant serves breakfast, snacks and dinner. Day trips to attractions around Nairobi can be arranged. **www.milimanibackpackers.com**

DOWNTOWN Kenya Comfort Hotel ⑤⑤
Corner Muindi Mbingu and Monrovia Streets **Tel** *020 317606* **Fax** *020 317610* **Rooms** *91*   **City Map** *1 B2*

This centrally-located hotel is popular with budget travellers and offers especially favourable single rates. Rooms are basic but all en suite with large beds and mosquito nets. There is a second floor restaurant, bar and Internet facilities. Taxis park right outside and the hotel itself organises tours around Nairobi. **www.kenyacomfort.com**

DOWNTOWN Meridian Court Hotel ⑤⑤
Murang'a Road **Tel** *020 3139911* **Fax** *020 317045* **Rooms** *85*   **City Map** *1 C2*

Affordable accommodation with balconies and satellite TV, and some triple and interconnecting rooms for families, plus great views of Nairobi's skyline from the rooftop swimming pool. The in-hotel Khyber Restaurant offers Chinese and Indian cuisine, and there are pool tables in the sports bar. **www.meridianhotelkenya.com**

DOWNTOWN Fairview Hotel ⑤⑤⑤
Bishops Road **Tel** *020 2881000* **Fax** *020 2721320* **Rooms** *113*

This renovated hotel, set in 5 acres (2 ha) of pretty gardens, represents good value. Guests can make use of the pool and gym, and its five restaurants including a sushi bar, plus a unique underground, stone-clad wine bar. There are comfortable communal lounge areas and Wi-Fi access in the rooms. **www.fairviewkenya.com**

DOWNTOWN Hotel Boulevard ⑤⑤⑤
Harry Thuku Road **Tel** *020 2227567* **Fax** *020 317825* **Rooms** *70*   **City Map** *1 A1*

With a great location at the foot of Museum Hill, this mid-range hotel is a little faded but popular with tour groups and offers excellent value for money. Set in expansive grounds with a pool and tennis courts, the hotel has a good restaurant and three bars to relax in. Spacious rooms have satellite TV and Wi-Fi. **www.hotelboulevardkenya.com**

DOWNTOWN Sarova Stanley Hotel ⑤⑤⑤
Corner Kenyatta Avenue and Kimathi Street **Tel** *020 2757000* **Fax** *020 2229388* **Rooms** *217*   **City Map** *1 C3*

Set in an eight-floor tower topped with a luxury penthouse, the Sarova Stanley offers comfortable, stylish rooms and facilities that include a health club and spa with a heated pool, the historic Thorn Tree Café *(see p382)* and the Exchange Bar where the Nairobi Stock Exchange ran for 37 years from 1954. **www.sarovahotels.com/stanley**

DOWNTOWN Fairmont The Norfolk Hotel ⑤⑤⑤⑤
Harry Thuku Road **Tel** *020 2265000* **Fax** *020 2216796* **Rooms** *165*   **City Map** *1 B2*

Built in 1904 and once frequented by early colonial adventurers, Fairmon The Norfolk still exudes old world charm and provides excellent service. It has plush rooms, several atmospheric bars and restaurants displaying early-Nairobi memorabilia and photographs on the walls and private tropical gardens. **www.fairmont.com/norfolkhotel**

DOWNTOWN Hilton Nairobi Hotel ⑤⑤⑤⑤
Mama Ngina Street **Tel** *020 2790000* **Fax** *020 2226477* **Rooms** *287*   **City Map** *1 C3*

Adhering to the usual Hilton standards, this landmark city centre hotel is set in a tall tower with excellent views from the upper floors and a shopping centre at its base. There are several restaurants and bars, a gym, large pool and sophisticated business centre. All rooms have soundproofed windows and Internet access. **www.hilton.com**

DOWNTOWN InterContinental Hotel Nairobi ⑤⑤⑤⑤
City Hall Way **Tel** *020 3200000* **Fax** *020 3200030* **Rooms** *376*   **City Map** *1 B4*

The Nairobi branch of this quality international chain lies within strolling distance of City Square and the Parliament buildings. A full range of amenities include a pool, health club and business centre, The Terrace buffet restaurant, good independent Indian and Italian restaurants, a casino and the popular Safari Bar. **www.ichotelsgroup.com**

Key to Symbols *see back cover flap*

DOWNTOWN Laico Regency

🏨 ⛱ 🍴 🛏 📋 W   ⑤⑤⑤⑤

Between Loita Street and Uhuru Highway **Tel** *020 2211199* **Fax** *020 2217120* **Rooms** *196*   **City Map** *1 B3*

A 12-storey hotel overlooking Central Park with a ground floor plant-filled atrium. Facilities include a shopping arcade, gym and popular casino. Several restaurants include the excellent Italian restaurant Roberto's and the top floor Panorama, which offers snacks and salads and great views. **www.laicohotels.com**

DOWNTOWN Nairobi Safari Club

🏨 ⛱ 🍴 🛏 📋 W   ⑤⑤⑤⑤

Corner of Koinange Street and University Way **Tel** *020 2821000* **Fax** *020 2215137* **Rooms** *146*   **City Map** *1 B2*

Popular with United Nations and World Bank employees, this all-suite hotel has good business facilities and a health centre. Food and entertainment come in the form of themed nightly buffets and live music in the Safari Restaurant, the Safari Terrace cocktail-and-piano bar and a Sunday poolside barbecue. **www.nairobisafariclub.com**

DOWNTOWN Nairobi Serena Hotel

🏨 ⛱ 🍴 🛏 📋 W   ⑤⑤⑤⑤

Kenyatta Avenue **Tel** *020 2725111* **Fax** *020 2725184* **Rooms** *183*   **City Map** *1 A4*

A flagship luxury hotel of the Serena group and member of Leading Hotels of the World, the individually-designed, spacious rooms and suites all have minibars and satellite TV. Facilities include the lavish Maisha Spa, a 25-m (80-ft) pool surrounded by palms, and excellent dining in a clutch of top-class restaurants. **www.serenahotels.com**

HURLINGHAM Silver Springs Hotel

🏨 ⛱ 🍴 🛏 📋 W   ⑤⑤⑤

Corner Valley and Argwings Kodhek Roads **Tel** *020 2722451* **Fax** *020 2720545* **Rooms** *160*

A professionally run three-star hotel 3 km (2 miles) to the west of the city centre. Rooms are bright, airy and modern with Wi-Fi and satellite TV. Superior rooms have air conditioning, four-poster beds and minibars. The restaurant serves buffet or à la carte meals and there is a large pool, gym and spa. **www.silversprings-hotel.com**

KAREN Karen Camp

🍴 W   ⑤

Marula Lane **Tel** *020 8833475* **Rooms** *20*

A good budget option close to the sights in Karen, offering basic but comfortable rooms with or without bath rooms and camping on the shady lawn. Showers are hot and there is a restaurant and lively bar. The camp can organise guided day trips, including Nairobi National Park and a climb of Mount Longonot. **www.karencamp.com**

KAREN Karen Blixen Coffee Garden and Cottages

🏨 ⛱ W   ⑤⑤⑤⑤

336 Karen Road **Tel** *020 882138* **Fax** *020 882508* **Rooms** *15*

Lovely stone cottages set in formal gardens of flowering shrubs and jacaranda trees, just up the road from the Karen Blixen Museum. Cottages feature high-beamed ceilings, wooden floors and fireplaces, plus satellite TV and minibars. Dining is at the adjoining restaurant. Can arrange horse riding. **www.karenblixencoffeegarden.co.ke**

KAREN Ngong House

🏨 ⛱ W   ⑤⑤⑤⑤⑤

Ndovu Lane **Tel** *020 2513331* **Fax** *020 890674* **Rooms** *9*

Very stylish and luxurious rooms in double-storey, thatched wooden treehouses with uninterrupted views of the Ngong Hills *(see p169)*. Houses are built on stilts in a patch of indigenous forest and decorated with African art. Delicious formal dinners are served by candle light. **www.ngonghouse.com**

KEGWA Windsor Golf Hotel and Country Club

🏨 ⛱ 🍴 🛏 📋 W   ⑤⑤⑤⑤

Ridgeways Road, off Kiambu Road **Tel** *020 8562300* **Fax** *020 8560160* **Rooms** *130*

Some 16 km (10 miles) to the north of the city, the luxurious rooms at the Windsor look out on an 18-hole championship golf course set in sweeping parkland. There are several high-class restaurants, bars and a popular nightclub. Outdoor activities include golf, tennis, squash and horse riding. **www.windsorgolfresort.com**

LANGATA Nairobi Campsite

🍴 W   ⑤

Magadi Road, Langata **Tel** *0728 333476* **Rooms** *14*

Not just a campsite – though tents and sleeping bags are available for hire – this excellent place also has single or double rooms and dormitories. Services include Internet, satellite TV and laundry, and there is a lively restaurant and bar. Also on offer are tours of the city, Nairobi National Park and other sights.

LANGATA Macushla House

🏨 ⛱ 🍴 🛏 W   ⑤⑤⑤

Nguruwe Road, off Gogo Falls Road **Tel** *020 891987* **Fax** *020 891971* **Rooms** *6*

Small, intimate and friendly guesthouse within walking distance of the Giraffe Centre *(see p168)* with a modern decor of zebra prints, wrought-iron furniture and *kilims* (Persian rugs) scattered on wooden floors. There are two cosy living rooms with open fires, bird-filled gardens, a pool and excellent wholesome food. **www.macushla.biz**

LANGATA The Giraffe Manor

🛏 W   ⑤⑤⑤⑤⑤

Koitobos Road **Tel** *020 891078* **Fax** *020 890949* **Rooms** *6*

A lovely red-tiled, ivy-clad, stone manor house with just six beautifully decorated rooms. The resident herd of giraffes from the nearby AFEW Giraffe Centre stalk the lawns and it is possibly the only place in the world where giraffes can be fed from the breakfast table. Rates full or half board. **www.giraffemanor.com**

NGURUMAN ESCARPMENT Shompole

🏨 ⛱   ⑤⑤⑤⑤⑤

Shompole Conservancy **Tel** *0722 656415* **Fax** *020 884135* **Rooms** *9*

An extremely isolated, super-luxurious eco-lodge overlooking the Nguruman Escarpment, 120 km (75 miles) or a 30-minute flight from Nairobi. Suites are in Bedouin-style tents under thatch, with local timber and stone decor and private plunge pools. Bush dinners, game drives and massages on offer. **www.wilderness-ventures.com**

SOUTHEASTERN SAVANNAHS

AMBOSELI NATIONAL PARK Amboseli Serena Lodge
🏨 🖼 Ⓦ   ⑤⑤⑤⑤
Southern area, near Road Junction 33 **Tel** *045 622361* **Fax** *045 622430* **Rooms** *96*   **Road Map** C6

The most luxurious of the larger lodges in Amboseli, the Serena is tucked away in lush forest at the south end of Enking Narok Swamp. The rooms make extensive use of red Maasai-style cloth, thatch, cane and traditional African artifacts. Excellent buffet meals and the shaded swimming pool is a joy. **www.serenahotels.com**

AMBOSELI NATIONAL PARK Amboseli Sopa Lodge
🏨 🖼   ⑤⑤⑤⑤
Outside Kimana Gate **Tel** *020 3750235* **Fax** *020 3751507* **Rooms** *102*   **Road Map** C6

Set in lush tropical gardens on a private Maasai conservancy bordering Amboseli, this smart chain lodge has a strong sense of place, with accommodation in scattered low-rise chalets and a generous use of organic building materials. There is a local Maasai craft market on site. **www.sopalodges.com**

AMBOSELI NATIONAL PARK Ol Tukai Lodge
🏨 🖼 🖼   ⑤⑤⑤⑤
Ol Tukai, near Park Headquarters **Tel** *045 622275* **Fax** *0456 22280* **Rooms** *80*   **Road Map** C6

This established lodge, set in a lush fever tree grove alongside the park headquarters, has a useful location at the heart of Amboseli. Accommodation is impressive, with wooden floors, tall thatch roofs and spacious rooms. The gardens support monkeys and 150-plus bird species, and elephants often pass right by. **www.oltukailodge.com**

AMBOSELI NATIONAL PARK Satao Elerai Camp
🏨   ⑤⑤⑤⑤
Elerai CCA, 11 km (7 miles) southeast of Kimana Gate **Tel** *0729 403566* **Fax** *041 473533* **Rooms** *14* **Road Map** C6

Along a rocky ridge in the remote Elerai Community Conservancy, this highly exclusive bush camp offers spacious accommodation in en suite chalets, with expansive views over the plains below Kilimanjaro. Well sited for drives into Amboseli, and guided game walks in the surrounding bush can be highly rewarding. **www.sataoeleraicamp.com**

AMBOSELI NATIONAL PARK Porini Amboseli Camp
🏨   ⑤⑤⑤⑤⑤
Selenkay Conservancy, 30 km (18 miles) north of Amboseli Airstrip **Tel** *020 7123129* **Rooms** *9*   **Road Map** C6

This eco-friendly, deluxe bush camp lies in a 60-sq km (15,000-acre) private conservancy on the community land of the Kisonko Maasai who staff the camp and offer game drives and escorted bush walks. The tents are large and comfortably furnished. Electricity is solar powered; hot showers to order. **www.porini.com**

AMBOSELI NATIONAL PARK Tortilis Camp
🏨 🖼   ⑤⑤⑤⑤⑤
Outside southern boundary, Kitirua **Tel** *045 6222195* **Rooms** *18*   **Road Map** C6

This ultra-exclusive tented camp lies in a hillside patch of acacia woodland on a private conservancy just outside Amboseli. It boasts the most spectacular views of Kilimanjaro imaginable. The chic tents are en suite and the Italian-influenced food is superb. Guided walks with local Maasai and game drives are on offer. **www.chelipeacock.com**

CHYULU HILLS NATIONAL PARK Ol Donyo Wuas
🏨 🖼   ⑤⑤⑤⑤⑤
Western foothills of Chyulu range, 29 km (19 miles) from Mbirikani **Tel** *020 6000457* **Rooms** *10*   **Road Map** C6

Overlooking savannah on which elephants are often seen, this deluxe lodge offers exceptionally large suites, each with a private balcony, plunge pool and roof terrace. Excellent meals are taken with the hosts, safari guide and pilot Richard Bonham and family. On offer are game drives, bush walks and horse-riding. **www.oldonyowuas.com**

LUMO COMMUNITY WILDLIFE SANCTUARY Lion Rock Safari Camp
📧 🏨   ⑤⑤⑤
50 km (30 miles) from Voi on the border of Tsavo West National Park **Tel** *0717 555498* **Rooms** *12*   **Road Map** D6

This small camp is run as part of a conservation project involving the local community. The furnished en suite tents have tall *makuti* roofs and are set on wooden platforms overlooking the plains towards Kilimanjaro. Set in private ranchland bordering Tsavo West, guided walks and night drives are offered.

NAMANGA Namanga River Lodge
📧 🏨   ⑤
Nairobi–Arusha Road, Namanga **Tel** *0734 591444* **Rooms** *20*   **Road Map** C6

This likeable riverside colonial relic is set in flowering gardens on the periphery of Namanga town. A little run-down these days, and seldom used by tour packages, it is still by far the best option in this colourful Maasai border town and makes a useful stopover between Nairobi and Amboseli.

TAITA HILLS WILDLIFE SANCTUARY Sarova Taita Hills Game Lodge
🏨 🖼   ⑤⑤⑤
Near Entrance Gate **Tel** *043 31271* **Fax** *043 30007* **Rooms** *62*   **Road Map** D7

Set in pretty, lansdcaped gardens with a small river flowing through, this elegant, colonial stone lodge is attractively draped in bougainvilleas. Rooms are large and very comfortable, and the service and food are excellent – though game drives in the sanctuary are the main attraction. **www.sarovahotels.com**

TAITA HILLS WILDLIFE SANCTUARY Sarova Salt Lick Lodge
🏨   ⑤⑤⑤⑤
Southern Sanctuary **Tel** *043 31271* **Fax** *043 30007* **Rooms** *96*   **Road Map** D7

Famous for its quirky architecture, this lodge in the heart of the sanctuary looks at first glance like a field full of oversized mushrooms. The in-house game viewing can be truly stunning, with thirsty elephants gathering to drink at the adjacent waterhole. Service is also attentive and buffet meals are excellent. **www.sarovahotels.com**

Key to Price Guide *see p362* **Key to Symbols** *see back cover flap*

TSAVO EAST NATIONAL PARK Ngutuni

$$$

Bordering the park, South of Voi **Tel** *043 30747* **Rooms** *48* **Road Map** *D6*

Situated on a large private estate, this is a well-priced and very pleasant, two-storey wood-and-thatch lodge facing a small waterhole rich in wildlife. The accommodation and public areas are very comfortable but rather cramped together. Unlike in the park itself, guided walks and night drives are offered. **www.rexresorts.com**

TSAVO EAST NATIONAL PARK Voi Safari Lodge

$$$

4 km (2 miles) from Voi Gate **Tel** *020 344201* **Fax** *020 2222661* **Rooms** *52* **Road Map** *D6*

This lodge boasts one of the most memorable locations of any Kenyan hotel, set on a rocky cliff and rustling with small wildlife, right above a waterhole that often attracts elephant and buffalo in their hundreds. The outmoded architecture aside, the lodge is well run, comfortable and very good value. **www.safari-hotels.com**

TSAVO EAST NATIONAL PARK Voi Wildlife Lodge

$$$

Immediately outside Voi Gate **Tel** *020 7125741* **Fax** *020 7125743* **Rooms** *88* **Road Map** *D6*

This modern lodge overlooks the park and a water hole that attracts plenty of elephants, birds and other wildlife. Low on bush atmosphere, the lodge compensates with excellent facilities, large comfortable rooms and superb vegetarian-friendly buffets with a strong Indian flavour. **www.voiwildlifelodge.com**

TSAVO EAST NATIONAL PARK Galdessa

$$$$$

West of Road Junction 111 **Tel** *040 3202217* **Fax** *040 3202431* **Rooms** *14* **Road Map** *D6*

Stunningly located on the palm-lined banks of the Galana river, Galdessa combines a genuine bush experience with world-class safari decor, cuisine and service. Game drives offer a good chance of sighting cheetah and large buffalo herds, while elephants and hippos pass by the camp daily. **www.galdessa.com**

TSAVO EAST NATIONAL PARK Satao Camp

$$$$$

Off Road Junction 144 **Tel** *043 30204* **Fax** *020 2039571* **Rooms** *20* **Road Map** *D6*

Set in a remote corner of the park, this low-key, eco-friendly tented camp is aimed at those looking for a genuine bush experience rather than modern facilities. Comfortably furnished tents all have private balconies for viewing the plentiful wildlife around, and the food and wine are world class. **www.sataocamp.com**

TSAVO WEST NATIONAL PARK Lake Jipe Bandas

$$

Just inside Jipe Gate **Tel** *020 6000800* **Fax** *020 6003792* **Rooms** *3* **Road Map** *C6*

Situated at the remote Jipe entrance to Tsavo West, these self-catering *bandas* are currently the best option in the Taveta area, wonderfully situated for watching birdlife and animals drinking at Lake Jipe. Simple but clean, each *banda* contains two beds with netting. A campsite is attached. **www.kws.go.ke**

TSAVO WEST NATIONAL PARK Tsavo Inn

$$

Mtito Andei, 1 km (half a mile) from Entrance Gate **Tel** *0720 379939* **Rooms** *20* **Road Map** *D6*

Entered through giant metallic tusks alongside the Caltex filling station, this veteran hotel is a useful budget base for exploring Tsavo West, though it is not actually in the park. The place has undoubtedly seen better days, but the nice swimming pool and keen service compensate. Rooms are usually available on the spot, even in peak season.

TSAVO WEST NATIONAL PARK Ngulia Safari Lodge

$$$

West of Tsavo Gate, off Road Junction 18 **Tel** *020 344201* **Fax** *020 2222661* **Rooms** *52* **Road Map** *D6*

This comfortable lodge, though a touch outmoded, has a wonderful location on the Ndewe Escarpment and is good for seeing the most elusive pair of the Big Five, with numerous black rhino in the adjacent Ngulia Rhino Sanctuary and leopards making regular nocturnal visits to a spotlit waterhole below the restaurant. **www.kenya-safari.co.ke**

TSAVO WEST NATIONAL PARK Kilaguni Serena Safari Lodge

$$$$

West of Mtito Andei Gate, off Road Junction 8 **Tel** *0734 699865* **Fax** *045 622470* **Rooms** *56* **Road Map** *D6*

Kilaguni is the oldest lodge in any Kenyan national park and combines classic safari decor with contemporary touches. Buildings overlook a water hole that attracts a steady stream of elephants and other animals. Kilimanjaro dominates the horizon above the water hole in clear weather. **www.serenahotels.com**

TSAVO WEST NATIONAL PARK Severin Safari Camp

$$$$

West of Mtito Andei Gate, off Road Junction 36 **Tel** *0722 650819* **Rooms** *35* **Road Map** *C6*

This attractive and well-managed tented camp lies in an area of animal-rich bush where close encounters with animals are guaranteed around the camp. Maasai guards are on hand to escort guests to their tents after dark. The camp offers game drives and bush walks, and has a spa and therapy centre and a large pool. **www.severin-kenya.com**

TSAVO WEST NATIONAL PARK Ziwani Voyager

$$$$

Ziwani Gate **Tel** *043 30506* **Fax** *043 31069* **Rooms** *25* **Road Map** *C6*

This friendly, unpretentious camp has a beautiful location in a glade of yellow fever trees flanking the Sante river. Plenty of wildlife passes through, notably hippos, monkeys and antelope. Guided morning bush walks and night drives are offered, and the candlelit dinner on the lawn is a real treat. **www.heritage-eastafrica.com**

TSAVO WEST NATIONAL PARK Finch Hatton's

$$$$$

16 km (10 miles) north of Road Junction 38 **Tel** *020 8030936* **Rooms** *31* **Road Map** *D6*

Named after the character played by Robert Redford in *Out of Africa*, this superb owner-managed tented camp is the most upmarket property in Tsavo West. The large standing tents are set on wooden stilts overlooking pools inhabited by hippos. The Continental cuisine is adventurous and there is a fine wine list. **www.finchhattons.com**

SOUTHERN COAST

CHALE ISLAND The Sands at Chale Island 🍴 ♨ 🛏 📺 W $\$\$\$\$$
10 km (6 miles) South of Diani **Tel** *040 3300269* **Rooms** *50* **Road Map** *E7*

This romantic luxury resort is set on a tiny, beautiful island with a lovely white-sand crescent beach. Accommodation is in a variety of thatched rooms and suites with Swahili decor, including two built on stilts over the ocean. There are two pools and a boutique, and spa treatments are available. Rates are all-inclusive. **www.hotelplan.co.ke**

DIANI BEACH Diani Marine Diver's Village 🍴 ♨ W $\$\$$
Diana Beach Road, Ukunda **Tel** *040-3202367* **Fax** *040 3203452* **Rooms** *13* **Road Map** *E7*

Set in well-tended tropical gardens, the village has a collection of attractive thatched chalets with verandas, one permanent self-catering tent under thatch suitable for a family of four and two fully-contained villas for groups. There is a five-star PADI dive school and deep-sea fishing can be arranged. **www.dianimarine.com**

DIANI BEACH Diani Sea Lodge 🍴 ♨ 🛏 📺 W $\$\$\$$
Diani Beach Road, Ukunda **Tel** *040 3203438* **Rooms** *162* **Road Map** *E7*

A German-run collection of modest double and family bungalows and cottages scattered around tropical gardens. Entertainment includes two pools, beach volleyball, table tennis, a children's playground and a TV room. Rates are all-inclusive except for windsurfing, diving and fishing. **www.dianisealodge.de**

DIANI BEACH Papillon Lagoon Reef 🍴 ♨ 📺 W $\$\$\$$
Diani Beach Road, Ukunda **Tel** *040 3202213* **Rooms** *119* **Road Map** *E7*

A friendly all-inclusive resort set in a landscaped garden, popular with British holiday-makers. Simple cottages sleep families of four, or there are beachfront rooms with extras like satellite TV and minibar. Windsurfing, snorkelling and one introductory dive in the pool are included in the price. **www.rexresorts.com**

DIANI BEACH Diani Reef Beach Resort & Spa 🍴 ♨ 🛏 🏋 📺 W $\$\$\$\$$
Diani Beach Road, Ukunda **Tel** *040 3202723* **Fax** *040 3202196* **Rooms** *143* **Road Map** *E7*

An upmarket resort with modern rooms looking on to either the gardens or the ocean, all with Internet and satellite TV. A broad range of facilities include two pools, a Jacuzzi, gym, casino and cinema, plus water sports and an extensive menu of spa treatments. This is a popular venue for weddings and honeymoons. **www.dianireef.com**

DIANI BEACH Indian Ocean Beach Resort 🍴 ♨ 🛏 🏋 📺 W $\$\$\$\$$
Diani Beach Road, Ukunda **Tel** *040 3203730* **Fax** *040 3203557* **Rooms** *100* **Road Map** *E7*

A beach resort notable for its Moorish architecture and accommodation in spacious rooms, some in whitewashed cottages with patios facing the beach. There is a buffet restaurant, informal beach bar with a live band and occasional cabaret shows, two pools and a water sports centre. Full- or half-board rates. **www.jacarandahotels.com**

DIANI BEACH Leopard Beach Resort & Spa 🍴 ♨ 🛏 🏋 📺 W $\$\$\$\$$
Diani Beach Road, Ukunda **Tel** *040 3202721* **Fax** *040 3203424* **Rooms** *158* **Road Map** *E7*

A fully contained beach resort with tastefully decorated rooms, suites and luxury cottages under thatch dotted around the tropical gardens. A good choice of restaurants and bars, relaxing treatments in the spa, evening entertainment, and close to Diani Beach's golf course. Rates are full or half board. **www.leopardbeachresort.com**

DIANI BEACH The Sands at Nomad 🍴 ♨ 🏋 📺 W $\$\$\$\$$
Diani Beach Road, Ukunda **Tel** *0724 262426* **Fax** *040 3203648* **Rooms** *37* **Road Map** *E7*

A luxury boutique hotel, beautifully designed by local artist Mario Scianna who has incorporated Swahili *objets d'art* and antiques into the decor. Includes a lovely restaurant under thatch and canvas, sushi bar, 24-hour cocktail lounge, beauty treatments and stunning rim-flow pool. **www.thesandsatnomad.com**

FUNZI ISLAND Funzi Keys 🍴 ♨ $\$\$\$\$\$$
South of Msambweni on the mainland **Tel** *073 3900446* **Rooms** *17* **Road Map** *E7*

A stunning, private island resort, consistently rated as one of the best beach hideaways in the world, Funzi Keys is especially popular with honeymooners. Features beautiful thatched rooms with stone baths, Jacuzzis and four-poster beds. Rates are all-inclusive of meals, drinks and certain activities. **www.thefunzikeys.com**

KILIFI Mnarani Club 🍴 ♨ 📺 W $\$\$\$$
Malindi Road **Tel** *020 8070501* **Fax** *020 8070505* **Rooms** *80* **Road Map** *E7*

Occupying a peaceful spot perched on a cliff overlooking Kilifi Creek and with a small beach and wonderful gardens, this South African-run resort is great value. Accommodation is in thatched blocks or smaller cabins, and there is a good restaurant. Bird-watching boat trips can be organised. **www.mnarani.co.za**

MOMBASA Lotus Hotel 🍴 🏋 📺 W $\$\$$
Cathedral Lane, off Nkrumah Road **Tel** *041 2313207* **Fax** *041 2311789* **Rooms** *35* **Road Map** *E7*

An atmospheric hotel that was once a favourite with white settlers visiting the coast. The building features wood panelling and Oriental arches, and there is a lovely tranquil courtyard full of exotic plants. Budget rooms include spacious bathrooms, and the restaurant serves Indian and Continental food. **www.lotushotelkenya.com**

Key to Price Guide *see p362* **Key to Symbols** *see back cover flap*

MOMBASA Royal Court Hotel
🍴🏊🍸🛗📺Ⓦ $$
Haile Selassie Avenue **Tel** *041 2223379* **Fax** *041 2312398* **Rooms** *42*   **Road Map** *E7*

Set in an eight-storey block with a spacious lobby of domed arches and stained glass, this hotel offers modern, comfortable rooms with balconies. The Rooftop Restaurant serves Italian and Indian dishes and affords good city views. There is a popular adjoining casino and bar. **www.royalcourtmombasa.co.ke**

MOMBASA Castle Royal Hotel
🍴🛗📺Ⓦ $$$
Moi Avenue **Tel** *041 2222682* **Fax** *041 230688* **Rooms** *58*   **Road Map** *E7*

A renovated colonial hotel in a whitewashed building with ornate stone balconies. The smart rooms have high ceilings, cool stone floors, satellite TV, refrigerators and Internet access – they are also soundproofed to keep out the noise from busy Moi Avenue. Visitors can enjoy the popular terrace bar and restaurant. **www.sentrim-hotels.com**

NORTHERN MOMBASA Bamburi Beach Hotel
🍴🏊🍸📺Ⓦ $$$
Bamburi Beach **Tel** *041 5485611* **Fax** *041 5485900* **Rooms** *150*   **Road Map** *E7*

A self-contained beach resort with facilities for diving, windsurfing and fishing, a kid's adventure club, two pools, squash and tennis courts, a beauty salon and fitness centre. Rates are inclusive of meals and drinks. Rooms are in three-storey blocks with TV and DVD, and most enjoy ocean views. **www.bamburibeachkenya.com**

NORTHERN MOMBASA Mombasa Serena Beach Hotel & Spa
🍴🏊🍸🛗📺Ⓦ $$$
Shanzu Beach **Tel** *041 5487220* **Fax** *041 5485453* **Rooms** *166*   **Road Map** *E7*

A superior spa hotel with architecture styled on an old Swahili town, all whitewashed arches and carved doors. Features several restaurants and bars, very pleasant rooms with Lamu-style furniture, satellite TV and Internet, and little extras such as bathrobes and bed turn-down service. Free shuttle to Mombasa. **www.serenahotels.com**

NORTHERN MOMBASA Nyali Beach Hotel
🍴🏊🍸🛗📺Ⓦ $$$
Nyali Beach **Tel** *041 471551* **Fax** *041 471987* **Rooms** *170*   **Road Map** *E7*

One of the coast's oldest hotels, built in 1946 and extensively expanded since then. Rooms are in blocks scattered around the garden, all with satellite TV and either balconies or patios. There are several bars and restaurants and an adjoining kite-surfing school. All-inclusive rates include beginner's scuba diving lessons. **www.nyalibeach.co.ke**

NORTHERN MOMBASA Reef Hotel
🍴🏊🍸🛗📺Ⓦ $$$
Fleet Road, Nyali **Tel** *041 471771* **Fax** *041 474194* **Rooms** *134*   **Road Map** *E7*

All rooms at this hotel come with balconies and are housed in attractive blocks set in lush gardens. Facilities include three pools, tennis courts and evening entertainment in the form of tribal shows or acrobatics. A variety of water sports can be organised, from kayaking to kite-surfing, and a dive school is on site. **www.reefhotelkenya.com**

NORTHERN MOMBASA Sarova Whitesands Beach Resort & Spa
🍴🏊🍸🛗📺Ⓦ $$$
Bamburi Beach **Tel** *041 2128000* **Fax** *041 5485652* **Rooms** *338*   **Road Map** *E7*

This comfortable hotel offers rooms with satellite TV, Wi-Fi facilities and ocean or pool views from a patio or balcony. Blocks are in whitewashed Arabian style and surrounded by palms. Water sports and diving are offered and one of the three swimming pools is exceptionally large and features a waterslide. Rates half-board. **www.sarovahotels.com**

NORTHERN MOMBASA Voyager Beach Resort
🍴🏊🛗📺Ⓦ $$$
Nyali Beach **Tel** *020 475114* **Fax** *020 4446600* **Rooms** *233*   **Road Map** *E7*

A large, family-friendly, nautically-themed resort with a full range of activities including deep-sea fishing, diving, windsurfing, kids' club, three pools and evening entertainment. Accommodation is in modern, comfortable cabins, with connected cabins for families. Package rates are good value. **www.heritage-eastafrica.com**

SHIMBA HILLS Sable Bandas
$$
Shimba Hills National Reserve, Kwale **Tel** *020 60008000* **Fax** *020 6003792* **Rooms** *4*   **Road Map** *E7*

Simple, cheap KWS accommodation in four circular thatched *bandas*, each sleeping four in two double beds, with solar power and a shared bathroom and kitchen with gas cooker. Bed linen and towels are provided but guests must bring their own food, firewood and drinking water. **www.kws.go.ke**

SHIMBA HILLS Travellers Mwaluganje Elephant Camp
🍴 $$$
Mwaluganje Elephant Sanctuary, Kwale **Tel** *041 5485121* **Fax** *041 5485678* **Rooms** *20*   **Road Map** *E7*

This camp offers spacious tents under thatched roofs built on elevated decks. There is a rustic restaurant overlooking a waterhole frequented by elephants and other wildlife, which can be followed by an evening's entertainment around the campfire. Game drives are also offered. **www.travellersbeach.com**

SHIMBA HILLS Shimba Lodge
🍴 $$$$
Shimba Hills National Reserve, Kwale **Tel** *0722 200952* **Fax** *041 2229121* **Rooms** *30*   **Road Map** *E7*

A lovely, rustic wooden lodge built on stilts and overlooking a waterhole in the heart of Shimba's forest. Rooms are simple and bathroom facilities are shared, but the setting is beautiful and game is regularly spotted from the elevated forest boardwalk and the open dining deck. No children under 5. **www.aberdaresafarihotels.com**

SHIMONI Shimoni Reef Lodge
🍴🏊 $$$
Shimoni Village **Tel** *0722 400476* **Fax** *041 473969* **Rooms** *10*   **Road Map** *E7*

A small, friendly lodge with just ten comfortable thatched cottages dotted around the grounds, each sleeping up to four. Lots of activities on offer including forest walks, canoeing, fishing and dhow trips to Kisite-Mpunguti Marine Reserve and Wasini Island. Relaxed restaurant, bar and sea water pool. **www.shimonireeflodge.com**

SHIMONI Pemba Channel Lodge

$$$$

Shimoni Village **Tel** *0722 205020* **Rooms** *6* **Road Map** *E7*

Relaxed all-inclusive lodge that is part of the Pemba Channel Fishing Club *(see p403)*, which has been operating deep-sea fishing trips for over 40 years. Prettily furnished cottages overlook the pool or ocean, and the atmospheric bar and lounge are adorned with fishing trophies. **www.pembachannellodge.com**

TIWI BEACH Amani Tiwi Beach Resort

$$$

Ukunda **Tel** *+44 (0)845 0772247* **Rooms** *210* **Road Map** *E7*

A large beachside resort with rooms in thatched blocks set in tropical gardens and arranged around a very attractive string of several swimming pools. Visitors can enjoy a full range of facilities including tennis and squash courts, water sports, kids' club, five restaurants, six bars and a disco. Rates are half-board. **www.amanitiwibeachresort.com**

NORTHERN COAST

LAMU ARCHIPELAGO Yumbe House

$

Next to the Swahili House Museum, Lamu Town, Lamu Island **Tel** *042 4633101* **Rooms** *12* **Road Map** *F6*

A good budget option right in the heart of the old town and set in a typical, four-storey narrow Swahili house arranged around a cool courtyard full of plants. Little wooden stairs lead to simple rooms, each with fans, four-poster beds and mosquito nets, but no hot water. The rooftop lounge affords good views.

LAMU ARCHIPELAGO New Lamu Palace Hotel

$$$

Waterfront, Lamu Town, Lamu Island **Tel** *042 4633164* **Fax** *042 4633104* **Rooms** *22* **Road Map** *F6*

Rooms are fairly small at this hotel but are air conditioned and arranged around lovely lounge areas, plus there are good views from the front over the dhow harbour. Visitors can eat at the pleasant terrace restaurant and bar, or on the rooftop deck. Offers day trips to Manda Bay and walking tours of the town. **www.lamuparadiseholidays.com**

LAMU ARCHIPELAGO Petley's Inn

$$$

Waterfront, Lamu Town, Lamu Island **Tel** *042 4633164* **Fax** *042 4633104* **Rooms** *12* **Road Map** *F6*

Occupying a traditional Lamu house with thatched roof and broad terraces, this is the sister hotel to the New Lamu Palace and offers similar facilities with the added advantage of a small swimming pool on the first floor. The delightful rooftop bar also serves alcohol. The best room is the tower room at the top. **www.lamuparadiseholidays.com**

LAMU ARCHIPELAGO Lamu House

$$$$

Waterfront, Lamu Town, Lamu Island **Tel** *042 4633491* **Fax** *042 4633492* **Rooms** *10* **Road Map** *F6*

Lamu House is actually two beautifully-restored, whitewashed Lamu houses featuring ten luxury rooms with terraces and great views over Lamu's rooftops. The stylish decor features plenty of antiques and modern art, and there are plunge pools surrounded by sofas. A luxury dhow is available for excursions. **www.lamuhouse.com**

LAMU ARCHIPELAGO Peponi Hotel

$$$$

Shela Village, Lamu Island **Tel** *020 8023655* **Rooms** *24* **Road Map** *F6*

Small and friendly family-run hotel with bright, airy rooms arranged in terraces overlooking the Lamu Channel. The atmospheric restaurant serves very good seafood and the public bar is one of the few places in Lamu that serves alcohol. Windsurfing, water-skiing and deep-sea fishing are offered. **www.peponi-lamu.com**

LAMU ARCHIPELAGO Kipungani Explorer

$$$$$

Southern tip of Lamu Island **Tel** *020 4446651* **Fax** *020 4446600* **Rooms** *13* **Road Map** *F6*

Peaceful, spacious thatched chalets in a coconut plantation overlooking the beach. There is a saltwater pool and plenty of chill-out areas with hammocks and giant cushions. Windsurfing, fishing and visits to the local village can be arranged. Rates are full-board. Closed March–June. **www.heritage-eastafrica.com**

LAMU ARCHIPELAGO Kiwayu Safari Village

$$$$$

Mainland, opposite Kiwayu Island **Tel** *020 600107* **Fax** *020 606990* **Rooms** *18* **Road Map** *F6*

Accessed by air and located on the mainland looking across to Kiwayu Island, this remote luxury lodge built of thatch and woven matting sits on an idyllic stretch of beach surrounded by palms. The honeymoon suite is so secluded it can only be reached by boat. Closed in March–April. Rates are full-board. **www.kiwayu.com**

LAMU ARCHIPELAGO Manda Bay

$$$$$

Manda Island **Tel** *020 2115453* **Rooms** *16* **Road Map** *F6*

This exclusive lodge on Manda Island is a 20-minute boat ride from Lamu town and offers an all-inclusive package of meals, drinks and water sports. Accommodation is in large, airy cottages with Lamu antiques and vast beds swathed in mosquito nets. Excellent three-course dinners are served under the stars or on a dhow. **www.mandabay.com**

MALINDI Malindi Beach Bandas and Campsite

$

Casuarina Point **Tel** *020 6000800* **Fax** *020 6003792* **Rooms** *4* **Road Map** *E6*

Basic KWS accommodation adjacent to the Malindi Marine National Reserve *(see p232)* with a shady campsite and *bandas* with bathrooms and double beds with mosquito nets. The communal kitchen is well equipped but guests will need to bring food, drinking water and firewood. **www.kws.org**

Key to Price Guide *see p362* **Key to Symbols** *see back cover flap*

MALINDI Driftwood Club

🍴 🏊 📋 W $$

Silversands Road, Malindi **Tel** *042 2120155* **Fax** *042 2130712* **Rooms** *34*   **Road Map** *E6*

This long-established family favourite right on the beach offers a variety of comfortable rooms in thatched cottages, as well as three villas and two larger cottages with their own private pool. The restaurant serves a set menu as well as à la carte meals, and the Sunday lunch curry buffets are very popular. **www.driftwoodclub.com**

MALINDI Eden Roc Hotel

🍴 🏊 🛁 📋 W $$

On the Lamu–Malindi Road **Tel** *042 2120480* **Fax** *042 2120333* **Rooms** *165*   **Road Map** *E6*

This affordable old hotel may look dated but the gardens of palms, flowering shrubs and lily ponds are pleasant, and there are four pools, tennis courts and an open-air disco. Two in-house restaurants include the Dhow Grill which serves excellent seafood. Windsurfing, water-skiing and deep-sea fishing are on offer. **www.edenrockenya.com**

MALINDI Tropical Beach Resort

🍴 🏊 🛁 📋 W $$$

Casuarina Road **Tel** *042 2120444* **Fax** *042 2131872* **Rooms** *109*   **Road Map** *E6*

Set in a double-storey, whitewashed thatched building, all rooms in this resort have balconies or patios and are decorated in Swahili furnishings, and there is a large buffet restaurant. Activities include the pool, archery, table tennis, water sports and diving. Local day trips can also be arranged. **www.planhotel.com**

MALINDI Diamonds Dream of Africa

🍴 🏊 📋 W $$$$

Casuarina Road **Tel** *042 2120444* **Fax** *042 2130747* **Rooms** *33*   **Road Map** *E6*

A member of Small Luxury Hotels of the World, this hotel boasts lavish rooms housed in Arabian-style blocks with cool arches and broad terraces, close to the beach and an attractive pool surrounded by palms and flowering shrubs. Italian-inspired cuisine and weekly seafood buffets. Rates are all-inclusive. **www.planhotel.com**

MALINDI Kilili Baharini Resort

🍴 🏊 🍽 📋 W $$$$

Casuarina Road **Tel** *042 2120169* **Fax** *042 2120634* **Rooms** *35*   **Road Map** *E6*

Kilili Baharini means "sofa by the sea" and this small, exclusive resort is certainly laid-back and comfortable. Rooms are stylishly decorated almost entirely white and overlook one of the five swimming pools. Breakfast is served on each private veranda. The luxury spa offering Italian-produced treatments is a highlight. **www.kililibaharini.com**

TANA RIVER Tana Delta Dunes

🍴 🏊 $$$$$

River estuary off the road to Garsen **Tel** *0721 322745* **Rooms** *6*   **Road Map** *E6*

An exclusive camp of just six partially-open thatched cottages perched on sand dunes. Each cottage boasts good views over the ocean and Tana river estuary and king-sized beds fashioned out of driftwood, while seafood meals are served in a communal tent. The camp is reached by 4WD transfer from Malindi. **www.africanterritories.co.ke**

WATAMU BEACH Turtle Bay Beach Club

🍴 🏊 🍽 🛁 📋 W $$$

Mida Creek Drive **Tel** *042 2332003* **Fax** *042 2332268* **Rooms** *145*   **Road Map** *E6*

An all-inclusive beach resort popular with European families, with good service and lots of activities for both children and adults, such as volleyball, football, bird-watching and village visits. Meals are buffet, plus guests can enjoy tribal dancing, quiz nights and a disco for evening entertainment. Good-value package rates. **www.turtlebay.co.ke**

WATAMU BEACH Blue Bay Club

🍴 🏊 🍽 W $$$$

Mida Creek Drive **Tel** *042 2332626* **Fax** *042 2332422* **Rooms** *118*   **Road Map** *E6*

This Italian-run resort offers spacious rooms decked in Persian rugs with vast beds and fans or air conditioning. The thatched chalets are double-storey and there is an attractive pool surrounded by ferns. Activities offered include water sports, archery and tennis, plus evening entertainment. Rates are full-board. **www.igrandiviaggi.it**

WATAMU BEACH Hemingways

🍴 🏊 🍽 🛁 📋 W $$$$

Mida Creek Drive **Tel** *042 2332052* **Fax** *042 2332656* **Rooms** *76*   **Road Map** *E6*

Another member of Small Luxury Hotels of the World, Hemingways has its own fleet of boats which makes it popular with big-game fishermen – the catch of the day is prepared to guests' liking for dinner. Rooms are spacious and individually designed, and there is a large pool, gym and dive school. **www.hemingways.co.ke**

SOUTHERN RIFT VALLEY AND MASAI MARA

LAKE BARINGO Roberts' Camp

📋 🍴 $$

Kampi ya Samaki **Tel** *0722 207772* **Rooms** *8*   **Road Map** *B3*

This place offers full-board accommodation in cottages and *bandas* or much cheaper self-catering rates, in addition to camping. The Thirsty Goat pub serves a wide range of drinks and good wholesome food, plus there is a small shop for provisions. Activities include camel rides, boat trips and guided bird walks. **www.robertscamp.com**

LAKE BARINGO Lake Baringo Club

🍴 🏊 🛁 W $$$

Kampi ya Samaki **Tel** *053 51401* **Rooms** *48*   **Road Map** *B3*

Built in the 1960s, this comfortable old hotel is perfect for bird-watchers, offering guided bird walks, as well as boat rides to see hippos and crocodiles. Guests can also enjoy the swimming pool and the attractive grounds shaded by bougainvillea. Service is good and the buffet meals excellent. **www.kenyahotelsltd.com**

LAKE BARINGO Island Camp
Ol Kokwe Island **Tel** *0735 919878* **Rooms** *23*   Road Map *B3*

This camp occupies a delightful and peaceful location in the middle of Lake Baringo. Tents under thatch are dotted around a hill in established gardens, with stone paths leading down from the swimming pool at the top to the informal restaurant and bar on the lakeshore. Walks, boat rides and water sports on offer. **www.islandcamp.co.ke**

LAKE BOGORIA Lake Bogoria Hotel
3 km (2 miles) before Loboi Gate **Tel** *051 2216687* **Rooms** *45*   Road Map *B4*

Set in expansive grounds full of acacia trees, rooms in the main block of this hotel are slightly old-fashioned and guests will find more modern accommodation in the garden cottages. Facilities include a terrace restaurant and bar, and two pools, one of which is fed by the Bogoria's hot springs. Guided bird walks offered.

LAKE ELMENTEITA Lake Elmentaita Lodge
Off the A104, 35 km (22 miles) SE of Nakuru **Tel** *050 50836* **Rooms** *33*   Road Map *B4*

Set in the former ranch house of an early settler family built in 1916, this hotel features wood-panelled walls, wide terraces overlooking the lake and a library with log fire. Popular with tour groups, rooms are comfortable if a little faded, though the ox-wagon rides with the Maasai are the main draw. **www.jacarandahotels.com**

LAKE NAIVASHA Fisherman's Camp
Moi South Lake Road, 20 km (12 miles) from Naivasha **Tel** *050 2030276* **Rooms** *5*   Road Map *B4*

Budget accommodation in either a self-catering cottage sleeping six, *bandas* for two to four or camping on beautiful lawns with acacia trees full of monkeys and birds, which lead down to Lake Naivasha. There are communal showers and a basic restaurant and bar, plus boat and mountain bike hire. **www.fishermanscampkenya.com**

LAKE NAIVASHA La Belle Inn
Moi Avenue, Naivasha Town **Tel** *050 3510404* **Rooms** *10*   Road Map *B4*

This old colonial inn was once a watering hole for white settlers coming to Lake Naivasha for the weekend. Rooms are simple but comfortable with piping hot showers, and there is a superb terrace restaurant with treats like grilled fish from the lake or home-made pies and quiches. Boat trips to Crescent Island *(see pp266–7)* are available.

LAKE NAIVASHA Crater Lake
Crater Lake Sanctuary, Moi South Lake Road **Tel** *050 2020613* **Rooms** *10*   Road Map *B4*

This intimate camp looks out to the milky-green waters of the lake in the Crater Lake Sanctuary. Accommodation is in spacious tents under thatch with four-poster beds and reproduction antique furniture. The honeymoon suite has a novel sunken bath. Nearby is the grave of Lady Diana Delamere *(see p269)*. **www.mericagrouphotels.com**

LAKE NAIVASHA Elsamere
Moi South Lake Road, 22 km (14 miles) from Naivasha **Tel** *050 2050964* **Rooms** *8*   Road Map *B4*

This former home of Joy Adamson *(see p333)* offers comfortable, airy rooms in chalets. The restaurant serves set communal dinners, though drinks are bring-your-own as there is no bar. Guests may also take a sumptuous afternoon tea on the lawn and there are boat trips to Crescent Island. Rates are full-board. **www.elsamere.com**

LAKE NAIVASHA Lake Naivasha Country Club
Moi South Lake Road, 5 km (3 miles) from Naivasha **Tel** *020 2370368* **Rooms** *51*   Road Map *B4*

A solid colonial hotel dating back to the 1930s, with English-style country decor and set in grounds full of giant acacia trees overlooking the lake. Rooms are arranged in single-storey wings or garden cottages, and guests can enjoy an atmospheric lounge and terrace. Boat rides can be arranged. **www.kenyahotelsltd.com**

LAKE NAIVASHA Lake Naivasha Sopa Resort
Moi South Lake Road, 12 km (7 miles) from Naivasha **Tel** *020 3750235* **Fax** *020 3751507* **Rooms** *84* Road Map *B4*

Built in 2003, this modern lakeside lodge is set in expansive grounds and offers rooms with balconies or patios in neat, two-storey garden cottages surrounded by flowering shrubs. There are two swimming pools, an attractive glass-enclosed restaurant and a bar. Popular venue for conferences and weddings. **www.sopalodges.com**

LAKE NAIVASHA Great Rift Valley Lodge
Moi North Lake Road, 11 km (7 miles) from Naivasha **Tel** *050 50021* **Fax** *050 50047* **Rooms** *30*   Road Map *B4*

Set on an 18-hole championship golf course with sweeping views of Lake Naivasha, this resort features modern, upmarket rooms, a driving range, swimming pool and clay tennis courts, and bird walks, horse riding and mountain biking in the grounds. Day trips to Hell's Gate and other attractions are also offered. **www.heritage-eastafrica.com**

LAKE NAIVASHA Chui Lodge
Oserian Wildlife Sanctuary, Moi South Lake Road **Tel** *050 2020792* **Fax** *050 2021059* **Rooms** *8*   Road Map *B4*

Well known for its excellent service and exquisite cuisine, this small lodge offers eight stunningly luxurious cottages featuring four-poster beds with opulent drapes, marble bathrooms and roaring log fires. Game drives are on offer and the sanctuary is home to white rhino, leopard, buffalo and antelope. **www.oserianwildlife.com**

LAKE NAIVASHA Malewa Wildlife Lodge
Kigio Wildlife Conservancy, on the A104 **Tel** *020 3742435* **Fax** *020 372435* **Rooms** *10*   Road Map *B4*

This lodge offers rooms in bright and airy cottages or riverside suites on stilts, and there is an imaginatively designed wood-and-thatch mess building with a restaurant, bar and lounges scattered with cushions. Rates are all-inclusive of meals, drinks and guided game walks and drives. Guests can also hire mountain bikes. **www.kigio.com**

LAKE NAKURU NATIONAL PARK Naishi House ⓈⓈⓈ

Near the airstrip and ranger's post **Tel** *020 6000800* **Fax** *020 6003792* **Rooms** *4*   **Road Map** B4

Kenya Wildlife Service park accommodation sleeping up to eight in a spacious house and adjacent cottage, with a fully-equipped kitchen, bedding and towels, and a generator for electricity in the evenings. Guests will need to bring their own food, firewood and drinking water. Good value for a group. **www.kws.go.ke**

LAKE NAKURU NATIONAL PARK Lake Nakuru Lodge ⓈⓈⓈⓈ

Close to Nderit Gate **Tel** *051 850518* **Fax** *051 216250* **Rooms** *68*   **Road Map** B4

Located in the southeast of the park, the original house was once part of Lord Delamere's estate and it now offers accommodation in a selection of cottages and *bandas* set in established gardens and with good views of the lake. There is a large swimming pool, and horse riding and bush barbecues can be arranged. **www.lakenakurulodge.com**

LAKE NAKURU NATIONAL PARK Sarova Lion Hill Game Lodge ⓈⓈⓈⓈ

East of Lake Nakuru, near Lion Cave **Tel** *051 852288* **Fax** *051 2210836* **Rooms** *67*   **Road Map** B4

Spread out on a hill with distant views to Lake Nakuru, rooms at this lodge are comfortable and with modern decor. Facilities include a swimming pool and sauna, and there is a beauty therapist. The restaurant can arrange private dinners in the gardens and guests are treated to traditional dancing in the evening. **www.sarovahotels.com**

MASAI MARA GAME RESERVE Basecamp Masai Mara ⓈⓈⓈⓈ

Concession east of Talek Gate **Tel** *020 3877490* **Rooms** *12*   **Road Map** B5

A relaxed, eco-friendly tented camp run by solar power and using recycled waste water. Tents are set in a loop of the Talek river with its resident hippos and crocodiles, and have verandas, hammocks and outdoor showers. Game drives, walks with Maasai guides and children's activities are offered. **www.basecampexplorer.com**

MASAI MARA GAME RESERVE Fig Tree Camp ⓈⓈⓈⓈ

Northern Mara, near Talek Gate **Tel** *050 22131* **Fax** *020 6003595* **Rooms** *70*   **Road Map** B5

This camp provides a modest standard of accommodation in tents or chalets located on the Talek river, with facilities including a pool, two dining decks and a curio shop. There are wildlife films and Maasai dancing in the evening, and champagne bush dinners can also be arranged. Base for balloon trips (*see p400*). **www.madahotels.com**

MASAI MARA GAME RESERVE Masai Mara Sopa Lodge ⓈⓈⓈⓈ

Eastern Mara **Tel** *050 22195* **Fax** *020 3751507* **Rooms** *100*   **Road Map** B5

An extensive lodge with communal areas decorated in a Maasai theme, including a large central fireplace in the restaurant topped with life-size carved figures of warriors. Comfortable rooms are arranged in round thatched buildings and there is a full range of facilities including a pool, gardens and gift shop. **www.sopalodges.com**

MASAI MARA GAME RESERVE Cottar's 1920 Camp ⓈⓈⓈⓈⓈ

Southeast Mara **Tel** *0733 4902343* **Rooms** *8*   **Road Map** B5

Run by renowned safari guide Calvin Cottar, this luxury bush camp with 1920s safari decor is in an excellent location near the Serengeti for watching the wildebeest migration. Each flowing white tent has its own butler, free-standing bath and dressing room. Excellent cuisine is served on silverware by candlelight. **www.chelipeacock.com**

MASAI MARA GAME RESERVE Elephant Pepper Camp ⓈⓈⓈⓈⓈ

Koiyaki Community Ranch, Northern Mara **Tel** *020 6004053* **Fax** *020 6004050* **Rooms** *8*   **Road Map** B5

An intimate bush camp set in a tract of shady forest with good views over the Mara Plains. Tents are spacious and comfortable each with a veranda and dressing room. Guests can enjoy bush breakfasts and guided walks and drives, then finish with "sundowner" safari cocktails followed by Italian-inspired cuisine for dinner. **www.chelipeacock.com**

MASAI MARA GAME RESERVE Governors' Camp ⓈⓈⓈⓈⓈ

Northern Mara **Tel** *020 2734000* **Fax** *020 2734023* **Rooms** *37*   **Road Map** B5

A classic luxury safari camp with tents on wooden platforms overlooking the game-rich Mara river or Mara Plains, and famous for being the base for the team of the BBC's *Big Cat Diary*. Apart from excellent service and good guides, the camp also offers walking safaris and visits with the Maasai. **www.governorscamp.com**

MASAI MARA GAME RESERVE Karen Blixen Camp ⓈⓈⓈⓈⓈ

Concession north of Musiara Gate **Tel** *0773 063863* **Rooms** *22*   **Road Map** B5

Tents at this camp are decorated in replicas of Karen Blixen's furnishings and feature large mahogany decks with day beds scattered with cushions, though showers are outdoor. The mess and dining area is attractively thatched, plus there is an open fire pit, pool and massage service. Located on the Mara river. **www.karenblixencamp.com**

MASAI MARA GAME RESERVE Keekerok Lodge ⓈⓈⓈⓈⓈ

Southeast Mara **Tel** *050 22680* **Fax** *020 650384* **Rooms** *101*   **Road Map** B5

This is the oldest lodge in the Mara and has comfortable rooms in chalets, a pool, garden, restaurant and three bars, including the unique Hippo Bar built at the end of an elevated walkway overlooking a hippo pool. Game drives, bird walks and Maasai dancing are on offer. **www.wildernesslodges.co.ke**

MASAI MARA GAME RESERVE Kichwa Tembo Tented Camp ⓈⓈⓈⓈⓈ

Concession northwest of Oloololo Gate **Tel** *050 22465* **Rooms** *58*   **Road Map** B5

Divided into two camps, the main camp offers spacious tents, a large swimming pool and a dining room with good views. Tents in the smaller, more exclusive adjoining Kichwa Tembo Bateleur Tented Camp have four-poster beds and a butler service. A member of Small Luxury Hotels of the World. **www.andbeyondafrica.com**

MASAI MARA GAME RESERVE Little Governors' Camp   🍴 📶   ⑤⑤⑤⑤⑤

Northern Mara **Tel** *020 2734000* **Fax** *020 2734023* **Rooms** *17*   **Road Map** *B5*

Accessed by boat across the Mara river and with just 17 tents clustered around a waterhole, this is a more intimate set-up than the main Governors' Camp, as the name would suggest. With no electricity, the flickering lights at night create a wonderful atmosphere. Three game drives per day are included in the price. **www.governorscamp.com**

MASAI MARA GAME RESERVE Mara Explorer   🍴 📶   ⑤⑤⑤⑤⑤

Central Mara **Tel** *050 22168* **Fax** *050 22327* **Rooms** *10*   **Road Map** *B5*

A small, luxury tented camp on the banks of the Talek river and the smartest of Heritage Hotels' trio of Mara lodges. The decor takes on an early explorer theme with old wooden chests, historical prints and open air claw-foot baths, and each tent comes with its own butler. Very good, delicately presented cuisine. **www.heritage-eastafrica.com**

MASAI MARA GAME RESERVE Mara Intrepids   🍴 🏊 🦓 📶   ⑤⑤⑤⑤⑤

Central Mara **Tel** *050 22168* **Fax** *050 22327* **Rooms** *30*   **Road Map** *B5*

A family-friendly camp that runs unique children's safaris teaching bush lore. Scattered around a riverside setting, some tents accommodate families in two rooms separated by a lounge and all include four-poster beds and wooden furniture. Several private dining decks in addition to the restaurant. **www.heritage-eastafrica.com**

MASAI MARA GAME RESERVE Mara Serena Safari Lodge   🍴 🏊 📶   ⑤⑤⑤⑤⑤

Western Mara **Tel** *050 22253* **Fax** *050 22382* **Rooms** *74*   **Road Map** *B5*

Built on a ridge with commanding views in the middle of the reserve, this established lodge features architecture emulating a Maasai *manyatta* (hut), with decor to match and a restaurant overlooking a waterhole. As well as two game drives a day, guests can try the beauty treatments and visit the gift shop. **www.serenahotels.com**

MASAI MARA GAME RESERVE Mpata Safari Club   🍴 🏊 📶   ⑤⑤⑤⑤⑤

Concession west of Oloololo Gate **Tel** *020 2217015* **Fax** *020 2229420* **Rooms** *23*   **Road Map** *B5*

Perched on top of the Oloololo Escarpment with commanding views of the Mara, this five-star lodge occupies an unusual structure of curves and glass designed by a Japanese architect, and is a particular favourite of the Japanese. Rooms have private plunge pools, while suites include additional kitchens and Jacuzzis. **www.mpata.com**

MASAI MARA GAME RESERVE Porini Lion Camp   🍴   ⑤⑤⑤⑤⑤

Olare Orok Conservancy, east of Musiara Gate **Tel** *020 7123129* **Rooms** *10*   **Road Map** *B5*

This exclusive camp on the 80-sq km (20,000-acre) Olare Orok Conservancy is run in association with the local Maasai community who own the conservancy and staff the camp. The area is renowned for its lion prides and is close to the annual migration route of the wildebeest herds. Maasai-escorted bush walks are available. **www.porini.com**

MASAI MARA GAME RESERVE Sarova Mara Game Camp   🍴 🏊 🦓   ⑤⑤⑤⑤⑤

Eastern Mara **Tel** *050 22386* **Fax** *050 22371* **Rooms** *73*   **Road Map** *B5*

This large camp with modern, comfortable tents is popular with families. The Club Tents have extended decks and minibars. Breakfast and lunch are buffet meals and there are barbecue dinners, as well as a bar. Two game drives are arranged each day and Maasai performances organised in the evening. **www.sarovahotels.com**

MASAI MARA GAME RESERVE Siana Springs Intrepids   🍴 🏊 🦓 📶   ⑤⑤⑤⑤⑤

Concession northeast of Sekenani Gate **Tel** *050 22553* **Fax** *020 2383085* **Rooms** *39*   **Road Map** *B5*

Another family-orientated camp from Heritage Hotels where extra activities are laid on for children by the fully supervised Adventurer's Club. Comfortable tents are set among woodland and bamboo, and there is a pool, boutique, large airy restaurant and Maasai dancing after dinner. **www.heritage-eastafrica.com**

NAKURU Midland Hotel   🍴   ⑤⑤

Geoffrey Kamau Highway **Tel** *051 2212125* **Rooms** *68*   **Road Map** *B4*

This is an adequate mid-range option and very friendly, with extras such as morning newspapers under the door, and an excellent, affordable restaurant and bar serving steaks, fish, pizzas and filled pancakes. Rooms are comfortable, though some are small and the best ones are in the new wing. There is a secure car park.

WESTERN KENYA

CHERANGANI HILLS Marich Pass Field Studies Centre   📖 🍴   ⑤

Marich Pass, 100 km (60 miles) north of Kitale, Kapenguria, West Pokot **Rooms** *23*   **Road Map** *B3*

Remote accommodation in simple huts for two–five people, with communal bathrooms, mosquito nets and hurricane lamps, plus a spacious campsite in a scenic forested spot. Buffet meals, beer and soft drinks are available. An ideal base for hiking in the Cherangani Hills and Pokot guides are available to hire. **www.gg.rhul.ac.uk/marichpass**

ELDORET Eldoret Wagon Hotel   🍴 🏊 🦓 📶   ⑤

Corner of Elgeyo and Oloo Roads **Tel** *053 2062270* **Fax** *053 2002400* **Rooms** *102*   **Road Map** *B4*

A local business hotel with somewhat worn rooms but nevertheless the best option in central Eldoret, favoured by NGOs and local politicians and a much better alternative to the other basic board-and-lodgings in town. Benefits from a professional staff, a pool and a decent restaurant and bar. **wagonhotel@africaonline.co.ke**

Key to Price Guide *see p362* **Key to Symbols** *see back cover flap*

ELDORET Naiberi River Campsite and Resort 🈁 🈁 🈁 Ⓦ ⑤

C54, 16 km (10 miles) northwest of Eldoret **Tel** *053 3550051* **Fax** *053 2062916* **Rooms** *7*   **Road Map** *B4*

A lovely rustic resort and overland stop with thatched en suite chalets and *bandas*, plus spacious camping sites with shared facilities. The on-site Stone Cave Pub is delightful, with streams and waterfalls running through it and a log fire. Visitors can also see the remains of some ancient Sirikwa dry-stone dwellings. **www.naiberi.com**

HOMA BAY Homa Bay Tourist Hotel 🈁 🈁 Ⓦ ⑤

Pier Road along the lakeshore **Tel** *059 22788* **Fax** *059 22044* **Rooms** *23*   **Road Map** *A4*

A friendly hotel in an ordinary brick-built block but with well-established gardens and excellent views of the lake. The affordable rooms have satellite TV, fans and fridges, and there is a pleasant terrace bar and restaurant. Bikes and boats can be hired and the hotel has a vehicle for trips to Ruma National Park. **www.homabaytouristhotel.com**

KAKAMEGA Isecheno Bandas 🈁 ⑤

Kakamega Forest National Reserve, road between Shinyalu and Chepsonoi **Rooms** *5*   **Road Map** *A4*

Run by the Kakamega Environmental Education Programme (KEEP), these simple traditional Luhya thatched huts are well hidden in the forest. Bathrooms and kitchen are communal and guests need to bring food, firewood and bedding. Excellent guides make for wonderfully informative forest walks. **keeporg@yahoo.com**

KAKAMEGA Golf Hotel 🈁 🈁 🈁 Ⓦ ⑤⑤

Khasakhala Road **Tel** *056 30150* **Fax** *056 30155* **Rooms** *62*   **Road Map** *A4*

Although old-fashioned, this hotel has comfortable rooms with mosquito nets, balconies and TV, and is set amid pleasant gardens. Excursions to Kakamega Forest can be organised and guests can play golf and tennis at the adjacent Kakamega Sports Club. Good restaurant with African, Indian and Continental dishes. **www.golfhotelkakamega.com**

KAKAMEGA Rondo Retreat 🈁 🈁 ⑤⑤

Kakamega Forest National Reserve, road between Shinyalu and Chepsonoi **Tel** *056 30268* **Rooms** *18*   **Road Map** *A4*

A Christian-run and very tranquil retreat in the heart of the forest, offering rooms in the old 1940s saw miller's house or garden cottages with polished wooden floors and antiques. The giant 500-year-old Elgon teak tree in the grounds is an impressive sight. Good wholesome food but no alcohol. Guided walks. **www.rondoretreat.com**

KAKAMEGA Udo's Bandas 🈁 ⑤⑤

Kakamega Forest National Reserve, access from the A2 **Tel** *020 6000800* **Fax** *020 6003792* **Rooms** *7* **Road Map** *A4*

This place offers very simple, two-bed thatched *bandas* with mosquito nets and hurricane lamps, plus camping. There is a partially-open kitchen but guests must bring all provisions, including cooking utensils, firewood, drinking water and bedding. Basic long-drop toilets and bucket showers. The start for many forest trails. **www.kws.go.ke**

KERICHO Tea Hotel 🈁 🈁 🈁 Ⓦ ⑤⑤

Moi Highway **Tel** *020 2050790* **Rooms** *45*   **Road Map** *B4*

A faded colonial hotel with old-fashioned rooms, but set in lush green lawns and surrounded by tea plantations. The restaurant is reasonable and guests can enjoy the pool, tennis courts and Kericho Golf Club next door. There is also a campsite with hot showers. Excellent guides offer tours of the tea plantations. **teahotel@africaonline.co.ke**

KERIO VALLEY Kerio View 🈁 🈁 🈁 ⑤⑤

C51, Elgeyo Escarpment near Iten **Tel** *0722 781916* **Rooms** *12*   **Road Map** *B3*

As the name suggests, the highlight here is the breathtaking view over the Kerio Valley from the main glass-fronted restaurant and the comfortable cottages and *bandas* spread over the hillside. The food is excellent and there is an outdoor barbecue. Mountain bikes are available for hire and there are plenty of hiking trails. **www.kerioview.com**

KISUMU Imperial Hotel 🈁 🈁 🈁 🈁 🈁 Ⓦ ⑤⑤

Jomo Kenyatta Avenue **Tel** *057 2020002* **Fax** *057 2022685* **Rooms** *70*   **Road Map** *A4*

Centrally located and popular with business travellers, this is Kisumu's best hotel with modern rooms and suites decorated with plush carpets and fittings – plus self-catering one-bedroom apartments. The staff are friendly, the restaurant serves good food, and there is a bar on the top floor. Secure parking. **www.imperialhotelkisumu.com**

KISUMU Kisumu Hotel 🈁 🈁 🈁 🈁 🈁 Ⓦ ⑤⑤

Jomo Kenyatta Avenue **Tel** *057 2024157* **Rooms** *80*   **Road Map** *A4*

Owned by Kisumu's university and set in a historic whitewashed building with an arched facade, rooms at this hotel are simply furnished but with newish bathrooms and satellite TV. Facilities include a modern restaurant and bar, and there is an adjoining casino.

KISUMU Milimani Resort 🈁 🈁 🈁 🈁 Ⓦ ⑤⑤

Busia Road **Tel** *057 2023245* **Fax** *057 2023242* **Rooms** *48*   **Road Map** *A4*

Located in one of Kisumu's quiet southern suburbs – though not on the lakeshore – this has comfortable, fairly modern rooms with satellite TV and 24-hour room service, a good restaurant serving African and Continental food, including tilapia fish from the lake, and a large pool with a bar in the middle of it.

KISUMU Sunset Hotel 🈁 🈁 🈁 🈁 Ⓦ ⑤⑤

Aput Lane **Tel** *057 2020464* **Rooms** *50*   **Road Map** *A4*

Despite the drab rooms and rather bland food in the restaurant, this hotel does have the advantage of being in a quiet area of town, with air conditioning (Kisumu can get very hot) and fantastic glass-fronted views from the higher rooms over Lake Victoria. Nice pool in pretty gardens, plus secure parking. **hotelsunset1977@yahoo.co.uk**

KISUMU Kiboko Bay Resort
$$
On the lakeshore, Dunga Village **Tel** 0733 532709 **Rooms** 9   **Road Map** A4

This resort offers the only accommodation in Kisumu on the lakeshore itself, with hippo grazing on the lawn, good birdlife and boats for fishing or to watch the sunset. Rooms are in comfortable en suite tents under thatch, there is a very good restaurant and a pool bar perched over the lapping waters of the lake. **www.kibokobay.com**

KITALE Karibuni Lodge
Off Hospital Road **Tel** 0735 573798 **Rooms** 11   **Road Map** A3

A fairly new family-run backpacker's lodge in a pleasant house set in a landscaped garden with views of the Cherangani Hills. Double and twin rooms, some en suite, and A-frame tents are available. Facilities include hot showers, a bar and communal dinners of good home cooking. Can organise local tours. **www.karibunikitale.com**

KITALE Kitale Club
Eldoret Road **Tel** 054 31338 **Fax** 054 30924 **Rooms** 16   **Road Map** A3

This is a good base for exploring Saiwa Swamp and Mount Elgon national parks, offering comfortable rooms with faded colonial charm at a golf club dating back to the 1930s. The 18-hole golf course is lovely and additional facilities include a pool and tennis courts. Good three-course set dinners and satellite TV in the bar.

MFANGANO ISLAND Mfangano Island Lodge
In the northeast of the island **Tel** 020 2734000 **Fax** 020 2734023 **Rooms** 6   **Road Map** A4

Part of the Masai Mara group of Governors' Camps with daily air links to the reserve, these six secluded, luxury thatched rooms with four-poster beds are shaded by gnarled fig trees and have sun decks overlooking the lake. Very good service, excellent cuisine, a spa and fishing for Nile perch on offer. **www.governorscamp.com**

MOLO Kembu Campsite and Cottages
Between Nakuru and Molo off the A104, 8 km (5 miles) W of Njoro **Tel** 0722 361102 **Rooms** 8   **Road Map** B4

An excellent option on a working old settler farm, with delightful cottages – one the former home of Beryl Markham, the English-born adventurer and first woman to fly solo East-to-West across the Atlantic – and a unique treehouse, plus a lovely campsite surrounded by bushes full of chameleons. Rustic bar and restaurant. **www.kembu.com**

MOUNT ELGON NATIONAL PARK Kapkuro Bandas
Near Park Headquarters, Chorlim Gate **Tel** 020 6000800 **Fax** 020 6003792 **Rooms** 4   **Road Map** A3

KWS accommodation in four basic en suite bandas in a pretty and peaceful forest glade. The communal kitchen has basic utensils and a gas cooker, and blankets and kerosene lights are provided, but guests need to bring other provisions such as firewood and drinking water. **www.kws.go.ke**

RUSINGA ISLAND Rusinga Island Lodge
In the northwest of the island **Tel** 020 882028 **Fax** 020 882868 **Rooms** 7   **Road Map** A4

Usually reached by private air charter, this remote island lodge is popular with fishermen in search of the giant Nile perch, though other activities include bird walks, boat-trips and spa treatments. The luxury stone and thatch cottages sit on sweeping lawns with giant fig trees, and are decorated with African cloth and baskets. **www.rusinga.com**

CENTRAL HIGHLANDS

ABERDARE NATIONAL PARK Fishing Lodge
In the south of the park, near Kiandongoro Gate **Tel** 020 6000800 **Fax** 020 6003792 **Rooms** 6   **Road Map** C4

This KWS lodge consists of two three-bedroom cottages set in high, rolling grassland along the Icharangathi river. Bedding, towels, lighting and lamps are provided, and cottages have a self-catering kitchen, but guests must bring food and drinks. Good trout fishing as well as scenic walks in areas still populated by big game. **www.kws.go.ke**

ABERDARE NATIONAL PARK The Ark
In the Salient, reached via Aberdare Country Club **Tel** 020 216940 **Fax** 020 216796 **Rooms** 60   **Road Map** C4

Built in 1969, this superb tree hotel overlooks a forest-fringed water hole and is the only tree hotel where all the Big Five are seen with regularity. The wooden exterior gives it a rustic atmophere, the set menus are hearty, and the rooms, though on the small side, are comfortable. No children under 7. **www.fairmont.com**

ABERDARE NATIONAL PARK Treetops
In the Salient on the eastern edge of the park **Tel** 061 2032425 **Fax** 061 2032286 **Rooms** 50   **Road Map** C4

Founded in 1932, Treetops is the original tree hotel and made headlines when Britain's Princess Elizabeth was staying there the night her father died and she became Queen. The lodge overlooks a waterhole that attracts wildlife. Rooms are small but comfortable. No children under 5. **www.aberdaresafarihotels.com**

EMBU Izaak Walton Inn
On the Meru Road, 1 km (half a mile) from the centre **Tel** 068 31128 **Fax** 068 31129 **Rooms** 50   **Road Map** C4

A charmingly frayed colonial relic, this inn on the northern outskirts of Embu was built in 1948 and lies in large grounds shaded by leafy tropical trees. The rooms all have TV, netting and telephones, but those in the new wing are in the best repair. Good restaurant attached and excursions can be organised.

Key to Price Guide see p362 **Key to Symbols** see back cover flap

LAIKIPIA PLATEAU Lewa Safari Camp

🅗 ▩ ⬜ $$$$$

Lewa Wildlife Conservancy **Tel** *020 6004053* **Rooms** *12* **Road Map** *C4*

On a private conservancy in the northern foothills of Mount Kenya, this exclusive camp offers luxurious tents near a waterhole. Activities include community visits, night drives, horseback safaris and game walks, while the varied wildlife includes Grevy's zebra, black and white rhino, African wild dog and sitatunga antelope. **www.chelipeacock.com**

LAIKIPIA PLATEAU Mukutan Retreat

🅗 ▩ $$$$$

Ol Ari Nyiro Conservancy **Tel** *0734 291710* **Fax** *062 31248* **Rooms** *3* **Road Map** *C4*

The remote field station and lodge lies in a vast private conservancy overlooking the Rift Valley in western Laikipia. Founded by the author Kuki Gallmann, who still lives there today, it offers bush accommodation in simple but comfortable furnished tents. Game drives and walks are offered to see the prolific wildlife. **www.gallmannkenya.org**

LAIKIPIA PLATEAU Ol Pejeta Ranch House

🅗 ▩ $$$$$

Ol Pejeta Conservancy **Tel** *062 32409* **Fax** *062 31965* **Rooms** *6* **Road Map** *C4*

Situated some 8 km (5 miles) from Sweetwaters Tented Camp and under the same management, this ultra-exclusive retreat consists of six luxury suites, with lush tropical gardens, two swimming pools and a waterhole for wildlife. Activities include day and night drives and visits to Sweetwaters Chimpanzee Sanctuary. **www.serenahotels.com**

LAIKIPIA PLATEAU Sabuk Camp

🅗 $$$$$

Northern Frontier District **Tel** *020 2663397* **Rooms** *7* **Road Map** *C4*

This superlative bush camp in the remote wilds of northern Laikipia has a stunning clifftop location above the Ewaso Nyiro river. The innovative wood, thatch, stone and canvas units are open-sided to make the most of the view. A holistic bush experience and the best chance anywhere in Kenya of seeing greater kudu. **www.africanterritories.co.ke**

LAIKIPIA PLATEAU Serena Sweetwaters Tented Camp

🅗 ▩ 🆃 🅱 ⬜ $$$$$

Southern end of the plateau **Tel** *062 32409* **Fax** *062 31965* **Rooms** *39* **Road Map** *C4*

This luxury camp has smartly-furnished tents with balconied wooden platforms overlooking a waterhole. Facilities include valet service and sumptuous five-course dinners. Popular trips to Ol Pejeta Chimpanzee Sanctuary are offered, along with day and night game drives and guided walks. **www.serenahotels.com**

MERU Pig & Whistle

$

Kenyatta Highway **Tel** *064 31411* **Rooms** *24* **Road Map** *C4*

Founded in 1934, this slightly rundown old hotel is the most characterful option for Meru town. Rooms have satellite TV and phone, a decent restaurant is attached and the garden is a pleasant spot for a cold beer. The original wooden cabins are a better choice than the more modern concrete cottages.

MERU NATIONAL PARK Murera Bandas

🗐 $

Near the Murera Entrance Gate **Tel** *020 6000800* **Fax** *020 6003792* **Rooms** *4* **Road Map** *D4*

The best budget option in Meru National Park is this complex of four en suite self-catering *bandas*. Each *banda* has one bedroom with single and double beds. Clean bedding is provided but towels are not and guests should also bring all their own food, which can be cooked at a communal barbecue area. **www.kws.go.ke**

MERU NATIONAL PARK Elsa's Kopje

🅗 ▩ $$$$$

Mughwango Hill in the centre of the park **Tel** *020 6004053* **Rooms** *10* **Road Map** *D4*

Among the most stunning lodges in Kenya, the hilltop Elsa's Kopje overlooks the former campsite of Joy and George Adamson and is named after the leonine star of *Born Free*. Open-fronted suites make the most of the wonderful view, and the food and service are top notch. Well positioned for game drives. **www.chelipeacock.com**

MERU NATIONAL PARK Leopard Rock Lodge

🅗 ▩ $$$$$

In the north of the park, close to Bisanadi Gate **Tel** *020 600031* **Fax** *020 600031* **Rooms** *15* **Road Map** *D4*

Running along the forested banks of the Bisanadi river, this lodge consists of a string of spacious stone-and-thatch cottages with private balconies and teak furniture. The lounge and dining area offers good bird and wildlife viewing as you dine, with hippo resident in the river. Excellent five-course meals. **www.leopardmico.com**

MOUNT KENYA NATIONAL PARK Serena Mountain Lodge

🅗 $$$$

In the Forest Reserve Area in the south of the park **Tel** *0771 109637* **Fax** *020 2718103* **Rooms** *42* **Road Map** *C4*

Enclosed in forest on the southern foothills of Mount Kenya, this lodge offers the best game viewing of the tree hotels of the Central Highlands, with elephant, bushpig and giant forest hog coming past most nights. Guided walks are a treat for bird-watchers. Large en suite rooms and excellent buffet meals. **www.serenahotels.com**

MWEA NATIONAL RESERVE Masinga Resort

🗐 🅗 $

Off the B7, 13 km (8 miles) from the reserve **Tel** *020 6000800* **Fax** *020 6003792* **Rooms** *40* **Road Map** *C4*

This pleasant resort lies in large, unkempt grounds sloping down towards the Masinga Dam Wall and can get busy when regattas or similar events are held at the dam, but otherwise runs at near-zero occupancy. En suite rooms are adequate and the pricier ones have private balconies. Decent restaurant and bar. **www.kws.go.ke**

NANYUKI Sirimon Bandas

🗐 $$

Sirimon Gate **Tel** *020 6000800* **Fax** *020 6003792* **Rooms** *4* **Road Map** *C4*

These cosy self-catering *bandas* are a popular starting point for hikes up Mount Kenya or for exploring the forested slopes. There are two *bandas*, each with one double and one twin room, and a shared bathroom. Bedding and towels are provided, and there is a gas cooker, but guests must bring their own food and drink. **www.kws.go.ke**

NANYUKI Sportsman's Arms
$$$

Outskirts of Nanyuki town **Tel** *062 32348* **Rooms** *84* **Road Map** *C4*

This long-serving hotel caters mainly to local business travellers, but it also makes a reasonably priced base for holiday-makers, offering comfortable accommodation in a variety of rooms, most with balcony and satellite TV. Good food and an excellent range of leisure and business facilities are offered.

NANYUKI Mount Kenya Safari Club
$$$$

8 km (5 miles) southeast of Nanyuki **Tel** *020 2216940* **Fax** *020 2216796* **Rooms** *120* **Road Map** *C4*

Set in vast grounds straddling the equator on the slopes of Mount Kenya, rooms here are luxurious and the excellent facilities range from a private golf course to horseback excursions. Views are superb and the attached wildlife conservancy protects the world's largest extant population of the endangered mountain bongo. **www.fairmont.com**

NARO MORU Mount Kenya Youth Hostel
$

8 km (5 miles) down the track to Mount Kenya National Park's Naro Moru Gate **Tel** *062 62412* **Road Map** *C4*

A cosy stone cottage set about halfway along the track between Naro Moru town and the national park entrance gate, this evergreen favourite with budget travellers has dormitory accommodation, camping facilities, cheap meals and a friendly pub. A great base for hikes up Mount Kenya and in the surrounding wildlife- and bird-rich forests.

NARO MORU Bantu Mountain Rock Lodge
$$

Along the Naro Moru–Nanyuki Road **Tel** *020 2242133* **Fax** *020 210051* **Rooms** *28* **Road Map** *C4*

Set in large forested gardens, this low-key lodge is a popular base for budget hikes up Mount Kenya. The place may have seen better days, but it is very affordable and the riverside setting is pleasant. It is worth paying extra for a superior room. For hikers, guides and provisions can be arranged on site. **www.mountainrockkenya.com**

NARO MORU Naro Moru River Lodge
$$$

2 km (1 mile) west of Naro Moru **Tel** *062 31047* **Rooms** *48* **Road Map** *C4*

This hotel has long served as a reliable and reasonably priced base for Mount Kenya climbs along the western ascent routes. The place has a time-warped aura, but modern facilities include a heated swimming pool, video room and squash courts. Horseback excursions, trout fishing and bird-watching are on offer. **www.naromoruriverlodge.com**

NYAHURURU Thomson's Falls Lodge
$

Next to Thomson's Falls on the outskirts of town **Tel** *065 22006* **Rooms** *32* **Road Map** *B4*

Set in rambling lawns overlooking the eponymous waterfall, this is a charming colonial-era hotel dating back to 1934. A little rundown but strong on period character, it makes for a refreshing highland stopover, and plenty of birds and monkeys can be seen in the garden and on the waterfall trail.

NYERI Sangare Ranch
$$$$

27 km (17 miles) north of Nyeri **Tel** *020 2722451* **Fax** *020 2720545* **Rooms** *14* **Road Map** *C4*

This exclusive tented camp overlooks a small lake in the Aberdare foothills. Spacious tents have four-poster beds with walk-in nets, and private verandas that offer great views over the lake. Daily game drives to Solio Game Ranch, while the grounds protect a varied birdlife and offer great views of Mount Kenya. **www.sangaretentedcamp.com**

NYERI The Outspan
$$$$

Baden-Powell Road **Tel** *061 2032424* **Fax** *061 2032286* **Rooms** *45* **Road Map** *C4*

Founded in 1927, this historic hotel stands in large grounds with a footpath to Chania river. A staging post for overnight visits to Treetops lodge *(see p374)*, it is also a charming old-fashioned colonial architecture and superb views of Mount Kenya. Best rooms are in the Chania Wing. **www.aberdaresafarihotels.com**

OLD DOINYO SABUK NATIONAL PARK Sabuk Guest House
$$

1 km (half a mile) inside the Park Entrance **Tel** *020 6000800* **Fax** *020 6003792* **Rooms** *4* **Road Map** *C5*

Formerly the warden's house, this KWS self-catering guesthouse is encircled by lush forest that offers plenty of walking and bird-watching opportunities. Although basic, the rooms are comfortable enough, but guests must bring all their own food, water and firewood. A campsite is nearby. **www.kws.go.ke**

THIKA Blue Posts Hotel
$$

2 km (1 mile) N of town on the Nairobi–Murang'a Road **Tel** *020 2080606* **Rooms** *32* **Road Map** *C5*

Older than the town itself, this iconic hotel stands in lush wooded grounds alongside a pair of pretty waterfalls. Accommodation is in charmingly old-fashioned ivy-clad cottages with TVs and private verandas. In addition to the birdlife, this family-friendly hotel has a small zoo and a good souvenir shop. **blueposthotel@africaonline.co.ke**

NORTHERN KENYA

BUFFALO SPRINGS NATIONAL RESERVE Buffalo Springs Simba Lodge
$$$$

Eastern end of the reserve **Tel** *0729 407162* **Rooms** *80* **Road Map** *C3*

With two pools and 80 rooms on a bluff above the river, this is the largest lodge in the Samburu area. The comfortably furnished rooms are well insulated against the region's heat and are arranged in blocks of six, with private balconies. On offer are game drives and visits to nearby springs. **www.simbalodges.com**

Key to Price Guide *see p362* **Key to Symbols** *see back cover flap*

LOIYANGALANI Oasis Lodge

⊞ ▦ ⑤⑤⑤

Centre of the village **Tel** *0722 810082* **Rooms** *24* **Road Map** *C2*

The closest thing to an upmarket resort on the shores of Turkana, this German-owned lodge lies in well-tended grounds with spring-fed streams that fill two swiming pools and help assuage the dust and the heat. Accommodation is in comfortable en suite cottages and the restaurant serves tilapia fresh from the lake. **www.oasis-lodge.com**

MARALAL Yare Camp

▨ ⊞ ⑤

Immediately south of the Town Centre **Tel** *072 2895126* **Rooms** *10* **Road Map** *C3*

Run by the eponymous safari company, which specialises in budget travel in Northern Kenya, Yare Camp has a large campsite, simple but clean bungalows and an occasionally lively bar and restaurant. It is a good place to meet local Samburu and is the focus of the idiosyncratic annual Maralal Camel Derby *(see p341)*.

MARALAL Maralal Safari Lodge

▨ ⊞ ▦ ⑤⑤⑤

Western outskirts of town **Tel** *0720 924523* **Rooms** *24* **Road Map** *C3*

The only lodge in Maralal National Reserve, offering accommodation in timber cottages. Rooms and common areas face a waterhole that attracts a steady stream of wildlife, ranging from eland and zebra to the more occasional hyena. Around 200 bird species have been recorded in the grounds.

MARSABIT NATIONAL PARK Marsabit Lodge

▨ ⊞ ⑤⑤⑤⑤

3 km (2 miles) west of Marsabit town **Tel** *0722 293216* **Rooms** *24* **Road Map** *D2*

One of Kenya's best-kept secrets, set in the heart of Marsabit National Park overlooking the steep Gof Sokorte Dika Crater and its permanent forest-fringed lake. Rooms are unpretentious but comfortable, with excellent views of the crater lake and passing wildlife, such as elephant and greater kudu. The restaurant and bar are adequate.

SAMBURU NATIONAL RESERVE Samburu Game Lodge

⊞ ▦ Ⓦ ⑤⑤⑤⑤

Near the reserve headquarters **Tel** *064 30781* **Fax** *020 650384* **Rooms** *61* **Road Map** *C3*

Built in 1963, this is the oldest lodge in Samburu and one of the nicest, with a prime location on the north bank of the river. The wood-and-shingle rooms in blocks run along the riverfront, offering good game viewing and excellent bird-watching. Buffet meals are reasonable and the gift shop is well stocked. **www.wildernesslodges.com**

SAMBURU NATIONAL RESERVE Samburu Sopa Lodge

⊞ ▦ ⑤⑤⑤⑤

Eastern end of the park **Tel** *020 3750235* **Fax** *020 3751507* **Rooms** *60* **Road Map** *C3*

The most affordable addition to Samburu's lodges sits on a hilltop away from the river. It is an excellent location for dry-country wildlife, especially birds, and a waterhole attracts plenty of game after dark, including the rarely seen striped hyena. Rooms are very large, with two queen-sized beds in each unit. **www.sopalodges.com**

SAMBURU NATIONAL RESERVE Elephant Watch Camp

⊞ ⑤⑤⑤⑤⑤

In the northwest of the reserve **Tel** *020 8891112* **Fax** *020 8890596* **Rooms** *6* **Road Map** *C3*

Owner-managed by the renowned elephant expert Oria Douglas-Hamilton, this small and highly exclusive camp lies along a part of the river known for its giant elephant bulls. Among the most eco-friendly of the upmarket camps, six stylish units combine Bedouin tents with natural building materials. **www.elephantwatchsafaris.com**

SAMBURU NATIONAL RESERVE Larsen's Camp

⊞ ▦ Ⓦ ⑤⑤⑤⑤⑤

Between the airstrip and Park Headquarters **Tel** *020 532329* **Fax** *020 650384* **Rooms** *20* **Road Map** *C3*

A luxury camp in an intimate wilderness setting on the forested north bank of the river. Simple but attractively decorated khaki tents are surrounded by riverine bush for privacy and enjoy shady balconies with river views. Unlike most safari camps, à la carte meals and snacks are served throughout the day. **www.wildernesslodges.co.ke**

SAMBURU NATIONAL RESERVE Samburu Intrepids

⊞ ▦ ⑤⑤⑤⑤

5 km (3 miles) from the West Gate **Tel** *064 30453* **Fax** *064 32022* **Rooms** *27* **Road Map** *C3*

A lovely tented camp along the north bank of the river. Tents are furnished in upmarket bush style with four-poster beds, linked by stilted walkways and shaded by tall ficus trees. The fabulous dining area and lounge feel like an extension of the woodland. Very child-friendly with a range of activities offered. **www.heritage-eastafrica.com**

SHABA NATIONAL RESERVE Sarova Shaba Lodge

⊞ ▦ ⑤⑤⑤⑤

1 km (half a mile) north of Natorbe Gate **Tel** *064 30638* **Fax** *020 2715566* **Rooms** *80* **Road Map** *C3*

The largest lodge in the area, Sarova Shaba still retains a bush feel thanks to its isolated location and superb grounds, run through by spring-fed streams and positively rustling with bird and monkey activity. The dining area is a row of double-storey buildings, all of which face the river. The dining and bar area is a delight. **www.sarovahotels.com**

SHABA NATIONAL RESERVE Joy's Camp

⊞ ▦ ⑤⑤⑤⑤⑤

Eastern sector **Tel** *020 6004053* **Rooms** *10* **Road Map** *C3*

Set in a little-visited part of the reserve, this remote tented camp lies on a site used by Joy Adamson. The spacious and airy tents show a Borana and Somali influence in the decor and overlook a spring-fed waterhole frequented by dry-country specials such as Grevy's zebra, reticulated giraffe, gerenuk and cheetah. **www.chelipeacock.com**

SOUTH HORR Desert Rose

⊞ ▦ ⑤⑤⑤⑤⑤

30-minute drive from Kowop airstrip **Tel** *020 3864831* **Rooms** *5* **Road Map** *C2*

This blissfully isolated and very exclusive lodge lies in a spring-fed forest grove on the footslopes of the sacred Mount Nyiru. Luxurious in an eco-friendly way, it is a great place just to hang out and appreciate the African wilderness. The main attraction is Samburu-led camel treks into the surrounding arid plains. **www.desertrosekenya.com**

WHERE TO EAT

Nairobi and Mombasa have a wide selection of restaurants offering international fare. Indian food is a firm favourite, although Italian, Chinese and Thai cuisines are also popular. There are some excellent specialist restaurants that make a fine addition to any visitor's itinerary. Safari lodges and beach resorts offer Continental buffets and à la carte menus. Kenyan food, usually stews, curries and some form of starch, can be found at local restaurants and

Sherlock's Den restaurant, Meru

cafés. Fast food chains are mushrooming all over Kenya and cater to the appetite for fried chicken and ice cream. Snacks such as samosas or fried sausages can be bought from any of the numerous vendors with simple charcoal burners at roadside stalls. Meat is eaten across the country, with the freshwater fish tilapia being preferred in Western Kenya and seafood a speciality along the coast. There is also an excellent choice of fruit and vegetables for vegetarian tastes.

PLACES TO EAT

Most hotels have restaurants. In fact, some in the upper bracket have several, which are also open to non-guests. At these, visitors can expect international standards, gourmet food and a good, albeit expensive, range of imported wines and champagne.

Some of the more exclusive lodges and tented camps are renowned for their cuisine, which is part and parcel of a luxury safari experience. Meals are often taken in the bush or around a crackling fire, and because of the early morning and late afternoon game drives, safaris often feature additional brunch and afternoon tea. On the coast, beach resorts offer sumptuous buffets featuring plenty of

seafood and tropical fruit, while smaller regional hotels will attempt some basic but adequate Continental dishes.

There are a number of fine individual restaurants. In Nairobi, Carnivore *(see p383)*, offers a gut-busting meat-eating frenzy, and in the mainland off Mombasa Island, Tamarind *(see p386)* provides a magical seafood banquet on board a dhow. A good choice for vegetarians is Indian cuisine, and Indian restaurants are prolific throughout Kenya and quite often offer good value all-you-can-eat buffets.

All towns feature simple cafés that offer steaming stews and curries to workers at lunchtime. However, these are rarely open in the evening. South African fast-food chains selling burgers,

fried chicken, pizzas and the like are starting to appear in Nairobi and Mombasa, including at some petrol stations.

PAYING AND TIPPING

Except at the larger hotels or tourist-orientated restaurants that accept credit cards, bills for meals need to be paid in cash. For a large group of customers, a restaurant may well add a 10–15 per cent service charge to the bill. Otherwise, a tip for good service is not usually expected but greatly appreciated. The amount is the prerogative of the customer, but 10 per cent is considered reasonable. Street vendors do not need to be tipped, but if they cannot give back change of a few shillings, it is polite not to insist.

Glorious views of the Indian Ocean from Tamarind restaurant in Nyali, Mombasa

A display of fresh fruit and vegetables at Nairobi's City Market

STREET FOOD

In urban areas, a number of food items can be purchased from street vendors who usually cook over charcoal burners in roadside shelters known as kiosks. Street food is safe to eat provided it is cooked thoroughly. Items to look out for include *nyama choma*, a feast of roast meat; *mandazi*, a sweet deep-fried dough; egg-bread, a wheat pancake filled with minced meat and fried eggs; samosas, deep-fried pastry triangles filled with meat or vegetables; roasted maize, similar to, but not as sweet as, corn on the cob; *mishkaki*, barbecued meat on skewers; hard boiled eggs and fried Farmers Choice sausages, a good and hugely popular local brand. Slices of watermelon, mango, papaya and oranges are also on offer, but visitors need to be wary of anything washed in local water. For those who are self-catering, all markets sell fruit and vegetables as well as eggs, meat and bread. Imported items can be found in supermarkets in the larger cities.

ALCOHOLIC DRINKS

Kenya Breweries, now part of East African Breweries, produces some very good beer under the labels Tusker, White Cap and Pilsner. The iconic award-winning Tusker lager is served chilled in brown half-litre bottles. Named when one of the Kenya Breweries founders was killed by an elephant in 1923, the

Kenya's Tusker lager

distinctive black-and-gold elephant logo can now be found on Tusker souvenirs such as T-shirts and caps.

Imported spirits are available but can be expensive. South African wines are fairly well priced, although these are rarely found away from tourist areas. Cheaper local brands include Kenya Cane, which is similar to rum, and Kenya Gold, a coffee liqueur. A popular and appetising local cocktail is *dawa*, a mixture of vodka, honey and lime. Home-brewed concoctions such as *pombe* or *chang'aa* are best avoided as they can be contaminated and the latter is also illegal.

OTHER DRINKS

Starting with the most global brands, Kenya has been literally branded by Coca-Cola and there are advertisements everywhere. Coke is sold from giant, bottle-shaped kiosks. Many different flavours of Fanta are also popular, and are sold in shops and on the street, even in remote areas. Soft drinks, or sodas as they are known in Kenya, come in reusable bottles that are returned when customers are done with their drinks. Bottled water is widely available, as is fresh fruit juice in season. *Chai* (tea) is usually served in small glasses. The tea, milk and sugar are boiled together, so the brew can be excessively sweet. Kenya is well known for its good coffee, but surprisingly, freshly ground coffee is hard to find and instant is often used.

VEGETARIANS

Most people in Kenya are non-vegetarians, and local meals often include red meat, chicken or fish. Sometimes the accompanying vegetable dishes are cooked in meat-based broths. Nevertheless, vegetarians will get by. Most upmarket restaurants offer vegetarian options. Indian food is a good bet, and even in the cheapest café, at the very least salads and chips are available.

Organised safaris cater specifically for vegetarians, as do buffets in hotels and lodges. Peanut butter is a popular addition to dishes, so people with a nut allergy need to enquire whether it has been used in their food.

Bar at the Colliers Shopping Centre in Diani Beach

The Flavours of Kenya

Kenyan food has a diversely international history. In the 15th century, the Portuguese introduced crops from newly discovered Brazil, including maize, cassava, bananas and pineapples, as well as citrus fruit from India and China, and pigs. Later, colonists brought potatoes, tomatoes and cucumbers, and indentured labour from India contributed curries and chapatis. The distinctive, spicy Swahili cooking of the coast stems from contact with Arab and other Indian Ocean traders. Tea and coffee were introduced in colonial times and are now important export crops for Kenya.

A pile of chapatis

Kebabs being grilled over a Kenyan barbecue cookstove (*jiko*)

KENYAN CUISINE

For Kenyans, a key objective of food is to fill one up as efficiently and cost-effectively as possible. Nevertheless, the food is tasty as well as filling. Take a liberal helping of starch, a roasted, grilled or stewed meat and a side dish such as *kachumbari* (a spicy relish) or *sukuma wiki* (stewed greens and tomatoes,

the name meaning "stretch the week" in Swahili since it helps to extend the weekly food budget), and you have the basic Kenyan meal.

Beer is the favoured accompaniment to meals, and Kenya Breweries has brewed good local bottled beer since 1922. Tusker is the most popular, with its slogan "Bia Yangu, Nchi Yangu", which in Swahili translates as "My Beer, My Country".

MEAT AND FISH

Kenyan beef, chicken, lamb and pork are all of good quality. Availability and preparation depend on the people and the region. The Maasai, for example, enjoy boiled goat soup, with the meat eaten separately afterwards, while the Kikuyu prefer stewed, boiled or roasted beef and mutton, served with vegetable dishes.

Watermelon   Pineapple   Bananas
Coconut   Passion fruits   Guavas
Mangoes   Papaya

Selection of tropical fruits grown in Kenya

KENYAN DISHES AND SPECIALITIES

Breakfast in Kenya is generally a simple affair consisting of sugary *chai* (tea), accompanied by *mandazi*, a sweet, doughnut-like flat bread. Another traditional breakfast dish is *uji*, a millet-based porridge served warm with lots of milk and sugar. Some sort of starch accompanies almost every main meal. This might be potato, rice, *matoke* (mashed plantain), *ugali* (a Kikuyu maize and water paste that varies in consistency from porridge-like to a firmish dough), or *irio*. Most are fairly bland on their own but absorb the flavour of the dish that they accompany. The most distinctive Kenyan food is the Swahili cooking found on the coast, in which spices such as cloves and cinnamon feature prominently. Desserts are simple, and include fruit salads, cakes and honey biscuits.

Cloves and cinnamon sticks

Irio, *a mashed potato, spinach and bean dish, is often used to accompany a vegetable stew such as* githeri.

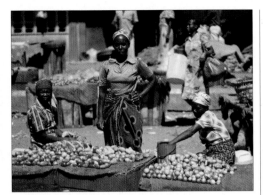

Stallholders and their wares at a market in Mombasa

Chicken is usually cooked in oil with tomatoes and onions. Surprisingly, game is not a traditional part of Kenyan cuisine, although meats such as ostrich and gazelle can be found on restaurant menus.

Coastal waters are rich in seafood, and a fragrant Swahili prawn or fish curry with coconut rice makes a perfect beachside dinner. Inland, freshwater tilapia is popular, and is usually split and dried in the sun. In the far west, Nile perch from Lake Victoria sometimes features on menus, while trout can be found in the Central Highlands.

FRUIT AND VEGETABLES

Kenyan cooking makes excellent use of the country's huge range of fresh vegetables and tropical fruits. The well-watered, fertile soil across the south and centre of the country ensures an endless supply, and every market offers a dazzling display of local produce. Cassava, maize, yams, plantains and pulses are among the all-important starch providers;

Swahili woman carrying freshly caught fish on the Kenyan shoreline

peppers, pumpkins and tomatoes give dishes flavour and colour; and greens such as kale are plentiful. On the coast, coconuts are abundant, and coconut milk is used in cooking. In the highlands, nuts such as cashews and macadamias are grown.

Right across the country, roadside shacks sell snacks such as barbecue-roasted corn cobs and hunks of cassava, pieces of sugar cane, or oranges and mangoes, halved and scored, to refresh parched travellers with their sweet and sticky juices.

ON THE MENU

Chapati Flat wheat bread, often served with *githeri*.

Githeri Boiled maize and beans or peas, cooked with tomatoes and onions to make a hearty vegetable stew.

Matoke Boiled and mashed plantains. When well prepared they taste like buttery, lightly whipped mashed potato.

Mukimo Mashed potatoes mixed with green corn, green peas and pumpkin leaves.

Mursik Milk that has been fermented and smoked in a gourd before consumption.

Kachumbari Spicy relish of chopped tomatoes, onions, cabbage, chillies, cucumber, coriander and lime juice.

Wali wa nazi Swahili dish of rice cooked with coconut milk until creamy.

Ugali with sukuma wiki *is a communal dish in which lumps of dough are used to scoop up the stewed greens.*

Nyama choma, *or marinated, spicy, barbecued chunks of meat, may be served with piquant* kachumbari *relish.*

Mchuzi wa kamba *is a prawn curry with a rich tomato and coconut-milk sauce, served with rice and fried plantain.*

Choosing a Restaurant

The restaurants in this guide have been selected for the quality of the food and atmosphere. However, in some parts of Kenya there are few restaurants that can be recommended. In such cases, places have been suggested that offer good value. For map references see pages 172–5 for Nairobi and the inside back cover for all others.

PRICE CATEGORIES
The price ranges are for a two-course meal with a bottle of beer, and include tax and service charges.

$ Under US$8
$$ US$8–$15
$$$ US$16–$25
$$$$ US$26–$35
$$$$$ Over US$35

NAIROBI

DAGORRETTI CORNER Mediterreneo $$$
Ngong Road **Tel** *020 3878608*

With branches at the trendy Junction Mall and Westlands, Mediterreneo serves a predictable but good range of pasta, pizzas, ground coffee and ice cream as well as excellent tiramisu. The chefs, all of whom are from Italy, will also prepare items not on the menu to please customers. The restaurant boasts an extensive range of Italian wines.

DOWNTOWN Discovery Sandwich Bar and Coffee Shop $
Corner Koinange and Banda Streets **Tel** *020 2241120*   *City Map 1 C3*

Inexpensive, centrally located café-bar on the second floor above the Kobil petrol station, offering generous salads, sandwiches made from home-made bread, coffees and freshly squeezed fruit juices. Pleasantly decorated in natural colours with African touches, it also has a deli counter and cocktail bar. Open from breakfast until 9.30pm.

DOWNTOWN Java House $
Mama Ngina Street **Tel** *020 4452273*   *City Map 1 C3*

The downtown venue for experiencing freshly ground Kenyan coffee, Java House also offers big breakfasts, light meals, cakes, ice-cream sundaes, milkshakes and yoghurt smoothies. Bags of its own coffee beans are on sale. Several other branches of this restaurant can be found around the city, including at shopping malls and the airport.

DOWNTOWN Pasara Café $
Lonrho House, Kaunda Street **Tel** *020 2338247*   *City Map 1 C3*

On the ground floor of the blue-glassed Lonrho House, this affordable daytime café is a popular lunch venue for office workers. One of the few places in downtown Nairobi to get freshly-made sandwiches using home-made baguettes, plus excellent soups and generous salads. Movie posters adorn the walls.

DOWNTOWN Thorn Tree Café $$
Sarova Stanley Hotel, Kimathi Street **Tel** *020 2757000*   *City Map 1 C3*

A pavement bistro café famous for its Thorn Tree message board, this is a focal downtown meeting point. The menu offers 15 types of coffee to accompany salads, pasta dishes, burgers and sandwiches, with more sophisticated main courses in the evening. Internet is available and there are big screen TVs for watching sport.

DOWNTOWN Trattoria $$$
Town House, corner of Kaunda and Wabera Streets **Tel** *020 340855*   *City Map 1 C3*

Long established and always busy, this traditional Italian restaurant-cum-delicatessen serves a huge range of pasta and sauces, grills, wood-fired pizzas, home-made ice cream and gooey desserts. Seating is spread over two floors bedecked with potted plants, with outside tables on the street and the mezzanine balcony.

DOWNTOWN Café Maghreb $$$$
Nairobi Serena Hotel, Kenyatta Avenue **Tel** *020 2725111*   *City Map 1 A4*

Upmarket restaurant next to the pool at the Nairobi Serena Hotel (*see p363*), with stunning Moroccan-themed decor and mud-styled architecture, and good views of Nairobi's skyline. There is a long international menu of North African, Indian, Italian, French and Creole dishes, with themed buffet nights. Coffee is poured from giant copper urns.

DOWNTOWN Thai Chi $$$$
Sarova Stanley Hotel, Kimathi Street **Tel** *020 316377*   *City Map 1 C3*

Best of the city's Thai restaurants, decorated with sculptures and artwork from Thailand and with atmospheric candlelit tables. There is a full menu of authentic dishes and the fragrant curries feature hot and sour flavours, peanuts and coconut milk. Grab a nightcap in the Stanley Hotel's Exchange Bar opposite.

DOWNTOWN Bhandini $$$$$
InterContinental Hotel, City Hall Way **Tel** *020 3200000*   *City Map 1 B4*

Justifiably expensive North Indian restaurant with impeccable service, pleasant decor and delicious, well-presented food. Dishes are fragrantly spiced and cooked from scratch by a well-regarded Indian chef who can be watched at work in the glass-fronted kitchen. The hotel also offers *nyama choma* (barbecued meat) on the pool deck.

Key to Symbols *see back cover flap*

DOWNTOWN Tamarind
□ 🎵 🖶 📺 �V   ⑤⑤⑤⑤⑤

National Bank Building, off Harambee Avenue **Tel** *020 2251811*   **City Map** *2 D4*

Award-winning restaurant and sister branch of the Tamarind Mombasa and Tamarind Dhow *(see p386)*. Renowned for its seafood which is flown up from the coast daily, plus good steak, venison and poultry, all served in very elegant surroundings. Try the crab claws or Swahili-style lobster with coconut rice.

GIGIRI Village Market Food Court
🖶 🖶 📺 V   ⑤

Village Market Mall, Limuru Road

Cheap eats can be found at the popular food court in this modern mall, where a cluster of outdoor tables are surrounded by dozens of restaurant counters offering ice cream, Chinese and Indian snacks, Kenyan *nyama choma*, pizzas and burgers, even German sausages and Mongolian "build-your-own" stir fries.

GIGIRI Tokyo
🖶 📺 📺 V   ⑤⑤⑤

Village Market Mall, Limuru Road **Tel** *020 7122512*

Japanese restaurant in the Village Market Mall. Simple decor with lots of fresh flowers and some tables outside. The preparation of sushi, sashimi and teppanyaki is overseen by a Japanese chef, and there are some à la carte dishes too. Sake is, of course, on offer and the takeaway sushi is reasonably priced.

KAREN Karen Blixen Coffee Garden
🎵 🖶 📺 V   ⑤⑤⑤

336 Karen Road **Tel** *020 882138*

Not far from the Karen Blixen Museum *(see p168)*, this restaurant is spread around an attractive garden, with an extensive international menu, including soup and seafood bisque of the day. Big screen TV in the bar attracts sports fans and on Sundays lunch is a barbecue with live music. Also offers good accommodation *(see p363)*.

KAREN Rusty Nail
🖶 📺 V   ⑤⑤⑤⑤

Dagoretti Road, close to the Karen roundabout **Tel** *020 882461*

A popular local expatriate haunt on the edge of Karen is set in a rambling old house surrounded by trees. The European cuisine is very good but a good reason to visit is to explore the paths through the beautiful gardens. Seating is on comfortable cushions, with big screen TV in the bar and alfresco eating at tables on the veranda.

KASARANI Nyama Choma Ranch
□ 🎵 🖶 📺 V   ⑤⑤⑤⑤

Safari Park Hotel, off Thika Road **Tel** *020 3633000*

One of several top-class restaurants at the Safari Park Hotel and a similar concept to Carnivore. As its name suggests, this restaurant specialises in barbecued meat. Acrobats and the resident band, The Safari Cats, provide entertainment and often get diners dancing in a chain around the restaurant.

LANGATA Rangers
🖶 📺 V   ⑤⑤⑤

Main Gate, Nairobi National Park, Langata Road **Tel** *020 2357470*

This attractive wooden restaurant built on boardwalks is located at the main gate of Nairobi National Park *(see pp162–5)* and has fantastic views right into the grassy enclosures of the animals in the Safari Walk. There is a wide Continental menu and the barbecue lunches are popular with tour groups.

LANGATA Carnivore
🎵 🖶 📺 V   ⑤⑤⑤⑤

Off Langata Road, behind Wilson Airport **Tel** *020 6005933*

With two restaurants, several bars, regular live music and a nightclub, Nairobi's best-known restaurant *(see p160)* is on most visitors' itineraries to Kenya. The gut-busting speciality is meat roasted on Maasai spears over hot coals and carved on to plates until customers can take no more. Drinks include a long list of cocktails.

MOMBASA ROAD Pampa Grill Churrascaria
□ 📺 V   ⑤⑤⑤⑤

1st Floor, Panari Centre **Tel** *020 828134*

Serving Brazilian cuisine of dozens of cuts of meat grilled over open flames and accompanied by fried onion rings, cassava, banana and French fries, all washed down with Brazilian wines. Also on offer is a buffet of hot vegetables and salads adequate for a vegetarian meal. Sarova Whitesands Resort *(see p367)*, Mombasa, has another branch.

MUTHAIGA Anghiti
□ 🎵 🖶 📺 V   ⑤⑤⑤⑤

Muthaiga Shopping Centre **Tel** *020 3740292*

One of Nairobi's best Indian restaurants serves a broad range of North Indian dishes at sensible prices. Service is attentive with waiters happy to make recommendations, and diners can watch the chefs at work behind glass walls. The restaurant offers free transport to and from hotels for groups of six or more.

NAIROBI HILL China Plate
🖶 📺 V   ⑤⑤

Chancery Building, Valley Road **Tel** *020 2719194*

Predominantly Chinese restaurant with a 25-year history and a long menu of mildly hot Szechwan cooking. The duck is especially good and there are also some Indian and Continental options, with a varied wine list. Guests sit at round tables for sociable, shared eating and there is a large outside veranda with a tent-like canopy.

RUNDA ESTATE Lord Erroll
🎵 🖶 📺 V   ⑤⑤⑤⑤⑤

89 Ruaka Road, off Limuru Road **Tel** *020 7122433*

This sophisticated gourmet restaurant named after the murdered earl of the 1940s Happy Valley set *(see p318)*, is located in lovely gardens where crowned cranes stalk the lawns and a pianist plays at weekends. Offering beautifully presented Continental, Italian and Oriental dishes, the Highlander British-style pub also serves afternoon tea.

WESTLANDS Pavement Club and Café 🎵 🖼 🍷 🅥   ⑤⑤
Westview Centre, Ring Road **Tel** *020 4441711*

A mixture of quality food is served at this café, from Thai and Japanese to traditional grills and pasta. The place has a buzzy atmosphere with funky decor of modern steel furniture and brightly painted walls. The bar is hugely popular and a nightclub with a spacious dance floor opens on Wednesdays and at weekends.

WESTLANDS Bangkok Chinese Restaurant 🍽 🖼 🍷 🅥   ⑤⑤⑤
Amcee Arcade, Parklands Road **Tel** *020 3751312*

Offers very good authentic Chinese cuisine but the service is rushed so this is not the place for a lingering meal. The decor is fairly typical with round tables and pictures of red Chinese dragons on the wall. Try the hot and sour vegetables, ginger and garlic crab or sautéed pepper prawns. Takeaways are available.

WESTLANDS Oasis 🎵 🖼 🍷 🅥   ⑤⑤⑤
Southern Sun Mayfair Hotel, Parklands Road **Tel** *020 3740920*

Popular and affordable restaurant with tables next to the swimming pool at the former Holiday Inn. Offers good value buffets and a snack menu for lunch, and themed dinner menus: African (Monday); fish (Wednesday); Indian (Saturday); Mongolian "build-your-own" stir fry (Tuesday, Thursday–Sunday).

WESTLANDS Orchid 🖼 🍷 🅥   ⑤⑤⑤
ABC Place **Tel** *020 4453372*

Affordable Thai restaurant with sleek red walls, teak floors and a long bar. Dishes are freshly prepared and well presented, cooked in large woks and served with bowls of rice and noodles. Try the green and red curries with giant prawns or the sweet and sour fish; there are also good vegetarian options. Great place for sharing meals.

WESTLANDS Pepper's Restaurant 🖼 🍷 🅥   ⑤⑤⑤
Parklands Road, opposite Holiday Inn **Tel** *020 3755267*

Set in a large, rambling house and garden with a huge menu of Continental, Chinese and Indian dishes and a long list of cocktails and wine. The grilled steaks, lobster and crab are especially good. The restaurant also caters to children during the day with a children's menu, playground, sandpit and child minders.

WESTLANDS The Phoenician 🎵 🖼 🍷 🅥   ⑤⑤⑤
Karuna Road, behind the Sarit Centre **Tel** *020 3744279*

Popular Lebanese restaurant with outside tables set in pretty gardens and a very comfortable lounge bar featuring Africa-print decor. It serves meze, falafel and grills, plus sushi and some Continental dishes including wood-fired pizza. There is also a deli selling olives and dips, a children's play area and occasional live music.

WESTLANDS Haandi 🖼 🍷 🅥   ⑤⑤⑤⑤
Mezzanine Floor, The Mall **Tel** *020 4448294*

Upmarket North Indian establishment with sister restaurants in London and Kampala. The place is renowned for its delicately flavoured and authentic food, freshly prepared from scratch by Indian chefs. Service is attentive and the candlelit tables are elegantly dressed. Reservations are essential at this deservedly popular restaurant.

WESTLANDS Alan Bobbe's Bistro 🖼 🍷 🅥   ⑤⑤⑤⑤⑤
Andrews Apartments, Rhapta Road **Tel** *020 4252000*

Named after a British intelligence officer who first opened the place in 1962, this restaurant offers fine dining with a French slant and accompanied by French wines. Decor features late 18th-century plates and paintings on the walls, and there is a swimming pool terrace. Try the crab claws or lobster thermidor.

SOUTHEASTERN SAVANNAHS

AMBOSELI NATIONAL PARK Ol Tukai Lodge 🖼 🍷 🅥   ⑤⑤⑤
Ol Tukai, near park headquarters **Tel** *045 622275*   **Road Map** *C6*

The most central lodge in Amboseli *(see pp194–7)* is also the obvious place to stop for a leisurely lunch between game drives. It serves the usual lodge-style buffet with a good selection of mostly meat-based dishes. The lush, shady grounds are great for a post-lunch stroll, with views across the plains and towards Kilimanjaro.

TAITA HILLS WILDLIFE SANCTUARY Sarova Taita Hills Game Lodge 🍷 🅥   ⑤⑤⑤
1 km (half a mile) off the Voi–Taveta Road **Tel** *043 31271*   **Road Map** *D7*

A visit to the Taita Hills Game Lodge *(see p364)* can easily be combined with a game drive in this excellent private wildlife sanctuary *(see p188)*. The lodge serves excellent buffet lunches, usually with at least one roast meat dish, some fish and great salad and dessert bars.

TSAVO EAST NATIONAL PARK Voi Safari Lodge 🖼 🍷 🅥   ⑤⑤⑤
4 km (2 miles) from Voi Gate **Tel** *020 2222661*   **Road Map** *D6*

Perched on a cliff edge overlooking a waterhole where elephant and buffalo reliably come past for a midday slurp and splash, this is the obvious place to stop for lunch in Tsavo East *(see pp184–5)*. Most days the lodge serves a typically expansive buffet, though it can switch to à la carte mode at quiet times.

Key to Price Guide *see p382* **Key to Symbols** *see back cover flap*

TSAVO WEST NATIONAL PARK Kilaguni Serena Safari Lodge 🔲 🍷 V $$$$

32 km (20 miles) from Mtito Andei Gate, off Junction 8 **Tel** *0734 699865* **Road Map** *D6*

The best place to stop for lunch in Tsavo *(see pp186–7)* is this well-run lodge offering views across a busy waterhole to distant Kilimanjaro, though the latter tends to be shrouded in clouds at midday. The excellent and very filling buffet here usually includes some good Indian and vegetarian dishes.

VOI Voi Wildlife Lodge 🔲 🍷 V $$

Just outside Tsavo East National Park Gate **Tel** *020 7125741* **Road Map** *D6*

This is a good lunchtime spot in Voi for those who do not intend to enter Tsavo East National Park and there is usually some wildlife on show for diners. It is owned and managed by Indian vegetarians, so lunchtime buffets are especially strong on both fronts, but meat dishes are also on offer.

SOUTHERN COAST

BAMBURI Il Covo 🔲 🎵 🔲 🍷 V $$$

Bamburi Beach **Tel** *041 5487460* **Road Map** *E7*

Boasting a fabulous beachfront terrace, Il Covo has a varied menu encompassing hearty breakfasts, pizzas, pasta, grills, sushi and other fresh seafood. Freshly ground coffee and home-made ice cream are also on the menu. Entertainment comes in the form of a disco held each night.

DIANI Shan E-Punjab 🔲 🔲 🍷 V $$

Diani Shopping Complex **Tel** *040 3202116* **Road Map** *E7*

This is the best Indian restaurant in Diani, though the location – in a shopping mall on the opposite side of the main road to the beach – does not quite match up to the excellent selection of meat and vegetarian dishes. There is a beer garden and you can ring ahead for a free lift from any of the nearby beach hotels.

DIANI Forty Thieves Beach Bar 🎵 🔲 🍷 V $$$

Diani Beachfront **Tel** *041 3202033* **Road Map** *E7*

Fitting somewhere between a beach bar and sports café in atmosphere, this relatively affordable sister café to Ali Barbour's serves a great range of grills, pizzas, seafood and snacks with a popular lunchtime carvery on Sundays. There is Internet access, a pool table and a nightly disco.

DIANI Ngiri Bar and Restaurant 🔲 🍷 V $$$

Diani Shopping Centre **Tel** *0727 970787* **Road Map** *E7*

This popular English-run pub-restaurant and sports bar is conveniently located mid-way along the Diani Beach road. Good breakfasts and a changing menu of freshly sourced dishes are available to eat in the garden or in front of the flatscreen TV. Open daily until late.

DIANI Nomad Beach Restaurant 🔲 🍷 V $$$

Diani Beach **Tel** *040 3203643* **Road Map** *E7*

Boasting a great beachfront location and chic decoration with Swahili influences, this is really two restaurants in one – the main restaurant concentrates on sumptuous Continental seafood, meat and pasta dishes, while the Red Pepper "enclave" serves sushi and other Japanese items.

DIANI Ali Barbour's 🍷 V $$$$$

Diani Beach **Tel** *041 3202033* **Road Map** *E7*

Founded in 1983, this famous Diani institution is among the most atmospheric eateries on the coast, situated as it is in a natural coral cave within a short walking distance of the beach. The focus is on seafood, but pasta, steaks and vegetarian options are also on the menu. Bookings are essential.

MOMBASA Recoda Restaurant 🔲 V $

Moi Avenue **Road Map** *E7*

Relocated from the Old Town, this stalwart Swahili eatery specialises in *pilau* (the Swahili equivalent of risotto) as well as grilled chicken and fish, and various vegetarian dishes. Aimed mainly at locals, it is also popular with backpackers but the food may be a bit greasy for the faint of heart.

MOMBASA Splendid View Café 🔲 🔲 🔲 V $

Mauongano Road **Road Map** *E7*

"Splendid" refers to the name of the rundown hotel opposite rather than the quality of the view, but it might equally describe the succulent and spicy grilled seafood and chicken tikka served on the pavement barbecue after dark. An excellent and long-serving budget eatery.

MOMBASA Castle Terrace 🔲 🍷 $$

Castle Royal Hotel, Moi Avenue **Tel** *041 2222682* **Road Map** *E7*

One of the city's top spots for people watching, the street-facing terrace of the Castle Royal Hotel *(see p367)* is a popular venue for a chilled beer in the early evening. The menu focuses on grilled dishes aimed primarily at those with more carnivorous tastes, though fish and seafood are also well represented.

MOMBASA Shehnai Restaurant 📋 Ⓥ ⑤⑤
Fatema House, Mauongano Road **Tel** *041 2312492* **Road Map** *E7*

This stylish North Indian restaurant specialises in Mughlai vegetarian and fish dishes. It is also famous for its excellent tandoori menu which includes dishes such as chicken and fish tikka baked in the traditional clay oven. No alcohol is served but the fresh fruit juices are great. Closed Mondays.

MOMBASA Singh Restaurant 📋 Ⓨ Ⓥ ⑤⑤
Mwembe Tayari Road **Tel** *0733 847562* **Road Map** *E7*

Spacious and very centrally located, this is one of the oldest restaurants in Mombasa, founded by its namesake Dalip Singh in 1962. It serves a varied selection of Punjabi dishes, with the chicken and seafood particularly recommended. Unlike many Indian restaurants in Mombasa, it has a full bar. Closed Mondays.

MOMBASA Galaxy Chinese 📋 Ⓥ ⑤⑤⑤
Archbishop Makarios Road **Tel** *020 2138611* **Road Map** *E7*

Situated a block from Moi Avenue south of the railway station, this popular and well-established eatery serves a very varied selection of tasty Chinese dishes. The extensive menu includes a good variety of meat and seafood selections, and vegetarians are especially well catered for.

MTWAPA La Marina 🏠 Ⓨ Ⓥ ⑤⑤⑤⑤
Mtwapa Creek **Tel** *020 2434726* **Road Map** *B6*

This beachfront restaurant has a fabulous, breezy deck on the creek front. Seafood is very much the speciality here, but vegetarians and meat-eaters are also catered for, and there is a cheaper snack menu too. They also offer dinner dhow cruises with on-board entertainment.

MTWAPA The Moorings 🎵🏠🍽️Ⓨ Ⓥ ⑤⑤⑤⑤
Off the Mombasa–Malindi Road **Tel** *041 5485045* **Road Map** *B6*

This floating restaurant, the only one of its kind on the coast, has a pretty location on mangrove-lined Mtwapa creek. Fresh seafood options are the speciality, and meat and other dishes are also on the menu, all served over a candlelit dinner – sea breeze permitting. Closed Mondays.

NYALI Café Mocha 📷📋🏠Ⓥ ⑤
Nyali Cinemax Complex **Road Map** *B6*

This excellent coffee shop situated in the largest mall along the north Mombasa coastline is a popular meeting spot and a great place for a coffee and light meal or sandwich. A varied selection of desserts, ice creams and cakes, along with great milkshakes, make the place a particular favourite with children.

NYALI Bollywood Bites Vegetarian 📋🏠Ⓥ ⑤⑤
Nyali Cinemax Complex **Tel** *041 470000* **Road Map** *B6*

One of the few dedicated vegetarian restaurants in the greater Mombasa area, Bollywood Bites – as the name suggests – is garishly decorated in a Bollywood Indian cinema theme. A wide variety of dishes are served with the speciality being 18 varieties of South Indian *dosas* (rice pancakes), fresh juices and ice cream.

NYALI Roberto's 🎵Ⓨ Ⓥ ⑤⑤
Nyali Cinemax Complex **Tel** *041 476559* **Road Map** *B6*

Known for its extensive and sensibly priced wine list, family-friendly Roberto's also serves a varied selection of pizzas, pasta and meat dishes in home-made Italian style. More substantial fare ranges from steaks and mixed meat grills to lobster, prawns and – if you want to splash out – a superb seafood platter.

NYALI Tamarind Dhow 🎵🏠 ⑤⑤⑤⑤⑤
Silo Road **Tel** *041 471747* **Road Map** *B6*

This floating companion to the Tamarind Mombasa offers perhaps the city's most romantic dining experience. Housed in a working dhow, the restaurant sets sail twice daily, passing Fort Jesus as it circles Mombasa Island, serving a set-menu seafood lunch and dinner accompanied by lively traditional Swahili music.

NYALI Tamarind Mombasa 📋🏠Ⓨ Ⓥ ⑤⑤⑤⑤⑤
Silo Road **Tel** *041 474600* **Road Map** *B6*

One of the top eateries in Kenya, the Tamarind Mombasa offers a choice of either eating on the leafy terrace overlooking the old dhow harbour or in the stylish Arab-influenced interior. Seafood is the main speciality, but meat, poultry, ostrich and quail are also on the menu.

SHIRAZI Paradise Lost 📷🏠Ⓨ Ⓥ ⑤⑤⑤
Shirazi Beach **Tel** *020 2333988* **Road Map** *E7*

This aptly named restaurant has a paradisal setting in lush, coastal gardens centred on the ruins of a medieval Swahili mosque and a large swimming pool. Set in complete isolation close to Shirazi Beach, it specialises in seafood lunches and caters mainly to groups. It is essential to book in advance.

WASINI Charlie Claws 🏠Ⓨ Ⓥ ⑤⑤⑤
Wasini Island **Tel** *040 3202331* **Road Map** *E7*

Most day tours from Diani to Shimoni and Wasini lunch at this attractive *makuti*-roofed seafood restaurant whose main dining area is carved into the coastal scrub, though the bar looks back towards the mainland across a mangrove-lined channel. Booking is recommended though room is usually found for day trippers from Shimoni.

Key to Price Guide *see p382* **Key to Symbols** *see back cover flap*

NORTHERN COAST

LAMU ARCHIPELAGO Coconut Juice Garden 🎴🔖Ⓥ Ⓢ

Harambee Avenue, Lamu Town, Lamu Island **Road Map** *F6*

Although not really a place for a filling meal, this venerable Lamu institution offers a wonderful selection of freshly pressed juices served in a leafy compound where travellers from all around the world come to chill out. Yoghurt, banana pancakes and a limited selection of light meals are also served. Open until 6pm daily.

LAMU ARCHIPELAGO Hapa Hapa 🎴🔖Ⓥ Ⓢ

Waterfront, Lamu Town, Lamu Island **Road Map** *F6*

The Bush Gardens' main competitor for seafront business, this restaurant has a similarly relaxed atmosphere but is slightly less expensive, reflected in the more variable quality in food. The fresh seafood platters are usually excellent, and it serves a great selection of fruit juices and pancakes, but no alcohol.

LAMU ARCHIPELAGO Bush Gardens 🎴🔖Ⓥ ⓈⓈ

Waterfront, Lamu Town, Lamu Island **Road Map** *F6*

In terms of quality, this is the pick of several likeable, locally-owned outdoor eateries that run along Lamu's characterful waterfront. Seafood dishes and fruit juice are the specialities, but a limited selection of meat and vegetarian fare is usually on offer too. Like most places in Lamu, speedy service and alcohol are in short supply.

LAMU ARCHIPELAGO Whispers 🎴📋Ⓥ ⓈⓈ

Harambee Avenue, Lamu Town, Lamu Island **Road Map** *F6*

Situated in the incongruously chic Baraka Gallery, Whispers is the only European-style coffee shop in Lamu, making it a popular spot to punctuate a walking tour of the town with freshly roasted coffee, refreshing fruit juice, and a great selection of cakes, pastries and other indulgent fare. Open until 6pm daily.

LAMU ARCHIPELAGO Lamu Palace 📋🔖Ⓥ ⓈⓈⓈ

Lamu Palace Hotel, Waterfront, Lamu Town, Lamu Island **Tel** *042 4633272* **Road Map** *F6*

The plushest hotel in Lamu town also houses its swankiest restaurant, which serves a good selection of Italian and other meat and seafood dishes, offering a break from the excellent but often rather similar Swahili-style food on offer elsewhere. One of the few places to serve beer and wine openly, but not on the otherwise attractive terrace.

LAMU ARCHIPELAGO Barbeque Grill 📋🔖ⓎⓋ ⓈⓈⓈⓈ

Peponi Hotel, Shela, Lamu Island **Tel** *042 8023655* **Road Map** *F6*

The top place to eat within walking distance of Lamu town, this restaurant in the owner-managed Peponi Hotel *(see p368)* serves a superb selection of imaginative seafood dishes, supplemented by a limited selection of meat and vegetarian fare. The drinks at the terrace bar are not the cheapest but it is a lovely beachfront hangout.

MALINDI Da Gama Restaurant 🎴🔖ⓎⓋ ⓈⓈ

Vasco da Gama Road **Tel** *042 2131942* **Road Map** *F6*

A stalwart of the Malindi restaurant scene, Da Gama has long been a favourite with budget-conscious visitors for its varied and affordable menu of Indian, Italian and seafood dishes. It has a pleasant beach-facing balcony and a good range of light snacks, making it a great lunch stop.

MALINDI Fermento Disco Bar 🎴📋🎵Ⓨ ⓈⓈ

Galana Shopping Centre, Lamu Road **Tel** *042 2131780* **Road Map** *E6*

Not quite so ghoulish as its moniker – "for those of the night" – might have you believe, this is one of the hottest nightspots in town and the cocktail bar is an absolute winner. Grilled meat and seafood dishes dominate the reasonably priced menu. Open 10pm until late Wednesday, Friday and Saturday, and other nights in high season.

MALINDI I Love Pizza 🎴📋🔖ⓎⓋ ⓈⓈⓈ

Vasco da Gama Road **Tel** *042 2120672* **Road Map** *E6*

As the name would suggest, pizzas are the main attraction of this affordable eatery opposite the craft market, but it also offers a good selection of pasta, meat and seafood dishes, and vegetarians will find that it caters better to their needs than most other competitors in Malindi.

MALINDI Old Man & The Sea 📋🔖Ⓥ ⓈⓈⓈ

Vasco da Gama Road **Tel** *042 2131106* **Road Map** *E6*

Named after the Hemingway novella but more fun than that might suggest, this is one of Malindi's oldest and most popular seafood restaurants, set in an old beachfront house with a homely atmosphere. It also serves a selection of grilled meat and chicken dishes. The balcony is particularly enjoyable for the view and sea breeze.

MALINDI Baby Marrow 🎴🔖ⓎⓋ ⓈⓈⓈⓈ

Vasco da Gama Road **Tel** *0727 581682* **Road Map** *E6*

Set back from the beachfront in large green gardens, the earthy decor and shady *makuti* roof make this place a favourite with the expat community. Imaginative home-made pasta dishes are the speciality, but seafood lovers will not be disappointed either. Service can be slow, so diners should come in a relaxed frame of mind.

MALINDI Tangeri   ▤ 🏨 🍸 Ⓥ   ⑤⑤⑤⑤
Vasco da Gama Road **Tel** *0722 785181*   **Road Map** *E6*

Another restaurant situated opposite the craft market, this boasts distinctive Arabic architecture and serves a great selection of cocktails. Vegetarians are well catered for by the mostly Italian menu, and seafood is also a clear speciality. Open 6pm till late in the low season and from 11am in high season.

WATAMU Hemingway's   ▤ 🏨 🍸 Ⓥ   ⑤⑤⑤
Watamu Beachfront **Tel** *042 2332052*   **Road Map** *E6*

This is probably the best bet in Watamu for a light lunch or more substantial buffet dinner, the latter following a different theme every night. Diners can eat alfresco around the pool, or in the handsome *makuti*-roofed dining room. The bar becomes very lively when major sporting events are being televised.

SOUTHERN RIFT VALLEY AND MASAI MARA

LAKE NAIVASHA Camp Carnelly's   🏨 🍸 Ⓥ   ⑤⑤
Moi South Lake Road **Tel** *0722 260749*   **Road Map** *B5*

This is a popular backpackers' camp, set in large grounds dominated by huge acacia trees and often visited by hippos. The relaxing bar and restaurant are furnished with sofas and cushions. On offer is an interesting and changing range of international dishes and snacks using local produce, as well as smoothies and milk shakes.

NAIVASHA La Belle Inn   🍽 🏨 🍸 Ⓥ   ⑤⑤
Moi Avenue **Tel** *020 3510404*   **Road Map** *B4*

The terrace at this fine old colonial relic has long been the place for a meal or snack in Naivasha town. The menu has expanded since the hotel's distant heyday, with traditional grilled fare such as steaks now supplemented by Italian and Indian food – and even salads – but the home-made pies remain the favourite of most regulars.

NAKURU Nakuru Sweet Mart   🍽 Ⓥ   ⑤
Gusii Road   **Road Map** *B4*

This inexpensive Indian eatery is a great choice for vegetarians. The lunchtime *thali* (vegetarian platter) is dauntingly filling and a variety of other snacks such as samosas and bhajis are on offer. No alcohol is served, but there is good passion fruit juice and masala tea. The bakery usually has fresh crusty baguettes, a rarity in Kenya. Open till 5pm.

NAKURU Taidy's Bar and Restaurant   🍸 Ⓥ   ⑤
Corner of Oginga Odinga Avenue and Gusii Road **Tel** *051 2211409*   **Road Map** *B4*

This is a very popular local restaurant and rendezvous in the centre of Nakuru, with TV screens showing live sport and music playing. You can eat inside or on the well-shaded verandah, separated from the street by tropical plants. It serves a wide-ranging menu of largely Continental dishes. The steaks and pizzas are recommended.

NAROK Kenol Petrol Station Restaurant   🏨 🍸 Ⓥ   ⑤
West side of Narok on the way to Masai Mara Game Reserve **Tel** *051 2213208*   **Road Map** *B5*

This popular truck stop and tourists' service station has a welcome, shady garden backing onto the banks of a river. The snacks include samosas, cookies and ice cream, and the drinks are cold. Also on offer are simple Kenyan, Chinese and Indian dishes. Picnic tables are available.

WESTERN KENYA

KERIO VALLEY Kerio View   🍽 🏨 🍸 Ⓥ   ⑤
C51, Elgeyo Escarpment near Iten **Tel** *0722 781916*   **Road Map** *B4*

The main glass-fronted restaurant has such a spectacular view of the Kerio Valley it is well worth making a detour up here. Huge menu from English breakfasts, hearty stews, curries and casseroles, fish and steaks and an outside barbecue offering grilled lamb and salads. Also offers accommodation *(see p373)*.

KISUMU Kiboko Bay Resort   🏨 🍸 Ⓥ   ⑤⑤
On the lakeshore, Dunga Village **Tel** *0733 532709*   **Road Map** *B4*

This popular resort right on the lake is open to day visitors and it is well worth spending time here. The delightful restaurant has outside tables with lovely views of the jetty and a separate pool bar. Good Indian and Swahili curries, steaks and fish, and snacks such as toasted sandwiches. Modern art is for sale on the walls.

KISUMU Kisumu Hotel   ▤ 🍸 Ⓥ   ⑤⑤
Jomo Kenyatta Avenue **Tel** *057 2024157*   **Road Map** *B4*

A fairly standard hotel dining room, but still one of the better of Kisumu's limited options. The place features a spotless white canteen with TVs showing CNN, and a popular bar serving large portions of stews, curries, lamb and pork chops and school dinner-type desserts of sponge and custard or fruit salad and ice cream.

Key to Price Guide *see p382* **Key to Symbols** *see back cover flap*

KISUMU Sunset Hotel
🍴 📶 🍷 Ⓥ   ⑤⑤

Aput Lane **Tel** *057 2020464*   **Road Map** *B4*

Another standard hotel restaurant serving the usual stews, grills and fish from Lake Victoria. Diners should try the fish masala or grilled tilapia. Eat downstairs in the bar or terrace, or upstairs in the more formal dining room with neatly dressed tables. Vegetarians are limited to salads, omelettes or vegetable stir-fries.

CENTRAL HIGHLANDS

NANYUKI Kentrout
📋 📶 Ⓥ   ⑤⑤⑤

Timau, 20 km (12 miles) east of Nanyuki **Tel** *0722 775881*   **Road Map** *C4*

Located next to a well-wooded river on the northern slopes of Mount Kenya, this trout farm serves wonderful buffet lunches with an emphasis on trout, but also caters to meat-eaters and vegetarians. The setting matches the food and diners can expect to see colobus monkeys and numerous forest birds while they dine. Open till 5pm.

NARO MORU Trout Tree Restaurant
📋 📶 Ⓥ   ⑤⑤⑤

Nanyuki Road **Tel** *062 62059*   **Road Map** *C4*

Clearly signposted along the main road between Naro Moru and Nanyuki, this isolated tree-shaded restaurant is set on a working trout farm, as reflected in a menu that ranges from the predictable grilled trout to the somewhat unexpected trout masala. A limited selection of meat and salad dishes is on offer too. Open till 4pm.

NYAHURURU Thomson's Falls Lodge
📋 📶 🍷 Ⓥ   ⑤⑤

Off Nyeri Road on the outskirts of town **Tel** *065 22006*   **Road Map** *B4*

Set in large, leafy grounds overlooking Kenya's most spectacular waterfall, this pleasant colonial hotel has seen better days but the setting is difficult to beat and the meals, though not exhibiting any discernible culinary flair, are filling and tasty. The place is certainly miles ahead of any other option in sleepy Nyahururu.

NYERI Green Oak Restaurant
📋 📶 🍷   ⑤

Kimathi Way   **Road Map** *C4*

This centrally located two-storey eatery serves decent local fare. Try the *ugali* (maize porridge) with *kuku* (chicken) stew for lunch or *nyama choma* (roast meat) in the evening. The first-floor terrace bar is a great place to watch the people of Nyeri go about their daily business. Food options are limited at the weekend.

NYERI Outspan Hotel
📶 🍷 Ⓥ   ⑤⑤⑤

Baden-Powell Road **Tel** *061 2032424*   **Road Map** *C4*

Even if staying elsewhere in town, it is well worth heading out to Nyeri's oldest and finest hotel for the lunchtime buffet, à la carte dinner or in-between snack. The hearty food reflects the lingering old-world atmosphere that permeates this leafy colonial relic. The bar is also a thing of time-warped wonder, and the garden is good for a stroll.

NORTHERN KENYA

ISIOLO Bomen Restaurant
📋 📶 🍷   ⑤

Bomen Hotel, Kanisani Road **Tel** *064 52272*   **Road Map** *C4*

Isiolo has limited options for quality hotels and eateries but this is easily the best choice, serving a selection of dishes typical of hotels catering to local businessmen – mostly grilled, fried or stewed meat with chips or rice. The lunchtime buffets and à la carte dinners are well above average, with friendly service and an enjoyable bar.

MARALAL Maralal Safari Lodge
📋 📶 🍷   ⑤⑤

Entrance to Maralal Wildlife Sanctuary **Tel** *0720 924523*   **Road Map** *C3*

Although a short drive from the town centre and with a menu that could display more imagination, there is no better place to enjoy lunch, dinner or a drink in Maralal than the patio of this lodge – with the added bonus of reliably good wildlife viewing at the waterhole. Meals and snacks are mostly grilled meat with rice or chips.

SAMBURU-BUFFALO SPRINGS NATIONAL RESERVES Samburu Lodge
📶 🍷 Ⓥ   ⑤⑤⑤

Close to Samburu Reserve Headquarters **Tel** *064 30781*   **Road Map** *C3*

Aside from a few undistinguished cafés in Archer's Post, there is nothing in the way of stand-alone eateries in Samburu-Buffalo Springs. However, this long-serving lodge welcomes day visitors to its excellent buffet lunch served between 12.30 and 2.30pm – and there is no more attractive setting overlooking the Ewaso Nyiro river.

SHABA NATIONAL RESERVE Surpelei Restaurant, Sarova Shaba Lodge
📶 🍷 Ⓥ   ⑤⑤⑤

1 km (half a mile) from Natorbe Gate **Tel** *064 30638*   **Road Map** *C3*

This stilted wood-and-thatch restaurant is strong on character, the buffet lunches are equally strong on choice, and it is the only lodge in the area with an à la carte snack menu. Do not miss out on the opportunity to wander through the lushly wooded riverfront grounds before or after your meal. Lunch served from 1–3pm.

SHOPPING IN KENYA

Kenya has a wide range of locally made items that are ideal as souvenirs and gifts. These include a number of traditional artifacts, precious stones and jewellery, wooden carvings, Maasai beads and blankets, *kikoys* (fabrics) and other textiles, baskets, batiks and paintings, and soapstone figurines and chess boards. There are well-stocked gift shops in Nairobi and along the coast, or dedicated bargain hunters can head for the many outdoor

Decorative ceramic plates from Nairobi

markets and street shops. Most tourist shops in Nairobi are clustered on Koinange Street. In Mombasa, souvenir shops and stalls are located on Moi Avenue and Nyerere Avenue. Hotels, lodges and camps that cater to holiday-makers have craft and curio shops. All airports have duty-free shops that sell high-quality, high-priced items. The art of bargaining has deep roots in Kenyan culture so visitors will often be treated to some good-humoured haggling.

OPENING HOURS

Business hours for shops and markets are usually 8am to 5 or 6pm, Monday to Saturday. The smaller shops close for an hour's lunch around 1 to 2pm. Muslim-owned establishments may stay closed all day on Fridays or at least in the afternoons. In Mombasa, opening hours are longer, but many shops and businesses close for a siesta between 2 and 4pm. In places where there are plenty of holiday-makers, such as the coast, shops also open on Sundays. In hotels and lodges, in-house shops usually have their opening times adapted to the times of the day when guests are around. Shopping malls in Nairobi and Mombasa and large supermarkets are also open on Sundays until 1pm.

HOW TO PAY

Most tourist-orientated shops as well as high-end lodges and hotels accept credit cards, US dollars and occasionally, cash in other currencies. When purchasing something on a credit card, a 2 to 5 per cent commission is often added, so in some instances it is cheaper to pay for items in cash. Kenya's economy is largely a cash-based one, and in small towns and villages, as well as local bus stations, markets, street-food stalls and other such places, only Kenyan shillings are accepted. Small denomination bills may

Swahili goods on display at a souvenir shop near Fort Jesus, Mombasa

not be readily available and are best kept handy as change or to pay for small items at markets and street stalls.

BARGAINING

Except in upscale shopping malls and shops, bargaining is the expected norm throughout Kenya, and for Kenyan traders it is an essential business skill. It is best to approach bargaining with a sense of humour and a friendly attitude, keeping in mind that it is not just a commercial transaction but a social encounter as well. Opening prices are almost always exaggerated and determined on what the seller thinks the customer can pay – the real price can sometimes be less than half the initial price. However, visitors should keep in mind that a lot of work has gone into making souvenir items, especially good quality carvings and

beaded jewellery. Traders make a living from their sales, so customers should not offer unreasonable prices. Generally, buyers get a good price after a little negotiation and the vendor a reasonable profit. Those who are unsure of what they should be paying should try walking away – if they are called back, there is still room for negotiation; if they are not, it means they did not offer enough and the trader is no longer interested.

CRAFTS AND CURIOS

A wide variety of indigenous crafts and curios is available in Kenya, and with careful searching, it is possible to find some of very high quality. Collectors of ethnic artifacts and objects of art will find plenty of traditional and tribal items. The Maasai and northern tribes such as the Gabbra, Turkana, Rendille, Oromo

Meru outlet of Nakumatt, Kenya's leading chain of supermarkets

DIRECTORY

SHOPS

Nakumatt Mega
Uhuru Highway, opposite
Nyayo Stadium.
Tel 020 551814.
www.nakumatt.net

Nakumatt Likoni
Nyerere Avenue, near
Likoni Ferry, Mombasa.
Tel 041 2228945.
www.nakumatt.net

and Samburu are all famous for their beautiful artifacts. Popular items include gourds, stools, neck pillows and drums. Other curios such as wooden salad servers, carved animals and batik paintings are specifically made for the tourist market. Deforestation is a major problem in Kenya. It is best to buy wooden items at high-end stores because cheap mass-produced objects present the greatest environmental threat, or to buy items that are made from renewable trees such as neem or blue gum.

A painted mask from Namanga

SHOPS

There are a number of gift shops in urban and tourist localities. Nairobi, in particular, has some fine upmarket galleries. For everyday items, most sizable towns have a supermarket. Nakumatt is the biggest chain of supermarkets and is expanding rapidly. It sells food, household goods, electronics, furniture and – of particular interest to holiday-makers – camping equipment. The **Nakumatt Mega** in Nairobi and **Nakumatt Likoni** in Mombasa are two of the largest shops in Kenya. Shopping malls are starting to feature all over Africa, and Nairobi now has several. These have cinemas, car parks, supermarkets, food courts, some international chain stores and speciality shops.

Since the building of the Lunatic Line *(see p299)*, Asian traders have been operating in the country. Today, many have small shops, selling a wide variety of things, generally clustered around markets or bus stations.

MARKETS

Every town in Kenya has a market while the cities have several. All of them feature an array of brilliantly coloured fresh produce, mounds of pulses and grains, pyramids of fresh eggs, live chickens and all sorts of practical items such as rope, plastic buckets, charcoal burners and brooms.

Some markets are housed in open concrete blocks built for the purpose, while others are nothing more than small congested grids of rickety stalls made from sticks and plastic sheeting. Prices are considerably lower in markets than in shops. They are also an ideal stop for visitors interested in absorbing the busy and lively atmosphere of the place where most Kenyans do their daily shopping.

Urban areas are also home to *mitumba* (second-hand clothes) markets. The clothing available here comes from the USA, Europe and Asia and is sold off in bales to traders – usually to make money for charities. Second-hand Western designer labels and well-known brands can be found here with a little rummaging, which makes these markets hugely popular with Kenyans.

One of the busy fish markets at Homa Bay, on the shores of Lake Victoria

Shopping in Nairobi

With its modern malls, galleries, downtown trading stores, specialist shops and outdoor markets, Nairobi offers the best shopping experience in Kenya. Apart from the usual wood carvings and soapstone souvenirs, there is a range of handicrafts, textiles, ornaments and paintings for sale here. In addition, there are good bookshops that sell maps of national parks and reference guides to wildlife and birds. The main shopping areas lie between Koinange Street and Moi Avenue, with the malls located further out in the more affluent suburbs of the city. Most shops can organise overseas shipping for larger items.

Souvenir shield

Busy corner outside a Nakumatt outlet in Downtown Nairobi

SHOPPING MALLS

Satellite shopping malls have mushroomed all over Nairobi and there are some 20 dotted around the suburbs. Most have a large supermarket serving the local community, specialist shops, restaurants, food courts, banks, bureaux de change, ATMs, post offices, large guarded car parks and additional entertainment such as cinemas. Nairobi's largest mall is **Sarit Centre**, which has hundreds of shops as well as a cinema, health club and an exhibition centre. It is close to the malls and shops in Westlands including Nakumatt Ukay, a 24-hour supermarket that is part of **Nakumatt**, Kenya's leading supermarket chain. Other shopping malls include **Yaya Centre**, which has a children's play area and a fitness centre, and **Village Market**, which has a very popular food court on the weekends, a cinema and is surrounded by gardens

with cascading waterfalls. Among the new malls are **Karen Crossroads** with a large branch of Nakumatt, and **The Junction**, which also features a Nakumatt, a cinema hall and a number of excellent restaurants.

MARKETS

For the visitor looking to buy crafts and curios, Nairobi's markets are the ideal places to head to. Among a colourful display of vegetables and fruit, the City Market *(see p156)* in Downtown Nairobi offers a full range of Kenyan souvenirs at reasonable prices, although customers may need to check quality. The **Maasai Market** is held every Sunday at Yaya Centre and every Friday on the roof of Village Market mall. Prices are good if customers bargain hard, and the selection of jewellery,

baskets, carvings and other artifacts is excellent. **Kariokor Market** is a huge sprawling open-air market selling everything from vegetables and fish to traditional fabrics and souvenirs. It also has a row of good, easily affordable eateries, which are popular at lunchtime with local workers.

The **Mitumba Market** is one of the best in the city and has stalls piled high with branded clothes from Europe and the USA. When visiting any of these busy markets, it is advisable to leave all valuables at the hotel and to watch out for pickpockets.

BOOKS AND MAPS

Nairobi has a number of bookshops selling Kenyan maps, souvenir books and guide books. These are, however, not especially cheap as most are imported. Located downtown, **Stanley Bookshop** covers a wide range of subjects despite being a modestly sized store, while **The Book Villa** offers a range of glossy hardbacks and **Prestige Booksellers** has plenty of field guides and maps. There are bookshops in all malls, the best of them being **Silverbird Lifestyle Store**, which also sells CDs and computer games, and **Bookstop** in Yaya Centre. The latter has a good selection of second-hand books including several on Africa. Outlets known as Books First can be found in all branches

Colourful cloth-paintings and soapstone chess boards at Maasai Market

of Nakumatt. The National Museum *(see pp158–9)* and Karen Blixen Museum *(see p168)* also have bookshops, which stock titles on a range of Kenyan and East African subjects, such as their wildlife, history, literature and culture. Most bookshops sell international newspapers and magazines, which can also be bought from street vendors.

Ceramic ware, bags and pottery items on display

SPECIALIST SHOPS

Downtown Nairobi has a dense assemblage of shops catering to visitors and holiday-makers along Muindi Mbingu Street and Kenyatta Avenue. Specialist shops are also scattered around the suburbs and can be visited on the way to attractions such as the Karen Blixen Museum. In town, **Collectors Den** and **Zanzibar Curio Shop** are both crammed with every imaginable Kenyan curio as well as safari clothes. **African Art Shoppe** offers a collection of antiques, furniture, carvings and paintings at the top end in terms of quality and price. On the outskirts of town, **Spinner's Web** has a good range of wool rugs, jewellery, crafts and weavings, which are outsourced from

women's groups. **Kamili Designs** produces a range of hand and screen paintings, many of which have animal designs on them. **Kazuri Beads** (Swahili for small and beautiful) employs destitute women who use clay-fired, hand-painted beads to make jewellery. These are now sold all over the world. **Kitengela Glass** is an open-air gallery selling wall panels, glasses and beads made out of recycled glass. They have outlets in The Junction and Village Market malls. **One Way** produces a range of high-quality products made from *kikoy* fabrics, including sarongs, tablecloths,

Contemporary wood carving

beach bags and clothing. They have several branches in Nairobi including in the Sarit and Yaya centres. **Matbronze** is a fine art foundry and gallery selling bronze wildlife statues. **Marula Studios** sells paintings, leather and beaded items and unusual crafts, including sculptures and jewellery, made from recycled plastic flip-flops. They also have a café and playground. Well worth a visit despite its distance from the city is The **House of Treasures** with its fine pieces of African art for sale as well as decor items from places as far away as Bali and Samarkand.

DIRECTORY

What to Buy

A Maasai drum

Kenya's bustling curio markets and small sidewalk stalls offer great bargains on a wide range of goods. Handmade items such as batik pictures, soapstone bowls, wood carvings and chess sets are made specifically for visitors. However, the country has a wealth of traditional textiles, artifacts and jewellery that make ideal souvenirs. Nairobi has some excellent upmarket boutiques and galleries selling quality products, with facilities for overseas shipment of large items. Its vibrant street-side stalls also offer the opportunity for some good-humoured bargaining.

Visitors browsing the wide array of handicraft items displayed in the City Market stalls, Nairobi

ART AND CRAFT

With a wide range of art and crafts produced by its myriad communities, Kenya has grown as a niche market for these items. Popular for interiors themes, African art is very versatile. For instance, a drum can alternate as a coffee table.

Lamu Chests
These intricately carved wooden boxes – some studded and inlaid with brass or copper – vary in size from small jewellery boxes to large chests.

Wooden Giraffes
One of Kenya's most popular souvenirs, these giraffes can be difficult to cart home. Herds of them, of varying heights, can be seen clustered in shops and markets.

Wood Carvings
Produced by the Akamba people of eastern Kenya, these carvings range from exquisite masks and bowls to carved animals and statues of Maasai warriors.

Handcrafted Toys
Local artisans shape wire or straw into toys often in the form of miniature vehicles with wheels and steering columns.

Batiks
These can be used as cushions, table cloths or wall hangings. Silk batiks are exclusive to Nairobi's chic galleries, while local markets stock the cheaper cotton ones with village scenes, ethnic and animal motifs.

Soapstone
Available in a range of colours such as cream, pink, lavender and black, soapstone is carved into soap dishes, animal statues, vases and unique chess sets with chess pieces fashioned after tribal figures.

CLOTHES, SHOES AND ACCESSORIES

With their primary colours, the traditional textiles of
Kenya are extremely versatile. Fabrics are adapted
into clothing, bags and cushions, while Maasai
beads are used to embellish a host of products.

Maasai Blankets
*Used by Maasai
herdsmen as robes,
these blankets have
red, blue and purple
stripes or checks.
They also make
good picnic table-
cloths and can be
used as wraps on a
morning safari.*

Kiondo Baskets
*Traditionally woven from sisal, these baskets
are now also lined with kikoy cloth and dyed
in bright colours to make stylish handbags.*

Tusker T-shirts
*Served in large
brown bottles, Tusker
is Kenya's premier
beer. The Tusker
logo with an
elephant's head
features in trendy
T-shirts sold as pop-
ular souvenirs.*

Swahili Sandals
*Found in coastal markets, these beautiful
women's sandals have leather straps in
floral shapes and are set with cowrie shells
or covered with tiny colourful beads.*

Kikoys
*These striped pieces
of cotton, worn by
Swahili men on
the coast as wrap-
around skirts, come
in bright primary
colours and make
good sarongs, bags
and cushions.*

Maasai Beaded Jewellery
*Jewellery, including the wide collars worn by
Maasai brides, earrings, bracelets, necklaces
and rings, is available in all tourist areas.
Maasai beading also adorns items such as
belts, cell phone covers and dog collars.*

TEA AND COFFEE

Tea and coffee are important cash crops
and form a substantial chunk of Kenya's
exports. Bags of coffee beans, ground
coffee, loose tea and locally produced
teabags can be bought in supermarkets
and even from shops at the airport.

Tea
*With a strong,
heady flavour, the
tea grown in
the fertile plains
of Western
Kenya is among
the finest in
the world.*

Coffee
*The acidic soil near
Mount Kenya yields
coffee that is easily
identified by its full
flavour and
pleasant aroma.*

WHAT NOT TO BUY

The purchase of any product
derived from wildlife, such as
animal pelts and skins, ivory,
lion teeth, coral and turtle
shell, should be avoided as
these are protected under the
Convention on International
Trade in Endangered Species
of Wild Flora and Fauna
(CITES). While such products
may be seen up for sale, it
is a punishable offence to
take them out of Kenya.
Buying these items also supports the illicit wildlife trade,
which is best discouraged.

ENTERTAINMENT IN KENYA

Nairobi and the coastal strip around Mombasa have the best choice of entertainment in Kenya. Local residents like to party and the popular Tusker beer flows freely at numerous laid-back pubs, upmarket wine bars and formal hotel lounges. There are plenty of nightclubs, and these do not get going until midnight and close only at dawn. Away from the cities, most small towns usually feature some basic bars or the town's main hotel may hold a discotheque on the

Tusker beer, a local favourite

weekends. Modern multi-screen cinema complexes are beginning to feature in Mombasa and Nairobi, as are a number of casinos that draw crowds. Live music can be enjoyed at many clubs. There are occasional theatre performances at venues such as the Kenya National Theatre or the foreign cultural centres in Nairobi. Many hotels and lodges provide evening entertainment such as tribal dancing and acrobatics. The Saturday edition of the *Daily Nation* has a selection of what is on.

BARS

Nairobi has a thriving bar culture and five-star hotels are hugely popular with locals and visitors alike. The Safari Bar in the InterContinental *(see p362)* has different music themes each night; the Jockey Pub in the Hilton *(see p362)* has a live duo band on weekends; while the Norfolk *(see p363)* has the Lord Delamere Terrace, made famous by the gin-and-tonic swilling settler set of early Nairobi. The Aksum Bar in the Nairobi Serena *(see p363)* offers cocktails and fine wines in elegant surroundings. Harry's Bar in the LAICO Regency *(see p362)* has an English pub atmosphere, while the Windsor Golf Hotel and Country Club *(see p363)* has several bars, including the elegant Library Bar, which has a good selection of single malt whiskies and cigars. Other popular bars include Spanish-themed **Gipsy**

Bar that serves tapas and plays flamenco and Latino music, and **Mercury Lounge**, which serves excellent cocktails and sometimes has live jazz nights. The **Sierra Lounge** is a subtle upmarket spot specialising in German beer that is brewed on site; **Tamambo** has a variety of cocktails and live music on Fridays.

Most hotels in Mombasa and along the coast have bars catering to holiday-makers. The exceptions are Lamu and downtown Mombasa, conservative Muslim areas, where alcohol is frowned upon. The spacious Castle Terrace bar at the Castle Royal Hotel *(see p367)* serves good food. A popular alternative to the hotel bars is **Forty Thieves Beach Bar** on Diani Beach, which has outdoor seating, dancing on some nights, pool tables and a good Sunday lunch buffet with live music. North of Mombasa, on Shanzu Beach, **Trekker's**

Entertainment Complex offers a cocktail bar, *nyama choma*, a large sports bar and an open-air discotheque.

A live band performance in one of several bars in Downtown Nairobi

NIGHTCLUBS

Most nightclubs are open Wednesday to Saturday from about 9pm to dawn, although some open every night, especially in peak season. Cover charges vary from 200–1,000 KSh. In Nairobi, **Martini's Ultra Lounge** is a sophisticated cocktail lounge and club with dance music, while the Windsor Room at the Windsor Golf Hotel and Country Club caters to an older crowd. The adventurous can head to Downtown Nairobi, where the **New Florida** and **Florida 2000** nightclubs, going strong since disco fever hit Kenya in the 1970s, are packed to the gills at weekends. **K1**, also called Klubhouse, is a rustically built club with a dance floor and pool hall, while the **Pavement Club and Café** is popular for

The cosy interior of Jockey Pub, Hilton Hotel, Nairobi

food, and DJs liven things up late at night. **CLUBarn** features a bar and dance floor with DJ. The Simba Saloon at Carnivore Restaurant *(see p383)* is Nairobi's largest club and can accommodate thousands of people. **Soho's** is a stylish club popular with an expat crowd, and has live jazz on Thursdays.

Mombasa and the coast have a host of clubs situated within close proximity to the major hotels, and many of the big hotels have their own clubs. With huge dance floors and five bars, **Pirates Beach Bar** is perhaps the most popular club along the north coast where virtually all kinds of music is played every night. The **Tembo Disco** has a dance floor, billiards lounge, restaurant and beer garden, while **Florida Nightclub and Casino** features 24-hour bars, a disco, casino and cabaret shows, and is best visited in a group.

CASINOS

There are many casinos dotted around Nairobi and Mombasa, most of them in the hotels, which offer bars, banks of slot machines and

A Maasai dance performance, Alliance Française, Nairobi

gaming tables. Nairobi's best and most sophisticated is the casino at the **InterContinental**. In Mombasa, the **Golden Key Casino** is located on the roof of the famous Tamarind Restaurant *(see p386)*, both of which offer impressive views of the city, its old dhow port and the Indian Ocean.

CINEMAS

Modern cinema complexes in Nairobi and Mombasa show mainstream Hollywood films. In Nairobi, cinema complexes can be found at the Village Market *(see p393)*, The Junction *(see p393)* and the Sarit Centre *(see p393)*. The most central cinema hall is the

Fox 20th Century. The best cinema hall in Mombasa is the **Nyali Cinemax**, which also has a sports bar and regularly showcases Bollywood films.

THEATRE

In Nairobi, occasional theatrical performances are held in the **Kenya National Theatre**. One of the longest-running performance groups is **Phoenix Players**, which has its own intimate, 110-seat theatre and offers a mixed bag of European and African plays. Another popular venue for theatre, comedy, films and art exhibitions is the **Alliance Française**, which has a garden stage popular for concerts.

DIRECTORY

BARS

Forty Thieves Beach Bar
Diani Beach, Ukunda.
Tel 040 3202033.

Gipsy Bar
Woodvale Grove, Westlands, Nairobi.
Tel 020 4440836.

Mercury Lounge
ABC Place, Waiyaki Way, Nairobi.
Tel 020 4451875.

Sierra Lounge
Mombasa Rd, Nairobi.
Tel 020 556960.

Tamambo
The Mall, Westlands, Nairobi. *Tel* 020 4448064.

Trekker's Entertainment Complex
Shanzu Beach, Mombasa.
Tel 0722 684176.

NIGHTCLUBS

CLUBarn
Ngong Racecourse, Nairobi. *Tel* 0723 224081.

Florida 2000
Commerce House, Moi Ave, Nairobi. **City Map** 2 D4. *Tel* 020 2229036.

Florida Nightclub and Casino
Mama Ngina Drive, Mombasa.
Tel 041 2313127.

K1 (Klubhouse)
Ojijo Rd, Parklands, Nairobi. *Tel* 020 3749870.

Martini's Ultra Lounge
China Centre, Ngong Rd, Nairobi. *Tel* 020 2727668.

New Florida
Koinange St, Nairobi.
City Map 1 B3.
Tel 020 2215014.

Pavement Club and Café
Westview Centre, Ring Rd, Westlands, Nairobi.
Tel 020 4441711.

Pirates Beach Bar
Mombasa–Malindi Rd, Nyali, Mombasa.
Tel 041 5487119.

Soho's
Maua Close, Westlands, Nairobi. *Tel* 020 3745710.

Tembo Disco
Mombasa–Malindi Rd, Bamburi, Mombasa.
Tel 041 5485074.

CASINOS

Golden Key Casino
Silos Rd, Nyali, Mombasa.
Tel 041 471071.

InterContinental
City Hall Way, Nairobi.
City Map 1 B4.
Tel 020 3200000.

CINEMAS

Fox 20th Century
Mama Ngina St, Nairobi.
City Map 1 C3.
Tel 020 2249672.

Nyali Cinemax
Nyali Rd, Mombasa.
Tel 041 470000.

THEATRE

Alliance Française
Loita St, Nairobi. **City Map** 1 B3. *Tel* 020 340054.

Kenya National Theatre
Harry Thuku Rd, Nairobi.
City Map 1 B2.
Tel 020 2086748.

Phoenix Players
Professional Centre Parliament Rd, Nairobi.
City Map 1 C4.
Tel 020 2225506.

OUTDOOR ACTIVITIES

Kenya has an incredible range of landscapes and as such offers plenty of outdoor activities. Most popular for its safaris, there are more ways to watch wildlife in Kenya than from a safari vehicle, such as game- and bird-walks, animal tracking and floating over herds of wildebeest in a balloon. Also popular is the Kenyan coast, with its full range of water sports as well as excellent snorkelling and scuba diving facilities. For the adventurous, there is camel trekking in the remote northern deserts with the Samburu, climbing Mount Kenya and whitewater rafting. There are many annual events, such as the Lewa (Safaricom) Marathon, that are open to international participants, and as a throwback to the colonial days, spectator sports are hugely popular. More relaxed activities include a round of golf on one of the many excellent courses, a gentle sail on a dhow or a relaxing massage in a health spa.

CULTURAL EXPERIENCES

One of the major highlights of travelling in Kenya is experiencing its immense cultural diversity. In Nairobi, the Bomas of Kenya *(see p161)* showcases tribal dance and music, and has mock-ups of typical villages and homesteads. Visitors on their way to the popular Masai Mara Game Reserve *(see pp262–5)* and Amboseli National Park *(see pp194–7)* will discover Maasai *manyattas* on the roads, where people still follow their traditional ways of life. On the coast, north of Mombasa, **Ngomongo Village Park** is a collection of working villages complete with crops and animals. Visitors to the north will be able to meet the seminomadic Samburu people – some of whom act as guides on camel treks – and the Pokot people, whose homesteads and markets can be visited from the **Marich Pass Field Studies Centre**.

Hikers to Mount Kenya making their way across Chogoria Route

HIKING AND CLIMBING

The most favourable areas for hiking in Kenya are Ngong Hills *(see p169)* near Nairobi, Chyulu Hills *(see p180)* in the Southeastern Savannahs, Menengai Crater and Mount Longonot in the Southern Rift Valley *(see pp252–83)*, Mount Elgon and Cherangani Hills *(see pp290–91)* in Western Kenya and the Aberdares *(see pp316–17)* in the Central Highlands. The most challenging trek in the country is to Mount Kenya *(see pp322–5)*. Of its three main peaks, Lenana can be reached by most trekkers, while Batian and Nelion are attempted only by serious climbers. The three main routes to Lenana – Chogoria, Naro Moru, and Sirimon – all penetrate forest and moorland. A leisurely 6 days are recommended but the mountain can be climbed in 4, and the best time to do so is during the dry season. Travellers arriving from the coast will need at least a couple of days to acclimatise at a temperate altitude such as Nairobi before attempting the climb. Some of the hotels and lodges around Mount Kenya can organise guided climbs, as can **Mount Kenya Guides and Porters Safari Club**, a community-based organisation of guides, porters and cooks in and around Naro Moru. Route details and general information can be found on the **Mountain Club of Kenya** website, which also has particulars on other more remote technical rock climbing destinations around the country. The club is located at Nairobi's domestic airport, and although it does not have a phone number – owing to regular changes in committee members – visitors can email and enquire about attending their weekly club night. Their library has a wide selection of mountaineering books, maps and useful resources for climbing in Kenya.

Traditional dance performance at the Bomas of Kenya, Nairobi

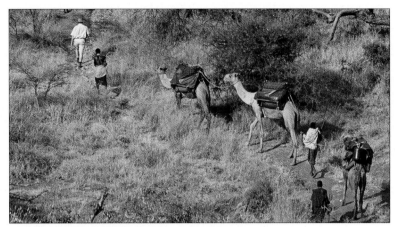

Camel trekking with the Samburu people across the semiarid plains of Maralal

CAMEL TREKKING

Adventurous camel trekking is available in the drier north and on some of Laikipia Plateau's private ranches (*see pp318–21*). Camels are used as pack animals for supplies and camping equipment, with travellers walking alongside. Treks are led by expert guides, usually the seminomadic Samburu who proudly show visitors everything of interest in the bush and desert landscape. Trips can last for a few hours from one of the lodges, to several days crossing remote wildernesses and camping out under the stars. Walking is done in the early morning or late afternoon when it is cool and distances of 8 to 20 km (5 to 12 miles) per day are not too strenuous. **Wild Frontiers**, **Desert Rose** and **Yare Safaris** can organise multiday treks.

BIRD-WATCHING

East Africa has one of the richest concentrations of birdlife in the world. Kenya alone is home to some 1,089 species, which represent 12 per cent of the world's bird-species count. Given these figures, it is not unusual to record more than 120 different birds at a particular site on a single day. Even a city such as Nairobi has over 600 resident and migratory species. **Nature Kenya** runs regular bird walks in Nairobi and produces checklists that cover the entire country.

There are also a number of tour operators that offer specialist bird-oriented tours. Bird-watching is good all year round, and birds of the bush, such as go-away birds, guinea fowl, rollers and barbets, are always active. For sheer numbers, however, the best time to visit is from October to April, when some 120 migrant species arrive from the northern hemisphere. During the rest of the year, the migrants are replaced by birds from the southern hemisphere, especially Madagascar, but these are no more than 10 or 12 species. Kenya's birding hotspots include the dry-country parks of Samburu (*see pp342–5*) and Tsavo (*see pp182–7*), the grasslands of the Masai Mara, the Rift Valley lakes and the highland and coastal forests. The coast is especially good during October and December when large flocks congregate at the estuaries.

HORSE RIDING

Horse riding is offered in Kenya by a number of country lodges and hotels. Rides vary from short trips for novices through local forests to multi day safaris in wilderness areas for those with experience in the saddle. Riding on the plains past herds of giraffe or zebra is an exhilarating experience and it is possible to get unusually close to wildlife. Most wildlife see horses as non-threatening and humans can go almost unrecognised on top of them. Kenya has a long tradition of rearing horses from the hunter-settler days, and horses reared in the bush are quite accustomed to the presence of wildlife. Usually, the longer trips for experienced riders utilise lodges or mobile tented camps for accommodation and riders are encouraged to look after their steed at night. Vehicles, and in some cases camels, are used to carry equipment and supplies. Popular regions for horseback safaris include the Masai Mara and Amboseli, the Chyulu Hills and the Laikipia Plateau. Most travel agents specialising in equestrian holidays will be able to book a horseback safari in Kenya, as can **Safaris Unlimited**, **Offbeat Safaris** or **Horseback in Kenya**.

Riders get close to a Maasai giraffe, Lewa Wildlife Conservancy

Hot-air balloons glide past grazing elephants at the Masai Mara

BALLOONING

Floating over wildlife on the misty plains of the Masai Mara is a magical experience. One of the highlights of a visit to Kenya, ballooning is offered by most of the Mara's lodges, and during the high season it is possible to see many candy-striped balloons drifting across the reserve at dawn. The ride usually lasts an hour and is followed by a champagne breakfast in the bush. The best time to go ballooning is during the wildebeest migration *(see pp124–5)* when the sight of thousands of plains animals from the air can be exhilarating, but a graceful and silent float over the Mara to watch the sun rise over the undulating plains is mesmerising at any time of year. **Transworld Safaris** and **Adventures Aloft** pick up passengers from several Mara lodges.

GOLF

Long sunny days are a feature of the typical Kenyan weather and are ideal for golf all year round. Thanks to its colonial history, Kenya has over 40 golf courses around the country, which have well-tended greens and popular clubhouses. Many are located in stunning settings where a round of golf can be combined with bird-watching. There are six courses within a 30-km (19-mile) radius of Nairobi, including the Windsor Golf and Country Club, Karen Golf and Country Club, Muthaiga Golf Club and the oldest course in Kenya, the Royal Nairobi Golf Club. The two principal courses along the coast are the Leisure Golf Course and the Nyali Golf and Country Club.

The **Kenya Golf Union**, established in 1928, organises several tournaments throughout the year, including the Kenya Open. It lists contact details of all Kenya's golf courses on its website, most of which offer temporary membership to visitors for a small fee. Most courses have the luxury of offering caddies who are usually very good players themselves. Unusually, many courses are at an altitude of over 1,500 m (5,000 ft), which gives an additional 10 per cent yardage to a golfer's stroke. **Kenya Golf Safaris** can organise golf packages.

WATER SPORTS

With soft white sands and a gentle sea breeze, the coast is a veritable playground for water sports. The warm water is ideal for swimming, with none of the health risks associated with Kenya's inland lakes, many of which are infected with the bilharzia parasite, or rivers where there may be the danger of crocodiles. As well as diving and snorkelling *(see*

p211) and boat trips on all manner of craft from traditional fishing boats to luxurious catamarans, the resorts along the coast offer parasailing, jet-skiing, sea-kayaking and rides on inflatable banana boats. With perfect cross-shore winds, the Kenyan coast is ideal for windsurfing and kiteboarding. **Prosurf Extreme** based at Nyali Beach and **Kite Surf Kenya** on Diani Beach offer professionally accredited courses.

Kite-surfing, an ever-popular water sport at the beaches of Kenya

DIVING AND SNORKELLING

The clear azure waters of Kenya's Indian Ocean are warm throughout the year and the shallow coral gardens, fringing reefs and blue-water drop-offs are home to some 3,000 species of marine animals and plants. Kenya's reefs, along with Egypt's Red Sea reefs and Australia's Great Barrier Reef, are ranked as some of the most diverse and beautiful in the world. There are a number of protected marine reserves that are alive with myriad species of marine life including manta rays, whale sharks, bottlenosed dolphins and turtles. Visibility is excellent for most of the year, though the best time to dive is from October to April before the long rains and subsequent silted river outflows.

Snorkelling can be done by simply walking into the sea or from small local sailing boats called *ngalawa*, while none of the dive sites are more than a 30-minute boat-ride away. Divers can also

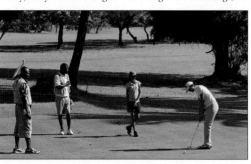

Game in progress at the well-tended greens of Nyali Golf and Country Club

Snorkelling off the Kenyan coast at Watamu Marine Park

explore a number of wrecks such as the MV *Dania* to the north of Mombasa, which was purposely sunk in 2002 to promote diving activities and has already become a thriving artificial reef.

Almost all hotels and resorts have diving and snorkelling facilities and rent out equipment. There are many dive schools that run recognised dive courses up to dive master level in several languages. These include **Diving the Crab** and **Diani Marine**, both of which operate from Diani Beach, and **Blue Fin Diving** which operates from hotels between Watamu and Malindi.

BOATING

There are a number of ways to enjoy a float on Kenya's innumerable rivers, lakes and even the ocean. On the coast, glass bottom boats are available from the large tourist hotels and lodges for viewing underwater life in the offshore coral reefs. A trip on one of the *ngalawa* boats is a relaxing way to be out on the water. Snorkelling is also offered. A popular day-excursion from Diani and Shimoni to the south of Mombasa is the dhow trip to **Wasini Island** *(see p220)* within the Kisite-Mpunguti Marine Park. This usually includes snorkelling and diving and a seafood lunch on the island. It is an ideal way to spend the day and dolphins often accompany the dhows through the reserve. A sail around Mombasa's harbour

on a traditional ocean-going **Tamarind Dhow** is also a lovely romantic way to enjoy a delicious seafood meal at sunset. Further inland, canoes can be taken out on many of the Rift Valley lakes and are a good way to go bird-watching or to get close to hippo. The more adventurous can go whitewater rafting with **Savage Wilderness Safaris** on the Tana river, which has rapids up to Grade V and is easily accessible as a day trip from Nairobi. There are longer 2- to 3-day trips on the Mathioya, Athi or Ewaso Nyiro rivers.

Weighing the catch

FISHING

The rich and deep waters off the East African coast are one of the best game-fishing territories in the world. Keen fishermen are permitted to go deep-sea fishing in the Pemba Channel for game fish such as marlin, yellowfin tuna, sailfish, shark, swordfish, barracuda and dorado, which are caught

on a tag and release system. Key departure places for boats include the coastal towns of Shimoni, Watamu, Malindi and Kilifi. There are two very definite fishing seasons – the yellowfin tuna season that lasts from August to October, and the marlin season, usually between December and March. Numerous hotels on the coast offer day and overnight trips out to sea. Established operators are, for example, the **Pemba Channel Fishing Club** and **Hemingway's Fishing Centre**.

Elsewhere in the country, fishing trips are available on motorised *ssese* canoes on Lake Victoria. These are frequently used to catch the giant Nile perch, and can be hired from the luxury fishing lodges on Mfangano and Rusinga islands *(see pp304–305)*. Some of the upmarket lodges in Aberdare National Park and the foothills of Mount Kenya can arrange trout fishing in nearby rivers and dams.

Brightly coloured fishing boats crowd the port at Mfangano Island

SPECTATOR SPORTS

Although the term athletics is synonymous with Kenyan sports and there is an active athletics calendar throughout the country, owing to its British and Asian legacy Kenya also features plenty of popular spectator sports. Cricket, for instance, was first played in Kenya in 1910 in a league known as Officials V Settlers that played up until 1964. A national team was formed in 1951 and the Kenya Cricket Association in 1953. Kenya has since gone on to play at international levels, including participating in the ICC World Cup – in fact, a few 2003 World Cup matches were hosted in Nairobi. The cricketing season lasts from June to February, when league and test matches can be watched at the **Nairobi Gymkhana Club**.

Rugby too, has its roots in colonial days. The **Kenyan Rugby Football Club** was established in 1923. Kenya's Safari Sevens is now a world-recognised tournament in the global sevens rugby series. Kenyans are serious football fans and matches attract plenty of fervent and vocal followers. The national team is the Harambee Stars, and other popular clubs include Oserian Fastac, Leopards FC, Gor Mahia FC and Mathere United. The local press carries news on when games are being held. Part of the European PGA Tour, the annual Kenya Open Golf Championship is usually held at Nairobi's prestigious **Muthaiga Country**

Athletes competing in the annual Lewa (Safaricom) Marathon

Club or **Karen Country Club** in March, and is also a popular event on the social calendar. Polo was introduced in Kenya at the beginning of the 20th century by officers of the King's Africa Rifles. It is still very popular and there are several clubs across the country, including the **Nairobi Polo Club** which celebrated its centenary in 2008. A popular Sunday excursion is the weekly horse race meetings at Nairobi's **Ngong Racecourse**. With three imposing grandstands, the turf course – laid out in the 1950s – also has a golf course at its centre. It is an enjoyable area with plenty of family entertainment, food stalls and a restaurant.

LEWA (SAFARICOM) MARATHON

Usually held in June, Kenya is host to one of the toughest and most unusual marathons in the world. The 42-km (26-mile) long Lewa (Safaricom) Marathon, which is open to international participants, is the only marathon in the world to run through a region inhabited by wildlife. It has become a hugely popular event and was conceived by the charity **Tusk Trust** in 1999. All funds raised by runners through sponsorship go towards various wildlife conservation projects in the Lewa–Il Ngwesi area. The event is now also sponsored by cell phone giant Safaricom.

The course is along dirt roads on the 251-sq-km (97-sq-mile) **Lewa Wildlife Conservancy** on Laikipia Plateau. This lies at an altitude of 1,670 m (5,500 ft) and is set in stunning scenery in the shadow of Mount Kenya. Lewa is home to all the Big Five and runners are very likely to encounter substantial numbers of rhino, elephant and plains game. To enhance the safety of the event, the course is patrolled by helicopters and armed rangers. Both the full and half marathons are open to runners of all abilities from walkers and fun runners to amateur athletes and international professionals. The event now attracts some 1,000 participants from over 20 countries. There is the added excitement of taking part with Kenya's famous long distance athletic superstars (*see p293*).

HEALTH AND WELLNESS

From a fitness course on the coast to a chilled-out yoga safari, Kenya's spa and wellness tourism is expanding fast and the country's scenic natural habitat is an ideal place to recharge. Many upmarket lodges and coastal resorts now have spas offering massages, scrubs, wraps, water treatments, facials, baths, manicures and pedicures and other beauty treatments. As in southern Africa, the term spafari is beginning to feature on tourists' itineraries. There are also a number of specialist operators offering fitness and yoga programmes. Based at Baraka House in Watamu,

Kenya's Maurice Ouma waits for a delivery

Wildfitness organises holidays on the beach combined with imaginative outdoor activities such as a 3-km (2-mile) swim across Mida Creek and a 6-km (4-mile) jog through Arabuko-Sokoke forest. **Chemoset Yoga** offers tailor-made mobile tented safaris in reserves such as Aberdare National Park, Masai Mara Game Reserve and Meru National Park that are accompanied by yoga and Pilates instructors. **Fatuma's Tower**, located in Lamu, is a popular yoga retreat, while **Shaanti Holistic Health Retreat** based on Diani Beach offers outdoor bubble baths, yoga, massages and a good variety of meditation facilities.

DIRECTORY

CULTURAL EXPERIENCES

Marich Pass Field Studies Centre
Kapenguria, West Pokot.
www.gg.rhul.ac.uk/
MarichPass

Ngomongo Village Park
Shanzu, Mombasa.
Tel 0718 939434.
www.ngomongo.com

HIKING AND CLIMBING

Mount Kenya Guides and Porters Safari Club
PO Box 128, Naro Moru.
Tel 020 3524393. www.
mtkenyaguides.com

Mountain Club of Kenya
Wilson Airport, Nairobi.
www.mck.or.ke

CAMEL TREKKING

Desert Rose
PO Box 76677,
Nairobi 00508.
Tel 020 3864831.
www.desertrosekenya.
com

Wild Frontiers
PO Box 24696, Nairobi.
Tel 020 884258.
www.prideofsafaris.com

Yare Safaris
PO Box 20600. 281
Maralal. **Tel** 0722 895126.

BIRD-WATCHING

Nature Kenya
www.naturekenya.org

HORSE RIDING

Horseback in Kenya
El Karama Ranch, Laikipia
Plateau. **Tel** 0727 532091.
www.horsebackinkenya.
com

Offbeat Safaris
PO Box 1146,
Nanyuki 10400.
www.offbeatsafaris.com

Safaris Unlimited
PO Box 24181,
Karen 00502, Nairobi.
Tel 020 8890435.
www.safarisunlimited.
com

BALLOONING

Adventures Aloft
Fig Tree Camp, Maasai
Mara. **Tel** 050 22131.
www.madahotels.com

Transworld Safaris
Former Agip House, Haile
Selassie Ave, PO Box
44690. Nairobi 00100.
City Map 1 C5.
Tel 020 4451620.

GOLF

Kenya Golf Safaris
PO Box 20146. Nairobi.
Tel 020 2710825. www.
kenya-golf-safaris.com

Kenya Golf Union
www.kgu.or.ke

WATER SPORTS

Kite Surf Kenya
Galu Kinondo,
Diani Beach.
Tel 0733 787336.
www.kitekenya.com

Prosurf Extreme
Nyali Beach Hotel,
Nyali, Mombasa.
Tel 0733 622882.
www.prosurfkenya.com

DIVING AND SNORKELLING

Blue Fin Diving
Tel 0722 261242.
www.bluefindiving.com

Diani Marine
PO Box 340, Ukunda.
Tel 040 3300213.
www.dianimarine.com

Diving the Crab
PO Box 5011, Diani Beach.
Tel 0722 990172.
www.divingthecrab.com

BOATING

Savage Wilderness Safaris
PO Box 1000. Sarit Centre
00606, Nairobi.
Tel 0733 735508.
www.whitewaterkenya.
com

Tamarind Dhow
Tamarind Restaurant jetty,
Silo Rd, Nyali, Mombasa.
Tel 041 474600.
www.tamarinddhow.com

Wasini Island
Kisite-Mpunguti Park.
Tel 040 3203154.
www.wasini.com

FISHING

Hemingway's Fishing Centre
Watamu.
Tel 042 2332052.
www.hemingways.co.ke

Pemba Channel Fishing Club
Shimoni.
Tel 0722 205020.
www.pembachannel.com

SPECTATOR SPORTS

Karen Country Club
Karen Rd, Karen, Nairobi.
Tel 020 3882802. www.
karencountryclub.org

Kenyan Rugby Football Union Club
Ngong Rd.
Tel 020 2370360.
www.kenyarfu.com

Muthaiga Country Club
Nguruwe Rd, Langata,
Nairobi. **Tel** 020 2326651.
www.mcc.co.ke

Nairobi Gymkhana Club
Forest Rd, Nairobi.
Tel 020 31150060.

Nairobi Polo Club
Ngong Rd, Nairobi.
Tel 020 31150060.

Ngong Racecourse
Ngong Rd, Nairobi.
Tel 020 3873994.

LEWA (SAFARICOM) MARATHON

Lewa Wildlife Conservancy
Lewa Downs.
Tel 064 31405.
www.lewa.org

Tusk Trust
4 Cheapside House,
High St, Gillingham,
Dorset, SP8 4AA.
Tel 01747 831005.
www.tusk.org

HEALTH AND WELLNESS

Chemoset Yoga
www.chemoset-
adventures.com

Fatuma's Tower
Shela, Lamu.
Tel 0722 277138.
www.fatumastower.com

Shaanti Holistic Health Retreat
Diani Beach.
Tel 020 3202064.
www.shaantiretreat.com

Wildfitness
Baraka House, Watamu.
Tel +44 (0)20 7734 2526
(UK).
www.wildfitness.com

Safari Tours and Bookings

Logo of the popular KATO

Kenya's single most popular outdoor activity for visitors is going on safari. Many tour operators offer multiday safaris and beach holidays in Kenya. There are essentially two choices. The first is to book with a home country tour operator or with one in Kenya and the second is to book a scheduled safari or a tailor-made tour to fit specific interests and budgets. Regardless of the various options available, selection should be based on good service and the operator's ability to understand the specific needs of a safarigoer in Kenya.

BOOKING OVERSEAS

The advantage of booking with an international agent is that a complete package can be easily organised including flights, safaris, hotel stays, even travel insurance and visa information. There are many specialist agents for travel in Africa who are passionately enthusiastic about their work. Some run their own safaris while others use reputable local ground handlers in Kenya. Another advantage is that many companies are bonded, ensuring that the payment the visitor makes is put in a trust fund until after the holiday is completed. So even if the company goes into liquidation at any time, the visitors' money is safe and can be returned. A good place to start looking is on the **African Travel and Tourism Association (ATTA)** website, which has a full list of operators and agents with plenty of experience of Kenya and good consultants. The list includes **Africa Adventure Company**, which

promotes sustainable tourism, and **Adventure Centre** – both in North America – luxury tour operators such as **Abercrombie & Kent**, specialised operators such as **Africa Travel Centre, Acacia Adventure Holidays, ResponsibleTravel.com** and **Tribes Travel** in UK. Other agents include **Go2Africa** and **Rhino Africa** in South Africa, and **Peregrine Adventures** and **Africa Safari Co** in Australia.

BOOKING IN KENYA

There are countless agents and tour operators in Kenya offering standard multiday safaris from Nairobi and Mombasa, with coastal add-ons. Usually, it is cheaper to book through a Kenyan operator than through an international agent. The advantage of booking directly is that more flexible itineraries can be organised, which can be changed at short notice to incorporate seasonal variations, of game movement for instance. Much of the money paid remains in Kenya and helps support its economy.

Valuable information on booking and itinerary planning can be found on the **Kenya Association of Tour Operators (KATO)** and **Kenya Association of Travel Agents (KATA)** websites. Although membership to these does not guarantee that the operator is a good one, it does guarantee that the operator follows a code of conduct and is properly licensed.

Once in Kenya, tourists are often approached in the street by safari company touts offering cheap deals. Avoiding such operators is wise as there is no way of knowing if they will provide value for money or whether they have licensing or insurance. Only established companies recommended by KATO or KATA are reliable. These include **Shoor Safaris, Gametrackers Safaris** and **Let's Go Travel** which specialise in East African safaris, **Spurwing Travel and Tours** and **Gamewatchers Safaris** which offer different kinds of safaris and other reputable operators such as **Suntrek Safaris, Acacia Safaris** and **Bunson Travel**.

TAILOR-MADE SAFARIS

Several companies, both in Kenya and overseas, offer regular scheduled safaris. These usually range from 3 to 10 days, from a short two-night fly- or drive-in package to Masai Mara Game Reserve, to longer trips covering many parks and reserves. On these, people booked together on the same package travel in a group and accommodation is in lodges or camps. Alternatively, all tour operators and agents

A light aircraft picking up visitors from the Masai Mara Game Reserve

offer tailor-made packages designed to suit a couple, a larger family or even a huge group of friends. However, they tend to be more expensive than scheduled safaris because of their exclusivity.

A specialised tour operator can carefully tailor a trip to suit special interests, budgets and preferred style of travel. To accommodate the client's specification, some also offer mobile luxury tented camps. Safari vehicles tend to be small 4WDs rather than the larger minibuses used on scheduled tours. Operators specialising in tailor-made safaris include **Origin Safaris**, which offers ornithological tours, **Basecamp Travel**, which promotes eco-tourism, **Ker Downey Safaris**, **Muthaiga Travel** and **Safari Travel**, which cater to smaller groups and others such as **Desert Rose**, **Richard Bonham Safaris** and **Southern Cross Safaris**, which offer a range of other services.

DIRECTORY

BOOKING OVERSEAS

Abercrombie and Kent
St George's House, Ambrose St, Cheltenham, Gloucestershire, GL50 3LG. *Tel 012 42547700.* www. abercrombiekent.com

Acacia Adventure Holidays
23 Craven Terrace, Lancaster Gate, London, W2 3QH. *Tel 0207 7064700.* www.acacia-africa.com

Adventure Centre
1311 63rd St, Suite 200, Emeryville, CA 94608. *Tel 0510 6541879.* www. adventurecenter.com

Africa Adventure Company
5353 North Federal Highway, Suite 300, Fort Lauderdale, FL 33308. *Tel 954 4918877.* www. africa-adventure.com

Africa Safari Co
Office 1, Commercial Suites, Illawong Shopping Village, 273 Fowler Rd, Illawong, NSW 2234. *Tel 02 95414199.* www. africasafarico.com.au

African Travel and Tourism Association (ATTA)
Mailbox 334, 56 Gloucester Rd, London, SW7 4UB. *Tel 020 79374408.* www.atta.co.uk

Africa Travel Centre
New Premier House, 150 Southampton Row, London WC1B 5AL. *Tel 0845 4501520.* www.africatravel.co.uk

Go2Africa
3rd Floor, Longkloof Studios, Darters Rd, Cape Town 8001. *Tel 021 4814900.* www.go2africa.com

Peregrine Adventures
380 Lonsdale St, Melbourne. *Tel 08601 4444.* www.peregrine adventures.com

ResponsibleTravel.com
6 Old Steine, Brighton BN1 1EJ. *Tel 01273 600030.*

Rhino Africa
81 St John's St, Cape Town 8001. *Tel 021 4692600.* www.rhinoafrica.com

Tribes Travel
12 The Business Centre, Earl Soham, Woodbridge, Suffolk IP13 7SA. *Tel 01728 685971.* www.tribes.co.uk

BOOKING IN KENYA

Acacia Safaris
College House, 4th Floor, University Way, Koinange St, Nairobi. **City Map** 1 B2. *Tel 020 341997.* www.acaciasafaris.co.ke

Bunson Travel
Southern House, Moi Ave, Mombasa. **City Map** 1 C3. *Tel 041 2311331.* www.bunsonkenya.com

Gametrackers Safaris
5th Floor, Nginyo Towers, Koinange St, Nairobi. **City Map** 1 B3. *Tel 020 2222703.* www. gametrackersafaris

Gamewatchers Safaris
PO Box 388-00621, Village Market, Nairobi. *Tel 020 7123129.* www.porini.com

Kenya Association of Tour Operators (KATO)
Longonot Rd, Upper Hill, Nairobi. *Tel 020 2713348.* www.katokenya.org

Kenya Association of Travel Agents (KATA)
Longonot Rd, Upper Hill, Nairobi. *Tel 020 2731475.* www.katakenya.org

Let's Go Travel
ABC Place, Waiyaki Way, Westlands. **City Map** 1 C3. *Tel 020 4447151.* www.uniglobelets gotravel.com

Shoor Safaris
Corner Plaza, Parklands Rd, Nairobi. *Tel 020 3745690.* www.shoortravel.com

Spurwing Travel and Tours
326 Dagoretti Rd, Karen, Nairobi. *Tel 020 3884412.* www.spurwing kenya.com

Suntrek Safaris
Safari Centre, Waiyaki Way, Nairobi. *Tel 020 4442982.* www.suntreksafaris.com

TAILOR-MADE SAFARIS

Basecamp Travel
Ole Odume Rd, Nairobi. *Tel 020 3877490.* www. basecampexplorer.com

Desert Rose
PO Box 76677-00508, Nairobi. *Tel 020 3864831.* www. desertrosekenya.com

Ker Downey Safaris
Ndalat Rd and Langata Rd Junction, Karen, Nairobi. *Tel 020 8890725.* www. kerdowneysafaris.co.ke

Muthaiga Travel
Muthaiga Shopping Centre, Limuru Rd, Nairobi. *Tel 020 2489985.* www.supersafari.com

Origins Safaris
5th Floor, Landmark Plaza, Argwings Khodek Rd, Nairobi. *Tel 020 2042695.* www.originsafaris.info

Richard Bonham Safaris
PO Box 24133, Nairobi 00502. *Tel 0720 737987.* www. bonhamsafaris.com

Safari Travel
2nd Avenue, Parklands, Nairobi. *Tel 020 3747276.* www.safaritravel.biz

Southern Cross Safaris
Symbion House, Karen Rd, Karen, Nairobi. *Tel 020 8070311.* www. southerncrosskenya.com

SURVIVAL GUIDE

PRACTICAL INFORMATION

Thanks to its unparalleled natural beauty, abundant wildlife and rich cultural tapestry, Kenya attracts a growing number of visitors each year. The country's tourism infrastructure falls into two extremes. Kenya's safari industry and coastal areas are booming with plenty of good accommodation, efficient tour operators and a range of outdoor activities to choose from. However, rural Kenya and the more remote regions in the north of the country suffer from bad roads, lack of quality accommodation and poor transport links.

Nevertheless, with a little advanced planning, Kenya can be explored relatively easily. Tour operators are particularly useful for making ground arrangements and internal air transport is good. Adventurous travellers have the option of getting around by public transport, although a 4WD is needed to get the most out of the national parks and game reserves. There are plenty of affordable safaris on offer from Nairobi and the various coastal resorts, and most visitors combine game viewing with some downtime at the beach.

Hikers on a trail as clouds gather above, Shimba Hills National Reserve

WHEN TO GO

Located on the equator, Kenya experiences subtropical temperatures in the coastal zone and more temperate conditions inland *(see pp40–41)*, with little variation over the year. There are generally two rainy seasons in Kenya, with the rain arriving in short, sharp thunderstorms in the afternoons. The longer rainy spell lasts from March to May and the shorter one from November to December, with two long intervening dry seasons. The long rains may hamper travel through parks as unpaved tracks can become impassable. Constant high temperatures and humidity on the coast are tamed by regular daytime breezes, though it can be sultry at night. The northern region features a typical desert climate with low rainfall and excessive heat. Temperatures are lowest in the Central

Highlands, where June to September is the coolest and cloudiest period. The western Rift Valley and Lake Victoria region receive the most rainfall and there is no real dry season as such, but rain seldom continues over long periods. Wildlife can be seen at all times of year, but the annual migration of wildebeest *(see pp124–5)* and other wildlife from the Masai Mara Game Reserve and Tanzania's Serengeti takes place only between June and September.

WHAT TO TAKE

On safari, comfortable cotton clothes in muted colours are most suitable although it is not necessary to wear the old-fashioned safari suits still sold in Nairobi. Evenings and early mornings can be chilly, so it is best to wear layers of clothing to stay warm. Beachgoers must take sunblock, sunglasses

and a wide-brimmed hat. Campers will need a sleeping bag, towel and flashlight. Long sleeves and trousers are advised to avoid mosquito bites. Specialised clothing is needed to climb Mount Kenya. Provisions can also be bought locally, but it is essential to carry a medical first aid kit if visiting remote areas.

VISA AND PASSPORTS

Passports must be valid for at least 6 months after the expected date of departure from Kenya. A visa is required from almost all nationalities, and these are available from Kenyan embassies or on arrival at all land borders and airports. Visitors may need to show a return ticket or proof of funds to buy one. They can use euros, British pounds and US dollars to pay for visas on arrival. The visa fee for adults is US$50, and visas for children under 16 are US$25. A transit visa is valid for 7 days; a standard single-entry visa is valid for 3 months and can be extended to six months by the **Kenya Immigration Department** once in the country. A multientry visa lasts 12 months but can only be applied for through embassies (not at entry points) and is only available to UK, US and Canadian passport holders. Visitors travelling to Tanzania and Uganda and returning to Kenya do not require a multientry visa. Most visitors need a visa for each country and all standard single-entry visas are valid for up to 3 months. However, if travelling from one country to another and returning to the original country within 3 months, visitors need not get another visa.

IMMUNISATIONS

Immigration officials will ask for proof of a yellow fever immunisation on arrival if you are coming from an infected region, including Tanzania. While other immunisations are not compulsory for Kenya, the following are recommended: hepatitis A, polio, typhoid and tetanus. The hepatitis B vaccine is essential for minors and healthcare workers.

VISITOR INFORMATION

The head office of the **Kenya Tourist Board (KTB)** in Nairobi and its offices overseas can provide a few general leaflets on Kenya. However, the KTB website is very comprehensive. While Kenya itself has very few tourist information offices, tour operators can provide local information, although travellers should remember that this advice may be biased if they are in the business of selling tours or accommodation. **Kenya Wildlife Service (KWS)** has an office at the entrance of Nairobi National Park *(see pp162–5)* and can provide information on national parks and camping fees and also issues and loads smart cards

A local waving his hand in greeting, Langoni Road, Mombasa

(see p69) for park entry. The website of the **Kenya Association of Tour Operators** is a good source of information on booking a safari.

OPENING HOURS

In larger towns, business hours are usually from 8.30am to 5pm, Monday to Friday, while shops stay open from 8am to 6pm from Monday to Saturday. Offices usually stay closed on Saturdays. Muslim-owned establishments may close all day on Friday or at least in the afternoons. In Mombasa, business hours are longer, but many shops and establishments close for a siesta from 2 to 4pm. In rural areas, small shops can have erratic opening hours. Most museums, galleries and curio markets stay open from 9am to 6pm daily. Outdoor attractions, such as parks and reserves, stay open from sunrise to sunset.

Logo, Kenya
Wildlife Service

ETIQUETTE

In general, Kenyans are exceptionally polite and helpful. Visitors will soon get used to hearing the Swahili words *jambo* (hello) and *hakuna matata* (no worries). It is important to respect local customs by not taking photographs of people without their approval, dressing fairly conservatively in Muslim areas and being sensitive to religious practices. It is illegal in Kenya to smoke in public places and for women to go topless on the beach. If visiting one of the cultural centres, a Maasai village for example, it is gracious to interact with the hosts and ask for permission if you want to take photographs. Kenya has a problem with begging, especially among children, but a better way of helping is to make a donation to a charity or school.

TIPPING

Tipping is not mandatory in Kenya but is customary for good service. Generally 10 per cent of a restaurant bill is considered normal, although in upmarket restaurants a service charge may already be added to the bill. Some lodges and resorts have boxes for tips, which are shared by the service staff. It is customary to tip safari guides and drivers; about US$10 a day for both is sufficient. Visitors must bear in mind that excessive tipping can make it difficult for the next customer. Taxi drivers generally do not need tipping and a flat fare is agreed upon before setting off.

A customer making a cash payment, Ol Tukai Lodge bar

Trekking with Samburu tribe in isolated wilderness, Northern Kenya

WOMEN TRAVELLERS

Women travellers should take normal precautions in Kenya such as avoiding secluded places, taking taxis after dark and locking hotel rooms. They may receive unsolicited attention from men, especially on the coast and smaller towns. This is best dealt with by being assertive. Women should dress conservatively in Muslim areas, although swimwear is fine on the beach.

DISABLED TRAVELLERS

Kenya, like many other African countries, has few specific facilities for the disabled. There are no provisions for the disabled on public transport. Having said that, a specialist tour operator will be able to make arrangements for wheelchair-bound travellers. Some hotels have easily accessible ground floor rooms. Tented camps are also a good option and safaris should not pose too many problems. Tour operators who cater to the disabled include Southern Cross Safaris *(see p405)*, **Go Africa Safaris and Travel** and **Victoria Safaris**. These operators have specially adapted vehicles and suitable accommodation for those with special needs.

TRAVELLING WITH CHILDREN

Kenya makes a good family destination. Seeing their first animal in the wild is exciting for children, and the beach with its warm, shallow sea and rock pools is ideal. Aside from the wildlife parks and reserves, there are a number of wildlife sanctuaries in Nairobi and along the coast where children can experience closer encounters with animals. However, on long, hot drives younger kids may get bored and irritable if there is no game activity, so bring additional items to keep them occupied and consider a tour operator who specialises in family safaris. In some cases, children under five are not permitted on safaris. Pay attention to the greater risk they run of getting heat exhaustion or diarrhoea and make sure that they drink plenty of water and wear high-factor sunscreen. Also consult a doctor about precautions to take when travelling with youngsters in a malarial zone. Items such as disposable nappies, ready-made puréed food and milk formula are available in the cities, but they are expensive, so consider bringing an adequate supply to last the trip. Most hotel accommodation has family or adjoining rooms and can provide high chairs for dining, cots and, in some cases, babysitting services if required. Away from the popular destinations, such facilities are not easily available.

Children taking a windsurfing lesson at Watamu Beach

LANGUAGE

Although there are many indigenous languages spoken in Kenya, almost everyone speaks English and Swahili, locally known as KiSwahili, the official language of Kenya. Only in the remote areas do people speak in their native tongue. Swahili was written down by the colonialists, so words are pronounced just as they are spelt, and as in any country, a few words spoken in the local language is much appreciated.

PHOTOGRAPHY

Photographing wildlife in Kenya is very rewarding, but a long lens is needed to get close-up shots of animals. Light in the middle of the day is harsh and is better in the early mornings and late afternoons, which coincide with the best times for game viewing. When photographing individuals or a crowd in a market or village, always ask for permission. In some cases, a payment is expected for taking photographs, but bargain for a better price. In cultural villages and other tourist attractions, a fee for photography is included in the entry fee. Digital cameras can be recharged in hotels but an adapter may be required. Batteries are expensive and not easily available in remote areas. It is forbidden to take photographs of government and military buildings.

ELECTRICAL SUPPLY

The standard voltage is 220-240 volts AC and square three-pin British-style plugs and sockets are used. For two-pin and other appliances a travel adapter is needed. Remote lodges and camps often rely on generators which are switched on for a fixed duration.

Standard switch panel

TIME

Kenya is 3 hours ahead of Greenwich Mean Time (GMT), 8 hours ahead of United States Eastern Standard Time and 6 hours behind Australia's Western Standard Time. As Kenya sits on the equator, there is very little change in the time for sunrise and sunset throughout the year (*see pp38–9*), usually between 6 and 7am and 6 and 7pm respectively.

CONVERSION CHART

Imperial to Metric
1 inch = 2.54 centimetres
1 foot = 30 centimetres
1 mile = 1.6 kilometres
1 ounce = 28 grams
1 pound = 454 grams
1 US pint = 0.473 litre
1 US quart = 0.947 litre
1 US gallon = 3.8 litres
Metric to Imperial
1 centimetre = 0.4 inch
1 metre = 3 feet 3 inches
1 kilometre = 0.6 mile
1 gram = 0.04 ounce
1 kilogram = 2.2 pounds
1 litre = 1.1 US quarts

DIRECTORY

VISAS AND PASSPORTS

Kenya Immigration Department
Nyayo House, Kenyatta Ave, Nairobi. **City Map** 1 B4. *Tel* 020 222022. www.immigration.go.ke

EMBASSIES

Australia
Tel 254 20 427 7100.
www.kenya.embassy.gov.au

Canada
Tel 254 20 3663000.
www.canadainternational.gc.ca/kenya

New Zealand
www.nzembassy.com

UK
Tel 254 20 2844000.
www.ukinkenya.fco.gov.uk

USA
Tel 254 20 3636000.
www.nairobi.usembassy.gov

VISITOR INFORMATION

Kenya Association of Tour Operators
Tel 020 2713348.
www.katokenya.org

Kenya Tourist Board
Kenya-Re Towers, Ragati Rd, Upper Hill, Nairobi.
Tel 020 2711262.
www.magicalkenya.com

Kenya Tourist Board in the US
www.magicalkenya.com

Kenya Tourist Board in the UK
www.magicalkenya.com

Kenya Wildlife Service
Nairobi National Park, Langata Rd, Nairobi.
Tel 020 6000800.
www.kws.go.ke

DISABLED TRAVELLERS

Go Africa Safaris and Travel
Tel 020 2353883.
www.go-africa-safaris.com

Victoria Safaris
City Map 2 D4. Cargen House, Harambee Avenue, Nairobi.
Tel 020 2252015.
www.victoriasafaris.com

Using a tele lens to shoot wildlife, Amboseli National Park

Personal Health

A number of tropical diseases are present in Kenya, but with immunisations and precautions, the risk of contracting these is fairly remote. The most serious health risk comes from malaria, against which protection is essential. More common conditions include upset stomachs, heat and sun exposure and bites and stings, all of which are easily treated. Nairobi and the coast have excellent hospitals, but facilities in remote areas are few and may be substandard. Treatment is expensive, so comprehensive travel insurance is needed, which should include medical repatriation. In the event of being hospitalised, check that the insurer is satisfied with hospital standards.

MEDICAL MATTERS

It is advisable to visit a doctor 6 weeks before departure to Kenya to get the necessary immunisations *(see p409)* and to discuss anti-malaria medication. For a small fee, **MASTA (Medical Advisory for Travellers Abroad)** provides an up-to-date health brief for Kenya. Items to take include insect repellent and sunscreen. Contact lens wearers need to bring enough solution and may want to take a pair of glasses as dust can be a problem on safari. If going off the beaten track, carrying a basic medical kit is recommended. In Kenya, HIV/AIDS rates are alarmingly high, so exercise caution in sexual matters and ensure that instruments are uninfected during medical procedures.

Antimalarial drugs

MALARIA

Except at extreme altitudes, malaria is widespread in Kenya and can be fatal within 24 hours of contracting it. It is transmitted by mosquitoes, which are particularly active after dark. A course of anti-malarial drugs should be started before arrival in Kenya and continued for the prescribed length of time after returning home. There is as yet no vaccine against malaria. Avoid getting bitten by mosquitoes by using insect repellent, covering exposed flesh and sleeping in an air conditioned room or under a fan and mosquito net. Symptoms, like lethargy, high fever and headaches, even after arriving back home, should be reported to a doctor immediately.

BITES AND STINGS

Mosquitoes can carry other diseases as well as malaria, and insect repellent should be applied every few hours throughout the day to avoid bites and stings. Use antiseptic and antihistamine creams on bites to stop them from itching and becoming infected.

Bites from dogs and monkeys can carry rabies and must therefore receive treatment immediately. Visitors travelling deep in the bush need to be wary of ticks and tsetse flies. For those who enjoy walking barefeet, jiggers and sandflies are the main hazard, as they can easily become embedded between the toes. On safari, sturdy shoes are necessary to avoid snake and scorpion bites, although these are rare occurrences. Snakes attack when they feel threatened, so when encountering a snake, it is best to stay put until it slithers away.

MEDICAL FACILITIES

Nairobi and the coast are well served with public and private hospitals, clinics and pharmacies. **Nairobi Hospital** is well known for its treatment of tropical diseases and has the best surgeon and specialist facilities in East Africa, with a 24-hour pharmacy. However, rural areas have more basic clinics and those who fall ill should try to reach the cities for medical treatment. It is best to take out medical insurance – covering death, dismemberment and repatriation – before travelling to Kenya. All costs of treatment are payable up front and receipts are required for medical insurance claims. City pharmacies stock a fairly good range of items, although brand names may be unfamiliar and expiry dates need to be checked. Visitors who are on regular medication should come prepared with enough for their stay.

Flying Doctors Service, providing medical support in remote areas

Freshwater streams and pools often carry water-borne diseases

DIRECTORY

EMERGENCIES

Ambulance
Tel 999.

MEDICAL MATTERS

MASTA (Medical Advisory for Travellers Abroad)
www.masta-travel-health.com

MEDICAL FACILITIES

Flying Doctors Service
AMREF Headquarters, Langata Rd, Nairobi. *Tel* 020 315454.
www.amref.org/flying-doctors

Nairobi Hospital
Argwings Kodhek Rd, Nairobi.
Tel 020 2845000.
www.nairobihospital.org

Kenya has a **Flying Doctors Service** run by the African Medical and Research Foundation (AMREF), which provides air ambulances and medical evacuations from remote destinations to hospitals, as well as medical repatriation to other countries. Visitors can take out a temporary subscription for the service, which covers most of East Africa and is worth considering by those who are not on an organised tour and going off the beaten track.

FOOD AND WATER

Most people get a bout of traveller's diarrhoea briefly when they arrive in a new country while their bodies adapt to the food and water and local conditions. There are a number of basic safeguards that help reduce the chances of succumbing to diarrhoea and other food- and water-borne diseases, such as typhoid and dysentery. These include washing your hands before a meal, ensuring that your food is prepared and cooked hygenically and avoiding salads and fruit washed in local water. It is best to stick to bottled water and not to take ice in drinks. Tea and coffee are safe to drink as the water is boiled, but unpasteurised milk and other dairy products should be avoided. Street food is not all risky provided it is fresh and cooked thoroughly and has not been standing around for a while covered in flies. The same can be said for buffets in hotel restaurants. Cooked foods that have been left at room temperature are particularly hazardous.

OUTDOOR HAZARDS

Being on the beach or on safari means a lot of time is spent outdoors. The sun is strong all year round, so hats and high-factor sunscreen are both indispensable. Ensure that children are lathered up regularly when they go swimming and snorkelling.

Beware of coral-cut infections, which can be nasty. Divers and snorkellers should wear plastic shoes. Swimming in the ocean or swimming pools poses no threat. However, drinking from or swimming in freshwater lakes and ponds can be hazardous owing to water-borne diseases such as bilharzia *(Schistosomiasis)*, which is transmitted by tiny worms in stagnant water. Lake Victoria and many smaller lakes are infected with this.

Most visitors to Mount Kenya choose a slow ascent to avoid altitude sickness. For those coming up from the coast, a couple of days acclimatising at over 1,000 m (3,200 ft) is necessary. Dress for the extreme cold to avoid developing hypothermia.

Hikers wearing hats to escape the scorching sun, Shimba Hills

Personal Security

Kenya has its fair share of security problems and is notorious for high rates of robbery, petty theft and more serious crimes such as armed carjacking and highway banditry. Tourists are easy targets, so they should remain vigilant throughout their stay. However, by taking sensible precautions, most visitors can have a safe and crime-free visit. On an organised tour, the risks are reduced considerably. In general, security is improving in the capital and the popular coastal tourist destinations. In Nairobi, the city centre is monitored by an increased police presence and there is an additional force of tourist police on the coast.

The crowded Mckinnon Market in Mombasa keeps up a frenetic pace

PERSONAL SAFETY

The golden rule is not to flash expensive items and to leave anything of monetary or sentimental value at home. Petty crime, bag snatching, mugging and pick-pocketing, can occur, but most are opportunist crimes. Money and passport are best kept in a slim money belt concealed beneath clothes. Visitors can make use of hotel safes to deposit cash or costly items. Avoid walking around wearing expensive jewellery, watches, or displaying phones and cameras. Day-packs or backpacks have been known to be slashed in crowded areas, so it is best to only take out exactly what you need and carry bags in front of you. It is not safe, specially for women, to walk alone or anywhere after dark, including on the beach.

Keeping bags in front

Follow local advice about what areas to avoid and be vigilant about the people around you. Hotel doors must be locked as noisy fans or air conditioning can provide cover for thieves. If travelling by public transport, especially buses and *matatus*, guard possessions fiercely and never accept food or drink from strangers as they may be drugged. Visitors should be cautious of con men posing as tour operators and ignore people who come up on the street offering their services.

INFORMATION

Located at the Kenya Wildlife Service (*see p411*) headquarters in Nairobi, at the entrance to Nairobi National Park, is the office of the **Safety and Communication Centre**. It is run by Kenya Tourism Federation, a body of tour operators, travel agents, hoteliers and airlines. The staff at this centre can provide information about issues of concern to visitors like road conditions, security, health and travel advisories for the various regions of the country. In the event of a security incident involving visitors to Kenya, the centre can arrange for assistance. It also operates a 24-hour control room and tourist helpline manned by well-trained staff, and has an excellent infrastructure in place, including a countrywide communications radio system. The centre works closely with KWS, the police and the Flying Doctors (*see p413*).

TRAVEL INSURANCE

It is essential to take out a comprehensive travel insurance policy when visiting Kenya. Insurance policies should cover all health requirements, such as treatment for injuries and illnesses, plus medical repatriation to the home country in case of an emergency, as well as provision for theft and loss of luggage. If unfortunate to be a victim of a crime, visitors must file a police report to make a travel insurance claim. The **Kenya Police** website lists all police stations and telephone numbers. Visitors can

Marine police keeping vigil along the coast, Lamu town

Heavy traffic on Digo Road, Mombasa

also contact the helpful tourist police, a division of the regular police that mainly patrols the coastal resorts.

ON THE ROAD

The number of road accidents in Kenya used to be alarmingly high, but the situation has improved greatly thanks to legislation in 2004 that has made wearing of seat belts compulsory and governed the road-worthiness of vehicles, speed limits and overcrowding on public transport. Despite these improvements, visitors should exercise caution on the road and not drive too fast as unexpected potholes or domestic animals on the road can cause accidents. To avoid theft from a parked vehicle, do not leave anything on display inside. Expensive looking 4WD are a favourite with carjackers and to avoid any such incident, keep windows rolled up and doors locked at all times. It is also not safe to travel late at night. Importantly, if carjacked at gunpoint, it is best not to resist.

Northern Kenya is known for lawlessness and is at its most dangerous near the Sudanese, Ethiopian and Somali borders, where localised incidents of violent cattle rustling, ethnic conflict and armed banditry occur. Take special precautions if travelling by road to this part of the country and always travel in a convoy of vehicles. The Safety and Communications Centre in Nairobi offers visitors useful and up-to-date information and advice on issues pertaining to security in all regions of Kenya.

ON SAFARI

Although incidents of attacks from animals are rare, Kenya's wildlife is exactly that – wild. Many animals are used to being admired by the army of safari vehicles that enter the national parks each day. However, it must never be forgotten that animal behaviour is unpredictable and it pays to have a healthy respect for wildlife. Use only signposted tracks or ones marked on official maps. Do not get out of a vehicle except in designated areas and never harass or feed the animals or get too close to them. Hippos are said to be among the most dangerous animals in Africa and they attack and trample when threatened or when their access to water is blocked. Buffalo and elephant are known to charge and attack, usually in self-defence when they are startled. Rhinos may charge when a vehicle blocks sight of their young. If camping in the wild, food should always be locked away from baboons and hyenas in vehicles and never left in tents. It is preferable not to leave your tent or *banda* during the night. When walking or hiking, it is best to wear sturdy boots and stick to existing paths or flat ground to avoid snakes, and carry a flashlight if it is necessary to move around the bush at night.

Visitors on safari maintaining safe distance from a grazing rhino

Banking and Currency

Banks and bureaux de change are plentiful in urban Kenya. Money can be obtained on arrival, as facilities at Nairobi and Mombasa airports stay open to meet all arriving flights. Small towns have at least one bank that will make foreign transactions, although service is often slow. Hotels, lodges and camps change money for their guests, but the exchange rate may not be competitive. US dollars are the easiest to change, and are accepted by Kenya Wildlife Service and tour operators. Owing to previous problems of fraud, many places do not take pre-2000 dollar bills. British pounds and euros are also accepted. All three currencies are used to pay for visas on arrival.

BANKS AND BUREAUX DE CHANGE

There are branches of **Barclays Bank**, **Kenya Commercial Bank** and **Standard Chartered Bank** across the country, and branch locators can be found on their websites. Banking hours are 8.30am to 3pm on weekdays and 8.30 to 11am on Saturdays. In Mombasa and on the coast, some banks open and close half an hour earlier. In small towns, banks may not open on Saturdays, or open only on one Saturday at the end of the month. Bureaux de change, also known as Forex (foreign exchange bureaus), have longer opening hours, and some, located in the cities and main tourist spots, also open on Sundays. At Nairobi's Jomo Kenyatta International Airport, banks are open 24 hours. Commission is usually charged on changing traveller's cheques and cash. Where commission is not charged, exchange rates are lower and travellers may want to weigh their options. When changing US dollars, lower denomination bills attract a lower exchange rate than higher denomination bills. Passports must always be presented when changing money and visitors should ensure that they get a competitive rate of exchange. The Kenyan shilling is fully convertible, so it can be taken both in and out of the country. On departure, excess currency need not be changed into US dollars or spent at the airport. There is no restriction on the amount of foreign currency that visitors can take into Kenya.

ATMs, a facility provided by most of the banks in the country

ATMS

Almost all banks now have ATMs that accept MasterCard, Visa, American Express, Cirrus and Diner's. Independent ATMs are also available at places such as petrol stations and modern shopping malls in Nairobi and on the coast. Withdrawals from ATMs offer the most competitive rate of exchange with no commission, but the account holder's bank at home may charge a fee for withdrawing cash from a foreign ATM and there may be a daily limit. Be vigilant if making a withdrawal from an ATM on the street.

TRAVELLER'S CHEQUES

It is possible to exchange traveller's cheques for Kenyan shillings, and in some cases US dollars, but this attracts a commission of 2 to 5 per cent, which is often lower in the bureaux de change than in the banks. Small town banks are less experienced with processing traveller's cheques, so the process can be painfully slow.

CREDIT CARDS

Credit cards are widely accepted to pay for accommodation, safaris and curios in upmarket shops. However, they are not taken in budget hotels, local markets and small shops, and few restaurants accept them. A 2 to 5 per cent commission is often added to a credit card purchase, so in some instances it is cheaper to pay in cash.

CURRENCY

The currency in Kenya is the Kenyan shilling. It is based on the decimal system, with one shilling comprising 100 cents. It is indicated either by the symbol KSh or by the /= notation after the amount, 1,000/= for instance. It is known locally as *bob*. While some hotels, tour operators and airlines often quote rates in US dollars, Kenyan shillings can also be used for paying. Kenyan shillings are needed in shops, markets and restaurants. It is best to keep the smaller bills for short taxi rides, drinks and inexpensive roadside curios.

The entrance to Barclays Bank at Voi

Coins

Kenyan coins come in denominations of 50 c (50 cents) and 1, 5, 10, 20 and 40 KSh. Jomo Kenyatta's head graces one side of the coin and Kenya's coat of arms the other. The word Harambee, *Swahili for unity, appears in the ribbon of the coat of arms.*

50 c

1 KSh

5 KSh

10 KSh

20 KSh

40 KSh

DIRECTORY

BANKS AND BUREAUX DE CHANGE

Barclays Bank
www.barclays.com

Kenya Commercial Bank
www.kcbbankgroup.com

Standard Chartered Bank
www.standardchartered.com

Banknotes

Kenyan bank notes come in denominations of 50, 100, 200, 500, and 1,000 KSh. After Kenya's independence, the face of its first president, Jomo Kenyatta, appeared on all notes and coins. In 1980, it was replaced by the face of the succeeding president, Daniel arap Moi. In 2005, a new series of notes and coins came out with Kenyatta's portrait restored.

50 KSh

100 KSh

200 KSh

500 KSh

1,000 KSh

Communications and Media

Kenya's communication facilities continue to improve in leaps and bounds and are, on the whole, modern and up-to-date. Mobile phones in particular are hugely popular with Kenyans, and in some cases many people and businesses have abandoned the landline network in favour of cell phones. Coverage, however, is restricted to

A typical postbox

urban areas, and is not usually available in the national parks, although this is improving all the time. Internet access is easily found in cities and tourist places, and even the smaller towns usually feature at least one public place for browsing the web. Much of the country is covered by high frequency radio, often used by the more remote lodges, as well as Nairobi's Safety and Communication Centre and the Flying Doctors. Postal services are fairly reliable. There is a well-organised Poste Restante in Nairobi, but it is always better to use a courier service for valuable items.

phone is the cheapest way to stay connected. Alternatively, roaming on international SIM cards is picked up automatically on arrival in Kenya. Visitors should check with Safaricom and Zain that their phone's network is compatible. Visitors need to check their insurance policy in case their phone gets stolen, and keep their network operator's helpline handy for emergencies. Depending on the model of the phone, an adapter may be needed for the charger.

Cell phone coverage is good in urban areas, on the coast, along the Nairobi–Mombasa Highway and on the loop around Mount Kenya. However, reception is limited in the remote areas and in reserves.

INTERNET

Most hotels and lodges in Nairobi and on the coast provide Internet access to their guests, and Wi-Fi is beginning to feature in public places including Nairobi's Jomo Kenyatta International Airport. Internet cafés are prolific and often double up as public phone and fax shops, and can

Telkom Kenya's public phones, a common sight in urban areas

TELEPHONES

Local and international calls can be made from public pay phones, operated by **Telkom Kenya**, that are housed in yellow or red booths on the street or in post offices. These accept coins or phone cards that are available from post offices. Rates are a minimum of 6 KSh per minute for a local call, and considerably more for a call to a cell phone from a landline. An international call costs US$ 0.60 per minute.

Off-peak times are 6pm to 8am on weekdays and all day at weekends. Calls from Kenya to the neighbouring states of Uganda and Tanzania are charged as long-distance calls

and not at international rates. Operator-assisted calls can be made from post offices (for a minimum of 3 minutes). There are also private phone shops in the cities, usually with additional Internet facilities. Most hotels add a hefty premium to phone calls, and it is best to avoid calling from satellite phones in remote lodges as they are very expensive.

CELL PHONES

Kenya has three cell phone providers, of which **Safaricom** alone has over eight million customers and **Zain** runs a rather unique network across borders that is considered to be a world first. Known as One Network, it is a single network with no roaming charges between 12 African countries. Phones can be topped up with local top-up cards, and local call rates are the same across a huge area that stretches from Burkina Faso in western Africa to Zambia in the south. Zain now has a staggering 24 million subscribers across Africa. Recently, the mobile phone network provider **Orange** launched its services in Kenya.

In Kenya, start-up packs with SIM cards and top-up cards for Safaricom and Zain are available everywhere, from shops to street stalls. Using a Kenyan SIM card in a cell

DIALING CODES

- To make a direct long-distance call, dial the area code, then the local number. Useful area codes include Nairobi 020, Mombasa 041, Voi 043, Uganda 007, Tanzania 006.
- To make a long-distance call via an operator dial 900, then follow the procedure given above.
- To make a direct international call, dial 000, then the country code.
- To make an operator-assisted international call, dial 0196.
- To make local calls, use area codes even if in the same area.
- For local operator assistance, dial 900.
- For international directory enquiries, dial 0196.
- For local directory enquiries, dial 991.

Roadside kiosk displaying popular dailies and magazines

vary from upmarket Internet cafés to small shops with just a couple of terminals. Access using regular landlines occasionally gets disconnected. Smaller towns usually have at least one facility that is often used by local students, although the places still using dial-up connections are slow. Internet access is not usually available in the park lodges.

Native flora on some of Kenya's colourful postage stamps

POST AND COURIERS

Postal services are relatively inexpensive and efficient. Run by Posta Kenya, there are post offices in most towns and urban areas. Postboxes are red and blue, and a letter sent via airmail costs 95 KSh. Post to Europe takes about a week to arrive, and about 10 days to Australia and the USA. Parcels need to be wrapped in brown paper and string. This needs to be done at the post office as contents are checked to see if export duty must be paid. Payment is not normally required for curios and souvenirs. Parcels sent by airmail can weigh up to 32 kg (71 lb) and there is a useful cost calculator to all countries on the website of Posta Kenya.

A courier service is recommended to send valuable items home. Most major international companies, such as **Fedex**, **DHL** and **TNT**, are represented

in Kenya. Post office hours are generally 8am to 5pm on weekdays and 9 to noon on Saturdays. Smaller post offices close during lunch hours. **Nairobi Post Office**, located near City Square, has an efficient Post Restante service, and post is held alphabetically.

NEWSPAPERS

The most popular English-language daily newspapers are the *Daily Nation* and the *East African Standard*. Both carry up-to-date news and listings, and the *Daily Nation* in particular has good entertainment and sports listings. The *Kenya Times* is the government-run newspaper, and it tends to have a pro-government bias. The weekly *East African* covers news from Kenya, Uganda and Tanzania. There are also two daily newspapers in Swahili. Day-old copies of newspapers from Europe and USA can be found at Nairobi's leading bookshops and the airport.

DIRECTORY

TELEPHONES

Telkom Kenya
www.telkom.co.ke

CELL PHONES

Orange
www.orange.co.ke

Safaricom
www.safaricom.co.ke

Zain
www.ke.zain.com

POST AND COURIERS

DHL
Tel 020 6925120.
www.dhl.co.ke

Fedex
Tel 020 3907000.
www.fedex.com/ke

Nairobi Post Office
Kenyatta Ave.
City Map 1 B3. *Tel 020 3242000.* **www**.posta.co.ke

TNT
Tel 020 2727382. **www**.tnt.com

TELEVISION AND RADIO

The Kenya Broadcasting Corporation (KBC) has many radio stations that transmit in English and Swahili. Nairobi's Kiss 100 FM station is popular for all kinds of music. KBC's Channel 1 shows sports, news and reruns of US television shows, while Digital Satellite TV is a paid-for channel found in most upmarket hotels.

The distinctive façade of a Posta Kenya office, Malindi

TRAVEL INFORMATION

Kenya is East Africa's air transport hub, so there is no shortage of airlines to choose from. Most people arrive in Nairobi on scheduled flights, but some on preorganised package holidays fly directly from Europe to Mombasa. Domestic flights connect the cities, regional airlines fly from Nairobi to safari destinations in Kenya and small planes ferry people in and out of

Logo of Air Kenya, a domestic carrier

reserves. The train between Nairobi and Mombasa is a slower alternative to flying to the coast. The best way to explore the sanctuaries is on organised safari. Self-drive is a good option on the coast, although roads elsewhere in the country are of varying standards. *Matatus* and buses are not for the timid as they can be driven rather recklessly; nevertheless, they link all the regional centres.

ARRIVING BY AIR

Most European carriers, including **British Airways** and **KLM**, and almost all the Asian, African and Middle Eastern airlines fly to Nairobi, which is 9 hours flying time from London. The national carrier, **Kenya Airways**, has direct links to London, Amsterdam and Paris as well as to destinations in the Middle and Far East, India and Africa. There are no direct flights with North America, however, and airlines fly to Kenya through partnerships with European airlines via London, Frankfurt, Amsterdam or other cities in Europe. Other options for North America visitors include flying through Johannesburg with **South African Airways**, through Dubai with **Emirates**, or through Addis Ababa with **Ethiopian Airlines**.

Owing to the large choice in airlines, air fares to Kenya are generally competitive and good deals can be had by booking well in advance.

INTERNATIONAL ARRIVALS

Nairobi's **Jomo Kenyatta International Airport** handles almost three and a half million passengers annually and there are plans to expand it, and possibly build a second runway. For now, all international departures and arrivals take place in one long building, with duty-free shops, bars, cafés and bookstores and airline lounges. Domestic flights have a separate terminal.

Visas *(see p408)* can be obtained on arrival at immigration before baggage collection and Customs. Visitors boarding connecting flights are directed through the transit procedures. Directly beyond the Customs are desks for car hire, tour operators and hotel bookings, plus bureaux de change and a branch of Barclays Bank with an ATM to exchange or obtain Kenyan shillings. Kenyan currency is required to pay for taxis to the city centre. For visitors

Kenya's flag flying near the Control Tower, Moi International Airport

moving on to safari in northern Tanzania, Nairobi is often the point of departure.

Mombasa's **Moi International Airport** is much smaller but has the same facilities, and banks stay open to meet incoming flights. It receives domestic flights and direct charter flights from Europe carrying people on package holidays to coastal resorts.

A Kenya Airways Airbus A310 rests at Jomo Kenyatta International Airport

Jomo Kenyatta International Airport, Nairobi

GETTING FROM AIRPORTS

Jomo Kenyatta International Airport is 15 km (9 miles) southeast of Nairobi and taxis can be obtained outside the main airport building. Visitors can expect to pay the equivalent of US$20 for a ride to the city centre. There is a public bus, but overcrowding leads to problems of luggage theft. Some hotels can arrange pick-ups but this needs to be organised in advance when booking accommodation.

Moi International Airport is on the mainland 10 km (6 miles) west of Mombasa's city centre. After Customs and in the main concourse, there is a row of shuttle bus companies with published rates that go to all the coastal resorts to the north and south of Mombasa. Regular taxis to the city centre are also available.

Border signpost on the south coast, Shimoni

ARRIVING BY ROAD

Kenya has road borders with Uganda, Ethiopia, Tanzania, Sudan and Somalia. Those most commonly used by visitors to Kenya are the Busia and Malaba borders with Uganda, through which regular daily buses run between Kampala and Nairobi, and the Namanga border with Tanzania, through which daily shuttle bus services operate the 273-km (170-mile) A104. Nairobi is popularly used as a base by tourists on organised safaris to southern reserves

and parks in Kenya as well as to the national reserves in Tanzania's Northern Circuit. Owing to the good shuttle bus links, independent travellers can make their own way between Nairobi and Arusha and organise safari options from each.

There is another border post between Kenya and Tanzania at Lunga Lunga, south of Mombasa, lying on the 518-km (322-mile) route between Dar es Salaam and Mombasa. Here again, daily buses operate between the two cities. Procedures at these land borders are generally very straightforward and visas are available for each country. Travellers in private vehicles are required to produce a Carnet de Passages en Douane (CPD) – a customs document that identifies a driver's motor vehicle – as well as third party insurance and other relevant paperwork to drive between countries. Most car hire companies allow

vehicles to go to Uganda and Tanzania after prior arrangements have been made. To take a Kenyan registered vehicle out of the country, a log book has to be filled out at the border and the registration documents of the vehicle need to be produced.

Border post in Tanzania, the point of entry into Kenya

Regional Air Travel

Flying around Kenya is an alternative to long journeys on bumpy and dusty roads. With over 500 airstrips and dozens of flight routes, it is a relatively safe and fairly affordable way to cover a lot of ground. Kenya Airways flies to major cities in Kenya as well as to neighbouring countries, and a number of airlines with smaller planes run scheduled services between Nairobi and the coast and parks. Charter flights operating out of Nairobi's Wilson Airport ferry small groups of people directly to lodges all over the country. All travellers on internal flights are required to carry their passport. Domestic departure taxes are included in ticket or charter costs.

Visitors disembarking at Lamu Airport on the Northern Coast

DOMESTIC AIRPORTS

The **Kenya Airports Authority (KAA)** oversees the management and administration of the airports and covers passenger services as well as cargo handling and freight services for horticultural and agricultural goods, which are a big export earner for Kenya. Information on all domestic airports can be found on the KAA website. While the bigger passenger airlines operate from Nairobi's Jomo Kenyatta International Airport (see p420), other charter flights and airlines from

Nairobi fly from **Wilson Airport** on Langata Road, 4 km (2 miles) south of the city centre. This is the heart of all private and commercial light aircraft activities in Kenya, and is also the base of the Flying Doctors (see p413) and has a flying school. The airport has an average traffic of 120,000 landings and take-offs annually. There are no central facilities as such, and the individual airlines have offices scattered around the hangars. Each year in October, the Wilson Airport hosts the enormously popular Nairobi

International Air Show (see p38), which features fly-bys, a variety of air acrobatics and plenty of on-the-ground entertainment.

Elsewhere, the other principal domestic airports are Mombasa's Moi International Airport (see p420), 10 km (6 miles) to the west of the city, where the small but orderly domestic terminal serves a regular stream of flights and has a café and shop. There are small airfields at **Malindi Airstrip**, 2 km (1 mile) west of the town on the west side of Mombasa Road, and also at **Kisumu Airport** on Busia Road about 4 km (2 miles) west of town. **Eldoret Airport**, 16 km (10 miles) south of town on Kisumu Road, was built in 1995. It has international status, but it is only served by scheduled domestic flights and its principal traffic is cargo which is in the form of flowers and vegetables from the Rift Valley and Western Kenya, destined for European supermarkets.

The delightful **Lamu Airport**, which is also known as Manda Airport owing to its location on the western side of Manda Island opposite Lamu town, has a simple open thatched terminal beneath numerous flowering bougainvillea bushes. Here, passengers can rest on characteristic Lamu-style antique furniture. From Manda Jetty, which is reached by a footpath from the edge of the airstrip, passengers are ferried across to Lamu town by motorised dhow, a trip which takes about 15 minutes.

Light aircraft parked near the terminal buildings of Wilson Airport, Nairobi

An Air Kenya De Havilland Dash 7 landing at Musiara, Masai Mara

DOMESTIC AND REGIONAL AIRLINES

From Nairobi's Jomo Kenyatta International Airport, Kenya Airways runs daily flights between Nairobi, Mombasa, Lamu and Kisumu, and further afield to Entebbe in Uganda and Dar es Salaam and Zanzibar in Tanzania. Also from Jomo Kenyatta, **Fly540**, a no-frills airline, offers daily flights between Nairobi and Eldoret, Kakamega, Kisumu, Kitale, Lamu, Lodwar, Malindi, Masai Mara and Mombasa. **Air Kenya**, based at Wilson Airport, partners with Regional Air in Tanzania to offer daily flights from Nairobi to Amboseli, Lamu, Lewa Downs, Malindi, several airstrips in Masai Mara, Samburu, and Nanyuki, plus destinations in Tanzania.

Safarilink flies daily between Nairobi and Amboseli, Diani Beach, Kiwayu, Lamu, Lewa Downs, Loisaba, Masai Mara, Naivasha, Nanyuki, Samburu, Shaba and Tsavo, as well as Kilimanjaro in Tanzania. It partners with Tanzania's Air Excel, which can provide onward links in Tanzania. **Mombasa Air Safari**, based on the coast, has daily flights from Mombasa, Diani Beach and Malindi to Masai Mara, Amboseli and Lamu; flights to Tsavo West can be arranged on request. **Tropic Air** is based in Nanyuki and has daily flights from there to Meru, Lewa Downs and airstrips in Masai Mara. Not all of these

routes are cheap, but it is worth shopping around the airlines for prices, and good deals can be found thanks to the strong competition. For instance, a one-way flight between Nairobi and Mombasa with Fly540 starts from as little as US$50.

CHARTER FLIGHTS

Apart from the destinations covered on scheduled flights, just about every corner of Kenya can be reached by charter flights. Many of East Africa's more remote tourist destinations, game reserves, ranches, camps and lodges have their own landing strips. There are over 30 charter companies based at Wilson Airport, and most charge a set rate for the flight regardless of the number of passengers. Usually Cessnas, these planes carry up to six people plus the pilot, so the cost can be shared among a group or family. Tour operators can arrange air charters or visitors can contact the airlines listed under scheduled flights. Some companies also offer helicopters.

SCHEDULED AIRLINE CIRCUITS

The smaller airlines generally run services in circuits. Flights may involve many intermediate stops, as the plane drops passengers off at different lodges on each circuit. For example, one of Mombasa Air Safari's routes from Mombasa

DIRECTORY

DOMESTIC AIRPORTS

Eldoret Airport
Tel 053 2063377.

Kenya Airports Authority (KAA)
Nairobi. *Tel* 020 6611000.
www.kenyaairports.co.ke

Kisumu Airport
Tel 057 2020811.

Lamu Airport
Tel 042 4631201.

Malindi Airstrip
Tel 042 2331201.

Wilson Airport
Off Langata Rd, Nairobi.
Tel 020 603260.

DOMESTIC AND REGIONAL AIRLINES

Air Kenya
Wilson Airport, Langata Rd, Nairobi. *Tel* 020 3916000.
www.airkenya.com

Fly540
Jomo Kenyatta International Airport, Nairobi. *Tel* 020 827521.
www.fly540.com

Mombasa Air Safari
Moi International Airport, Mombasa. *Tel* 0734 400400.
www.mombasaairsafari.com

Safarilink
Wilson Airport, Langata Rd, Nairobi. *Tel* 020 6000777
www.safarilink.com

Tropic Air
Nanyuki. *Tel* 020 2033032.
www.tropicairkenya.com

Logo of the Fly540 airline

touches down at Diani Beach, Tsavo West, Amboseli and Masai Mara, and returns in the same way. Within Masai Mara itself, there can be several "drops", at each of the lodges.

BAGGAGE

There are no special baggage restrictions on the larger planes, but on smaller ones baggage is restricted to 15 kg (33 lb) and soft-sided bags are preferable. It is possible to leave excess baggage at hotels in Nairobi, and storage can also be arranged with airlines and tour operators.

Travelling by Bus and Train

All regional centres in Kenya are connected by regular buses and *matatus* (minibuses), once considered unsafe due to chronic overcrowding, poor maintenance and speeding. Things have improved considerably since 2004 when tough new legislation governing public transport was implemented. However, safety problems persist with the possibility of theft on public transport, not only in the vehicles but also at the bus stands (or stages, as they are known), which are often located in rough areas of the cities, and vehicles are still driven rather recklessly. Passenger trains run between Nairobi and Mombasa.

MATATUS

A *matatu* is a Toyota or Nissan minibus that usually carries about 15 people. The name derives from the Swahili word *tatu* (three), as at one time a flat fee of three coins was charged for the ride. Before the 2004 legislation implemented by Member of Parliament John Michuki – and hence referred to as the Michuki Rules – all kinds of vehicles could serve as *matatus* and they were famously painted and decorated with colourful murals. These older vehicles are now off the road and have been replaced with fleets of white minibuses with yellow stripes. Now, every seat in a *matatu* has to have a seat belt that must be worn by law. The traffic police can, and do, issue on-the-spot fines to violators. *Matatus* can only carry the correct number of passengers the vehicle is designed for and are speed governed not to exceed 80 kmph (50 mph). Some drivers may still drive irresponsibly, but in general these moves have considerably reduced the number of road accidents in Kenya.

There are set fares and *matatus* running between cities and towns depart only when all the seats have been occupied. They are usually run by a staff of two – the driver and the tout who collects fares and competes with other *matatu* touts over passengers. After all, the sooner a vehicle fills up, the sooner it can depart. However, because of the risk of theft and the necessity to fiercely guard their possessions, most visitors to Kenya still do not use *matatus* very frequently.

BUSES

There are dozens of privately owned buses, and like *matatus*, the stringent traffic rules also apply to them. Standing in the aisle is also no longer permitted. Large buses cover the longer distances, timetables are fairly reliable and fares are cheap, although they are slower than *matatus*. The large buses also link Nairobi with Kisumu, Eldoret and Mombasa, and there are bus services across the borders. Tickets are sold at kiosks and should be bought a day in advance to be assured of a seat. Buses generally share the same stages as *matatus*, so again theft can be a problem.

Several companies run shuttle bus services between Nairobi and Arusha in Tanzania, a trip of about 6 hours, including the border crossing. Some services continue further to Moshi for those going to Kilimanjaro. **Riverside Shuttles** offers a good daily service.

A local bus outside the National Archives building, Nairobi

TRAINS

The 930-km (578-mile) Mombasa to Kisumu railway was completed in 1901 and extended to Kampala in 1931. Chronic underinvestment has since left the railway a shadow of its former self, with ageing locomotives and carriages and frequent breakdowns. The coming years may see an improvement, as a new consortium has taken over the management of the railways and plans to upgrade its tracks and rolling stock.

For now, overnight passenger trains run three times a week between Nairobi and Mombasa. In theory, the Nairobi–Mombasa run should take 13 hours. However, frequent stops and breakdowns can

***Matatus*, a popular means of getting around**

Tuk-tuks or three-wheel buggies, suitable for short rides within town

DIRECTORY

BUSES

Riverside Shuttles
Monrovia St, Nairobi. **City Map**
1 B2. *Tel 020 2229618.*
www.riverside-shuttle.com

TRAINS

Mombasa Railway Station
Haile Selassie Ave, Mombasa.
www.krc.co.ke

Nairobi Railway Station
Moi Ave, Nairobi. **City Map** 2 D5.
www.krc.co.ke

make the actual journey much longer. Indeed, locals have been known to get off the train and hitch a ride the rest of the way.

First class offers two-person compartments, Second Class offers four-person and Third Class is seated and can get very crowded. Travellers should also bear in mind that some carriages may be more than 85 years old, and facilities such as washbasins or even lights may not function. The First Class carriages are the best bet, and the fare is inclusive of breakfast and dinner. There is a dining car that serves simple dishes, such as soup, beef stew and sponge pudding.

Tickets are available at **Nairobi Railway Station** and **Mombasa Railway Station**, but can also be arranged in advance via a tour operator. Although visitors can fly the distance in an hour for very little more than the cost of a First Class ticket, the journey will appeal to anyone with an interest in rail travel. Daylight hours offer excellent views of the countryside along the way.

CITY TRANSPORT

Matatus also ply the streets of any sizable town and city for short distance trips. To hail one, visitors need to just wave with their palm down and a vehicle will pull over to let them in if it is not already full. Again, drivers can be reckless and drive up pavements, footpaths or on the wrong side of the road to jump traffic queues.

Nairobi has a fleet of buses, including the green Citi Hoppas, which use a system of numbers and locations to indicate their destination. The main bus terminals are outside the Hilton Hotel *(see p362)* and Nairobi Railway Station. Nairobi has a fleet of London-style Hackney cabs. Mombasa too has new red Metro buses that crisscross the island. Taxis are easily available everywhere, some new and some barely serviceable. Some have meters, but for others, it is best to negotiate a fare before getting in.

The latest entrant into the transport scene are *tuk-tuks*, motorised three-wheel buggies seating three people behind the driver. They are cheap over short distances, but not very fast, so it is best to take a taxi for long distance trips. *Tuk-tuks* are especially prolific along the coast and cost half the price of a taxi.

Boda-bodas are bicycle taxis with one padded seat over the rear wheel. They are popular in Western Kenya for ferrying people across the Kenya-Uganda border. While they are very cheap, they are not suitable for passengers carrying heavy baggage.

The overnight train from Nairobi to Mombasa crossing the Athi Plains

Travelling by Road

The obvious advantage of self-driving is that visitors can explore at their own pace. However, driving in Kenya can be challenging, and for those without sufficient experience, it is best to stick to organised safaris. The tarred roads in southern Kenya are marred by potholes and crumbling edges but are passable in a normal car. Elsewhere in the country, roads are gravel or dirt and, in the parks, little more than dusty tracks that get muddy in wet weather. A 4WD is essential for off-road driving. Apart from bad road conditions, the biggest threat of road accidents comes from reckless *matatu* drivers racing each other, but this situation has improved considerably since the 2004 laws were put in place.

HIRING A CAR

Car hire services are available in Nairobi and Mombasa. Most of the international companies are represented, including **Avis** and **Budget**, which have offices at the airports as well as downtown locations in both cities. There are numerous local car hire companies, and hotels and tour operators can make recommendations. In Nairobi try **Uniglobe Let's Go Travel**, **Central Car Hire** or **Concorde Car Hire**. The former can also supply vehicles in Mombasa and Malindi and rents out safari vehicles with roof hatches and, if required, even chauffeurs. Companies with offices in Mombasa allow people to hire a car in Nairobi and drop it off in Mombasa, or vice versa, for an extra fee.

Depending on the planned itinerary, car hire companies can advise on whether a 4WD is needed. These should be a minimum of 1300cc and in good condition. Land Rovers,

A 4WD, highly recommended on muddy forest tracks

Suzuki jeeps or Pajeros are the favoured vehicles. Visitors must remember to ask what services the company provides in the event of a breakdown or emergency.

INSURANCE AND OTHER DOCUMENTS

Drivers need to be over 23 years of age and have a driving licence printed in English or a translation, or an international driver's permit and a passport. A credit card will be needed for a deposit. Rates are set per day and per

kilometre after the daily limit, usually 100 km (60 miles). Alternatively, drivers can choose an unlimited mileage option for long distance trips, in which case they should ensure that the quote includes 16 per cent VAT charge.

It is advisable to check the small print of the contract and consider paying extra over the standard insurance that is included in the rate for collision damage, theft protection and excess liability waivers. Also consider personal accident and personal effects cover against having items stolen from a vehicle, although these may already be covered under personal travel insurance policies. With prior arrangement, and for an extra fee required to organise the paperwork, hire cars can be taken into Tanzania and Uganda. Note that some contracts state that if drivers take regular cars off tarred roads or into the game parks and reserves, all waivers may be nullified and the driver held financially responsible for any damage caused.

RULES OF THE ROAD

All vehicles are right-hand drive and driving is on the left, but on potholed stretches it is customary to drive all over the road if there is no oncoming traffic. It is not safe to drive after dark as other vehicles may have missing headlights and there is the danger of people and animals on the road or missing signposts indicating sharp bends or steep hills. Driving through closed roads or areas in parks is not safe as fallen trees or a flood may obstruct the way. Drivers should note that speed bumps, often spaced very closely, are found in even the tiniest of settlements.

Speed limits are 80 kmph (50 mph) for rental vehicles and 100 kmph (62 mph) for other vehicles outside of urban areas, and 40–80 kmph (25–50 mph) in towns and cities. In parks and reserves, the speed limit is 40 kmph (25 mph).

Police road blocks are common, but unless a driver is actually breaking the law,

Organised traffic in one of Nairobi's major thoroughfares, Kenyatta Avenue

A safari vehicle with a roof hatch for game viewing, Amboseli National Park

such as by not wearing a seat belt, in most cases the vehicle will be waved through. If fined for any reason, insist on going to the nearest police station to make the payment and get a receipt to ensure that it is a genuine fine and not a request for a bribe.

At petrol stations attendants fill up tanks and check oil and water. Most will accept only cash. When parking on the street in any sizable town, a small fee must be paid to a municipal parking attendant, who issues a ticket that must be displayed prominently on the windscreen.

ROAD CONDITIONS

The tarred roads linking the urban centres in the south of the country are generally passable by all cars. The coastal stretch south of Malindi is especially easy to negotiate for those wanting to explore in a hire car for a couple of days. The loop around the Rift Valley lakes from Nairobi is feasible in a regular car. Drivers should watch out for potholes, corrugations and, on hills, deep ruts in the tar made by heavy traffic crawling up and down.

The north of the country is intersected by stony gravel roads and it is best to travel in a convoy of at least two vehicles carrying adequate fuel and spares. It is worthwhile to remember that all roads deteriorate in the wet season and some become impassable. Dirt tracks in the parks are very rough so be wary of getting stuck.

Traffic is heavy in Nairobi and Mombasa and drivers must get used to the Kenyan mindset of "me first" to get anywhere at all.

ROAD ASSISTANCE

For roadside assistance it may be worth considering taking a temporary membership with the **Automobile Association**

(AA) of Kenya. In the event of a breakdown, it is customary in Africa to deposit a bundle of leaves or grass a few metres behind and in front of the vehicle to warn other motorists. To get up-to-date information on road conditions off the beaten track visit the Safety and Communication Centre *(see p415)* in Nairobi before setting out.

A local bus travelling on the dusty track leading to Mbita Point, on Lake Victoria

General Index

Page numbers in **bold** refer to
main entries

A

Aardvark 61, 81, 83, **122**
 Masai Mara Game Reserve 265
 Laikipia Plateau 319
Aardwolf **109**
Abbott's duiker 191
 See also Ader's duiker; Blue duiker;
 Common duiker; Harvey's red
 duiker
Aberdare National Park (Central
 Highlands) 11, **316–17**
 accommodation 77, 374
 what to see 76
 when to go 76
Aberdare, Lord 316
Aberdare Range 20, 21, 83, 309, 312
Acacia forest (Lake Nakuru National
 Park) 276
Accommodation **358–77**
 beach resorts 360–61
 booking 359, 361
 budget lodging 358, 360
 Central Highlands **374–6**
 children 359, 361
 choosing 358
 facilities 358–9
 hotel groups 359, 361
 hotels *see* Hotels
 lodges *see* Lodges and guesthouses
 Nairobi 358, **362–3**
 Northern Coast **368–9**
 Northern Kenya **376–7**
 on safari 361
 pricing 358
 self-catering cottages and
 homestays 360, 361
 Southeastern Savannahs **364–5**
 Southern Coast **366–8**
 Southern Rift Valley and Masai
 Mara **369–72**
 tree hotels *see* Tree hotels
 Western Kenya **372–4**
 See also Safari
Acrobats *see* Music and dance
Adamson, George 37, 330, **333**
Adamson, Joy 37, 260, 331, **333**,
 346
 art 35
 Elsamere (Lake Naivasha) 268–9
 Joy's Camp (Shaba National
 Reserve) 343, 346, 377
Adamson's Falls (Meru National Park)
 333
Adders and vipers **135**
Ader's duiker 132, 214, 236
 See also Abbott's duiker; Blue
 duiker; Common duiker; Harvey's
 red duiker
AFEW Giraffe Centre (Nairobi) 152,
 168
African baobab 86
African buffalo 63, **118–19**
 Amboseli National Park 197
 Hell's Gate National Park 60, 270,
 271
 Lake Naivasha 268, 269
 Masai Mara Game Reserve 262
 Meru National Park 75, 330, 331,
 332
 Nairobi National Park 162, 164
 Shimba Hills National Reserve 218,
 219

African buffalo (cont.)
 Tsavo East National Park 184, 185
 Tsavo West National Park 182, 186
African bullfrog **134**
African bush elephant 62, 81, 97,
 114–15
 Aberdare National Park 316, 317
 Amboseli National Park 10, 21, 74,
 149, 177, 192, 193, 194, 196, 197
 David Sheldrick Wildlife Trust 10,
 161
 Lake Jipe 189
 Masai Mara Game Reserve 258,
 262, 264, 265
 Meru National Park 75, 332
 Mwaluganje Sanctuary 214, 215
 poaching 65, 165, 185
 Shimba Hills National Reserve 218,
 219
 Taita Hills Wildlife Sanctuary 178,
 188
 Tsavo East and West National Parks
 10, 21, 75, 161, 177, 182, 184, 185
African Children's Choir 33
African civet 110
African darter **138**, 187, 264
African Diary (Bill Bryson) 37
African fish eagle **140**, 187, 266, 282,
 283, 348
African firefinch **144**
African grey parrot **142**
African Heritage Centre (Nairobi) 34,
 160
African hoopoe **142**
African jacana 92, **142**
African literature 36
African Medical and Research
 Foundation 413
African paradise flycatcher **145**, 187
African pied wagtail **144**
African spoonbill 279
African water rail 189
African wild cat **100**
African wild dog 64, 65, **109**, 265, 318
Afro-montane forests 88, 91
Afro-montane habitats 83, **90–91**
Afro-Alpine moorland
 Aberdare National Park 316
 Mount Kenya National Park 323,
 324, 325
Agamas 83, 97, **134**, 184
Ahmed, the elephant (Marsabit) 348
 Nairobi National Museum 158
Air travel 420, 421, **422–3**
Akalas 29
Akamba *see* Indigenous peoples
Albino zebra (Nairobi National Park)
 162, 164
 See also Grevy's zebra; Plains zebra;
 Zebra
Alia river 355
Alpine swift 184
Amboseli Elephant Research Project
 197
Amboseli National Park (Southeastern
 Savannahs) 10, 21, 60, 69, 74, 81,
 82, 97, 149, 177, 178, **194–7**
 accommodation 76, 364
 restaurants 384
 visitors' checklist 195
 what to see 76
 when to go 68, 76
Amboseli Plains (Amboseli National
 Park) 196
Amphibians and reptiles **134–7**

Anglican Cathedral (Mombasa) 204
Angola colobus 210, 214, 218, 220
 See also Black-and-white colobus
Animal Orphanage (Nairobi National
 Park) 162, 164–5
Antelopes 97, **128–33**
 large **130–33**
 spiral-horned **128–9**
Arabuko Sokoke National Park
 (Northern Coast) 10, 88, **234–7**
 visitors' checklist 235
Arabuko Swamp and Treehouse
 (Arabuko Sokoke National Park)
 236
Arawale Hirola Reserve 99
Archer's Post (Samburu-Buffalo
 Springs National Reserves) 345
Arid and semiarid habitats *see* Habitats
Ark (Aberdare National Park) 317, 374
Arts and crafts **34–5**
 African Heritage Centre (Nairobi)
 160
 City Market *see* City Market
 Crafts Fair (Nairobi) 38
 Malindi Tourist Market (Malindi) 240
 See also Carving; Shopping
Aruba Dam (Tsavo East National
 Park) 184
Athi Plains and Kitengela corridor
 (Nairobi National Park) 163, 165
Athi river 162, 165, **170**, 314
Athi River town (Nairobi) 170
Athi river track (Nairobi National
 Park) 163
ATMs 416
Augur buzzard **140**, 270
August 7th Memorial Park (Nairobi)
 155, **156**
Automobile Association of Kenya 427

B

Baboon Cliff (Lake Nakuru National
 Park) 276, 279
Baboon Escarpment (Nairobi National
 Park) 163, 165
Baboons 113, 163
 olive *see* Olive baboons
 yellow *see* Yellow baboons
Baden-Powell, Lord Robert 312, **315**
Baden-Powell, Olave **315**
Baggage 423
Ballooning 17, 60, 356–7, 400, 403
 Masai Mara Game Reserve 61, 262,
 264, 358
Bamburi Beach (Southern Coast) **224**
 accommodation 367
 restaurants 385
Banded mongoose **111**
Banking and currency **416–17**
Bantu linguistic group 18, 24, 26, 43
Bao board game 273
Baobabs 214
Baragoi (Northern Kenya) **341**
Barbets 83
Bargaining 240, 390
Barghash, Sultan 221, 222
Baringo cliffs (Lake Baringo) 283
Basheikh Mosque, Old Town
 (Mombasa) 206
Bat-eared fox **108**
 Masai Mara Game Reserve 262, 265
Bateleur eagle 85
Batian and Nelion Peaks (Mount
 Kenya National Park) 322
Batik 35, 390, 391, 394

Acknowledgments

Dorling Kindersley would like to thank the many people whose help and assistance contributed to the preparation of this book.

Main Contributors

Philip Briggs was born in the UK and raised in South Africa, and first backpacked between Nairobi and Cape Town in 1986. In the 1990s, he wrote a series of pioneering Bradt guides to destinations that were then – and in some cases still are – practically uncharted by the travel publishing industry, including South Africa, Ghana, Uganda, Ethiopia, Malawi, Mozambique, Tanzania and Rwanda. Philip has visited more than two dozen African countries and written about most of them, whether for guidebook publishers such as AA, Berlitz, Dorling Kindersley, Frommers, Camerapix, Struik-New Holland, APA-Insight and 30 Degrees South, or magazines such as *Africa Birds & Birding, Africa Geographic, BBC Wildlife, Travel Africa* and *Wanderlust.* He still spends at least 4 months on the road every year, and the rest of his time at home in the mountainous uKhahlamba-Drakensberg region of South Africa.

Lizzie Williams, who originally hails from the UK, worked for several years as a tour leader on overland trucks across Africa before settling in Cape Town to write guide books. She is the author of Footprint guides to Namibia, Kenya and Tanzania. She also wrote the only city guide to Johannesburg and the first country guide to Nigeria for Bradt. Her additional work includes updating the Rough Guide to Egypt and Turkey, and writing travel content on Africa for websites.

Fact Checker Matt Brown

Proofreader Deepthi Talwar

Indexer Jyoti Dhar

Design and Editorial

Publisher Douglas Amrine
List Manager Vivien Antwi
Managing Art Editor Jane Ewart
Project Editor Michelle Crane
Senior Project Designer Paul Jackson
Project Designer Kate Leonard
Senior Cartographic Editor Casper Morris
Managing Art Editor (jackets) Karen Constanti
Jacket Design Tessa Bindloss
DTP Designer Natasha Lu
Picture Researcher Ellen Root
Production Controller Linda Dare

Design and Editorial Assistance

Fay Franklin, Camilla Gersh, Sylvia Goulding, Maite Lantaron, Rada Radojicic, Marisa Renzullo, Julie Thompson, Richard Trillo.

Additional Photography

Trish Gant, Frank Greenaway, Mathew Kurien, Harry Taylor, Jerry Young.

Special Assistance

Dorling Kindersley would like to thank the following for their assistance:

Bike Treks, Dr Dame Daphne Sheldrick at David Sheldrick Wildlife Trust, Alex Millar at Governors' Camp, Peter Kimani at Heritage Hotels, Craig Hilton-Taylor at the IUCN, Raphael Mwangi at Kenya National Archives, Betty Ichan at Kenya Tourist Board, Michael Kipkeu, Evelyn Oroni, Andrew Toboso at Kenya Wildlife Service, LAICO Regency Hotel, Nairobi, Freddie Maruk and Iris Hunt at Mount Kenya Wildlife Conservancy's Animal Orphanage, Simon Gatheru at Nairobi National Museum, Dr Idle Omar Farah, Esther Keige, Dr Mzalendo Kibunjia and Ibrahim Mohamud at National Museums of Kenya, Eve Onduru at Sarova Hotels, Sanjay Shoor at Shoor Travel, Fatma Muses at Sopa Hotels, Torben Rune at Southern Cross Safaris, Mombasa.

Picture Credits

Placement Key: a = above; b = below/bottom; c = centre; f = far; l = left; r = right; t = top.

Photography Permissions

Dorling Kindersley would like to thank the following for their assistance and kind permission to photograph at their establishments:

African Heritage Centre, Nairobi, Borana Lodge at Laikipia Plateau, Carnivore Restaurant, Colliers Shopping Centre, Elsa's Kopje at Meru National Park, Grand Regency Hotel, Nairobi, Shemina at Galdessa Camp at Tsavo East National Park, Giraffe Manor at Nairobi National Park, Kicheche Camp at the Masai Mara Game Reserve, Kisumu Museum, Lamu Guest House, Nairobi Railway Museum, Ol Tukai Lodge Bar, Rondo Retreat at Kakamega Forest National Reserve, Satao Elerai Camp at Amboseli National Park, Serena Beach Hotel, Serena Mountain Lodge, Elizabeth Nguraru at Shimba Lodge at Shimba Hills National Reserve, Bhavni Satish at Voi Wildlife Lodge.

Works of art have been reproduced with the kind permission of the following copyright holders:
Wings of Love (1998) © Gakunju Kaigwa 35cb,

Dancing with the Enemy (2000) © Jimmy Ogonga 35clb; Portrait of Naisuaki Enole Kosen Sarbabi by Joy Adamson, © National Museums of Kenya, Joy Adamson Collection 35cr; *World-Class Black Rhino, Aberdare Forest* (1972) © Peter Beard 35bc.

The publisher would like to thank the following individuals, companies, and picture libraries for their kind permission to reproduce their photographs:

4CORNERS IMAGES: Schmid Reinhard 177b.
ABERDARE SAFARI HOTELS LTD: 77tl, 317clb.
AERO CLUB OF EAST AFRICA: Athol Frantz 38cl.
AFRICA IMAGE LIBRARY: Ariadne Van Zandbergen 25cla, 30crb, 83tc, 83cr, 86crb, 89tl, 94tr, 103br, 107br, 112cla, 119cr, 123cr, 126cl, 126cla, 129tl, 132c, 133tc, 136-37t, 139br, 143cr, 148clb, 183bc, 229bl, 254br, 257crb, 271bl, 271cr, 279c, 332cr, 342bl, 343crb, 354bl.
AKG-IMAGES: 47t, 51tr.
ALAMY: A & J Visage 99tr; Ace Stock Limited 102bc; Africa/Tina Manley 28cl, 127cra, 201bl; AfriPics.com 66bl, 85cr, 119clb; Arco Images GmbH 108br, 111cla,/Dolder, W. 20cr, 124tr,/ Wothe, K 45cb; Robert E. Barber 66cr; Peter Barritt 20crb, 107clb, 145tr; Blickwinkel 66tc, 100cr, 131tl, 144tl,/Dolder 20cb, 20bc,/Katz 86br,/ Layer 111ca,/McPHOTO/BIO 84tr,/ZAD 216br, 229cr, 255cra, 337cb,/Poelking 15c, 121bl,/ Trutnau 64tc,/Wisniewski 65tl; David Boag 108clb, 140clb, 144c, 144tc; Bon Appetit/Kröger/ Gross 93bc; Mark Boulton 29c, 92br, 230cl, 295bc; James de Bounevialle 121br; Penny Boyd 114cla, 129cr; Yvette Cardozo 115cr, 317tl; Gordon Chambers 21fbr, 145tl, 297tc; Nick Cobbing 33cb; Gary Cook 345bl; Neil Cooper 257cra; Corbis Premium RF/Michele Burgess 29cr, 395crb; CreativeAct - Toys/Games series 394br; Dacorum Gold 138br; Danita Delimont 347cl,/David Northcott 98crb; Tim Davies 132tl,/Gavriel Jecan 29tr; Reinhard Dirscherl 118cla; Discpicture 87bc; Ulrich Doering 191clb; EcoPic 138cr; EggImages 95br; Chad Ehlers 425tb; Elvele Images Ltd/B J Gadie 310cla,/Fritz Poelking 4-5t, 264cl; Mark Eveleigh 63br, 115br, 262bl; Alissa Everett 109tl; F1 online/Harald Trinkner 123tl; F323/Juniors Bildarchiv 94br; David Fleetham 110ca; FLPA 95cr, 139clb, 276cla, 355tr; Fotoshoot 380cla; Fotosonline/Klaus-Peter Wolf 343tl; Franzfoto.com 62b; Chris Fredriksson 87cr, 113cr; G&B Images/ Gustav Gonget 92cla; Jason Gallier 143tr; Gallo Images/Daryl Balfour 68b; Eddie Gerald 295br; Angelo Giampiccolo 163tl; Simon de Glanville 134clb; Ken Hackett 20cl; Martin Harvey 114-115; Kevin Henshaw 130br; David Hodges 60tc; Peter Horree 34cr, 395tr; Friedrich von Hörsten 142tr; David Hosking 145cr; Andre van Huizen 143tc, 143cl; Imagebroker/Stefan Auth 32cr, 91tl,/Klaus-Peter Wolf 145cl; Images & Stories 44bc,135cla; Images of Africa Photobank/Friedrich von

Hörsten 88cla, 295crb,/David Keith Jones 26crb, 27cl, 30cl, 30cr, 32bc, 61tr, 63cb, 70b, 86tr, 110crb, 114clb, 115bl, 122clb, 123br, 126-127, 127bl, 127br, 132cl, 155tr, 161clb, 229cb, 257tl, 265t, 279br, 298tl, 298b, 302br, 311crb, 319crb, 320bl, 322cla, 330cl, 331br, 336tr, 336c, 336-37c, 337tr, 337cra, 337bl, 347crb, 347clb, 347bl, 349tc, 353tl, 392cl, 394cl, 400tl, 401br , 420cr, 422b,/ Jeremy van Riemsdyke 79cra,/Carla Signorini 254bl, 256tr, 342cl,/Charlotte Thege 25crb; ImageState /Georgette Douwma 211bl,/ Jonathan&Angie Scott 138clb; INTERFOTO Pressebildagentur 311bl; Paul Ives 211crb; James Davis Photography 60bl; John Warburton-Lee Photography / Nigel Pavitt 300-1; Juniors Bildarchiv 124cla, 142c; Marion Kaplan 103cra, 333cb, 341cb, 352bc; Mike Lane 144cr,187bc; Zute Lightfoot 5clb, 172tc, 323bl, 325t; Andrew Linscott 354c; LMR Group 142cr; Tina Manley 21bc; Mary Evans Picture Library 49tr, 310tr; Michael Matthews 33cl; Mike Mckavett 295fbr; Mediacolor's 89cr; Mooch Images 394bl; Nature Picture Library/Jose B. Ruiz 281ca,/Bernard Castelein 112clb; Nordicphotos/Jörgen Larsson 235bc; North Wind Picture Archives 48bc; Chris Pancewicz 394crb; Trevor Payne 133cr; Peter Arnold, Inc./Martha Cooper 255bl; Photodisc 113clb,/Anup Shah 107bl,144cl; Phototake Inc./ Carolina Biological Supply Company 349cr; Pictorial Press Ltd 36c, 37bl, 109cr; Picture Contact/Jochem Wijnands 82tl, 111cb, 267tl; Vic Pigula 134cla; Peter Pinnock 137bl; Pixonnet. com/Bo Jansson 88tr; Stu Porter 137cr; Robert Estall Photo Agency/Angela Fisher 29clb,/Ariadne Van Zandbergen 242-43,/David Coulson 23cr; Robert Harding Picture Library Ltd/Charles Bowman 208br; Malcolm Schuyl 111tr, 138cla, 140br, 142tc; Sean Sprague 51c; Frantisek Staud 310cb; Stephen Frink Collection 211tc; Steve Bloom Images 41tr, 121bc, 133tl, 194cla; Stockbyte/Tom Brakefield 130clb,133c,305cr; Stuwdamdorp 54c; Sue Cunningham Photographic 254tr, 254-55c; Trevor Smithers ARPS 381tl; Jack Sullivan 31br; Bjorn Svensson 24bl; Dawn Swift 113tl; Sylvia Cordaiy Photo Library/Kjell Sandved 86cla ,130cla,/Massimo Piacentino 163bl; Jim Tampin 128br, 131br; Tbkmedia.de 256cl; Terry Harris just Greece photo library 404b; David Tipling 280br; Peter Titmuss 122cla; TNT Magazine 266clb; Charles Tomalin 106bc; Top-Pics TBK 92tr; Travel Ink/Dave Saunders 207tl; Travelshots.com 227b; Nick Turner 22br, 73t, 285b; David Uney 145c; Miroslava Vilimova 21cl; Vintage Images 44tr; Visions of America, LLC/Joe Sohm 14, 64br, 162clb, 310bl, 319ca, 399br; Ross Warner 108cr; Maximilian Weinzierl 59b, 62c; Westend 61/Martin Rietze 255br; Terry Whittaker 91cr, 100bl, 109clb, 129bl; Wild Places Photography/Chris Howes 170b; Wildviews/Charles Tomalin 107bc; World Pictures 127bc; World Religions Photo Library/

Christine Osborne 33cr; WorldFoto 61bl, 93crb, 124-125, 135cb, 191br; Karsten Wrobel 90tr; Wyrdlight 89bc; Ariadne Van Zandbergen 143tl, 244tr, 246b, 257bl, 263tl, 317cra, 337tl, 337br.
ALLIANCE FRANÇAISE DE NAIROBI: Christian Randrianampizafy 397tr.
KARL AMMANN: 246cl.
ARDEA: Mark Boulton 94cla; Piers Cavendish 17bl; Kenneth W. Fink 99cl, 297br; Clem Haagner 110cb; Michael Neugebauer 349cl.
ART + COMMERCE: 35bc.
TOM ASHTON: 211cra.
BIRD WATCHING EAST AFRICA: Chege Wa Kariuki 90cla
THE BRIDGEMAN ART LIBRARY: Vasco da Gama (1469-1524) (gouache on paper), Baraldi, Severino (b.1930)/Private Collection/© Look and Learn/The Bridgeman Art Library 42, 200-201c, Sloane 197 f.9 Francisco de Almeida, illustration from 'Historical Accounts of Portuguese Settlements', 1646 (vellum), Barretto de Resende, Pedro (fl.1646)/British Library, London, UK,/The Bridgeman Art Library 201cra, Sloane 197 f.225v-6 Portuguese exploration map of Mombassa, illustration from 'Historical Accounts of Portuguese Settlements' 1646 (vellum), Barretto de Resende, Pedro (fl.1646)/British Library, London, UK,/The Bridgeman Art Library 201cb, Kibuya Nahoe Market, Kenya, 1932 (pencil, w/c & bodycolour on paper), Mimpriss, Violet Baber (1895-1987)/Private Collection/The Bridgeman Art Library 357c.
CAMERAPIX: 25tr, 26cla, 27tr, 31tr, 31clb, 235cra.
CORBIS: 52crb, 191crb; Yann Arthus-Bertrand 119br, 293c, 352clb, 412b; Bettmann 45bl, 53tc, 53crb, 311tr, 349cla; Tom Brakefield 104cla, 104bc, 105tl, 107cra, 120-121, 255tl; Ralph A. Clevenger 140tl; Brandon D. Cole 112br; John Conrad 102-103, 125bl; Corbis Sygma/Orban Thierry 44cla; Alissa Crandall 71br; Tim Davis 192-93; DLILLC 1c, 21cr, 28crb, 102cla, 103cb, 104clb, 117cr, 120clb, 127tl, 195tl; Ecoscene/ Chinch Gryniewicz 284,/Sally A. Morgan 185tl; Epa 18bl,/Nic Bothma 95bc,/Jon Hrusa 17c,/ Stephen Morrison 55tr; Stephen Frink 211cl, 245tl; Gallo Images 101bl,/Martin Harvey 105cr,/Nigel J. Dennis 110clb,/Roger De La Harpe 103ca; Louise Gubb 37tc; Martin Harvey 126bc; Rob Howard 126crb; Hulton-Deutsch Collection 52t, 52bc, 315cb; JAI/Demetrio Carrasco 16bl; Chen Jianli 19bl; Barbra Leigh 106br; Renee Lynn 93tl; Joe McDonald 102br, 120cl, 126tl, 128cr, 134ca; Mary Ann McDonald 101tr; Momatiuk - Eastcott 103bc; Micheline Pelletier 55bc; Carl & Ann Purcell 395tl, 415br; Jeffrey L. Rotman 211cb; Kevin Schafer 121tc; Paul Souders 72bl, 104-105; Wendy Stone 410t; Keren Su 18tr; Sygma/William Campbell 54bc; Roger Tidman 89br; Brian A. Vikander 29bl, 124clb; Inge Yspeert 10br; Zefa/Michael Fiala 20tr,/Gabriela Staebler 15b, 102crb, 105br,/ Winfried Wisniewski 105bc,/Wolfgang Meier 176.

DANITA DELIMONT STOCK PHOTOGRAPHY: John Warburton-Lee 2-3, 334
DK IMAGES: Ian O'Leary 380tr, 380cb, 380bl, 380br, 381bl, 381bc, 381br; courtesy of the Natural History Museum, London 43bc, 297cb; courtesy of the National Museum of Kenya 44br.
EAST AFRICAN EDUCATIONAL PUBLISHERS LTD.: 36bl
FLPA: Neil Bowman 144tr; Peter Davey 93br; Alan Detrick/Linda Detrick 91crb; David Hosking 92clb, 115tl; Imagebroker/Frank Stober 114bc; Frans Lanting 84clb, 115bc; Minden Pictures/Tim Fitzharris 114br; Fritz Polking 84cla; Malcolm Schuyl 84br, 115cb; Jurgen & Christine Sohns 85bc; Martin B Withers 143bc; Ariadne Van Zandbergen 29cla, 244bc.
STEVE GARVIE: 98bl.
GETTY IMAGES: Afp/Stringer/Deshakalyan Chowdhury 32cl,/Gianluigi Guercia 311tc,/Simon Maina 311cra,/Olivier Morin 293crb; Aurora/ Robert Caputo 28tr; Steve Bloom 116tl; Digital Vision 67bl,/Paul Souders 67tr; DigitalGlobe 13cr; Gallo Images - Daryl Balfour/Photographer's Choice 10c,/Heinrich van den Berg 127cb; Hulton Archive/Anwar Hussein 37cr; Peter Lilja 258cl; S Purdy Matthews 103bl; Minden Pictures/Mark Moffett 85tl; National Geographic/Kenneth Garrett 45cr; Stan Osolinski 191c; Photodisc/Anup Shah 105cb, 118br, 119bc; Photographer's Choice/ James Warwick 108cla; Peter Pinnock 20fclb; Robert Harding World Imagery/Storm Stanley 80; Staff/John Gichigi 293clb; Kim Steele 381cb ;Stone/ Art Wolfe 262tr,/Peter/ Stef Lamberti 118bc; Time & Life Pictures/Dmitri Kessel 310-11c,/William F. Campbell 310bc,/Stringer/Mansell 51br,/Terrence Spencer 305cb; Ami Vitale 119tl.
THE GRANGER COLLECTION, NEW YORK: 9c, 50crb, 52bl, 169crb, 221cl.
HAMILL GALLERY OF AFRICAN ART, BOSTON: 3c.
HILTON NAIROBI HOTEL: 396bl.
JAMHURI WEAR: 395cra.
JOHN WARBURTON-LEE PHOTOGRAPHY: 21tr, 318cl, 322br, 355bl, 399t; Nigel Pavitt 5c, 21cla, 24crb, 27bl, 30bl, 34cb, 38tc, 39tc, 128clb, 171tr, 171br, 228-29c, 229tr, 249tl, 267br, 270cla, 281tl, 303br, 336clb, 350-51, 394cra; Susanna Wyatt 402tr.
THE KENYA ASSOCIATION OF TOUR OPERATORS (KATO): 404tl.
KENYA NATIONAL ARCHIVES: 50br, 53bc, 53bl.
KENYA WILDLIFE SERVICE: 79cla; Kakamega Forest National Reserve 295tl.
LAST REFUGE: Adrian Warren 23fbl.
RICHARD LEAKEY: 349bc.
LEBRECHT MUSIC AND ARTS: African Pictures 32tr, 33tr, 33cla, 33bl, 33br.
LUC LENS: 99bl.
LONELY PLANET IMAGES: Casey & Astrid Mahaney 211br; Mitch Reardon 149tl.
MARY EVANS PICTURE LIBRARY: 49cb, 50tl, 147c, 221cr, 221crb, 221br; Illustrated London News Ltd 49br.

MASTERFILE: George Calef 104br; Albert Normandin 16t; Radius Images/Horst Klemm 335b.
RONALD MULWA: 99crb.
NAIROBI NATIONAL MUSEUM: 158tr, 158tl, 158cla, 158clb, 158br, 159tl, 159cr, 159crb.
NATIONAL GEOGRAPHIC STOCK: 45tl, 111cra; Gordan Gahan 44-5c; Kenneth Garrett 44clb, 349bl.
NATIONAL MUSEUMS OF KENYA: Fort Jesus Museum/Steve Okoko Ashikoye 229cra.
NATUREPL.COM: Karl Ammann 321br; Peter Blackwell 122br, 135ca, 325c; Bernard Castelein 122cr; Bruce Davidson 141cr, 142cl; Jurgen Freund 95tl; Tony Heald 120br, 120bc, 132cr; Luiz Claudio Marigo 234clb; Hugh Maynard 294clb; Tony Phelps 135tr; Premaphotos134cra; Mike Read 145tc; Jeff Rotman 95cl; Keith Scholey 21bl, 107tl; Anup Shah 105bl, 106crb, 112cr, 119bl, 124br, 125cra, 133cl; Lynn M. Stone 106cla; Jeff Vanuga 126br.
NORTH WIND PICTURE ARCHIVES: 48tl.
JIMMY OGONGA: 35clb.
OHIORUNNER.COM: 293br.
JOCHEN OTT: 295ca.
PAN MACMILLAN PUBLISHERS: Author: Charles Miller, 1971 299cr.
DOUGLAS B. PATTERSON: 33cra.
PHOTOLIBRARY: 318 tr; Abpl/Daryl Balfour 356-57,/Gerald Hinde 118-119; Roderick Edward Edwards 141br; Nabil Ezz 123cl; Gallo Images-Daryl Balfour/Photodisc 125crb,/Anup Shah 96; Juniors Bildarchiv 11tl, 252; Robert Mackinlay 308; Martin Moxter 406-407; Kenneth Murray 166-67; Oxford Scientific (OSF)/Ariadne Van Zandbergen 198,/David W Breed 91bc,/Derek Bromhall 291br,/Elliot Neep 65bl, 106-107, 274-75,/Steve Turner 56-57; Photononstop/M & C Denis-Huot 11br,/Yves Talensac 149br; Robert Harding Travel 146-47,/Jack Jackson 326-27,/Julia Bayne 81b.
PHOTOSHOT: Hemis.fr/Frances Stéphane 212-13; NHPA/Daryl Balfour 87tl, 88br,/Anthony Bannister 110cla, 110cra, 118clb, 135clb, 295fbl,/Gerald Cubitt 85br,/Nigel J Dennis 111crb, 132tc,/Nick Garbutt 111clb,/Martin Harvey 121cb,/Daniel Heuclin 87br, 297bl,/Chris Mattison134cb,/Jean-Louis Le Moigne 21ca,/Christophe Ratier 352cla,/Kevin Schafer109br,/Jonathan & Angela Scott 349br,/John Shaw 113br,/James Warwick 133tr, 139cr; Talking Sport 293bc; World Pictures 336br.
THE PICTURE DESK: The Kobal Collection/Umbrella/BBC/Brit Screen 319tl.
PRIVATE COLLECTION: 30cra, 48c.
RAHIMTULLA MUSEUM OF MORDERN ART: 35c.
REUTERS: EPA 19tc; Barry Moody 264br; Antony Njuguna 162br, 402bl, 420b; Radu Sigheti 121cra.
RHINO ARK CHARITABLE TRUST: 39bl.
DR. FRANCESCO ROVERO: 132tr.
RUSINGA ISLAND LODGE: www.private wilderness.com 302cl.
SARAKASI TRUST: 32cb.
SAROVA LION HILL LODGE: 77cb.
SASINI TEA & COFFEE LTD: 395cb.
MICHAEL SMITH: 421br.
ST. MARTIN'S PRESS: Author: John Henry Patterson, 1907 36tr.
RONALD SYDNEY STARLING: 35cr.
SAM W STEARMAN: 34crb, 421tl.
DR. JULIE WIECZKOWSKI: 98cl, 98cra.
www.africanpictures.net: Drum Social Histories/Baileys African History 54cb, 55c.
www.bmpix.org: Archives mission 21: Basel Mission 48bl.
Front Endpaper: CORBIS: Ecoscene/Chinch Gryniewicz ftl, Zefa/Wolfgang Meier fbr;
DANITA DELIMONT STOCK PHOTOGRAPHY: John Warburton-Lee ftr; PHOTOLIBRARY: Juniors Bildarchiv fl, Oxford Scientific (OSF)/Ariadne Van Zandbergen br, Photodisc/Anup Shah bc, Robert Mackinlay cr; GETTY IMAGES: Robert Harding World Imagery/Storm Stanley bl.
Jacket: Front – CORBIS: Frans Lanting.
Back – AWL IMAGES: Nigel Pavitt t; CORBIS: Randy Wells cla; DORLING KINDERSLEY: Nigel Hicks bl; Linda Whitwam cl. Spine – CORBIS: Frans Lanting.

All other images © Dorling Kindersley
For further information see: www.dkimages.com

Phrase Book

Kenya's official language Swahili, more formally called KiSwahili, belongs to the Bantu group of languages from the Niger-Congo family. Originally spoken by the indigenous people along the East African coast, Swahili was greatly influenced by Arabic as well as Persian, Portuguese and English. Standard Swahili developed from Zanzibar and although there are many regional variations and dialects present, it is generally recognised throughout East Africa.

Written in the Roman alphabet, the language is spoken in a straightforward manner, the pronunciation of most words being similar to the English equivalent. The stress is nearly always on the penultimate syllable and all vowels in a word are sounded. The consonant **ng** is possibly the only unfamiliar sound for English speakers. There is also a clear distinction between the English **r** and the softer Swahili **r**, which is closer to the sound **d**.

The Swahili system of telling time varies from the international system. Swahili time (*saa za kiswahili*) begins 6 hours after international time and consists of two 12-hour segments – sunrise to sunset and sunset to sunrise.

This phrase book gives the English word or phrase, followed by Swahili, then the romanisation adapted to aid pronunciation.

In an Emergency

Help!	**Saidia!**	*sa-ee-dee-a*
Stop!	**Simama!**	*see-ma-ma*
Fire!	**Moto!**	*mob-toh*
Call a doctor!	**Mwite daktari**	*m-wee-tay dak-ta-ree*
Call an ambulance!	**Ita gari la hospitali!**	*ee-ta ga-ree la ho-spee-ta-lee*
Call the police!	**Waite polisi!**	*wa-ee-tay poh lee see*
I've been robbed	**Niliibiwa**	*nee-lee-ee-bee-wa*
Where is the nearest telephone?	**Simu hapo karibuni iko wapi?**	*see-moo ha-poh ka-ree-boo-nee ee-koh wa-pee?*
Where is the nearest hospital?	**Hospitali hapo karibuni iko wapi?**	*boh-spee-ta-lee ha-poh ka-ree-boo-nee ee-koh wa-pee?*

Communication Essentials

Yes	**Ndiyo**	*n-dee-yoh*
No	**Hapana**	*ba-pa-na*
Please	**Tafadhali**	*ta-fa-dha-lee*
Thank you	**Asante**	*a-san-tay*
Excuse me	**Samahani**	*sa-ma-ha-nee*
Sorry	**Pole**	*pob-lay*
Hello	**Habari**	*ha-ba-ree*
Goodbye	**Tutaonana**	*too-ta-oh-na-na*
Good night	**Usiku mwema**	*oo-see-koo mway-ma*
Morning	**Asubuhi**	*a-soo-boo-hee*
Afternoon	**Mchana**	*m-cha-na*
Evening	**Jioni**	*jee-oh-nee*
Yesterday	**Jana**	*ja-na*
Today	**Leo**	*lay-oh*
Tomorrow	**Kesho**	*kay-shoh*
Here	**Hapa**	*ha-pa*
There	**Hapo**	*ha-poh*
How?	**Vipi?**	*vee-pee*
What?	**Nini?**	*nee-nee*
When?	**Lini?**	*lee-nee*
Why?	**Kwa nini?**	*kwa nee-nee*
Where?	**Wapi?**	*wa-pee*
Pleased to meet you	**Nafurahi kuku-fahamu**	*na-foo-ra-hee koo-koo fa-ha-moo*

Useful Phrases

How are you?	**Hujambo?**	*hoo-jam-boh*
I'm fine	**Sijambo**	*si-jam-boh*
See you later	**Baadaye tutaonana**	*ba-ada-yay too-ta-oh-na-na*
That's fine	**Ni sawa**	*nee sa-wa*
Where is/are...?	**...iko wapi?**	*ee-koh wa-pee*
How far is it to...?	**Ni umbali gani**	*nee oom-ba-lee ga-nee kwyn-da*
Do you know a good restaurant?	**Unajua hoteli nzuri kula?**	*oo-na-joo-ahoh-tay-lee n-zoo-ree koo-la*
Do you speak English?	**Unasema Kiingereza?**	*oo-na-say-ma kee-een gay ray-za*
I don't understand	**Sielewi**	*see-ay-lay-wee*
Could you speak slowly please?	**Tafadhali sema pole pole?**	*ta-fa-dha-lee say-ma pob-lay pob-lay*
You're welcome	**Karibu**	*ka-ree-boo*

May I take your picture?	**Ni sawa nikipiga picha ya wewe?**	*nee sa-wa nee-kee-pee-ga pee-cha ya way-way*

Useful Words

big	**kubwa**	*koob-wa*
small	**dogo**	*dob-goh*
hot	**joto**	*job-toh*
cold	**baridi**	*ba-ree-dee*
good	**nzuri**	*n-zoo-ree*
bad	**mbaya**	*m-ba-ya*
enough	**ya kutosha**	*ya koo-toh-sha*
open	**wazi**	*wa-zee*
closed	**ya kufungwa**	*ya koo-foon-gwa*
opening hours	**masaa ya kufunguliwa**	*ma-sa ya koo-foon-goo-lee-wa*
right	**kulia**	*koo-lee-a*
left	**kushoto**	*koo-shob-toh*
straight on	**moja kwa moja**	*moh-ja kwa mob-ja*
near	**karibu**	*ka-ree-boo*
far	**mbali**	*m-ba-lee*
up	**juu**	*joo*
down	**chini**	*chee-nee*
in front of	**mbele ya**	*m-bay-lay-ya*
opposite	**kinyume**	*kee-nyoo-may*
behind	**nyuma**	*nyoo-ma*
woman	**mwanamke**	*mwan-am-kay*
man	**mwanamume**	*mwa-na-moo-may*
early	**mapema**	*ma-pay-ma*
late	**ya kuchelewa**	*ya koo-chay-lay-wa*
now	**sasa**	*sa-sa*
soon	**sasa hivi**	*sa-sa hee-vee*
more	**zaidi**	*za-ee-dee*
less	**chache**	*cha-chay*
little	**chache**	*cha-chay*
very	**sana**	*sa-na*
entrance	**mwingilio**	*mween-gee-lee-oh*
exit	**kutoka**	*koo-toh-ka*
toilet	**choo**	*choh*
free, unoccupied	**kupatikana**	*koo-pa-tee-ka-na*
bathroom	**bafu**	*ba-foo*
toilet paper	**karatasi ya choo**	*ka-ra-ta-see ya choh*
camera	**kemra**	*kaym-ra*
batteries	**betri**	*bay-tree*
health certificate	**cheti cha afya**	*chay-tee cha af-ya*
passport	**pasipoti**	*pa-see-poh-tee*
visa	**visa**	*vee-sa*

Making a Telephone Call

I'd like to place a long-distance call	**Nataka kupiga simu ya mbali**	*na-ta-ka koo-pee-ga see-moo ya m-ba-lee*
I want to make a local call	**Nataka kupiga simu jirani**	*na-ta-ka koo-pee-ga see-moo-jee-ra-nee*
I'll call again later	**Nitajaribu tene baadaye**	*nee-ta-ja-ree-boo tay-na ba-a-day-yay*
Can I leave a message?	**Naomba niache ujumbe?**	*na-ohm-ba nee-a-chay oo-joom-bay*
The number is...	**Namba ni...**	*nam-ba ni*
Can I speak to...?	**Nataka kuongea na...?**	*na-ta-ka koo-ohn-gay-a na*

Shopping

How much is it?	**Ni bei gani...?**	*ni bay ga-nee*
I would like...	**Nataka...**	*na-ta-ka*
Do you have...?	**Mna...?**	*m-na*
I'm just looking	**Naangalia tu**	*na-an-ga-lee-a-too*
Do you take credit cards?	**Mnakubali kadi ya benki?**	*m-na-koo-ba-lee ka-dee ya bayn-kee*
Do you take traveller's cheques?	**Mnakubali hundi ya msafiri?**	*m-na-koo-ba-lee boon-dee ya m-sa-fee-ree*
Can I have it sent overseas?	**Naweza kuipostia kwenye nchi za nje?**	*na-way-za koo-ee-eepoh-stee-a kway-nyay n-chee za n-jay*
What time does the shop open?	**Inafungua duka saa ngapi?**	*ee-na-foon-goo-a doo-ka sa n-ga-pee*
What time does the shop close?	**Inafunga duka saa ngapi?**	*ee-na-foon-ga doo-ka sa n-ga-pee*
This one	**Hii**	*hee*
That one	**Hiyo**	*hee-yoh*
expensive	**ghali**	*ga-lee*
cheap	**rahisi**	*ra-hee-see*

bargain	bei nafuu	bay na-foo
size	saizi	sa-ee-zee
white	nyeupe	nyay-oo-pay
black	nyeusi	nyay-oo-see
red	nyekundu	nyay-koon-doo
yellow	manjano	man-ja-noh
green	kijani	kee-ja-nee
blue	buluu	boo-loo
antique shop	duka la vitu vya	doo-ka la vee-too vya
	kizamani	kee-za-ma-nee
shop	duka	doo-ka
bakery	duka la mkate	doo-ka la mkate
bank	benki	bayn-kee
book shop	duka la vitabu	doo-ka la vee-ta-boo
chemist	duka la dawa	doo-ka la da-wa
department store	duka lenye vitu vingi	doo-ka lay-nyay vee-too veen-gee
delicatessen	duka la vyakula	doo-ka la vya-koo-la
	tayari	ta-ya-ree
fishmonger	duka la samaki	doo-ka la sa-ma-kee
gift shop	duka la vitu vya	doo-ka la vee-too vya
	zawadi	za-wa-dee
greengrocer	duka la mboga	doo-ka la m-boh-ga
grocery	duka la vyakula	doo-ka la vya-koo-la
hairdresser	mususi	m-soo-see
market	soko	soh-koh
store	vitu vingi	vee-too veen-gee
newsagent	shirika la habari	shee-ree-ka la ha-ba-ree
post office	posta	poh-sta
supermarket	duka kubwa	doo-ka koob-wa
shoe shop	duka la viatu	doo-ka la vee-a-too
tobacconist	duka la tumbaku	doo-ka la tumbaku
travel agent	uwakala wa safari	oo-wa-ka-la wa sa-fee-ree

Sightseeing

avenue	barabara	ba-ra-ba-ra
art gallery	nyumba ya sanaa	nyoom-ba-ya sa-na
beach	ufukwe	oo-fook-way
boat trip	safari ya boti	sa-fa-ree ya boh-t
cathedral	kanisa kuu	ka-nee-sa koo
church	kanisa	ka-nee-sa
garden	bustani	boo-sta-nee
guide	kiongozi	kee-ohn-goh-zee
house	nyumba	nyoom-ba
highway	barabara	ba-ra-ba-ra
map	ramani	ra-ma-nee
museum	makumbusho	ma-koom-boo-shoh
national park	hifadhi ya wanyama	hee-fa-dhee ya wa-nya-ma
night drive	kuzamia wakati	koo-za-mee-a wa-ka-tee wa oo-see-koo
	wa usiku	
park	hifadhi	hee-fa-dhee
road	barabara	ba-ra-ba-ra
square	uwanja	oo-wan-ja
street	njia	n-jee-a
tourist bureau	uwakala wa safari	oo-wa-ka-la wa sa-fa-ree

Safari

safari/tour	safari	sa-fa-ree
day trip	safari ya siku moja	sa-fa-ree ya see-koo moh-ja
game park	hifadhi ya wanyama	hee-fa-dhee ya wa-nya-ma
camel safari	safari ya ngamia	sa-fa-ree ya n-ga-mee-a
walking safari	safari ya kutembea	sa-fa-ree ya koo-taym-bay-a
park entrance fees	ada za hifadhi	a-da za hee-fa-dhee
buffalo	nyati	nya-tee
cheetah	duma	doo-ma
elephant	ndovu	n-dor-voo
leopard	chui	choo-ee
lion	simba	seem-ba
rhinoceros	kifaru	kee-fa-roo

Post Offices and Banks

bank	benki	bayn-kee
Bureau de change	mahali pa kubadilisha pesa	ma-ba-lee pa koo-ba-dee-lee-sha pay-sa
What is the exchange rate?	Kiwango cha kubadilisha ni nini?	kee-wan-goh cha koo-ba-dee-lee-sha nee nee-nee
I want to send	Nataka kupeleka	na-ta-ka koo-pay-

a letter	barua	lay-ka ba-roo-a
parcel	kifurushi	kee-foo-roo-shee
postcard	postkadi	pohst-ka-dee
stamp	stempu	staym-poo
draw out money	kuondoa hela	koo-ohn-doh-a bay-la

Transport

When does it leave?	Itaondoka saa ngapi	ee-ta-ohn-doh-ka saa ngapi?
When's the next train/bus?	Basi/treni ijayo itaondoka lini?	ba-see/tray-nee ee-ja-yoh ee-ta-ohn-doh-ka lee-nee
Could you call a taxi for me?	Niitie teksi	nee-ee-tee-ay yay tayk-see
airport	uwanja wa ndege	oo-wan-ja wa n-day-gay
railway station	stesheni ya treni	stay-shay-nee ya tray-nee
bus station	stendi ya basi	staym-dee ya ba-see
customs	forodha	foh-roh-dha
boarding pass	pasi ya kuingilia	pa-see ya koo-een-geee-lee-a
car hire	gari za kukodi	ga-ree za koo-koh-dee
bicycle	baisikeli	ba-ee-see-kay-lee
rate	kiasi	kee-a-see
insurance	bima	bee-ma
fuel station	kituo cha mafuta	kee-too-oh cha ma-foo-ta
garage	gereji	gay-ray-jee
I have a flat tyre	nina pancha	nee-na pan-cha

Health

I don't feel well	Mimi ni mgonjwa	mee-meee nee m-gohn-jwa
I have a stomach ache	Nina maumivu ya tumbo	nee-na ma-oo-mee-voo ya toom-boh
headache	maumivu ya kichwa	ma-oo-mee-voo ya kee-chwa
I've been injured	Nimejeruhiwa	nee-may-jay-roo-hee-wa
clinic	kliniki	klee-nee-kee
insect repellent	dawa la kufukuza wadudu	da-wa la koo-foo-koo-za wa-doo-doo

Staying in a Hotel

I have a reservation	Nina buking	nee-na boo-keeng
Are there any rooms available?	Una nafasi ya chumba?	oo-na na-fa-see ya choom-ba
How much is per...?	Ni bei gani kwa?	nee bay ga.ne kwa
day	siku	see-koo
person	mtu	m-too
week	wiki	wee-kee
double room	chumba cha watu wawili	choom-ba cha wa-too wa-wee-lee
double bed	kitanda cha watu wawili	kee-tan-da cha wa-too-wa-wee-lee
twin beds	vitanda viwili	vee-tan-da vee-wee-lee
single room	chumba kwa mtu mmoja	choom-ba kwa m-too m-moh-ja
bath, shower	bafu	ba-foo
soap	sabuni	sa-boo-nee
warm/cold	ya joto/baridi	ya job-toh/ba-ree-dee
water	maji	ma-jee
key	ufunguo	oo-foon-goo-oh

Eating Out

I want to reserve a table	Nataka kuhifadhi meza	na-ta-ka koo-hee-fa-dhee may-za
Can I see the menu, please?	Naweza kuona, menyu, tafadhali?	na-way-za koo-or-na may-nyoo ta-fa-dha-lee
The bill please	Lete bili	lay-tay bee-lee
I am a vegetarian	Mimi ni mlaji wa mboga za majani tu	mee-mee nee m-la-jee wa m-boh-ga za ma-ja-nee too
menu	menyu	may-nyoo
cover charge	bei ya kuingia	bay ya koo-een-gee-a
wine list	orodha ya mvinyo	oh-roh-dha ya

		m-vee-nyob
glass	glasi	gla-see
bottle	chupa	choo-pa
knife	kisu	kee-soo
fork	uma	oo-ma
spoon	kijiko	kee-jee-koh
breakfast	chai ya asubuhi	cha-ee ya a-soo-boo-hee
lunch	chakula cha mchana	cha-koo-la cha m-cha-na
dinner	chakula cha jioni	cha-koo-la cha jee-oh-nee
main course	chakula kikuu	cha-koo-la kee-koo
starter, first course	kiamsha hamu	kee-am-sha ha-mu
appetisers	kiamsha hamu	kee-am-sha ha-moo
main courses	chakula kikuu	cha-koo-la-kee-koo
bar	baa	baa
café	mgahawa	m-ga-ba-wa
rare	ya kuiva kidogo	ya koo-ee-va kee-doh-gob
medium	ya kuiva wastani	ya koo-ee-va wa-sta-nee
well done	ya kuiva sana	ya koo-ee-va sa-na

Menu Decoder

tofaa	to-fa	apple
ndizi	n-dee-zee	banana
nyama m'gombe	nya-ma mg-ohm-bay	beef
wa nyama	wa nya-ma	beef stew
bia	bee-a	beer
ya kuchemshwa	ya koo-chaym-shwa	boiled
mkate	m-ka-tay	bread
siagi	see-a-gee	butter
keki	kay-kee	cake
flat, round Indian bread	cha-pa-tee	chapati
jibini	jee-bee-nee	cheese
kuku	koo-koo	chicken
chipsi	chee-psee	chips
dafu	da-foo	coconut (green)
kahawa	kab-ba-wa	coffee
kitindamlo	kee-teen-da-m-loh	dessert
maandazi	man-da-zee	deep-fried doughnut
kavu	ka-voo	dry
yai	ya-ee	egg
samaki	sa-ma-kee	fish
samaki ya kupaka	sa-ma-kee ya koo-pa-ka	fish cooked in a delicate coconut sauce
tunda safi	toon-da sa-fee	fresh fruit
nyama ya wanyama pori	nya-ma ya wa-nya-ma pob-ree	game meat
kitunguu saumu	kee-toon-goo sa-oo-moo	garlic
sukuma wiki	soo-koo-ma wee-kee	green vegetables (such as spinach)
ya kuchomwa	ya koo-chohm-wa	grilled ham
aiskrimu	a-ee-skree-moo	ice, ice cream
mwanakondoo	mwa-na-kohn-doh	lamb
limau	lee-ma-oo	lemon
maji ya ndimu	ma-jee ya n-dee-moo	lime juice
kamba	kam-ba	lobster, crayfish
ugali	oo-ga-lee	maize/cassava flour cooked like porridge
nyama	nya-ma	meat
nyama choma	nya-ma chob-ma	meat grilled over charcoal
maziwa	ma-zee-wa	milk
uji	oo-jee	millet staple served as a breakfast dish
maji ya madini	ma-jee ya ma-dee-nee	mineral water
mastadi	ma-sta-dee	mustard
tambi	tam-bee	noodles
omlet	ohm-layt	omelette
mafuta	ma-foo-ta	oil
zaituni	za-ee-too-nee	olives
kitunguu	kee-toon-goo	onions
chungwa	choon-gwa	orange
maji ya machungwa	ma-jee ya ma-choon-gwa	fresh orange juice
pilipili	pee-lee-pee-lee	pepper
nyama nguruwe	nya-ma n-goo-roo-way	pork
matoke	ma-toh-kay	a staple dish of boiled/steamed and mashed plantains
kiazi	kee-a-zee	potatoes

kamba	kam-ba	prawns
sambusa/samosa	sam-boo-sa/sa-mob-sa	puffed pastry stuffed with meat or vegetables and deep-fried
mchele	m-chay-lay	rice (uncooked)
wali	wa-lee	rice (cooked)
skonzi	skohn-zee	roll
chumvi	choom-vee	salt
sandwichi	sand-wee-chee	sandwich
soseji	sob--say-jee	sausage
konokono	kob-nob-kob-nob	snails
supu	soo-poo	soup
mchuzi	m-choo-zee	spicy sauce served with ugali
mnofu	m-nob-foo	steak
sukari	soo-ka-ree	sugar
chai	cha-ee	tea
slaisi	sla-ee-see	toast
mboga	m-bob-ga	vegetables
siki	see-kee	vinegar
maji	ma-jee	water
mwekundu	mway-koon-doo	red wine
mweupe	mway-oo-pay	white wine

Numbers

0	sifuri	see foo ree
1	moja	mob ja
2	mbili	m bee lee
3	tatu	ta too
4	nne	n nay
5	tano	ta nob
6	sita	see ta
7	saba	sa ba
8	nane	na nay
9	tisa	tee sa
10	kumi	koo mee
11	kumi na moja	koo mee na mob ja
12	kumi na mbili	koo mee na m bee lee
13	kumi na tatu	koo mee na ta too
14	kumi na nne	koo mee na n nay
15	kumi na tano	koo mee na ta nob
16	kumi na sita	koo mee na see ta
17	kumi na saba	koo mee na sa ba
18	kumi na nane	koo mee na na nay
19	kumi na tisa	koo mee na na tee sa
20	ishirini	ee shee ree nee
30	thelathini	thay la thee nee
40	arobaini	a rob ba ee nee
50	hamsini	ham see nee
60	sitini	see tee nee
70	sabini	sa bee nee
80	themanini	thay ma nee nee
90	tisini	tee see nee
100	mia moja	mee a mob ja
1,000	elfu	ayl foo
1,000	laki	la kee

Time

one minute	dakika moja	da-kee-ka mob-ja
one hour	saa moja	sa mob-ja
half an hour	nusu saa	noo-soo sa
Monday	Jumatatu	joo ma ta too
Tuesday	Jumanne	joo ma n nay
Wednesday	Jumatano	joo ma ta nob
Thursday	Alhamisi	al ba mee see
Friday	Ijumaa	ee joo ma
Saturday	Jumamosi	joo ma mob see
Sunday	Jumapili	joo me pee lee

Swahili Time (saa za kiswahili)

6am (sunrise)	12 (ST)	saa kumi na mbili asubuhi
12pm (noon)	6 (ST)	saa sita mchana
6pm (sunset)	12 (ST)	saa kumi na mbili jioni
12am (midnight)	6 (ST)	saa sita usiku
morning	asubuhi	asubuhi
afternoon	mchana	m-cha-na
evening	jioni	jee-oh-nee
night	usiku	oo-see-kuu

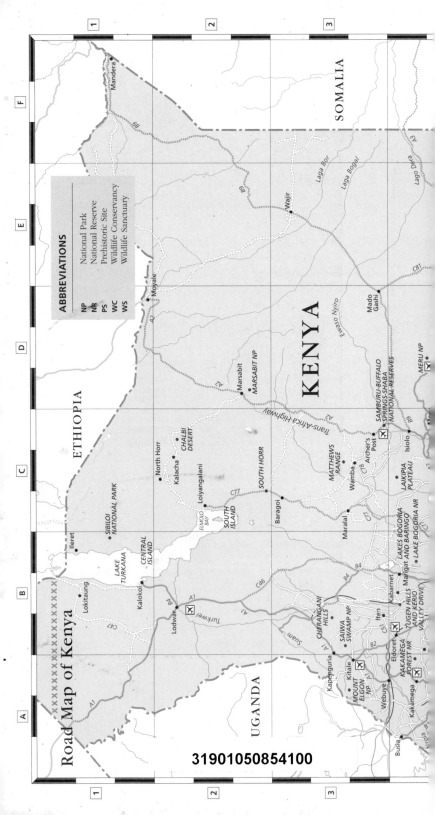

Road Map of Kenya

ABBREVIATIONS

NP	National Park
NR	National Reserve
PS	Prehistoric Site
WC	Wildlife Conservancy
WS	Wildlife Sanctuary

KENYA

ETHIOPIA

SOMALIA

UGANDA

Mandera

Wajir

Moyale

Mado Gashi

Marsabit
MARSABIT NP

North Horr
CHALBI DESERT
Kalacha
Loiyangalani
ELMOLO BAY
SOUTH ISLAND

Ileret
SIBILOI NATIONAL PARK
CENTRAL ISLAND
LAKE TURKANA

SOUTH HORR

Baragoi
Maralal
MATTHEWS RANGE
Wamba
Archer's Post
SAMBURU-BUFFALO SPRINGS-SHABA NATIONAL RESERVES
Isiolo
LAIKIPIA PLATEAU
MERU NP

Lokitaung
Kalokol
Lodwar
Turkwel

CHERANGANI HILLS
SAIWA SWAMP NP
Kapenguria
Kitale
MOUNT ELGON NP
Webuye
KAKAMEGA FOREST NR
Kakamega
Busia

Kabarnet
Iten
Eldoret
LAKES BOGORIA AND BARINGO
Marigat
LAKE BOGORIA
TUGEN HILLS AND KERIO VALLEY DRIVE
LAKE BOGORIA NR

Trans-Africa Highway

Ewaso Nyiro

Laga Bor
Laga Bogal
Lago Dera

Suam

31901050854100